RETRACING
THE
PAST

RETRACING THE PAST

Readings in the History of the American People

VOLUME TWO · SINCE 1865

GARY B. NASH

EDITOR

University of California, Los Angeles

Generously Donated to

The Frederick Douglass Institute

By Professor Jesse Moore

Fall 2000

1817

HARPER & ROW, PUBLISHERS, New York

Cambridge, Philadelphia, San Francisco,
London, Mexico City, São Paulo, Singapore, Sydney

Sponsoring Editor: Marianne J. Russell
Development Editor: Johnna G. Barto
Project Editor: Jo-Ann Goldfarb
Text and Cover Design: Robert Bull/Design
Photo Research: Elsa Peterson
Production: Willie Lane
Compositor: ComCom Division of Haddon Craftsmen, Inc.
Printer and Binder: R. R. Donnelley & Sons Company

Cover Illustration: W. Louis Sonntag, Jr., *The Bowery at Night,* 1895. Museum of the City of New York.

Part-Opening Illustrations: (Part One) John Ferguson Wier, *Forging the Shaft: A Welding Heat,* 1877. Metropolitan Museum of Art, New York, gift of Lyman G. Bloomingdale.   (Part Two) John Sloan, *Gloucester Trolley,* 1917. Canajoharie Library and Art Museum, Canajoharie, N.Y.   (Part Three) Jack Beal, *Harvest,* 1979–1980. Galerie Claude Bernard, Paris.

RETRACING THE PAST: Readings in the History of the American People, Volume Two, Since 1865

Library of Congress Cataloging-in-Publication Data
Main entry under title:

Retracing the past.

Contents: v. 1. To 1877—v. 2. Since 1865.
1. United States—History.   I. Nash, Gary B.
E178.1.R37   1986   973   85–24893
ISBN 0–06–044719–2 (v.1)
ISBN 0–06–044721–4 (v.2)

85 86 87 88 9 8 7 6 5 4 3 2 1

CONTENTS

Preface vii

PART ONE
AN INDUSTRIALIZING PEOPLE

1. Forming a Free Black Community ELIZABETH R. BETHEL   2
2. Power and Politics in Upcountry Georgia STEVEN HAHN   16
3. The Chinese Link a Continent and a Nation JACK CHEN   34
4. The Great Upheaval of 1877 JEREMY BRECHER   44
5. Boss Cox's Cincinnati: A Study in Urbanization and Politics, 1880–1914
   ZANE L. MILLER   58
6. Women in the Southern Farmers' Alliance: The Role and Status of
   Women in the Late Nineteenth Century JULIE ROY JEFFREY   67
7. Populist Dreams and Negro Rights: East Texas As a Case Study
   LAWRENCE C. GOODWYN   80
8. Thomas Edison: The Most Useful American HAROLD C. LIVESAY   93
9. The Military Occupation of Cuba, 1899–1902: Workshop for American
   Progressivism HOWARD GILLETTE, JR.   109

PART TWO
A MODERNIZING PEOPLE

10. William Haywood and the IWW MELVYN DUBOFSKY   120
11. Samuel M. Jones and the Golden Rule in Action PETER J. FREDERICK   139
12. Woman's Place Is at the Typewriter: The Feminization of the Clerical
    Labor Force MARGERY W. DAVIES   157
13. Welfare, Reform, and World War I ALLEN F. DAVIS   168
14. W. E. B. Du Bois: Dusk of Dawn LERONE BENNETT   177
15. Birth Control and Social Revolution LINDA GORDON   186
16. What the Depression Did to People EDWARD R. ELLIS   203
17. The New Deal: The Conservative Achievements of Liberal Reform
    BARTON BERNSTEIN   222

PART THREE
AN ENDURING PEOPLE

18. The Decision for Mass Evacuation of the Japanese-Americans
    ROGER DANIELS   234
19. The Atomic Bomb and the Origins of the Cold War
    MARTIN J. SHERWIN   253
20. American Politics and the Origins of "McCarthyism"
    ROBERT GRIFFITH   268
21. The New Freedom: Los Angeles since 1920 SAM BASS WARNER   276
22. From Harlem to Montgomery: The Bus Boycotts and Leadership of
    Adam Clayton Powell, Jr., and Martin Luther King, Jr.
    DOMINIC J. CAPECI, JR.   290
23. Miracle in Delano DICK MEISTER AND ANNE LOFTIS   300
24. The Vietnam War, the Liberals, and the Overthrow of LBJ
    ALLEN J. MATUSOW   315
25. The New Feminism and the Dynamics of Social Change
    JANE DeHART MATHEWS   327

PREFACE

This two-volume reader has been constructed to accompany *The American People: Creating a Nation and a Society* (New York: Harper & Row, 1986), but I hope it will also prove a useful supplement to other textbooks in American history. The essays have been selected with three goals in mind: first, to blend political and social history; second, to lead students to a consideration of the role of women, ethnic groups, and laboring Americans in the weaving of the nation's social fabric; and third, to explore life at the individual and community levels. The book also means to introduce students to the individuals and groups who made a critical difference in the shaping of American history or whose experience reflected key changes in their society.

A few of the individuals highlighted are famous—Benjamin Franklin, Abraham Lincoln, and Thomas Edison, for example. A number of others are historically visible but not quite household names—Daniel Shays, Tecumseh, "Big Bill" Haywood, W. E. B. Du Bois, and Margaret Sanger. Some will be totally obscure to students, such as "Long Bill" Scott, a revolutionary soldier, and Mayo Greenleaf Patch, whose early nineteenth-century misfortunes mirror some of the changes occurring in rural society after the American Revolution. Sometimes the focus is on groups whose role in history has not been adequately treated—the Chinese in the building of the transcontinental railroad, the women of the Southern Farmers Alliance in the late nineteenth century, and the Hispanic agricultural laborers of this century.

Some of the essays chosen take us inside American homes, farms, and factories, such as the essays on the beginnings of industrialization before the Civil War, the transcontinental migrants of the nineteenth century, and the upcountry yeoman farmers of Georgia after the Civil War. Such essays, it is hoped, will convey an understanding of the daily lives of ordinary Americans, who collectively helped shape society. Other essays deal with the vital social and political movements that transformed American society: the revolutionary movement of the eighteenth century; abolitionism in the antebellum period; populism and progressivism in the late nineteenth and early twentieth centuries; and the civil rights and feminist movements of our own times. Finally, some of the essays treat technological and scientific advances that greatly affected society, such as electricity and birth control.

Readability has been an important criterion in the selection of these essays. An important indicator of readability, in turn, is how vividly and concretely the past has been brought alive by the author. The main objective has been a palpable presentation of the past—one that allows students to sense and feel the forces of historical change and hence to understand them.

GARY B. NASH

PART ONE
AN INDUSTRIALIZING PEOPLE

1

FORMING A FREE BLACK COMMUNITY

ELIZABETH R. BETHEL

The end of the Civil War in 1865 opened the question of the position of the freedman in American society. Now that they were no longer slaves, would black Americans be allowed the same rights as white citizens? Should black males be allowed to vote? To serve on juries? To hold office? To own property? The Fourteenth and Fifteenth Amendments to the Constitution provided one answer to these questions; they gave the freedman all the rights of American citizenship including the right to vote.

But constitutional principle was one thing and southern practice another. Through intimidation and violence, southern whites sought to maintain the old system of racial domination and white supremacy that had prevailed in the prewar South. As Elizabeth Bethel documents in this essay, southern blacks were beaten for attempting to vote, black political leaders were assassinated, and the Ku Klux Klan was organized with the object of keeping blacks "in their place." By the late 1860s it was clear that white southerners were determined to prevent any change in their system of racial privilege and power.

But the history of Reconstruction was not only a story of black suppression and white domination. Individually and collectively, southern blacks challenged the power and racialist assumptions of their white neighbors. Wherever they could, freedmen reestablished the family and kinship ties they had lost during slavery. Thousands of ex-slaves flocked to urban areas to find employment and establish their economic independence. Others, such as those whose story is told in this essay, purchased land, established communities, and provided for their family's well-being. The story of black reconstruction, as Bethel ably shows, is a story of courage and a single-minded search for freedom.

What do you think accounts for the solidarity shown by the people of Promised Land in the face of white terrorism? How do the political struggles of the small farmers of Promised Land compare with those of the white yeomen of upcountry Georgia as described by Steven Hahn in Reading 2?

Promised Land was from the outset an artifact of Reconstruction politics. Its origins, as well, lie in the hopes, the dreams, and the struggles of four million Negroes, for the meaning of freedom was early defined in terms of land for most emancipated Negroes. In South Carolina, perhaps more intensely than any of the other southern states, the thirst for land was acute. It was a possibility sparked first by General William T. Sherman's military actions along the Sea Islands, then dashed as quickly as it was born in the distant arena of Washington politics. Still, the desire for land remained a goal not readily abandoned by the state's freedpeople, and they implemented

Reprinted from Elizabeth R. Bethel, *Promiseland: A Century of Life in a Negro Community* (Philadelphia: Temple University Press, 1981), 17–40. © 1981 by Temple University. Reprinted by permission of Temple University Press.

a plan to achieve that goal at the first opportunity. Their chance came at the 1868 South Carolina Constitutional Convention.

South Carolina was among the southern states which refused to ratify the Fourteenth Amendment to the Constitution, the amendment which established the citizenship of the freedmen. Like her recalcitrant neighbors, the state was then placed under military government, as outlined by the Military Reconstruction Act of 1867. Among the mandates of that federal legislation was a requirement that each of the states in question draft a new state constitution which incorporated the principles of the Fourteenth Amendment. Only after such new constitutions were completed and implemented were the separate states of the defeated Confederacy eligible for readmission to the Union.

The representatives to these constitutional conventions were selected by a revolutionary electorate, one which included all adult male Negroes. Registration for the elections was handled by the Army with some informal assistance by "that God-forsaken institution, the Freedman's Bureau." Only South Carolina among the ten states of the former Confederacy elected a Negro majority to its convention. The instrument those representatives drafted called for four major social and political reforms in state government: a statewide system of free common schools; universal manhood suffrage; a jury law which included the Negro electorate in county pools of qualified jurors; and a land redistribution system designed to benefit the state's landless population, primarily the freedmen.

White response to the new constitution and the social reforms which it outlined was predictably vitriolic. It was condemned by one white newspaper as "the work of sixty-odd Negroes, many of them ignorant and depraved." The authors were publicly ridiculed as representing "the maddest, most unscrupulous, and infamous revolution in history." Despite this and similar vilification, the constitution was ratified in the 1868 referendum, an election boycotted by many white voters and dominated by South Carolina's 81,000 newly enfranchised Negroes, who cast their votes overwhelmingly with the Republicans and for the new constitution.

That same election selected representatives to the state legislature charged with implementing the constitutional reforms. That body, like the constitutional convention, was constituted with a Negro majority; and it moved immediately to establish a common school system and land redistribution program. The freedmen were already registered, and the new jury pools remained the prerogative of the individual counties. The 1868 election also was notable for the numerous attacks and "outrages" which occurred against the more politically active freedmen. Among those Negroes assaulted, beaten, shot, and lynched during the pre-election campaign months were four men who subsequently bought small farms from the Land Commission and settled at Promised Land. Like other freedmen in South Carolina, their open involvement in the state's Republican political machinery led to personal violence.

Wilson Nash was the first of the future Promised Land residents to encounter white brutality and retaliation for his political activities. Nash was nominated by the Republicans as their candidate for Abbeville County's seat in the state legislature at the August 1868 county convention. In October of that year, less than two weeks before the general election, Nash was attacked and shot in the leg by two unidentified white assailants. The "outrage" took place in the barn on his rented farm, not far from Dr. Marshall's farm on Curltail Creek. Wilson Nash was thirty-three years old in 1868, married, and the father of three small children. He had moved from "up around Cokesbury" within Abbeville County, shortly after emancipation to the rented land further west. Within months after the Nash family was settled on their farm, Wilson Nash joined the many Negroes who affiliated with the Republicans, an alliance probably instigated and encouraged by Republican promises of land to the freedmen. The extent of Nash's involvement with local politics was apparent in his nomination for public office; and this same nomination brought him to the forefront of county Negro leadership and to the attention of local whites.

After the attack Nash sent his wife and young children to a neighbor's home, where he probably believed they would be safe. He then mounted his mule and fled his farm, leaving behind thirty bushels of recently harvested corn. Whether Nash also left behind a cotton crop is unknown. It was the unprotected corn crop that worried him as much as his concern for his own safety. He rode his mule into Abbeville and there sought refuge at the local Freedman's Bureau office where he reported the attack to the local bureau agent and requested military protection for his family and his corn crop. Captain W. F. De-Knight was sympathetic to Nash's plight but was powerless to assist or protect him. DeKnight had no authority in civil matters such as this, and the men who held that power generally ignored such assaults on Negroes. The Nash incident was typical and followed a familiar pattern. The assailants remained unidentified, unapprehended, and unpunished. The attack achieved the desired end, however, for Nash withdrew his name from the slate of legislative candidates. For him there were other considerations which took priority over politics.

Violence against the freedmen of Abbeville County, as elsewhere in the state, continued that fall and escalated as the 1868 election day neared. The victims had in common an involvement with the Republicans, and there was little distinction made between direct and indirect partisan activity. Politically visible Negroes were open targets. Shortly after the Nash shooting young Willis Smith was assaulted, yet another victim of Reconstruction violence. Smith was still a teen-ager and too young to vote in the elections, but his age afforded him no immunity. He was a known member of the Union League, the most radical and secret of the political organizations which attracted freedmen. While attending a dance one evening, Smith and four other League members were dragged outside the dance hall and brutally beaten by four white men whose identities were hidden by hoods. This attack, too, was an act of political vengeance. It was, as well, one of the earliest Ku Klux Klan appearances in Abbeville. Like other crimes committed against

politically active Negroes, this one remained unsolved.

On election day freedmen Washington Green and Allen Goode were precinct managers at the White Hall polling place, near the southern edge of the Marshall land. Their position was a political appointment of some prestige, their reward for affiliation with and loyalty to the Republican cause. The appointment brought them, like Wilson Nash and Willis Smith, to the attention of local whites. On election day the voting proceeded without incident until midday, when two white men attempted to block Negroes from entering the polling site. A scuffle ensued as Green and Goode, acting in their capacity as voting officials, tried to bring the matter to a halt and were shot by the white men. One freedman was killed, two others injured, in the incident which also went unsolved. In none of the attacks were the assailants ever apprehended. Within twenty-four months all four men—Wilson Nash, Willis Smith, Washington Green, and Allen Goode—bought farms at Promised Land.

Despite the violence which surrounded the 1868 elections, the Republicans carried the whole of the state. White Democrats refused to support an election they deemed illegal, and they intimidated the newly enfranchised Negro electorate at every opportunity. The freedmen, nevertheless, flocked to the polls in an unprecedented exercise of their new franchise and sent a body of legislative representatives to the state capitol of Columbia who were wholly committed to the mandates and reforms of the new constitution. Among the first legislative acts was one which formalized the land redistribution program through the creation of the South Carolina Land Commission.

The Land Commission program, as designed by the legislature, was financed through the public sale of state bonds. The capital generated from the bond sales was used to purchase privately owned plantation tracts which were then subdivided and resold to freedmen through long-term (ten years), low-interest (7 percent per annum) loans. The bulk of the commission's transactions occurred along the coastal areas of the state where land was readily available. The labor and financial problems of the rice planters of the low-country were generally more acute than those of the up-country cotton planters. As a result, they were more eager to dispose of a portion of the landholdings at a reasonable price, and their motives for their dealings with the Land Commission were primarily pecuniary.

Piedmont planters were not so motivated. Many were able to salvage their production by negotiating sharecropping and tenant arrangements. Most operated on a smaller scale than the low-country planters and were less dependent on gang labor arrangements. As a consequence, few were as financially pressed as their low-country counterparts, and land was less available for purchase by the Land Commission in the Piedmont region. With only 9 percent of the commission purchases lying in the up-country, the Marshall lands were the exception rather than the rule.

The Marshall sons first advertised the land for sale in 1865. These lands, like others at the eastern edge of the Cotton Belt, were exhausted from generations of cultivation and attendant soil erosion; and for such worn out land the price was greatly inflated. Additionally, two successive years of crop failures, low cotton prices, and a general lack of capital discouraged serious planters from purchasing the lands. The sons then advertised the tract for rent, but the land stood idle. The family wanted to dispose of the land in a single transaction rather than subdivide it, and Dr. Marshall's farm was no competition for the less expensive and more fertile land to the west that was opened for settlement after the war. In 1869 the two sons once again advertised the land for sale, but conditions in Abbeville County were not improved for farmers, and no private buyer came forth.

Having exhausted the possibilities for negotiating a private sale, the family considered alternative prospects for the disposition of a farm that was of little use to them. James L. Orr, a moderate Democrat, former governor (1865 to 1868), and family son-in-law, served as negotiator when the tract was offered to the Land Commission at the grossly inflated price of ten dollars an acre.

Equivalent land in Abbeville County was selling for as little as two dollars an acre, and the commission rejected the offer. Political promises took precedence over financial considerations when the commission's regional agent wrote the Land Commission's Advisory Board that "if the land is not bought the (Republican) party is lost in this district." Upon receipt of his advice the commission immediately met the Marshall family's ten dollar an acre price. By January 1870 the land was subdivided into fifty small farms, averaging slightly less than fifty acres each, which were publicly offered for sale to Negro as well as white buyers.

The Marshall Tract was located in the central sector of old Abbeville County and was easily accessible to most of the freedmen who were to make the lands their home. Situated in the western portion of the state, the tract was approximately sixty miles northwest of Augusta, Georgia, one hundred and fifty miles northeast of Atlanta, and the same distance northwest of Charleston. It would attract few freedmen from the urban areas. Two roads intersected within the lands. One, running north to south, linked those who soon settled there with the county seat of Abbeville to the north and the Phoenix community, a tiny settlement composed primarily of white small-scale farmers approximately eighteen miles to the south. Called New Cut Road, Five Notch Road, and later White Hall Road, the dirt wagon route was used primarily for travel to Abbeville. The east-west road, which would much later be converted to a state highway, was the more heavily traveled of the two and linked the cluster of farms to the village of Greenwood, six miles to the east, and the small settlement of Verdery, three miles to the west. Beyond Verdery, which served for a time as a stagecoach stop on the long trip between Greenville and Augusta, lay the Savannah River. The road was used regularly by a variety of peddlers and salesmen who included the Negro farmers on their routes as soon as families began to move onto the farms. Despite the decidedly rural setting, the families who bought land there were not isolated. A regular stream of travelers brought them news of events from well beyond their limited geography and helped them maintain touch with a broader scope of activities and ideas than their environment might have predicted.

The Marshall Tract had only one natural boundary to delineate the perimeter of Negro-owned farms, Curltail Creek on the north. Other less distinctive markers were devised as the farms were settled, to distinguish the area from surrounding white-owned lands. Extending south from White Hall Road, "below the cemetery, south of the railroad about a mile" a small lane intersected the larger road. This was Rabbit Track Road, and it marked the southern edge of Negro-owned lands. To the east the boundary was marked by another dirt lane called Lorenzo Road, little more than a trail which led to the Seaboard Railroad flag stop. Between the crossroads and Verdery to the west, "the edge of the old Darraugh place" established the western perimeter. In all, the tract encompassed slightly more than four square miles of earth.

The farms on the Marshall Tract were no bargain for the Negroes who bought them. The land was only partially cleared and ready for cultivation, and that which was free of pine trees and underbrush was badly eroded. There was little to recommend the land to cotton farming. Crop failures in 1868 and 1869 severely limited the local economy, which further reduced the possibilities for small farmers working on badly depleted soil. There was little credit available to Abbeville farmers, white or black; and farming lacked not only an unqualified promise of financial gain but even the possibility of breaking even at harvest. Still, it was not the fertility of the soil or the possibility of economic profit that attracted the freedmen to those farms. The single opportunity for landownership, a status which for most Negroes in 1870 symbolized the essence of their freedom, was the prime attraction for the freedmen who bought farms from the subdivided Marshall Tract.

Most of the Negroes who settled the farms knew the area and local conditions well. Many were native to Abbeville County. In addition to Wilson Nash, the Moragne family and their in-laws, the Turners, the Pinckneys, the Letmans, and the Williamses were also natives of Abbeville, from "down over by Bordeaux" in the southwestern rim of the county which borders Georgia. Others came to their new farms from "Dark Corner, over by McCormick," and another nearby Negro settlement, Pettigrew Station—both in Abbeville County. The Redd family lived in Newberry, South Carolina before they bought their farm; and James and Hannah Fields came to Promised Land from the state capitol, Columbia, eighty miles to the east.

Many of the settlers from Abbeville County shared their names with prominent white families —Moragne, Burt, Marshall, Pressley, Frazier, and Pinckney. Their claims to heritage were diverse. One recalled "my granddaddy was a white man from England," and others remembered slavery times to their children in terms of white fathers who "didn't allow nobody to mess with the colored boys of his." Others dismissed the past and told their grandchildren that "some things is best forgot." A few were so fair skinned that "they could have passed for white if they wanted to," while others who bought farms from the Land Commission "was so black there wasn't no doubt about who their daddy was."

After emancipation many of these former bondsmen stayed in their old neighborhoods, farming in much the same way as they had during slavery times. Some "worked for the marsters at daytime and for theyselves at night" in an early Piedmont version of sharecropping. Old Samuel Marshall was one former slave owner who retained many of his bondsmen as laborers by assuring them that they would receive some land of their own—promising them that "if you clean two acres you get two acres; if you clean ten acres you get ten acres" of farmland. It was this promise which kept some freedmen on the Marshall land until it was sold to the Land Commission. They cut and cleared part of the tract of the native pines and readied it for planting in anticipation of ownership. But the promise proved empty, and Marshall's death and the subsequent sale of his lands to the state deprived many of those who labored day and night on the land of the free farms they hoped would be theirs. "After they had cleaned it up they still had to pay for it." Other freedmen in the county "moved off after slavery ended but couldn't get no place" of their own to farm. Unable to negotiate labor or lease arrangements, they faced a time of homelessness with few resources and limited options until the farms became available to them. A few entered into labor contracts supervised by the Freedman's Bureau or settled on rented farms in the county for a time.

The details of the various postemancipation economic arrangements made by the freedmen who settled on the small tracts at Dr. Marshall's farm, whatever the form they assumed, were dominated by three conscious choices all had in common. The first was their decision to stay in Abbeville County following emancipation. For most of the people who eventually settled in Promised Land, Abbeville was their home as well as the site of their enslavement. There they were surrounded by friends, family and a familiar environment. The second choice this group of freedmen shared was occupational. They had been Piedmont farmers throughout their enslavement, and they chose to remain farmers in their freedom.

Local Negroes made a third conscious decision that for many had long-range importance in their lives and those of their descendents. Through the influence of the Union League, the Freedman's Bureau, the African Methodist Church, and each other, many of the Negroes in Abbeville aligned politically with the Republicans between 1865 and 1870. In Abbeville as elsewhere in the state, this alliance was established enthusiastically. The Republicans promised land as well as suffrage to those who supported them. If their political activities became public knowledge, the freedmen "were safe nowhere"; and men like Wilson Nash, Willis Smith, Washington Green, and Allen Goode who were highly visible Negro politicians took great risks in this exercise of freedom. Those risks were not without justification. It was probably not a coincidence that loyalty to the Republican cause was followed by a chance to own land.

Land for Sale to the Colored People

I have 700 acres of land to sell in lots of from 50 to 100 acres or more situated six miles from Abbeville. Terms: A liberal cash payment; balance to be made in three annual payments from date of purchase.

J. Hollinshead, Agent
(Advertisement placed by the Land Commission in Abbeville Press, 2 July 1873)

The Land Commission first advertised the farms on the Marshall Tract in January and February 1870. Eleven freedmen and their families established conditional ownership of their farms before spring planting that year. They were among a vanguard of some 14,000 Negro families who acquired small farms in South Carolina through the Land Commission program between 1868 and 1879. With a ten-dollar down payment they acquired the right to settle on and till the thin soil. They were also obliged to place at least half of their land under cultivation within three years and to pay all taxes due annually in order to retain their ownership rights.

Among the earliest settlers to the newly created farms was Allen Goode, the precinct manager at White Hall, who bought land in January 1870, almost immediately after it was put on the market. Two brothers-in-law, J. H. Turner and Primus Letman, also bought farms in the early spring that year. Turner was married to LeAnna Moragne and Letman to LeAnna's sister Francis. Elias Harris, a widower with six young children to raise, also came to his lands that spring, as did George Hearst, his son Robert, and their families. Another father-son partnership, Carson and Will Donnelly, settled on adjacent tracts. Willis Smith's father Daniel also bought a farm in 1870.

Allen Goode was the wealthiest of these early settlers. He owned a horse, two oxen, four milk cows, and six hogs. For the other families, both material resources and farm production were modest. Few of the homesteaders produced more than a single bale of cotton on their new farms that first year; but all, like Wilson Nash two years earlier, had respectable corn harvests, a crop essential to "both us and the animals." Most households also had sizable pea, bean, and sweet potato crops and produced their own butter. All but the cotton crops were destined for household consumption, as these earliest settlers established a pattern of subsistence farming that would prevail as a community economic strategy in the coming decades.

This decision by the Promised Land farmers to intensify food production and minimize cotton cultivation, whether intentional or the result of other conditions, was an important initial step toward their attainment of economic self-sufficiency. Small scale cotton farmers in the Black Belt were rarely free agents. Most were quickly trapped in a web of chronic indebtedness and marketing restrictions. Diversification of cash crops was inhibited during the 1870's and 1880's not only by custom and these economic entanglements but also by an absence of local markets, adequate roads, and methods of transportation to move crops other than cotton to larger markets. The Promised Land farmers, generally unwilling to incur debts with the local lien men if they could avoid it, turned to a modified form of subsistence farming as their only realistic land-use option. Through this strategy many of them avoided the "economic nightmare" which fixed the status of other small-scale cotton growers at a level of permanent peonage well into the twentieth century.

The following year, 1871, twenty-five more families scratched up their ten-dollar down payment; and upon presenting it to Hollinshead obtained conditional titles to farms on the Marshall Tract. The Williams family, Amanda and her four adult sons—William, Henry, James, and Moses—purchased farms together that year, probably withdrawing their money from their accounts at the Freedman's Savings and Trust Company Augusta Branch for their separate down payments. Three of the Moragne brothers—Eli, Calvin, and Moses—joined the Turners and the Letmans, their sisters and brothers-in-law, making five households in that corner of the tract soon designated "Moragne Town." John Valentine, whose family was involved in A.M.E. organizational work in Abbe-

ville County, also obtained a conditional title to a farm, although he did not settle there permanently. Henry Redd, like the Williamses, withdrew his savings from the Freedman's Bank and moved to his farm from Newberry, a small town about thirty miles to the east. Moses Wideman, Wells Gray, Frank Hutchison, Samuel Bulow, and Samuel Burt also settled on their farms before spring planting.

As the cluster of Negro-owned farms grew more densely populated, it gradually assumed a unique identity; and this identity, in turn, gave rise to a name, Promised Land. Some remember their grandparents telling them that "the Governor in Columbia [South Carolina] named this place when he sold it to the Negroes." Others contend that the governor had no part in the naming. They argue that these earliest settlers derived the name Promised Land from the conditions of their purchase. "They only promised to pay for it, but they never did!" Indeed, there is some truth in that statement. For although the initial buyers agreed to pay between nine and ten dollars per acre for their land in the original promissory notes, few fulfilled the conditions of those contracts. Final purchase prices were greatly reduced, from ten dollars to $3.25 per acre, a price more in line with prevailing land prices in the Piedmont.

By the end of 1873 forty-four of the fifty farms on the Marshall Tract had been sold. The remaining land, less than seven hundred acres, was the poorest in the tract, badly eroded and at the perimeter of the community. Some of those farms remained unsold until the early 1880's, but even so the land did not go unused. Families too poor to consider buying the farms lived on the state-owned property throughout the 1870's. They were squatters, living there illegally and rent-free, perhaps working a small cotton patch, always a garden. Their condition contrasted sharply with that of the landowners who, like other Negroes who purchased farmland during the 1870's, were considered the most prosperous of the rural freedmen. The freeholders in the community were among the pioneers in a movement to acquire land, a movement that stretched across geographical and temporal limits. Even in the absence of state or federal assistance in other regions, and despite the difficulties Negroes faced in negotiating land purchases directly from white landowners during Reconstruction, by 1875 Negroes across the South owned five million acres of farmland. The promises of emancipation were fulfilled for a few, among them the families at Promised Land.

Settlement of the community coincided with the establishment of a public school, another of the revolutionary social reforms mandated by the 1868 constitution. It was the first of several public facilities to serve community residents and was built on land still described officially as "Dr. Marshall's farm." J. H. Turner, Larkin Reynolds, Iverson Reynolds, and Hutson Lomax, all Negroes, were the first school trustees. The families established on their new farms sent more than ninety children to the one-room school. Everyone who could be spared from the fields was in the classroom for the short 1870 school term. Although few of the children in the landless families attended school regularly, the landowning families early established a tradition of school attendance for their children consonant with their new status. With limited resources the school began the task of educating local children.

The violence and terror experienced by some of the men of Promised Land during 1868 recurred three years later when Eli and Wade Moragne were attacked and viciously beaten with a wagon whip by a band of Klansmen. Wade was twenty-three that year, Eli two years older. Both were married and had small children. It was rumored that the Moragne brothers were among the most prominent and influential of the Negro Republicans in Abbeville County. Their political activity, compounded by an unusual degree of self-assurance, pride, and dignity, infuriated local whites. Like Wilson Nash, Willis Smith, Washington Green, and Allen Goode, the Moragne brothers were victims of insidious political reprisals. Involvement in Reconstruction politics for Negroes was a dangerous enterprise and one which addressed the past as well as the future. It was an activity suited to young men and those

who faced the future bravely. It was not for the timid.

The Republican influence on the freedmen at Promised Land was unmistakable, and there was no evidence that the "outrages" and terrorizations against them slowed their participation in local partisan activities. In addition to the risks, there were benefits to be accrued from their alliance with the Republicans. They enjoyed appointments as precinct managers and school trustees. As candidates for various public offices, they experienced a degree of prestige and public recognition which offset the element of danger they faced. These men, born slaves, rose to positions of prominence as landowners, as political figures, and as makers of a community. Few probably had dared to dream of such possibilities a decade earlier.

During the violent years of Reconstruction there was at least one official attempt to end the anarchy in Abbeville County. The representative to the state legislature, J. Hollinshead—the former regional agent for the Land Commission—stated publicly what many local Negroes already knew privately, that "numerous outrages occur in the county and the laws cannot be enforced by civil authorities." From the floor of the General Assembly of South Carolina Hollinshead called for martial law in Abbeville, a request which did not pass unnoticed locally. The Editor of the *Press* commented on Hollinshead's request for martial law by declaring that such outrages against the freedmen "exist only in the imagination of the legislator." His response was probably typical of the cavalier attitude of southern whites toward the problems of their former bondsmen. Indeed, there were no further reports of violence and attacks against freedmen carried by the *Press,* which failed to note the murder of County Commissioner Henry Nash in February 1871. Like other victims of white terrorists, Nash was a Negro.

While settlement of Dr. Marshall's Farm by the freedmen proceeded, three community residents were arrested for the theft of "some oxen from Dr. H. Drennan who lives near the 'Promiseland.'" Authorities found the heads, tails, and feet of the slaughtered animals near the homes of Ezekiel and Moses Williams and Colbert Jordan. The circumstantial evidence against them seemed convincing; and the three were arrested and then released without bond, pending trial. Colonel Cothran, a former Confederate officer and respected barrister in Abbeville, represented the trio at their trial. Although freedmen in Abbeville courts were generally convicted of whatever crime they were charged with, the Williamses and Jordan were acquitted. Justice for Negroes was always a tenuous affair; but it was especially so before black, as well as white, qualified electors were included in the jury pool. The trial of the Williams brothers and Jordan signaled a temporary truce in the racial war, a truce which at least applied to those Negroes settling the farms at Promised Land.

In 1872, the third year of settlement, Promised Land gained nine more households as families moved to land that they "bought for a dollar an acre." There they "plow old oxen, build log cabin houses" as they settled the land they bought "from the Governor in Columbia." Colbert Jordan and Ezekiel Williams, cleared of the oxen stealing charges, both purchased farms that year. Family and kinship ties drew some of the new migrants to the community. Joshuway Wilson, married to Moses Wideman's sister Delphia, bought a farm near his brother-in-law. Two more Moragne brothers, William and Wade, settled near the other family members in "Moragne Town." Whitfield Hutchison, a jack-leg preacher, bought the farm adjacent to his brother Frank. "Old Whit Hutchison could sing about let's go down to the water and be baptized. He didn't have no education, and he didn't know exactly how to put his words, but when he got to singing he could make your hair rise up. He was a number one preacher." Hutchison was not the only preacher among those first settlers. Isaac Y. Moragne, who moved to Promised Land the following year, and several men in the Turner family all combined preaching and farming.

Not all of the settlers came to their new farms as members of such extensive kinship networks as the Moragnes, who counted nine brothers, four sisters, and an assortment of spouses and children among the first Promised Land residents. Even those who joined the community in relative isolation, however, were seldom long in establishing kinship alliances with their neighbors. One such couple was James and Hannah Fields who lived in Columbia before emancipation, While still a slave, James Fields owned property in the state capitol, which was held in trust for him by his master. After emancipation Fields worked for a time as a porter on the Columbia and Greenville Railroad and heard about the up-country land for sale to Negroes as he carried carpet bags and listened to political gossip on the train. Fields went to Abbeville County to inspect the land before he purchased a farm there. While he was visiting, he "run up on Mr. Nathan Redd," old Henry Redd's son. The Fieldses' granddaughter Emily and Nathan were about the same age, and Fields proposed a match to young Redd. "You marry my granddaughter, and I'll will all this land to you and her." The marriage was arranged before the farm was purchased, and eventually the land was transferred to the young couple.

By the conclusion of 1872 forty-eight families were settled on farms in Promised Land. Most of the land was under cultivation, as required by law; but the farmers were also busy with other activities. In addition to the houses and barns which had to be raised as each new family arrived with their few possessions, the men continued their political activities. Iverson Reynolds, J. H. Turner, John and Elias Tolbert, Judson Reynolds, Oscar Pressley, and Washington Green, all community residents, were delegates to the county Republican convention in August 1872. Three of the group were landowners. Their political activities were still not received with much enthusiasm by local whites, but reaction to Negro involvement in politics was lessening in hostility. The *Press* mildly observed that the fall cotton crop was being gathered with good speed and "the farmers have generally been making good use of their time." Cotton picking and politics were both seasonal, and the newspaper chided local Negroes for their priorities. "The blacks have been indulging a little too much in politics

but are getting right again." Iverson Reynolds
and Washington Green, always among the community's Republican leadership during the
1870's, served as local election managers again
for the 1872 fall elections. The men from Promised Land voted without incident that year.

Civic participation among the Promised
Land residents extended beyond partisan politics when the county implemented the new jury
law in 1872. There had been no Negro jurors for
the trial of the Williams brothers and Colbert
Jordan the previous year. Although the inclusion of Negroes in the jury pools was a reform
mandated in 1868, four years passed before
Abbeville authorities drew up new jury lists
from the revised voter registration rolls. The
jury law was as repugnant to the whites as
Negro suffrage, termed "a wretched attempt at
legislation, which surpasses anything which has
yet been achieved by the Solons in Columbia."
When the new lists were finally completed in
1872 the *Press,* ever the reflection of local white
public opinion, predicted that "many of [the
freedmen] probably have moved away; and the
chances are that not many of them will be forthcoming" in the call to jury duty. Neither the
initial condemnation of the law nor the optimistic undertones of the *Press* prediction stopped
Pope Moragne and Iverson Reynolds from responding to their notices from the Abbeville
Courthouse. Both landowners rode their mules
up Five Notch Road from Promised Land to
Abbeville and served on the county's first integrated jury in the fall of 1872. Moragne and
Reynolds were soon followed by others from the
community—Allen Goode, Robert Wideman,
William Moragne, James Richie, and Luther
(Shack) Moragne. By 1874, less than five years
after settlement of Dr. Marshall's farm by the
new Negro landowners began, the residents of
Promised Land remained actively involved in
Abbeville County politics. They were undaunted
by the *Press* warning that "just so soon as the
colored people lose the confidence and support
of the North their doom is fixed. The fate of the
red man will be theirs." They were voters, jurors, taxpayers, and trustees of the school their

children attended. Their collective identity as an
exclusively Negro community was well established.

Only Colored Down in This Old Promised Land

Abbeville County, South Carolina
Mr. John Lomax passed through the Promised Land
yesterday, and he thinks the crops there almost a failure. The corn will not average two bushels to the acre,
and the cotton about 300 pounds [less than one bale]
to the acre. A large quantity of sorghum cane was
planted. It was almost worthless. The land appeared as
if it had been very well cultivated.
Abbeville Press
30 September 1874

The forty-eight men and women who established conditional ownership of the farms at
Promised Land between 1870 and 1872 were required by law to place at least half of their land
under cultivation within three years of their purchase. There was, however, no requirement about
the crops to be planted. The men who established
that cultivation standard probably assumed that
cotton would be the major cash crop, as it was
throughout the Piedmont. At Promised Land
cotton was indeed planted on every one of the
farms, but not in overwhelming amounts. The
relatively small cotton fields were overshadowed
by fields of corn, peas, and sorghum cane; and the
sense of permanence among the settlers was
clearly evident when "they planted peach trees
and pear trees and had grape vines all over" the
land, which only a few years before was either
uncleared of native pine forests or part of the
upcountry plantation system. Cotton, the antebellum crop of the slaves, became the cash crop
of freedom. It would never dominate the lives of
the farmers at Promised Land.

The 1870's were economically critical years
for the new landowners. They had mortgage payments to meet and taxes to pay, but they also had
families to feed. In 1870, when the price of cotton
reached twenty-two cents a pound, all this was
possible. In the following years, however, cotton
prices declined dramatically. This, combined
with generally low cotton yields, resulted in eco-

nomic hardship for many of the farmers. Poverty was their constant neighbor, and their struggle for survival drew them into a cycle of indebtedness to white "lien men."

In those depression years there was little credit in the Piedmont. "The poor people wasn't able to buy their fertilize. That's what makes your cotton." Storekeepers and merchants reserved their resources for the local white planters, and the Negro farmers were forced to find credit from other sources. They turned to their white landowning neighbors and in some cases their former masters, the Devlin family in Verdery; the Tuck family, nearby farmers; and the Hendersons, Verdery merchants. To them the Promised Land farmers paid usurious interest rates for the fertilizer they needed "to make a bale of cotton" and the other supplies and foodstuffs they required to survive the growing season.

It was during this decade that the community farmers learned to maintain a skillful balance between a small cotton cash crop and their subsistence fields. Careful in the management of debt, most landowners probably used their cotton crop to meet their mortgage payment to the Land Commission and their tax bill to the county. There was never any surplus on the small farms, and a crop failure had immediate and personal consequences. At best a family would go hungry. At worst they would lose their farm.

Times were hard; and, despite generally shrewd land and debt management, twenty of the original settlers lost title to their land during the early 1870's. All migrated from Promised Land before the 1875 growing season. An advertisement in the *Press* attracted some new purchasers to the vacated farms, but most buyers learned of the land through friends and relatives. New families once again moved on to the land. Wilson Nash bought the farm originally purchased by John Valentine; both men were church leaders and probably discussed the transaction in some detail before the agreement was finalized.

Allen Goode, Wells Gray, and James Fields added to their holdings, buying additional farms from discouraged families who were leaving. Moses Wideman's younger brothers, William

and Richmond, together bought an eighty-five-acre farm and then divided it, creating two more homesteads in the community. J. H. Turner, who secured a teaching position in an Edgefield County public school, sold his farm to his brother-in-law Isaac Y. Moragne. Each of the landowners had a brother, a cousin, or a friend who was eager to assume the financial burden of landownership; and none of the twenty vacated farms remained unoccupied for long. Promised Land quickly regained its population. The new arrivals strengthened and expanded the kinship bonds, which already crisscrossed and united individual households in the community.

Marriage provided the most common alliance between kinship groups. The Wilson and Wideman families and the Fields and Redds were both so related. The use of land as dowry, first employed by James Fields to arrange his granddaughter's marriage to Nathan Redd, provided a convenient and viable bargaining tool. When Iverson Reynolds bought his thirty-acre farm he also purchased a second, twenty-acre tract in his daughter's name, looking forward to the time of her marriage. "When Oscar Pressley married Iverson Reynolds' daughter, Janie, Iverson Reynolds give him that land or sold it to him. But he got that farm from old Iverson Reynolds when he got married." The Moragnes, Turners, Pinckneys, and Letmans were also united through land-based dowry arrangements. "The Moragne women is the ones that had the land. All them, the Turners, the Pinckneys, and the Letmans— all them got into the Moragnes when the women married these men."

Marriage did not always accompany kinship bonds, for at Promised Land, like every place else, "some folks have childrens when they not married. Things get all mixed up sometimes." Still, the community was a small and intimate place, woven together as early as the 1880's by a complex and interlocking series of kin ties, which were supplemented by many other kinds of personal relationships. The separation of public and private spheres blurred; and, married or not, "when the gals get a baby" everyone was aware of the heritage and family ties of new babies.

"Andrew Moragne supposed to been his daddy, but his momma was a Bradley so he took the name Bradley." Even so, promiscuity and illegitimacy were not casually accepted facts of life. Both were sinful and disgraceful not just to the couple but to their families as well. For women a pregnancy without marriage was particularly painful. "Some might be mean to you then," and many refused to even speak publicly to an unmarried women who became pregnant. "All that stop when the baby is born. Don't want to punish an innocent baby." Legitimate or not, babies were welcomed into families and the community, and the sins of the parents were set aside. Ultimately, the bonds of kinship proved more powerful than collective morality, and these bonds left few residents of the community excluded from an encompassing network of cousins, aunts, uncles, and half-brothers and sisters.

As the landowning population of Promised Land stabilized, local resources emerged to meet day-to-day needs. A molasses mill, where the farmers had their sorghum cane ground into molasses by Joshuway Wilson's oldest son Fortune, opened in the community. Two corn and wheat grist mills opened on Curltail Creek. One, the old Marshall Mill, was operated by Harrison Cole, a Negro who subsequently purchased a vacant farm in the community. The other, the former Donalds Mill, was owned and operated by James Evans, an Irish immigrant whose thirst for land equaled that of his Negro neighbors. North Carter, the youngest son of landowner Marion Carter, opened a small general store at the east-west crossroads, where he sold candy, kerosene, salt, and other staples to his neighbors, extending credit when necessary, knowing that they would pay when they could. Long before the final land purchase was completed, the freedmen at Promised Land had established a framework for economic and social self-sufficiency.

The farms, through hard work, decent weather, and an eight-month growing season, soon yielded food for the households. A pattern of subsistence agriculture provided each Promised Land family a degree of independence and self-reliance unknown to most other Negro families in the area. Cows produced milk and butter for the tables, and chickens eggs and fresh poultry. Draft animals and cash money were both scarce commodities, but "in them days nobody ever went hungry." Hogs provided the major source of meat in the community's subsistence economy. "My mother and them used to kill hogs and put them down in salt in wood boxes and cover them so flies couldn't get to them for about five or six weeks. Take it out and wash it, put on red pepper and such, hang it up to dry, and that meat be *good.*" The absence of an abundant cotton crop was not a sign of lack of industry. Prosperity, as well as productivity, was measured against hunger; and, in the never-ending farm cycle, fields were planted according to the number of people in each household, the number of mouths to be fed.

Community and household autonomy were firmly grounded in the economic independence of the land. Both were strengthened with the establishment of a church in Promised Land. In 1875, fully a decade before the final farms were settled, James Fields sold one acre of his land to the Trustees of Mt. Zion A.M.E. Church. It was a sign of the times. At Promised Land, as elsewhere in the South, freedmen withdrew from white churches as quickly as possible. Membership in the Baptist and Methodist denominations increased tenfold between 1860–1870 as the new Negro churches in the South took form. Mt. Zion was relatively late in emerging as a part of that movement for independence from white domination, but the residents of Promised Land were preoccupied for a time with more basic concerns. The fields had to be established as productive before community residents turned their energies to other aspects of community development.

The Field's land, located squarely in the geographical center of Promised Land, was within a two-mile walk of all the houses in the community. On this thinly wooded tract the men carved out a brush arbor, a remnant of slavery days; and Isaac Y. Moragne led everybody in the young settlement in prayers and songs. From the beginning of their emancipation schools and churches were central components of Negro social life; and at Promised Land religion, like education, was established as a permanent part of community life while the land was still being cleared.

Newcomers and Community Growth

Most families survived those first settlement years, the droughts and crop failures, Ku Klux Klan attacks, and the violent years of Reconstruction. They met their mortgage payments and their taxes, and the years after 1875 were relatively prosperous ones. Promised Land was well established before the Compromise of 1877, the withdrawal of federal troops from the state, and the election of Wade Hampton as governor. The political squabbles among the white Democrats during the years after Hampton's redemption of South Carolina touched the folks at Promised Land only indirectly. The community was, for the most part, preoccupied with internal events.

By 1880 the community had expanded from forty-nine to eighty-nine households, an average growth of four new families each year for the previous decade. Fifty of those families were landless, attracted to Promised Land for a combination of reasons. Probably at least some of them hoped to acquire land there. Promised Land was the only place in the area where Negroes had even minimal hope of buying land after 1877. Local farmers and planters, never eager to sell land to Negroes, now grew even more recalcitrant as Democratic white rule was re-established. Sharecropping dominated farming arrangements between whites and Negroes throughout the Cotton Belt. The landowners at Promised Land, "well, they was wheels. They *owned* their farms." And the respect and prestige they commanded within the county's landless Negro population were another kind of attraction for landless families.

The violence of Reconstruction was moderated only slightly, and a concern for personal safety was surely another reason Negroes moved to Promised Land. Few of the early settlers, those who came before the mid-1880's, could have escaped that violence, even if their contact was indirect. Wilson Nash, Willis Smith, Allen Goode, Washington Green, Wade and Eli Moragne all

headed landowning households. For any who might forget, those men were constant reminders of the dangers which lay just beyond the community's perimeter.

The men at Promised Land still exercised their franchise, fully aware of both the dangers and the benefits which they knew accompanied political activity. Together they walked the three miles to Verdery and collectively cast their ballots at the post office "where Locket Frazier held the box for the niggers and Red Tolbert for the whites." Perhaps they walked together as a symbolic expression of their solidarity, but much more likely it was because of a practical concern for their own safety. They were less vulnerable to attack in a group. As it had in the past, however, this simple exercise of citizenship enraged the local whites; and, once again, in the early 1880's the men at Promised Land faced the threat of violence for their partisan political activities.

> Them old Phoenix rats, the Ku Klux, come up here to beat up the niggers 'cause they went to Verdery and voted. Them old dogs from Phoenix put on red shirts and come up here to beat the poor niggers up. Old George Foster, the white man, he told them "Don't go down in that Promiseland. Josh Wilson and Colbert Jordan and them got some boys up there, and they got shotguns and Winchesters and old guns. Any white man come in to Promiseland to beat the niggers up, some body going to die. They'll fight 'til hell freezes over. You Phoenix rats go back to Phoenix." So they went on down to Verdery, and they told them the same thing.

Their reputation, their readiness, and their willingness to defend their land were clearly well-known facts about the people at Promised Land. The "Red Shirts" heeded the warning, and white terrorists never again attempted to violate Promised Land. This, too, must have been a part of the community's attraction to landless families who moved there.

Promised Land in 1880 was a community which teemed with activity. Most of the newcomers joined in the brush arbor worship services and sent their children to the community schools. Liberty Hill School and the white schoolmaster were replaced by "schools scattered all around the woods" taught by Negro men and women who lived at Promised Land. Abbeville County maintained a public school. Crossroads School for Colored was taught by H. L. Latimer. The Mill School, maintained by the extensive Moragne family for their children, was held in James Evans' mill on Curltail Creek and was taught by J. H. Turner, Moragne brother-in-law. The Hester School, located near the southern edge of the community, was so named because it met in the Hester family's home. All three private schools supplemented the meager public support of education for Negro children; and all were filled to capacity, because "folks had big families then—ten and twelve childrens—and them schools was crowded."

The representatives to the 1868 South Carolina Constitutional Convention who formulated the state's land redistribution hoped to establish an economically independent Negro yeomanry in South Carolina. The Land Commission intended the purchase and resale of Dr. Marshall's farm to solidify the interests of radical Republicanism in Abbeville County, at least for a time. Both of these designs were realized. A third and unintended consequence also resulted. The land fostered a socially autonomous, identifiable community. Drawing on resources and social structures well established within an extant Negro culture, the men and women who settled Promised Land established churches and schools and a viable economic system based on landownership. They maintained that economic autonomy by subsistence farming and supported many of their routine needs by patronizing the locally owned and operated grist mills and general store. The men were actively involved in Reconstruction politics as well as other aspects of civil life, serving regularly on county juries and paying their taxes. Attracted by the security and prestige Promised Land afforded and the possible hope of eventual landownership, fifty additional landless households moved into the community during the 1870's, expanding the 1880 population to almost twice its original size. Together the eighty-nine households laid claim to slightly more than four square miles of land, and within that small territory they "carved out their own little piece of the world."

2

POWER AND POLITICS IN UPCOUNTRY GEORGIA

STEVEN HAHN

Reconstruction involved more than reintegrating the South into the American nation and creating a place in American life for several million former slaves. Reconstruction also involved the rising power of white yeoman farmers. These small farmers had been an integral part of the southern slave system since the late seventeenth century. Living at the margins of the section's large plantations, the small farmers provided both food for the plantation system and a zone of protection for the plantation owners against wandering or escaping slaves.

These yeoman farmers had long been tied to the plantation system through bonds of economic interest and paternalistic patronage. Plantation owners served both as purchasers of small farmers' crops and as their marketing agents in a rural region lacking commercial towns. In return yeoman farmers had given their votes to the plantation elite and their candidates. The cement of this entire system, which kept at bay the often competing interests of yeoman and plantation owner, was an ideology of racial supremacy through which plantation owners drew small white farmers to themselves as members of a "superior" race.

With the breakdown of the plantation system during the Civil War these bonds between yeoman farmer and plantation owner were broken. As a result, small farmers began a search for economic and political independence that placed them at odds with the remnants of the plantation-owning class. In this essay Steven Hahn traces the struggles of one group of these farmers, the yeomen of upcountry Georgia, as they sought to establish a place for themselves in postwar politics. It was in local struggles of this sort that the nature of the postwar South was decided.

How do the actions of the yeoman farmers of Georgia compare with those of the Southern Farmers' Alliance described by Julie Roy Jeffrey in Reading 6? Compare the role of white racial ideology in the yeoman's quest for political power in Georgia and in the Texas Populist movement discussed by Lawrence C. Goodwyn in Reading 7?

Jesse Wade, a white tenant farmer from Cobb County, who "was a Union man . . . like my daddy befo'e me" and suffered more than his share of abuse during the war, believed that justice demanded a far-reaching policy of Reconstruction. "We should tuk the land, as we did the niggers, and split it, and gin part to the niggers and part to me and t'other Union fellers," he told the English traveler J. T. Trowbridge in late 1865, feeling confident that "they'd have to submit to it, as they did to the niggers." And, according to Trowbridge, a number of freedmen listening in on the conversation "were unanimously of this opinion." To Southern planters, Wade's sentiments and the enthusiastic response they elicited from the blacks nurtured their deepest fears that

Reprinted from *The Roots of Southern Populism: Yeoman Farmers and the Transformation of the Georgia Upcountry, 1850–1890* by Steven Hahn. (New York: Oxford University Press, 1983), pp. 204–38. Copyright © 1983 by Oxford University Press, Inc. By permission of the publisher.

Emancipation began rather than concluded a convulsive era of social change. One wealthy landowner fretted that there was "bound to be another revolution of some sort" for "seven tenths of the people of the South would vote for . . . confiscation of Southern property." "Every negro would vote for such a proposition," he insisted, "and a vast number of the whites." Another planter envisioned a similar nightmare: "Negroes and Tories will form a government for us [and bring about] Repudiation—abolition of poll tax division of land disfranchisement of Rebels regulation of the price of labor and rent of land—all to the benefit of the negro and the poor."

The specter of a biracial coalition of poor Southerners long weighed ominously on the mind of the planter class. The proslavery argument, in its appeal for the allegiance of the white lower classes, tacitly acknowledged the planters' uneasiness. Social tensions during the secession crisis and, especially, during the war hardly offered solace. But Reconstruction held out dramatic new possibilities. The prospect of extensive land reform, anticipated by General Sherman's field order reserving much abandoned coastal land in Georgia and South Carolina for exclusive black settlement, suggested that a truly revolutionary transformation might be the price of sectional reconciliation. Although Southerners acquainted with the temper of national politics, like Alexander Stephens, could rest assured that conservative instincts would circumscribe congressional policy, others saw in the radical stances of Charles Sumner, Thaddeus Stevens, and George Julian the mainstream of "Black Republicanism." If radical measures did indeed falter in the halls of Congress, the creation of a Republican party in the South shifted the arena of political contention and gave added dimensions and vitality to major social questions. This potential challenge to the very fabric of Southern society fueled the political turbulence of the postwar years.

From the first, Republican efforts to forge an electoral majority in the South threatened a new political departure. Whether or not they shared a commitment to radical reforms, Republicans

recognized that the freedmen would constitute a significant element in a nascent Southern wing. Yet only in South Carolina and Louisiana were blacks likely to account for more than half of the eligible voters. Success, thereby, hinged on the ability to attract a considerable number of native whites, and the Upcountry seemed to hold special promise for such an undertaking. There, a longstanding distaste for planter prerogatives saw expression in Unionism, if not outright hostility to the Confederacy; there, the largest concentration of whites loyal to the federal government might be found at war's end. The counties of north Georgia "were all strongly opposed to secession in 1860–61, and this Congressional district furnished several hundred soldiers to our armies," Sidney Andrews observed from Atlanta in November 1865. "Its disposition toward the government is now, as a whole, probably better than that of any district in the state." Numerous witnesses before Congress's Joint Committee on Reconstruction the next year issued similar reports.

Republicans faced a formidable task in cementing the coalition. The Upcountry in Georgia, as well as in other states of the Lower South, had been antebellum strongholds of the Democratic party. Partisan loyalties had deep generational roots. There was, furthermore, little love lost between resident yeomen and blacks. As one federal officer noted in 1866, "The poorer classes of white people . . . have a most intense hatred of the negro, and swear he shall never be reckoned as part of the population." Developments during the immediate postwar years served only to exacerbate animosities, for if abolition itself did not shake smallholders severely, its consequences quickly did. As an initial response to liberation, many Upcountry blacks, like their counterparts in the Black Belt, left the plantations and farms and wandered through the countryside. Those finding employment were frequently dismissed without pay after harvest. Hunger often drove them to kill hogs foraging in the woods and, at times, to steal from white homesteads. Complaints of such offenses poured into the local offices of the Freedmen's Bureau. While the planters may have viewed this petty thievery simply as a manifestation of the freed-men's "natural disposition," yeomen desperately struggling to feed themselves and their families were not entertained. The "depredations" committed by the blacks seemed to offer hard evidence for the warnings of proslavery theorists that Emancipation would cast the property of all white Southerners in jeopardy. Small farmers, therefore, occasionally joined vigilante bands organized by members of the local elite, who were primarily concerned with reestablishing labor controls, in an effort to discipline the freedmen. It was a lesson neither white nor black would easily forget.

The dire straits that many Upcountry yeomen found themselves in did provide an opening for the Republicans, however. Cries for debtor relief sounded throughout the region within a short time after the surrender, and little satisfaction came from the planter-dominated state legislature of 1866. Governor Charles Jenkins, a Whig turned Democrat, vetoed the one measure designed to alleviate distress—the stay law, which would have postponed the settlement of private debts—charging that "no state shall pass any law impairing the obligation of contracts." When the assembly enacted a second stay law later that year, this time over Jenkins's veto, the State Supreme Court, presided over by Chief Justice Hiram Warner, a Democrat, struck it down as unconstitutional. Thus, a meeting in Jackson County, viewing efforts "by the last legislature [as] insufficient," demanded "relief according to what the people estimate and value," and called upon recalcitrant assemblymen to "resign their position that representative men may be . . . sent to serve the people." Should the legislature balk, the meeting warned, "the people know their rights . . . and will take up their own work, and in convention do it . . . effectually." Another Jackson County resident went so far as to predict mob violence if action was not taken.

Propelled by the Reconstruction Acts of 1867, which enfranchised the ex-slaves, and by growing resentment toward planter conservatives, Republicans seized their opportunity. The Georgia party's Radical wing, based in Augusta and

guided by John E. Bryant, Foster Blodgett, Rufus Bullock, and Benjamin F. Conley, had already spurred the formation of the Georgia Equal Rights Association, a politically inspired organization of freedmen. Now, anticipating the upcoming elections for a state constitutional convention, they spelled out a program tailored to attract disaffected yeomen. At an Atlanta gathering in July dominated by the Radicals, the party approved the congressional plan of Reconstruction, assured "equal rights" for all citizens, and pledged support for relief, homestead laws, and free schools.

As early as the summer of 1866, Loyal Leagues—the organizational predecessors of the Republican party—had established a foothold in north Georgia, and by the winter of 1867 a conservative inhabitant of Marietta could groan that "Leagues are being formed all over the country. . . ." A few months thereafter, a Freedmen's Bureau agent in Carroll County announced that "The different Loyal Leagues of this county held a very large meeting" attended by "over one thousand of the loyal voters of the county." But the new registration laws and the campaign for constitutional reform gave the movement added momentum. Rallies in Cobb, Clayton, Campbell, Bartow, and Cherokee counties that August brought out voters of both races and ratified the Republican planks. As the editor of the Democratic Cartersville *Express* sneered, "Early Saturday morning last, our streets were alive with sable citizens—male and female—of African descent, and now and then a sprinkling of whites [for the Republican mass meeting]." Henry P. Farrow, a party leader from the Upcountry, felt "exceedingly encouraged by the reports of progress made in organizing the Union Republican party in North Georgia" and proclaimed that "the question of convention will carry by an overwhelming majority. . . ."

The November election bore out Farrow's assessment. A landslide of voters cast ballots in favor of the convention. But the turnout statewide amounted to just a hair over the requisite 50 percent of those eligible: many Democrats, particularly in the Black Belt, voiced their dissatisfaction with congressional Reconstruction simply by refusing to participate. And while native Republicans clearly commanded the ensuing convention, serious divisions within their own ranks soon came to the surface. The well-organized Radicals, standing squarely on the platform drawn up the previous summer and committed to black suffrage and officeholding, encountered resistance from a loose, though sizable, Moderate faction. With politics and political alignments in flux, many of the Moderates had joined the Republican party intending to exercise a conservative influence; others merely had axes to grind with the Augusta leadership. In the convention, they opposed debtor relief and homestead exemptions while expressing grave doubts about the extension of full political rights to blacks. Although the Radicals, with the aid of Democratic defectors from the Upcountry, managed to push through the relief and homestead measures, Moderates whittled down the homestead's coverage and then succeeded in blocking efforts to disfranchise former Confederates and to guarantee black officeholding. In this, the Moderates won the support of north Georgia delegates. Recognizing that a fight on the question of political participation would cost Upcountry votes, the Radicals gave in.

The dissension among Georgia Republicans had close parallels in other Southern states and, in an important sense, reflected a national party debacle. Sharing a commitment to the resurrection of a Union based on equality of opportunity under law, congressional Republicans nonetheless divided over how that vision should unfold and what its meaning should be. The Radical-Moderate schism emerged in debates over Southern policy as well as over issues of money, banking, and tariffs. Racism and a complementary concern about broadening party appeal did not alone shape the terrain of discussion; divergent notions about the dimensions of freedom and Union loomed throughout. The most far-reaching proposals for Reconstruction equated freedom with control over productive resources and saw economic independence as a prerequisite of political democracy in a smallholders' republic.

Thus, the preoccupation of some Radicals with breaking the back of the planter class and initiating land reform. Congressional Moderates, on the other hand, who increasingly held ideological sway, viewed freedom of contract in the marketplace as the foundation of a national economic system in which a revitalized cotton South would be a significant component. Linking moral and material progress, and convinced—by direct and indirect evidence—that the freedmen favored subsistence farming, they believed that black economic power could threaten national development. Hence they grew committed to the encouragement of entrepreneurial elements in rural and urban areas and gradually abandoned the party's Radical Southern wing.

If the split between Radicals and Moderates in Georgia had somewhat different features from the one in Congress, it also highlighted internal social tensions. The Radicals may have welcomed the accession of men like the former governor Joseph E. Brown, especially because of his Upcountry following, but Brown had his own ideas about party goals. Despite solemn pronouncements in support of the Republican platform, he, along with a handful of industrial promoters and a larger contingent of ex-Whigs who together formed the core of the Moderate faction, had greater interest in smooth reconciliation and economic growth than in social and political reform. Wishing to attract outside capital and diversify the economy, they pressed for a broader constituency than one of freedmen or poor Southerners generally. At the same time, the task of maintaining a coalition which included yeomen and blacks presented the Radicals with delicate problems that the constitutional convention did little to resolve.

The campaigns for ratification of the newly drawn constitution and for state and congressional offices, which occurred simultaneously during the late winter and early spring of 1868, displayed a clever short-run strategy that could promise only disastrous long-term consequences. Taking the support of blacks for granted and focusing their energies on the Upcountry, Republicans hoped to court yeomen by playing, at once, to class and racial resentments. An "Appeal by Republicans to the Poor White Men of Georgia," for example, proclaimed, "Be a man! Let the Slaveholding aristocracy no longer rule you," and counseled a vote "for a constitution which educates your children free of charge; relieves the poor debtor from his rich creditor; allows a liberal homestead for your families; and more than all, places you on a level with those who used to boast that for every slave they were entitled to three-fifths of a vote in congressional representation." The Republican Atlanta *New Era* similarly urged "poor men" to cast their ballots for the party promising "Relief, Homesteads, and Schools for the people," while the gubernatorial aspirant Rufus Bullock publicly styled himself the "workingman's candidate."

Coupled with this emphasis on the economic benefits of a Republican victory came assurances that "negro rule" was not in the offing. Party faithfuls had long admonished "the negroes to banish from their minds the idea of Confiscation," but spokesmen touring the Upcountry in 1868 took special care in raising the matter of the freedmen's potential political power. While Black Belt Republican leaders insisted that the new constitution protected the freedmen's right to hold office, their counterparts in the Upcountry issued a rather different message. Joseph Brown, in particular, who appeared at several north Georgia rallies, claimed that although the blacks were legally enfranchised, nowhere was their access to officeholding guaranteed.

Yet, however much such appeals to racism may have eased yeoman acceptance of the Republican program, they ultimately weakened the party's prospects by shattering the foundation of the very coalition that could make the program viable. The Republicans had a difficult enough row to hoe in creating a durable organizational structure. Accommodating as the Moderates might have been, the party retained its image as the agent of disruptive social change. If not in Georgia, then in Virginia, the Carolinas, and Maryland, "confiscation radicals"—overwhelmingly black—maintained a significant bearing and forced conservative elements to make good on the

issue of civil and political rights for the freedmen. "By the presence of armed soldiers and continued threats of confiscation and the halter," the Cartersville *Express* warned in 1868, the Republicans "design to awe us into submission." It was "the Radical party," the paper reminded its readers, "which associates the negro and the poor white man together as a class in common . . . break[ing] down all distinction between white and black . . . mingl[ing] the two together on terms of equality." For the Southern elite, "Black Republicanism" symbolized more than a new system of race relations; it symbolized a new system of class relations.

And so commenced the "reign of terror." Georgia Democrats were in disarray, unable to formulate a strategy capable of unifying their forces. But local leaders played a hand in enforcing a special kind of discipline. Vigilante violence, employed since the war in an effort to control black laborers and to even scores with white Unionists, took on new political dimensions. It was no accident that the Ku Klux Klan spread through much of the South in the spring of 1868, after a series of Republican victories the preceding November, and in Georgia the Klan's reputed leader was none other than John B. Gordon, the Democratic gubernatorial hopeful. Reports of the Klan's social composition varied, but few doubted that men of "property and standing" associated with Democratic or "Conservative" clubs figured prominently. As one Upcountry Republican asserted, "the order was gotten up and is kept up, as a rule, by the men who are disfranchised."

With the Reconstruction Acts stacking the electoral cards against them, Democrats launched a campaign of intimidation. "I learn that a secret Democratic meeting held . . . at [Cartersville] . . . resolved that there should be no more than one ballot box opened," a Freedmen's Bureau agent complained shortly before the national election of 1868, "and that every colored voter shall be challenged if he has not paid all his taxes his vote shall not be taken and that the white man shall not be challenged. . . ." In Jackson County another bureau agent found "that large bodyes of armed men are roving through the districts . . . halting and hailing all col'd men they see and compelling them [with] threats of violence . . . to sign . . . an oath that they will vote the democratic ticket in November 1868." "[N]o white radical or col'd man will be allowed to vote in the next president elections unless he vote the democratic ticket," the agent added.

Indeed, local Republican leaders and sympathizers of both races faced constant harassment, if not narrow brushes with death. "[T]he Rebs is working hard against the Rads in this place troping letter saying to leve or tak 300 Lashes on the Bare Back," one white Madison County denizen told the governor. "I received 2 to that effect sum time agow. . . ." Joseph Addison, a small white farmer from western Haralson County, suffered similar treatment from the "Ku Klux," being ordered to leave the area under threat of death. "I just think it was on account of politics—that it was because I was radical," he reckoned. J. R. Holliday of Jackson County, a self-proclaimed Union man, was administered a beating; Cherokee County's James McCoy saw his house burned to the ground. "[F]or some weeks previous to the election the leading members of the democratic party . . . resorted to every imaginable means to intimidate the poor white man, as well as the colored man," the Hart County craftsman J. A. Bowers testified in 1868. "These threats so much intimidated both white and colored voters that many republicans did not go out to the election."

That much of the politically inspired violence was directed against Upcountry blacks suggests the extent of the freedmen's response to the promise of Reconstruction. And, in an important way, their very self-activity and enthusiasm for politics, coinciding with the Republicans' racist appeal to white yeomen, created further obstacles to the establishment of an organized party. As early as 1865, J. T. Trowbridge found a large number of ex-slaves in Atlanta assembled, dressed in their "Sunday clothes," and engaged in an "animated discussion of their political rights." For Trowbridge the gathering seemed an "outdoor convention of the freed people." When the Reconstruction Acts extended the franchise to

blacks, those in the Upcountry registered in large numbers and wasted little time in displaying their partisanship. The Cartersville *Express* could note derisively that at a local Republican meeting "about two hundred negroes formed themselves in a line—*à la militaire*—marched through [the streets]—up and down and back and forth during the whole evening . . . and filled the air almost incessantly with yells and screams without significance, to the annoyance of all quiet population." Henry P. Farrow could feel relief when party rallies began drawing more than a smattering of whites. Twenty-four freedmen could send written protest of Klan abuse as members of the "Union Republican Party." In many Upcountry counties, blacks constituted the most significant Republican element.

Attracted to the Republican program of debtor relief yet circumscribed in their partisanship by deeply rooted political loyalties, the threat of physical retribution, and black assertiveness, yeoman whites seemed of divided minds. The results of the spring 1868 elections bore ample testimony to this condition. The Upcountry provided much needed support for the new constitution, which won ratification by a margin of about 18,000 votes; it provided somewhat less support for the gubernatorial candidate Rufus Bullock, who eked out a victory despite the disadvantages hampering Democrats; and it sent only a small delegation of Republicans to the state legislature. By a very conservative estimate, the Republican party could expect to receive the votes of between 15 and 25 percent of the eligible whites regionwide, and perhaps near majorities in counties with the fewest blacks or in relatively poor, almost exclusively white county districts. For this, party leaders might have felt some satisfaction. While these areas had been strongholds of the Democracy, economic issues appeared capable of cutting them loose from their political moorings. So, at least, the conservative Athens *Southern Watchman* surmised in explaining the Republican vote in northeastern Georgia: "[I]t was not Radicalism, but relief, that played mischief there. . . . Thousands of our people who, on a square fight between Democracy and Radicalism, would always vote the Dem-

ocratic ticket, were induced to vote for the constitution on account of relief, and also for the Radical candidates."

Had the Georgia Republicans pressed forward
with their social and economic program, they
might have been able to hold on to their new
Upcountry yeoman adherents and then win new
ones. They also might have begun to build some
bridges across racial lines. But this did not come
to pass. Propped by an unwieldy coalition of
groups with divergent interests and expectations,
Republicans quickly found themselves embroiled
in heated squabbles over patronage, black officeholding, and economic reforms. Though
achieving some success, the party never fully
delivered on its promises, and by the presidential
contest in the fall of 1868, under added strains of
violence and intimidation, its electoral strength
had eroded substantially. Ulysses S. Grant mustered a scant 32 percent of the ballots cast in the
state and fared even more poorly in the Upcountry, as the white vote shrank to a trickle. Some
Upcountry counties occasionally favored a Republican for the legislature through the early
1870s. Carroll County elected the Republican
Benjamin M. Long in 1872, although it appears
that his personal popularity in the traditionally
Democratic Carrollton district proved decisive.
As a political alternative capable of vying for or
maintaining state power in Georgia, however, the
Republican party was dead.

In 1869, a Cobb County Republican bitterly
assailed the emergence of "jo Brown and his
Satillites . . . in the first rank as leaders" of the
party, branding them as "traitors." His stinging
rebuke captured the disenchantment of Upcountry supporters who found the party's conservative
drift and the growing influence of industrial promoters hard to swallow. For other yeoman
whites, aversion to the Republican standard reflected different social antagonisms. Whatever
their economic tribulations and resentments toward Black Belt planters, they were small property holders who feared that Republican political
power might pose a threat to their way of life.
That Upcountry blacks quickly aligned with the
party of Emancipation only made that threat

seem more immediate. Planter concerns notwithstanding, the Jesse Wades, who hoped for radical
land reform, had a decidedly limited presence.
The new political departure held out by Reconstruction thus foundered on the rocks of class and
racial tensions. It would have another day as the
Upcountry was swept into the vortex of the cotton economy.

When, in early 1868, an effort to defeat the
Republican state constitution and gubernatorial
candidate spawned the formation of a "Conservative party" in Jackson County, members of the
local elite played a leading role. Especially prominent in the movement for "white unity" were
James E. Randolph, J. B. Silman, W. B. J. Hardman, W. C. Howard, J. D. Long, W. I. Pike, W.
F. Stark, J. H. Rhinehardt, and W. J. Colquitt.
What distinguished these men were their residences and occupations: Randolph was a merchant living in the county seat of Jefferson; Silman an attorney; Hardman a merchant and
doctor in the town of Harmony Grove; Howard
a Jefferson lawyer; Long a Jefferson physician;
Pike a Jefferson attorney; and Colquitt a planter
closely linked to Jefferson. Similar profiles could
be claimed by a number of Carroll County inhabitants actively organizing to meet the Republican
challenge in their locale. Joining R. L. Richards
and Oscar Reese, two attorneys from the town of
Carrollton, were the Carrollton merchants J. Y.
Blalock and J. W. Merrill, the Bowdon merchant
J. W. Adamson, the Villa Rica merchandiser S.
C. Candler, the editor of the Carrollton-based
weekly newspaper E. R. Sharp, and two large
landowners living within the Carrollton district,
M. R. Russell and J. L. Cobb.

The influence of town-associated interests on
Upcountry politics was not entirely new. Because
poor means of transportation and the demands of
family farming limited regular mobility, the inhabitants of and around the small antebellum
towns and villages had more immediate access to
county government and sundry political activities. The county seat served, at once, as the meeting place of the court and local officialdom, as the
marketplace, and as the staging ground for parti-

san assemblies, rallies, and conventions. The handful of professionals and storekeepers often appeared on party executive committees and grand juries. But during the prewar period the farming population held sway. Most county officeholders made their homes in the rural districts, and while substantial farmers and planters figured large in the political process, yeomen filled county posts in considerable numbers. If indicative of the relative unimportance of towns and commerce, this pattern also reflected a specific set of social relations.

The war and Emancipation began to change the local political landscape much as it did the social and economic. Although slavery did not have the significance in the Upcountry that it had in the Black Belt, its demise disrupted the region's economy and seemed to create widespread chaos nonetheless. Freedmen leaving the farms and plantations not only wandered in the countryside; they frequently headed to the towns, which at least offered some refuge from the drudgeries and close supervision of farm labor. Village residents complained of "unruly" blacks congregating in the streets and "grog shops" and disturbing the peace. Dr. Robert Battey of Rome bemoaned the influx of "idle negroes . . . lounging in town . . . in the prime of their manhood," who, he believed, sustained themselves by stealing. "[M]y dogs keep me awake at night running persons out of my garden and orchard," he grumbled. To men like Battey, the Republican party, greeted with unmistakable enthusiasm by the blacks, must have appeared an ominous threat. Small wonder that white townspeople joined with wealthy landowners to "redeem" their counties. The "Conservative party" in Jackson County, and similarly designated organizations elsewhere in the Upcountry, constituted bridges to a revitalized Democratic party; cries for "white unity" expressed the desire to stabilize social relations along broadly traditional lines.

Other war-related dislocations, coupled with methods of decision making, further contributed to the towns' growing influence in the Democratic party. Residents of rural districts, who normally had a difficult time attending to political

affairs, faced even greater obstacles as hardships on the home front turned their energies to the matter of basic subsistence as never before. And the system of candidate selection, involving a day-long meeting at the county seat rather than a primary, limited their impact on the party slate. But postwar economic developments proved perhaps the greatest spur, for they lent the towns a new importance and vitality. Railroad construction and the extension of commercial agriculture activated once sleepy villages and nurtured an elevated civic awareness among dwellers whose well-being increasingly depended on the cotton plant. In Carrollton, for example, storekeepers and professionals organized a Masonic lodge, a debating club, and an "Industrial, Scientific, and General Improvement Society," where they hoped "to foster honest and manly pride in the growth and prosperity of the entire county."

A greater town voice in party circles soon had more concrete manifestations. With Republican voting strength largely confined to blacks by the early 1870s, Democratic candidates for county office had a relatively easy time, and those candidates came increasingly from the town districts. Thus in 1873 almost half of the elected officials in Jackson County hailed from Jefferson alone, and by the end of the decade the county seat could boast a decided majority. When officeholders from Harmony Grove and the wealthiest rural district which bordered Jefferson are added, the proportion climbed from 50 per cent in 1873 to 63 percent in 1875, to 70 percent in 1877, to 85 percent in 1879, and finally to 100 percent in 1881. The trend was even more pronounced in Carroll County, where citizens of Carrollton saw a railroad arrive in 1872, after several years of eager promotion. The next year, seven of eight county officials came from the town's district, the remaining officer being an inhabitant of the wealthiest rural precinct. While an exception to the pattern appeared occasionally, town dominance of the county government continued through the 1870s and into the 1880s. In 1877, representatives from Carrollton occupied every county post, and it was a rare year when more than one official could claim a different residency (see Table 1).

Table 1
Residences of County Officers, Jackson and Carroll Counties, 1873–1881

| | Jackson County | | Carroll County | |
	No.	Percentage	No.	Percentage
Town district	13	44.8%	36	87.8%
Wealthiest rural district	7	24.1	1	2.4
Other rural districts	9	31.1	4	9.8
Total	29	100.0%	41	100.0%

The emergence of the towns as a political force in the Upcountry symbolized changing dimensions of power wider in scope. Town districts embraced not only urban incorporations but the immediately surrounding countryside as well, which often included some of the choicest, most highly improved land in the county. Real-estate values normally exceeded those for any other district. The local Democratic leadership mirrored the growing links between landed and commercial wealth. Consider an aggregation of prominent Jackson County Democrats listed by the Jefferson *Forest News* in 1876. Of thirty individuals, fully one-third were professionals, merchants, or members of families engaged in merchandising; the other two-thirds were large landowners, almost all of whom employed white or black farm hands. Indeed, their landholdings averaged nearly 450 acres. Some, like W. B. J. Hardman, combined occupations. Hardman sold goods in Harmony Grove while owning 950 acres close by. Leading Democrats from Carroll County had similar backgrounds.

Wealth had long commanded political power in the Upcountry, much as it had in the Black Belt. But the meaning of political power altered significantly as the region was absorbed into the cotton economy. If, during the antebellum period, small farmers had direct voices in local affairs, they usually did so by virtue of elite backing, and the more prestigious offices such as ordinary, sheriff, state representative, and state senator generally fell to the well-to-do. This democratically sanctioned structure of patronage and deference was made possible by a wide, though unequal, distribution of property and by the relative unimportance of exploitative relations between different groups of whites. What-

ever their political muscle, substantial farmers and planters simply did not hold much economic leverage over their poorer white neighbors. And their political success, aside from enhancing personal followings, served the interests of their settlements, districts, and counties.

As the expansion of commercial agriculture began to rupture white class relations, politics took on a new aspect. No easy road welcomed the system of credit and labor relations upon which postwar cotton culture boomed. State law and local custom protected the productive property of smallholders, limited the repercussions of debt, and often subordinated the will of the marketplace to the larger concerns of the community. Local officials and county courts played key roles in legitimizing and enforcing the "rules of the game." They adjudicated contracts and other financial obligations, assessed taxes for county services and projects, administered mortgaging, and carried out foreclosures and public sales. Postbellum landlords, merchants, and town professionals, whose livelihoods came to rest on the institutionalization of market relations, thus saw political preferment as a springboard to reshaping Upcountry society. It was not merely a self-conscious process of manipulation; they believed the commercialization of agriculture a vital stepping-stone to economic and moral progress. The town boosterism of the 1870s, seeking to promote railroad development and attract other capital, gave vivid expression to these sentiments. That "progress" increasingly jeopardized the welfare and independence of a growing segment of the white population turned political contention into far more than a matter of personal and local pride.

The political alliance of large landowners and

merchants was neither tension free nor complete. Social and economic changes that drew elements of the elite together also generated conflicts. The lien system fostered competition over control of the cotton crop and, thereby, over the surpluses produced by tenants and sharecroppers. Rich and poor farmers alike felt squeezed by the combination of inflated credit and declining commodity prices. If the burdens fell most heavily on yeomen and the landless, landlords were by no means immune from "financial distress." Appeals for the establishment of county agricultural societies, which resounded through the Upcountry during the late 1860s and early 1870s, cited the need for "cooperation among farmers" to defend their interests and blamed economic woes on the designs of "middlemen." "It was the duty [of farmers] to act in concert for their own protection," the president of the Gwinnett County Agricultural Society declared in 1873, reminding his audience that the "planters were the only class of laborers in the country who allowed purchasers to fix the price of their productions." Only "by such cooperation," a Floyd County landowner proclaimed, can we "protect ourselves against the exactions and speculations of middle men in commercial relations."

The Grange, which spread across the South beginning in 1872, gave these efforts their widest organizational expression. It planted its firmest foothold in the Black Belt, where the struggle between planters and merchants was most intense. Indeed, despite the accession of many small farmers, large landowners clearly dominated the order. Interest in cooperative purchasing and the "labor question," along with advocacy of a deflationary monetary policy, "pay as you go" buying and habits of thrift and industry reflected the outlook of a landed elite hoping to stabilize labor relations and curtail the inroads of merchandisers. Connections between the Grangers and conservative Democrats became apparent, if not openly admitted, and facilitated the passage of measures prohibiting traffic in produce at night and providing for more stringent enforcement of contracts.

Granges sprouted in the Upcountry within a short time after their appearance in the Black Belt. Floyd and Gwinnett counties saw initial gatherings in 1873, Bartow County did in 1874, and by 1875, organizations could be found throughout the region. Although yeomen were more conspicuous here, wealthy landowners again played the major role. "The new order called the Patrons of Husbandry have established a Grange . . . [and] among its members are found some of our best citizens," the Cartersville *Standard and Express* reported. The Gwinnett *Herald* also noted that the local Grange "is composed of many of our leading farmers. . . ." While railing against "speculators," "monopolists," and "all combinations operating against the farmers," Grangers insisted that they "make no war upon any body or class." Anticipating later activities of the Southern Farmers' Alliance, some Granges made trading arrangements with receptive mercantile firms. But for the most part, meetings involved little more than debates over various methods of agricultural improvement and speeches on the necessity of "raising supplies at home," leading small farmers to wonder whose interests were being served. One Carroll County yeoman interrupted a discussion on the "merits of guano" with the blast that "he didn't want any guano and while it might pay to use it, it wouldn't pay to buy it, and it caused production of too much surplus." The only extensive campaign waged by the Grange took on, not the local merchant, but "manufacturers and general agents of commercial fertilizers [who] have combined together in fixing the price . . . beyond remunerative value to the planter." Thus, the Jefferson *Forest News* could applaud the "wisdom . . . [of] the Grange movement," which it once feared would be controlled by "communistic influences."

Town elements continued to express concern that organizations like the Grange did, in fact, array "farmers against all other nonagricultural occupations, especially merchants," while numerous planters remained steadfast in their suspicion of all "middlemen," particularly as declining cotton prices made trying circumstances chronic. Yet, tensions eased over time as broader class interests began to mitigate the divisions and nagging quarrels among the Upcountry elites. Prosperous merchants amassed real estate and became landlords; large landowners employing tenants and croppers occasionally moved into the supply business. And whether or not such a "merger" was effected, both groups faced common problems of labor discipline and surplus extraction in a society in which social relations were increasingly mediated by the marketplace. If unity was never fully achieved, the rise of the towns as the leading force in the region's Democratic party symbolized the social and cultural metamorphosis of the newly aggressive ruling class.

Other developments made the association of political and economic power clearer for Upcountry Georgians by the mid-1870s. Leading Democrats, enlisting the aid of county newspapers which sprang up over the region during the decade, agitated for the abolition of usury laws and for a state constitutional convention primarily to reform the homestead statute. "[A] man has the same right to put a price upon his money that he has to price his horse or his lands," they charged; the "inviolability of contracts" must be assured, they announced. Little wonder that disaffection from the Democratic party focused, in part, on such issues. As one independently inclined Floyd County inhabitant warned, if the usury laws and homestead exemption were repealed, "the producing classes" would be "shaved." "The producing classes must have their work tools; they must have something of real and personal property to produce," he cried. "Their wives and children must know in the future, as they have in the past, what 'home' means."

Local issues also began to heighten awareness of the dimensions of political power. In 1878 the Jackson County grand jury recommended construction of a new courthouse in Jefferson to be funded by a bond issue. The Jefferson *Forest News* and other town interests threw their weight behind the proposal, only to be greeted by staunch popular resistance. Some objected to the method of finance, others to the location, but most questioned the entire undertaking. "We

have been taught that the people were their own rulers . . . but [the Jefferson ring] has dictated contrary to the wishes of 2/3 of the people, or perhaps more, that we shall build a new courthouse," one opponent protested, adding that "the people of Jackson do not wish to be taxed . . . for the benefit of Jefferson." Another like-minded spokesman claimed that "the people do not, as a mass, like the way they were forced into the matter, altogether against their wishes; so they feel hurt and that their rights have been invaded and trampled upon." At a time when farmers increasingly fell under the burden of debt and encumbrance and increasingly faced the specter of the auction block, the courthouse seemed to embody the very forces of distress, and they joined to hand the project a stiff rebuke when it came to a vote. Only the Jefferson district cast a majority of favorable ballots. Most Upcountry counties witnessed a similar contest on various occasions during the next decade.

The charge of "ring rule" was familiar to the region's politics. Antebellum Democrats, chafing under the Black Belt's dominance in party circles, had blamed the intrigues of, say, the Athens "clique." But in the 1870s the cry had a new immediacy and reflected new conditions. No longer was an abstract principle—fear of the potential consequences of excessive influence and power brought home by the institution of slavery—at issue. No longer were social tensions and political battles drawn primarily along regional lines. Emancipation, the expansion of commercial agriculture, and the development of market relations of production and exchange in the postwar Upcountry transformed the nature and reality of power and conflict: they became more localized, more direct, and arrayed different social groups. The rumblings of discontent, signaled by complaints of "ring rule," gave notice that "white unity" and the "solid South" would be long in coming.

The failure of the Southern Republican party to marshal a constituency sufficiently large to vie for political power without the assistance of federal authorities left a vacuum that Democrats could fill only with difficulty. The Republicans, of course, maintained a distinct presence well after Reconstruction, as freedmen and Mountain whites helped the party muster a substantial percentage of the vote in many states. Hopes of attracting former Whigs on a program of economic development, though, proved at best short-lived. Scattered Republican support among wealthy planters faded as freedmen and yeoman whites pressed for political and economic reforms with the sympathies and aid of congressional Radicals. By the time that a "union of the propertied" became national Republican policy, most of these Whiggish elements had left the fold. Yet the Democracy did not afford them the most comfortable of homes. Partisan loyalties died hard, and while the threat of radical social change encouraged ex-Whigs to unite with their old adversaries under the Democratic banner and to reap more than their share of political offices, the coalition was uneasy.

Democratic troubles were caused by more than the Whig accession. Real divisions among Southern elites over what the postwar world would be like and who would command it also provoked party tensions. Black Belt landlords and merchants battled for control of the black labor force; aspiring industrialists struggled with planters over the issues of economic diversification and agricultural reform—and all the jousting took place, virtually by necessity, within Democratic ranks. To these conflicts can be added the long-standing animosities between plantation and non-plantation regions that often factionalized the Democracy of the antebellum era. The Southern version of the "Great Barbecue" only made matters worse. If Redemption toppled the Radical regimes, it did not end the most egregious features of financial corruption—however exaggerated by Southern apologists—that marred Republican rule. Joseph Brown, who returned to the Democrats, along with John B. Gordon and Alfred H. Colquitt, together composing Georgia's "Bourbon Triumvirate," found healthy profits in political machinations. Conservatives like Robert Toombs could but reel in disgust at men seeking to live off rather than for politics. "There is no

principle involved in politics since the war," a planter of similar instincts wrote. "It is only a contest between the *ins* and the *outs* for place and power for the privilege and opportunity to rob the U.S. treasury." And so it was for those who found principle less imposing and grew frustrated when unable to share the spoils.

By the early 1870s, these varied strands of discontent saw political manifestation in a loosely coordinated challenge of Independents. Complaining, in particular, of "packed" nominating conventions which excluded the public and concentrated power in the hands of a few "professional politicians," candidates in several congressional districts bolted the Democratic party and ran independently. Perhaps most prominent among them was William H. Felton, a well-to-do farmer and Methodist minister residing in Bartow County, who had previously aligned with the Whigs. Following a heated six-way battle for the northwestern Seventh District congressional nomination in 1874, he struck off on his own, even declining the promise of a second contest if he would remain faithful. Three years later the northeastern Ninth District witnessed a similar showdown when Emory Speer took on the Democratic nominee Hiram W. Bell for the congressional seat vacated by Benjamin H. Hill. Speer, much like Felton, cited "the so-called Congressional conventions" as "unjust and unfair . . . a fraud on [the people's] rights—which cheats them of their preference and serves, year to year, to perpetuate the political power of the district in the hands of a ring of politicians."

Felton and Speer, among others, availed themselves of an Independentism that first emerged in local politics. No clear regional lines defined its impact, but the Upcountry seemed especially active. When, in 1872, the Democratic convention in Jackson County selected T. C. Williams for the state legislature, a disappointed Green R. Duke bolted. A candidate for ordinary in Cherokee County followed a similar tack that same year when informed that the party nomination "was a family concern." In Bartow County, another aspiring ordinary charted an Independent route, calling the local convention "anti-Democratic."

"I concluded to submit my case to the Democracy of the people rather than the oligarchy of sixty men," he explained. A former Republican in Carroll County, proclaiming that he had "lived in Carroll 54 years and [was] fully identified with the people of the county," sought a legislative seat as an Independent in 1876.

Self-righteousness and political purity, to be sure, were often the garbs of self-aggrandizement. For men facing bleak prospects on the farm, political preferment at least offered a steady income, if not more lucrative rewards. A veritable flood of office-seekers appeared in the years after Reconstruction. "It has been said that Carroll has no less than a dozen candidates for the [legislative] nomination," one resident moaned in 1872, "each one feeling called not by his fellow citizens, but by himself. . . ." The Cartersville *Standard and Express* found that local elections in neighboring Cherokee County caused a great "state of excitation" because of the "many candidates in the field." "The county is overrun with candidates, some 12 or 14 for the legislature, 8 or 10 for sheriff, 6 or 8 for tax collector, all trying to reach soft places," Floyd County's John Dent scowled.

Yet, if mere office seeking or factional disputes initially led aspiring politicians down the Independence road, their candidacies soon tapped developing social antagonisms and growing resentments of the countryside toward the towns. One Felton supporter explained his preference by noting that all members of Georgia's congressional delegation were lawyers while Felton stood "as an admirable representative of the farmers." Charging that "After the war a set of cunning politicians got into power when honest men's hands were tied," another north Georgian proclaimed that Felton "does not belong to the legal fraternity . . . [but] stands by the farmer, the producer." An independently oriented Carroll County denizen attributed the Democratic congressional nomination in the Fourth District to "a few little plug hat fellows [who] got together in the towns and manipulated the thing. The great mass of the people, the wool hat boys had nothing to do with it." "This was not democracy but aristocracy," he thundered. In Bartow

County, the Democratic Cartersville *Express* bore the accusation of being the "organ of the cotton ring," while in Floyd County a disgruntled resident later declared that "by heavy taxation" and other "unjust burdens . . . Rome rule[d] the county."

Conservative ex-Whigs of the Toombs-Stephens ilk may have looked favorably upon Independentism as the true representative of "Democratic principles" and "local government" against centralizing tendencies and the power of "gigantic corporations." They spoke for planters who feared the designs of the Democratic party's industrial wing and saw the decentralization of wealth and authority as their best means for securing control of the black labor force. Indeed, numerous Independents took occasion to announce their ultimate fealty to what they believed proper Democratic doctrine. But in the Upcountry, at least, an emerging constituency of small producers disenchanted with the social relations and economic consequences of commercial agriculture pushed party bolters leftward.

The Independent career of William Felton, who represented a large section of Georgia's Upcountry, is a case in point. Striking out in opposition to the nominating process controlled by the "Atlanta ring," Felton initially evinced a clear conservatism. In a speech before the Cartersville Grange, he bemoaned "the senseless requirements of [Northern] Trades' Unions" in "demanding of the national and municipal governments 'work or bread' " and in "asserting their right to reduce their hours of labor without a corresponding reduction of wages." "It is the old leaven of Red Republicanism and Constitutionalism; of Internationalism," he cried, praising instead the farmers as the vanguard "of the conservative and Christian hosts." Yet, once in public office, he responded to popular sentiment by pressing for currency and banking reform, railroad regulation, an end to the poll tax, and the abolition of the convict-lease system. Corresponding with the Georgia Greenbacker Ben E. Green, Felton denounced a "privileged class of creditors" and maintained that "Congress shall provide . . . money adequate to the full employment of labor, the equitable distribution of its produce, and the requirements of business, fixing a minimum amount per capita."

Local Independents also sought to ride a growing tide of popular unrest. One aspirant for county office, accusing the incumbent of financial mismanagement, blamed the situation on "a class of men, mostly in town," and pledged "to be economical with the people's money . . . [and] to do exact justice to all without regard to riches or poverty, race or color. . . ." A Floyd County Independent urged limitations on the public debt and on state liability for corporations, while railing against efforts to abolish usury laws and the homestead. And in Carroll County, a candidate for the legislature exclaimed that "there are little if any differences between the two national parties on major issues," and favored "correcting the abuses existing in the state government like exempting a large amount of property over $100,-000 from taxation while taxing the poor heavily."

Yet for Democrats, this issue orientation proved perhaps less disconcerting than did other potential ramifications of the Independent challenge. Loyal partisans occasionally admitted that "the Democratic party in the state has grown too big to accommodate all the aspirants for office," that "there are real grievances," and that reform in nominating procedures was necessary. But they counseled fidelity to the party standard for fear that a divided vote would permit a Republican victory. "There is an apprehension, founded upon what appears to be sound reason and common sense," the Jefferson *Forest News* warned, "that the hope of the Republican party . . . lies in what is called the Independent movement." The chairman of the Democratic executive committee in the northeastern Ninth Congressional District fretfully issued a similar forecast: "Our enemies are organizing. . . . The Radical party [intends] . . . to support Independent candidates . . . with a view of dividing the solid South, increasing their numbers in Congress and thus controlling the General Government." "Independent Democracy in the South must inevitably lead to Republicanism," the fiery Benjamin Hill declared. As he saw it, "no Independent can get the

Republican support . . . without giving himself over absolutely, definitely, and finally to that party." Independentism, in short, marked "an attempt to Africanize the South. . . ."

Both the Republican party's stance toward the Independents and the Independents' stance toward the Republicans remained ambiguous for much of the 1870s. Still hopeful of maintaining at least a share of political power in the state, many Republicans were reluctant to jettison their own ticket in favor of Independent candidates whose loyalties were often unclear. And numerous Independents, either serious in styling themselves true Democrats or fearful that a coalition with Republicans would cost votes, approached the matter with great caution, if at all. After suffering a sound beating in the elections of 1876, the Republican state leadership recommended "support for Independent candidates . . . in those districts in which it is thought best," but not until 1881 were formal steps taken. In a confidential letter to William Felton, Henry P. Farrow suggested "getting up a political combination in Georgia to run through 1884" with the objects of securing "the recognition of the right element of Republicanism in Georgia by the powers that be in Washington . . . [and] the recognition of the Independents," and of promoting Felton's "interests as the leader of the Independents to whom we must look for success." Shortly thereafter, Farrow, Felton, and a small group of other Republicans and Independents met in Atlanta and drew up an agreement based on a platform calling for "a free ballot and a fair count," repeal of internal-revenue laws, internal improvements, redemption of silver and greenbacks, state-supported free public schools, and an end to "monopolies" and the convict-lease system.

On the local level, however, Republicans and Independents often made a separate peace earlier on. While denying "private" arrangements with the powerful Atlanta faction, Felton hoped to attract Republican votes from the first—and with obvious success. One Floyd County Democrat sneered in 1876 that "the Radical of the District, Major Zack Hargrove of Rome made a political speech at Cave Spring—his audience was composed of 30 niggers and all the Feltonites of the village. To the Niggers he extolled Grant and his administration to the skies . . . and to his white audience he remarked [that] . . . Felton was his man." Indeed, this Democrat blamed Felton's initial victory in 1874 on the support "of the Radicals and niggers." Elsewhere in the Upcountry similar, though perhaps more tentative, developments unfolded. In the Ninth Congressional District race for a vacated seat in 1877, a Democrat, a Republican, and an Independent entered the field, with success falling to the Democrat by a small margin. The next year, district Republicans chose not to put up a candidate, and the Independent emerged triumphant. In Carroll County a Republican ran for the state legislature under the banner of Independentism.

Men like Felton may have dismissed the charge that their Independent political course threatened to "Africanize" the state, but courting Republicans in the Upcountry, much as in the Black Belt, meant repudiating the plea for "white unity." For while the Republicans retained a small white constituency, by the mid-1870s the party's rank and file was overwhelmingly black. Independent overtures testified to the persistence of black political participation and mobilization. Even under intimidation, the region's blacks continued to go to the polls. As one Floyd County landlord could grumble in 1876, "all business suspended for the election today, a full nigger vote cast in the county. . . ." Such resolve emanated from developing Afro-American communities that provided networks for mutual interaction, organization, and protection. Building upon customs and institutions forged under slavery, Upcountry blacks strengthened bonds among themselves and, in so doing, became a force to be reckoned with, however outnumbered they were in the population as a whole.

It was an impressive achievement and one that renders inappropriate the categorical dualities of "accommodation" or "resistance," "integration" or "racial solidarity," political or apolitical. The most common manifestations of community life did, to be sure, seem to mark a turn inward, a defensiveness, a shift away from political con-

frontation to the cultivation of racial pride and self-help after Reconstruction: social gatherings and celebrations, religious meetings, musical groups, fire companies, and educational associations. But these were never fully divorced from, and were often thoroughly infused with, politics. When, for example, Paulding County blacks "enjoyed a grand festival" one May, they not only feasted and heard two brass bands; they also listened to "plenty of speeches." A large camp meeting of Floyd County blacks in 1873 served, according to the landlord John Dent, as both a spiritual convocation and a forum to discuss "getting higher wages—more privileges—and greater liberties." Blacks in Jackson County established seventeen schools for their children during the 1870s while pressing the state government for increased funding.

Such activities were the foundation of a more formal political structure which sought to link racial improvement with the acquisition of full citizenship rights. Despite the violence of Redemption and the ascendancy of the "lily-white" faction in what was left of the state Republican party, Upcountry blacks kept local Republican organization alive. Under the direction of their own county executive committees, they held meetings, sent delegates to state party conventions, and occasionally ran black candidates for local office. In this way, black leaders mitigated political demoralization, drew black voters to the polls, and rallied opposition to white discrimination and injustice. Thus, "a large crowd of colored citizens of [Jackson] county" could gather at the courthouse one afternoon to protest their exclusion from grand juries. "Their intention," the local paper reported, "was to ask humbly and respectfully for the right which they thought they were entitled to enjoy as much as any other privilege of citizenship." Elsewhere blacks called for reform of the convict-lease system, more effective support for black education, and elimination of the new poll tax.

The Independents did little to address the specific concerns and grievances of the black community. They hardly spoke for equality between the races, nor did they pledge many political favors. Yet, with the fortunes of Upcountry Republicans in unmistakable decline and with state patronage in the hands of the "lily-white" faction, the Independent offer of a "free ballot and a fair count" served as an attractive alternative to Democratic attacks on black political rights. Felton's initial campaign, in fact, drew an enthusiastic response. "The negroes assembled [in Cartersville] today," the Atlanta *Daily Herald* reported. "The notorious negro Crumley . . . made a bitter speech against [Felton's Democratic opponent], denouncing him as the candidate of an odious party of outrages and Ku Kluxism . . . [and] spoke strongly in favor of Dr. Felton." Two years later, a disconcerted Floyd County Democrat found that local blacks cast ballots in large numbers "for Hays, Wheeler, and Felton." In 1878, the Gwinnett *Herald* attributed the defeat of the Democratic nominee in the Ninth Congressional District to "overconfidence," lack of "organization," and "underrating the strength of the opposition." "We did not count on the negro vote going solid," the paper explained, "but . . . nine-tenths of them voted the Independent ticket."

Black support for Independent candidates formed part of a developing political alignment that Radical Republicans hoped to forge for their own benefit and that would become more apparent in the 1880s and 1890s. The Upcountry long displayed an independent spirit in state politics, whether in the antebellum Democratic party, in the secession crisis, or during the Civil War. Thus, it is not surprising that the region proved receptive to Democratic bolters thereafter. William Felton fared well from the beginning, winning a narrow victory in 1874, when he carried six of eight Upcountry counties by overwhelming majorities. Reelection came more easily in 1876, and in 1878 he won in every Upcountry county in the district, as well as in two Mountain counties previously in the Democratic camp. The Independent Emory Speer got off to a slower start in the northeastern Ninth District, losing to the Democrat in a three-way race for a vacated congressional seat in 1877. But the next year, when the Republican dropped out, Speer turned the tables in a closely fought contest.

Election returns from districts within Upcountry counties, however, reveal emerging divisions between town and countryside and between rich and poor farmers. In Gwinnett County, for example, the Democratic congressional candidate rolled up sizable majorities in the three town districts and in two of the wealthier rural districts in 1878; the Independent, on the other hand, swept six of the nine remaining rural districts, including most of the poorest by measure of per capita wealth. A similar, though somewhat less distinct, trend was evident in Jackson County that same year. The Democrat carried the town and five of the rural districts, including the more well-to-do. The Independent won three rural districts, two of which were among the poorest in the county (see Table 2). In Carroll County, the Independent candidate for the Fourth Congressional District received the support of four relatively poor rural districts while sustaining a sound defeat elsewhere.

These results, to be sure, failed to demonstrate a clear-cut convergence of social and political antagonisms. Some poor rural precincts remained within the Democratic fold, while wealthier counterparts occasionally threw their support to Independents. Partisan loyalties did not unravel easily; small farmers, tenants, and croppers of both races might face the coercion of merchants and landlords; and many voters continued to follow the lead of well-known political figures. Still, Democratic hegemony appeared to be shaken in the countryside. In 1878 roughly half of the voters in all rural districts cast ballots for Independent congressional candidates in Gwinnett and Jackson counties. In 1880 well over half chose the Independent alternative. As poor white farmers increasingly joined blacks in protest at the ballot box, a new political day seemed to be dawning in Georgia and other Southern states.

The Democrats recognized as much, resorting to the tactics of fraud and intimidation that proved successful during Reconstruction. If men like Felton came under fierce verbal assault, Independent constituents frequently encountered more trying episodes. One Feltonite complained

Table 2
District Voting Returns in Congressional Races, Gwinnett and Jackson Counties, 1878

District	Gwinnett County Per capita* wealth	Dem.	Ind.	District	Jackson County Per capita* wealth	Dem.	Ind.
Town Dist.:				*Town Dist.:*			
Lawrenceville	$1,436	401	364	Jefferson	$977	464	404
Duluth	973	101	52	Harmony Grove	1,090	183	147
Norcross	?	103	33	Maysville	619	67	20
Rural Dist.:				*Rural Dist.:*			
Hog Mountain	649	14	25	Clarksboro	557	86	48
Bay Creek	792	24	21	Newtown	622	150	149
Cates	692	17	49	Miller	640	50	0
Martins	779	27	54	Cunningham	497	37	14
Rockbridge	653	51	33	Randolph	661	83	117
Harbins	614	23	0	House	646	83	82
Ben Smith	522	81	55	Chandler	530	51	71
Berkshire	774	81	9	Santafe	397	28	37
Buford	?	114	128	Total		1,282	1,088
Cains	545	36	38				
Suwanee	?	31	85				
Total		1,104	946				

*Total wealth divided by total number of persons on tax rolls.

of several forms of electoral corruption practiced by local Democrats: "whiskey brought in and distributed, illegal voting, closing polls early, and voting all the negroes." Carroll County denizens spoke of widespread "bulldozing," and in the eastern Upcountry, Democrats waged a multisided campaign to unseat Emory Speer. "Candler clubs [the Democratic candidate] were organized all over the district, nightly meetings were held, committeemen traveled through the country for weeks and money was spent freely," the Independent Gainesville *Southron* charged. "Banners were painted, voting places were hung with all sorts of devises, mottoes, and bulldozing insults. . . . Three clubs took possession of the polls here, at Athens, Madison, Jefferson, and Toccoa . . . and every Speer man knows it was difficult to get to the polls and back without being insulted. . . ." For other Democrats, electoral "reform" promised the best solution to political unrest. It was no accident that the new state constitution, written under Democratic auspices in 1877, included a retroactive poll tax and stiffer residency requirements for voting; Felton, along with numerous local Independents, had already tri-

umphed over Democratic "rings." And additional measures soon merited consideration. "There is a good deal of talk among some of the papers about a general registration law . . . [which] would undoubtedly have a good effect towards purifying the ballot box," the Carroll County *Times* sympathetically reported.

The Democratic counterattack wore heavily on the Independents, who never developed an organized party or coherent program to unify and discipline favorably inclined voters. This failure, in part, attested to the divergent motivations of Independent politicians, many of whom expected to return to the Democratic house. Attempting to lure Alexander Stephens into the gubernatorial race in 1882 hardly represented a radical initiative, and even the formal Independent-Republican coalition of 1881, which issued a platform, came from the efforts of a handful of political leaders unable to command the clear loyalties of a mass following. Furthermore, those Independents hoping to forge a new party faced a formidable task in organizing small farmers, whose collective experiences within settlements fostered a profound localism and whose racism continued to hamper an essential political alliance. Thus, by the early 1880s, Democrats had recaptured the two Upcountry congressional seats and the Independents were generally in disarray.

Yet the spirit of Independentism lived on in the Upcountry. Democratic congressional nominees still had to weather challenges capable of amassing substantial votes, and numerous counties, including Jackson, Carroll, Heard, Bartow, Cherokee, and Campbell, sent an occasional Independent to the state legislature. More than this, the Independent upsurge, whatever its origins, began to offer a political focus for rising social antagonisms; divisions within the postbellum elite created a significant opening for movements from below. Though it may not have been of the radical, biracial brand that the tenant farmer Jesse Wade espoused, political insurgency expressed developing class conflicts which threatened to bridge the racial chasm. Trapped in a cycle of indebtedness and ultimate dispossession, yeoman landholders increasingly shared the fate of the region's blacks. Joseph Brown could only agree with his fellow Democrat L. N. Trammell's bleak assessment "of the condition of popular sentiment." "There is a growing feeling among our people of opposition to all accumulation of capital," Brown answered him in 1883. "There is an agrarian tendency among our people." Events of the 1880s in the Georgia Upcountry would give ample credence to Brown's forecast.

3

THE CHINESE LINK
A CONTINENT AND A NATION

JACK CHEN

It is an historical commonplace that America is a nation of immigrants. From the original settlers of Jamestown in 1607 to the Hispanic and Asian immigrants of the 1980s new Americans have loomed large in the national experience. But while immigration has always played an important role American life, its impact was perhaps greatest during America's industrial revolution of the nineteenth century. From the 1820s, when 100,000 men, women, and children entered the United States, to the first decade of the twentieth century, when 8.2 million landed on American shores, more than 33 million immigrants came to the United States and helped build it into the world's premier industrial power.

Among these millions of immigrants, one group has received scant attention— the Chinese peasants, almost entirely males, who came to America as contract laborers to provide agricultural labor for California's central valley and to build railroads and levees in the West. Unlike European immigrants who arrived as free men and women in New York and other eastern cities, the Chinese who landed in San Francisco were bound to the mercantile companies that acted as labor contractors and had advanced them the cost of their fare. Under this contract system, one of the Six Companies in San Francisco negotiated with an employer and agreed to provide workers at an agreed-upon rate. The Companies were then responsible for the supply, supervision, and discipline of the contract laborers.

As Jack Chen shows in this essay, these Chinese contract laborers braved the harshest of conditions to fulfill their contract to build America's first transcontinental railroad. Employing skills in excavation and the use of explosives which they had brought from China, these Chinese workingmen carved a path through the solid granite of the Sierra Nevada range that opened the West to the remainder of the nation.

How does the racial discrimination experienced by the Chinese compare with that experienced by the freedmen of Promised Land, discussed by Elizabeth Bethel in Reading 1? Do you think the Chinese workingmen would have agreed with William Haywood's radicalism as presented by Melvyn Dubofsky in Reading 10?

The expansion of the railroad system in the United States was astonishingly swift. England had pioneered the building of railways and for a time was the acknowledged leader in the field, but from the moment the first locomotive was imported into the United States in 1829 the far-sighted saw railways as the obvious solution for transport across the vast spaces of the American continent. By 1850, 9,000 miles of rails had been laid in the eastern states and up to the Mississippi. The California Gold Rush and the opening of the American West made talk about a transcontinental line more urgent. As too often happens, war spurred the realization of this project.

The West was won. California was a rich and influential state, but a wide unsettled belt of desert, plain, and mountains, separated it and Oregon from the rest of the states. As the economic separation of North and South showed, this situation was fraught with danger. It could lead to a political rift. In 1860, it was cheaper and quicker to reach San Francisco from Canton in China—a sixty-day voyage by sea—than from the Missouri River, six months away by wagon train. The urgent need was to link California firmly with the industrialized eastern states and their 30,000 miles of railways. A railway would cut the journey to a week. The threat of civil war loomed larger between North and South over the slavery issue. Abraham Lincoln's Republican administration saw a northern transcontinental railway as a means to outflank the South by drawing the western states closer to the North. In 1862, Congress voted funds to build the 2,500-mile-long railway. It required enormous resourcefulness and determination to get this giant project off the drawing boards. Not much imagination was required to see its necessity, but the actual building presented daunting difficulties. It was calculated that its cost would mount to $100 million, double the federal budget of 1861.

It was Theodore Judah, described by his contemporaries as "Pacific Railroad Crazy," who began to give substance to the dream. An eastern engineer who had come west to build the short Sacramento Valley Railroad, he undertook a preliminary survey and reported that he had found a feasible route crossing the Sierra by way of Dutch Flat. But the mainly small investors who supported his efforts could not carry through the whole immense undertaking. With rumors of civil war between North and South, San Francisco capitalists, mostly Southerners, boycotted the scheme as a northern plot, and pressed for a southern route. Then the Big Four, Sacramento merchants, took up the challenge: Leland Stanford as president, C. P. Huntington as vice-president, Mark Hopkins as treasurer, and Charles Crocker, in charge of construction, formed the Central Pacific Railway Company. Judah was elbowed out.

The Big Four came as gold seekers in 1849 or soon after but found that there was more money to be made in storekeeping than in scrabbling in the rocks in the mountains. As Republicans, they held the state for the Union against the secessionists. Leland Stanford, the first president of the Central Pacific, was also the first Republican governor of California.

The beginnings were not auspicious. The Union Pacific was building from Omaha in the East over the plains to the Rockies, but supplies had to come in by water or wagon because the railways had not yet reached Omaha. The Civil War now raged and manpower, materials and funds were hard to get. The Indians were still contesting invasion of their lands. By 1864, however, with the Civil War ending, these problems were solved. The UP hired Civil War veterans, Irish immigrants fleeing famine and even Indian women, and the line began to move westward.

The Central Pacific, building eastward from Sacramento, had broken ground on January 8, 1863, but in 1864, beset by money and labor problems, it had built only thirty-one miles of track. It had an even more intractable manpower problem than the UP. California was sparsely populated, and the gold mines, homesteading, and other lucrative employments offered stiff competition for labor. Brought to the railhead, three out of every five men quit immediately and took off for the better prospects of the new Nevada silver strikes. Even Charles Crocker, boss of construction and raging like a mad bull in the railway camps, could not control them. In the winter of 1864, the company had only 600 men working on the line when it had advertised for 5,000. Up to then, only white labor had been recruited and California white labor was still motivated by the Gold Rush syndrome. They wanted quick wealth, not hard, regimented railway work. After two years only fifty miles of track had been laid.

James Strobridge, superintendent of construction, testified to the 1876 Joint Congressional Committee on Chinese Immigration: "[These] were unsteady men, unreliable. Some would not go to work at all. . . . Some would stay until pay day, get a little money, get drunk and clear out." Something drastic had to be done.

In 1858, fifty Chinese had helped to build the California Central Railroad from Sacramento to Marysville. In 1860, Chinese were working on the San Jose Railway and giving a good account of themselves, so it is surprising that there was so much hesitation about employing them on the Central Pacific's western end of the first transcontinental railway. Faced with a growing crisis of no work done and mounting costs, Crocker suggested hiring Chinese. Strobridge strongly objected: "I will not boss Chinese. I don't think they could build a railroad." Leland Stanford was also reluctant. He had advocated exclusion of the Chinese from California and was embarrassed to reverse himself. Crocker, Huntington, Hopkins, and Stanford, the "Big Four" of the Central Pacific, were all merchants in hardware, dried goods, and groceries in the little town of Sacramento. Originally, they knew nothing about railroad building, but they were astute and hard-headed businessmen. Crocker was insistent. Wasted time was wasted money. The CP's need for labor was critical. The men they already had were threatening a strike. Finally fifty Chinese were hired for a trial.

Building the Transcontinental Railroad

In February 1865, they marched up in self-formed gangs of twelve to twenty men with their own supplies and cooks for each mess. They ate a meal of rice and dried cuttlefish, washed and slept, and early next morning were ready for work filling dump carts. Their discipline and grading—preparing the ground for track laying—delighted Strobridge. Soon fifty more were hired, and finally some 15,000 had been put on the payroll. Crocker was enthusiastic: "They prove nearly equal to white men in the amount of labor they perform, and are much more reliable. No danger of strikes among them. We are training them to all kinds of labor: blasting, driving horses, handling rock as well as pick and shovel." Countering Strobridge's argument that the Chinese were "not masons," Crocker pointed out that the race that built the Great Wall could certainly build a railroad culvert. Up on the Donner Pass today the fine stonework embankments built by the Chinese are serving well after a hundred years.

Charles Nordhoff, an acute observer, reports Strobridge telling him, "[The Chinese] learn all parts of the work easily." Nordhoff says he saw them "employed on every kind of work. . . . They do not drink, fight or strike; they do gamble, if it is not prevented; and it is always said of them that they are very cleanly in their habits. It is the custom, among them, after they have had their suppers every evening, to bathe with the help of small tubs. I doubt if the white laborers do as much." As well he might. Well-run boarding-houses in California in those days proudly advertised that they provided guests with a weekly bath.

Their wages at the start were $28 a month (twenty-six working days), and they furnished all their own food, cooking utensils, and tents. The headman of each gang, or sometimes an American employed as clerk by them received all the wages and handed them out to the members of the work gang according to what had been earned. "Competent and wonderfully effective because tireless and unremitting in their industry," they worked from sun-up to sun-down.

All observers remarked on the frugality of the Chinese. This was not surprising in view of the fact that, with a strong sense of filial duty, they came to America in order to save money and return as soon as possible to their homes and families in China. So they usually dressed poorly, and their dwellings were of the simplest. However, they ate well: rice and vermicelli (noodles) garnished with meats and vegetables; fish, dried oysters, cuttlefish, bacon and pork, and chicken on holidays, abalone meat, five kinds of dried vegetables, bamboo shoots, sea-weed, salted cabbage, and mushroom, four kinds of dried fruit, and peanut oil and tea. This diet shows a considerable degree of sophistication and balance compared to the beef, beans, potatoes, bread, and butter of the white laborers. Other supplies were purchased from the shop maintained by a Chinese merchant contractor in one of the railway cars that followed them as they carried the railway line forward. Here they could buy pipes, tobacco, bowls, chopsticks, lamps, Chinese-style shoes of cotton with soft cotton soles, and ready-made clothing imported from China.

On Sundays, they rested, did their washing, and gambled. They were prone to argue noisily, but did not become besotted with whiskey and make themselves unfit for work on Monday. Their sobriety was much appreciated by their employers.

Curtis, the engineer in charge, described them as "the best roadbuilders in the world." The once skeptical Strobridge, a smart, pushing Irishman, also now pronounced them "the best in the world." Leland Stanford described them in a report on October 10, 1865, to Andrew Johnson:

> As a class, they are quiet, peaceable, patient, industrious, and economical. More prudent and economical [than white laborers] they are contented with less wages. We find them organized for mutual aid and assistance. Without them, it would be impossible to complete the western portion of this great national enterprise within the time required by the Act of Congress.

Crocker testified before the congressional committee that "if we found that we were in a hurry for a job of work, it was better to put on Chinese at once." All these men had originally resisted the employment of Chinese on the railway.

Four-fifths of the grading labor from Sacramento to Ogden was done by Chinese. In a couple of years more, of 13,500 workers on the payroll 12,000 were Chinese. They were nicknamed "Crocker's Pets."

Appreciating Chinese Skills

The Chinese crews won their reputation the hard way. They outperformed Cornish men brought in at extra wages to cut rock. Crocker testified,

> They would cut more rock in a week than the Cornish miners, and it was hard work, bone labor. [They] were skilled in using the hammer and drill, and they proved themselves equal to the very best Cornish miners in that work. They were very trusty, they were intelligent, and they lived up to their contracts.

Stanford held the Chinese workers in such high esteem that he provided in his will for the permanent employment of a large number on his estates. In the 1930s, some of their descendants were still living and working lands now owned by Stanford University.

The Chinese saved the day for Crocker and his colleagues. The terms of agreement with the government were that the railway companies would be paid from $16,000 to $48,000 for each mile of track laid. But there were only so many miles between the two terminal points of the projected line. The Union Pacific Company, working with 10,000 mainly Irish immigrants and Civil War veterans, had the advantage of building the line through Nebraska over the plains and made steady progress. The Central Pacific, after the first easy twenty-three miles between Newcastle and Colfax, had to conquer the granite mountains and gorges of the Sierra Nevada and Rockies before it could emerge onto the Nevada-Utah plains and make real speed and money. The line had to rise 7,000 feet in 100 miles over daunting terrain. Crocker and the Chinese proved up to the challenge. After reaching Cisco, there was no easy going. The line had to be literally carved out of the Sierra granite, through tunnels and on rock ledges cut on the side of precipices.

Using techniques from China, they attacked one of the most difficult parts of the work: carrying the line over Cape Horn, with its sheer granite buttresses and steep shale embankments, 2,000 feet above the American River canyon. There was no foothold on its flanks. The indomitable Chinese, using age-old ways, were lowered from above in rope-held baskets, and there, suspended between earth and sky, they began to chip away with hammer and crowbar to form the narrow ledge that was later laboriously deepened to a shelf wide enough for the railway roadbed, 1,400 feet above the river.

Behind the advancing crews of Chinese builders came the money and supplies to keep the work going. This was an awesome exercise in logistics. The Big Four, unscrupulous, dishonest, and ruthless on a grand scale, were the geniuses of this effort. The marvel of engineering skill being created by Strobridge and his Chinese and Irish workers up in the Sierra was fed by a stream of iron rails, spikes, tools, blasting powder, locomotives, cars, and machinery. These materials arrived after an expensive and hazardous eight-month, 15,000-mile voyage from East Coast ports around Cape Horn to San Francisco, thence by river boat to Sacramento, and so to the railhead by road.

The weather, as well as the terrain, was harsh. The winter of 1865–1866 was one of the severest on record. Snow fell early, and storm after storm blanketed the Sierra Nevada. The ground froze solid. Sixty-foot drifts of snow had to be shoveled away before the graders could even reach the roadbed. Nearly half the work force of 9,000 men were set to clearing snow.

In these conditions, construction crews tackled the most formidable obstacle in their path: building the ten Summit Tunnels on the twenty-mile stretch between Cisco, ninety-two miles from Sacramento and Lake Ridge just west of Cold Stream Valley on the eastern slope of the summit. Work went on at all the tunnels simultaneously. Three shifts of eight hours each worked day and night.

The builders lived an eerie existence. In *The Big Four,* Oscar Lewis writes,

Tunnels were dug beneath forty-foot drifts and for months, 3,000 workmen lived curious mole-like lives, passing from work to living quarters in dim

passages far beneath the snow's surface. . . . [There] was constant danger, for as snows accumulated on the upper ridges, avalanches grew frequent, their approach heralded only by a brief thunderous roar. A second later, a work crew, a bunkhouse, an entire camp would go hurtling at a dizzy speed down miles of frozen canyon. Not until months later were the bodies recovered; sometimes groups were found with shovels or picks still clutched in their frozen hands.

On Christmas Day, 1866, the papers reported that "a gang of Chinamen employed by the railroad were covered up by a snow slide and four or five [note the imprecision] died before they could be exhumed." A whole camp of Chinese railway workers was enveloped during one night and had to be rescued by shovelers the next day.

No one has recorded the names of those who gave their lives in this stupendous undertaking. It is known that the bones of 1,200 men were shipped back to China to be buried in the land of their forefathers, but that was by no means the total score. The engineer John Gills recalled that "at Tunnel No. 10, some 15–20 Chinese [again, note the imprecision] were killed by a slide that winter. The year before, in the winter of 1864–65, two wagon road repairers had been buried and killed by a slide at the same location."

A. P. Partridge, who worked on the line, describes how 3,000 Chinese builders were driven out of the mountains by the early snow. "Most . . . came to Truckee and filled up all the old buildings and sheds. An old barn collapsed and killed four Chinese. A good many were frozen to death." One is astonished at the fortitude, discipline and dedication of the Chinese railroad workers.

Many years later, looking at the Union Pacific section of the line, an old railwayman remarked, "There's an Irishman buried under every tie of that road." Brawling, drink, cholera, and malaria took a heavy toll. The construction crew towns on the Union Pacific part of the track, with their saloons, gambling dens, and bordellos, were nicknamed "hells on wheels." Jack Casement, in charge of construction there, had been a general in the Civil War and prided himself on the discipline of his fighting forces. His work crews worked with military precision, but off the job they let themselves go. One day, after gambling in the streets on payday (instigated by professional gamblers) had gotten too much out of hand, a visitor, finding the street suddenly very quiet, asked him where the gamblers had gone. Casement pointed to a nearby cemetery and replied, "They all died with their boots on." It was still the Wild West.

It is characteristic that only one single case of violent brawling was reported among the Chinese from the time they started work until they completed the job.

The Central Pacific's Chinese became expert at all kinds of work: grading, drilling, masonry, and demolition. Using black powder, they could average 1.18 feet daily through granite so hard that an incautiously placed charge could blow out backward. The Summit Tunnel work force was entirely composed of Chinese, with mainly Irish foremen. Thirty to forty worked on each face, with twelve to fifteen on the heading and the rest on the bottom removing material.

The Donner tunnels, totaling 1,695 feet, had to be bored through solid rock, and 9,000 Chinese worked on them. To speed the work, a new and untried explosive, nitroglycerin, was used. The tunnels were completed in November 1867, after thirteen months. But winter began before the way could be opened and the tracks laid. That winter was worse than the preceding one, but to save time it was necessary to send crews ahead to continue building the line even while the tunnels were being cut. Therefore, 3,000 men were sent with 400 carts and horses to Palisade Canyon, 300 miles in advance of the railhead. "Hay, grain and all supplies for men and horses had to be hauled by teams over the deserts for that great distance," writes Strobridge. "Water for men and animals was hauled at times 40 miles." Trees were felled and the logs laid side by side to form a "corduroy" roadway. On log sleds greased with lard, hundreds of Chinese manhandled three locomotives and forty wagons over the mountains. Strobridge later testified that it "cost nearly

three times what it would have cost to have done it in the summertime when it should have been done. But we shortened the time seven years from what Congress expected when the act was passed."

Between 10,000 and 11,000 men were kept working on the line from 1866 to 1869. The Sisson and Wallace Company (in which Crocker's brother was a leading member) and the Dutch merchant Cornelius Koopmanschap of San Francisco procured these men for the line. Through the summer of 1866, Crocker's Pets—6,000 strong—swarmed over the upper canyons of the Sierra, methodically slicing cuttings and pouring rock and debris to make landfills and strengthen the foundations of trestle bridges. Unlike the Caucasian laborers, who drank unboiled stream water, the Chinese slaked their thirst with weak tea and boiled water kept in old whiskey kegs filled by their mess cooks. They kept themselves clean and healthy by daily sponge baths in tubs of hot water prepared by their cooks, and the work went steadily forward.

Crocker has been described as a "hulking, relentless driver of men." But his Chinese crews responded to his leadership and drive and were caught up in the spirit of the epic work on which they were engaged. They cheered and waved their cartwheel hats as the first through train swept down the eastern slopes of the Sierra to the meeting of the lines. They worked with devotion and self-sacrifice to lay that twenty-odd miles of track for the Central Pacific Company in 1866 over the most difficult terrain. The cost of those miles was enormous—$280,000 a mile—but it brought the builders in sight of the easier terrain beyond the Sierra and the Rockies. Here costs of construction by veteran crews were only half the estimated amount of federal pay.

By summer 1868, an army of 14,000 railway builders was passing over the mountains into the great interior plain. Nine-tenths of that work force was Chinese. More than a quarter of all Chinese in the country were building the railway.

When every available Chinese in California had been recruited for the work, the Central Pacific arranged with Chinese labor contractors in

San Francisco to get men direct from China and send them up to the railhead. It was evidently some of these newcomers who fell for the Piute Indian's tall tales of snakes in the desert "big enough to swallow a man easily." Thereupon "four or five hundred Chinese took their belongings and struck out to return directly to Sacramento," reports the *Alta California.* "Crocker and Company had spent quite a little money to secure them and they sent men on horseback after them. Most of them came back again kind of quieted down, and after nothing happened and they never saw any of the snakes, they forgot about them." At least one Chinese quit the job for a similar reason. His daughter, married to a professor of Chinese art, told me that her father had worked on the railway but quit because "he was scared of the bears." He later went into domestic service.

By September 1868, the track was completed for 307 miles from Sacramento, and the crews were laying rails across the plain east of the Sierra. Parallel with the track layers went the telegraph installers, stringing their wires on the poles and keeping the planners back at headquarters precisely apprised of where the end of the track was.

The Great Railway Competition

On the plains, the Chinese worked in tandem with all the Indians Crocker could entice to work on the iron rails. They began to hear of the exploits of the Union Pacific's "Irish terriers" building from the east. One day, the Irish laid six miles of track. The Chinese topped this with seven. "No Chinaman is going to beat us," growled the Irish, and the next day, they laid seven and half miles of track. They swore that they would outperform the competition no matter what it did.

Crocker taunted the Union Pacific that his men could lay ten miles of track a day. Durant, president of the rival line, laid a $10,000 wager that it could not be done. Crocker took no chances. He waited until the day before the last sixteen miles of track had to be laid and brought up all needed suplies for instant use. Then he

unleashed his crews. On April 28, 1869, while Union Pacific checkers and newspaper reporters looked on, a combined gang of Chinese and eight picked Irish rail handlers laid ten miles and 1,800 feet more of track in twelve hours. This record was never surpassed until the advent of mechanized track laying. Each Irishman that day walked a total distance of ten miles, and their combined muscle handled sixty tons of rail.

So keen was the competition that when the two lines approached each other, instead of changing direction to link up, their builders careered on and on for 100 miles, building lines that would never meet. Finally, the government prescribed that the linkage point should be Promontory, Utah.

Competition was keen, but there seems to be no truth in the story that the Chinese and Irish in this phase of work were trying to blow each other up with explosives. It is a fact, however, that when the two lines were very near each other, the Union Pacific blasters did not give the Central Pacific men timely warning when setting off a charge, and several Chinese were hurt. Then a Central Pacific charge went off unannounced and several Irishmen found themselves buried in dirt. This forced the foremen to take up the matter and an amicable settlement was arranged. There was no further trouble.

On May 10, 1869, the two lines were officially joined at Promontory, north of Ogden in Utah. A great crowd gathered. A band played. An Irish crew and a Chinese crew were chosen to lay the last two rails side by side. The last tie was made of polished California laurel with a silver plate in its center proclaiming it "The last tie laid on the completion of the Pacific Railroad, May 10, 1869." But when the time came it was nowhere to be found. As consternation mounted, four Chinese approached with it on their shoulders and they laid it beneath the rails. A photographer stepped up and someone shouted to him "Shoot!" The Chinese only knew one meaning for that word. They fled. But order was restored and the famous ceremony began; Stanford drove a golden spike into the last tie with a silver hammer. The news flashed by telegraph to a waiting nation. But no Chinese appears in that famous picture of the toast celebrating the joining of the rails.

Crocker was one of the few who paid tribute to the Chinese that day: "I wish to call to your minds that the early completion of this railroad we have built has been in large measure due to that poor, despised class of laborers called the Chinese, to the fidelity and industry they have shown." No one even mentioned the name of Judah.

The building of the first transcontinental railway stands as a monument to the union of Yankee and Chinese-Irish drive and know-how. This was a formidable combination. They all complemented each other. Together they did in seven years what was expected to take at least fourteen.

In his book on the building of the railway, John Galloway, the noted transportation engineer, described this as "without doubt the greatest engineering feat of the nineteenth century," and that has never been disputed. David D. Colton, then vice-president of the Southern Pacific, was similarly generous in his praise of the Chinese contribution. He was asked, while giving evidence before the 1876 congressional committee, "Could you have constructed that road without Chinese labor?" He replied, "I do not think it could have been constructed so quickly, and with anything like the same amount of certainty as to what we were going to accomplish in the same length of time."

And, in answer to the question, "Do you think the Chinese have been a benefit to the State?" West Evans, a railway contractor, testified, "I do not see how we could do the work we have done, here, without them; at least I have done work that would not have been done if it had not been for the Chinamen, work that could not have been done without them."

It was heroic work. The Central Pacific crews had carried their railway 1,800 miles through the Sierra and Rocky mountains, over sagebrush desert and plain. The Union Pacific built only 689 miles, over much easier terrain. It had 500 miles in which to carry its part of the line to a height of 5,000 feet, with another fifty more miles in which to reach the high passes of the Black Hills.

With newly recruited crews, the Central Pacific had to gain an altitude of 7,000 feet from the plain in just over 100 miles and make a climb of 2,000 feet in just 20 miles.

All this monumental work was done before the age of mechanization. It was pick and shovel, hammer and crowbar work, with baskets for earth carried slung from shoulder poles and put on one-horse carts.

For their heroic work, the Chinese workmen began with a wage of $28 a month, providing their own food and shelter. This was gradually raised to $30 to $35 a month. Caucasians were paid the same amount of money, but their food and shelter were provided. Because it cost $0.75 to $1.00 a day to feed a white unskilled worker, each Chinese saved the Central Pacific, at a minimum, two-thirds the price of a white laborer (1865 rates). Chinese worked as masons, dynamiters, and blacksmiths and at other skilled jobs that paid white workers from $3 to $5 a day. So, at a minimum, the company saved about $5 million by hiring Chinese workers.

Did this really "deprive white workers of jobs" as anti-Chinese agitators claimed. Certainly not. In the first place, experience had proved that white workers simply did not want the jobs the Chinese took on the railroad. In fact, the Chinese created jobs for white workers as straw bosses, foremen, railhandlers, teamsters, and supervisors.

The wages paid to the Chinese were, in fact, comparable to those paid unskilled or semiskilled labor in the East (where labor was relatively plentiful), and the Chinese were at first satisfied. Charles Nordhoff estimated that the frugal Chinese could save about $13 a month out of those wages. The *Alta California* estimated their savings at $20 a month and later, perhaps, as wages increased, they could lay aside even more. With a bit of luck, a year and a half to two years of work would enable them to return to China with $400 to buy a bit of land and be well-to-do farmers.

But the Chinese began to learn the American way of life. On one occasion in June 1867, 2,000 tunnelers went on strike, asking for $40 a month, an eight-hour day in the tunnels, and an end to beating by foremen. "Eight hours a day good for white man, all same good for Chinese," said their spokesman in the pidgin English common in the construction camps. But solidarity with the other workers was lacking, and after a week the strike was called off when the Chinese heard that Crocker was recruiting strikebreakers from the eastern states.

When the task was done, most of the Chinese railwaymen were paid off. Some returned to China with their hard-earned savings, and the epic story of building the Iron Horse's pathway across the continent must have regaled many a family gathering there. Some returned with souvenirs of the great work, chips of one of the last ties, which had been dug up and split up among them. Some settled in the little towns that had grown up along the line of the railway. Others took the railway to seek adventure further east and south. Most made their way back to California and took what jobs they could find in that state's growing industries, trades, and other occupations. Many used their traditional and newly acquired skills on the other transcontinental lines and railways that were being swiftly built in the West and Midwest. This was the start of the diaspora of the Chinese immigrants in America.

The Union and Central Pacific tycoons had done well out of the building of the line. Congressional investigation committees later calculated that, of $73 million poured into the Union Pacific coffers, no more than $50 million could be justified as true costs. The Big Four and their associates in the Central Pacific had done even better. They had made at least $63 million and owned most of the CP stock worth around $100 million and 9 million acres of land grants to boot.

Ironically, the great railway soon had disastrous results for the Chinese themselves. It now cost only $40 for an immigrant to cross the continent by rail and a flood of immigrants took advantage of the ease and cheapness of travel on the line the Chinese had helped to build. The labor shortage (and resulting high wages) in California turned into a glut. When the tangled affairs of the

Northern Pacific line led to the stock market crash of Black Friday, September 19, 1873, and to financial panic, California experienced its first real economic depression. There was devastating unemployment, and the Chinese were made the scapegoats.

Building Other Lines

The expansion of the railroads was even faster in the following decade. In 1850, the United States had 9,000 miles of track. In 1860, it had 30,000. In 1890, it had over 70,000 miles. Three years later, it had five transcontinental lines.

The first transcontinental railway was soon followed by four more links: (1) the Southern Pacific-Texas and Pacific, completed in 1883 from San Francisco to Texas by way of Yuma, Tucson, and El Paso; (2) the Atchison, Topeka, and Santa Fe, completed in 1885 from Kansas City to Los Angeles via Santa Fe and Albuquerque; (3) the Northern Pacific completed in 1883 from Duluth, Minnesota, to Portland, Oregon, and the Great Northern (1893). The skill of the Chinese as railroad builders was much sought after, and Chinese worked on all these lines. Some 15,000 worked on the Northern Pacific, laying tracks in Washington, Idaho, and Montana; 250 on the Houston and Texas line; 600 on the Alabama and Chattanooga line; 70 on the New Orleans line. Nearly 500 Chinese were recruited for the Union Pacific even after the lines were joined. Many worked in the Wyoming coal mines and during the summer months doubled as track laborers. They carried the Southern Pacific lines over the burning Mojave Desert. They helped link San Francisco with Portland in 1887.

The Canadian Pacific seized the chance to enlist veteran Chinese railwaymen from the Southern Pacific and Northern Pacific railroads and also brought Chinese workers direct from China. In 1880, some 1,500 were working on that line, increasing to 6,500 two years later. Casualties were heavy on this line. Hundreds lost their lives while working on it.

Chinese railwaymen helped on the Central and Southern Pacific's main line down the San Joaquin Valley in 1870 and 1871. They worked on the hookup to Los Angeles and the loop with seventeen tunnels over the Tehachapi Pass completed in 1876. On this line, 1,000 Chinese worked on the 6,975-foot San Fernando Tunnel, the longest in the West. This rail link between San Francisco and Los Angeles, tapping the rich Central Valley, played a major role in the development of California's agriculture, later its biggest industry. They worked on the line north from Sacramento along the Shasta route to Portland, which was reached in 1887. In 1869, the Virginia and Truckee line employed 450 Chinese, veterans of the Central Pacific, to grade its track. When the Virginia and Truckee's Carson and Colorado branch line was planned from Mound House to Benton, its tough manager Yerington arranged with the unions for the grading to be done by white labor to Dayton and by Chinese from Dayton on south. "If the entire line had to be graded by white labor, I would not think of driving a pick into the ground, but would abandon the undertaking entirely," he said.

Chinese laborers worked on the trans-Panamanian railway, which linked the Pacific and the Atlantic before the Panama Canal was completed. This railway played a major role in speeding up the economic development of the United States, but it was not built without sacrifice: hundreds of the Chinese builders died of fever and other causes during its construction.

This by no means completes the list of contributions of the Chinese railway workers. The transcontinental lines on which they worked "more than any other factor helped make the United States a united nation," writes the *Encyclopedia Britannica* ["Railways"]. They played a major role in building the communications network of iron roads that was the transport base of American industrial might in the twentieth century.

Speaking eloquently in favor of the Chinese immigrants, Oswald Garrison Villard said,

> I want to remind you of the things that Chinese labor did in opening up the Western portion of this country. . . . [They] stormed the forest fastnesses, endured cold and heat and the risk of death at hands of hostile Indians to aid in the opening up of our northwestern empire. I have a dispatch from the chief engineer of the Northwestern Pacific telling how Chinese laborers went out into eight feet of snow with the temperature far below zero to carry on the work when no American dared face the conditions.

And these men were from China's sun-drenched south, where it never snows.

In certain circles, there has been a conspiracy of silence about the Chinese railroadmen and what they did. When U.S. Secretary of Transportation John Volpe spoke at the "Golden Spike" centenary, not a single Chinese American was invited, and he made no mention in his speech of the Chinese railroad builders.

4

THE GREAT UPHEAVAL OF 1877

JEREMY BRECHER

Spurred by war contracts and the rapid expansion of railroads in the years immediately following the Civil War, the United States experienced a prolonged period of heavy industrialization. In rapid succession the small prewar steel, oil, and railroad industries became giant enterprises, employing thousands of workers and spreading their influence throughout the nation. After the end of the Civil War in 1865 thousands of rural Americans and foreign immigrants flocked to the nation's industrial centers, finding there new kinds of work and new rhythms of labor.

As these new workers quickly learned, however, their new jobs required more concentration, discipline, and unremitting labor than any they had experienced before. Gone were the more human rhythms of the farm or the artisan's shop, where work was part of a whole way of life. In the giant factories, workers found themselves without any control over the pace of work, the tasks they would perform, or the hours they would work. Unlike the intimate contact they had experienced with employers on farms or in small shops, the new industrial workers found that all decisions in their new workplaces were made by owners and managers whom they were unlikely ever to see.

Not all workers accepted this new way of working, however. From the beginning, they resisted the domination and dehumanization that factory life implied. Workers formed unions to defend themselves and fought long and hard to gain a degree of control over their worklife. As the events of 1877 show, these workers were ready to take to the streets and battle both their employers and the police for their rights as citizens and workers. As Jeremy Brecher shows, the "Great Upheaval" of 1877 was no mere series of riots, but was rather a serious and planned attempt by American workers to claim a place for themselves in the new industrial society of the late nineteenth century.

What do you think accounts for the differences between the response to industrialization of Chinese workers and those discussed in this selection? Do you find any parallels between the goals of American workers in 1877 and those—portrayed by Melvyn Dubofsky in Reading 10—who joined the International Workers of the World in 1905?

In the centers of many American cities are positioned huge armories, grim nineteenth-century edifices of brick or stone. They are fortresses, complete with massive walls and loopholes for guns. You may have wondered why they are there, but it has probably never occurred to you that they were built to protect America, not against invasion from abroad, but against popular revolt at home. Their erection was a monument to the Great Upheaval of 1877.

July, 1877, does not appear in many history books as a memorable date, yet it marks the first great American mass strike, a movement which was viewed at the time as a violent rebellion. Strikers stopped and seized the nation's most important industry, the railroads, and crowds defeated or won over first the police, then the state militias, and in some cases even the Federal troops. General strikes stopped all activity in a dozen major cities, and strikers took over social authority in communities across the nation.

It all began on Monday, July 16th, 1877, in the little railroad town of Martinsburg, West Virginia. On that day, the Baltimore and Ohio Railroad cut wages ten percent, the second cut in eight months. In Martinsburg, men gathered around the railroad yards, talking, waiting through the day. Toward evening the crew of a cattle train, fed up, abandoned the train, and other trainmen refused to replace them.

As a crowd gathered, the strikers uncoupled the engines, ran them into the roundhouse, and announced to B&O officials that no trains would leave Martinsburg till the pay cut was rescinded. The Mayor arrived and conferred with railroad officials. He tried to soothe the crowd and was booed; when he ordered the arrest of the strike leaders they just laughed at him, backed up in their resistance by the angry crowd. The Mayor's police were helpless against the population of the town. No railroad workers could be found willing to take out a train, so the police withdrew and by midnight the yard was occupied only by a guard of strikers left to enforce the blockade.

That night, B&O officials in Wheeling went to see Governor Matthews, took him to their company telegraph office, and waited while he wired Col. Charles Faulkner, Jr., at Martinsburg, to have his Berkeley Light Guards preserve the peace "if necessary, . . . prevent any interference by rioters with the men at work, and also prevent the obstruction of the trains."

Next morning, when the Martinsburg Master of Transportation ordered the cattle train out again, the strikers' guard swooped down on it and ordered the engineer to stop or be killed. He stopped. By now, hundreds of strikers and townspeople had gathered, and the next train out hardly moved before it was boarded, uncoupled, and run into the roundhouse.

About 9:00 A.M., the Berkeley Light Guards arrived to the sound of a fife and drum; the crowd cheered them. Most of the militiamen were themselves railroaders. Now the cattle train came out once more, this time covered with militiamen, their rifles loaded with ball cartridges. As the train pulled through the yelling crowd, a striker named William Vandergriff turned a switch to derail the train and guarded it with a pistol. A soldier jumped off the train to reset the switch; Vandergriff shot him and in turn was fatally shot himself.

At this, the attempt to break the blockade at Martinsburg was abandoned. The strikebreaking engineer and fireman climbed down from the engine and departed. Col. Faulkner called in vain for volunteers to run the train, announced that the Governor's orders had been fulfilled, dismissed his men, and telegraphed the governor that he was helpless to control the situation.

With this confrontation began the Great Upheaval of 1877, a spontaneous, nationwide, virtually general strike. The pattern of Martinsburg—a railroad strike in response to a pay cut, an attempt by the companies to run trains with the support of military forces, the defeat or dissolution of those forces by amassed crowds representing general popular support—became that same week the pattern for the nation.

With news of success at Martinsburg, the strike spread to all divisions of the B&O, with engineers, brakemen, and conductors joining with the firemen who gave the initial impetus. Freight traffic was stopped all along the line, while the men continued to run passenger and mail cars without interference. Seventy engines and six hundred freight cars were soon piled up in the Martinsburg yards.

The Governor, resolved to break the strike, promised to send a company "in which there are no men unwilling to suppress the riots and execute the law." He sent his only available military force, sixty Light Guards from Wheeling. But the Guards were hardly reliable, for sentiment in Wheeling supported the strike strongly. They marched out of town surrounded by an excited crowd, who, a reporter noted, "all expressed sympathy with the strikers"; box and can makers in Wheeling were already on strike and soon people would be discussing a general strike of all labor. When the Guards' train arrived in Martinsburg, it was met by a large, orderly crowd. The militia's commander conferred with railroad and town officials, but dared not use the troops, lest they "further exasperate the strikers." Instead, he marched them away to the courthouse.

At this point the strike was virtually won. But hardly had the strike broken out when the president of B&O began pressing for the use of the U.S. Army against the strikers in West Virginia. "The loss of an hour would most seriously affect us and imperil vast interests," he wrote. With Federal troops, "the rioters could be dispersed and there would be no difficulty in the movement of trains." The road's vice-president wired his Washington agent, saying that the Governor might soon call for Federal troops, and telling him "to see the Secretary of War and inform him of the serious situation of affairs, that he may be ready to send the necessary force to the scene of action at once." Although a newspaperman on the scene of action at Martinsburg reported "perfect order," and other correspondents were unable to find violence to report, the Colonel of the Guards wired the Governor:

> The feeling here is most intense, and the rioters are largely cooperated with by civilians. . . . The disaffection has become so general that no employee could now be found to run an engine even under certain protection. I am satisfied that Faulkner's experiment of yesterday was thorough and that any repetition of it today would precipitate a bloody conflict, with the odds largely against our small force. . . .

On the basis of this report, the Governor in turn wired the President:

> Owing to unlawful combinations and domestic violence now existing at Martinsburg and at other points along the line of the Baltimore and Ohio Railroad, it is impossible with any force at my command to execute the laws of the State. I therefore call upon your Excellency for the assistance of the United States military to protect the law abiding people of the State against domestic violence, and to maintain supremacy of the law.

The president of the B&O added his appeal, wiring the President that West Virginia had done all it could "to suppress this insurrection" and warning that "this great national highway [the B&O] can only be restored for public use by the interposition of U.S. forces." In response, President Hayes sent 300 Federal troops to suppress what his Secretary of War was already referring to publicly as "an insurrection."

This "insurrection" was spontaneous and unplanned, but it grew out of the social conditions of the time and the recent experience of the workers. The tactics of the railroad strikers had been developed in a series of local strikes, mostly without trade union support, that occurred in 1873 and 1874. In December, 1873, for example, engineers and firemen on the Pennsylvania Railroad system struck in Chicago, Pittsburgh, Cincinnati, Louisville, Columbus, Indianapolis, and various smaller towns, in what the *Portsmouth* [Ohio] *Tribune* called "the greatest railroad strike" in the nation's history. Huge crowds gathered in depot yards and supported the strikers against attempts to run the trains. State troops were sent into Dennison, Ohio, and Logansport, Indiana, to break strike strongholds. At Susquehanna Depot, Pennsylvania, three months later, shop and repair workers struck. After electing a "Workingmen's Committee," they seized control of the repair shops; within twenty minutes the entire works was reported "under complete control of the men." The strike was finally broken when 1,800 Philadelphia soldiers with thirty pieces of cannon established martial law in this town of 8,000.

The strikes were generally unsuccessful; but, as Herbert Gutman wrote, they "revealed the power of the railroad workers to disrupt traffic on many roads." The employers learned that "they had a rather tenuous hold on the loyalties of their men. Something was radically wrong if workers could successfully stop trains for from two or three days to as much as a week, destroy property, and even 'manage' it as if it were their own." And, Gutman continued, ". . . the same essential patterns of behavior that were widespread in 1877 were found in the 1873–1874 strikes. Three and a half years of severe depression ignited a series of local brush fires into a national conflagration . . ."

The more immediate background of the 1877 railroad strike also helps explain why it took the form of virtual insurrection, for this struggle grew out of the failure of other, less violent forms of action.

The wage cut on the B&O was part of a general pattern which had started June 1st on the Pennsylvania Railroad. When the leaders of the Brotherhoods of Engineers, Conductors, and Firemen made no effort to combat the cut, the railroad workers on the Pennsylvania system took action themselves. A week before the cut went into effect, the Newark, New Jersey division of the Engineers held an angry protest meeting against the cut. The Jersey City lodge met the next day, voted for a strike, and put out feelers to other workers; by the day the cut took effect, engineers' and firemen's locals throughout the Pennsylvania system had chosen delegates to a joint grievance committee, ignoring the leadership of their national union. Nor was the wage cut their only grievance; the committee proposed what amounted to a complete reorganization of work. They opposed the system of assigning trains, in which the first crew into town was the first crew out, leaving them no time to rest or see their families; they wanted regular runs to stabilize pay and working days; they wanted passes home in case of long layovers; they wanted the system of "classification" of workers by length of service and efficiency—used to keep wages down—abolished.

But the grievance committee delegates were easily intimidated and cajoled by Tom Scott, the masterful ruler of the Pennsylvania Railroad, who talked them into accepting the cut without consulting those who elected them. A majority of brakemen, many conductors, and some engineers wanted to repudiate the committee's action; but, their unity broken, the locals decided not to strike.

Since the railroad brotherhoods had clearly failed, the workers' next step was to create a new, secret organization, the Trainmen's Union. It was started by workers on the Pittsburgh, Fort Wayne and Chicago. Within three weeks, lodges had sprung up from Baltimore to Chicago, with thousands of members on many different lines. The Trainmen's Union recognized that the privileged engineers "generally patched things up for themselves," so it included conductors, firemen, brakemen, switchmen, and others besides engineers. The union also realized that the various railroad managements were cooperating against the workers, one railroad after another imitating the Pennsylvania with a ten percent wage cut. The union's strategy was to organize at least three-quarters of the trainmen on each trunk line, then strike against the cuts and other grievances. When a strike came, firemen would not take engineers' jobs, and men on non-striking roads would not handle struck equipment.

But the union was full of spies. On one railroad the firing of members began only four days after the union was formed, and others followed suit: "Determined to stamp it out," as one railroad official put it, the company has issued orders to discharge all men belonging to "the Brotherhood or Union." Nonetheless, on June 24th, forty men fanned out over the railroads to call a general railroad strike for the following week. The railroads learned about the strike through their spies, fired the strike committee in a body, and thus panicked part of the leadership into spreading false word that the strike was off. Local lodges, unprepared to act on their own, flooded the union headquarters with telegrams asking what to do. Union officials were denied use of railroad telegraphs to reply, the companies ran their trains, and the strike failed utterly.

Thus, the Martinsburg strike broke out because the B&O workers had discovered that they had no alternative but to act completely on their own. Not only were their wages being cut, but, as one newspaper reported, the men felt they were "treated just as the rolling stock or locomotives" —squeezed for every drop of profit. Reduced crews were forced to handle extra cars, with lowered pay classifications, and extra pay for overtime eliminated.

A similar spontaneous strike developed that same day in Baltimore in response to the B&O wage cut, but the railroad had simply put strikebreakers on the trains and used local police to disperse the crowds of strikers. What made Martinsburg different? The key to the strike, according to historian Robert Bruce, was that "a conventional strike would last only until strikebreakers could be summoned." To succeed, the strikers had to "beat off strikebreakers by force, seize trains, yards, roundhouses . . ." This was possible in Martinsburg because the people of the town so passionately supported the railroad workers that they amassed and resisted the state militia. It was now the support of others elsewhere which allowed the strikers to resist the Federal troops as well.

On Thursday, 300 Federal troops arrived in Martinsburg to quell the "insurrection" and bivouacked in the roundhouse. With militiamen and U.S. soldiers guarding the yards, the company was able to get a few trains loaded with regulars through the town. When 100 armed strikers tried to stop a train, the Sheriff and the militia marched to the scene and arrested the leader. No one in Martinsburg would take out another train, but with the military in control, strikebreakers from Baltimore were able to run freights through unimpeded. The strike seemed broken.

But the population of the surrounding area also now rallied behind the railroad workers. Hundreds of unemployed and striking boatmen on the Chesapeake and Ohio Canal lay in ambush at Sir John's Run, where they stoned the freight that had broken the Martinsburg blockade, forced it to stop, and then hid when the U.S. regulars attacked. The movement soon spread

into Maryland, where at Cumberland a crowd of boatmen, railroaders, and others swarmed around the train and uncoupled the cars. When the train finally got away, a mob at Keyser, West Virginia, ran it onto a side track and took the crew off by force—while the U.S. troops stood helplessly by. Just before midnight, the miners of the area met at Piedmont, four miles from Keyser, and resolved to go to Keyser in the morning and help stop trains. Coal miners and others—"a motley crowd, white and black"—halted a train guarded by fifty U.S. regulars after it pulled out of Martinsburg. At Piedmont a handbill was printed warning the B&O that 15,000 miners, the united citizenry of local communities, and "the working classes of every state in the Union" would support the strikers. "Therefore let the clashing of arms be heard . . . in view of the rights and in the defense of our families we shall conquer, or we shall die."

The result was that most of the trains sent west from Martinsburg never even reached Keyser. All but one, which was under heavy military escort, were stopped by a crowd of unemployed rolling-mill men, migrant workers, boatmen, and young boys at Cumberland, Maryland, and even on the one that went through a trainman was wounded by a gunshot. When two leaders of the crowd were arrested, a great throng went to the Mayor's house, demanded the release of the prisoners, and carried them off on their shoulders.

Faced with the spread of the strike through Maryland, the president of the B&O now persuaded Governor Carrol of Maryland to call up the National Guard in Baltimore and send it to Cumberland. They did not reckon, however, on the reaction of Baltimore to the strike. "The working people everywhere are with us," said a leader of the railroad strikers in Baltimore. "They know what it is to bring up a family on ninety cents a day, to live on beans and corn meal week in and week out, to run in debt at the stores until you cannot get trusted any longer, to see the wife breaking down under privation and distress, and the children growing up sharp and fierce like wolves day after day because they don't get enough to eat."

The bells rang in Baltimore for the militia to assemble just as the factories were letting out for the evening, and a vast crowd assembled as well. At first they cheered the troops, but severely stoned them as they started to march. The crowd was described as "a rough element eager for disturbance; a proportion of mechanics [workers] either out of work or upon inadequate pay, whose sullen hearts rankled; and muttering and murmuring gangs of boys, almost outlaws, and ripe for any sort of disturbance." As the 250 men of the first regiment marched out, 25 of them were injured by the stoning of the crowd, but this was only a love-tap. The second regiment was unable even to leave its own armory for a time. Then, when the order was given to march anyway, the crowd stoned them so severely that the troops panicked and opened fire. In the bloody march that followed, the militia killed ten and seriously wounded more than twenty of the crowd, but the crowd continued to resist, and one by one the troops dropped out and went home, and changed into civilian clothing. By the time they reached the station, only 59 of the original 120 men remained in line. Even after they reached the depot, the remaining troops were unable to leave for Cumberland, for a crowd of about 200 drove away the engineer and firemen of the waiting troop train and beat back a squad of policemen who tried to restore control. The militia charged the growing crowd, but were driven back by brickbats and pistol fire. It was at that stage that Governor Carrol, himself bottled up in the depot by the crowd of 15,000, in desperation wired President Hayes to send the U.S. Army.

Like the railroad workers, others joined the "insurrection" out of frustration with other means of struggle. Over the previous years they had experimented with one means of resistance after another, each more radical than the last. First to prove their failure had been the trade unions. In 1870, there were about thirty-three national unions enrolling perhaps five percent of non-farm workers; by 1877, only about nine were left. Total membership plummeted from 300,000 in 1870 to 50,000 in 1876. Under depression conditions, they were simply unable to withstand the organized attack levied by lockouts and blacklisting. Unemployment demonstrations in New York had been ruthlessly broken up by police. Then the first major industrial union in the United States, the Workingmen's Benevolent Association of the anthracite miners, led a strike which was finally broken by the companies, one of which claimed the conflict had cost it $4 million. Next the Molly Maguires—a secret terrorist organization the Irish miners developed to fight the coal operators—were infiltrated and destroyed by agents from the Pinkerton Detective Agency, which specialized in providing spies, agents provocateurs, and private armed forces for employers combatting labor organizations. Thus, by the summer of 1877 it had become clear that no single group of workers—whether through peaceful demonstration, tightly-knit trade unions, armed terrorism, or surprise strikes—could stand against the power of the companies, their armed guards, the Pinkertons, and the armed forces of the Government.

Indeed, the Great Upheaval had been preceded by a seeming quiescence on the part of workers. The general manager of one railroad wrote, June 21st: "The experiment of reducing the salaries has been successfully carried out by all the Roads that have tried it of late, and I have no fear of any trouble with our employees if it is done with a proper show of firmness on our part and they see that they must accept it cheerfully or leave." The very day the strike was breaking out at Martinsburg, Governor Hartranft of Pennsylvania was agreeing with his Adjutant General that the state was enjoying such a calm as it had not known for several years. In less than a week, it would be the center of the insurrection.

Three days after Governor Hartranft's assessment, the Pennsylvania Railroad ordered that all freights eastward from Pittsburgh be run as "double-headers"—with two engines and twice as many cars. This meant in effect a speed-up—more work and increased danger of accidents and layoffs. The trains were likely to break and the sections collide, sending fifty or sixty men out of work. Then Pennsylvania trainmen were sitting in the Pittsburgh roundhouse listening to a fireman read them news of the strike elsewhere when the order came to take out a "double-header." At the last minute a flagman named Augustus Harris, acting on his own initiative, refused to obey the order. The conductor appealed to the rest of the crew, but they too refused to move the train. When the company sent for replacements, twenty-five brakemen and conductors refused to take out the train and were fined on the spot. When the dispatcher finally found three yard brakemen to take out the train, a crowd of twenty angry strikers refused to let the train go through. One of them threw a link at a scab, whereupon the volunteer yardmen gave up and went away. Said flagman Andrew Hice, "It's a question of bread or blood, and we're going to resist."

Freight crews joined the strike as their trains came in and were stopped, and a crowd of mill workers, tramps, and boys began to gather at the crossings, preventing freight trains from running while letting passenger trains go through. The company asked the Mayor for police, but since the city was nearly bankrupt the force had been cut in half, and only eight men were available. Further, the Mayor was elected by the strong working-class vote of the city, and shared the city's upper crust's hatred for the Pennsylvania Railroad and its rate discrimination against Pittsburgh. At most the railroad got seventeen police, whom it had to pay itself.

As elsewhere, the Trainmen's Union had nothing to do with the start of the strike. Its top leader, Robert Ammon, had left Pittsburgh to take a job elsewhere, and the president of the Pittsburgh Division didn't even know that trouble was at hand; he slept late that morning, didn't hear about the strike until nearly noon—his first comment was "Impossible!"—and he busied himself primarily at trying to persuade his colleagues to go home and keep out of trouble.

The Trainmen's Union did, however, provide a nucleus for a meeting of the strikers and representatives of such groups as the rolling-mill workers. "We're with you," said one rolling-mill man, pledging the railroaders support from the rest of Pittsburgh labor. "We're in the same boat. I heard a reduction of ten percent hinted at in our

mill this morning. I won't call employers despots, I won't call them tyrants, but the term capitalists is sort of synonymous and will do as well." The meeting called on "all workingmen to make common cause with their brethren on the railroad."

In Pittsburgh, railroad officials picked up the ailing Sheriff, waited while he gave the crowd a *pro forma* order to disperse, and then persuaded him to appeal for state troops. That night state officials ordered the militia called up in Pittsburgh but only part of the troops called arrived. Some were held up by the strikers, others simply failed to show up. Two-thirds of one regiment made it; in another regiment not one man appeared. Nor were the troops reliable. As one officer reported to his superior, "You can place little dependence on the troops of your division; some have thrown down their arms, and others have left, and I fear the situation very much." Another officer explained why the troops were unreliable. "Meeting an enemy on the field of battle, you go there to kill. The more you kill, and the quicker you do it, the better. But here you had men with fathers and brothers and relatives mingled in the crowd of rioters. The sympathy of the people, the sympathy of the troops, my own sympathy, was with the strikers proper. We all felt that those men were not receiving enough wages." Indeed, by Saturday morning the militiamen had stacked their arms and were chatting with the crowd, eating hardtack with them, and walking up and down the streets with them, behaving, as a regular army lieutenant put it, "as though they were going to have a party." "You may be called upon to clear the tracks down there," said a lawyer to a soldier. "They may call on me," the soldier replied, "and they may call pretty damn loud before they will clear the tracks."

The *Pittsburgh Leader* came out with an editorial warning of "The Talk of the Desperate" and purporting to quote a "representative workingman": "'This may be the beginning of a great civil war in this country, between labor and capital. It only needs that the strikers . . . should boldly attack and rout the troops sent to quell them— and they could easily do it if they tried. . . . The workingmen everywhere would all join and help . . . The laboring people, who mostly constitute the militia, will not take up arms to put down their brethren. Will capital, then, rely on the United States Army? Pshaw! These ten or fifteen thousand available men would be swept from our path like leaves in the whirlwind. The workingmen of this country can capture and hold it if they will only stick together. . . . Even if so-called law and order should beat them down in blood . . . we would, at least, have our revenge on the men who have coined our sweat and muscles into millions for themselves, while they think dip is good enough butter for us.' "

All day Friday, the crowds controlled the switches and the officer commanding the Pittsburgh militia refused to clear the crossing with artillery because of the slaughter that would result. People swarmed aboard passenger trains and rode through the city free of charge. The Sheriff warned the women and children to leave lest they be hurt when the army came, but the women replied that they were there to urge the men on. "Why are you acting this way, and why is this crowd here?" the Sheriff asked one young man who had come to Pittsburgh from Eastern Pennsylvania for the strike. "The Pennsylvania has two ends," he replied, "one in Philadelphia and one in Pittsburgh. In Philadelphia they have a strong police force, and they're with the railroad. But in Pittsburgh they have a weak force, and it's a mining and manufacturing district, and we can get all the help we want from the laboring elements, and we've determined to make the strike here." "Are you a railroader?" the Sheriff asked. "No, I'm a laboring man," came the reply.

Railroad and National Guard officials, realizing that the local Pittsburgh militia units were completely unreliable, sent for 600 fresh troops from its commercial rival, Philadelphia. A Pittsburgh steel manufacturer came to warn railroad officials not to send the troops out until workingmen were back in their factories. "I think I know the temper of our men pretty well, and you would be wise not to do anything until Monday. . . . If there's going to be firing, you ought to have at least ten thousand men, and I doubt if even that

many could quell the mob that would be brought down on us." These words were prophetic. But, remembering the 2,000 freight cars and locomotives lying idle in the yards, and the still-effective blockade, the railroad official replied, "We must have our property." He looked at his watch and said, "We have now lost an hour and a half's time." He had confidently predicted that "the Philadelphia regiment won't fire over the heads of the mob." Now the massacre he counted on—and the city's retaliation—was at hand.

As the imported troops marched toward the 28th Street railroad crossing, a crowd of 6,000 gathered, mostly spectators. The troops began clearing the tracks with fixed bayonets and the crowd replied with a furious barrage of stones, bricks, coal, and possibly revolver fire. Without orders, the Philadelphia militia began firing as fast as they could, killing twenty people in five minutes as the crowd scattered. Meanwhile, the local Pittsburgh militia stood on the hillside at carry arms and broke for cover when they saw the Philadelphian's Gatling gun come forward. Soon they went home or joined the mob.

With the crossing cleared, the railroad fired up a dozen doubleheaders, but even trainmen who had previously declined to join the strike now refused to run them, and the strike remained unbroken. Their efforts in vain, the Philadelphia militia retired to the roundhouse.

Meanwhile, the entire city mobilized in a fury against the troops who had conducted the massacre and against the Pennsylvania Railroad. Workers rushed home from their factories for pistols, muskets and butcher knives. A delegation of 600 workingmen from nearby Temperanceville marched in with a full band and colors. In some cases the crowd organized itself into crude armed military units, marching together with drums. Civil authority collapsed in the face of the crowd; the Mayor refused to send police or even to try to quiet the crowd himself.

The crowd peppered the troops in the roundhouse with pistol and musket fire, but finally decided, as one member put it, "We'll have them out if we have to roast them out." Oil, coke, and whiskey cars were set alight and pushed downhill toward the roundhouse. A few men began systematically to burn the yards, despite rifle fire from the soldiers, while the crowd held off fire trucks at gunpoint. Sunday morning, the roundhouse caught fire and the Philadelphia militia were forced to evacuate. As they marched along the street they were peppered with fire by the crowd and, according to the troops' own testimony, by Pittsburgh policemen as well. Most of the troops were marched out of town and found refuge a dozen miles away. The few left to guard ammunition found civilian clothes, sneaked away, and hid until the crisis was over. By Saturday night, the last remaining regiment of Pittsburgh militia was disbanded. The crowd had completely routed the army.

Sunday morning, hundreds of people broke into the freight cars in the yards and distributed the goods to the crowds below—on occasion with assistance from police. Burning of cars continued. (According to Carroll D. Wright, first U.S. Commissioner of Labor, "A great many old freight cars which must soon have been replaced by new, were pushed into the fire by agents of the railroad company," to be added to the claims against the country.) The crowd prevented firemen from saving a grain elevator, though it was not owned by the railroad, saying "it's a monopoly, and we're tired of it," but workers pitched in to prevent the spread of the fire to nearby tenements. By Monday, 104 locomotives, more than 2,000 cars, and all of the railroad buildings had been destroyed.

Across the river from Pittsburgh, in the railroad town of Allegheny, a remarkable transfer of authority took place. Using the pretext that the Governor was out of the state, the strikers maintained that the state militia was without legal authority, and therefore proposed to treat them as no more than a mob. The strikers armed themselves—by breaking into the local armory, according to the Mayor—dug rifle pits and trenches outside the Allegheny depot, set up patrols, and warned civilians away from the probable line of fire. The strikers took possession of the telegraph and sent messages up and down the road. They took over management of the railroad, running

passenger trains smoothly, moving the freight cars out of the yards, and posting regular armed guards over them. Economic management and political power had in effect been taken over by the strikers. Of course, this kind of transfer of power was not universally understood or approved of, even by those who supported the strike. For example, a meeting of rolling-mill men in Columbus, Ohio, endorsed the railroad strikers, urged labor to combine politically and legislate justice, but rejected "mobbism" as apt to destroy "the best form of republican government."

The strike spread almost as fast as word of it, and with it the conflict with the military. In Columbia, Meadville, and Chenago, Pennsylvania, strikers seized the railroads, occupied the roundhouses, and stopped troop trains. In Buffalo, New York, the militia was stoned on Sunday but scattered the crowd by threatening to shoot. Next morning a crowd armed with knives and cudgels stormed into the railroad shops, brushed aside militia guards and forced shopmen to quit work. They seized the Erie roundhouse and barricaded it. When a militia company marched out to recapture the property, a thousand people blocked and drove them back. By Monday evening, all the major U.S. roads had given up trying to move anything but local passenger trains out of Buffalo. Court testimony later gave a good picture of how the strike spread to Reading, Pennsylvania. At a meeting of workers on the Reading Railroad, the chairman suggested that it would not be a bad idea to do what had been done on the B&O. "While it is hot we can keep the ball rolling," someone chimed in. After some discussion, men volunteered to head off incoming trains. Next day a crowd of 2,000 assembled while twenty-five or fifty men, their faces blackened with coal dust, tore up track, fired trains, and burned a railroad bridge. That evening seven companies of the National Guard arrived. As they marched through a tenement district to clear the tracks, the people of the neighborhood severely stoned them, wounding twenty with missiles and pistol shots. The soldiers opened fire without orders and killed eleven. As in Pittsburgh, the population grew furious over the killings. They plundered freight cars, tore up tracks, and broke into an arsenal, taking sixty rifles. Next day the companies which had conducted the massacre marched down the track together with newly arrived troops; the crowd stoned the former and fraternized with the latter. When the hated Grays turned menacingly toward the crowd, the new troops announced that they would not fire on the people, turned some of their ammunition over to the crowd, and told the Grays, "If you fire at the mob, we'll fire at you."

Such fraternization between troops and the crowd was common. When the Governor sent 170 troops to Newark, Ohio, they were so unpopular that the county commissioners refused to provide their rations. Thereupon the strikers themselves volunteered to feed them. By the end of the day strikers and soldiers were fraternizing in high good humor. Similarly, when the Governor of New York sent 600 troops to the railroad center of Hornellsville, in response to the strike on the Erie, the troops and strikers fraternized, making commanders doubtful of their power to act. When the entire Pennsylvania National Guard was called up in response to the Pittsburgh uprising, a company in Lebanon, Pennsylvania, mutinied and marched through town amidst great excitement. In Altoona, a crowd captured a westbound train carrying 500 militiamen. The troops gave up their arms with the best of will and fraternized with the crowd. The crowd refused to let them proceed, but was glad to let them go home—which one full company and parts of the others proceeded to do. A Philadelphia militia unit straggling home decided to march to Harrisburg and surrender. They entered jovially, shook hands all around, and gave up their guns to the crowd.

Persuasion worked likewise against would-be strikebreakers. When a volunteer started to take a freight train out of Newark, Ohio, a striking fireman held up his hand, three fingers of which had been cut off by a railroad accident. "This is the man whose place you are taking," shouted another striker. "This is the man who works with a hand and a half to earn a dollar and a half a day,

three days in the week, for his wife and children. Are you going to take the bread out of his mouth and theirs?" The strikebreaker jumped down amidst cheers.

By now, the movement was no longer simply a railroad strike. With the battles between soldiers and crowds drawn from all parts of the working population, it was increasingly perceived as a struggle between workers as a whole and employers as a whole. This was now reflected in the rapid development of general strikes. After the burning of the railroad yards in Pittsburgh, a general strike movement swept through the area. At nearby McKeesport, workers of the National Tube Works gathered early Monday morning and marched all over town to martial music, calling fellow workers from their houses. From the tube workers the strike spread first to a rolling mill, then a car works, then a planing mill. In mid-morning, 1,000 McKeesport strikers marched with a brass band to Andrew Carnegie's great steel works, calling out planing-mill and tin-mill workers as they went. By mid-afternoon the Carnegie workers and the Braddocks car workers joined the strike. At Castle Shannon, 500 miners struck. On the South Side, laborers struck at Jones and Laughlin and at the Evans, Dalzell & Co. pipe works.

In Buffalo, New York, crowds roamed the city trying to bring about a general strike. They effectively stopped operations at planing mills, tanneries, car works, a bolt and nut factory, hog yards, coal yards, and canal works. In Harrisburg, Pennsylvania, factories and shops throughout the city were closed by strikes and crowd action. In Zanesville, Ohio, 300 unemployed men halted construction on a hotel, then moved through town shutting down nearly every factory and foundry and sending horse-cars to the barns. Next morning a meeting of workingmen drew up a schedule of acceptable wages. In Columbus, a crowd growing from 300 to 2,000 went through town spreading a general strike, successfully calling out workers at a rolling mill, pipe works, fire clay works, pot works, and planing mill. "Shut up or burn up" was the mob's slogan. An offshoot of a rally to support the railroad workers in Toledo,

Ohio, resolved to call a general strike for a minimum wage of $1.50 a day. Next morning a large crowd of laborers, grain trimmers, stevedores, and others assembled and created a committee of safety composed of one member from every trade represented in the movement. Three hundred men formed a procession four abreast while a committee called on the management of each factory; workers of those not meeting the demands joined in the strike.

In Chicago, the movement began with a series of mass rallies called by the Workingman's Party, the main radical party of the day, and a strike by forty switchmen on the Michigan Central Railroad. The switchmen roamed through the railroad property with a crowd of 500 others, including strikers from the East who had ridden in to spread the strike, calling out other workers and closing down those railroads that were still running. Next the crowd called out the workers at the stockyards and several packinghouses. Smaller crowds spread out to broaden the strike; one group, for example, called out 500 planing-mill workers, and with them marched down Canal Street and Blue Island Avenue closing down factories. Crews on several lake vessels struck. With transportation dead, the North Chicago rolling mill and many other industries closed for lack of coke and other supplies. Next day the strike spread still further: streetcars, wagons and buggies were stopped; tanneries, stoneworks, clothing factories, lumber yards, brickyards, furniture factories, and a large distillery were closed in response to roving crowds. One day more and the crowds forced officials at the stockyards and gasworks to sign promises to raise wages to $2.00 a day, while more dock and lumber yard workers struck. In the midst of this, the Workingman's Party proclaimed: "Fellow Workers . . . Under any circumstances keep quiet until we have given the present crisis a due consideration."

The general strikes spread even into the South, often starting with black workers and spreading to whites. Texas and Pacific Railroad workers at Marshall, Texas, struck against the pay cut. In response, black longshoremen in nearby Galves-

ton struck for and won pay equal to that of their white fellow workers. Fifty black workers marched down the Strand in Galveston, persuading construction men, track layers and others to strike for $2.00 a day. The next day committees circulated supporting the strike. White workers joined in. The movement was victorious, and $2.00 a day became the going wage for Galveston. In Louisville, Kentucky, black workers made the round of sewers under construction, urging a strike for $1.50 a day. At noon, sewer workers had quit everywhere in town. On Tuesday night a march of 500 stoned the depot of the Louisville and Nashville Railroad, which was refusing a wage increase for laborers. By Wednesday, most of Louisville's factories were shut down by roving crowds, and Thursday brought further strikes by coopers, textile and plow factory workers, brickmakers, and cabinetworkers.

The day the railroad strike reached East St. Louis, the St. Louis Workingman's Party marched 500 strong across the river to join a meeting of 1,000 railroad workers and residents. Said one of the speakers, "All you have to do, gentlemen, for you have the numbers, is to unite on one idea—that the workingmen shall rule the country. What man makes, belongs to him, and the workingmen made this country." The St. Louis General Strike, the peak of the Great Upheaval, for a time nearly realized that goal.

The railroad workers at that meeting voted for a strike, set up a committee of one man from each railroad, and occupied the Relay Depot as their headquarters. The committee promptly posted General Order No. 1, forbidding freight trains from leaving any yard.

That night, across the river in St. Louis, the Workingman's Party called a mass meeting, with crowds so large that three separate speakers' stands were set up simultaneously. "The workingmen," said one speaker, "intend now to assert their rights, even if the result is shedding of blood. . . . They are ready to take up arms at any moment."

Next morning, workers from different shops and plants began to appear at the party headquarters, requesting that committees be sent around to "notify them to stop work and join the other workingmen, that they might have a reason for doing so." The party began to send such committees around, with unexpected results. The coopers struck, marching from shop to shop with a fife and drum shouting, "Come out, come out! No barrels less than nine cents." Newsboys, gasworkers, boatmen, and engineers struck as well. Railroadmen arrived from East St. Louis on engines and flatcars they had commandeered, moving through the yards enforcing General Order No. 1 and closing a wire works.

That day, an "Executive Committee" formed, based at the Workingman's Party headquarters, to coordinate the strike. As one historian wrote, "Nobody ever knew who that executive committee really was; it seems to have been a rather loose body composed of whomsoever chanced to come in and take part in its deliberations."

In the evening, 1,500 men, mostly molders and mechanics, armed themselves with lathes and clubs and marched to the evening's rally. To a crowd of 10,000 the first speaker, a cooper, began, "There was a time in the history of France when the poor found themselves oppressed to such an extent that forbearance ceased to be a virtue, and hundreds of heads tumbled into the basket. That time may have arrived with us." Another speaker called upon the workingmen to organize into companies of ten, twenty, and a hundred, to establish patrols to protect property, and to "organize force to meet force." Someone suggested that "the colored men should have a chance." A black steamboatman spoke for the roustabouts and levee workers. He asked the crowd would they stand behind the levee strikers, regardless of color? "We will!" the crowd shouted back.

The general strike got under way in earnest the next morning. The employees of a beef cannery struck and paraded. The coopers met and discussed their objectives. A force of strikers marched to the levee, where a crowd of steamboatmen and roustabouts "of all colors" forced the captains of boat after boat to sign written promises of fifty percent higher pay. Finally everyone assembled for the day's great march. Six hundred factory workers marched up behind a brass band; a company of railroad strikers came with coupling pins, brake rods, red signal flags and other "irons and implements emblematic of their calling." Strikers' committees went out ahead to call out those still working, and as the march came by, a loaf of bread on a flag-staff for its emblem, workers in foundries, bagging companies, flour mills, bakeries, chemical, zinc and white lead works poured out of their shops and into the crowd. In Carondolet, far on the south side of the city, a similar march developed autonomously, as a crowd of iron workers closed down two zinc works, the Bessemer Steel Works, and other plants. In East St. Louis, there was a parade of women in support of the strike. By sundown, nearly all the manufacturing establishments in the city had been closed. "Business is fairly paralyzed here," said the *Daily Market Reporter.*

But economic activities did not cease completely; some continued under control or by permission of the strikers. The British Consul in St. Louis noted how the railroad strikers had "taken the road into their own hands, running the trains and collecting fares"; "it is to be deplored that a large portion of the general public appear to regard such conduct as a legitimate mode of warfare." It was now the railroad managements which wanted to stop all traffic. One official stated frankly that by stopping all passenger trains, the companies would cut the strikers off from mail facilities and prevent them from sending committees from one point to another along the lines. Railroad officials, according to the *St. Louis Times,* saw advantage in stopping passenger trains and thus "incommoding the public so as to produce a revolution in the sentiment which now seems to be in favor of the strikers." From the strikers' point of view, running non-freights allowed them to coordinate the strike and show their social responsibility.

The strikers had apparently decided to allow the manufacture of bread, for they permitted a flour mill to remain open. When the owner of the Belcher Sugar Refinery applied to the Executive Committee for permission to operate his plant for forty-eight hours, lest a large quantity of sugar spoil, the Executive Committee persuaded the refinery workers to go back to work and sent a guard of 200 men to protect the refinery. Concludes one historian of the strike, "the Belcher episode revealed . . . the spectacle of the owner of one of the city's largest industrial enterprises recognizing the *de facto* authority of the Executive Committee."

But the strikers here and elsewhere failed to hold what they had conquered. Having shattered the authority of the status quo for a few short days, they faltered and fell back, unsure of what to do. Meanwhile, the forces of law and order—no longer cowering in the face of overwhelming mass force—began to organize. Chicago was typical: President Hayes authorized the use of Federal regulars; citizens' patrols were organized ward by ward, using Civil War veterans; 5,000 special police were sworn in, freeing the regular police for action; big employers organized their reliable employees into armed companies—many of which were sworn in as special police. At first the crowd successfully out-maneuvered the police in the street fighting that ensued, but after killing at least eighteen people the police finally gained control of the crowd and thus broke the back of the movement.

Behind them stood the Federal government. "This insurrection," said General Hancock, the commander in charge of all Federal troops used in the strike, must be stifled "by all possible means." Not that the Federal troops were strong and reliable. The Army was largely tied down by the rebellion of Nez Perce Indians, led by Chief Joseph. In the words of Lieutenant Philip Sheridan, "The troubles on the Rio Grande border, the Indian outbreak on the western frontier of New Mexico, and the Indian war in the Departments of the Platte and Dakota, have kept the small and inadequate forces in this division in a constant state of activity, almost without rest, night and day." Most of the enlisted men had not been paid for months—for the Congress had refused to pass the Army Appropriations Bill so as to force the withdrawal of Reconstruction troops from the South. Finally, the Army included many workers driven into military service by unemployment. As

one union iron molder in the Army wrote, "It does not follow that a change of dress involves a change of principle." No mutinies occurred, however, as the 3,000 available Federal troops were rushed under direction of the War Department from city to city, wherever the movement seemed to grow out of control. "The strikers," President Hayes noted emphatically in his diary, "have been put down by *force.*" More than 100 of them were killed in the process.

The Great Upheaval was an expression of the new economic and social system in America, just as surely as the cities, railroads and factories from which it had sprung. The enormous expansion of industry after the Civil War had transformed millions of people who had grown up as farmers and self-employed artisans and entrepreneurs into employees, growing thousands of whom were concentrated within each of the new corporate empires. They were no longer part of village and town communities with their extended families and stable, unchallenged values, but concentrated in cities, with all their anonymity and freedom; their work was no longer individual and competitive, but group and cooperative; they no longer directed their own work, but worked under control of a boss; they no longer controlled the property on which they worked or its fruits, and therefore could not find fruitful employment unless someone with property agreed to hire them. The Great Upheaval grew out of their intuitive sense that they needed each other, had the support of each other, and together were powerful.

This sense of unity was not embodied in any centralized plan or leadership, but in the feelings and action of each participant. "There was no concert of action at the start," the editor of the *Labor Standard* pointed out. "It spread because the workmen of Pittsburgh felt the same oppression that was felt by the workmen of West Virginia and so with the workmen of Chicago and St. Louis." In Pittsburgh, concludes historian Robert Bruce, "Men like Andrew Hice or Gus Harris or David Davis assumed the lead briefly at one point or another, but only because they happened to be foremost in nerve or vehemence." In Newark, Ohio, "no single individual seemed to command the . . . strikers. They followed the sense of the meeting, as Quakers might say, on such proposals as one or another of them . . . put forward. Yet they proceeded with notable coherence, as though fused by their common adversity."

The Great Upheaval was in the end thoroughly defeated, but the struggle was by no means a total loss. Insofar as it aimed at preventing the continued decline of workers' living standards, it won wage concessions in a number of cases and undoubtedly gave pause to would-be wage-cutters to come, for whom the explosive force of the social dynamite with which they tampered had now been revealed. Insofar as it aimed at a workers' seizure of power, its goal was chimerical, for the workers as yet still formed only a minority in a predominantly farm and middle-class society. But the power of workers to virtually stop society, to counter the forces of repression, and to organize cooperative action on a vast scale was revealed in the most dramatic form.

It was not only upon the workers that the Great Upheaval left its mark. Their opponents began building up their power as well, symbolized by the National Guard Armories whose construction began the following year, to contain upheavals yet to come.

Certain periods, wrote Irving Bernstein, bear a special quality in American labor history. "There occurred at these times strikes and social upheavals of extraordinary importance, drama, and violence which ripped the cloak of civilized decorum from society, leaving exposed naked class conflict." Such periods were analyzed before World War I by Rosa Luxemburg and others under the concept of mass strikes. The mass strike, she wrote, signifies not just a single act but a whole period of class struggle.

Its use, its effects, its reasons for coming about are in a constant state of flux . . . political and economic strikes, united and partial strikes, defensive strikes and combat strikes, general strikes of individual sections of industry and general strikes of entire cities, peaceful wage strikes and street battles, uprisings with barricades—all run together and run alongside each other, get in each other's way, overlap each other; a perpetually moving and changing sea of phenomena.

The Great Upheaval was the first—but by no means the last—mass strike in American history.

5

BOSS COX'S CINCINNATI: A STUDY IN URBANIZATION AND POLITICS, 1880–1914

ZANE L. MILLER

The rush of foreign immigrants and rural migrants into America's industrial cities after the Civil War posed new problems for municipal administrations. As wave after wave of these new urban dwellers came in search of jobs, American cities literally exploded. Before midcentury New York, America's largest city, contained less than a half million people; by 1870 it had passed the million mark. In 1850 only 3.5 million Americans lived in municipalities containing 2,500 or more people; a half century later that number stood at 30 million, a tenfold increase.

This enormous population increase changed the nature of the American city. At midcentury cities were small enough that most people walked to work, to shop, or to play. There was little residential segregation and rich, middle-income, and poor families lived near each other. After the Civil War population density increased dramatically, causing overcrowding and a myriad of social problems. As the street railway and streetcar came into general use in the 1870s, providing cheap and reliable transportation from outlying areas to workshops and business districts, prosperous middle- and working-class families began to move away from the city center to new suburban developments.

The explosion of America's urban areas and the dispersion of its population gave birth to a new political animal: the city "boss." As Zane L. Miller details in this essay, urban bosses, like George B. Cox of Cincinnati, fashioned powerful political machines that appealed to the diverse nature of the new urban electorate. By dispensing patronage throughout the city on an organized basis and opening city government to rich and poor alike, Boss Cox created an effective, if corrupt, form of city government. Where no national social welfare system existed before, his machine provided a measure of protection to poor and working-class residents who found themselves cast adrift in the new urban wilderness.

What do you think accounts for the popularity of machine politics in the late-nineteenth and twentieth centuries? Were the people as ill-served by men like Boss Cox as Progressive reformers suggest? How does the attitude of the urban boss compare with that of Progressive reformers, such as those discussed by Howard Gillette in Reading 9 and Allen F. Davis in Reading 13.

Many observers of the turn-of-the-century urban scene have depicted bossism as one of the great unmitigated evils of the American city, as a ty- rannical, authoritarian, relentlessly efficient and virtually invulnerable political system. Between 1904 and 1912, for example, George B. Cox was

Reprinted from *Journal of American History,* 54 (1968): 823–38, by permission of the *Journal of American History.*

castigated by writers in four national magazines. Gustav Karger called him the "Proprietor of Cincinnati." Lincoln Steffens declared that "Cox's System" was "one great graft," "the most perfect thing of the kind in this country." Frank Parker Stockbridge claimed that "The Biggest Boss of Them All" had an organization "more compact and closely knit than any of the political machines which have dominated New York, Philadelphia, Chicago, St. Louis or San Francisco." And George Kibbe Turner concluded that in the 1890s "the man from Dead Man's Corner . . . seated himself over the city of Cincinnati. For twenty years he remained there—a figure like no other in the United States, or in the world." Yet these knowledgable and sensitive journalists obscured as much as they revealed about the nature of Queen City politics in the Progressive era. A new kind of city had developed, and "the boss" comprised only a fraction of its novel political system.

Paradoxically, Cox and his machine were produced by, fed on, and ultimately helped dispel the spectacular disorder which engulfed Cincinnati in the late-nineteenth century and threatened the very survival of the democratic political process. In these years, increasing industrialization, technological innovations in communication and transportation—especially the coming of rapid transit—and continued foreign and domestic migration had reversed the physical pattern of the mid-century walking city and transformed Cincinnati into a physically enlarged, divided, and potentially explosive metropolis.

Old citizens were shocked as familiar landmarks and neighborhoods vanished. By 1900, railroads and warehouses had monopolized the Ohio River bottoms. The financial and retail districts had moved up into the Basin around Fountain Square, the focus of the street railway system; new club, theater, and tenderloin districts had developed; and industries had plunged up Mill Creek Valley, converting Mohawk-Brighton into "the undisputed industrial bee-hive of the Great Queen City of the West," surrounding once fashionable Dayton Street, creating a new community called Ivorydale, and reaching out to the villages of Norwood and Oakley in search of cheap land, ready access to railroads, and less congested and more cheerful surroundings.

The Over-the-Rhine entertainment section along Vine Street became tawdry with commercialism. It now had, complained one habitué, "all the tarnished tinsel of a Bohemianism with the trimmings of a gutter and the morals of a sewer" —a repulsive contrast, he felt, to "the old-time concert and music halls . . . where one could take wife, sister, or sweetheart and feel secure . . . that not one obnoxious word would profane their ears."

The fashionable residential districts which had flanked the center of the walking city began to disintegrate. One family after another fled the East End for the hills around the Basin, leaving only a small coterie led by the Charles P. Tafts to stave off the advance of factories and slums. The elite West End seemed to disappear overnight. It "did not go down imperceptibly," recalled one old resident. "It went to ruin almost as if a bombshell sent it to destruction."

The Hilltops, at mid-century the private preserve of cemeteries, colleges, and a handful of wealthy families, became the prime residential district in the new city. The crush to get in generated new tensions. In 1899 one observer acidly remarked: "when rapid transit came the Hebrews . . . flocked to" Walnut Hills

until it was known by the name of New Jerusalem. Avondale was then heralded as the suburb of deliverance, but again rapid transit brought the wealthy Hebrews . . . in numbers greater than the flock of crows that every morning and evening darkens her skies, until now it has been facetiously said that the congregation has assembled in force and . . . when Avondale is roofed over the synagogue will be complete.

The diffusion of wealthy families, the reduction in casual social and business contacts, and the construction of new communities made ardent joiners of the Hilltops elite. Each neighborhood had an improvement association, and between 1880 and 1905 five new businessmen's

organizations devoted to boosting the city's le-
thargic economy had appeared. In the same period six social clubs opened downtown facilities,
and three country clubs were started. By 1913,
moreover, there were twenty-two exclusive clubs
and patriotic societies and innumerable women's
groups. These developments helped counteract
the disruptive effects of the "country movement,"
as one visitor labeled it, which was "so general
that church-going became an affair of some difficulty" and "society itself . . . more or less disintegrated."

But not all those moving out were affluent.
Liberated by rapid transit, skilled and semiskilled
workers and moderately prosperous professional
and white-collar men with life savings, the courage to take out a mortgage, an equity in a building
and loan association, or a willingness to rent a flat
in a double or triple decker, also fled the Basin.
They took refuge in a no-man's-land between the
center of the city and the Hilltops frontier which
was similar to an area dubbed the Zone of Emergence by Boston social workers.

Zone residents formed what the Cincinnati
Post referred to as "the so-called middle class
. . . , the class that makes any city . . . what it is
. . . [,] the class that takes in the great body of
people between wealth and poverty" and builds
up "many organizations, societies, associations,
fraternities and clubs that bring together people
who are striving upward, trying to uplift themselves, and hence human society."

They, too, found life in the new city a novel
experience. A retired leather factory porter who
moved into the Zone lamented:

> When I lived down on Richmond in a little house
> we cooked the corn beef and cabbage in the house
> and ate in there, and when we wanted to go to the
> toilet we went out into the yard, now I live in a fine
> house, I am made to eat . . . out in the yard, and
> when I want to go to the toilet I have to go into the
> house.

Graham R. Taylor had noted that since most
Zone residents commuted they suffered a severe
"dislocation of the normal routine of factory and

home": they had to adjust to "the need for travel
and its curtailment of leisure and income . . . ,"
to eating lunches away from home, to doing without "customary city facilities," and to knowing
the feeling of "isolation from their fellows." Price
Hill—like the rest of the Zone a heavily Catholic
area—felt itself conspicuously cut off. In the
1890s the editor of the *Catholic-Telegraph,* denouncing the traction company as the "octopus,"
joined the Price Hill Improvement Association in
begging both city and traction company officials
to bring the area "within range of the civilized
world" and suggested secession as a means of
dramatizing to the "people east of Millcreek"
that a new public school, "granted by the un-
bounded munificence of the City of Cincinnati,"
did not amount to a redemption of the city's annexation pledges.

The exodus, however, did not depopulate the
Basin. Instead, a great residential Circle formed
around the central business district. It filled with
newcomers and those who lacked the means to
get out—rural whites and Negroes from the
South, Germans, Irish, Greeks, Italians, and Jews
from eastern Europe. Working at the poorest
paying jobs available, they were jammed into the
most congested quarters. The Circle led all other
areas of the city in arrests, mortality, and disease.

Although the pressure to escape was enormous, the barriers were formidable. Ignorant of
the ways of the city, as an Associated Charities
report put it, Circle dwellers had to be "shown
how to buy, how to cook, how to make the home
attractive, how to find employment." Many, "utterly friendless and discouraged," succumbed to
"the damnable absence of want or desire" and
grew "indifferent . . . to their own elevation."
Plagued by "physical bankruptcy," they found it
difficult to find and hold jobs, let alone form and
maintain the kind of organizations which enabled
Zone residents to shield themselves from economic disaster, legal pitfalls, social isolation, and
apathy.

The immediate impact of the emergence of the
new city pushed Cincinnati to the brink of
anarchy. In March 1884, the *Enquirer* complained that the police had failed to choke off a

crime wave although, in the last year alone, there had been twelve arrests for malicious shooting, twenty-nine for malicious cutting, forty-seven for cutting with intent to wound, 284 for shooting with intent to kill, ninety-two for murder and manslaughter, and 948 for carrying a concealed weapon. The total number of arrests came to 56,-784. The city's population was 250,000. Later that same month, a lynch mob descended on the county jail. While police and militia fought off the mob, gangs looted stores and shops on the fringe of the downtown district. In three days of riot the courthouse was burned to the ground, fifty-four people were killed, and an estimated 200 people wounded.

During the fall elections, violence erupted in the lower wards; two policemen and one Negro were killed. Congressman Benjamin Butterworth remarked that he had "never witnessed anywhere such coarse brutality and such riotous demonstrations. . . ." Cincinnati, he concluded, "seems . . . doomed to perdition."

Less than two years later the city faced another major crisis. On May 1, 1886, Cincinnati workers joined in nationwide demonstrations for the eight-hour day. These were followed by a series of strikes. The militia was called out, and for two weeks the city resembled an armed camp. Only the show of force and, perhaps, the memory of the courthouse catastrophe prevented another riot.

Yet labor remained restive, and a rash of strikes followed. By 1892, the paternalistic system which had dominated the breweries was smashed. And in 1894, Judge William Howard Taft spent the hot days of June and July "trying to say nothing to reporters" and "issuing injunctions" in an effort to control and prevent the railroad strike from leading to mass violence.

The Sunday-closing question was another explosive issue. The *Post,* the *Catholic-Telegraph,* a Committee of Five Hundred, and many Protestant clergymen all leveled scathing attacks on the continental Sabbath. "Sunday in Cincinnati," asserted one Methodist minister, "is a high carnival of drunkenness, base sensuality, reeking debauchery and bloody, often fatal crime." Other spokesmen tied the open Sunday to anarchism, atheism, corrupt politicians, a decadent daily press, indifferent public officials, and the ruthless exploitation of labor. "The modern Puritan," insisted Charles P. Taft, "intends to rise up and oppose to the uttermost this kind of Sunday."

When, in 1889, the mayor announced his intention to enforce the Sunday-closing law for saloons, the city almost faced another riot. Some 1,000 saloonkeepers vowed to ignore the new policy. When a cadre of police and firemen marched over the Rhine to close Kissell's saloon, an unruly crowd gathered, epithets were hurled, but no violence occurred. Kissell's was closed; the "era of the back door," with "front doors locked and curtains up, but back doors widened," had opened.

These spectacular outbreaks plus other pressures overwhelmed city hall. Indeed, scarcely a residential area, economic interest, or social or occupational group was left unscathed by the multidimensional disorder. As the physical area of the city expanded, officials were besieged by demands for the extension, improvement, and inauguration of public services of all kinds and for lower taxes. Simultaneously, the relative decline of the city heightened the urgency of the agitation. Municipal institutions and agencies, established to meet the needs of the walking city, became overburdened, outmoded, and dilapidated.

The new city, with old ways shattered, provided a fertile breeding ground for turmoil and discontent and, as it turned out, for innovation and creative reconstruction. Initially, however, this unprecedented change accompanied by unprecedented demands for government action produced only the hope of reform. In 1885, on the eve of the repudiation of a Democratic administration, William Howard Taft predicted that "the clouds are beginning to break over this Sodom of ours and the sun of decency is beginning to dispel the moral miasma that has rested on us now for so many years. It's the beginning of an era of reform."

Yet for almost a decade no party could put together a decisive ruling majority. The city's political processes seemed frozen by a paralyzing factionalism. The division of the city into residential districts which roughly coincided with socio-economic lines made it difficult for the wealthy and well-educated to keep in contact with and control ward politics. As a result, extreme factionalism developed which could, apparently, be surmounted only by appealing to a host of neighborhood leaders and by constructing alliances which crossed party lines.

According to close observers, the chief products of this system were the use of money in city conventions and the rise of what Charles P. Taft called the "bummer," a "queer creature" who "evolves somehow from the slums. . . ." In youth "a bootblack, a newsboy or a general loafer," he matured into "an Arab" who needed only "a good standing with a saloon that has a fine layout during the day." A "hustler at the polls and conventions," the bummer was in such demand that he could accept money from competing candidates, thus lengthening the convention and contributing to interfactional dealing. After studying the influence of the "bummer," Tat gloomily concluded that the "day of pure politics can never be . . . until a riot, a plague or flood kills off all the ward bummers."

By 1897, however, and without divine intervention, all this had changed. In January of that year, three months before the city election, the *Post* gravely announced its intention to describe "impassionately and without bias the means employed" in Cincinnati's "superior and unrecorded government." It was controlled by "the boss, whose power is absolute"—George B. Cox.

The *Post*'s analysis closely paralleled those made after the turn of the century. It dissected the patronage system, outlined the sources of financial support, and noted the attempted appeasement of the city's various special groups—the soldiers, the Germans, the Republican clubs, the Reform Jews, the legal and medical professions, the socially prominent Hilltops businessmen, and certain cooperative Democrats. It excitedly reported the effectiveness of the organization's intelligence system, the way the "plugger" and the "knocker" wore "beaten paths to the office of the boss to urge the appointment of this

man, the discharge of that [,] or to report some feature of misconduct or expression. . . ." The paper noted that Cox was always available for consultation with any citizen regardless of station or status and that he had been little more than one of several important factional leaders until, in 1886, Governor Joseph B. Foraker selected him to serve as chief adviser on patronage and political affairs in Hamilton County.

Foraker made a shrewd choice; Cox had grown up with the new city and received a liberal education in its ways. The son of British immigrants, he was born in 1853 and reared in the Eighteenth Ward, a district which by the 1880s contained fashionable as well as slum housing, factories, and its share of saloons and brothels. His father died when Cox was eight. Successively, Cox worked as a bootblack, newsboy, lookout for a gambling joint, grocery deliveryman, bartender, and tobacco salesman. His school principal, who later became superintendent of schools, claimed that Cox was frequently in boyish trouble in classes, exhibited an "undisguised love for his mother," and "never lied . . . bore malice, sulked, whined or moped." Cox had also been exposed to religion. Although not a churchgoer, as an adult he had, according to one journalist, "dormant powerful sentiments, which rest on foundations of the firmest faith."

In the mid-1870s Cox acquired a saloon in his home neighborhood. He entered politics and served on the city council from 1878 until 1885 when, after joining forces with the Republican reform mayoralty candidate, he ran unsuccessfully for county clerk. He tried for the same post in 1888, failed, and never again stood for public office.

At that time, moving away politically from the Circle, Cox worked with George Moerlein, perhaps the strongest of the GOP professionals in the Zone. In 1890, he and Moerlein quarreled over patronage; and in the city convention of 1891, Cox was able, with the support of the Blaine Club, a kind of political settlement house that he had helped to establish, to defeat Moerlein's candidate for police judge and nominate his own man. Moerlein men now became Cox men.

So, too, did Charles P. Taft and the *Times-Star,* which had been one of the last, the most influential, and the most outspoken of Cox's critics in the Hilltops Republican ranks. It accepted Cox, the paper announced, to secure a "New Order" for Cincinnati. And the president of the gas company, sensing the political drift, confided to his diary that he had "concluded [an] arrangement with Geo. B. Cox for services at $3500 per year quarterly to last for three years." In the spring election of 1894 the Republicans carried the city with a plurality of over 6,500 votes, the first decisive municipal election in a decade. In 1897, Cox was the honest broker in a coalition composed of Circle and Zone Negroes, Zone politicians, the gas and traction companies, and Hilltops Republican reformers.

Election returns after 1885 disclose a clear pattern. The GOP won five successive contests by uniting powerful Hilltops support with enough strength in the Zone to overcome the Democratic grip on the Circle. Until 1894 the margins of victory were perilously thin. The substantial triumph of that year merely marked the completion of the alliance which pitted a united periphery against the center of the city.

The heart of the Republican "New Order" coalition, and the critical factor in the election of 1894, was its appeal to voters in the Hilltops fringe who demanded order and reform. To satisfy the Hilltops, Cox and his associates eliminated the bummer, provided brief and decorous conventions, enfranchised Negroes by suppressing violence at the polls, reduced the rapid turnover in office, and cut down the incidence of petty graft and corporation raiding.

Moreover, the "machine" heeded the advice of its reform allies from the Hilltops. Cox accepted the secret ballot, voter registration, and a series of state laws which, though retaining the mayor-council form of government with ward representation, were designed to give the city a stable and more centralized government. The administrations which he indorsed started to build a professional police force, expanded and reequipped the fire department, pushed through a $6,000,000 water-works program, renovated municipal institutions, supported the growth of the University of Cincinnati, launched extensive street-paving and sewer-constructing projects, and tried to reduce the smoke problem and expand the city's park acreage. They also opened the door to housing regulation, suppressed the Sunday saloon, flagrant public gambling, and disorderly brothels (the city was never really closed), began to bring order into the chaotic public-utilities field by favoring privately owned, publicly regulated monopolies under progressive management, and succeeded in keeping the tax rate low. The Republican regime, in short, brought positive government to Cincinnati.

While this program also won votes in the Zone, it was not the sole basis for the party's popularity there. Many of the lieutenants and captains closest to Cox were Zone residents. They composed a colorful group known variously as "the gang," "the sports," or the "bonifaces"—a clique which met nightly Over-the-Rhine either at Schubert and Pels, where each had a special beer mug with his name gilded on it, or at the round table in Wielert's beer garden. Three of them owned or operated combination saloons, gambling joints, and dance halls; one was prominent in German charitable associations and the author of several textbooks used in the elementary schools; another served twenty consecutive terms as president of the Hamilton County League of Building Associations; and one was a former catcher for the Cincinnati Redlegs.

Their tastes, behavior, and attitudes were conveniently summarized in the biographical sketches of ward leaders and city officials in the 1901 *Police and Municipal Guide.* All were characterized as friendly, well-known, "All Around Good-Fellows" who liked a story, belonged to several social and fraternal groups, gave generously to charity, and treated the poor and sick with special kindness. They were all among the most ardent supporters of any project to boost the city.

Cox is pictured in the *Guide* as an adherent to the code of the Zone who had risen to the top. He was a *bon vivant* who enjoyed good cigars and good jokes, a man of wealth whose recently completed Clifton mansion was luxuriously decorated and adorned with expensive works of art, a man of impressive but quiet and private charity. Above all, he was true to his word, loyal to his friends, yet quick to reprimand and replace those who betrayed his trust by misusing public office.

Cox and his top civil servants—surrounded by a motley crowd of newspaper reporters, former boxers and ball players, vaudeville and burlesque performers, and other Vine Street characters—provided an attractive model for men awed by the glamor, wealth, and power which was so visible yet so elusive in the new city. Cox's opponents in the Zone seldom attacked him or this inside group directly. Even in the heat of the 1897 campaign, the *Volksfreund,* the German Catholic Democratic daily, carefully described Cox as an "amiable man" who had to be "admired" for his "success" and, either ignoring or unaware of the process of negotiation and mediation by which he ruled, criticized him only for his illiberality in imposing "dictatorial methods" on the GOP. Indeed, most Zone residents, like those of the Hilltops, found it difficult to object to a government which seemed humane, efficient, and progressive.

Yet it would be a mistake to overestimate the strength of the "New Order" Republican coalition. Its victories from 1885 to 1894 were won by perilously close pluralities. The organization, moreover, failed to carry a referendum for the sale of the city-owned Southern Railroad in 1896 and lost the municipal contest in 1897 to a reform fusion ticket, and the fall elections of 1897, 1898, and 1899 to the Democrats. In all these reversals, crucial defections occurred in both the Hilltops and the Zone. Skittish voters grew indignant over alleged corruption, outraged by inaction on the traction and gas questions, piqued by the rising cost of new city projects, annoyed by the slow expansion of the educational program, or uneasy over the partial sacrifice of democracy to efficiency within the Republican organization.

Thereafter, however, the Republicans rallied and won three of the next four city elections by unprecedented margins. The strategy and tactics remained essentially the same. Although not wholly averse to raising national issues, Cox's group gave local affairs the most emphasis. The organization was occasionally purged of its less savory elements. Cox and his Zone advisors continued to consult with their Hilltops allies on nominations. The party promised and, in fact, tried to deliver order and reform. Without abolishing ward representation in the city council, it strengthened the mayor and streamlined the administration. The party also broadened and deepened its program as civic associations, women's clubs, social workers, social gospellers, and spokesmen for the new unionism—all novel forces in urban politics—expanded and elaborated their demands.

But voting patterns underwent a fundamental and, for the GOP, an ultimately disastrous change. By 1903 the Republicans dominated the entire city, carrying not only the Zone and Hilltops but also the center. The Circle was now the invincible bulwark of Cox's power.

There were several factors involved in the conversion of Circle Democrats to Republicanism. First, Cox had extensive personal contacts with them which dated back to his unsuccessful races for county clerk in the 1880s. Second, the Democrats had been unable to put down factionalism. By the late 1890s there were two reform elements in the party, both of which belabored the regulars from the center of the city as tainted with corruption, too cozy with Cox, and perhaps worst of all, as a discredit and burden to the party because they wore the charred shirt of the courthouse riot.

In the wake of the fusionist victory of 1897, Mike Mullen, the leader of a riverfront Democratic ward, explained why he would henceforth work with the Republican party.

I have worked hard [for the Democratic party] have suffered much and have won for it many victories. Yet all the while there was a certain element . . . that looked on me with distrust. . . . [L]eaders of the Fusionist Party did not think enough of me to let me look after the voting in my own ward, but sent down a lot of people to watch the count. That decided me.

He was later joined by Colonel Bob O'Brien who, like Mullen, specialized in Christmas turkey, soupline, and family-service politics. These Democrats led their constituents into the Republican fold.

It was this alliance with the Circle which ultimately destroyed Cox. Anti-machine spokesmen were convinced that they had to educate the city before they could redeem it. They felt, too, that politics was a potent educational tool. But campaigns had to be spectacular in order to engage the voters' attention and participation. As A. Julius Freiberg notes, the "psychology" of the electorate was such that years of "speaking, writing, explaining, even begging and imploring" had been "to no purpose." The "reformer and his fellow students may sit about the table and evolve high principles for action, but the people . . . will not be fed by those principles unless there is a dramatic setting, and the favorite dramatic setting is the killing of a dragon." And all the people "love the dramatic; not merely the poor, but the rich, and the middle class as well." All that was needed was a situation which would enable the right man to "bring to book the boss himself."

Reformers hammered relentlessly at the theme that Cox was not a good boss; he was the head of a "syndicate" which included the worst products of slum life. In "that part of the city where vice and infamy hold high revel," went one version of the charge, "the boss-made ticket finds its most numerous supporters. Every dive keeper, every creature who fattens upon the wages of sin . . . , all the elements at war with society have enlisted." Men "who claim to be respectable," the chief "beneficiaries of this unholy alliance . . . , go down into the gutter and accept office from hands that are reeking with the filth of the slums." Worse still, this "alliance of the hosts of iniquity with the greed of special privilege and ambition for power and place" plays so successfully "upon the prejudices and . . . superstition of the many that wrong is often espoused by those who in the end are the victims of the wrong."

The reformers also inpugned Cox's personal integrity. Democratic County Prosecutor Henry T. Hunt secured evidence that Cox had perjured himself in 1906 when he said he had not received a cent of some $250,000 of interest on public funds which Republican county treasurers had been paid by bankers. In the spring of 1911, Hunt and the grand jury indicted Cox and 123 others during a broad investigation of politics, corruption, and vice.

Finally, Hunt, stressing the issue of moral indignation, ran for mayor in the fall of 1911 on a Democratic reform ticket. Using the moral rhetoric of the muckraker, Hunt and his associates tied bossism, the chaos, poverty, and vice of the slums, and the malefactors of great wealth together and pictured them as a threat to the welfare of the whole city. Once again the Hilltops and Zone voted for order and reform. Hunt's progressive coalition swept the periphery, lost only in the Circle wards, and won the election.

By that time, however, Cox was no longer boss. President Taft and Charles P. Taft had wanted Cox to step aside as early as 1905, but they found him indispensable. After the grand jury revelations, however, they were able to convince the "bonifaces" that Cox was a liability. With the organization against him, Cox retired. For a time, he insisted that his two chief assistants, August Herrmann and Rudolph Hynicka, should also quit, apparently convinced that they, like himself, could no longer command the confidence of the periphery. Charles P. Taft's *Times-Star* agreed. The two men, backed by the Blaine Club, merely resigned their official party positions but refused to get out of politics entirely.

What, then, was Cox's role in politics and government in the new city? He helped create and manage a voluntary political-action organization which bridged the racial and cultural chasms between the Circle, Zone, and Hilltops. He and his allies were able to bring positive and moderate reform government to Cincinnati and to mitigate the conflict and disorder which accompanied the emergence of the new city. With the crisis atmosphere muted, ardent reformers could develop

more sophisticated programs and agitate, educate, and organize without arousing the kind of
divisive, emotional, and hysterical response
which had immobilized municipal statesmen in
the 1880s. In the process, while battering at the
boss, the slums, and the special-privilege syndicate, they shattered the bonds of confidence
which linked the Zone "bonifaces" and the moderate reformers of the Hilltops to Cox's organization. Cox, it seems, said more than he realized
when, in 1892, he remarked that a boss was "not
necessarily a public enemy."

6

WOMEN IN THE SOUTHERN FARMERS' ALLIANCE: THE ROLE AND STATUS OF WOMEN IN THE LATE NINETEENTH CENTURY

JULIE ROY JEFFREY

Early in the nineteenth century southern writers and publicists developed a mythology to explain the uniqueness of the southern experience. This "code of ethics," as one recent historian describes it, was formed around the concept of male chivalry and military honor such as was popularized by Sir Walter Scott's contemporary novels. A critical aspect of this southern code was the elevation of the white woman (black women, as slaves, were exempt from consideration by the code) to represent the purest essence of virtue, morality, and innocence. If the southern man represented the knight, the southern woman was his damsel, untouched by worldly affairs and dependent upon her knight for protection.

In this essay Julie Ray Jeffrey recounts one way in which this southern ethic was dissolved. By the 1880s southern farmers were beginning to feel the effects of a worldwide glut in the cotton market. In the face of falling prices and stiff international competition many farmers began to organize themselves in order to better their competitive position and to diversify their single-crop system. The Southern Farmers' Alliance grew to dominate this movement for agrarian change.

The Alliance, as Jeffrey shows, needed more than farmers for its success however: it also needed the active support and participation of farming women. Slowly and haltingly at first, farming women began to speak publicly and to write for the Alliance paper, *The Progressive Farmer.* From these new experiences Alliance women began to gain a sense of self-importance and utility that the old southern code denied them. It was a first step toward a fuller realization of the potential that had been long repressed in women.

Jeffrey makes the point that women's participation in the Farmers' Alliance elevated their public standing, but failed to lead on to further claims for the political participation of women. How does this compare with the experiences of northern women who developed their own self-understanding in other social movements? How does the experience of southern women in the late nineteenth century compare with that of American women of other regions and times as discussed in essays by Lois Green Carr and Lorena S. Walsh, Catherine M. Scholten, and John M. Faragher in *Retracing the Past: Readings in The History of The American People, Volume One?*

Reprinted by permission of the author from *Feminist Studies,* 3 (Fall 1975): 72–91. Copyright (c) 1975 by Julie Roy Jeffrey.

In the spring of 1891, Mrs. Brown, secretary of the Menola Sub-Alliance in North Carolina, welcomed an audience of delegates to the quarterly meeting of the Hertford County Farmers' Alliance. After introductory remarks to both the women and men in the audience, Brown addressed her female listeners directly.

> Words would fail me to express to you, my Alliance sisters, my appreciation of woman's opportunity of being co-workers with the brethren in the movement which is stirring this great nation. Oh, what womanly women we ought to be, for we find on every hand, fields of usefulness opening befor us. Our brothers . . . are giving us grand opportunities to show them, as Frances E. Willard says, that "Drudgery, fashion and gossip are no longer the bounds of woman's Sphere."

So enthusiastically was Brown's speech received, that the County Alliance unanimously requested its publication in the official paper of the Farmers' Alliance, the *Progressive Farmer.* In a similar fashion, the Failing Creek Alliance asked the *Progressive Farmer* later that year to reprint a speech Katie Moore had delivered to them. Moore had also spoken before an audience of women and men, and she too had had some special words for the women. " 'Tis not enough that we should be what our mothers were," she told them. "We should be more, since our advantages are superior. . . . This is the only order that allows us equal privileges to the men; we certainly should appreciate the privilege and prove to the world that we are worthy to be considered on an equal footing with them."

That the two audiences had approved of these speeches to the point of urging their wider circulation was not surprising. For the slogan of the Southern Farmers' Alliance itself was, "Equal rights to all, special privileges to none." As one Alliance publication explained, "The Alliance has come to redeem women from her enslaved condition, and place her in her proper sphere. She is admitted into the organization as the equal of her brother . . . the prejudice against woman's progress is being removed."

Such statements about the condition of Alliance women were important, for they came from an organization which had millions of members and which was a significant force on the regional and national level in the 1880s and 1890s. In part, the Alliance was a rural protest against the inferior social, economic, and political position its members felt farmers occupied in the emerging urban-industrial society. But, like civil service reformers and other protest groups in the Gilded Age, the Farmers' Alliance argued that the finely balanced two-party system responded only to the demands of special interest groups and political machines rather than to the needs of the people. Alliance members first tried to change this situation by pressing at the state level for control of monopolies and other unfriendly interests and for favorable legislation. Better public schools for rural children, state agricultural colleges, colleges for women, laws controlling the railroads, better prices for farm products were some of the goals the Alliance sought to enable rural classes to survive within a new world. As this strategy proved frustrating, about half of the Alliance membership moved into the Populist party which ran its first presidential candidate in 1892. Although the Populist party ultimately failed, it offered the most serious challenge to the two-party system in the late nineteenth century and contributed to the reshaping of the American political system.

These exhortations and demands emphasizing female equality and opportunity were important, then, because the Alliance was important, but they have an unfamiliar ring in the context of what has generally been known about sex roles and relationships in the post-Civil War South. The accepted interpretation of late nineteenth-century southern society has argued that the model of the southern lady, submissive and virtuous, "the most fascinating being in creation . . . the delight and charm of every circle she moves in," still marked the parameters of appropriate behavior for middle-class women, though the model had been predictably weakened by the traumatic experience of civil war. As for lower-class women, this interpretation suggests, they were "not much affected by role expectations,"

although "farmers' wives and daughters and illit-
erate black women . . . in some inarticulate way
doubtless helped to shape [society]" and its standards.

Yet an investigation of the Farmers' Alliance
in North Carolina, where the Alliance had great
success, indicates this explanation does not hold
true for that state. If the North Carolina experience is at all typical of other southern Alliance
states, and there is little reason to think it is not,
the reality of southern attitudes toward women
was more complex than recent analyses have allowed. The Civil War had been the initial catalyst
for women entering new areas of activities; after
the war, poverty and loss of fathers, brothers,
husbands, and other male relatives forced many
women to run farms, boarding houses, to become
seamstresses, postmistresses, and teachers. As the
traditional view of woman's sphere crumbled
under the impact of the post-war conditions, at
least one alternative to the older view emerged in
the South—one exemplified by the case of North
Carolina. Responsive to social changes stemming
from war and defeat, the Alliance in the 1880s
and 1890s urged women to adopt a new self-
image, one that included education, economic
self-sufficiency, one that made a mockery of all
false ideas of gentility. The activities and behavior
that the Alliance sanctioned were not only considered appropriate for middle-class women but
for women on all social levels. Although evidence
on the social class composition of the Alliance is
limited, recent work suggests that approximately
55 percent of the North Carolina membership
owned their land, about 31 percent were tenants,
and 14 percent rural professionals. Since many
wives and daughters joined the Alliance, it seems
reasonable to assume that female membership,
like male membership, crossed class lines. Certainly, the new female role was applicable to all
of them. Finally, although it was not actually
created by Alliance women, the new cultural
model was consciously elaborated by some of
them, thus offering one way of understanding
how middle-class farming women, later deemed
"inarticulate" because they left so few written
records, perceived and shaped their social role.

Furthermore, a case study of the North Carolina Farmers' Alliance shows that the Alliance
also offered numerous rural women the rare privilege of discussing important economic and political issues with men and of functioning as their
organizational equals. Few southern institutions
offered women similar opportunities. The political party barred them altogether. The Methodist
and Baptist churches, which with the Presbyterian claimed a majority of church members, still
supported the traditional view that women ought
to remain at home although they had allowed
women a new area of activity in establishing female missionary societies. This expansion of their
sphere was considered to be "no compromise
. . . [to] female modesty and refinement," although in reality, women could and did acquire
political experience and skills in them. After
1883, North Carolina women also gained valuable organizational knowledge through their involvement in the Women's Christian Temperance Union. But the W.C.T.U., the church
missionary societies and women's clubs of the
1880s were all-female organizations and thus did
not offer women the chance to establish a pragmatic working relationship with men as the Alliance would do.

One other rural organization in the South, the
Grange, which reached its height of popularity in
North Carolina between 1873 and 1875, admitted
both sexes before the Alliance did so. Unlike the
Alliance, however, the Grange made clear distinctions between most of the offices and ranks
women and men could hold. Nevertheless, the
Grange clearly provided women with some practical organizational experience with men and,
presumably, offered some kind of rough equality.
Still, partly because of its Northern origins, the
impact of the Grange was limited in the South. In
North Carolina, the Grange's total membership
never surpassed the 15,000 mark, and by the
1880s, numbers had dwindled. Moreover, since
the Grange was primarily an educational body, it
failed to provide the same kind of experience for
southern women as the Alliance would in the
1880s and 1890s. Ostensibly apolitical, the Alliance was actually devoted to a discussion of the

"science of economical government" and was deeply involved in political questions. Within the North Carolina Alliance, the spheres of women and men drew closer as both sexes voted, held office, and discussed together the stirring issues of the day as they had rarely done before.

Within the framework of the Alliance, then, southern women had the opportunity to discuss pressing economic, political, and social questions, to try out ways of behaving in mixed groups and to gain confidence in newly acquired skills. One might expect that a group of women, and perhaps men, would eventually emerge whose Alliance experience would lead them ultimately to demand or sympathize with the greater expansion of woman's role that the organization officially supported. Yet this never happened. At the same time that the Alliance offered new roles and organizational possibilities for women, the meaning of equality for women was constricted by the organization's major goal of reviving southern agriculture. Political rights within the Alliance were not seen as the first step toward political rights outside of the Alliance. The career of the North Carolina Alliance and its inclusion of women in its membership thus offers another kind of study of the slow progress of the women's rights movement in North Carolina and perhaps gives additional clues for its uncertain course in the South as a whole.

The evidence for this study comes from many sources. Most useful is the State Alliance paper, the *Progressive Farmer,* whose policy it was to publish the views of the Alliance membership. Few of these rural correspondents provided the leading articles for the paper, but rather they contributed letters to the correspondence page. Since these long forgotten farm women and men left virtually no other personal records, their letters, some literary, most artless, provide a crucial insight into the grassroots level of the Alliance and an important view of their responses to the opportunities the Alliance held out to them.

Initial interest in a farmers' organization in North Carolina resulted from the depressed state of southern agriculture in the 1880s. By 1886, Colonel Leonidas Polk, editor of the new agricul-

tural weekly, the *Progressive Farmer,* was vigorously urging the paper's readers to organize local farmers' clubs as the basis for a future state wide organization. From the beginning he visualized at least some women in the clubs, for he advised they could be "elected as honorary members." Yet farmers' clubs were not to have a long life in North Carolina. By May 1887 Alliance organizers from Texas, where the agricultural order had originated, had begun to establish local Alliances in North Carolina, while a Carolinian, J. B. Barry, also began recruiting. Polk, aware of the growth potential of the Alliance, joined one of Barry's Alliances in July 1887, and was soon meeting with Texas Alliance leaders to discuss a merger between the Alliance and his farmers' clubs. After the merger was made the North Carolina Alliance grew by leaps and bounds. In the summer of 1888 the membership stood at 42,000. By 1891 the Alliance claimed 100,000 members in over 2,000 local chapters.

Requirements for membership in the Alliance, formalized in the state constitution adopted in October 1887, were far more positive to female members than Polk's farmers' clubs had been. Membership was open to rural white women and men over sixteen years of age who had a "good moral character," believed in "the existence of a Supreme Being," and showed "industrious habits." While men were to pay fifty cents as an initiation fee in addition to quarterly dues of twenty-five cents, women had no required fee or dues, no doubt a recognition of their marginal economic status and their desirability as members. Membership of both sexes was essential to Alliance goals as state Alliance president, Captain Sydenham B. Alexander, indicated. The purpose of the Alliance, Alexander wrote in 1887 was "to encourage education among the agricultural and laboring classes, and *elevate to higher manhood and womanhood* those who bear the burdens of productive industry."

Alliance leaders did not leave the issue of female participation in the organization to chance but stressed it forcefully. Harry Tracy, a National Lecturer of the order, urged *"the ladies to come out and hear him,"* and warned Alliance members: "The ladies eligible must join the order before we can succeed." Despite emphatic support from the top, however, letters from local Alliances to the *Progressive Farmer,* now the official organ of the North Carolina Alliance, indicate some male resistance to the idea of female members. As the Secretary of the Davidson College Alliance explained: "I think that the ladies are best suited to home affairs." Verbal opposition to female members led one woman to comment, "They don't want us to join, and think it no place for us." Other, more subtle techniques of discouraging female membership seem to have existed. Holding meetings in places where women would be uncomfortable or feel out of place kept the number of female members down. As the correspondent from Lenoir Alliance noted, his Alliance had fifty men and one woman because meetings were held in the court house. As one frequent contributor to the *Progressive Farmer* who favored female members pointed out: "Each Sub-Alliance needs a hall. . . . We cannot urge the ladies to attend until we can seat them comfortably."

Numerous questions addressed to Polk, now secretary of the state Alliance as well as editor of the *Progressive Farmer* indicated that even if not opposed to female membership, men were often hesitant and confused about the membership of women. A variety of questions focused on what women were eligible for membership and, if elected, what their rights should be. Were women, in fact, to have the same "rights and privileges of the male members"? Over and over again Polk replied that women were to have equal rights and privileges; they were to vote on new members, participate in all Alliance business and to know "all the secret words and signs" of the order.

If some men were unenthusiastic about female members, so too were some of the women. As one Allianceman explained: "Our female friends seem to repose great confidence in our ability to conduct the affairs of the Alliance without their direct union and assistance. Indeed, our wives, mothers and sisters have as much as they can do to attend their own business." Other letters from men more enthusiastic about female members agreed that women refused to join because they were "too modest, or think it out of their line." There was even some outright female opposition to Alliance membership as one "bright and energetic young lady," the first woman to join the Alliance in Vance County, discovered when her friends ridiculed "the idea of young ladies joining." The traditional view of woman's sphere, then, constituted a barrier to active female participation in the Alliance, and it was one which female members consciously tried to undermine. When Alliancewomen wrote to the *Progressive Farmer* they frequently urged the other women to overcome feelings of timidity. "Dear Sisters, go to work; don't stay home and die, then say I have something else to do; that will never do," wrote Addie Pigford. "Sisters, what are you doing?" asked Mrs. Carver. "There is work for us to do, and we shall not be found wanting. We can help in many ways, and we must do it."

Opposition and hesitation on the subject of female members obviously existed as the reports of local and county Alliances and male and female correspondents to the *Progressive Farmer* show. But evidence suggests that the message that women were to be encouraged as vigorous participants of the Alliance eventually came through clearly to most local groups. By 1889, for example, the State Line Alliance reported it was planning to discuss the desirability of female members. Rather ruefully, the writer commented: "That indicates *how far we are behind,* but we do not intend to remain there." Questions about membership requirements and privileges, membership breakdowns sent into the *Progressive Farmer,* and local minute books, indicate that women were presenting themselves for membership. Not only did the wives and daughters of male members join but so too did unattached women. As the Alliance grew so did the number of women in the organization. In some cases, women comprised one-third to one-half of local groups. "We can work just as well as the brethren," pointed out one Alliance woman. "If we want to derive good from the Alliance, we must work in love and harmony with our fellow-man."

As thousands of women responded to the Alliance's invitation to join "the great army of reform," there were hints that women felt increasingly at ease in their new organizational role. Although it is difficult to recover the perceptions of these rural women, their letters to the *Progressive Farmer* from 1887 through 1891 can serve as an imperfect measure for their thoughts and feelings about their participation in the Alliance.

One of the most striking aspects of the women's correspondence is the initial hesitation about writing to a newspaper at all. Only one woman communicated to the editor in 1887. Gradually, however, women began to send letters, many of them conscious of departing from past patterns of behavior. "Being a farmer's wife, I am not in the habit of writing for the public prints," wrote the first female correspondent of 1888, a certain Mrs. Hogan who was concerned about stray dogs. Replied the second, "Mr. Editor:—I have never written anything for the public to read, but I feel just now, after reading Mrs. Hogan's trouble . . . that I want to tell her I truly sympathize with her." Other correspondents in 1888 and 1889 often began their letters with the polite request for a "small space" for a few words from a farm woman or with the phrase, "I am but a female." "I suppose your many subscribers will not expect much from a female correspondent," wrote one corresponding secretary, "and if so, they will not be disappointed when they read this article, but if I can be of any service to the Alliance by putting in my little mite, I am willing to do what I can." By 1890 such protestations and expressions of humility had disappeared. A series of letters from Evangeline Usher exemplifies the growing confidence on the part of women that their letters and reports on Alliance activities were appropriate and acceptable. In an early letter, Usher urged other women to write to the paper, with the typical hope that Polk would "give us a little space somewhere." Describing herself as fearful that her letter would go into the wastebasket, she further explained that her feelings of delicacy would prevent her from contributing her Alliance's news regularly. "I already imagine I see Brother 'R' smiling ludicrously at the idea." Within a few months, however, Usher wrote again, confessing "a kind of literary pride in seeing my name in print." By 1889, she could begin her letter, "I feel like I must intrude again, and as I am quite independent of all disfavor, I do not care whether you like the intrusion or not." Though Usher was unusually outspoken, her growing boldness correlates with the straightforward and secure tone women gradually adopted in writing to the paper and suggests their greater feelings of confidence within the organization.

Local reports, letters, and records also give information on another crucial consideration concerning women's involvement in the Alliance. If women only sat on the back benches during Alliance meetings, listening silently while men discussed the great economic and political issues of the day, their membership would have been insignificant. If, on the other hand, women actually helped to run the organization and helped contribute to its success, even if they were not equal in every respect to men, then the Alliance was an important departure from the typical southern organization.

Although there is no indication that women were ever elected to the office of president of local Alliances, they were occasionally, at least, voted into important positions. The Jamestown Alliance Minute Book, for example, records that a year after the subject of female members was first discussed, a woman was elected as assistant secretary; she declined, but two months later was elected as treasurer. Other women held the office of secretary, with the responsibility not only for making "a fair record of all things necessary to be written," but also for "receiving all moneys due" and for communicating with Secretary Polk. Still others became lecturers or assistant lecturers, both crucial positions since they were to give addresses, lead discussions, and furnish "the material of thought for the future consideration of the members." Women as well as men read papers "on subjects of importance for the benefit of the order." In one Alliance, records show that women conducted the business on an Alliance meeting day. At the county level where meetings were held quarterly, women were included in the membership count on which representation was based, were delegates, and at least one was elected vice-president. Others gave key addresses to large audiences. Women could also be found at the annual meetings of the state Alliance. As the *Progressive Farmer* warmly replied to two women who had written to ask if they could go to the meeting, "You are not only *allowed*, but you will be most cordially welcomed to a seat." Though such evidence is fragmentary, it does imply that many women took an active part in running Alliance affairs.

Women participated in the Alliance in a variety of other areas too. Several letters to the *Progressive Farmer* noted that women subscribed to the State Business Agency Fund, an important Alliance effort aimed at eliminating middlemen in purchasing fertilizers, groceries, and agricultural goods. Alliance leaders urged local groups to donate at least fifty cents a member to the fund. A few reports show women carrying their financial share. Women also sent in news to the paper, wrote articles, and worked to increase the subscription list, a job which Polk and other leaders saw as vital to Alliance success since they argued that earlier efforts to arouse farmers had foundered on ignorance and lack of proper information.

If not all women were active members of the Alliance, enough were to be reported and praised in the *Progressive Farmer*. Clearly, many women welcomed the chance to work in the organization. Moreover, as their letters indicate, they shared men's interest in the compelling subjects of the day: agricultural cooperation, the role of combines and trusts in creating the farming crisis, the need to diversify southern agriculture, all standard themes for discussion and instruction in Alliance meetings and reading material. But as much as women were involved with such topics, as much as they enjoyed the social conviviality of the Alliance, many must have agreed with the woman who reminded her Alliance, "This is the only order that allows us equal privileges to the man; we certainly should appreciate the privilege."

North Carolina Alliance's support of "equal rights" for women within the organization and of the new role described for them outside it may seem startling, yet it corresponded to the reality of life for southern women in the late 1880s and early 1890s. It would have been surprising if the changes in southern society following the Civil War had failed to result in some ideological reconsideration of women's status. Yet the Alliance's stance was not merely a response to social change in the South. The National Alliance upheld the concept of equal rights. State leaders recognized that the farmer and his wife worked as an agricultural unit. It made sense to involve both in the Alliance for as one farmer pointed out, "We know we can scarcely dispense with the labor of our wives and children on the farm." Furthermore, leaders reasoned that the Alliance could not count on continued enthusiasm and good attendance unless women as well as men came to meetings. "Meetings must be interesting" to spur membership and attendance, one pamphlet pointed out, "and the first step in this direction is to get more women and young people into the Order." At least one member agreed. The presence of women, he wrote, "cheers us on." Clearly, if the Alliance and its work were to prosper, both sexes would have to be involved.

The social composition of the leadership suggests another important reason for the Alliance support for women. Although men like Colonel Polk and Sydenham Alexander, president of the state Alliance, had been or were farmers genuinely concerned with agricultural problems, they were also members of the rural upper-class. Polk had had a long career as planter, army officer, legislator, commissioner of agriculture, and editor. Alexander had headed the state Grange in the 1870s. Other leaders were teachers, doctors, and clergymen. As members of North Carolina's elite, these men partially accepted the traditional view of woman as the beacon of social morality. "If our organization means anything," one prominent supporter of female members wrote, "it means a moral reformation, morality must be our guide. The ladies are and always have been the great moral element in society; therefore *it is im-*

possible to succeed without calling to our aid the greatest moral element in the country."

This was how Alliance leaders conceived of the role and importance of women within their organization. But women themselves had their own ideas about their role, as an examination of their letters to the *Progressive Farmer* reveal. The writers stressed their pride in farm life, the need to throw off female passivity, the vital importance of women to the Alliance effort. "While it has been remarked that women are necessary evil," wrote Fannie Pentecost, "let us by our untiring energy, and zeal show them that it is a mistake. . . . We should devise plans and means by which we can assist those who have to bear the burdens of life." In the Alliance, another woman pointed out, women had the unique opportunity of helping men "in the thickest of the fight" by encouragement, prayers, self-denial, and endurance. Some correspondents clearly saw their role as one of moral support, but others visualized a more active role, using words like helpmate or companion to describe how they saw themselves. One woman shaped the female role curiously: "Let us all put our shoulders to this great wheel, the Alliance. We, as sisters of this Alliance may feel we are silent factors in this work; we know we constantly need something to lean upon. . . . Let us so entwine ourselves around our brothers that *should we be taken away* they will feel they are *tottering.*" Here, encouragement and support had become the vital activity for women. So, too, one woman from Fair Grove commented that women must be "ready to hold the hands of the strong, should they become weak."

That women perceived themselves occasionally as the major support for men corresponds with the way in which Alliance leaders visualized them. But there was a sharp edge to the role of moral guide as some correspondence revealed. Again, Evangeline Usher provides an insight into this kind of thinking. In a letter of September 1890, Usher wrote that someone had recently sent her a compliment, "saying they were just as strong an Alliance boy as I was an Alliance girl." Evangeline's rather surprising comment was "Brother . . . I only hope you are, for I am one

that believes in working and not talking." Other letters and articles convey a similar scepticism of men. "Why," asked assistant lecturer Lizzie Marshburn, "is it that the farmer and laboring class generally, have got no self-will or resolution of their own? . . . as a general rule they have been ever ready to link their destinies with any political aspirant who can get up and deliver a flowerly address of misrepresentation." Allie Marsh told her audience at a Randolph County meeting, "We come to these meetings with an unwritten agreement to take things as they are." Women, she said, were "perfectly content" that men exercise political rights "as long as you are vigilant in making [the ballot box] as efficient as possible." Yet the remainder of her speech suggested that she had found the men "wanting." A letter from still another woman acidly observed, "Some men can't see beyond their nose."

Although most women and men probably agreed upon the function of women's participation within the Alliance, it appears that some Alliance women saw the matter differently and that they suspected that the commonly accepted view of women as the quiet impetus behind male reformers was inadequate. Their letters convey misgivings about the ability of men to persist in their support of reform and implicitly suggest that these women perceived themselves as steadier leaders than the men. As one Alliance woman explained: "My sisters, this is something we should know, that our names are on this list [of reformers] and [we should] regret we could not be allowed this opportunity years ago, for no doubt our country would be in a much better condition to-day had we taken this step." Added another, apparently filled with misgivings about men: "I would earnestly *beg the brethren* when they put their hands to the plow *not to look back . . . if they do,* they will not reap the harvest we all desire. *We must work* and *wait,* and not grow discouraged." Yet, despite these indications that women suspected that they rather than men were possibly the most steadfast and reliable leaders of reform, they were hardly ready to challenge openly the Alliance's basic assumptions because of the positive support the Alliance was already providing for southern women in many areas of life.

Indeed, women's rights within the organization was only part of the Alliance's reformulation of women's status. A woman's role in the Alliance was understood to parallel the more significant role the Alliance suggested women could enjoy in society at large. The *Progressive Farmer*'s policy of reporting on the achievements of women who were doctors, surgeons, journalists, lawyers, government workers, even pastors, indicated the wide range of possibilities beyond the conventional one of marriage and motherhood. These career options, of course, depended on educating women, a goal that the Alliance and its official newspaper consistently supported as part of the general attempt to improve all educational facilities for "farmers and laborers."

"The ability of girls," the *Progressive Farmer* stated flatly, "has been found equal to that of boys." As the resolutions of the 1890 State Alliance meeting show, the Alliance went on record that year not only in favor of public schools for boys and girls but also in support of "ample [state] appropriations [for] the training and higher education of females." The paper explained, "The lopsided system of education in North Carolina . . . provides for the education of men and neglects that of women. Gentlemanly instinct, to say nothing of justice and mercy, requires that women should be given as good a chance for education as men possess. . . . Give the noble girls of the State—those who are not able to go to our expensive colleges a chance to get an education," the paper urged. Responding to pressure from the Alliance and other interested groups, the legislature of 1891 appropriated $10,-000 a year to establish a normal and industrial training school for girls.

The reason for the Alliance's concern with women's education becomes obvious in the *Progressive Farmer*'s discussions of private girls' schools, traditionally, these schools had stressed teaching female accomplishments to the would-be southern lady of means. But now the *Progressive Farmer* enthusiastically reported, Salem Female Academy had expanded its offering by establishing a business course featuring music, telegraphy, phonography (shorthand), typing and bookkeeping. Such a course, the *Progressive Farmer* pointed out, was most desirable with its "studies of a practical character, fitting the learners for active avocations when required to depend upon their own efforts in the battle of life." Other schools, the paper urged, ought to follow Salem Academy's example. The fundamental point, the paper emphasized, was that *all* young women of *all* social classes should be prepared for jobs. It was true, of course, that education would help poor girls by enabling them "to make an honest living," but all women ought to learn to be self-sufficient and self-supporting.

Women themselves stressed the importance of economic self-sufficiency. They did not want to "be entirely dependent upon the bounties of others" if they lost their protectors. And, as an additional point in favor of education, one Alliance woman brought up the important question of marriage. Self-sufficiency would allow women to marry because they wanted to, not because they needed financial support. Thus education of a certain kind would help women avoid the "fatal blunder," incompatibility in marriage.

Alliance support for practical education for women was based on a rejection of the concept of gentility which had been such a fundamental component of the idea of the southern lady. The search for a "pale and delicate" complexion, the interest in elaborate clothing and accomplishments were all denounced in the pages of the *Progressive Farmer*. These traditional female concerns were misguided since they undermined the importance of hard work and, thus, the opportunities for female independence. The idea that labor was degrading, the *Progressive Farmer* reminded its readers, was just another unfortunate remnant of slavery, and, in fact, contributed in an important way to poverty itself. True Alliance men and women wanted young people "to see that it is no disgrace, but a high honor, to know how to work and to be able to do it." The feminine ideal was the woman who was independent and practical, educated either to support herself or to marry wisely.

Better education for both sexes was an issue with which many Alliance members sympathized, hoping their children's future would be more promising than their own. Yet the Alliance could not concern itself exclusively with the new options for young women who still had their lives ahead of them. With so many adult female members, the Alliance also considered how to reshape life styles for those women who would never leave the farm for school or a job. "Is the life of the Farmer's wife under present systems, calculated to give her virtue and intelligence full play," asked the Southern Alliance paper, the *National Economist*. "Is she not a slave and a drudge in many cases?" The *Progressive Farmer* gave the answer: there were "thousands and tens of thousands" of farmers' wives "worked to their graves." Improving this dreary situation necessitated a multipronged approach. First, the paper's scientific articles on housekeeping and cooking could show the farm wife how to lighten her work load. Then, too, her husband was to be prodded into helping her out. As one correspondent to the *Progressive Farmer* explained, men needed tough words. "Our Lecturer, in trying to discuss the social feature [of the Alliance], handles husbands quite roughly, but it is received in the proper spirit. If country life is ever made more attractive, there must be more congeniality in spirit and aggressiveness between the one that follows the plow handles and the one of all beings earthly that acts as a helpmeet to man." What were "the conveniences for the good and faithful wife?" asked Colonel Polk. How far did she have to walk to the woodpile or the spring? Had the bloom on her cheeks faded prematurely? These were the subjects, he urged, that ought to be discussed in Alliance circles so that "new life, new energy, new action . . . and new views of life and living" might emerge for both sexes.

The Alliance's concern with helping hard working farmwomen fused with the order's major objective, the overall improvement of agricultural life. To this end, the Alliance sought to discover "a remedy for every evil known to exist and afflict farmers and other producers." The remedy of improved farming methods was especially impor-

tant as the number of articles in the *Progressive Farmer* attest. The paper argued that the one-crop system was the obvious and basic cause of the state's agricultural depression. Over and over again, the paper and Alliance meetings focused on the need to farm properly and to stay out of debt. Consider the two kinds of farmers, the *Progressive Farmer* urged. One raised cotton on his land, bought milk, bread, hay and fertilizers on credit. The other chose the Alliance route and would prosper. And "his wife, dear devoted woman, instead of wearing out her life in cooking for a lot of negroes to work cotton, has time to look after the adornment and the beautifying of her home, to attend to her milk and butter, eggs, garden, bees, chickens and other poultry, and with all this they have a little time to spare socially with their neighbors and to go to church."

The *Progressive Farmer* might describe the tasks of the wise farmer's wife enthusiastically, but the list of her activities highlights a crucial problem in the Alliance's approach to women. Although the Alliance supported expanding women's rights and privileges, its over-all objective was to put farmers on an economic, social, and political parity with other occupations. To do so, or to try to do so, had definite implications for women's lives and shaped the Alliance's conception of equality. If the home was to be made attractive enough to discourage children from abandoning farm life, if it was to be "a place of rest, of comfort, of social refinement and domestic pleasure," then women would have to make it so. If the farm was to stay out of debt, if the farmer was to remain free of the supply merchant by raising as many of his necessities as he could, his wife must help. Woman's "judgement and skill in management may be essential to the success of her husband," one article reminded Alliance readers. "And this responsibility . . . continues to the close of her life."

The Alliance proposed a position for women that embodied an equality of sorts, the economic equality of a diligent coworker. In its recognition of the importance and difficulty of woman's work, the role model differed from that of the southern lady. Nor did the model merely update the characters of the yeoman farmer's family. The Alliance's concern with diversifying southern agriculture, with eliminating the disastrous dependency on the one-crop system, was not an attempt to recreate the small farm and agricultural myth of an idealized past but to create a new kind of farm and a new cast of characters. Agricultural reform, in fact, was seen as part of a modernizing process, and it was favored not only by the Alliance but also by leaders of the New South movement. Spokesmen for each group agreed that the South had to end its colonial status both through substantial industrial growth and through agricultural diversification.

But what were the implications of such a view for women? "The housewife, who, by her industry, transforms the milk from her dairy into butter . . . is as truly a manufacturer as the most purse-proud mill-owner of Britain," explained the *National Economist.* Labeled manufacturers or helpmates, women were to carry a heavy burden in creating the new order. The truth was that even though the Alliance talked of a variety of opportunities available for women, most women in North Carolina would continue to live on the farm, and Alliance leaders thought this right in terms of the world they wished to create. Farm women were important for they would share in the task of restoring agriculture to its rightful position in the economy. Even the Alliance's interest in women's education was partially tied to this goal. If women were to become efficient, modern coworkers in the task of agricultural reconstruction, they needed an education. As Polk explained: "The great and imperative need of our people and our time, is the practical education of the masses. . . . It will be a glorious day for the South when her young ladies, educated in all the higher and refined arts of life, shall boast and without blushing of equal proficiency in the management of the household and the flower-garden."

Moreover, women needed to be educated so that, in turn, they could teach Alliance children, first at home and then at school. Rural children, many Alliance members were convinced, needed a special kind of education, one that embraced "the moral, physical and industrial, as well as the mental training of our children." By providing such an education, women could offer an "invaluable service." For "this system will strengthen the attachment of these classes [to agricultural life] instead of alienating [them] from it . . . it will better qualify them for success and happiness in life . . . increase the opportunity and inclination to adorn the home and practice the social virtues."

Other pragmatic considerations led to the support of women's education. Education could provide poor girls with the opportunity "to make an honest living." Most, but not all, women would marry. To prepare for the possibility of spinsterhood, every careful mother must see not only that daughters were trained in their domestic and spiritual responsibilities, but would also "have them taught a trade or profession and thus equip them fully to 'face the world' if this need shall come to them." No one, not even a woman, ought to be an economic drain on others. Teaching provided one means of support. So too would factory work, which the Alliance leaders, like spokesmen of the New South movement, hoped would be a growing field of employment. North Carolina's piedmont region, the *Progressive Farmer* enthusiastically suggested, should be covered with factories. "Then we could have money because our boys and girls and women who are now consumers would find constant, honorable and remunerative employment and would thus become self-supporting." Women not only had the option but, indeed, the duty of being self-supporting and of adding "to the general wealth of the place." The more educated and useful women became, "the better for them and for our State."

The part that the Alliance encouraged women to play in southern life was more expansive than the traditional role of the southern lady at the same time that it had definite limitations. Women need no longer cultivate the appearance of genteel passivity; they required education as the preparation for a useful life. But the Alliance defined utility in terms of the organization's over-all objectives, the profitability of agriculture, the prosperity of the state. Thus, it was vital that women learn to be skilled managers or teachers. Whether spinsters or widows, women must never be parasites on their families or on their state. Beneath the rhetoric, the lifestyle the Alliance supported for women was one of constant hard work and low wages, if women were to be paid for their labor at all. These limitations, harsh though they seem, were realistic both in terms of the Alliance's major goals and in terms of available options in the South. As one northern observer testified, "There is yet no rapid development of opportunity for profitable labor for young white women in the South."

There may be yet another reason for the contradictory meaning of equality that the Alliance proposed for women. Despite the support the Alliance gave to an expanded life style for women, Alliance leaders were affected by the circumstances of time, place, and class. Like other well-born Southerners, they had not rejected the traditional view of women as the source of morality and goodness. Because of their moral qualities, women had to participate in the Alliance, but it is doubtful whether North Carolina Alliance leaders would have supported enlarging women's sphere in any way that might threaten their own social or political position.

As the *Progressive Farmer* firmly acknowledged, it had no sympathy with "that spirit which could encourage class feeling or class prejudice. . . . It is . . . *subversive of the social order.*" Leaders wanted changes, but not at the expense of social stability. Thus women might share in a kind of social and economic equality with men but they would hardly be offered political rights.

There are few indications that this strategy was unacceptable to the majority of Alliance women. Most letters from women indicate that the new parameters for female behavior were thankfully welcomed. Only occasionally can one discern an undercurrent of unrest, when women remarked on men's failure to be vigorous Alliance fighters or when they pointed out how much better a place the world would be had women, long ago, taken a more active part in shaping it. Then, too, a few women dared to write on political matters, giving their own opinions and urging

men to take notice. At least one woman realized how far she had stepped out of her place. After mocking Alliance men who were "willing to wave Alliance principles and swallow the whole Democratic party," she observed, "I could say a good deal more on this line, but will stop, for fear some fool will ask: 'Are you a woman?' "

The *Progressive Farmer* not surprisingly steered away from the explosive issue of women's participation in politics. In two unusual references to the question of women's political rights, however, it is clear that the issue had come up in local meetings. At one county rally, the lecturer told the women, "He did not invite them to suffrage, though it was gaining rapidly in public favor and if they had the ballot they would drive out the liquor traffic of this country and other evils." In Almance County, the Alliance lecturer warned his female listeners, "Do not spend your time in longing for opportunities that will never come, but be contented in the sphere the Lord hath placed you in. If the Lord had intended you for a preacher or lawyer He would have given you a pair of pantaloons."

But the desire to maintain the *status quo* did not automatically succeed. Though Alliance leaders delineated definite boundaries to the theoretical and actual position women might occupy in the world, the fact that suffrage was mentioned at all may indicate a turbid undercurrent of half conscious challenge to the leadership. The way the two Alliance speakers spoke of the suffrage issue suggests that some Alliance circles had discussed it. A few letters to the *Progressive Farmer* and other fragmentary evidence point to the same conclusion. On a visit to North Carolina in 1893, for example, a Mrs. Virginia Durant who had established a suffrage organization in South Carolina, reported she found "suffrage sentiment" of an unfocused kind in the state. Perhaps she sensed incipient interest among those women exposed to the Alliance.

Yet there is not enough evidence to resolve the issue. If there were some support for the further expansion of women's activities through the Alliance, however, it never had the time to grow strong and vocal. For although the Alliance lingered on into the twentieth century, by the mid-1890s it had ceased to be an institution of importance. The failure of Alliance cooperative economic ventures, continued hard times, and a split within the organization over the support of the Populist party all contributed to a decline in membership. A changing political climate brought new issues, new questions to the fore; many of them would have conservative implications. By the end of the decade, the shape of southern life would be set. After the Populist challenge, franchise for both poor whites and blacks would be limited and the question of political participation closed. Voting was a privilege, not a right. "Equal rights for all, special privileges for none" was a slogan best forgotten.

Though the Alliance did not survive long enough to dislodge the traditional ideas of woman's sphere, its spirited attempt to work out a new place for her both in theory and practice shows greater complexity in late nineteenth-century attitudes and behavior with respect to sex roles than previously recognized, and suggests that there may have been other attempts to create new roles for women in the South. The Alliance alternative, it is true, fell short of offering women equality in all spheres of life. Primary Alliance goals and the nature of the leadership limited the meaning of equal rights for women. Yet to expect the Alliance to propose full equality for women would be to ignore the influence of both time and place and to expect consistency of thought and action when such consistency rarely exists.

7

POPULIST DREAMS AND NEGRO RIGHTS: EAST TEXAS AS A CASE STUDY

LAWRENCE C. GOODWYN

The last decade of the nineteenth century was a time of upheaval in a century marked by unprecedented change. In the Northeast mammoth factories and the immigrants who labored in them dominated the cities of America's industrial heartland. Throughout the country an ever-growing network of railroads connected even outlying regions to the burgeoning metropolises of the nation. And in these metropolises financial and industrial cartels, monopolies, and holding companies exercised an economic and political influence unparalleled in American life.

Facing these changes were workers and farmers. American workers responded to the growing power of industrial capitalism with the collective power of their numbers and struggled with their employers over control of the workplace and the process of production itself. For their part the small farmers of the South and Midwest responded by forming organizations to fight discriminatory railroad freight rates and to challenge the power of eastern banks to yoke them to a cycle of unending indebtedness.

In the South the farmer's protest was embodied in the Southern Farmers' Alliance and its successor, the Populist or People's party, which sought to forge an alliance between black and white small farmers that would reinstate the power of the small producer in American society. As Lawrence C. Goodwyn shows in this essay, this Populist ideal followed a path fraught with danger. Faced with a resurgent white supremacist movement and southern terrorism directed against black Populists, the Populist movement found itself unable to protect its members in their interracial coalition. Racism had again triumphed in America. Yet the idea of an interracial radical movement did not die with the decline of populism; it was continued after 1910 by the southern and western branches of the Socialist party, which elected local and state officials as had the Populists before them.

What do you think accounts for the different outcomes of white terrorism in Grimes County and in Promised Land, discussed above by Elizabeth R. Bethel in Reading 1? What similarities and differences do you find in the form of racial hostility directed against blacks in East Texas and the Chinese in gold-rush California, discussed by Jack Chen in Reading 3?

Nearly a century later the Populist decade lingers in historical memory as an increasingly dim abstraction. The very word "Populism" no longer carries specific political meaning. It is now invoked to explain George Wallace, as it was used to explain Lyndon Johnson in the six-

Reprinted from the *American Historical Review*, 76 (1971), by permission of the author and the American Historical Association.

ties, Joe McCarthy in the fifties, and Claude Pepper in the forties. Though afflicting principally the popular mind, this confusion is at least partly traceable to those historians who have insisted on concentrating on Populism as exhortation, so that Ignatius Donnelly's utopian novels or Mary Lease's pronouncements on the respective uses of corn and hell become the explanatory keys to agrarian radicalism. For scholars who mine political movements with a view to extracting cultural nuggets, the focus has been chiefly upon the word, not the deed; in the process the agrarian crusade has become increasingly obscure.

Much of the difficulty centers on the subject of race. There is essential agreement that, on economic issues, Populists were men of the Left, primitive to some, prophetic to others, but leftists to all. But did their banner indicate a highly selective nativist radicalism for whites only, or did they grapple with the inherited legacies of the caste system as part of an effort to create what they considered a more rational social and economic order? The analysis of Populist rhetoric has left us with contradictory answers.

While party platforms can be useful tools in determining professed attitudes, the gap between asserted ideals and performance is sufficiently large to defeat any analysis resting on the implicit assumption that political manifestos have an intrinsic value apart from the milieu in which they existed. In America the distance between assertion and performance is especially evident in matters of race; as a result, on this issue above all, the context of public assertions is central to the task of their political evaluation. An inquiry into the murkiest corner of Populism, interracial politics, should begin not merely with what Populists said but what they did in the course of bidding for power at the local level. What was the stuff of daily life under Populist rule in the rural enclaves where the third party came to exercise all the authority of public office, including police authority? What can we learn not only about Populist insurgency but also about the orthodoxy the third party opposed?

Grimes County, Texas, was one of many counties scattered across the South and West where the People's party achieved a continuing political presence in the latter part of the nineteenth century. Located some sixty miles north of Houston in the heart of what the natives call the Old South part of Texas, Grimes County displayed the cotton-centered economy typical of rural East Texas in 1880. Its largest town, Navasota, contained 1,800 persons in 1890 and its second largest town, Anderson, the county seat, only 574 persons as late as 1900. Farms in Grimes County ranged from plantation size in the rich bottomland country of the Brazos River on the county's western border to small, single-family agricultural units on the poorer land of the northern part of the county. The 1890 census revealed a county population of 21,312, of which 11,664 were black.

Populism in Grimes County is the story of a black-white coalition that had its genesis in Reconstruction and endured for more than a generation. In time this coalition came to be symbolized by its most enduring elected public official, Garrett Scott. The Scotts had roots in Grimes County dating back before the Civil War. Their sons fought for the Confederacy and returned to face a postwar reality by no means unique in the South; possessing moderately large holdings of land but lacking necessary capital to make it productive, the Scotts did not achieve great affluence. During the hard times that continued to afflict undercapitalized Southern agriculture through the 1870s Garrett Scott became a soft-money agrarian radical. His stance was significant in the political climate of Grimes County in the early 1880s. During Reconstruction Negroes in the county had achieved a remarkably stable local Republican organization, headed by a number of resourceful black leaders. When Reconstruction ended and white Democrats regained control of the state governmental machinery in Texas, Grimes County blacks retained local power and sent a succession of black legislators to Austin for the next decade. The local effort to end this Republican rule took the usual postwar Southern form of a political movement of white solidarity under the label of the Democratic party. In supporting the Greenback party Garrett Scott not only was disassociating himself from the politics of white racial solidarity, he was undermining it.

In 1882 a mass meeting of various non-Democratic elements in Grimes County nominated a variegated slate for county offices. Among the candidates were black Republicans, "lily-white" Republicans, and Independent Greenbackers. Garrett Scott was on the ticket as the Independent Greenback candidate for sheriff. Not much is known about the racial climate in Grimes County in 1882, but it must not have been wholly serene, because the "lily-white" nominee for county judge, Lock MacDaniel, withdrew from the ticket rather than publicly associate with black candidates. Garrett Scott did not withdraw, and in November he was elected. Also elected, as district clerk, was a black man who became a lifelong political ally of Scott, Jim Kennard. Thus began an interracial coalition that endured through the years of propagandizing in Texas by the increasingly radical Farmers Alliance and through the ensuing period of the People's party. The success of the coalition varied with the degree of white participation. After the collapse of the Greenback party in the mid-eighties visible white opposition to the Democratic party declined for several years before Grimes County farmers, organized by the Alliance, broke with the Democracy to form the nucleus of the local People's party in 1892. Scott and Kennard were the most visible symbols of the revitalized coalition, but there were others as well. Among them were Morris Carrington, a Negro school principal, and Jack Haynes, both staunch advocates of Populism in the black community, as well as J. W. H. Davis and J. H. Teague, white Populist leaders. These men led the People's party to victory in the county elections of 1896 and again in 1898.

A subtle duality creeps into the narrative of events at this point. To the world outside Grimes County in the 1890s, to both Populists and Democrats, Garrett Scott was simply another Populist officeholder, distinguished for his antimonopoly views and his generally radical approach to monetary policy. To his white support-

ers within Grimes County he was doubtless respected for the same reasons. But to the Democrats of Grimes County the sheriff symbolized all that was un-Southern and unpatriotic about the third party. Under Populist rule, it was charged, Negro school teachers were paid too much money; furthermore, in Scott's hands the sheriff's office hired Negro deputies. The two Democratic newspapers in Navasota were fond of equating Populist rule with Negro rule and of attributing both evils to Scott. The Navasota *Daily Examiner* asserted that "the Negro has been looking too much to political agitation and legislative enactment. . . . So long as he looks to political agitation for relief, so long will he be simply the means of other men's ambition." To the Navasota *Tablet* Scott was simply "the originator of all the political trouble in Grimes County for years." Both these explanations oversimplify Grimes County politics. The political presence and goals of blacks were definite elements of local Populism, as was, presumably, the personal ambition of Garrett Scott. But the Populists' proposed economic remedies had gained a significant following among the county's white farmers, and this was of crucial importance in inducing white Populists to break with Democrats and ally themselves with blacks. Garrett Scott was a living embodiment of white radicalism; he did not cause it. Beyond this the political cohesion of blacks was a local phenomenon that had preceded Scott's entry into Grimes County politics and had remained relatively stable since the end of the war. The ease with which Democratic partisans saw the fine hand of Garrett Scott in Negro voting was more a reflection of their own racial presumptions than an accurate description of the political dynamics at work in the county.

Through the election of 1898 Democrats in Grimes County had labored in vain to cope with the disease of Populism among the county's white farmers. Finally, in the spring of 1899, the Democrats moved in a new direction. The defeated Democratic candidate for county judge, J. G. McDonald, organized a clandestine meeting with other prominent local citizens and defeated Democratic office seekers. At this meeting a new and

—for the time being—covert political institution was created: the White Man's Union. A charter was drawn providing machinery through which the Union could nominate candidates for county offices in elections in which only White Man's Union members could vote. No person could be nominated who was not a member; no person could be a member who did not subscribe to these exclusionary bylaws; in effect, to participate in the organization's activities, so adequately expressed in its formal title, one had to support, as a policy matter, black disfranchisement. Throughout the summer and fall of 1899 the White Man's Union quietly organized.

Writing years later McDonald explained that care was taken not to launch the organization publicly "until the public attitude could be sounded." By January 1900 the covert organizing had been deemed sufficiently successful to permit the public unveiling of the White Man's Union through a long story in the *Examiner.* During the spring the *Examiner*'s political reporting began to reflect a significant change of tone. In April, for example, the *Examiner*'s report of a "quiet election" in nearby Bryan noted that friends of the two mayoral candidates "made a display of force and permitted no Negroes to vote. All white citizens went to the polls, quietly deposited their ballots for whom they pleased and went on about their business." The *Examiner* had progressed from vague suggestions for disfranchisement to approval of its forcible imposition without cover of law.

The first public meetings of the White Man's Union, duly announced in the local press, occupied the spring months of 1900 and were soon augmented by some not-quite-so-public night riding. The chronology of these events may be traced through the denials in the local Democratic press of their occurrence. In July the *Examiner* angrily defended the county's honor against charges by the Negro Baptist State Sunday School Conference that the county had become unsafe for Negroes. The Austin *Herald* reported from the state's capital that the Sunday School Board, "after mature thought and philosophical deliberation," had decided to cancel its

annual meeting scheduled for Navasota. The *Examiner* cited as "irresponsible slush" the charge that Negroes were being threatened and told to leave the county, but within weeks reports of just such events began cropping up in the *Examiner* itself. One example of terrorism left no one in doubt, for it occurred in broad daylight on the main street of the county seat: in July Jim Kennard was shot and killed within one hundred yards of the courthouse. His assailant was alleged to be J. G. McDonald.

Intimidation and murder constituted an even more decisive assault on the People's party than had the ominous bylaws of the White Man's Union. The Populist leadership recognized this clearly enough, and Scott went so far as to attempt to persuade Southern white farmers to shoulder arms in defense of the right of Negroes to vote. Beyond this we know little of the measures attempted by the local Populist constabulary to contain the spreading terrorism. A well-informed member of the Scott family wrote a detailed account of these turbulent months, but the manuscript was subsequently destroyed. In the early autumn of 1900 members of the White Man's Union felt sufficiently strong to initiate visits to white farmers with a known allegiance to the People's party. Under such duress some of these farmers joined the White Man's Union.

In August the Union, aided by a not inconsiderable amount of free publicity in the local press, announced "the Grandest Barbecue of the Year," at which the "workings of the White Man's Union" would be explained to all. The leadership of the People's party objected to announced plans to include the local state guard unit, the Shaw Rifles, in the program. After some discussion the Texas adjutant general, Thomas Scurry, placed at the discretion of the local commander the question of the attendance of the Shaw Rifles in a body. The commander, Captain Hammond Norwood, a leading Navasota Democrat and a member of the White Man's Union, exercised his option, and the Shaw Rifles appeared en masse at the function. Populist objections were brushed aside.

Shortly after this well-attended barbecue had

revealed the growing prestige of the White Man's Union as well as the inability of the People's party to cope with the changing power relationships within the county, a black exodus began. People left by train, by horse and cart, by day and by night. The *Examiner,* with obvious respect for the new political climate its own columns had helped engender, suggested elliptically that the exodus could produce complications. Some citizens, said the *Examiner,* "are beginning to feel a little nervous as the thing progresses, and lean to the idea that the action will bring on detrimental complications in the labor market."

The next day, however, the paper printed a public address that it said had been "ordered published by the executive committee of the White Man's Union in order to combat the many reports that are calculated to injure the Union." After reaffirming the Union's intent to end "Negro rule" in the county, the report concluded with a message "to the Negroes":

> Being the weaker race, it is our desire to protect you from the schemes of those men who are now seeking to place you before them. . . . Therefore, the White Man's Union kindly and earnestly requests you to keep hands off in the coming struggle. Do not let impudent men influence you in that pathway which certainly leads to trouble. . . . In the future, permit us to show you, and convince you by our action, that we are truly your best friends.

Fourteen days later a black Populist leader, Jack Haynes, was riddled with a shotgun blast by unknown assailants. He died instantly in the fields of his cotton farm.

The White Man's Union held a rally in Navasota two nights later that featured a reading of original poetry by one of the Union's candidates, L. M. Bragg. The verse concluded:

> Twas nature's laws that drew the lines
> Between the Anglo-Saxon and African races,
> And we, the Anglo-Saxons of Grand Old Grimes,
> Must force the African to keep his place.

Another White Man's Union rally held in Plantersville the same week displayed other Union candidates whose conduct won the *Examiner*'s editorial approval: "They are a solid looking body of men and mean business straight from the shoulder." Apparently this characterization of the Plantersville speakers was not restricted to approving Democrats; Populists, too, responded to events initiated by the men who "meant business." In October the Plantersville school superintendent reported that only five white families remained in his school district and that all the Negroes were gone. The superintendent stated that twelve white families had left that week, and "the end is not in sight."

Amid this wave of mounting terror the People's party attempted to go about its business, announcing its nominating conventions in the local press and moving forward with the business of naming election judges and poll watchers. But there were already signs of a fatal crack in Populist morale. The People's party nominee for county commissioner suddenly withdrew from the race. His withdrawal was announced in the *Examiner,* and no explanation was offered.

Throughout the late summer and autumn of 1900 the demonstrated power of the White Man's Union had protected McDonald from prosecution in the Kennard slaying. Nothing short of a war between the Populist police authority and the White Man's Union could break that extralegal shield. An exasperated and perhaps desperate Garrett Scott angrily challenged a White Man's Union official in October to "go and get your Union force, every damn one of them, put them behind rock fences and trees and I'll fight the whole damn set of cowards." That Scott had to use the first person singular to describe the visible opposition to the Union underscores the extent to which terror had triumphed over the institutions of law in Grimes County. By election eve it was clear that the Populist ticket faced certain defeat. The third party had failed to protect its constituency. White Populists as well as black were intimidated. Many would not vote; indeed, many were no longer in the county.

Over 4,500 votes had been cast in Grimes in 1898. On November 6, 1900, only 1,800 persons ventured to the polls. The People's party received exactly 366 votes. The Populist vote in Planters-ville fell from 256 in 1898 to 5 in 1900. In the racially mixed, lower-income precinct of south Navasota the Populist vote declined from 636 to 23. The sole exception to this pattern came in a geographically isolated, lower-income precinct in the extreme northern part of the county that contained few Negroes and thus, presumably, fewer acts of terrorism. The Populist vote in this precinct actually increased from 108 to 122 and accounted for one-third of the countywide vote of 366. In north Navasota, also almost all white but not geographically isolated from the terror, the Populist vote declined from 120 to 3. An additional element, nonstatistical in nature, stamped the election as unusual. The underlying philosophy of the South's dominant political institution, the Democratic party, has perhaps never been expressed more nakedly than it was in Grimes County in 1900 when "the party of white supremacy," as C. Vann Woodward has called the Southern Democracy, appeared on the official ballot as the White Man's Union.

On the way to its landslide victory the Union had grown more self-confident in its willingness to carry out acts of intimidation and terrorism in defiance of the local Populist police authority. Now that that authority had been deposed and a sheriff friendly to the White Man's Union had been elected, would terrorism become even more public?

On November 7, 1900, the morning after the election, a strange tableau unfolded on the streets of Anderson, the tiny county seat. Horsemen began arriving in town from every section of the county, tied their horses all along the main street, and occupied the second floor of the courthouse. In a nearby house Garrett Scott's sister, Cornelia, and her husband, John Kelly, watched the buildup of Union supporters on the courthouse square, not fifty yards from the sheriff's official residence on the second floor of the county jail. They decided the situation was too dangerous to permit an adult Populist to venture forth, so the Kellys sent their nine-year-old son with a note to warn Scott not to appear on the street.

At about the same time that this mission was carried out Garrett Scott's younger brother, Emmett Scott, came into town from the family farm, rode past the growing clusters of armed men, and reined up in front of the store belonging to John Bradley, his closest friend in town. Bradley was a Populist but, as befitting a man of trade, a quiet one. His store was adjacent to the courthouse.

Cornelia Kelly's son found the sheriff at Abercrombie's store across the street from the jail and delivered the warning note. As Scott read it an outbreak of gunfire sounded from the direction of Bradley's store. Scott stepped to the street and peered in the direction of the fusillade. Rifle fire from the second floor of the courthouse immediately cut him down. Upon hearing the gunfire Cornelia Kelly ran out of her house and down the long street toward the courthouse. The gunsights of scores of men tracked her progress. Seeing her brother's body in the street she turned and confronted his attackers. "Why don't you shoot me, too," she yelled, "I'm a Scott." She ran to her brother and, with the assistance of her son, dragged him across the street to the county jail. He was, she found, not dead, though he did have an ugly wound in his hip. Inside Bradley's store, however, three men were dead—Emmett Scott, Bradley, and Will McDonald, the son of a Presbyterian minister and a prominent member of the White Man's Union. McDonald had shot Scott shortly after the latter had entered the store; the two men grappled for the gun, and the fatally wounded Scott fired one shot, killing McDonald. Bradley was killed either by a shot fired from outside the store where Union forces had gathered near the courthouse or by a stray bullet during the struggle inside.

The siege of Anderson continued for five days, with the wounded sheriff and his deputies—black and white—in the jail and the White Man's Union forces in the courthouse. Shots crossed the fifty yards between the two buildings intermittently over the next several days. On the evening of the fatal shooting another member of the Scott clan, Mrs. W. T. Neblett, had left Navasota for Austin to plead with the governor, Joseph D. Sayers, for troops. On Friday she returned, accompanied by the adjutant general of the State of

Texas, Thomas Scurry—the same official who had earlier acquiesced in the participation of the state guard in the White Man's Union barbecue. After conferring with the contending forces Scurry pondered various methods to get the wounded Scott out of town and into a hospital; gangrene had set in. For protection, Scurry suggested that he be authorized to select a group of twenty prominent citizens of Navasota to escort the sheriff from the jail to the railroad station. Since most of the "prominent citizens" of Navasota were members of the White Man's Union, it is perhaps understandable that Scott declined this offer. The adjutant general then suggested that the Shaw Rifles be employed as an escort. This idea was respectfully declined for the same reason. Asked what he would consider a trustworthy escort, the wounded sheriff suggested a state guard unit from outside the county.

On Saturday, four days after the shooting, a company of Houston light infantry of the Texas Volunteer State Guard detrained at Navasota and marched the eleven miles to Anderson. On Sunday morning Garrett Scott was placed on a mattress, the mattress put in a wagon, and the procession began. In the wagon train were most of the members of the large Scott clan—Emmett Scott's widow and children, the Kelly family, and the Nebletts, all with their household belongings piled in wagons. A file of infantrymen marched on either side as the procession formed in front of the jail, moved past hundreds of armed men at the courthouse and onto the highway to Navasota, and then boarded a special train bound for Houston.

Thus did Populism leave Grimes County. From that day in 1900 until well after mid-century Negroes were not a factor in Grimes County politics. J. G. McDonald regained his judgeship and served for many years. The White Man's Union continued into the 1950s as the dominant political institution in the county. None of its nominees, selected in advance of the Democratic primary, was ever defeated. The census of 1910 revealed the extent of the Negro exodus. It showed that Grimes County's Negro population

had declined by almost thirty per cent from the 1900 total. School census figures for 1901 suggest an even greater exodus.

To this day the White Man's Union, as a memory if no longer as an institution, enjoys an uncontested reputation among Grimes County whites as a civic enterprise for governmental reform. In this white oral tradition the general events of 1900 are vividly recounted. Specific events are, however remembered selectively. The exodus of Negroes from the county is not part of this oral tradition, nor is the night riding of the White Man's Union or the assassination of the Negro Populist leaders.

As for Garrett Scott, he endured a long convalescence in a San Antonio hospital, regained his health, married his nurse, and moved to a farm near Houston. He retired from politics and died in his bed. He is remembered in the oral tradition of the black community as the "best sheriff the county ever had." Kennard and Haynes were killed because they "vouched" for Scott among Negroes. In this black oral tradition the Negro exodus plays a central role. It is perhaps an accurate measure of the distance between the races in Grimes County today that two such contradictory versions of famous events could exist side by side without cross-influence.

To these two oral traditions a third must be added—the Scott tradition. The Scotts were, and are, a proud family. One by one, as they died, they were brought home to be buried in the family plot in the Anderson cemetery, little more than a mile from the site of the bloody events of 1900. Tombstones of female members of the clan bear the Scott middle name, defiantly emblazoned in marble. Edith Hamilton of Richards, Grimes County, was ten years old in November 1900 and remembers vividly the day her nine-year-old brother carried her mother's message to Garrett Scott. She remembers the defiance of her mother, the political commitment of her father, the acts of intimidation by the White Man's Union, the Negro exodus, and what she calls the "intelligence of Uncle Garrett." "They said that Uncle Garrett was a nigger-lover," recalls Mrs. Hamilton. "He wasn't a nigger-lover, or a white-lover, he just believed in being fair to all, in justice."

The Scott oral tradition—similar to the black oral tradition and at odds with the white tradition—is virtually the only legacy of the long years of interracial cooperation in Grimes County. Beyond this the substance of political life that came to an end in Grimes County in 1900 cannot be measured precisely from the available evidence. Very little survives to provide insight into the nature of the personal relationship that existed between Garrett Scott and Jim Kennard, between any of the other Populist leaders of both races, or between their respective constituencies. Scott and his third-party colleagues may have been motivated solely by personal ambition, as the White Man's Union charged; on the other hand, the impulses that made them Populists in the first place may have led them toward public coalition with blacks. It is clear that such stridently white supremacist voices as the Navasota *Tablet* were unable to project any reason other than personal ambition to explain the phenomenon of white men willingly associating themselves politically with black men. To what extent this attitude reflected Populist presumptions is another question. White Populists and black Republicans shared an animosity toward the Southern Democracy that grew in intensity during the bitter election campaigns of the 1890s. Democratic persistence in raising the cry of "Negro domination" to lure Populist-leaning voters back to the "party of the fathers" was effective enough to keep white Populists on the defensive about the race issue throughout the agrarian revolt in the South. The circumstance of a common political foe nevertheless provided Populists and Republicans with a basis for political coalition that was consummated in a bewildering variety of ways—and sometimes not consummated at all. The stability of local black organizations and their demonstrated capacity to withstand Democratic blandishments or acts of intimidation were only two of the factors governing the complex equation of post-Reconstruction interracial politics. A stable, local black political institution existed in Grimes County, and its enduring qualities obviously sim-

plified the organizational task confronting Garrett Scott. What might be regarded as "normal" Bourbon efforts to split blacks from the Populist coalition—mild intimidation, petty bribery, campaign assertions that the Democrats were the Negroes' "best friends," or a combination of all three—failed to achieve the desired results in Grimes County in the 1890s. The precise reasons are not easily specified. The Navasota *Tablet,* seeing the world through lenses tinted with its own racial presumptions, ascribed the credit for Negro political cohesion solely to the white sheriff. In the face of all Democratic stratagems, the third party's continuing appeal to Negroes was, in the *Tablet*'s view, a thing of "magic." A white supremacist view does not automatically exclude its holder from rendering correct political analyses on occasion, and it is possible that the *Tablet*'s assessment of the cause of Negro political solidarity was correct; however, such an analysis does not explain how the Negro Republican organization was able to send a succession of black legislators to Austin in the 1870s and 1880s, before Garrett Scott became politically active. It seems relevant that when Grimes County Democrats decided upon an overt campaign of terrorism, the men they went after first were the leading black spokesmen of Populism in the county rather than the third party's white leadership. To this extent the actions of Democratic leaders contradicted their public analysis of the causal relationships inherent in the continuing Populist majorities.

Before they indulged in terrorism the Democrats already possessed another method of splitting the Populist coalition: regaining the loyalty of white Populists. Against the historic Democratic campaign cry of white supremacy, the People's party had as its most effective defense the economic appeal of its own platform. The persuasiveness of Populism to white farmers in Grimes County was confirmed by newspaper accounts of the public reaction to the Populist-Democratic debates that occurred during the years of the agrarian uprising. While the reports in the *Examiner* were uniformly partisan and invariably concluded that Democratic spokesmen "won" such debates hands down, the papers conceded that Populist speakers also drew enthusiastic responses from white residents. The absence of reliable racial data by precincts renders a statistical analysis of the Populist vote in Grimes County impossible; however, the fragmentary available evidence suggests that the People's party was generally able to hold a minimum of approximately thirty per cent of the county's white voters in the four elections from 1892 to 1898 while at the same time polling approximately eighty to ninety per cent of the Negro electorate. The inability of the Democratic party to "bloc vote" the county's white citizenry, coupled with the party's failure to win black voters by various means or, alternatively, to diminish the size of the Negro electorate, combined to ensure Democratic defeat at the polls. The fact merits emphasis: both the cohesion of black support for the People's party and the maintenance of substantial white support were essential to the local ascendancy of Populism.

This largely deductive analysis, however, reveals little about the internal environment within the third-party coalition during the bitter struggle for power that characterized the decade of Populist-Democratic rivalry. However scrutinized, the bare bones of voting totals do not flesh out the human relationships through which black and white men came together politically in this rural Southern county. In the absence of such crucial evidence, it seems prudent to measure the meaning of 1900 in the most conservative possible terms. Even by this standard, however, a simple recitation of those elements of Grimes County politics that are beyond dispute isolates significant and lasting ramifications.

An indigenous black political structure persisted in Grimes County for thirty-five years following the Civil War. Out of his own needs as a political insurgent against the dominant Southern Democratic party, Garrett Scott decided in 1882 to identify his Greenback cause with the existing local Republican constituency. Once in office as sheriff he found, among other possible motives, that it was in his own self-interest to preserve the coalition that elected him. It is clear that the style of law enforcement in Grimes County under

Scott became a persuasive ingredient in the preservation of black support for the People's party. The presence of black deputy sheriffs and Scott's reputation within the black community seem adequate confirmation of both the existence of this style and its practical effect. The salaries paid Negro school teachers constituted another element of third-party appeal. Comparisons with white salaries are not available, but whatever black teachers received, partisans of the White Man's Union publicly denounced it as "too much." It is evident that Grimes County Negroes supported the People's party for reasons that were grounded in legitimate self-interest—an incontestable basis for political conduct. The point is not so much that the county's Negroes had certain needs, but that they possessed the political means to address at least a part of those needs.

From this perspective the decisive political event of 1900 in Grimes County was not the overwhelming defeat of the local People's party but the political elimination of that part of its constituency that was black. Scott was valuable to Negroes in short-run terms because he helped to translate a minority black vote into a majority coalition that possessed the administrative authority to improve the way black people lived in Grimes County. In the long run, however, it was the presence of this black constituency—not the conduct of a single white sheriff nor even the professed principles of his political party—that provided the Negroes of the county with what protection they had from a resurgent caste system. As long as Negroes retained the right to cast ballots in proportion to their numbers they possessed bargaining power that became particularly meaningful on all occasions when whites divided their votes over economic issues. Disfranchisement destroyed the bargaining power essential to this elementary level of protection. Arrayed against these overriding imperatives for Negroes such questions as the sincerity of Garrett Scott's motives fade in importance. Whatever the sheriff's motives, both the political realities that undergirded the majority coalition and Scott's ability to respond to those realities shaped a course of government conduct under the People's party that was demonstrably of more benefit to Negroes than was the conduct of other administrations before or since. The permanent alteration of those realities through black disfranchisement ensured that no other white administration, whether radical, moderate, or opportunistic, would be able to achieve the patterns in education and law enforcement that had come to exist in the county under Populism. Stated as starkly as possible, after 1900 it was no longer in the interest of white politicians to provide minimal guarantees for people who could not help elect them.

Beyond this crucial significance for the county's black people, disfranchisement also institutionalized a fundamental change in the political environment of whites. More than a third party passed from Grimes County in 1900; in real political terms an idea died. Though a new political idea invariably materializes in democratic societies as an expression of the self-interest of a portion of the electorate, the party that adopts the idea in the course of appealing for the votes of that sector of the electorate inevitably is placed in the position of having to rationalize, defend, explain, and eventually promote the idea. If the concept has substance, this process eventually results in the insinuation of the idea into the culture itself. In this sense it is not necessary to know the precise depth of the commitment to Negro rights of the Grimes County People's party to know that the *idea* of Negro rights had a potential constituency among white people in the county as long as black people were able to project its presence through their votes. Given the endurance of this real and potential constituency, one could reasonably intuit that twentieth-century politics in Grimes County would have contained one, or a dozen, or a thousand Garrett Scotts—each more, or less, "sincere" or "ambitious" than the Populist sheriff. Disfranchisement destroyed the political base of this probability. A political party can survive electoral defeat, even continuing defeat, and remain a conveyor of ideas from one generation to the next. But it cannot survive the destruction of its constituency, for the party itself then dies, taking with it the possibility of transmitting its political concepts to those as yet un-

born. It is therefore no longer possible to speak of two white political traditions in Grimes County, for the White Man's Union succeeded in establishing a most effective philosophical suzerainty. Seventy years after disfranchisement Mrs. Hamilton can recall the racial unorthodoxy of Uncle Garrett; she cannot participate in such activity herself. "The Negro people here don't want this school integration any more than the whites do," she now says. "They're not ready for it. They don't feel comfortable in the school with white children. I've talked to my maid. I know."

While Garrett Scott's memory has been preserved, the local presence of the creed of his political party died with the destruction of that party. There has been literally no political place to go for subsequent generations of Scotts and Teagues, or Kennards and Carringtons. This absence of an alternative political institution to the Democratic party, the party of white supremacy, has been a continuing and unique factor in Southern politics. The circumstance is based on the race issue, but in its long-term political and social implications it actually transcends that issue.

The Populist era raises a number of questions about the interaction of the two races in the South, both within the third party and in the larger society. It is widely believed, by no means merely by laymen, that after the failure of Reconstruction meaningful experiments with the social order were finished in the South and that the aspirations of blacks were decisively thwarted. The example of Grimes County suggests, however, the existence of a period of time—a decade perhaps, or a generation—when nascent forms of indigenous interracial activity struggled for life in at least parts of the old Confederacy. Was some opportunity missed and, if so, how? How widespread through the South, and the nation, was this opportunity?

The White Man's Union was organized and led by men who considered themselves the "best people" of the South. If this attitude was typical, major adjustments must be made in our understanding of precisely how, and for what reasons, the antebellum caste system, in altered form, was

reinstitutionalized in Southern society a generation after the formal ending of slavery. Was the
"red-neck" the source of atrocity, or was he
swept along by other stronger currents? And
what of the Populist role? To what extent was
agrarian racial liberalism in Texas traceable to an
overall philosophy within the third-party leadership? Through what intuition of self-interest did
the radical organizers of the Farmers Alliance,
the parent institution of the People's party, accept the political risks of public coalition with
blacks? What were their hopes and fears, and
where did they falter? And, finally, what does the
substance of their effort tell us about the Democrats in the South and the Republicans in the
North who opposed them?

Answers to these questions rest, in part, on
detailed knowledge of such events as those in
Grimes County, but they require more than com-
pilations of local histories, just as they assuredly
require more than cultural assessments based on
novels, speeches, and party manifestoes considered apart from their organic milieu. These answers will not provide much of a synthesis—
Populism was too diverse, too congregational,
and too ideologically thin—but they should tell
us more about the larger society that, along with
the Populists, failed to erect the foundations for
a multiracial society in the nineteenth century.
As the inquiry proceeds, it should be remembered
that Populism perished before developing a mature philosophy—on race, on money, or on socialism. One must generalize, therefore, not only
from contradictory evidence but, more important, from incomplete evidence. An analogy,
doubtless unfair, could be made with the plight
that would face modern historians of Marxism
had that movement been abruptly truncated at
the time, say, of the Brussels Conference in 1903.
Who could have predicted on the evidence available to that date the Stalinist reign of terror that
evolved from the mature, victorious revolutionary party of 1917? By the same token sweeping
generalizations about what Populist radicalism
could have become are not only romantic but
historically unsound.

It should be sufficient to observe that in the
long post-Reconstruction period—a period not

yet ended—during which the social order has
been organized hierarchically along racial lines,
Populism intruded as a brief, flickering light in
parts of the South. For a time some white Southerners threw off the romanticism that has historically been a cover for the region's pessimism and
ventured a larger, more hopeful view about the
possibilities of man in a free society. Under duress
and intimidation this public hope failed of persuasion at the ballot box; under terrorism it vanished completely.

The Grimes County story dramatically illustrates this failure, but in the insight it provides
into the underlying politics of black disfranchisement and the achievement of a monolithic one-
party political environment in the American
South it is not unique. Other Populists in East
Texas and across the South—white as well as
black—died during the terrorism that preceded
formal disfranchisement. In Texas the extrapar-
liamentary institutions formed by white Democrats to help create the political climate for disfranchisement bore a variety of local names: the
Citizens White Primary of Marion County; the
Tax-Payers Union of Brazoria County; the Jay-
bird Democratic Association of Fort Bend
County; and the White Man's Union of Wharton,
Washington, Austin, Matagorda, Grimes, and
other counties. The available historical material
concerning each of these organizations comes
largely from the founders themselves, or their
descendants, reflecting an incipient or a mature
oral tradition—one oral tradition. The secondary
literature based on these accounts, including
scholarly works used in graduate schools as well
as primary and secondary textbooks, is corre-
spondingly inadequate.

A surprising amount of uninterpreted material
from violently partisan white supremacist
sources has found its way into scholarly literature. One example from the Grimes experience
pertains directly to the scholarly characterization
of Negro political meetings during the Populist
era. It is worth attention as an illustration of the
impact of white supremacist modes of thought on
modern scholarship. The sunup-to-sundown
work routine of Southern farm labor obviously
precluded daytime political meetings. Accord-

ingly, Kennard, Haynes, and Carrington campaigned among their black constituents by holding political meetings in each of the towns and hamlets of the county at night. Democratic partisans termed these rallies "Owl Meetings" and characterized black Populist leaders as " 'fluence men." Drawing upon their own party's time-honored campaign technique with Negroes, Democrats further asserted that owl meetings were more concerned with sumptuous banquets and whisky than with politics. If partisans of white supremacy had difficulty finding reasons for white acceptance of political coalition with blacks, they were culturally incapable of ascribing reasons for Negro support of the third party to causes other than short-run benefits in terms of money and alcohol. The point is not that Democrats were always insincere in their descriptions (as white supremacists they were quite sincere), but that scholars have subsequently accepted such violently partisan accounts at face value. The darkly sinister picture of " 'fluence men" corrupting innocent blacks with whisky at surreptitious owl meetings served to justify, at least to outsiders, the use of terrorism as the ultimate campaign technique of Democratic interracial politics. This sequential recording of events has found its way into scholarly monographs that otherwise demonstrate no inherent hostility to the Populistic inclinations of Southern farmers, black or white. In *The People's Party in Texas* Roscoe Martin precedes his brief allusion to the White Man's Union with a resumé of owl meetings and " 'fluence men" that reflects in detail the bias of white supremacist sources. Other scholars writing broadly about Gilded Age politics have routinely drawn upon such monographs as Martin's, and by this process " 'fluence men" have materialized as an explanation of Negro political insurgency in the nineties. In the heat of local political combat, however, Democratic leaders often were able to face a wholly different set of facts in the course of persuading their followers, and the citizenry as a whole, to adjust to the necessity of terrorism. As the time approached for actual precinct campaigning in Grimes County in the autumn of 1900, the executive board of the White Man's Union published a no-

tice of the Union's intentions, climaxed by a "fair distinct warning" to the county's Negro leadership. The statement is revealing—not only of the transformation visited upon normal campaign practices when they were viewed through the cultural presumptions of white supremacy but also of the dangers of uncritical acceptance of such perspectives by scholars relying upon monoracial sources. The notice read in part:

> The Union is largely composed of the best citizens of the county. . . . They are the tax payers, representing the worth, the patriotism, the intelligence, and the virtues of the county. . . . We are not fighting any political party or individuals, but only those who band together under any name, who seek to perpetuate negro rule in Grimes County. [Good citizens] are astounded at the manner in which the children's money has been expended. Colored teachers with fat salaries and totally incompetent have been appointed for political "fluence." Our white teachers, male and female, enjoy no such fat salaries as these colored politicians or these sweet colored girls. . . . One of the most corrupting practices in the past has been the system of Owl Meetings which has been in vogue for years. . . . This is the school and hot bed where the negro politician received his inspiration, and riding from one end of the county to the other as an apostle of his race, corrupting his own people who may be in the honest pathway of duty. We give fair warning that any effort to continue these Owl Meetings—by the appointment of special deputies sheriffs to organize and carry them on—will be prevented. No threat of shotguns will deter us from the discharge of this duty.

Even without recourse to other perspectives this view of the existing political situation in Grimes County contains serious internal contradictions. Black Populist leaders were "incompetent" but as "apostles of their race" they had been so effective that their efforts needed to be stopped. Black teachers were paid "fat salaries" solely for political reasons, but among those receiving such gross patronage were "sweet colored girls," who obviously were not conducting owl meetings. The assertion that black teachers were actually paid more than white teachers must be rejected out of hand. In addition to the compelling fact that such an arrangement would have constituted poor political behavior on the part of a third party strenuously endeavoring to hold a substantial portion of the white vote and the further reality that such expenditures were unnecessary since parity for blacks in itself would have represented a notable accomplishment in the eyes of Negro leaders, Democrats had access to the records of all county expenditures and no such charge was ever leveled, much less documented, at any other time during the Populist decade. Whites complained that Negro teachers received "too much," not that they received more than white teachers. In any case, it seems necessary only to observe that American political parties have routinely utilized night gatherings without having their opponents characterize them as owl meetings and that persons who benefited from incumbency were not presumed to be acting in sinister ways when they campaigned for their party's re-election. The only thing "special" about Garrett Scott's deputies was that some of them were black. Viewed as some sort of black abstraction Jim Kennard might appear convincing as a shadowy " 'fluence man," but as an intelligent and determined voice of the aspirations of Negro people he merits scholarly attention from perspectives not bounded by the horizons of those who murdered him. To an extent that is perhaps not fully appreciated, decades of monoracial scholarship in the South have left a number of Jim Kennards buried under stereotypes of one kind or another. They sometimes intrude anonymously as " 'fluence men," but they simply do not appear as people in books on Southern politics.

This circumstance suggests that not only the broad topic of interracial life and tension but the entire Southern experience culminated by disfranchisement needs to be tested by a methodology that brings both black and white sources to bear on the admittedly intricate problem of interpreting a free society that was not free. At all events, evidence continues to mount that monoracial scholarship, Northern and Southern, has exhausted whatever merit it possessed as an instrument of investigating the variegated past of the American people. The obvious rejoinder—

that written black sources do not exist in meaningful quantity—cannot, of course, be explained away; at the same time, this condition suggests the utility of fresh attempts to devise investigatory techniques that offer the possibility of extracting usable historical material from oral sources. The example of the erroneous report in the Navasota *Examiner* of Morris Carrington's death illustrates, perhaps as well as any single piece of evidence, not only the dangers inherent in relying on such "primary sources" for details of interracial tension in the post-Reconstruction South but also the value of received oral traditions in correcting contemporary accounts. Nevertheless, the problem of evaluating such source material remains; white and black versions of the details of racial conflicts are wildly contradictory. When they are measured against other contemporary evidence, however, the interpretive problem becomes considerably less formidable; indeed, the task of penetrating the substance behind partisan contemporary accounts may be lessened through recourse to available oral sources, as I have attempted to demonstrate.

Since much of the *Realpolitik* of the South, from Reconstruction through the modern civil rights movement, rests on legal institutions that, in turn, rest on extralegal methods of intimidation, the sources of political reality may be found less in public debate than in the various forms of intimidation that matured in the region. However determined a historian may be to penetrate the legal forms to reach this extralegal underside of the political culture of the South he is, in our contemporary climate, blocked off from part of his sources by his skin color. For black scholars there are limits to the availability both of courthouse records in the rural South and of responsive white oral sources. There are corresponding limits to the information white scholars can gain from interviews in black communities. Here, then, is fertile ground for scholarly cooperation. Methods of achieving this cooperation need to be explored. In its fullest utilization the subject is not black history or Southern history but American history.

8

THOMAS EDISON: THE MOST USEFUL AMERICAN

HAROLD C. LIVESAY

In 1800 America was an agrarian nation that lay largely outside the movements of international economic development. But by the end of the nineteenth century the United States was fast becoming the industrial giant of the world with American steel, machinery, electrical, and consumer goods dominating international markets from Europe to Asia. In part this growing international economic dominance was due to America's vast population, size, and resources, which provided a large and stable domestic market along with cheap and plentiful raw materials.

But as important as these factors were, more important still were the unique American methods of industrial production developed during the nineteenth century. The earliest component of the American system of manufacturing was the development of interchangeable parts and their production on a mass scale. Pioneered between 1830 and 1850 at the federal armory at Harper's Ferry, Virginia, the introduction of interchangeable parts allowed a speed and uniform quality of production unparalleled in the industrial world.

The second component of the American system, as Harold C. Livesay demonstrates in this essay, was the joining of capital and scientific research to create new products and new production techniques. To more than any other individual this modern idea of research and development can be attributed to Thomas A. Edison. An inventor more than a scientist, Edison early realized the value of "practical"—that is, profitable—research. In his Menlo Park, New Jersey, workshop Edison brought together craftsmen and other inventors such as himself to seek ways of creating useful goods that could draw large profits. His success with such inventions as the incandescent light paved the way for others, and by the early twentieth century applied research was an integral part of large business organizations in every industrial nation.

Livesay notes that many of Edison's inventions were developed in competition with other inventors of his time. In what do you think Edison's originality and success lay? How does Edison's inventiveness and creativity compare with that of the Chinese railroad builders discussed by Jack Chen in Reading 3?

Travel has a lot of advantages, including the opportunity to engage in a variety of social analyses, ranging from the acute to the crackpot. To the latter category I add my superficial observation that a higher percentage of habitual airplane passengers send their children to college than do people who ride trains. When I flew a great deal, I met lots of college parents and spent considerable time arguing that when the fate of the universe passed into the hands of their children things could be expected to improve rather than collapse. I admire my students; I think they com-

From Harold C. Livesay, *American Made: Men Who Shaped the American Economy,* pp. 127–156. Copyright © 1979 by Harold C. Livesay. Reprinted by permission of Little, Brown and Company.

prise the most decent generation of people this country has yet produced. I am not alarmed that they watch a lot of bad TV; their parents passed through childhood reading terrible books and wasted many a Saturday afternoon gazing rapturously at movie screens filled with unimaginably puerile nonsense.

It's stylish to bemoan young people's supposed inability to read, write, or conjure with numbers and then predict dire consequences ahead. The Cassandras usually document their auguries with statistics that show declining scores on standardized tests that supposedly measure a student's aptitude for college, graduate school, medical school, law school, business school, and I know not what all else. None of this apparatus nor the results it produces impresses me, although I personally have benefited enormously by it. The tests prove little except how well a student does on the tests, and no one has the vaguest idea what any of it means in any other context, despite elaborate pretensions to the contrary. One potent precedent for my skepticism was established long ago by Thomas Edison, who thought such tests absurd, and mockingly devised one of his own entitled the "ignoramometer."

It simply isn't true that today's students cannot read. Students in fourth-rate colleges today read more than students in citadels of intellectuality did a generation ago, and while the worst of them can't write any more than the worst of them ever could, the best of them write so well that I'm repeatedly dazzled by their skills. If in fact, they know no arithmetic (and I personally couldn't care less; calculators are dirt cheap), the fault lies far more with those who inflicted the "new math" upon them than on the students themselves. If every student in the United States rose up and refused categorically to submit to any further standardized testing, we'd all be better off. Today's college students simply come prepared in a different way from the generations that preceded them. Not worse, different. Calling them uneducated is silly. As I told one of my sneering colleagues, it's all very well for us to rejoice in the elegance of our intellectual preparation, but Coleridge would have dismissed us as barbarians.

My students have provided me with a lot of rewarding surprises, not least of which has been the discovery that many of them truly love history for its own sake. Among the more passionate I've encountered was one who worked as a guide at the Greenfield Village and Henry Ford Museum in Dearborn, Michigan. Among other relics of the American past, Henry Ford had Thomas Edison's Menlo Park laboratory brought intact to Greenfield Village. And I do mean intact: every plank, every nail, every bottle, every machine, indeed the very earth on which it sat was dug up, and the whole collection brought to Michigan. When Ford triumphantly presented his handiwork to Edison, the inventor, who had not seen the laboratory in forty years, said, "You got it ninety-nine percent perfect." "What's wrong with it?" asked the crestfallen Ford. "We never kept the floor this clean," replied Edison.

My student, whose sense of the drama of the past together with her considerable thespian abilities made her a favorite with the visiting throngs, particularly liked to show people through Edison's laboratory. Steering her charges through the labyrinth of mysterious apparatus, shelved chemicals, and workbenches and tables on which Edison had often napped, she would sometimes abandon the prepared script, carefully researched by the Museum's staff, in favor of an extemporaneous discourse, the author of which, or so she claimed, was Edison himself. The living Edison, blunt, cranky, and deaf, had relied heavily on shouts and obscenities when communicating to his subordinates; however, his pneuma displayed both a gentler temperament and more subtle methods, inspiring his cicerone by spiriting his thoughts into her mind. Fascinated visitors often asked their guide what use Edison had made of this or that mysterious apparatus, now squatting obscurely in some dusty nook or cranny. Invariably, she rendered an explanation, often in elaborate detail, only afterward realizing that she had never noticed the relic before and had no personal knowledge of it whatever.

So where did she get her information? "From Edison," she told me; "I'm just his amanuensis."

Well, who's to say otherwise? In 1920 Edison, then in his seventies, explored the possibility of communication between the quick and the dead. The subject generated widespread interest in the era following a war that had killed millions. Edison, having tried nearly everything else (and perhaps thinking that he himself would need celestial contact in the near future), began searching for an appropriate technology. "I don't claim," Edison told a reporter from *Scientific American,* that:

> Our personalities pass on to another existence or sphere. I don't claim anything because I don't know anything. . . . But I do claim that it is possible to construct an apparatus . . . so delicate that if there are personalities in another existence or sphere who wish to get in touch with us . . . this apparatus will at least give them a better opportunity to express themselves than the tilting tables and raps and ouija boards and mediums and the other crude methods now purported to be the only means of communication.

One of his assistants, Edison observed, had died while working on the apparatus, and "he ought to be the first man to use it if he is able to do so."

If Edison ever received news from the other world, he kept it to himself. The whole business may have been a hoax, for Edison's character included a wide streak of perversity. Genuinely iconoclastic in scientific matters, Edison enjoyed spreading consternation in other areas as well. The fundamentalist clergy and their fervent followers formed a particularly attractive target, since Edison, like many another inventor before and after him, had often stirred the wrath of the faithful by carrying worldly business into the precincts of the Heavenly City. Samuel Morse's telegraph, for instance, had provoked many a sermon and letter to Congress on the lines of "If God had intended words to be sent over wire, He would have . . ." This opposition Morse tried to negate through his choice of "What hath God wrought" as the first official message.

In 1910, when asked what a personal God meant to him, Edison replied, "Nothing," a statement he repeated at suitable intervals. What he really believed in is anyone's guess, but he unquestionably enjoyed spreading distress among archenemies of the inventive mind. Suggesting the possibility of an apparatus delicate enough to communicate with the departed may have been just another excursion in provocative posturing. But maybe not. He didn't get the job done in his lifetime, but Edison the ghost may have finished what Edison the man began. If so, it wouldn't be the only time that Edison succeeded where others failed, and it wouldn't be the only revolution Edison ever facilitated.

Americans have evinced an ambivalent view toward things revolutionary. In the political sphere we have embraced the notion that the first revolution did the job so well that there has been neither excuse nor justification for one since; consequently, we've neither wanted, needed, nor had any more.

While steadfastly resisting political overturn in either thought or deed, however, Americans have celebrated the interrelated revolutions in transportation, communication, and energy that remade their society. As technological advancements broke the shackles that had limited transportation and communication to the velocity of wind and water and accelerated them to the speed of sound and light, most Americans rejoiced and called it progress. Fundamental to this change and to the expansion of manufacturing capacity, was a two-stage revolution in the ways by which man converted potential energy to power. In the first stage, steam supplanted human and animal muscle, wind, and water as the source of power to drive tool and machine; in the second, electricity and the internal combustion engine took over. In retrospect these momentous changes seem easy, logical, and even inevitable to most Americans, a smug perspective reinforced if one restricts one's travels to those countries favored by American Express Company tours, but quickly shattered by a detour to Niger or the Panamanian outback.

American industry has thus developed in three distinct periods, demarked by the prevalent energy source of the time. Eli Whitney belonged to the first era. The first cotton gin was a machine "which required the labor of one man to turn it" and could also "be turned by water or with a horse." On the other hand, manufacturing cotton gins, muskets, or anything else in volume, required "machinery moved by water," and this imperative dictated the location of his works where there was "a good fall of Water in the Vicinity." Above all, in the early days these waterfalls had to be in close proximity to the point where the stream became navigable to the sea, for only water transportation was economically feasible for heavy materials. It also greatly facilitated matters if these riparian resources could be found near settled areas where labor and markets were available.

In Whitney's day this happy combination could best be found on rivers from the Susquehanna northward. There the mountains lay close to the sea and ribbed the land between with rocky spines that eroded into a staircase of waterfalls ideal for powering machinery. Many rivers compressed a great vertical fall into a short lateral distance. In twenty miles of Pennsylvania and Delaware countryside, for example, the Brandywine River has a bigger drop than Niagara Falls. In some cases—the Brandywine at Wilmington, Delaware, the Passaic at Paterson, New Jersey—the last fall drops into tidewater. South of the Susquehanna, the fall line lies hundreds of miles from the coast in a region that was, in Whitney's time, largely a wilderness. From there to the ocean the rivers flow lazily through soft southern soil and limestone.

Since American manufacturing was born in this era of water power, its cradles were the valleys of the Brandywine, Connecticut, Merrimack, and other rivers of the north, not the James, Cape Fear, Savannah, or Chattahoochee. Southern cotton became cloth at mills in Lowell, Waltham, and Chicopee, Massachusetts, far removed from the raw material source, and Whitney, retreating from Georgia to a suitable locale familiar to him, manufactured cotton gins and muskets in New Haven, Connecticut, for markets that lay far away.

Steam power liberated Cyrus McCormick and

Andrew Carnegie from some of these locational restrictions. Although both men situated their works on navigable waterways and used them to transport raw materials and finished products, the railroads played a crucial role in their firms' massive expansion. Railroads created much of McCormick's market, carrying settlers to the land and their produce away from it, while making it possible for McCormick to distribute his machines in the huge landlocked regions of the wheat belt. Carnegie Steel used railroads so extensively to bring raw materials in and carry finished products away that it became the largest single railroad customer in the world.

In deciding where to build his plant, neither McCormick nor Carnegie had to consider access to water power. Steam engines worked anywhere you could get fuel to them, and Chicagoans rightly regarded McCormick's steam-powered plant as a symbol of the new industrial age. A visit to McCormick's factory in 1851 moved a local newsman to a baroque burst of rhetorical elegance:

An angry whir, a dronish hum, a prolonged whistle, a shrilled buzz and a panting breath—such is the music of the place. You enter—little wheels of steel attached to horizontal upright and oblique shafts are on every hand. They seem motionless. Rude pieces of wood without form or comeliness are hourly approaching them upon little railways, as if drawn thither by some mysterious attraction. They touched them, and *presto,* grooved, scalloped, rounded, on they go, with a little help from an attendant who seems to have an easy time of it, and transferred to another railway, when down comes a guillotine-like contrivance—they are sawn, bored, and whirled away, where the tireless planes without hands, like a boatswain, whistle the rough plank into polish and it is turned out smooth shaped and fitted for its place in the Reaper or the Harvester. The saw and the cylinder are the genii of the establishment. They work its wonders, and accomplish its drudgery. But there is a greater than they. Below, glistening like a knight in armor, the engine of forty-horse power worked as silently as the "little wheel" of the matron; but shafts plunge, cylinders revolve, bellows heave, iron is twisted into screws like wax, and sawed-off at the rate of forty rounds a second, at one movement of [the engine's] mighty muscles.

There, in Cyrus McCormick's factory in 1851, with its power tools turning out interchangeable parts and its "little railways" moving components from one operation to another, stood a fulfillment of the system of manufacturing that Eli Whitney had envisioned. Driven by its power plant that could be erected almost anywhere, McCormick's establishment was a rudimentary but unmistakable prototype of the modern factory that lies at the heart of American industrial productivity. Carnegie's Edgar Thomson steel works, which opened a quarter of a century later, carried the evolution one step further. Steam-powered machinery made it possible to expand volume and speed up production so much that by the end of the nineteenth century Carnegie's mill produced as much in one day as an 1850 Pittsburgh establishment could produce in a year. Steam drove the fans that put the blast in the hard-driven furnaces; steam-powered rollers shaped the rails and beams; steam cranes and locomotives moved the material from one operation to another and from the plant to its customers.

Outside the factory, however, the world progressed more slowly. For all the impact they had on American business, steam engines had little effect on life in the American home, whether city or farm. There, human muscle and horseflesh, as always, supplied the power that got the chores done. Before electricity most urban Americans lived dark, smelly, tattletale gray, washed-by-hand lives in the homes and streets lit by guttering wicks and flickering gaslamps, suffused with the reek of coal smoke, human excretion, and horse manure. Farm families, enduring numbing toil and embittering isolation, struggled with the realities of an existence far removed from the romantic Jeffersonian myth of the happy yeoman, an existence starkly chronicled in the novels of Willa Cather and Ole Rölvaag, and graphically depicted in *Wisconsin Death Trip*.

How much impact Edison's work had on these daily American lives is suggested by a partial list of the projects in which he involved himself as inventor, manufacturer, perfecter, or promoter. These included: the electric light and all the associated apparatus needed to generate and distribute electricity, first for lighting and then for the whole paraphernalia of electrical appliances; the phonograph; motion pictures; electric traction motors and storage batteries that powered streetcars and delivery wagons and got horses and their droppings off the streets; the "Edison effect," the phenomenon that led to the vacuum tube, the keystone of wireless telegraphy, radio broadcasting, and television. Small wonder that the public acclaimed Edison as the "most useful American."

Edison also contributed directly and significantly to America's industrial development by perfecting a system to send multiple telegraph messages in both directions over the same telegraph wire, by lighting up factories as well as homes, by devising new methods to manufacture and pour cement, by developing the prototype of the modern industrial research laboratory, by inventing the mimeograph machine, and by innumerable other contributions to technology. So active was Edison that, on the average, he produced a patentable device every two weeks of his adult life. Together he, his colleagues, his rivals, and his imitators literally and figuratively electrified America by devising a power source, driven by falling water, steam, or the internal combustion engine to generate a cheap, flexible energy whose voltage could be stepped up to drive the heaviest industrial machinery, or down for every household.

Edison, along with those who perfected the internal combustion engine, thus presided over the last energy revolution we have so far had, though he suspected that others lay ahead. Today, groping for new sources of energy, we travel paths that Edison surveyed speculatively long ago. In 1922, he noted in his diary the possibility of atomic energy: "It may come someday. As a matter of fact, I am already experimenting along the lines of gathering information at my laboratory here. . . . So far as atomic energy is concerned there is nothing in sight just now. Although tomorrow some discovery might be made." On this subject, as on many others, Edison displayed his uncommon faculty ("a pipeline to God," some called it) for sensing that a thing might be done without at the moment seeing how. Some of his visions—helicopters and hovercraft, for example—remained just that, visions, in his lifetime. But many became realities that changed American life; indeed, few men could claim to have witnessed so much change or to have contributed so much to the process.

When Thomas Edison was born in 1847, James K. Polk was President; there were 29 states containing 21 million people (85 percent of them living in rural areas), served by 5,000 miles of railroad. When he died in 1931, Herbert Hoover was President; there were 48 states, with a population of 124 million (56 percent of it urban), and 430,000 miles of track. In addition, industries unheard of at Edison's birth had reshaped American lives by the time of his death. In 1931, 26 million motor vehicles traveled 216 billion miles over 830,000 miles of paved highway; scheduled airlines flew 43 million revenue miles; Americans had 20 million telephones and made 83 million calls a day on them; 17 million families had radios, and there were 612 broadcasting stations; 68 percent of American households had electricity and had purchased more than 300 million dollars' worth of electrical appliances and radios every year since 1925; altogether, Americans consumed 110 billion kilowatt hours of electricity, almost half of it in factories, where electric motors furnished more than half the total horsepower used.

Almost at its beginning Edison's life was buffeted by the tempest of change stirred by the introduction of steam power. He was born in Milan, Ohio, a town that owed its prosperity to a canal that carried Ohio farmers' produce to Lake Erie and thence to eastern markets. In 1854 the Lake Shore Railroad, building west, bypassed Milan. The canal dried up and the town with it; Edison's father's timber business collapsed. Samuel Edison removed his family to Port Huron, Michigan, set up a new business and sent his son off to school. The local school-

master (no Eli Whitney he) pronounced young Thomas "addled," enraging Edison's mother, who declared the teacher a fool and carried the boy home determined to teach him herself (a temptation I've often resisted). This exercise of parental discretion which, in our more enlightened age, would, unless excused on grounds of religious idiosyncrasy, land its perpetrator in the hoosegow, or worse, in the arms of a lawyer, rescued Edison from a style of learning he found "repulsive."

Under his mother's supervision Edison escaped from the rote learning of the schoolhouse to an early exposure to classics like Gibbon and Shakespeare. He read Thomas Paine and experienced a revelation similar to Carnegie's encounter with Spencer:

> It was a revelation to me to read [Paine's] views on political and theological subjects. Paine educated me then about many matters of which I had never before thought. I remember very vividly the flash of enlightenment that shone from Paine's writings. . . . I went back to them time and time again, just as I have done since my boyhood days.

Newton's *Principia,* however, proved heavier going; young Edison soon found himself lost in "the wilderness of mathematics," for which he developed "a distaste . . . from which I never recovered." In fact, mathematics roused his perversity throughout his life and he continued to dismiss it as merely a necessary adjunct to his trade. "I look upon figures as mathematical tools," he declared, "which are employed to carve out the logical results of reasoning, but I do not consider them necessary to assist one to an intelligent understanding of the result." Later he added, "I am not a mathematician, but I can get within ten percent in the higher reaches of the art." Besides, he concluded with savage satisfaction, "I can always hire mathematicians, but they can't hire me." (Stung by the truthful arrogance of these and other sallies, his critics coined the pejorative term "Edisonian" to denote the trial and error methods forced on Edison and others by their lack of theoretical background.)

The books that most fired young Edison's imagination, however, were Richard Parker's *Natural and Experimental Philosophy,* and a *Dictionary of Science.* Spending all his pocket money on chemicals, bottles, and other apparatus, Edison lay below stairs to carry out the experiments described in these magical books. According to his father, Edison "never knew a real boyhood like other boys" because "he spent the greater part of his time in the cellar." Like most sorcerers' apprentices, Tom produced some jarring results, leading his father to predict, "He will blow us all up!" Edison's mother, like Carnegie's, stood behind him. "Let him be," she urged; "[he] knows what he's about." "My mother was the making of me," Edison later recalled, "She understood me; she let me follow my bent."

In 1859 fate in the form of the railroad boom once again took a hand in young Edison's life. It found him, like Carnegie, toiling away in his cellar. The Grand Trunk Railroad, building a line from Portland, Maine, through Canada and across Michigan to Chicago, reached Sarnia, Ontario, across the St. Clair River from Edison's hometown, Port Huron. The railroad established a car ferry to shuttle its trains across the river and built a branch line from Port Huron to Detroit. Finding himself this time squarely in the path of railroad-borne progress, young Edison swiftly climbed aboard.

Declaring himself grown and independent at the age of twelve, Edison became a "train butcher," selling candy, fruit, and vegetables on the morning trip from Port Huron to Detroit and the evening Detroit newspapers on the return journey. This was no commuter train, bounding from stop to stop as quickly as possible so as to get workers to and from suburbs and city, but rather a now-extinct species known as the "way passenger train." The train left Port Huron at 7 o'clock in the morning and took 4 hours to cover the 63 miles to Detroit; in the evening it left Detroit at 5:30 P.M. and arrived back at Port Huron at 9:30. The train paused at each station, loading and unloading passengers, baggage, and express parcels before sauntering on down the line.

Thus at an age when, nowadays, children are thought capable of little more independent action than flicking on a television set, Edison developed the pattern, continued throughout his life, of working sixteen-hour days and making the most of them. In Port Huron he set up a garden and hired boys to tend it to supply him with produce to sell on the train. In Detroit he used the six-hour layover to peruse the scientific volumes in the Detroit library. In the train baggage car he set up a printing press and published a sheet called the *Grand Trunk Herald,* containing local news and gossip, which he peddled to the passengers. In 1862 he found a way to enlist the telegraph as an aid to his entrepreneurial energies. Hearing that a bloody battle had been fought at Shiloh, Edison persuaded the editor of the Detroit *Free Press* to supply him with 1,500 newspapers on credit. He then cajoled the railroad's Detroit telegraph operator into sending the headlines to all the stations down the road, where the stationmasters chalked the bulletins up on the train board. As the evening train worked its way north, Edison found a mob at each station so eager to buy his newspapers that he was able to raise the price from five cents to a quarter and sold out his entire stock. "You can understand," he recalled, "why it struck me then that the telegraph must be about the best thing going, for it was the telegraphic notices on the bulletin boards which had done the trick. I determined at once to become a telegraph operator."

The chance came through an incident worthy of Horatio Alger's imagination. Standing on the platform at Mt. Clements, Michigan, Edison saw that the station telegrapher's son was about to be run over by a passing freight train. Edison, the boy's father remembered, threw

his papers . . . upon the platform, together with his . . . cap, and plunged to the rescue, risking his own life to save his little friend, and throwing the child and himself out of the way. . . . They both landed face down in sharp, fresh gravel ballast with such force as to drive the particles into the flesh, so that, when rescued, their appearance was somewhat alarming.

Unlike Alger's characters, the relieved father had neither fortune nor daughter to bestow upon his benefactor, but he gave what he had, teaching Edison the telegrapher's art.

Soon mastering the rudiments of the craft, Edison easily secured a regular job because operators left the railroads and telegraph companies in droves for the higher pay and greater excitement of the Military Telegraph Corps. In 1863 Edison began an eight-year career as a "boomer," an itinerant telegraphist who, like similar-minded brethren among railroad brakemen and locomotive firemen, worked for a while at one place and then restlessly moved on to another, motivated by an independent spirit that Jimmy Rogers, Leadbelly, and others wove into American folklore:

> I went down to the depot and I looked up on the board;
> It said, "There's good times here, but there's better down the road."

Joining this mobile brotherhood (also, like the passenger train, now largely extinct), Edison traveled far and wide, working in Louisville, Nashville, Memphis, New Orleans, Fort Wayne, Indianapolis, Cincinnati, Detroit, and a dozen other, smaller towns in the United States and Canada. Serving a variety of railroads and telegraph companies, Edison became a first-class operator and developed a style of his own. One of his colleagues later recalled that

> a memorable experience of this episode [of my life] was to listen to what might be called the autograph of a certain operator . . . at Indianapolis named Edison. The telegraphic style of the great inventor that was to be was unique, and was detected by its lightning-like rapidity. It was the despair even of expert telegraphers, who often had to break into his narrative to ask him to repeat.

Like most boomers, Edison had idiosyncrasies that made him something less than an ideal employee and often got him fired. For some, the weakness was drink; for others, a tendency to leave the apparatus unattended while they pursued gambling or more pernicious weaknesses of

the flesh. For Edison the snare was his scientific curiosity, which often led him to conduct experiments on the telegraphic apparatus itself, or to be involved with his bottles and chemicals when he should have been dispatching trains or forwarding telegrams.

Finally, in 1868, Edison wandered to Boston, where he took a job with the Western Union Telegraph Company. Now twenty-one and wise in the ways of the road (though woefully naïve about cities and the business carried on in them), Edison manifested personal traits that never subsequently changed: slovenly dress, a tireless indifference to night and day that made his work habits the despair of those who tried to keep up with him, a gaudy vocabulary (as essential as good eyesight to survival around a railroad, as Carnegie also had learned), and a national reputation for his skill matched only by his cockiness. Ace telegraphers, like gunfighters, confronted challenges at every turn, but Edison, who could send faster than anyone else could transcribe and transcribed faster than anyone else could send, proved hard to shoot down.

On his first night in Boston, his fellow operators manipulated their assignments so that Edison had to take a message from "the fastest man in New York." The New Yorker began slowly, but "soon," Edison said,

> the New York operator increased his speed, to which I easily adapted my pace. This put my rival on his mettle, and he put on his best powers, which, however, were soon reached. At this point I happened to look up, and saw the operators all looking over my shoulders, with their faces shining with fun and excitement. I knew then that they were trying to put a job on me, but kept my own counsel and went on placidly with my work, even sharpening a pen at intervals by way of extra aggravation.

After some minutes of this, Edison "thought the fun had gone far enough . . . [so I] opened the key and remarked: 'Say, young man, change off, and send with your other foot.' "

Working at night, studying in the daytime, Edison delved into Michael Faraday's *Experi-*

mental Researches in Electricity. Bristling with confidence, armed with a thorough knowledge of the practical and theoretical aspects of telegraphy, Edison decided to become an inventor. Logically enough, he looked for some situation in which the application of telegraph technology might improve the status quo. In the factory of Charles Williams, who later made Alexander Graham Bell's first telephone, Edison devised an apparatus to record votes in legislative assemblies instantaneously. To his amazement he soon discovered that his potential customers, both in the Massachusetts legislature and the federal Congress, reacted with horror to this device that threatened to accelerate the traditional, glacial pace of their proceedings. "Young man," they told him in Washington, "if there is any invention on earth that we don't want down here, it is this." With his feathers thus singed, Edison determined to waste no further time inventing things that, however useful, did not have an immediate commercial application.

The incident of the automatic vote recorder taught Edison a lesson often disregarded by otherwise prescient individuals before and since: the man who deals in ideas that are ahead of his time is destined for oblivion, not success. Success most often goes to those who perfect innovations that are long overdue. After his first failure, Edison concentrated his efforts on developing equipment to improve telegraphic services where they had already proved useful and profitable. In January, 1869, he placed a notice in *The Telegrapher* announcing that "T. A. Edison has resigned his situation in the Western Union office, Boston, and will devote his time to bringing out inventions." The first of these was an improved stock ticker that supplied current market quotations to brokerage houses. This device found a ready market and made Edison some money, which, establishing another lifelong pattern, he immediately plowed back into other experiments. When these new enterprises failed, Edison decided to emulate the American capital market and migrated from Boston to New York, arriving, penniless, in May, 1869.

In New York, Edison for a time fell upon lean days, existing largely on a diet of apple dumplings until fate once again rescued him. Poor but not unknown in his own field, Edison was befriended by Franklin L. Pope, chief engineer of the Laws Gold Reporting Company, one of two firms that had a stranglehold on the lucrative service of furnishing gold and stock market quotations to brokers in New York. Pope let Edison sleep on a cot in the company's battery room. Edison thus chanced to be on hand one day when the central transmitting machine broke down. Pandemonium at once ensued as runners from dozens of brokerage houses rushed into the office demanding instant information. Both Pope and Dr. S. S. Laws, the firm's proprietor, succumbed to the hysteria of the moment. Edison, keeping his head, located the trouble and soon repaired it. Impressed and relieved, Laws hired Edison at a salary of $300 a month, two and a half times his wage as a first-class telegraph operator. But Edison, who had no more mind than Carnegie to restrict himself to the "narrow field" delineated by "the beck and call of others," soon resigned and set up a partnership with Pope. Pope, Edison & Company advertised its services as electrical engineers, specializing in "the application of electricity to the Arts and Sciences." Edison offered to design instruments "to order for special telegraphic services," and to perfect "the application of Electricity and Magnetism for Fire-Alarms, Thermo-Alarms, Burglar-Alarms, etc."

Despite this grandiose advance billing, Edison in fact continued to concentrate on a narrow range of telegraphic instruments. By this time the principle had become well established that patents were something that capitalists either bought or evaded. As a man whose fertile mind spun off a series of practical improvements for an industry embroiled in cutthroat competition, Edison soon found himself courted by the emerging titans of telegraphy, particularly the moguls at Western Union, who wanted nothing less than a monopoly of the industry in the United States.

It was easier to plan such a monopoly than to accomplish it, even for Western Union, masterminded by Ezra Cornell and Amos J. Kendall, and backed by the vast financial resources of a

Vanderbilt-Morgan syndicate. An industry that offered glittering prospects for profits, a national market of continental dimensions, plentiful supplies of capital, and new technology that improved almost daily, invited competitors. They appeared from far and wide to challenge Western Union's hegemony. Western Union mounted a two-handed counterattack, gathering in rivals with one hand while reaching out with the other to snap up new inventions before they could help the competition. Thus, when Edison designed an improved stock printer and organized a service to rent it to subscribers, Western Union bought him out for $5,000. The company then proceeded to add Edison to its stable of inventors, which included among others Elisha Gray (who subsequently created a working telephone simultaneously with Alexander Graham Bell).

Edison did not become a formal employee of Western Union, but General Marshall Lefferts, one of Western Union's executives, gave him a series of practical problems to tackle and supplied the money to finance his research. With the money from the sale of his stock ticker supplemented by Western Union's subsidy, Edison could afford to become a free-lance inventor, a scientific soldier of fortune, free to pursue any problem that intrigued him, as well as to accept specific assignments from Lefferts. While Edison operated under an informal understanding that Western Union would have first refusal on any patents he might obtain, he could in fact double-cross his patron by selling his inventions to anyone he chose.

Some months and several inventions later, Lefferts called him in and offered him $40,000 for the work done so far. Edison accepted and, knowing nothing of banks (or so his version of the story goes), sat up all night in his Jersey City boarding-house, fearful that some footpad might relieve him of his new-found wealth. The next day, with a friend's help, Edison penetrated the mysteries of banking sufficiently to open a deposit account, but to his dying day he retained the deep-seated suspicion of bankers and banking that characterized many Americans (Henry Ford a spectacular example) of rural midwestern origins.

Now possessed of more wealth than he had ever dreamed possible, Edison moved across the river to Newark, New Jersey, and opened a factory to manufacture the new stock tickers for Western Union. Earlier, when he had received the $5,000, Edison had written home to his irascible father, "Don't do any hard work and get mother anything she desires. You can draw on me for money. Write me . . . how much money you will need . . . and I will send the amount on the first of [the] month." Old Sam's astonishment at finding his vagabond son rich enough to pension off his parents increased when Thomas, now ensconced in his Newark factory, wrote, "I have one shop which employs 18 men and am fitting up another which will employ over 150 men. I am now what you Democrats call a 'Bloated Eastern Manufacturer.' "

Between 1869 and 1875, the inventor-cum-bloated-manufacturer continued to improve the telegraph. Financed by Western Union and by the Mephistopheles of late nineteenth-century American finance, Jay Gould, Edison churned out improvements, patented them, and then set up factories to produce the equipment. Inevitably he became embroiled in the suits and countersuits with which the corporate rivals battered one another. He had to endure character assaults in and out of the witness box, hearing himself branded as a man who had "basely betrayed" his Western Union patrons, as a "rogue inventor," a "professor of duplicity and quadruplicity," and as a "young man [with] a vacuum where his conscience ought to be."

Since Edison sometimes accepted support from several companies simultaneously to work on the same problem, and then sold the results to the highest bidder, some of these accusations bore an element of truth. Since he considered himself more swindled than swindling, Edison's conscience emerged relatively unscathed. "Everybody steals in commerce and industry," he reflected. "I've stolen a lot myself. But I knew *how* to steal. They don't know *how* to steal—that's all that's the matter with them." His excursions into the freebooting world of high finance, which included a fleecing at the hands of Gould and a particularly ferocious courtroom denunciation by a master of legalistic histrionics, Roscoe Conkling, did, however, persuade him that the denizens of Wall Street were an even more rascally lot than small-town bankers, a view later vehemently espoused by his disciple, Henry Ford.

However reprehensible these characters might have been, Edison had to deal with them, for in the late nineteenth century technology became so complex and so expensive that no inventor could hope to progress far without access to capital markets and the men who manipulated them. The day when an Eli Whitney could create a revolutionary machine using hand tools to shape bit of wood and wire, and could then test his creation by turning a crank, had not entirely passed, as Edison later proved with the phonograph. But most electrical apparatus required months of experimentation to perfect expensive, precision equipment to manufacture, elaborate facilities to test (the only way to try a system of long-distance transmission was to have a far-flung network to transmit on), and a well-financed factory to manufacture. Consequently, Edison and other inventors found themselves clutching at financiers, however distasteful the embrace.

Many brilliant inventors had a business sense that would have embarrassed children. Edison, who started shrewdly enough in his days as a railroad vendor, apparently lost his somewhere along the way. For years, he admitted, he kept nothing but payroll accounts. "I kept no books," he said. Sometimes he simply handed clerks fistfuls of cash with which to pay bills, but usually he settled his debts with personal notes. When the notes came due he "had to hustle around and raise the money." This chaotic system avoided "the humbuggery of bookkeeping, which," he said, "I never understood." Later, when his empire grew so large that some form of financial organization became unavoidable, he put his affairs in the hands of Samuel Insull, a bounder with ideas so original that in later life his handiwork helped precipitate the Great Crash of 1929 and inspired a whole new category of preventive legislation.

In the wide-open booming economy of the late nineteenth century, fortunes could be made by alliances of capitalists and technicians. The prospects were alluring enough to bring forth an endless stream of innovations across the whole spectrum of business activity. Unsurprisingly, the inventors often came out on the short end; promoters Ezra Cornell, Theodore Vail, and J. P. Morgan made fortunes out of the telegraph, the telephone, and the electric light that dwarfed the returns to Samuel F. B. Morse, Alexander Graham Bell, and Edison, who invented them. As the golden stream flowed by, Edison did, however, manage to siphon off enough to finance projects that filled even his monumental working hours. On an upper floor of his Newark factory, Edison established a laboratory, filled it with apparatus and staffed it with technicians. Their enthusiasm for the work, or for Edison himself (some of his most talented associates migrated to Newark specifically to associate themselves with the great man), was such that they thrived on working conditions that Edison himself summarized by saying, "We don't pay anything and we work all the time."

Work all the time they did, as Edison, driven by inspiration or financial necessity, turned his team onto one project after another. Some of these quests were original, including one that produced the first mimeograph machine. (These personal projects gave him special satisfaction. After completing one of them, he noted in his journal that it was "invented by & for myself and not for any small-brained capitalist.") Some involved improving upon the work of other inventors, such as the automatic telegraph, invented by George D. Little and brought to Edison by Edward H. Johnson, an entrepreneur who had bought Little's patent. Others, including the telephone, were suggested by corporate sponsors like Western Union. Whatever the inspiration, the approach was the same. Rounding up everything known on the subject, Edison listed all the alternatives that he and his staff could conjure up, then set his team to work creating the apparatus necessary to test them all. Edison was a driving master of the hunt. Once, when confronted with a breakdown in a new model stock ticker, Edison summoned his staff: "Now, you fellows," he told them, "I've locked the door, and you'll have to stay here until this job is completed." It took sixty hours, and while this admittedly was an extreme case, Edison commonly expected his men to work until they could work no more, then nap on a workbench, the floor, or in some out-of-the-way corner until they could rouse themselves enough to work again.

The employees tolerated this regimen because the boss worked as hard or harder. In addition, his charismatic, pyrotechnic character generated excitement and kept the staff entertained. "Mr. Edison had his desk in one corner," one of his workers said, "and after completing an invention he would jump up and do a kind of Zulu war dance. . . . He would swear something awful. We would crowd round him and he would show us the new invention and explain it to the pattern maker and tell us what to do about it." Once, returning from a day spent in negotiations with New York lawyers and capitalists, who used a language Edison described as "as obscure as Choctaw," he rushed into "the workshop with a whoop, fired his silk hat into an oil pan, and was preparing to send his fine coat after it, when someone laughingly pinned him down." Edison then gladly resumed his normal persona, "as dirty as any of the other workmen, and not much better dressed than a tramp."

By 1876, America's centennial year, Edison's combined labors as inventor and manufacturer brought him solvency, even modest wealth. The hard-won principles of modern manufacturing—repetitious reproduction of undifferentiated components, constantly monitored by cost-control accounting—always bored Edison. Nevertheless he understood them and applied them to his own enterprises, despite his public pronouncements on the boredom of bookkeeping. Even the magic of economies of scale, which Andrew Carnegie, across the mountains in Pittsburgh, was about to teach the iron trade of the world, held no mystery for Edison. When he first began to manufacture light bulbs, for example, they cost $1.40 each to produce, but Edison priced them at 40¢, knowing that volume production would soon bring costs down.

But manufacturing, which demanded constant attention to a single project, could not long absorb a man with Edison's cast of mind: "I never think about a thing any longer than I want to," he said. "If I lose my interest in it, I turn to something else. I always keep six or eight things going at once, and turn from one to the other as I feel like it." In 1876, therefore, Edison abandoned his manufacturing ventures, moved his equipment and his staff to the hamlet of Menlo Park, New Jersey, twenty-five miles south of Newark and then a remote spot. At the Menlo Park laboratory, Edison institutionalized his role as creative inventor, establishing what amounted to an invention factory, where he planned to produce technology to order while simultaneously pursuing his own interests.

At Menlo Park, Edison continued to restrict his organization to projects that promised to make money and make it quickly. As one commentator observed, Edison was "the first great scientific inventor who clearly conceived of inventions as subordinate to commerce." By adhering to this maxim, Edison became, as German economist Werner Sombart observed, "the outstanding example of a man who made a business of invention itself." As such he contributed to the dynamic blend of technology and capital that drove American manufacturing to world prominence in the late nineteenth century.

Edison himself made no bones about his role:

I do not regard myself as a pure scientist, as so many persons have insisted that I am. I do not search for the laws of nature, and have made no great discoveries of such laws. I do not study science as Newton and Faraday and Henry studied it, simply for the purpose of learning truth. I am only a professional inventor. My studies and experiments have been conducted entirely with the object of inventing that which will have commercial utility.

He insisted upon a similar focus among the members of his staff. Criticizing one of his subordinates, Edison said:

I set him at work developing details of a plan. But when he [notes] some phenomenon new to him, though easily seen to be of no importance in this apparatus, he gets sidetracked, follows it up and loses time. *We can't be spending time that way!* You got to keep working up things of commercial value —that is what this laboratory is for. We can't be like the old German professor who as long as he can get his black bread and beer is content to spend his whole life studying the fuzz on a bee!

At Menlo Park this pragmatic formula brought dynamic results and considerable income, which Edison, as always, reinvested in new apparatus and further research. He continued to enjoy corporate patronage. Western Union, for example, concluded in 1876 that the telephone was not just a gadget but a dangerously competitive form of communication. It once again engaged Edison, this time to create a system that evaded the patents held by Alexander Graham Bell and his backers. Edison soon produced one that, after the inevitable, protracted legal wrangles, brought him $300,000. It also required a second trip to England (he had gone once before in an unsuccessful attempt to sell his telegraphic apparatus to the British post office), where he supervised its installation and testing. Unlike so many of his countrymen—McCormick, Carnegie, T. S. Eliot, Henry James, to name a few— who found European society sophisticated and invigorating, Edison thought the English slow and unimaginative. "The English," he said, "are not an inventive people." This shortcoming he explained by one of the crackpot formulas that so endeared him to the American press and public: "They don't eat enough pie. To invent, your system must be all out of order, and there is nothing that will do that like good old-fashioned American pie."

The phonograph, which Edison and his helpers constructed late in 1877, exemplified Edison's dedication to the profit motive. The talking machine excited the public imagination, bringing newspaper reporters, scientists, and other interested parties on pilgrimages to the wilds of New Jersey. Edison enjoyed showing visitors around

and performing parlor tricks to convince the many skeptics that his apparatus did not depend on some chicanery like ventriloquism, but actually reproduced the human voice. Arthur Clarke, coauthor of *2001: A Space Odyssey,* a man who predicted communications satellites twenty years ahead of time, claims that "any sufficiently advanced technology is indistinguishable from magic." The public reaction to the phonograph certainly mirrored such a viewpoint. Edison was dubbed "the Wizard of Menlo Park," a title reaffirmed in the public imagination by subsequent sorceries, particularly the electric light.

Edison basked in the publicity generated by the phonograph, but didn't let it blind him to the needs of his purse. He set the phonograph aside for some years in favor of the telephone and the electric light, which offered superior commercial possibilities.

The invention of the incandescent electric light, which brought Edison enduring, worldwide fame, resulted from his belief that electricity could be harnessed to tasks other than communication. Steam engines could generate plenty of power, but it was not easily transmitted beyond the confines of a factory. In addition, the country contained many remote areas, where a shortage of fuel or a small market made steam power uneconomical. Edison thought that electricity, which flowed through wires like water through pipes, might be generated at a central location and then transmitted to operate branch-line railroads, or to do the heavy work at isolated mines and quarries. Edison turned his attention to the potential of electric lighting during a visit to the workshop of William Wallace, a dynamo manufacturer in Ansonia, Connecticut. After watching Wallace's experiments with arc lights, Edison left Wallace with this parting shot: "I believe I can beat you making electric lights. I don't think you are working in the right direction."

Edison's boast flowed from one of his intuitive perceptions. The arc light had been in use since the 1850s, illuminating streets and lighthouse beacons, but had inherent disadvantages—glare, obnoxious fumes, and the need for frequent adjustment—that made it impractical for use indoors. Inventors on both sides of the Atlantic struggled to eliminate these quirks, but Edison's nimble mind leapt to another track altogether. He would make light not through an electrical arc— that is, passing a current across a gap from one conductor to another—but by incandescence: that is, passing a current through a continuous conductor of sufficient resistance to glow. Other men had tried this idea before and were trying it then, but none so far had succeeded in overcoming the practical problems involved. Edison returned to Menlo Park and set to work at once, for here lay an idea with a huge and waiting market.

When Edison started his search, indoor lighting depended on the burning of candles, coal gas, or kerosene. Only the latter two were economical on a large scale, but both had objectionable features. They shed a feeble light and smelled. Both were fire hazards. The business of distributing gas, furthermore, had been cartelized by a combination of local companies. This aroused the traditional venomous American response to such situations and opened a lucrative market for kerosene that John D. Rockefeller was busily exploiting in the interests of his own growing monopoly. Kerosene refiners, moreover, had access to a large market where no competition existed, for kerosene lanterns could be carried to the darkened dwellings of rural America, where half the population lived and where no gas company, not even a monopoly, could operate profitably. Nowadays, our reflexive association of petroleum and the automobile obscures the fact that Rockefeller built his empire and his fortune on kerosene, not gasoline, that the United States was the Saudi Arabia of the nineteenth century, and that Rockefeller's machinations excited hostile suspicions around the world ("that greedy little prune-faced peasant," one Frenchman called him) as great as the trepidations with which we now await the latest bulletin from the Organization of Petroleum Exporting Countries.

So, the market was there and Edison went after it. Difficulties there were in plenty: the right-shaped bulb had to be found; a filament that would glow without breaking had to be perfected; pumps had to be developed to create a near-per-

fect vacuum in each bulb. Once successful, laboratory methods had to be translated into manufacturing practice that would permit mass production. A system to supply electricity had to be developed from scratch. Not a single generating station existed; not a foot of wire had been strung.

Edison confidently predicted that he would succeed "in six weeks." But the weeks became months and, as time and equipment ate up money, Edison had to seek outside help. In the fall of 1878 the Edison Electric Light Company was founded to finance research, take out patents, and license their use. Among the new firm's backers were Western Union and, almost inevitably, a Morgan partner. With adequate financial backing, and with the marathon labors of his laboratory team guided by the calculations of a theoretical mathematician, Francis R. Upton, whom Edison had grudgingly hired, the Wizard ultimately fulfilled his own prophecy. In the last week of 1879, Edison put on a spectacular display of incandescence at Menlo Park, lighting the grounds and the laboratory with long strings of bulbs. Special Pennsylvania Railroad trains brought newspaper reporters and throngs of pilgrims to witness the miracle.

Electricity went on to light much of the world, but that week in December, 1879, was the high point for Edison. Thereafter his own role in it declined. The tremendous amount of capital required to manufacture equipment, generate electricity, and distribute it forced Edison to yield more and more control of his electrical company to financiers like Morgan. In addition, his initial demonstration of electricity's potential led to a swiftly ramifying technology so complex that Edison could not keep up with it. Hundreds of other experimenters were attracted, one of whom, George Westinghouse, developed a system of alternating current that supplanted Edison's direct-current method. Within a few years, Edison's technical skills no longer had any relevance to the booming American electrical industry.

J. P. Morgan soon combined the bulk of American electrical manufacturing firms (most of which bore Edison's name in some combination) into one of his pet behemoths. He called his new creation "General Electric," thus erasing even the inventor's name from the masthead. A few weeks later Edison exposed his bitterness when his secretary, Alfred Tate, asked him a question about electricity: "Tate," Edison replied, "if you want to know anything about electricity, go out to the galvanometer room and ask [Arthur] Kennelly. He knows far more about it than I do. In fact, I've come to the conclusion that I never did know anything about it. I'm going to do something now so different and so much bigger than anything I've ever done before, people will forget that my name ever was connected with anything electrical."

People of course did not forget, nor did Edison do anything much bigger than he'd done before, but he kept trying. The fortune he made in electricity disappeared into a fruitless attempt to separate low-grade iron ore by magnetism. When the money was spent, he said, "Well, it's all gone, but we had a hell of a good time spending it." Undiscouraged, he returned to the phonograph, perfected it, made another fortune, and yet another in motion pictures. He devised a practical electrical storage battery, which he manufactured profitably. Although he continued his driving pace at work, he found more time for his personal life. His first marriage, in 1871 to Mary Stilwell, a worker in his Newark factory, suffered from his neglect; it produced three children, two of whom came to unhappy ends. In 1884, his first wife died of typhoid fever. Two years later he remarried. His new bride, Mina, though only nineteen (Edison, like Whitney, McCormick, and Carnegie, apparently preferred young women), was made of sterner stuff. She forced Edison's life into a semblance of order, demanded companionship, and insisted that he fulfill his family responsibilities, a regimen that he increasingly enjoyed as the years passed. In these more normal family circumstances, the children of the second marriage thrived. (One of them, to Edison's wry amusement, became a theoretical physicist.)

As the first quarter of the twentieth century passed, Edison found himself revered as an American folk hero, a role he relished. Newspapermen, as always, found him excellent copy. Like Carnegie, he was almost always good for some iconoclastic statement. When a clergyman asked him if he should install lightning rods on his church spire, Edison answered, "By all means, as Providence is apt to be absentminded." Edison also supplied reporters with quotable aphorisms: "Genius is one percent inspiration and ninety-nine percent perspiration."

In his declining years, Edison found an increasing fascination in nature's miraculous powers. He gloried in the perfection of an oak leaf and enjoyed showing a burned thumb that had healed perfectly, observing that "the life entities rebuilt that thumb with consummate care." He enjoyed camping trips with Ford, Harvey Firestone, naturalist John Burroughs, and the entourage of reporters that accompanied their caravan. Tutored by Burroughs and encouraged by Ford and Firestone, Edison developed a strain of giant goldenrod, searching for a source of raw rubber that could be raised in the United States. As he grew older, the driving force of creativity wound down into more relaxed forms of puttering and rumination. When asked, as he often was, when he planned to retire, he usually responded, "When the doctor brings in the oxygen tank." After the First World War, however, he retired in fact, if not in name.

When he died in 1931, the world mourned the passage of an original mind and Americans the loss of their "most useful citizen." During his lifetime, theoretical scientists had deprecated the contributions of men like Edison and Alexander Graham Bell. The latter had been caustically described by theoretical physicist James Clerk Maxwell as an elocutionist who "to gain his private ends [became] an electrician." Professor Emory A. Rowland of Johns Hopkins University said that "he who makes two blades of grass grow where one grew before" might do mankind some good, but "he who labors in obscurity to find the laws of such growth is the intellectual superior as well as the greater benefactor of the two." Perhaps, but in Edison's lifetime and to a large extent through the force of his own efforts, practical science became inextricably intertwined with American industry, nourishing its growth by the constant infusion of updated technology. Edison's example persuaded progressive corporate managers that their firms must have "invention factories" of their own. From General Electric, the Bell System, and Du Pont, the idea of integrated research facilities spread across the spectrum of American industry and ultimately into the government. With its complex of individual, corporate, and government-sponsored facilities, the American economy has channeled a higher percentage of its income into research and development than any other in the world. Science tied to industry has facilitated prodigious (if often wasteful) growth, created terrifying weaponry, and given mankind a powerful ally in its eternal combat with darkness, isolation, and hunger.

Today we ponder these awesome consequences with mixed emotions, but our predecessors welcomed the convergence of science and industry, seeing it as evidence of America's superior contribution to the elevation of mankind. Scientific change meant human progress, and practical scientists were American heroes. Americans needed no Kants or Spinozas to transcribe the music of the spheres, but practical men who could

> Bring the balloon of the mind
> That bellies and drags in the wind
> Into its narrow shed

where it could do some useful work.

In the tradition of earlier Americans who had dubbed a mechanic "the artist of his country" and a reaper manufacturer a "hero in the classical mold," one of Edison's contemporaries celebrated a society in which "the chemist, the mineralogist, the botanist, and the mathematician are fellow laborers with the practical farmer and the manufacturer," and "vain and unprofitable theories no longer engrossed the attention of men of science." Other peoples might view "an active and feverish imagination . . . as [a] distinguishing mark of [the] philosopher," but not hardheaded Americans. For them, "philosophers

are businessmen," and Edison, who made invention a business, was repeatedly named "America's most useful citizen" by his countrymen.

It was said when Edison died, and it has been said often since, that the world would never see his like again. In a world run by huge bureaucracies and staffed by scientists trained for years in arcane disciplines, so these lamentations go, such individualists have no place, and useful scientific perceptions are beyond the reach of minds not formally trained. I think such obituaries for individualism were and are premature. On April 17, 1978, *Newsweek* magazine carried a story about an obscure inventor named Stanford Ovshinsky. In 1968, Ovshinsky had predicted that the use of solar energy would eventually become feasible through the development of cheap, electronic switches that would convert the sun's heat into electrical current. "Electronics experts," *Newsweek* reported, "were highly skeptical on two counts. Theorists could not imagine how the amorphous semiconductors could possibly work. And they and others regarded Ovshinsky as a scientific outsider. He had no college degree, let alone one in physics; his only apparent talent seemed to be publicizing [himself]. Ten years later, Professor David Adler of the Massachusetts Institute of Technology admitted, 'Almost every statement Ovshinsky made in 1968 has now turned out to be true.' " The role of individuals in the making of history, even scientific history, may not have died with Thomas Edison.

The Edison heritage surely lives on, most obviously in the American Lifestyle, which he transformed, but equally dynamically (if less visibly) in American industry. During Edison's lifetime, and partially because of his work, applied science became a permanent component of American manufacturing. Like so many of the techniques developed by nineteenth-century individualists, systematic industrial research and development departments and sequestered them in places like the Bell System Laboratories and the Du Pont Experimental Station. But, as we shall see in the case of Edwin Land, here and there Tom Edison's notion of an "invention factory" has survived and waxed mighty.

9

THE MILITARY OCCUPATION OF CUBA, 1899–1902: WORKSHOP FOR AMERICAN PROGRESSIVISM

HOWARD GILLETTE, JR.

The years from 1890 to 1920 witnessed a renewed debate by American reformers on the merits of industrial capitalism. As with early nineteenth-century reformers, these latter-day reformers drew upon a wide range of doctrines to attack monopolies, trusts, and large corporations and the social problems such as poverty, government corruption, and industrial pollution that followed in their train. The Progressives, as these new reformers came to be called, offered a solution to mounting social problems that their earlier counterparts would never have countenanced. Recognizing the immense power wielded by corporate capitalism because of its enormous resources and effective bureaucratic organization, progressives sought a counterweight in the resources and power of government. The notion of government intervention as a means to tame the corporations separated the Progressives from all previous reformers who saw government as a means of insuring the safety and liberty of its citizens and little else.

In articulating their new ideas about the place of government in social reform the Progressives were inspired by their contemporaries in the British social welfare movement and by the success of Bismarck's welfare state in Germany. But as Howard Gillette demonstrates in this essay, many of the ideas of the progressive reformers had a different origin: they were worked out during the American occupation of Cuba following the Spanish-American War. It was in Cuba, where American administrators exercised virtually unopposed power, that Progressive ideas about civil administration, public schooling, and proper sanitation could be tested and refined without the interference of corporate interests or domestic politics.

Was the Progressive attitude toward business entirely negative? What was the proper role of business in the Progressive creed? How does Gillette's view of Progressive reform compare with the view of Allen F. Davis in Reading 13? Why do you think the Progressives were so insensitive to the needs of the Cubans themselves?

The Spanish-American War marked an important turning point in American domestic as well as foreign policy. The intervention on behalf of Cuban independence generated a national sense of mission, not only to uplift the oppressed people of other countries, but also to improve domestic conditions at home. The war and the resulting policy of extraterritorial expansion, according to such a major contributor to progressivism as Herbert Croly "far from hindering the process of domestic amelioration, availed, from the sheer force of the national aspirations it aroused, to

Reprinted from the *American Quarterly*, 25 (October 1973): 410–425. Copyright © 1973, Trustees of the University of Pennsylvania. Reprinted with the permission of the author and the *American Quarterly*.

give a tremendous impulse to the work of national reform."

The agents of the occupation of Cuba brought the prospects of American civilization—good government, education and business efficiency. In this sense the occupation was profoundly conservative, a reflection of already well-established American values and programs. On the other hand Leonard Wood, the second military governor of the island, established an overall pattern of political action which contrasted sharply with previous reform movements of both populists and Mugwumps. Rejecting both the populist appeal to the masses and the negative Mugwump commitment to laissez-faire and puritan moralism, the Wood administration provided a model of new government powers in the hands of "responsible" leadership. It combined the Mugwump bias for elitism with the belief of populists in government activism. As such it serves as an important, previously neglected, link between old and new reform movements in America. In a real sense the occupation of Cuba served as a workshop for progressivism.

The issues surrounding the early occupation emerged out of the long-term conflict between Mugwump reformers and their opponents. Indeed, John R. Proctor, president of the U.S. Civil Service Commission, could not resist moralizing on Cuba's fate on the occasion of its transfer to American control:

> We do not feel personally responsible for misgovernment in New York or Philadelphia, but every American citizen will feel a personal responsibility for misgovernment in Havana, Santiago, and Manila, and will hold any party to a strict accountability, and any party daring to apply the partisan spoils system to the government of our colonies or dependencies will be hurled from power by the aroused conscience of the American people.

Following as it did the excesses of the Gilded Age, the war inevitably inspired charges from anti-imperialists that it was only the product of greedy business interests wishing to exploit Cuba's natural resources. Such charges made

Congress sensitive enough to declare its own good intention through the Teller amendment to the Paris peace treaty: "That the United States hereby disclaims any disposition or intention to exercise sovereignty, jurisdiction, or control over [Cuba] except for the pacification therein and asserts its determination, when that is accomplished, to leave the government of the Island to its people." To insure that the new territory would not be subject to economic exploitation, Congress passed the Foraker Amendment to the Army Appropriations bill in February 1899, prohibiting the granting of franchises or concessions in Cuba to American companies during the period of military occupation. President McKinley himself stressed America's good intentions in an effort to distinguish his foreign policy from the prevailing drive among European nations for colonial possessions. The Spanish territories, McKinley claimed in a recurrent theme of his administration, "have come to us in the providence of God, and we must carry the burden, whatever it may be, in the interest of civilization, humanity and liberty."

Cuba's first military governor, John Brooke, a career soldier who made his reputation in the Spanish War by leading invading columns through the virtually bloodless conquest of Puerto Rico, did his best to effect the outlines of good government promised in Washington. He initiated programs to build new schools and to provide basic sanitation facilities for the island. Among his appointees he counted as military governor of Havana William Ludlow, a man who had already established a credible record in the United States as a good government reformer. During his tenure as director of the Water Department in Philadelphia, according to a New York *Times* report, "political heelers who had won sinecures by carrying their wards were discharged and their places filled by efficient men. Political bosses stood aghast at such independence and after trying all kinds of 'influence' and 'pulls' were compelled to leave the Water Department alone as long as Colonel Ludlow remained at its head." Ludlow expressed his confidence in the effectiveness of transporting America's campaign against corruption to the island, claiming in his first annual report in 1900 that, "For the first time, probably in its history, Havana had an honest and efficient government, clean of bribery and speculation, with revenues honestly collected and faithfully and intelligently expended."

But the problems facing Brooke required more than basic services and clean government. The devastation and near anarchy of the island suggested immediately the need for extensive social, economic and political reconstruction. Yet lacking both administrative experience and any philosophical commitment to government activism, Brooke dampened every effort to provide government services whose need he did not find absolutely compelling. At one point he rejected a plan for long-term low-interest loans to destitute farmers, calling the program a kind of paternalism which would destroy the self-respect of the people.

The prospect for more comprehensive reform was discouraged by the lack of direction from Washington. Despite his repeated promise to carry out an American mission in Cuba, President McKinley outlined no general policy for the island. Henry Adams complained in January 1899, that "the government lets everything drift. It professes earnestly its intention to give Cuba its independence, but refuses to take a step toward it, and allows everyone to act for annexation." Fully a year after the military occupation began, McKinley admitted, "Up to this time we have had no policy in regard to Cuba or our relations therewith, for the simple reason that we have had no time to formulate a policy." Under the circumstances Brooke was forced, as he said, to conduct the government by induction.

Without clear direction from Washington, Brooke lapsed into a narrow strain of reform directed at purifying Cuba's social system. Among his first circulars were orders to abolish gambling, to close business houses on Sunday and to prohibit public games and entertainments on Sunday. In perhaps his most misguided effort at reform he ordered in the interest of public safety the confiscation of all machetes on the island, not realizing that the law, if executed faithfully,

would ruin the island's sugar business. Brooke's announced restrictions on theaters and dance halls led the Washington *Post* to editorialize: "Our first duty in Cuba is not morals or customs, but the establishment of institutions of law and order . . . if we begin by interference in their private lives, with puritanical compulsion and missionary irritation, the problem of Cuban rehabilitation will be set back twenty years."

The Brooke administration provoked its first serious internal criticism from Leonard Wood, past commander of the Rough Rider brigade Teddy Roosevelt made famous and military governor of the province of Santiago. As a young activist who felt well-tested by the war, Wood bridled at Brooke's timidity. "The condition of the Island is disheartening," he wrote his friend Roosevelt in August 1899. "I tell you absolutely that no single reform has been initiated which amounts to anything to date." Publicly he made no effort to conceal his discontent, telling a New York *Times* reporter, "The Cuban problem can easily be solved. With the right sort of administration everything could be straightened out in six months. Just now there is too much 'tommy-rot.' What is needed is a firm and stable military government in the hands of men who would not hesitate to use severe measures should the occasion arise."

Roosevelt took Wood's complaints seriously and launched a campaign to promote him to Brooke's position. Five days after Wood penned his scathing report on Brooke Roosevelt replied: "Your letter makes me both worried and indignant . . . I am going to show it privately and confidentially to [Secretary of War Elihu] Root. I do not know what to say. Root is a thoroughly good fellow and I believe he is going to steadily come around to your way of looking at things." As early as July 1 Roosevelt had touted Wood for Military Governor, writing Secretary of State John Hay that he doubted whether "any nation in the world has now or has had within recent time, anyone so nearly approaching the ideal of military administrator of the kind now required in Cuba." Wood, Roosevelt argued, "has a peculiar facility for getting on with the Spaniards and

Cubans. They like him, trust him, and down in their hearts are afraid of him." Roosevelt's campaign had its effect, for in December 1899, Wood succeeded to Brooke's position.

Wood accepted his appointment as no ordinary assignment. "He is further impressed with the idea he has a mission—is charged with a great reformation," Brooke's retiring chief of staff noted. Such a mission demanded not just the establishment of civil order as sought by Brooke but reconstruction of the island as a thriving nation state. Though he showed some sensitivity to differences between Latin and Anglo-Saxon cultures, Wood could not resist promoting Americanization of the island—in the administration of justice, the training of police and general administrative practice—where proven methods could speed up goals of efficiency and uplift. As he wrote President McKinley explaining his ultimate objective, "We are going ahead as fast as we can, but we are dealing with a race that has steadily been going down for a hundred years and into which we have got to infuse new life, new principles and new methods of doing things."

Unlike Brooke, Wood established the administrative credibility to effect the changes he sought. He assiduously avoided imposition of puritanical social reforms on the Cuban people. "The main thing," he wrote, "is to avoid the appearance of correcting abuses which do not exist." Instead he emphasized adoption of "a business-like way of doing things," which he had complained was missing from the Brooke administration. His interest in corporate administrative efficiency drew sustenance and support from McKinley's new Secretary of War Elihu Root who had left his job as a New York corporate lawyer to take responsibility both for administering the Spanish possessions and modernizing the Army along efficient corporate lines. Together they shared the goals of an emerging social type in America which stressed organization and efficiency as touchstones of the progress of civilization.

As a start new lines of organization were drawn for the entire administrative system of the island. Wood revamped Brooke's educational program, for example, because it lacked preci-

sion. Though Brooke's minister of education succeeded in building new schools and increasing enrollment, he developed no institutional controls over the system. With the application of a new approach fashioned after Ohio law, school administration was divided according to function. A commissioner of education handled all executive matters, including purchasing supplies and making appointments, while a superintendent of schools developed educational policy. Together with six provincial commissioners he formed a board of education authorized to determine and introduce proper methods of teaching in the public schools. Each school district was granted local autonomy, though individual teachers were held responsible to central authority through a system of reports. The school board required teachers to complete reports monthly and yearly. Salaries were withheld for failure to comply. All teachers were also required to spend the first two summers of the American occupation in school and pass a certification exam at the end of their second year. The rigorous system was completely new to Cuba, where no public school system had previously existed and where teaching standards had never been defined.

Next to education, Cuban law was the most important object of Wood's administrative reorganization. In his annual report for 1900, Wood said that no department was "more in need of thorough and radical reform, rigid inspection, and constant supervision," than the department of justice which "was lacking in efficiency, energy and attention to duty." He complained that the Cuban judiciary and legal body had "surrounded itself with a cobweb of tradition and conservatism and adopted a procedure so cumbersome and slow of execution as to render impossible a prompt administration of justice." But he believed progress had been made under his administration. "Incompetent and neglectful individuals have been dismissed, the number of correctional courts has been very greatly increased, the audiencias supplied with necessary material, and very much done to improve the court houses."

Wood also launched a massive program of public works to reconstruct the island's cities.

This municipal reform effort started under the crudest conditions. Wood's sanitary engineer in Santiago wrote that when he took office "not a shovel or a broom [was available], and for several days, pieces of oil cans and brushes of trees, and palm branches, were the only implements available." By the close of 1900 chief engineer William Black could report that the streets of the island's major cities were sprinkled and swept nightly. In 1901 Black reported a wide range of services planned for the island, including new sewer systems; modern street pavements; construction of water mains to new buildings; water pollution controls; public parks; construction of new schools and public buildings; a modern slaughterhouse designed after the best Chicago examples and a system of subways for wires for transmission of electricity for light power, telegraph and telephone service.

The Department of Public Works not only provided a wide range of public services, but under Black it reorganized its internal operation to promote efficient conduct of city business. Cuban street cleaners could no longer be haphazard in their work or their dress. Each man was assigned a particular district responsibility and was uniformed smartly in white cotton-duck suits with brown cord trimmings, white metal badges and brown hats. In addition, the department prepared codes for municipal operations, including a list of plumbing specifications that set standard requirements for every class of pipe and fitting.

In order to institutionalize the improved efficiency of municipal departments in particular, Wood urged adoption of a new city charter in Havana. Soon after his promotion, Wood appointed a commission of American and Cuban experts to draw up a model city charter. The commission was given copies of recent American charters, in which the fundamental principles encouraged were "simplicity, effectiveness, responsibility, and the largest measure of autonomy that could with safety be authorized." Following the argument for home rule in the United States, the new charter prevented the central and provincial governments from intervening in municipal affairs, granting the city control of "all matters within its boundary." Specifically city government was held responsible for "the comfort and health of the inhabitants, and the security of their persons and property." Significantly the charter provided for regulation of all public utilities at a time when municipal reformers in America were attempting to write the same provision into law. The charter also incorporated an order previously adopted on the island which simplified the tax system by eliminating the ill-defined system of shared responsibility between city and province and making a direct connection between the tax rate and benefits received from city government.

The new city charter pointed the way to the best of American municipal reform. It established the dictum, which would be stated most precisely by Herbert Croly, that government must be efficient and to be efficient its powers must equal its responsibilities. Not only was the city authorized to use broad powers in the public interest, it was held responsible to promote that interest. As such, the charter reflected the general enthusiasm for positive government intervention in public affairs shared by Wood, Root, Roosevelt and Croly. Wood worked to define similar powers of public responsibility at a national level in Cuba through the creation of a railroad commission. He was offended, as he said, that the railroads "have always been able to buy the government and run things about as they saw fit." But much more he felt the state had a responsibility to protect public welfare. "I'm going to insist on state intervention in regulating rates," he wrote President Roosevelt in 1902, "when it is evident that such rates are prejudicial to the public interest."

When the railroads balked at possible state regulation Wood received encouragement from E. H. Moseley, Secretary of the U.S. Interstate Commerce Commission. "The demand of the railroads of Cuba that they should be allowed to control at pleasure, consulting their own interest only, the arteries of the internal commerce of the country is preposterous," he wrote Wood in January 1902. "I'm convinced that the railroad commission, composed of men of high character, is determined to follow the reasonable and correct course, dealing fairly with all, and while having the interest of the State and welfare of the people fully in view, do no act of injustice to the railroads."

The Cuban railroad law enacted a month later incorporated all the major features of the Interstate Commerce Act adopted in the United States in 1887. It forbade railroads to engage in discriminatory practices, required them to publish their rate schedules, prohibited them from entering pooling arrangements to keep rates high and declared that rates should be "reasonable and just." The Cuban law attempted to avoid the major pitfall of its predecessor by holding a ruling valid until revoked by the Supreme Court. Under the American law, where the I.C.C. relied on the Supreme Court for enforcement, fifteen of the first sixteen cases appealed had been decided in favor of the railroads against the commission.

Recent scholarship has revealed how legislation for the I.C.C., though stimulated by agrarian discontent, ultimately reflected the concerns of commercial interests, which wished to rationalize the system for their own profits. Taken out of the American context the Cuban reform represented an ideal in itself divorced from the factions which originally shaped the bill. Significantly, Wood gave it new purpose in protecting middle-class producers and planters for whom, he wrote Root, lower rates would be "a very substantial gain."

Indeed Wood built his program around the establishment of a conservative middle-class ruling elite. He distrusted the Cuban politicians who had gained office in the first elections and who, he said, appeared to be "in a certain sense doctors without patients, lawyers without practice and demagogues living in the subscription of the people and their friends." Planters and producers, on the other hand, appealed to him as "an honest, warm-hearted class of people," who were most appreciative of good order and protection of life and property. Wood often called the planter class conservative in a positive sense, consciously identifying them with the better class of citizens in America who unfortunately, he thought, had bypassed public service. He continued to believe, however, that their success, both political and commercial, was essential to the future of Cuba,

for ultimately they would have to provide both the tax revenues to pay for needed services on the island and the leadership to effect those services. Wood underscored his belief in working hard for reciprocal trade agreements:

> The resources on which Cuba must depend for the income necessary to establish a stable government, requiring, as any government does, good schools, good courts, a system of public works, means of communication, hospitals, charities, etc., are those which will be derived from the sale of her two most stable products, and, if we continue to legislate against these, we cannot, with any degree of sincerity, expect the new government to be able to maintain such conditions as constitute stable government.

Ultimately Wood revealed the kind of commitment to conservative political capitalism which Gabriel Kolko has described as characteristic of progressivism. His hope for Cuba lay in a working relationship of responsible businessmen in both countries. He assigned highest priority to sanitation measures, for instance, largely because he believed adequate safeguards against disease were a prerequisite for American investment in the island. Part of his desire to standardize Cuban law derived from reports from American businessmen that the principal reason for the lack of confidence in Cuban investments was the threat of costly time-consuming litigation in native courts. Wood risked criticism from Cuban patriots for limiting popular suffrage because, as he wrote Root, "if it were known to be a fact that we were going to give universal suffrage, it would stop investments and advancement in this island to an extent which would be disastrous in its results."

Wood clearly opposed outright business exploitation, but he could not avoid a bias for conservative middle-class business ideology. In the final year of his administration he worked actively for a stipulation gained in the controversial Platt Amendment to the Army Appropriations bill which guaranteed the preservation of American commercial interests through the right of intervention. All orders of the military government were granted permanence in Article IV which declared that "all acts of the United States in Cuba during its military occupancy thereof are ratified and validated, and all lawful rights acquired thereunder shall be maintained and protected." Americanization of the island was thus completed, with legal assurance that it would not be quickly or easily overturned.

By every American standard the occupation had been a tremendous success. In guiding Cuba to its independence without succumbing to colonialism, business exploitation or government corruption, Wood rested the worst fears of the Mugwump reformers. Jacob Riis, the New York social reformer, granted the occupation that degree of success, in terms widely adopted by the press at the time:

> Cuba is free, and she thanks President Roosevelt for her freedom. But for his insistence that the nation's honor was bound up in the completion of the work his Rough-Riders began at Las Guasimas and on San Juan hill, a cold conspiracy of business greed would have left her in the lurch, to fall by and by reluctantly into our arms, bankrupt and helpless, while the sneer of the cynics that we were plucking that plum for ourselves would have been justified.

Beyond these essentially negative results, however, the administration provided a positive achievement through government activism which separated Wood and his contemporaries from the Mugwumps. Wood himself stressed this activism, in contrast to Brooke's timid administration, in summarizing his record. He had, as he wrote in 1903, completed work "which called for practically a rewriting of the administrative law of the land, including the law of charities, hospitals and public works, sanitary law, school law, and railway law; meeting and controlling the worst possible sanitary conditions; putting the people to school; writing an electoral law and training the people in the use of it, establishing an entirely new system of accounting and auditing." Not without pride he concluded that the work called for and accomplished "the establishment, in a

little over three years, in a Latin military colony, in one of the most unhealthy countries of the world, a republic modeled closely upon the lines of our own great Anglo-Saxon republic."

Our understanding of the special nature of the Wood reform ethic is heightened through a brief analysis of its reception in Cuba. For a country whose economic and social identity lay largely in the countryside, Wood could well have concentrated government expenditures in a program of agricultural reconstruction modeled after methods being instituted in the American South and suggested by Governor James Wilson of Matanzas Province. "I do not consider the future of Cuba depends chiefly upon schools, road-making, improved sanitation or judiciary reform," Wilson said. "The best the United States can do for Cuba and the Cubans is to give every opportunity for improving the value of the land by putting it to the best uses. In this way capital could do an immense amount of good here as well as get returns." Wood rejected Wilson's plea, resting his hopes for Cuba's future not in small farms but in the cities. He stressed this urban orientation when he wrote Roosevelt in August 1899, "All we want here are good courts, good schools and all the public work we can pay for. Reform of municipal government and a business way of doing things."

Wood's emphasis on urban development ran counter to established Cuban tradition. While his work in Havana drew praise in America, it received a less welcome reception among Cubans. The Havana ayuntamiento (city council) overwhelmingly rejected the charter commission report, although the proposal purportedly incorporated the best features of American law. According to one councilman, the new plan was but one more of the great many fancies which had been thrust on the Cubans by force.

Beyond Wood's urban orientation lay a bias for government authority which again rankled the Cubans. As governor of Santiago, Wood had gained tremendous popularity by criticizing the centralization of authority in Havana. When Brooke decreed that all customs revenues would be distributed from Havana, Wood took the case for decentralized distribution to Washington and became a hero among Cubans. Wood's act struck a responsive chord with a people who hoped for a substitution of American decentralized administration for the highly centralized Spanish system. The Spanish law of 1878 governing local administration outwardly allowed local autonomy. But a provision making the alcalde (mayor) removable at will placed the executive authority and the towns generally at the mercy of the central government. The Cubans moved toward greater local independence with the Autonomist Constitution of 1897 which stipulated that the ayuntamientos and not the central government made the final selection of alcaldes.

Wood's reputation as champion of Santiago's independence encouraged the Cubans to believe that he would complete the decentralization begun by the Autonomist Constitution. Wood did encourage municipal autonomy. He eliminated many municipalities which had been created during the war solely to act as agents of the Spanish government, making the remaining cities real functioning units with their own taxing and spending power. But with a lack of administrative experience at the local level, cities repeatedly exceeded their budgets, depending on national revenues to remain solvent. Wood's own personal vigor and the fact that he was so insistent on his directives helped sustain all final authority in Havana. As one sensitive observer of America's overseas policy, Leo S. Rowe, said, "The leaders in the work of civic reorganization were determined to put an end to the highly centralized administration of Spanish times, but in actual development of the system the force of tradition has proved stronger than conscious purpose. Although the municipalities enjoy more extensive powers in law, in fact they remain subservient to the central government."

Wood's authoritarian bent must have reflected a military man's desire to get a job done. He recognized, for instance, no restraints in effecting sanitation measures in Santiago. According to President McKinley's special commissioner to the island, Robert Porter, "The doors of houses had to be smashed in; people making sewers of

the thoroughfares were publicly horsewhipped in the streets of Santiago; eminently respectable citizens were forcibly brought before the commanding general and sentenced to aid in cleaning the streets they were in the habit of defiling." As A. Hunter Dupree has pointed out, Wood managed to institute his sanitation program in Cuba because island administrators held powers which "would have been entirely unavailable to the President of the United States had the infected city been New Orleans instead of Havana." Wood himself credited his success in Cuba to the wide scope of his power, indicating that if he were to take a role in administering the Philippines "I should like to have a go at the situation with the same authority I have had here. Without such full authority I believe the Islands will be the burial ground of the reputation of those who go there."

Had Wood shared the philosophical restraints of Brooke or other Mugwump leaders of his generation on the limited use of government power he might not have aroused the kind of opposition in Cuba he did. The important factor for the historian of American reform, however, lies in the example Wood held up to his countrymen back home and its reception there, whatever his own motivations for seeking government authority in Cuba. By carefully selecting among existing precedents in the United States those models which allowed the greatest government activism, Wood presented fellow reformers in America with a new spirit of administrative technique and law. His reforms emphasizing administrative efficiency served as a bridge between Root's reorganization of the Army and Gifford Pinchot's program for a professionally managed forest system and later administrative reforms instituted by Theodore Roosevelt as president.

In a general sense Wood's administration, undertaken as it was in the full glare of national publicity, provided a visibility for reform which had been badly lacking in earlier good government movements. The emergence of Roosevelt, Root and Wood from virtual obscurity to national heroes helped dramatize a new spirit of reform and suggested to the public at large the dawn of a new moral leadership for America.

"The war with Spain," Secretary of the Navy William H. Moody claimed in a speech in 1902, "disclosed the enormous resources of this country, its wealth, its power, its strength, but it disclosed more. It disclosed the character of our people, and we know that where the Tafts, and the Roots, and the Days, and the Woods, and the Roosevelts came from, there are many more like them to come to the service of the country when their country calls." Wood's heralded decision to turn down a $25,000-a-year street railway presidency offered during his term as military governor set him apart from public figures of the Gilded Age and gave substance to a new leadership ideal, articulated by Roosevelt as early as 1897 when he was still Assistant Secretary of the Navy that: "The fight well fought, the life honorably lived, the death bravely met—those count far more in building a fine type of temper in a nation than any possible success in the stockmarket, than any possible prosperity in commerce or manufactures."

In a more direct sense the philosophical connection between the occupation and emerging progressivism was tied through personal links, the most important of which was Wood's close relationship with Theodore Roosevelt. Among more specialized progressive leaders, Leo Rowe of the University of Pennsylvania recognized immediately the importance of administrative innovation in the Spanish possessions. Though recognized as an expert on municipal reform in America, Rowe found the study of the Spanish possessions irresistible. He wrote not only extensive articles on the administration of Cuba and the Philippines but also a book on the occupation of Puerto Rico, where he served as chairman of the island's code commission. He predicted in March 1899, that the workshop provided by the Spanish possessions would turn America's political philosophy away from limited protection of individual liberties to one of activist intervention for national development. "The readjustment of the country's international relations, which must follow the recent struggle with Spain, will supply the connecting link between economic and political development," he wrote in *The Forum*. "Its

influence, however, will extend far beyond these limits. It will modify our political ideas, develop a broader view of the country's relation to the larger affairs of the world, and react upon domestic politics, with the result of raising the level of public life."

In his urban work Rowe reached theoretical conclusions which Wood coincidentally put into pragmatic effect. In 1897 Rowe argued that even though American cities had reached a nadir in the American experience they would have to serve nonetheless as the chief agent of civilization. The reformer's role, then, lay clearly in upgrading the urban environment, precisely the approach Wood took in Cuba. Indeed, Wood's administration both reflected Rowe's philosophy and gave it sustenance through the apparent triumph of urban-oriented programs to give the island the services sought in America through the city beautiful movement, particularly good schools, grand public buildings and clean streets.

On another level the experiments in the Caribbean served to inspire activists among two other major elements of the emerging reform movement, the journalists who would soon become known as muckrakers and the social welfare activists. Robert Bannister cites the tremendous impact the activism of Wood and Roosevelt had on Ray Stannard Baker in converting him from a Mugwump to a progressive. Indeed Baker seems to have absorbed himself the chief principles of Roosevelt's strenuous life, writing in his journal, "A warrior is not made by the battles he avoids but by the battles he fights." Another entry suggests a parallel drive with Roosevelt, Wood and Rowe to take up the challenge of remaking society: "What we must be thankful for is not perfection, not the solution of all our problems; this condition we can never hope to attain—but let us praise God for the struggle! Completeness we can not attain, but where there is restless activity, there is also health and hope. Not beautification, perfection: that is heaven, but turmoil and struggle, progress; that is human life." For the social reformer Jacob Riis, the example of the American occupation was no less inspiring. "How jolly it is to think of you and Roosevelt being both where you are," he wrote Wood in February 1900. "This is a good world anyway, and the pessimists lie like the Dickens."

Despite our recognition today that Wood's specific programs as well as his desire to civilize Cuba generally reflected already established American values, we should not underestimate the impact of the overall reform effort on the United States. For a country in which administrative reform had not yet emerged as a national goal and in which urban reconstruction remained rather a hope than a reality, Wood's achievement must have provided, as Croly said, a tremendous stimulus for domestic reform. The Cuban occupation provided progressives not only with a programmatic cohesion which had been lacking in earlier reform movements but also the kind of favorable national publicity which could give new efforts momentum at home. The success of the occupation, by American standards, underscored the belief that the United States had fulfilled its mandate to lift the Cuban people into the forward stream of Western civilization, and in so doing, it provided for a new generation of progressives faith in man's ability to remake and reform the world around him.

PART TWO
A
MODERNIZING
PEOPLE

10

WILLIAM HAYWOOD AND THE IWW

MELVYN DUBOFSKY

The American labor movement began among independent skilled artisans who sought to protect their way of life from the incursions of industrial capitalism. But while the craft focus of American labor unions was a source of real strength, it also proved to be a liability. As industrial capitalism expanded rapidly after the Civil War, the ranks of the unskilled, immigrant worker also expanded. Often possessing neither skill nor craft tradition, these workers performed the most menial and repetitious tasks under the worst conditions while receiving the lowest pay. By the turn of the century, America supported a segmented labor market in which native-born and northern European immigrant workers held the best and highest paying jobs while southern European, Asian, black, and women workers occupied the lowest rungs of the occupational ladder.

The craft orientation of the labor movement served to reinforce this segmented labor market. By limiting membership to those holding traditional skills, craft unions were able to obtain high wages and good working conditions for the upper tier of the industrial workers, but only at the expense of those at the bottom, who were left without effective organization. More than any labor organization, the American Federation of Labor (AFL) came to symbolize this exclusive, craft-oriented form of unionism. Rather than bringing the millions of second-tier workers into the union ranks the AFL fought to maintain the privileges of its members by limiting its goals to purely economic issues and, after the turn of the century, by joining in partnership with the developing American state.

There had always been critics of this drift toward exclusiveness on the part of the labor movement, but perhaps no organization was so vocal in the quest for industrial unionism as the Industrial Workers of the World (IWW). As Melvyn Dubofsky's essay suggests, the IWW was the union of the dispossessed. Starting with the assumption that all workers needed and deserved to be part of the American labor movement, IWW organizers sought out workers in the poorest paying and most degraded industries and gave them a voice in their own destiny. While as Dubofsky shows, their rough rhetoric often collided with the practicalities of organization, the IWW represented hope and potential power for those caught at the bottom of the occupational ladder. Although suppressed as subversive by the government during World War I, the IWW left a legacy that would be used by the Congress of Industrial Organizations during the 1930s and 1940s to bring the unskilled and semiskilled into the mainstream of the labor movement.

The late nineteenth and twentieth centuries have seen many movements of the

Reprinted from Alfred F. Young, ed., *Dissent: Explorations in the History of American Radicalism* (DeKalb: Northern Illinois University Press, 1968), with permission of the publisher.

dispossessed. Compare the goals and ideology of the IWW with that of the Southern Farmers' Alliance discussed by Julie Roy Jeffrey in Reading 6. How do the organizations of the IWW and the SFA compare?

Clio's fickleness never ceases to amaze. The man who made so strong an impression upon Mary Gallagher and Ramsay MacDonald, and the labor organization he personified, aroused dreadful anxieties among most "respectable" middle-class Americans early in the twentieth century. But few people today know anything about the man and the movement which once frightened a less affluent America.

That man—William D. Haywood—and his organization, the Industrial Workers of the World, represented America's early twentieth-century generation of dispossessed workers. Little remembered today and less understood, the IWW and Haywood tell us much about the nature of radicalism in America, the limits of dissent in a purportedly free society, and the prospects, if any, for radical transformations in American society. For the IWW, like the Negro militants and the "New Left" of the 1960's, despised the "power structure" and confronted established authority with nonviolent direct action. "Wobblies" also preached power and promised revolution, beliefs which sometimes involved their organization in riots and violence. Moreover, Wobblies, like today's young radicals, practiced an anti-organizational, semi-utopian, almost anarchistic radicalism. To understand where the new radicalism is today, and where it is headed tomorrow, we might well look back to see where it was only yesterday.

But it is difficult to come to grips with the IWW's place in American history. Posing a threat to the American establishment just before and during the First World War, after Versailles the IWW survived only on the fringes of society. Some of its leaders had been lynched or imprisoned; others had died or joined livelier causes; and the organization itself vanished into what Dan Wakefield has called "haunted halls." In 1923 federal agents added insult to injury when they incinerated the IWW files they had used to persecute and prosecute Wobblies, thereby denying scholars of a later generation an opportunity to perform a decent autopsy.

With the IWW no longer a threat to constituted authority after 1919, and its papers destroyed, novelists and folklorists seized upon the travails of prewar Wobblies to weave a legendary web around their very real exploits. John Dos Passos, earlier than most other novelists, utilized the Wobbly myth in *The 42nd Parallel,* in which the hero, Mac, deserted the girl he loved to join the IWW class war in Nevada. Thirty years later, James Jones also introduced the IWW into fiction; in *From Here to Eternity* an army old-timer lectures a young recruit: "You don't remember the Wobblies. You were too young. Or else not born yet. There has never been anything like them before or since. They called themselves materialist-economists but what they really were was religion. They were workstiffs and bindlebums like you and me, but they were welded together by a vision we don't possess." The religion and the vision gave Wallace Stegner material for his novel, *The Preacher and the Slave,* and Barrie Stavis material for his play, *The Man Who Would Not Die,* both of which were based upon the life of the Swedish-born IWW organizer, bard, and martyr Joe Hill, who melodramatically declaimed before facing a Utah firing squad, "Don't mourn for me. Organize."

Folklorists and folksingers also discovered a usable past in their version of the IWW legend. For Wobblies had sung as they organized, their bards composing lyrics on picket lines and in prison cells. The IWW put its songs together in the *Little Red Song Book,* where a later generation of folksingers could rediscover them to sharpen discontent among protesting civil rights marchers—not oppressed workers as the Wobblies had intended.

Scholars who have investigated the IWW, however, have not been as kind as literary folk. Where novelists discovered an admirable Wobbly tradition, scholars, with one or two exceptions, have been either patronizing or hostile. Either devotees of the American Federation of Labor's official line or products of post-World War II prosperity, euphoria, and Cold War conservatism, these scholars have deprecated the IWW as an association of gun-slinging frontiersmen more famous for its singing than for its accomplishments and for its oratory rather than its organizing—an organization which offered "merely an over-simplified, anti-political Marxism" and therefore "quietly withered on the radical vine without leaving many tangible fruits."

Left-wing scholars have also been critical of the Wobblies. Notwithstanding the IWW's commitment to working-class solidarity and industrial unionism, the Marxist historian Philip Foner and the Communist Party chairman William Z. Foster (himself a wobbly *ca.* 1909–12) derogate it as an infantile disorder inflicted upon the more mature, realistic Marxian left. They indict the IWW for failing to participate adequately in politics and for dividing the American labor movement, thereby weakening radical influences within the house of labor. Foner in particular, measuring the IWW against his version of Marxism-Leninism, naturally finds the Wobblies wanting. Even Ray Ginger, a non-communist scholar, castigates the IWW for splitting the labor movement. Only William D. Haywood escaped the full wrath of the IWW's left-wing critics. He seemed more committed politically than the organization he led, and he later followed the road to Moscow, becoming a Communist Party member in 1919 and an exile to Russia in 1921—unlike most Wobblies, who after 1920 chose to ridicule Soviet communism as industrial autocracy under a new name.

Distorted by the romanticism of novelists and the antipathy of most scholars, the history of the IWW remains unreal, misunderstood, and relatively meaningless. Almost the same can be said of William D. Haywood, its most famous personality. If little is known about the IWW as a labor organization, less is known about Haywood as a person. If the IWW story is encrusted in legend, Haywood's life is pure myth.

Haywood contributed to this myth. Allowing Communist Party hacks to ghost-write his 1927 autobiography, Haywood, by then a gravely ill man, produced a book telling of the exploits of a Western frontiersman. Homesteader, gun-slinger, advocate of the homemade justice of the Colt .45, organizer of a cowboys' union, Haywood leaps from the pages to duel with sheriffs and deputies at pistol point. The picture in *Bill Haywood's Book* is that of a rugged frontiersman who ended his life believing in Karl Marx and communist revolution, not in the rugged individualism of Horatio Alger.

But the real William Haywood differed as drastically from the "Big Bill" of autobiographical recollection as the historical IWW differed from the Wobblies of novelists, playrights, and poets. The real man and the real organization matured in an America in which the primitive frontier was giving way to an urban and industrial environment. The workers Haywood knew and the IWW organized lived in cities and worked for corporations. The agricultural workers they spoke for toiled in "factories in the field," not on small farms. Wage workers, not frontiersmen, followed the call of Haywood and the IWW.

Haywood's America counted its dispossessed by the millions: workers whose skills had been rendered obsolete by technological innovation; Negroes emancipated by law but denied the social and economic freedom to make emancipation meaningful; European immigrants drawn to the land of promise only to dwell in urban slums and to work in dark mills; sons of farmers forced off the land and searching for work wherever it could be had.

The America of Haywood's youth and early manhood also fit the historical context out of which Oscar Lewis sees the "culture of poverty" emerging. It featured, in the four decades after 1877: (1) a cash economy, wage labor, and production for profit; (2) a persistently high rate of unemployment and underemployment for unskilled labor; (3) low wages; and (4) a paucity of social, political, and economic organization, whether on a voluntary basis or by government imposition, for the low-income population. Its values, imposed by the dominant class, stressed the accumulation of wealth and property and the possibility of upward mobility through thrift, and attributed low economic status to personal inadequacy.

Haywood's life, as much as we know of it, was that of an individual who experienced "family disruption, violence, brutality, cheapness of life, lack of love, and lack of education." Born in the American West, to be sure, he was neither rugged frontiersman, frustrated homesteader, nor gunslinger. Rather, he led what—based upon his own testimony, twice offered under oath—must have been a typical Western working-class life.

His life, at least as much of it as can be reconstructed accurately because of the paucity of Haywood's papers and the inaccuracies with which friends and scholars have surrounded it, developed in five distinct phases which flowed smoothly one into the other. He was born in Salt Lake City in 1869. Beginning with few advantages of family, education, or wealth, Haywood had to earn his own way at an early age. By age 15, he had become a hardrock miner; for the next twelve years he worked in Western mining camps, seldom remaining in one place long enough to establish roots. From these early work experiences in an industry unusual for its labor solidarity and violence he probably derived his beliefs about the worker's place in American society and the irrepressibility of conflict between capital and labor. During the next decade (1896–1905), after settling down in one community, Haywood served first as a local union official and then as an officer in his international union. Service in the cause of trade unionism taught him the limitations as well as the advantages of the American labor movement. Aware of its inadequacies, he became a crusader for industrial unionism and socialism.

The third phase of his life saw his role as labor leader diminish as his activities as a Socialist Party politician rose. But seven years of Socialist Party struggles (1906–13) left Haywood disillusioned with the ability of American Marxists to make a revolution in his native land. Recalled from the party's National Executive Committee

in 1913, he began a new phase in his career: national leader of the apolitical, syndicalist, and revolutionary IWW. At last finding full satisfaction in his work, Haywood again became a diligent and efficient union administrator, as well as a fire-eating, spell-binding advocate of revolution. But his success ended in federal repression of the IWW, which brought Haywood's life to its final phase: political exile in the Soviet Union, unable to promote radicalism in the land of his birth or to build the new society in the land of his exile. Such, in brief, is a summary of the various phases through which Haywood's life passed.

Little is known about Haywood's family antecedents. Salt Lake City, his first home, with its well-planned streets, carefully tended gardens, and superior public services, may have been a terrestrial paradise for its Mormon founders; it was anything but that for Haywood. His father died when Haywood was only three, and the boy had little home or school life. Moving with his mother back and forth between Salt Lake City and his stepfather's home in the mining camp of Ophir, where he suffered the childhood accident that cost him an eye, young Haywood soon began to earn his own way. As an adolescent in Salt Lake City he spent his days scrambling for the various jobs open to an uneducated, working-class youth. By fifteen he was a strapping young man with broad shoulders, stout legs and bulging muscles, ready to go down into Nevada's mines with his stepfather, who introduced him to work in the hardrock mining industry.

Haywood's life is hardest to reconstruct during the years 1888 to 1894, when he drifted around the widely scattered mining camps of Utah, Colorado, Nevada, and Idaho. His autobiography said that he had cowboyed and homesteaded during this period (a claim given credence by scholars who were attracted to the portrait of Haywood as a frustrated frontiersman), yet in sworn testimony about his life Haywood never mentioned either a homestead or life as a cowboy. Nor can his associates offer evidence to substantiate such assertions. We do know that about this time Haywood married and began to raise a family. His wife, "Nevada Jane" Minor—

as described in her husband's autobiography—was the classic frontier woman, waging a losing struggle against the forces of nature, drudgery, and loneliness when the man of the family was absent from home for long stretches. Few photographs exist of "Nevada Jane," but one that was taken after she had been invalided and separated from her husband shows a slender woman with penetrating eyes, a homely, unexpressive face, and clear signs of having lived a hard life. Possibly wanting sons, like most workingmen, Haywood had only daughters, but his two girls, Vern Florence and Henrietta Ruth, though clearly their father's daughters, and even more handsome, were never close to their father.

On the skimpy evidence available, one can only conclude that Haywood had a family but was not a family man. His wife, invalided as a result of childbirth and attracted to the mysteries of Christian Science, grew more frail and less attractive as the years passed—hardly the sort of woman to keep a virile husband at home. By 1900, when he had become a national union official, Haywood's marriage was failing. By the time he had become a national celebrity, after his arrest for murder in the notorious Steunenberg assassination case of 1906, it was a fiasco. Indeed, Pinkerton detectives seized their prime suspect in a Denver brothel, almost within walking distance of the family home where his wife lay ill in bed.

In the ensuing trial the advice of the defense counsel, Clarence Darrow, brought a family reconciliation, and "Nevada Jane" and the two girls played a prominent role in court. It was hard for a jury to believe that a defendant with a frail wife and two attractive children, all of whom professed their man's absolute innocence, could be a cold-blooded mass murderer as the prosecution charged. The purpose of the courtroom charade accomplished, Haywood was acquitted and the family separated, this time permanently. Haywood would make his career and establish his fame as a radical labor leader unencumbered by wife or children.

Whatever Haywood did between 1888 and 1895, in 1896 he worked in the mines of Silver City, Idaho, where he met Ed Boyce and the Western Federation of Miners and began a new phase of his life. The WFM had grown directly out of the corporatization of the Western mining frontier and the efforts of large corporations, backed by state and federal power, to "discipline" the previously powerful and independent Western workers. Founded in 1893, the WFM barely survived infancy; the 1893 depression and incompetent leadership made the union's first three years perilous. Prosperity returned in 1896, however, and an effective leader, Ed Boyce, assumed the WFM's presidency. That same year Boyce came to Silver City to organize a WFM local in which Bill Haywood became a charter member, finally finding a career for himself and a purpose in life.

Haywood rose rapidly within the union's ranks. As secretary of the Silver City local he organized a determined campaign to win the union shop in local mines. So successful was he that only two Silver City miners remained outside the union. He cautiously led his fellow unionists along the accepted route of American trade unionism, concentrating upon job security, higher wages, shorter hours, and union-sponsored protection and benefits against illness, injury, and death. His successful administration of local union affairs enhanced Haywood's reputation as an effective "business unionist" within the high echelons of the Western Federation. Elected secretary-treasurer of the WFM at its 1900 convention (a position he would hold for almost eight years), he looked forward to repeating his local triumphs on a national scale.

When Haywood assumed national union office in 1900 the WFM had already left the labor movement's mainstream. Confronted by the united power of capital and the state during an industrial conflict at Leadville, Colorado, in 1896–97, the WFM, as a recent American Federation of Labor affiliate, had vainly pleaded with President Samuel Gompers and the AFL's 1896 convention for assistance. Boyce's experience at this convention so convinced him of the failure of traditional trade union tactics that, in a bitter exchange with Gompers, Boyce even denied that he was a trade unionist as Gompers defined the term.

By 1896 Gompers and the AFL were moving to make their peace with the American system. Although the AFL had once preached the inevitability of class conflict and the need to abolish the "wage-slave" system, it now proclaimed the beauties of class harmony and the possibilities inherent in a beneficent capitalism. By 1900 Gompers faithfully served the needs of the AFL's rank and file—men who possessed valuable and scarce skills, belonged to powerful craft unions, were treated better than the mass of workers, and quarreled over their share of what capitalism produced rather than with the system itself.

Vehemently disagreeing with Gompers' approach to trade unionism, Boyce led the WFM in establishing the Western Labor Union, a dual, schismatic labor federation. Formed in 1898 largely by Boyce with Western Federation funds, it claimed that the AFL emphasized the needs of labor's skilled elite whereas the WLU stressed a policy "broad enough in principle and sufficiently humane in character to embrace every class of toil, from the farmer to the skilled mechanic, in one great brotherhood." Where the AFL stressed the absolute autonomy of the national craft union, the Westerners favored the industrial union, free transfer from union to union, and union solidarity. Where the AFL sought to close America's gates to newcomers, the Westerners welcomed them. Where the AFL preferred such traditional trade union tactics as strikes, boycotts, and collective bargaining, the WLU insisted that industrial technology and corporate concentration had made the traditional tactics obsolete, leaving the working class but one recourse: to vote socialist.

This was the labor environment in which Haywood matured as a union official, keeping the WFM's books and for a time editing its official journal, the *Miner's Magazine.* Haywood's editorials in the *Miners' Magazine* reflected a growing disenchantment with "business unionism" and an increasing distaste for many aspects of American society. From his early pieces extolling the value of union labels and promoting coop-

eration with AFL affiliates, he moved on—in awkward metaphors—to compose passionate pleas for union ownership of mines, to celebrate the eventual triumph of socialism, and to issue vitriolic comments on Gompers and the AFL. As secretary-treasurer he managed the international's affairs as efficiently as he had once handled those of his Silver City local.

Under the combined leadership of Boyce and Haywood the WFM thrived; radicalism proved no impediment. The WFM chartered more new locals and recruited more new members from 1900 to 1903 than at any other time in its history. Between 1900 and 1902 it added 55 locals and ten thousand members; and during 1903 it increased its total membership by a third, raising it to between thirty-five thousand and forty thousand. In 1902, when Boyce retired from the union's presidency, he left behind him an organization which seemed secure.

Up to this point in his life Haywood had proved himself an able union official, one who had traveled ideologically from the pure and simple policies employed at Silver City to the industrial unionism and political socialism of the Western Federation, the Western Labor union, and the American Labor Union. As early as February, 1902, however, he had a premonition that his career as an ordinary union official would soon end. In an editorial he wrote for the *Miners' Magazine,* and which seemed to refer directly to its author's ambitions, Haywood commented: The agitator "is the advance agent of social improvement and fully realizes that reforms are not achieved by conservative methods."

Within a year of this remark events in Colorado transformed Haywood from a rhetorical radical into a revolutionary activist. Until 1903 he had maintained that social change would come to the working class through organization, education, and legislation. He even derided the need for class conflict, informing Colorado officials and businessmen: "We [the WFM] are not opposed to employers . . . it is our purpose and aim to work harmoniously and jointly with the employers as best we can under this system, and

we intend to change the system if we get sufficiently organized and well enough educated to do
so."

One year later Haywood would drastically reverse himself, for class warfare in Colorado in
1903 and 1904 taught him the limitations inherent in seeking to cooperate with private employers and public officials. Before engaging in industrial conflict the WFM had offered to negotiate
with Colorado employers, but the businessmen
preferred to smash the union—an "un-American," seditious, even criminal organization. And
a pliant governor who had no scruples about authorizing illegal searches and seizures, unwar-
ranted arrests, and suspension of due process,
taught Haywood and the WFM just how "impartial" government was.

The militia that was sent to the Cripple Creek
and Telluride strike districts by the Colorado
governor, James H. Peabody, made its purpose
clear. "To hell with the Constitution," an officer
proclaimed; "we aren't going by the Constitution." In Colorado the state was indistinguishable
from private capitalism. The governor provided
the troops and the mine owners paid for them; the
governor employed and paid Pinkerton detectives, and the mine owners supervised their work
in the field.

The Western Federation went into the
Colorado labor conflict a dynamic and growing
organization; it came out a crushed and declining
one. Haywood went into the conflict as a full-time
union official, part-time agitator, and equivocal
revolutionary; he came out a part-time union official, a full-time agitator, and a committed revolutionary.

The Colorado experience made Haywood and
the WFM cynical about the value of education
and legislative reforms, and they now began to
emphasize direct labor action. Colorado had convinced them that America's disinherited had to
discover new weapons to win social change. Traditional trade unions, political action, even radical politics had been found wanting. Haywood
later told the United States Commission on Industrial Relations: "It was during the period of
those strikes that the Western Federation of Min-

ers realized the necessity of labor getting together
into one big union. . . . There seemed to be no
hope for such a thing as that [solidarity] among
any of the existing labor organizations." To find
new weapons Haywood and the WFM, together
with other discontented American radicals,
created the Industrial Workers of the World.

Chairman of the IWW's founding convention,
the keynoter, and afterward the eulogizer of its
accomplishments, Haywood epitomized the spirit
of the convention of June, 1905. He spoke to
delegates who represented the Socialist Trades
and Labor Alliance, splinter labor unions,
"paper" labor unions, a few real unions (his own,
of course), and to delegates who represented only
themselves (Debs, Mother Jones, Lucy Parsons,
and Algie Simons, for example) as an experienced, successful union official. Also, he
stood above the nasty and petty sectarian socialist
squabbles many delegates had brought with them
to Chicago as he stressed the convention's essential purpose. From the opening moment, when
Haywood called to order "the Continental Congress of the Working Class," he spoke of the need
to emancipate America's working-class masses
from capitalism through the power of an organization that could destroy the existing system and
the prevailing relationships of production. Haywood advised the assembled delegates to create a
new labor organization as the voice of the unskilled, the unorganized, the powerless. "What I
want to see from this organization," he said, "is
an uplifting of the fellow that is down in the
gutter . . . realizing that the society can be no
better than its most miserable." Following Haywood's sentiment, the IWW opened its doors to
all workers, skilled and unskilled, native and immigrant, child and adult, male and female, black,
white, and even yellow. It provided for low uniform initiation fees, still lower dues, and free universal transfer of union cards.

In order to train the powerless in the uses of
power the IWW vested ultimate organizational
authority in the rank and file, establishing—on
paper—the most democratic decision-making
procedures in the history of American trade unionism. All actions taken by IWW national offi-

cials were made subject to appeal to the general convention, whose decisions, in turn, might be put to a general-membership referendum. In practice, the IWW's anti-organizational, implicitly anarchic spirit hindered the effective functioning of its general headquarters and allowed IWW affiliates even more local autonomy and freedom than the organization's constitution offered them in theory. Even the locals usually practiced a form of rotation of officials that was so effective it would have shocked Andrew Jackson himself.

The delegates at the IWW's founding convention must have found Haywood impressive. Well over six feet tall, broad shouldered, with ample girth and a pock-marked but handsome face set off by a patch over his right eye, Haywood's features bore witness to the battles he had waged and the suffering he had endured. His appearance proclaimed his strength. Neither stamping, pounding, bellowing, nor bullying, he used simple, direct, working-class expressions. Listening to "Big Bill" speak, an observer commented, and "stripping Haywood of all the attributes which usually enable labor leaders to lead, we end by finding in him two qualities, rare ones: genuine power and genuine simplicity."

Haywood, however, had less endearing qualities by American Victorian standards. He was as much "at home" in the saloon and brothel as on the speaker's platform or in the union office. Whoring and drinking, however, added to the image of his virility and apparently did not lessen his appeal to workingmen, although this may have diminished his ability to serve the labor movement. At any rate, Haywood never had a chance to put his strength or his imagination to work for the IWW; he would be isolated in an Idaho prison for the next two years.

On the afternoon of December 30, 1905, ex-Idaho Governor Frank Steunenberg was assassinated. Two days later, on January 1, 1906, local police apprehended the presumed assassin, Harry Orchard, who after several weeks of subtle interrogation by famed Pinkerton agent James McParland (the man who had brought Pennsylvania's notorious Molly Maguires to "justice"

thirty years earlier) confessed to the governor's murder and to countless other crimes, all of which he alleged he performed at the behest of the Haywood-dominated "inner circle of the WFM." McParland's men then kidnapped Haywood, George Pettibone (a former WFM member, close friend of Haywood and Moyer, and then a small businessman in Denver), and WFM President Charles Moyer on February 17, 1906. Unable to communicate with friends, family, or attorney, the three abductees were sped to Idaho on a special train, where a month later they would be indicted on murder charges. They remained in jail, without bond, for more than a year while McParland unsuccessfully searched for evidence to corroborate Orchard's confession.

Meanwhile, Wobblies and members of the Western Miners organization fought among and between themselves; indeed, an open factional battle erupted at the 1906 IWW convention about whether the IWW should be an uncompromising revolutionary organization, or whether it should concentrate upon unionism and the achievement of improved working conditions. The majority at this second Wobbly convention, calling themselves revolutionists, purged their opponents, even abolishing the office of president. During the convention struggle the Western Federation's delegates divided, bringing the Wobblies' civil war into their own union. The western miners disagreed about whether to endorse the new "revolutionary" IWW, or whether to create a non-revolutionary industrial union federation, until the 1907 WFM Convention voted to withdraw from the IWW.

The struggle raged even within the prison walls. Moyer, after the WFM's 1904 defeat in Colorado, had begun to rethink his support of radical socialism, dual unionism, and constant industrial conflict. His arrest and confinement hastened the reassessment. In the future, he decided, he would lead his union toward the AFL —that is, toward less radicalism and more cooperation with employers. Many WFM members who had never taken to radical unionism or to socialism or who had fought the IWW "revolutionists" at the 1906 convention could be counted upon to support Moyer. No discernible shift toward the right could be detected in Haywood, however; if anything, arrest and imprisonment impelled him toward more radical views. Haywood claimed in his autobiography that reading radical literature while in prison had reinforced his own intuitive judgments. More likely, however, Haywood's personality was more rebellious than Moyer's, and perhaps he had a desire for martyrdom—what a Freudian might call a death wish. Further research into Haywood's early life would doubtless turn up many more examples of his rebellious nature inasmuch as several documents suggest Haywood's strong assertiveness well before the founding of the IWW and his formal break with Moyer (who apparently was a contented family man).

Thus divided, Moyer and Haywood could do nothing to bind the IWW's wounds nor, for that matter, to temper the conflict within the miners' union. Moyer threw in his lot with the dominant WFM faction, which by 1907 was on the road to a reconciliation with the AFL. Haywood, however, found himself alone. Although critical of the men who had dominated the 1906 IWW convention, he could not endorse their opponents. Still a member of the Socialist Party and a believer in political action, Haywood was leery of an IWW dominated by Daniel De Leon's Socialist Labor Party and Vincent St. John's apolitical direct actionists.

In May, 1907, Haywood was finally brought to trial, and was acquitted (partly because Orchard's confession was uncorroborated and partly because Orchard's testimony during cross-examination was contradictory). But he left prison a union leader without an organization, an agitator without an immediate cause. The Western Federation, which by then had withdrawn from the IWW and restored Moyer to the presidency, wanted no part of the radical Haywood, and early in 1908 it unceremoniously dropped him. Contrary to the version of Charles Madison, Patrick Renshaw, and Carl Hein, Haywood's attitude toward the feeble IWW was similarly cool. A Denver IWW official complained: "So much

does Haywood think of the IWW that he has never been near our headquarters or our meetings, here in Denver, since his acquittal."

The Idaho incident, however, had opened a new phase in Haywood's life. Converted into a national celebrity by his trial, he proved exceedingly useful to the Socialist Party, and he was accommodating. Even while he had been in prison he had run for the governorship of Colorado on the Socialist Party ticket in 1906. Rejecting the lucrative lecturing and writing offers that awaited him on his release, he chose instead to speak for the party. In 1908 he took a prominent part in Debs' "Red Special" campaign for the presidency.

Even among Socialists, who elected him to the party's National Executive Committee in 1909, Haywood proved a dissenter. His experiences had convinced him that no capitalist law was worth a laborer's respect, no capitalist's property was worth a worker's life; and he increasingly counseled law-breaking, sabotage, and direct nonpolitical action. On one occasion Haywood defiantly informed an audience of Socialists: "I despise the law, and I am not a law-abiding citizen." To American Socialists who, unlike Debs, feared imprisonment, Haywood said: "Those of us who are in jail—those of us who have been in jail—all of us who are willing to go to jail—care not what you say or do! We despise your hypocrisy. . . . We are the Revolution!" Yet he represented a party that by and large respected the law and opposed the destruction of property. In 1913 his continued advocacy of sabotage would lead to his recall from the party's National Executive Committee.

Sent to Europe in 1910 as an American delegate to that year's Copenhagen Congress of the Second International, Haywood spent most of his time with trade union activists and his European contacts influenced him to end the phase of his life that had been dominated by Socialist Party politics and oratory. Like William Z. Foster, who visited the continent at the same time and whom Haywood met in Paris (the two American radicals, however, were never close friends), Haywood became intrigued with the militancy of

European labor, its appeal to the less skilled workers, and its effective use of direct-action tactics. It was in Europe that Haywood decided to resume his connection with the IWW. Interviewed in a French syndicalist paper, Haywood declared his belief in industrial unionism as represented by the IWW. Returning to America, he appeared on the rostrum at New York City's Yorkville Casino in December, 1910, as an accredited IWW speaker. The enthusiastic audience welcomed the lost son back to the fold.

The IWW and Haywood now thought alike and acted alike. In 1908 the IWW had suffered a second purge that expelled Daniel De Leon, the self-proclaimed high priest of revolutionary socialism, and those who shared his belief in the primacy of political over economic action. Vincent St. John, a former WFM official who had allied himself with the IWW "revolutionists" in 1906 and later had left the Western Federation, now took firm control of the IWW. Under his leadership the organization divorced itself from all political parties and concentrated upon direct economic action that would deliver "the goods" to America's underpaid and overworked but unorganized laborers. Like Haywood, St. John stressed direct action and militant tactics in his leadership of the IWW, disdaining to hide his abomination of the law and private property. Finally finding an organization that was suited to his personality and in need of his unique talents, Haywood entered upon the most significant phase of his life.

Haywood, St. John, and the IWW created a derivative but distinctly American radicalism. IWW beliefs must be understood in terms of those to whom the organization appealed and those whom it tried to organize. After 1908 the IWW concentrated upon workers who had been neglected by the mainstream American labor movement. To "timber beasts," hobo harvesters, itinerant construction hands, the exploited East and South European immigrants, racially excluded Negroes, Mexican, and Asian Americans the IWW promised a new day. As Haywood told an inquisitive reporter: "Here were millions and

millions of people working desperately and barely able to exist. All I needed was to stir those millions into a sense of their wrongs."

Rexford G. Tugwell aptly described the kind of worker to whom the IWW carried its radical gospel. Writing about the Pacific Northwest logger, Tugwell noted:

"His eyes are dull and reddened; his joints are stiff with the rheumatism almost universal in the wettest climate in the world; his teeth are rotting; he is wracked with strange diseases and tortured by unrealized dreams that haunt his soul. . . . The blanket-stiff is a man without a home. . . . The void of his atrophied affections is filled with a resentful despair and bitterness against the society that self-righteously cast him out."

Wobbly recruits were Marx's *Lumpenproletariat,* individuals who felt marginal, helpless, dependent, inferior. Impotent and alienated, they harbored deep-seated grievances against the institutions of the ruling class: police, government, and church. Although IWW leaders did not come from the ranks of these disinherited, they shared their alienation.

The disinherited joined the IWW by the thousands because it offered, in the words of Carleton Parker, "a ready-made dream of a new world where there is a new touch with sweetness and light and where for a while they can escape the torture of forever being indecently kicked about." To migratory workers the IWW promised "the only social break in the harsh search for work that they have ever had: its headquarters the only competitor of the saloon in which they are welcome."

More important, the IWW also promised its followers a way out of their "culture of poverty." It endowed them with class consciousness, organization, solidarity, hope for the future; that is, with a sense of identification with larger social groups that might destroy the psychological and social core of their marginality, dependence, and impotence. It tried to give them what revolutionaries the world over usually see as an absolute necessity: a sense of self-respect, importance, and power—a feeling that the disinherited were humanity's last best hope.

IWW ideology visualized the downtrodden emerging from the abyss. They would seize industry for themselves; mere crumbs from their masters' tables were not enough. "We are many," proclaimed the IWW's newspapers. "We are resourceful; we are animated by the most glorious vision of the ages; we cannot be conquered, and *we shall conquer the world for the working class.*" Simply put in the IWW's favorite revolutionary hymn, the *Internationale:* "We have been *naught*—We shall be All!"

But Wobblies did not expect their revolution to make itself. It was inevitable, but they would help the course of history. "Our organization is not content with merely making the prophecy," insisted *Solidarity,* "but acts upon industrial and social conditions with a view to shaping them in accord with the general tendency." To help history, the Wobblies followed the pattern of all modern revolutionaries: they proposed a program, developed a doctrine concerning the transfer of power, and elaborated a system of organization. Unlike most other modern revolutionaries, however, with the exception of the anarcho-syndicalists whom they resembled, Wobblies rejected purely political tactics and organizations. The Wobblies believed they could best make history by obtaining power. Who held power ruled society!

The IWW proposed to transfer power from the capitalists, who held it and used it for antisocial purposes, to the proletariat, who would exercise power for the benefit of humanity. Jack London in *The Iron Heel,* a novel referred to often and lovingly by Wobblies, expressed better than any IWW editorial or pamphlet the organization's feelings about power. London's hero, Ernest Everhardt—a fictional Haywood—affirmed that "Power . . . is what we of the working class preach. We know and well we know by bitter experience, that no appeal for the right, for justice, for humanity, can ever touch you. . . . So we have preached power." And he concluded, as coldly as London's capitalist, "Power will be the arbiter, as it has always been the arbiter. . . . We

of the labor hosts have conned that word over till our minds are all a-tingle with it. Power. It is a kingly word."

The doctrine had Darwinian overtones. In its widely circulated organizing pamphlet for lumber workers the IWW emphasized: "It is the law of nature that the strong rule and the weak are enslaved." George Speed, a veteran West Coast trade unionist and charter member of the IWW, expressed the IWW concept tersely: "Power is the thing that determines everything today . . . it stands to reason that the fellow that has got the big club swings it over the balance. That is life as it exists today." Thus workers had to develop their own sources of power; nobody could do it for them—neither Socialists, political action, nor legislation. "That is my contention," argued Speed. "They have to learn to do it themselves, and they are going to suffer until they do learn."

IWW antipathy toward political action reflected the status of its members. Migratory workers moved too often to establish legal voting residences. Millions of unnaturalized immigrants lacked the franchise. So did Negroes, and women, and children, to whom the IWW opened its doors. As Haywood informed the Commission on Industrial Relations: "The wage earner or producing classes are in the minority; second . . . they are not educated to the game of politics . . . their life is altogether industrial." Even immigrants and the native born who had the right to vote nourished a deep suspicion of government. The state, symbolized by the policeman's club and the magistrate's edict, hardly treated the poor kindly. Wobblies realized that the power of the state was used against them. Who knew better than an IWW, who had been imprisoned for exercising his right of free speech or clubbed by a cop while peacefully picketing for higher wages? Wobblies never believed that stuffing pieces of paper, even socialist ones, into a ballot box would transform this repressive state into a humane one.

If the workers could not use political power to alter the rules of the game, what remained? Wobblies thought they had the answer. "Political power," said one, "is a reflex of economic power, and those who control economic power control the political power of the state." Another concluded: "Without economic power working-class political action is like a house without a foundation or a dream without substance."

IWW leaders therefore taught their followers how to achieve economic power. "Get it through industrial organization." "Organize the workers to control the use of their labor power." "The secret of power is organization." "The only force that can break . . . tyrannical rule . . . is one big union of all the workers."

Through organization the IWW could exert direct action, its essential means of bringing the new society into existence. By direct action it meant "any economic step taken by the workers. . . . It includes sabotage . . . passive resistance . . . and covers the ordinary strike, the intermittent strike, the silent strike, and the death blow to capitalism in the form of the social general strike." "Shall I tell you what direct action really means?" another IWW manifesto asked. "The worker on the job shall tell the boss when and where he shall work, how long, and for what wages and under what conditions." Direct action, according to Haywood, would eventually reach the point where workers were strong enough to say: " 'Here, Mr. Stockholder, we won't work for you any longer. You have drawn dividends out of our hides long enough; we propose that you shall go to work now, and under the same opportunities that we have had.' "

Wobblies, in their emphasis on direct action, liked to compare themselves to antebellum abolitionists, who had also defied the laws that sanctioned human bondage and who had publicly burned the American Constitution. "We are the modern abolitionists fighting against wage slavery," proclaimed general organizer James Thompson. Wobblies were willing to unsheath the Lord's terrible swift sword.

Although the IWW employed the vocabulary of violence, more often than not it utilized passive resistance and was itself the victim of violence that was instigated by law-enforcement officials, condoned by the law-abiding. The IWW, in fact, sought through organized activities to channel the frustrations and antisocial rage of the dispos-

sessed into constructive courses. Even Haywood, whose career with the Western Federation had been associated with labor violence, told a reporter during the 1912 Lawrence textile strike: "I should never think of conducting a strike in the old way. . . . I, for one, have turned my back on violence. It wins nothing. When we strike now, we strike with our hands in our pockets. We have a new kind of violence—the havoc we raise with money by laying down our tools. Pure strength lies in the overwhelming power of numbers."

Wobblies also looked to nonviolent tactics in order to expose the brutality of their enemy and to win sympathy for their suffering. Passive resistance, editorialized *Solidarity,* "has a tremendous moral effect; it puts the enemy on record; it exposes the police and city authorities as a bunch of law breakers; it drives the masters to the last ditch of resistance. 'Passive resistance' by the workers results in laying bare the inner workings and purposes of the capitalist mind. It also reveals the self-control, the fortitude, the courage, the inherent sense of order, of the workers' mind. As such, 'passive resistance' is of immense educational value."

But IWW passive resistance should not be confused with pacifism. Nonviolence was only a means, never an end, and if passive resistance led only to beatings and deaths, the IWW threatened to respond in kind. Arturo Giovanitti, a sometime poet, sometime Wobbly, put the IWW's position bluntly: "The generally accepted notion seems to be that to kill is a great crime, but to be killed is the greatest." And Haywood cited Abraham Lincoln's alleged advice to citizens who suffered from hunger as a result of wartime food speculation: "Take your pick-axes and crowbars and go to the granaries and warehouses and help yourselves." That, said Haywood, "is a good IWW doctrine."

In keeping with its commitment to nonviolence (at least when lacking the power to employ violence), the IWW even saw its revolution coming peaceably. It would come, according to Haywood, when "labor was organized and self-disciplined [so] it could stop every wheel in the United States . . . and sweep off your capitalists and State legislatures and politicians into the sea." The only violence involved, he added, would occur after labor had drained the capitalists' pocketbooks.

The nonviolent overthrow of capitalism would result from a general strike. Neither Haywood nor any other Wobbly, however, ever precisely defined the general strike, but Haywood explained it as the stoppage of all work and the destruction of the capitalists through a peaceful paralysis of industry. Ben Williams insisted that it was no strike at all—simply "a 'general lockout of the employing class' leaving the workers in possession of the machinery of distribution and production." Whatever the exact definition of the general strike, Haywood wrote, whenever its day came "control of industry will pass from the capitalists to the masses and capitalists will vanish from the face of the earth." This utopian day would come peaceably if workers had their way, and violently if capitalists attempted to postpone it with "roar of shell and whine of machine-guns."

In Haywood's dream of his utopia, "there will be a new society sometime in which there will be no battle between capitalist and wage earner, but . . . every man will have free access to land and its resources. In that day . . . the machinery can be made the slave of the people instead of a part of the people being made the slave of machinery." Another Wobbly's utopia would have no room for poverty, jails, police, the army and marines, Christians, churches, heaven and hell. Its cities would be clean and beautiful, with wide streets, parks, flowers, and fine homes and its workers "no longer stoop shouldered and consumptive looking." Prudery would disappear, along with heaven and hell, and naked children would frisk on the grass and bask in the sunshine. With economic freedom in this utopia and an abundance of food, shelter, clothing, and leisure, and education for everyone, "all hearts and minds [would be] turned towards solving the mysteries of the Universe."

Wobblies never quite explained how this paradise would be governed; they agreed, however, that the state—as most Americans knew it—

would be nonexistent. "There will be no such thing as the State or States," Haywood said. "The industries will take the place of what are now existing States." "Whenever the workers are organized in the industry, whenever they have a sufficient organization in the industry," added St. John, "they will have all the government they need right there."

Somehow, each industrial union would possess and manage its own industry. Union members would elect superintendents, foremen, secretaries, and managers. The separate industrial unions would then meet jointly to plan for the welfare of society as a whole. This system, "in which each worker will have a share in the ownership and a voice in the control of industry, and in which each shall receive the full product of his labor," was variously called "the Cooperative Commonwealth," "the Workers' Commonwealth," "the Industrial Commonwealth," "Industrial Democracy," and "Industrial Communism." Unsure of its proposed system, the IWW could not label it definitively.

Like European syndicalists, the Wobblies aimed to abolish capitalism by nonpolitical means; and, like them, they also emphasized direct action. In the IWW's new society, as in that projected by European syndicalism, the political state would not exist; workers would administer industry directly through their industrial unions. The IWW even took over the French syndicalist concept of the militant minority. "Our task," said an IWW paper, "is to develop the conscious, intelligent minority to the point where they will be capable of carrying out the imperfectly expressed desires of the toiling millions." As a perceptive Socialist theorist noted, notwithstanding superficial variations caused by different economic and political conditions in different countries, "this living spirit of revolutionary purpose unifies French and British syndicalism and American Industrial Unionism (the IWW)."

Industrial unionism, Haywood once stated, was socialism "with its working clothes on." After 1913, however, when Haywood was recalled from the Socialist Party's highest council, IWW industrial unionists and American Social-

WILLIAM HAYWOOD AND THE IWW   **133**

ists had little in common. When Socialists talked of capturing control of the government through the ballot box and of transforming the capitalist state into the "Cooperative Commonwealth," the IWW responded: "A wise tailor does not put stitches into rotten cloth."

Wobblies might obey the law, use the voting booth, and temporize on their revolutionism, but they could never—despite the intellectuals among them—entirely forego anti-intellectualism. To Socialists who prided themselves on their intellectual abilities, Haywood said: "Socialism is so plain, so clear, so simple that when a person becomes intellectual he doesn't understand socialism." IWW ideology always remained that of the poor, not of the educated; it was intended to motivate the disinherited, not to satisfy the learned. As an IWW member noted, reviewing John Graham Brooks' *American Syndicalism:* "It is not the Sorels . . . the Wallings, LaMontes and such figures who count for the most—it is the obscure Bill Jones on the firing line, with stink in his clothes, rebellion in his brain, hope in his heart, determination in his eye and direct action in his gnarled fist."

In the last analysis, the Wobblies and Haywood must be remembered more for what they did than for what they thought, more for what they fought for than what they learned. In 1914, the year he became the IWW's top official, Haywood succinctly explained the organization's role. "It has developed among the lowest strata of wage slaves in America a sense of their importance and capabilities such as never before existed. Assuming control and responsibility of their own affairs, the unorganized and unfortunate have been brought together, and have conducted some of the most unique strikes, fights for free speech and battles for constitutional rights." And that is just what the organization did both before and after Haywood took command of the IWW. From 1909 to 1917 it led workers who were neglected by other labor organizations in struggles that raised their self-esteem and improved their conditions of life.

By fighting for free speech in Spokane, Fresno,

Missoula, Sioux City, and Minot (among other cities), the IWW proved to long-brutalized migratories that authority could be defeated through direct action and passive resistance. Taking to the streets in defense of their civil liberties, Wobblies courted arrest, and those arrested were quickly replaced on soap boxes by other free-speech speakers. Wobblies flooded the jails, paralyzed the courtrooms, and strained the purses of the cities they confronted. Most civic authorities, unable to cope with such passive resistance on a mass scale, succumbed to IWW demands; but some authorities, like San Diego's dealt with the IWW "menace" by methods later made infamous in Mussolini's Italy and Hitler's Germany. The IWW also achieved reforms in private employment agencies that had traditionally exploited migratories, and improved working conditions in farming and forestry.

In industrial centers such as McKees Rocks (steel, in 1909), Lawrence (textiles, in 1912), Paterson (textiles, in 1913), and Akron (rubber, in 1913), the IWW showed mass-production workers the possibilities of industrial unionism. It also tempered ethnic divisions by organizing without regard to distinctions of national origin. Most important, the IWW taught previously unorganized mass-production workers how to wage their own struggles for improvement. IWW members learned industrial warfare and union tactics in the manner Marxist theorists and even John Dewey prescribed—by doing! If Wobbly strikers wanted higher wages, shorter hours, and better conditions, their organizers let them fight for them. If workers wanted agreements with their employers, IWW leaders let their followers negotiate them. The IWW organized, agitated, advised; but it was the workers themselves who led and decided. When authorities queried IWW strikers about their leaders, the men and women could respond in a single voice: "We are all leaders."

After the Wobblies' surprising strike victory at Lawrence in 1912, the revolution seemed near at hand. Commentators forgot about the rising tide of socialism and began to worry about the more dangerous threat of revolutionary industrial unionism. Such intellectuals as Max Eastman and the young John Reed saw in the IWW the agency that would accomplish the Nietzschean transvaluation of the values of existing society. And they saw William Haywood as the archetypal Nietzschean superman, as Jack London's Ernest Everhardt come to life. Haywood became the darling of New York's Greenwich Village rebels, enjoying the role of star proletarian performer in Mabel Dodge Luhan's Fifth Avenue salon.

But the IWW's revolutionary threat disappeared as quickly as it had come; victory in Lawrence was followed by defeat in Paterson, Akron, and other Eastern cities. Economic adversity aggravated organizational ills. When the American economy declined in 1913 and 1914, IWW membership, never more than thirty thousand before 1916, fell to about fifteen thousand in 1915. By December, 1914, Haywood reported a bankrupt treasury and the IWW seemed on the verge of extinction. No longer did leading journals warn about the dangers of industrial unionism.

From 1909 to 1915, although the IWW had demonstrated to a segment of the American proletariat the virtues of organization, solidarity, and direct action, it could not keep them organized or united. It contended against forces that were simply too powerful to defeat. Employers, supported by local, state, and federal authorities, could vitiate IWW organizing efforts either through outright repression, or with the aid of progressive reforms, could offer workers immediate palliatives.

Throughout its history the IWW faced paradoxes the organization never resolved. If it offered only perpetual industrial warfare, how could it maintain its membership, let alone increase it? But if it won better contracts, and union recognition, and improved life for its members, what was to keep them from forswearing revolutionary goals and from following the established AFL pattern? If it declared a truce in the class war, how could it bring about the ultimate revolution? In the end, IWW leaders, including Haywood, subordinated reform opportunities to revolutionary necessities; the

rank and file, when it could, took the reforms and neglected the revolution.

In adversity and decline, however, the IWW learned important lessons. In the summer of 1914 it began to concentrate upon the hard-core disinherited—the migrant workers who harvested the nation's wheat, picked its hops, cut its lumber, built its railroads, and mined its copper. To these men the IWW offered a purpose in life and a sense of identity and value; to the IWW they, in turn, gave allegiance and strength.

Migratories joined the IWW in increasing numbers as the organization demonstrated that it could improve their conditions of work. When Haywood took over the general headquarters in November, 1914, the IWW was almost broke. A year later, after its Agricultural Workers' Organization had begun an organizing campaign in the wheat belt, the IWW had a surplus in its treasury and thousands of new members on its roster, and it paid organizers to carry its word to lumber and construction workers and hardrock miners. The message Wobbly organizers carried in 1915 and 1916 emphasized organization, not revolution, and immediate gains, not utopian ideology. The new message was heard. Membership rose between 1915 and early 1917 to between sixty thousand and one hundred thousand. By 1916 the Wobblies could charter new industrial unions for lumber workers, hardrock miners, and construction hands.

As its membership and treasury increased, the IWW's tone seemed to alter. The 1916 convention was the first convention that fully asserted the authority of general headquarters; separate industrial unions were to be subject to closer supervision by Haywood's new, centralized Chicago office. Those who disagreed with the new emphasis or disliked Haywood's predominant influence left the IWW or were relegated to obscurity within the organization. After 1916 Elizabeth Gurley Flynn, Joseph Ettor, Arturo Giovanitti, and Carlo Tresca (among others)—leaders who had once shared the headlines and national publicity with Haywood—were pushed into the background. They were replaced by a new breed of Wobblies, those who propagandized less and organized more. Over this new IWW, which flourished as never before, presided William D. Haywood.

Sitting behind his large roll-type desk at the new IWW headquarters on Chicago's West Madison Street, Haywood never seemed happier than early in 1917. Ralph Chaplin, then the editor of *Solidarity,* later remembered that Haywood, his boss and close friend, appeared more self-assured, more firm of voice, and more youthful as he worked among busy clerks and secretaries. Haywood seemed "a revolutionary tycoon whose dream was coming true." His enthusiasm infected everyone at IWW headquarters, which, in its effort "to build the new society within the shell of the old," became one of the liveliest places in Chicago. But Haywood's happiness and enthusiasm would prove short-lived; so, too, would the IWW's success and growth. The factors that had brought the IWW prosperity presaged its death, and Haywood's exile.

The European conflict contributed greatly to IWW resurgence under Haywood, as war orders poured into the American market. Rising production brought rising profits and increasing labor scarcity. In a tight labor market the IWW could not only organize successfully, it could also win material improvements for its members inasmuch as employers were loath to sacrifice wartime profits to anti-union principles. But when America intervened in April, 1917, employers discovered how they could have profits without the IWW.

The IWW had long preached antimilitarism and antipatriotism as basic principles, and the war did not make any changes in this, but the IWW now concentrated upon organization, direct action, and on-the-job activities. It was too busy organizing harvest hands, lumber workers, and miners to lead antiwar campaigns. It was too busy fighting for higher wages and shorter hours to waste its time in an anti-conscription drive. The IWW did nothing directly to interfere with the American war effort, but it did organize and strike in industries that were vital to that effort.

In the spring of 1917 IWW strikes threatened the lumber industry, copper mining, and the wheat harvest. Stories were spread which received credence in the Justice and War Departments, that IWW strikes were German-inspired and German-financed. Western employers pleaded with state and national authorities to suppress the IWW in the interest of national security; they also took direct action of their own, organizing Citizens' Alliances and Vigilante Leagues, some of these with the sanction of the Justice Department. These vigilantes hunted out every worker who threatened war profits.

Everywhere the IWW found itself beset by enemies. Local and state officials joined private businessmen in persecuting Wobblies. If their action proved ineffective, officials demanded federal intervention, and before long federal troops patrolled West Coast docks, Northwest woods and farmlands, and the mining towns of Arizona and Montana. Simultaneously, the Justice Department and Military Intelligence infiltrated agents into the IWW. Between Pinkertons, Thiel detectives, and federal agents, spies had the IWW under constant surveillance. Even the Labor Department, less anxious and more realistic about Western labor conflicts than the War and Justice Departments, did its part to curb the IWW. Labor Department agents, however, also tried to use the war crisis to improve working conditions, as well as to induce IWW laborers to join AFL affiliates. With Gompers' hearty approval and direct cooperation, the Labor Department attacked the IWW menace, promoting the AFL cause.

When these efforts failed to end the IWW's threat to Western industries, the federal government—pressured by private business, state governors, United States attorneys, and influential congressmen—took the final step. With presidential approval, the Justice Department proscribed the IWW. In a nationwide series of raids on September 5, 1917, the department's agents invaded every important IWW headquarters, seizing everything they could lay their hands on (including rubber bands, paper clips, and Ralph Chaplin's love letters). Sorting through tons of confiscated material, the Justice Department assembled the evidence to indict IWW leaders for sedition, espionage, and interference with the war effort.

By the end of 1917 almost every important IWW official, including Haywood, was in prison. In the interests of national security, industrial harmony, and business profits, the government put the IWW under lock and key. Due process followed, but what happened in the courtrooms in which Wobbly leaders were tried, convicted, and sentenced was only a legal charade. Whether in Chicago, Wichita, or Sacramento, the trial evidence was always the same, as were the results. In every case the IWW—as an organization, not its individual leaders or members—was placed on trial. In every case the IWW was judged not for what it had done but for what it said and wrote, although most of the "seditious" writings and speeches antedated America's overseas involvement and, to a great extent, 1914.

Some subordinates in the Justice Department realized that the government did not have a valid case against the IWW. They suggested that, in the interest of justice, trials be postponed until wartime hysteria subsided, but the Justice Department would not listen to such an argument. To its top officials, many drawn from Wall Street law offices, and often associates of leading businessmen, the IWW represented a real menace, both to America's war effort and to business profits. The trials went on and Wobbly leaders were sent to Leavenworth.

Thus ended the IWW's threat to the prevailing order. New and inexperienced Wobbly leaders took to fighting among themselves, becoming easy prey to the Pinkertons and military intelligence agents who continued to infiltrate the organization. And thus ended Haywood's role in the history of American radicalism. In 1917 he had led a dynamic organization that posed a growing threat to the established order. In 1918, after smashing the IWW, the United States government in effect said to Haywood and his fellow Wobblies what Leon Trotsky had said to Martov and the Russian Mensheviks after the Bolsheviks' November revolution: "You are miserable isolated individuals. You are bankrupt. You have played out your role. Go where you belong, to the dustheap of history."

Most convicted Wobblies, accepting their punishment and what they thought of as martyrdom, went to Leavenworth, but Haywood refused to surrender. Plagued by a history of ulcers and diabetes, and perhaps by cirrhosis of the liver, and fearful of another prison term, he jumped bail and turned up in the Soviet Union in 1921. Neither his close friends nor inveterate critics knew why he declined martyrdom and chose political exile. Whatever the reason, that decision betrayed Haywood's bail backers, brought them financial loss (and in one case suicide), and turned most of his former IWW comrades against him.

Escape to Russia, however, did not save Haywood from history's dustheap. Not really a Bolshevik, he did not fit into Lenin's or Trotsky's schemes for a new and better world. Expecting to find the Wobblies' utopian workers' state—or nonpolitical anarcho-syndicalist society—he found instead a system busily constructing its own political and industrial bureaucracy. The IWW's anti-organizational approach proved as unacceptable to Russia's new rulers as it had to America's. For a time Haywood directed a labor project in the Kuznets district, but by 1923 his dream of building a Wobbly utopia in Russia had soured.

Tired, sick, the strength draining from his huge body, Haywood retired to a room in Moscow's Lux Hotel. He later married a Russian national, but almost nothing of substance can be discovered about this marriage. Haywood usually kept to his Moscow hotel at the time Alexander Trachtenberg, an American Communist leader, made his pilgrimages to Moscow in the 1920's. Later, Trachtenberg remembered Haywood as a desperately lonely man, alien to Moscow's new society, who found solace only in the bottle and in the companionship of old Wobblies who somehow drifted into his hotel room. They would join their former chief in drink and song, going through the *Little Red Song Book* from cover to cover interminably, until they collapsed in a drunken stupor.

Such was Haywood's Moscow exile; he played no part in the construction of Soviet society. Ailing and frequently hospitalized, he tried to keep abreast of labor developments at home, and he found time to complete his unsatisfactory and distorted autobiography. On May 28, 1928, he died unmourned in a Moscow hospital. Russian officials placed part of his ashes alongside those of John Reed beneath a plaque in the Kremlin wall, and the remaining ashes were shipped to Waldheim Cemetery in Chicago for burial beside the graves of the Haymarket Riot martyrs.

To President Theodore Roosevelt, Haywood was an undesirable citizen; to Frank P. Walsh, reform Democrat and chairman of Woodrow Wilson's Commission on Industrial Relations, he was the "rugged intellectual, with his facility of phrasing, his marvelous memory and his singularly clear and apt method of illustration." To conservatives, Haywood was the voice of anarchy; to friends and admirers, he was the epitome of sweet, simple reason. To such labor foes as Samuel Gompers, he was an inept propagandizer and a smasher of trade unions; to his supporters, he was an effective administrator and a talented organizer. To Mary Gallagher, who directed the campaign to free Tom Mooney, he was a great leader in every way; to Ramsay MacDonald, he was a rough-hewn agitator, splendid with crowds but ineffectual as an administrator.

Scholars have done little to interpret Haywood's character other than allude to his rebellious spirit and frontier heritage. The essays of Charles Madison and Carl Hein tell us nothing that cannot be found in Haywood's autobiography; and in Patrick Renshaw's recent history of the IWW his treatment of Haywood is notable for the number of errors he makes in only three pages. Haywood's grossly inaccurate autobiography is a masterpiece of precise history compared to Renshaw's summary. Perusing the comments of Haywood's contemporaries and the analyses of scholars gives us no understanding of his personality. Unfortunately there is little evidence to support any of the differing versions of Haywood's life.

The only comment one can make with certainty is that Haywood, like most Wobblies, was neither an original thinker nor a theoretician. Haywood, in short, was not plagued by the "hob-goblin of little minds": consistency; his life is a tale of inconsistency.

During his early years with the WFM he displayed outstanding ability as an administrator and organizer. Willing to work long hours and to drive himself furiously, Haywood mastered the intricacies of trade unionism. From 1914 to 1917, in a later and vastly different environment, he also proved to be an industrious union official. During those years, when the IWW experienced its most rapid growth, Haywood gave the Wobblies their first taste of effective administration under a rationalized central office. Between these tours of duty as a union official he devoted himself to agitation and to freewheeling revolutionary oratory in which he impressed many observers with his anti-disciplinarian, anti-organizational, anarchistic personality.

The inconsistencies abound. In a life that was shadowed by violence, few radicals ever expressed the doctrine of passive resistance so forcefully or played so prominent a part in nonviolent labor demonstrations. A denigrator of effete intellectuals, Haywood nevertheless had intellectual pretensions of his own. He harangued strikers in the working-class vernacular, but he also read widely (and deeply), and wrote with considerable skill. It is impossible to pinpoint the time when he began to read serious fiction and nonfiction, but during his incarceration in 1917–18 he wrote movingly to Frank Walsh about the latest Mark Twain he had read. As a writer—he was temporary editor of the *Miners' Magazine,* a contributing editor to the *International Socialist Review,* and a regular commentator in the IWW press—Haywood developed from an immature and awkward stylist into a master of the caustic comment and the philippic phrase, if not an author of graceful and closely reasoned economic and social treatises. In his writings and speeches on economics, politics, sex, and religion he wielded one pen in the modern camp of harsh realism and the other in maudlin Victorian romanticism. Haywood appealed to immigrant workers in the East and to migrant workers in the West, as well as to such bohemian intellectuals as John Reed and Max Eastman.

In the last analysis, Haywood fits no pattern. Unlike the typical labor leader, who begins his career as a radical, finds success, and becomes more conservative, Haywood began his union career as a conservative, discovered success, and became a radical. A man of many talents—administrator, organizer, agitator, speaker, writer —he developed none of these to its utmost, which was perhaps his gravest failing. A labor leader who was at home both with wage workers and intellectuals (an unusual combination in the United States), he led a labor organization that was out of touch with most workers and he frustrated many intellectuals by his refusal to accept martyrdom in 1921. In Russia, he neither served American radicalism nor built the new utopia.

Haywood's life and the history of the Wobblies support an ambivalent conclusion about the results of dissent in America. Dissenting at the outset, Wobblies maintained that poor immigrants and dispossessed native Americans could be organized, given a sense of purpose, and taught to confront authority nonviolently. As they proceeded to do just this, American society accommodated the Wobbly-induced radicalism within the existing system. Rexford Tugwell, commenting upon the IWW's ability to organize casual workers, remarked in 1920: "No world regenerating philosophy comes out of them and they are not going to inherit the earth. When we are a bit more orderly they will disappear."

Tugwell was right. During World War I the federal government influenced Western employers to be more "orderly"; lumbermen established company unionism and the eight-hour day, and owners of copper mines improved working conditions and created grievance machinery. Many Wobblies watched American society vitiate their radicalism by accommodating to it, and ended up by joining that society. Ralph Chaplin is the best example of this process: he became a member of the Congregational church, an ardent patriot, and an even more ardent anti-Communist.

Wobblies who did not opt for reform capitalism lost the faith for other reasons. The IWW's anti-organizational credo, its utter abomination of existing institutions, and its refusal (or, perhaps, inability) to conceptualize an alternative of its own to the structural arrangements of American society (so much like the dilemma of the contemporary New Left) resulted in internal anarchy and recurrent secessions, divisions, and organizational collapses. Thus some Wobblies— Elizabeth Gurley Flynn, James P. Cannon, William Z. Foster are good examples—eventually located the disciplined organization they craved in the Communist Party. Others kept the original faith, never losing their belief in a utopian society bereft of a coercive state. When their dissent moved from speech to action, from criticism to resistance, they felt the heavy hand of a repressive state. If America was capable of domesticating its radicals by offering them reforms, it could also smash them with a vengeance.

Never able to forget his 1915 utopian dream, yet unable to adjust to Communist discipline, Haywood's ashes were divided between the land of his miserable exile and America, among an earlier generation of martyred dissenters.

11

SAMUEL M. JONES AND
THE GOLDEN RULE IN ACTION

PETER J. FREDERICK

As the United States entered the twentieth century, increasing numbers of Americans began to take stock of the immense social changes that industrialization and urbanization had brought to their country. Among these were men and women who used as their social yardstick neither small town values nor the tenets of American republicanism, but looked instead to the social teachings of nondenominational Christianity.

Religious values had long been an integral part of American reform movements. From the Great Awakening of the 1730s and 1740s to the temperance crusades of the nineteenth century, Americans had drawn upon religious principles to criticize the drift of their society. But while many of these earlier reforms were products of institutionalized churches, by the turn of the twentieth century many of those same churches had become integrated into the power structure of America and were busying themselves promulgating the Gospel of Wealth and Social Darwinism, both of which equated material success with social superiority. In the first decades of the new century this acceptance of secular values by organized religion would be met with a religious movement known as the Social Gospel. Developed by religious reformers such as Walter Rauschenbusch, the Social Gospel sought to make Christianity once again the religion of the common people by applying the teachings of Christ to the everyday world.

But anticipating the Social Gospel movement itself was another movement that sought to apply the Sermon on the Mount to the world of monopoly capitalism. As Peter Frederick details in this essay, Samuel K. Jones and other "Knights of the Golden Rule" took seriously the dictum "Do unto others as you would have them do unto you" and attempted to order their public and private lives in accordance with it. The story of Jones provides eloquent testimony to the importance of moral concerns in the shaping of American life.

How do Samuel Jones' methods in the running of Toledo compare with those of "Boss" Cox in Cincinnati, as described by Zane L. Miller in Reading 5? Do you think that Jones's approach to city government and the running of his business would work today?

In the late spring of 1904 the Common Council of Toledo, Ohio, extended the franchise of a private street railway company for twenty-five years. The mayor of Toledo, Samuel Milton Jones, who had opposed the extension, promptly vetoed the action. For several years Jones had advocated a

---

Reprinted from Peter J. Frederick, *Knights of the Golden Rule: The Intellectual as Christian Social Reformer in the 1890s* (Lexington, Ky.: University Press of Kentucky, 1976), by permission of the publisher. (c) 1976 by the University Press of Kentucky.

public street railway system, and this last of many skirmishes with the city council and the private interest groups of the city was bitterly contested. Five councilmen were on the railway company's payroll in 1903 and the general manager of the *Toledo Times* spent $75,000 to combat the mayor's influence. On the night of July 12, Jones died; the next day the railway company's stock rose twenty-four points. What other reformer in this study could claim such an immediate and practical impact of his death, much less his life? Samuel Jones put the golden rule into action. In death, as in life, he had a singular influence on the people and events of his age.

On the same day as the railway stock was rising, an estimated 55,000 persons filed past Jones's coffin. His funeral on July 15 was equally impressive. Some 15,000 mourners gathered in front of Jones's home to hear a eulogy delivered by his friend and successor as mayor, Brand Whitlock. "I know not how many thousands were there," Whitlock recalled, for "they were standing on the lawns in a mass that extended across the street and into the yards on the farther side. Down to the corner, and into the side streets, they were packed, and they stood in long lines all the way out to the cemetery." Of more significance than the numbers, however, was the diverse character of those who attended Jones's funeral: "In that crowd there were all sorts of that one sort he knew as humanity without distinction —judges, and women of prominence and women he alone would have included in humanity, there were thieves, and prizefighters—and they all stood there with the tears streaming down their faces." Whitlock spoke eloquently of Jones's massive sympathy for the poor, the oppressed, and the outcast. Affectionately called "the Golden Rule man" by his many friends, Jones "saw that in the gentleness of love lay the mightiest power in the world." Although accused of being a dreamer by friends and enemies alike, which indeed he was, Jones's aspirations for a society founded on love, equality, brotherhood, and dignity were—in his Toledo environment—partly fulfilled. "With him religion, politics, business and life were one," Whitlock said, and "he could not separate them nor distinguish them." As Whitlock and many others understood, in Jones the dream and deed were one.

Jones was a rare kind of intellectual reformer. He read widely in European and American literature and philosophy, but the knowledge and insights he acquired were used not to torment his own soul but to improve others' lives. He quoted texts, not in obscure little journals, but in city parks, Polish halls, and police courts. He wrote books, pamphlets, poetry, and songs, not for other intellectuals, but for factory and oil field workers. Because Jones applied his intellectual ideals and dreams to his life and deeds as businessman and mayor, he suffered less guilt and fewer self-doubts than the other reformers in the new religious movement. He was influenced by the same sources as they, notably Tolstoy, Mazzini, Whitman, and Emerson, but did not, like so many others, take refuge in the comforts of idealism. These inspirations caused Jones to dream, with the other knights, of the Altrurian millennium. But he knew well that until he put himself "into just relation with my fellow-men," as he wrote in his annual Christmas message to his workers in 1902, it would be "absolutely impossible for me to know perfect happiness." He therefore took small, concrete steps, an approach that enabled him to see the practical accomplishments of his work. In 1894 he "resolved to make an effort to apply the Golden Rule as a rule of conduct," and in 1897 proudly reported that "after nearly three years of a test I am pleased to say the golden rule works." He not only yearned for a world as he believed it ought to be but also was able to understand and deal with it as it was. Rather than engaging in self-reproach for failing to be the reformer he thought he ought to be, he generally accepted himself for the man that he was.

Unlike the other members of the new religious movement, Jones was not bothered by any conflict between collectivist institutions and individual freedom. On the one hand, he recognized, like Bellamy and Lloyd, that since "the trust is here, and here to stay," the only way to overcome it was to own it; "we must all be in the trust . . .

whereby through the organized love of the municipality, state, and nation, we can minister to one another better than we can in our individual capacity." But on the other hand, like his good friend Ernest Crosby, he revered the freedom of the individual. He told a crowded hall of immigrants in Toledo: "I don't want to rule anybody. . . . Nobody has a right to rule anybody else. Each individual must rule himself." The apparent contradiction of achieving self-rule within a collective people's trust did not trouble him, nor did an inconsistency of political beliefs. In his Fifth Annual message to the Common Council of Toledo, he called for municipal ownership of all public utilities and for expanded municipal responsibilities at the same time as he asserted that "they are governed best who are governed least." His constituency, he once said, was "the whole human family." He believed in the "unity of the entire race" and was "content to be one in the mass." Like Emerson, whom he admired, his reverence for both the "one" and the "mass" was thoroughly consistent.

Nor was Jones bothered by a conflict between the principle of widespread democratic participation and the need for bringing exceptional talents to bear on social problems. "The idea that a few of us are endowed with the 'divine right of kings,' and are especially fitted to govern or rule what we have called the lower classes, is undemocratic, as well as unchristian and of course unbrotherly. . . . If we are a democracy, we must believe in the people; there is no escape from that conclusion." And yet, his whole later life was one of using his privileged positions as employer and mayor to do good, as he interpreted it, for the people of his city. Despite his prominence, however, there was absolutely no pretense or intellectual elitism about him. When a visitor chided him for taking off his hat to a scrubwoman in the Toledo City Hall, he commented that "if I should not take off my hat . . . to a scrubwoman who does the dirty work that I don't want to do, then I will not take it off to any one." Whitlock wrote that Jones was "always going down to the city prisons, or to the workhouses, and talking to the poor devils there, quite as if he were one of them, which indeed he

felt he was." Jones himself wrote: "I like the 'common people' because they are most democratic. They believe in one another. They are neighborly and helpful. The rich man has no neighbors—only rivals and parasites." Jones trusted the average citizen to rule himself and sought only to remove artificial obstacles to his freedom and happiness. There were no rules in his factory except the golden rule. He loved the workers in his factory and oil fields, and the tramps, vagrants, and prostitutes of Toledo. They returned his love with loyalty to his business, with votes in his four mayoralty campaigns, and with tears at his funeral.

Samuel Jones was born in a humble cottage in North Wales in 1846. At the age of three he came to the United States in steerage with his family, settling near Utica, New York, where his father was a tenant farmer. In his youth Sam worked successively as a farm laborer, in a stone quarry, in a sawmill, and as a wiper and greaser on a steamship. He recalled in 1899 that he had had less than thirty months of formal schooling in his life. At the age of eighteen he traveled with fifteen cents in his pocket to the new oil fields near Titusville, Pennsylvania. He struggled for several years in the fields as a tool sharpener and dresser, pipe liner, pumper, and driller. Gradually, he acquired enough savings to go into business for himself, as did so many others in the early years of the oil boom in the United States. In 1886 Jones moved to Lima, Ohio, where he drilled the first large oil well in Ohio, and became one of the original incorporators of the Ohio Oil Company. Shortly thereafter, however, he sold out to Rockefeller's Standard Oil. He never criticized Rockefeller's business practices, for Jones rarely, if ever, blamed individuals for evils which he believed intrinsic to a corrupt system. "Our trouble is not with the bosses, with the aristocrats, with the corporations or the Standard Oil Company," he wrote, "but with a system that denies brotherhood and makes a weaker brother the legitimate prey of every strong man." Although lacking the predator instinct, Jones continued to prove that he was a strong man in the oil business. He formed the Acme Oil Company, which drilled oil in new fields in northwest Ohio, and in 1892 and 1893 he invented a number of labor-saving devices for oil wells. For the manufacture of his many inventions, Jones opened the Acme Sucker Rod Company in Toledo in the depression year of 1894. As the owner of a factory and oil wells for the next ten years until his death, and as mayor of Toledo for seven of those years, he consistently embodied, as Brand Whitlock said, "the greatest original practical example" of the golden rule in action.

The awakening of Jones's social conscience coincided with the launching of his career as a factory owner. As Jones began in 1894 to manufacture clasp joint couplings, pull-rods, clamp stirrups, sucker rods, and other oil-well appliances, he also discovered his social obligations for improving the quality of life for others. He had felt some sympathy for the degraded human condition before 1894, but he was shocked by the sight of unemployed men begging for work during the depression. "I never had seen anything like it. Their piteous appeals and the very pathos of the looks of many of them stirred the very deepest sentiments of compassion within me." That same year he read George Herron's "Philosophy of the Lord's Prayer," which made a lasting impression on his understanding of brotherhood and the duties of man. These insights, his sense of the hopelessness of the socioeconomic situation, directly influenced Jones to apply the golden rule in his business. Three years later he wrote to W. T. Stead, "I have been a close reader of all that George D. Herron has ever written, and believe he is a prophet of a better era." Jones also read *Wealth against Commonwealth* in 1894. At the memorial meeting in Chicago after Lloyd's death, Jones recalled the notable impact that reading and meeting Lloyd in 1894 had had on him. "Lloyd's great idea of a Golden Rule government for America unfolded itself before my vision" and made him, as he said, a "Golden Rule man."

Jones's initial impetus to reform was prompted by Herron and Lloyd and by depression conditions of unemployment and suffering. His social thought continued to be influenced by the familiar inspirational sources of the new religious movement, most significantly the Bible, Whitman, and Tolstoy. Jones was an avid reader, though hardly a sophisticated intellect, and had a remarkable facility for quoting poems and passages from memory. In a statement in 1901 of the intellectual influences on his life, he cited the New Testament, Isaiah, Job, and Psalms as the primary "help to the development of my life." Among poets he named only Whitman, "the greatest poet of democracy"; among other writers, he most admired Emerson, Edward Carpenter, and Tolstoy. In other lists he also mentioned Ruskin, Morris, Mazzini, Francis of Assisi, and Lamennais. Finally, as an integral member of the new religious movement, Jones frequently cited Crosby, Markham, and Howells, as well as Lloyd and Herron, as contributing to his social thought.

His favorite poet-philosophers were Carpenter, Emerson, and Whitman. Under the advice of Ernest Crosby, Jones began reading Carpenter in 1897 and three years later wrote to the Tolstoyan Englishman to praise his books, all of which he owned, as "some of the loftiest and most helpful things that I have thus far read." Shorly before writing this letter, Jones had officiated at the wedding of two single-taxers. In an unorthodox ceremony, conducted as the couple wished, he read from Genesis and from Carpenter's *Love's Coming of Age*. Emerson's essays in Jones's personal book collection were well marked, particularly "The Over-Soul" and "Self-Reliance." These two essays helped Jones to see the unity of life without having to sacrifice his faith in individual integrity and freedom. Although he never renounced his commitment to self-reliance, Jones gradually inclined, as he wrote to Eugene Debs in 1899, "more and more to Walt Whitman's idea . . . that there is no possible way of saving a fragment of society, but the *whole thing* must be raised altogether." Jones therefore ardently believed both in individual regeneration and in collective salvation.

The primary source for his faith in individual regeneration, other than Emerson, was the ethic of Jesus. Jones's copy of the Bible and a volume of selections from the teachings of Jesus were both abundantly and vigorously underscored.

Among the passages which he not only marked but also frequently quoted in his speeches were those on nonresistance to evil, not judging others, being like little children, and the rich man's obligations and difficult path to heaven. After the nonresistance passage, he wrote: "our rule"; elsewhere in the Sermon on the Mount he added in the margin: "all life is one" and "Jesus the Iconoclast." Next to the Bible on his desk in the mayor's office lay a volume of Whitman's *Leaves of Grass.* Whitlock reported that the book was heavily underscored in red and that Jones often was so excited over a Whitman passage that he would call him up to read it to him. Two pictures of Whitman hung in his office, and many visitors to the mayor could not leave until they had consented to listen to him quote from Whitman. Like Jesus and Emerson, Whitman confirmed Jones's understanding of democracy by celebrating both the individual and the individual *en masse.* After praising Emerson, Carpenter, and Mazzini in a letter to a minister in 1900, Jones wrote that "the one who has led me to see further into the meaning of a perfect Democracy than any of the others —perhaps all—is Walt Whitman." Two years earlier, while bedridden with illness for four days, Jones was reading the Gospels, the *Social Gospel,* Howells's *A Traveller from Altruria,* Lloyd's *Labor Copartnership,* and "a whole lot of Walt Whitman." Six months later he wrote Horace Traubel agreeing enthusiastically to join the Walt Whitman Fellowship and said that he would "always wish to be counted as one thoroughly and hopelessly gone in 'Whitmania.' "

Whitman helped Jones develop his concept of democratic politics, which he applied as mayor; John Ruskin and William Morris helped him develop his concept of cooperative economics, which he applied as factory owner. One of Jones's central beliefs was that art was a necessary and pleasurable part of work. In his book, *The New Right,* he quoted no less than four times Ruskin's statement that "the wealth of a nation may be estimated by the number of happy people that are employed in making useful things." Another of Jones's favorite quotations was Morris's conviction that "art is the expression of a man's joy in labor." He owned many volumes of the works of both English reformers and frequently recommended them to his friends. Jones's "letters of labor and love" to his workers were strikingly similar to Ruskin's letters to English workingmen in *Fors Clavigera.* Soon after Ruskin's death in 1900, Jones delivered a talk on him at Golden Rule Hall, reading from Ruskin's *Unto This Last* to his workers on the proper (paternal) relationship of an employer to his employees. Ruskin was, Jones said, "one of the greatest, noblest, and purest men of our generation. . . . He loved the beautiful and artistic, and indeed gave to the world superb, artistic ideals." Jones's response to Ruskin was not only aesthetic but also practical. His conduct as an employer was dedicated to insuring joyful labor for his workers in the making of "useful things." He introduced profit-sharing in his factory and treated his workers with an ambiguous mixture of paternalism and fraternity. Ultimately, the chief object of the Acme Sucker Rod Company, he wrote, was not making money but making men, which was identical with Ruskin's (and Emerson's) definition of wealth.

The influence of Mazzini helped Jones incorporate his personal responsibilities as factory owner and mayor into a larger view of progress toward a collective utopian society. Jones often quoted Mazzini's assertion that "the next great word is 'Association.' " Mazzini's vision of the oneness of humanity, as well as his emphasis on the duties rather than the rights of man, were central to Jones's social thought. He concluded *The New Right* with a distinctly Mazzinian chapter on the Brotherhood of Man, which was prefaced by a long quotation from the Italian. "America's task," Jones wrote, "is to teach larger views of life and duty." After his book was published, he regretted his choice of title, which had been formulated because his depression experiences had convinced him of man's inalienable right to work. This was "the new right" which Jones deemed imperative. But in a letter written a year after publication, he said that there had been "too much about *rights* to the neglect and hurt of *duties;* there are no rights except as they flow from duties performed. So I am more inclined to call attention to the NEW DUTY than to the NEW RIGHT." Two days before writing the letter, Jones had written another indicating that he was thoroughly absorbed in the writings of Mazzini: "I do not know anything loftier . . . than his chapter on the duties of men." Despite his enthusiasm, Jones's admiration for Mazzini was not unqualified. He opposed the Italian's revolutionary militancy. In the margin of a chapter on Mazzini's organization of the "Young Italy" movement, Jones wrote: "1898 I don't believe in this at all. . . . I don't believe in fighting by physical force." He much preferred the gentler, nonresistant doctrines of Francis of Assisi, William Lloyd Garrison, and Tolstoy.

Portraits of Tolstoy were the only ones, other than Whitman's, to hang in two places in Jones's cluttered office. The mayor often wrote to the Russian and adopted many of his ideas. Jones's understanding and literal application of the Sermon on the Mount, his repudiation of institutionalized religion, his relationship with his employees, his pacifism and opposition to the use of force by government, and his yearning for the simple life all bore the imprint of Tolstoy's influence. He apparently knew about him even before his contacts in the mid-1890s with Crosby and other Tolstoy enthusiasts like Whitlock, who wrote that Jones "was full of Tolstoy at that time." In September 1898 Jones wrote to Tolstoy to say that he had been reading his books for many years and that they had been of great help. He told the Russian that as mayor of Toledo he had "tried to hold up the doctrine of overcoming evil with good as the only scientific doctrine that we could tie to and expect anything from." He expressed the hope that he might visit him someday as Crosby and Jane Addams had done. In an excess of enthusiasm he told Tolstoy that his teachings on war "have had much to do" with ending the American war with Spain and signed the letter "with very tender love." Tolstoy expressed appreciation for Jones's friendship and good wishes in his reply, which Jones proudly included next to a letter from Howells in his book *The New Right.*

Jones's library contained most of the works of Tolstoy, and most were copiously underscored and marked with innumerable marginal comments. In *What to Do?, Resurrection,* and a collection of Tolstoy's essays, for example, Jones reacted with exclamation points and enthusiastic assents to Tolstoyan statements of love, nonresistance, the evils of the penal system, the responsibilities of the wealthy, and the need to follow literally the commandments of Jesus. After an injunction to obey Jesus' law of love, Jones added "the law of my being." Wherever Tolstoy rationalized his conscience for his inability to assist all the poor who sought his help, Jones responded with pained agreement. In two places, for example, he wrote: "the universal experience" and "as I do." These are only three of scores of appended comments by the ardent reader. The only places he apparently disagreed with the Russian were where Tolstoy indicated a lack of complete trust and faith in the common people. In *What to Do?* Tolstoy remarked that the rural peasants could not survive well in the city, and Jones, himself an ex-ruralite, commented, "not altogether true." Where Tolstoy asserted that all workingmen could not appreciate high culture, Jones added, "almost all." These, however, were rare qualifications.

By 1899, with the English publication of *Resurrection,* Tolstoy's novel condemning capital punishment and penal practices, Jones's indebtedness to him was unqualified. The mayor talked more and more about Tolstoy in his letters. He wrote to Washington Gladden in April 1900, saying that if the current rumor that Admiral Dewey was going to run for president as an anti-imperialist were true, he would surely support him. Jones compared Dewey to Tolstoy, who had also been a soldier he pointed out, before his great change in middle age. In the early years of the new century, Tolstoy's name appeared with regularity in Jones's lists of "the best minds of today" with whom he agreed on the subjects of war, nonresistance, penal reform, love, and simplicity. In July 1903 Jones arranged to have a picture done of Tolstoy, painted for his office by an artist from Hull House. Beneath the painting, as Jones requested, was an inscription from *Resurrection:*

"Men think there are circumstances when one may deal with human beings without love, and there are no such circumstances. One may deal with things without love, one may cut down trees, make bucks, hammer iron, without love, but you cannot deal with men without it." The selection was an appropriate one. For almost ten years Jones had been dealing with people with love. His ethic of putting the golden rule to action required no other guide.

Samuel Jones had only one rule—the golden rule law of love—in his oil fields and factory. As owner of the Acme Oil Company and the Acme Sucker Rod Company, he initiated measures that were far ahead of their time. In 1897 he introduced the eight-hour day for oil well drillers, a first in Ohio, if not the nation, and sought to persuade the Western Oil Men's Association to do the same. His rationale was that to divide the day into three segments of eight hours rather than into two segments of twelve hours would be both more humane for the workers and potentially more profitable for employers. He showed how labor-saving devices (made at Acme Sucker Rod), in conjunction with dividing the day, not only enabled more men to work but also increased production. His practice of increasing from four to six the number of men working on each well during each shift in his oil fields, he admitted, had lowered profits; he had, however, hired more men, lightened the work of all, and insured that "the men who did the work got the money." These were, he insisted, more worthy achievements. In his Christmas message to the workers of the Acme Oil Company in 1897, Jones announced that the company "will never go back to the twelve hour plan." While hundreds of oil drillers were having difficulty finding even one hour's work, it made no sense, he said, to ask others to work twelve hours. "The Acme Oil Company has not yet *made any money. We may never make any.* No matter; we will continue to *stand flat* on the Golden Rule."

Jones's factory employees in Toledo fared even better than his oil workers under the same rule. He frequently wrote inspiring, sentimental poems which were set to music for his workers to sing.

One of his songs was "Divide the Day," a "practical" solution to the problem of unemployment:

Divide up the day! divide up the day!
In more ways than one 'tis a plan that will pay,
    Then all who desire will have work for their
    hand,
    And the problem is solved that darkens our land.
With millions of idle in fruitful employ,
The homes of the workers will echo with joy;
    Then want and distress will flee far away,
    We can bring it about just by splitting the day.

In addition to his poems and songs, he also wrote annual Christmas letters and even weekly "letters of love and labor" for his employees. At the end of the year in 1900 and again in 1901 he compiled the weekly messages into a small book and added a quotation before each letter from authors "whom I believe to be preaching the Christ principle." All the letters were written in plain, simple, yet unpatronizing language. They generally, though not always, followed his commitment to discuss, rather than to preach. "I wish to write as friend to friend; I wish to have with you simple heart to heart talks, as brother to brother." The several topics of the talks touched on specific reforms introduced by Jones into his factory, as well as his beliefs about trade unionism (he approved, but had a contented company union), democracy, liberty, and fellowship. It was fitting that a letter on "Service Brings Its Own Reward," in which Jones mused somewhat vaguely about equality and helping others, was followed by "A Word on Vacations," in which he announced the continuation of a week's paid vacation for all employees of six months or more. Jones often paired a statement of principle with an announced practical reform, which is what the golden rule in action was all about.

In December 1901 Jones took stock by reporting on the progress of the Acme Sucker Rod Company since 1894. His employees worked eight hours instead of ten; they were paid a $2.00 minimum wage per day for eight hours instead of the Toledo average of $1.25 to $1.50 per day for ten hours. They received a week's vacation and enjoyed two company picnics each year with pay. There were no bosses or timekeepers in the factory ("every man his own boss," "every man his own timekeeper"), and there were no lists of rules: "just the Golden Rule—that's all." In the company cafeteria a worker could get a hot lunch for fifteen cents (the "Golden Rule Dinner") which cost the company twenty-one cents to prepare. The rationale for the dinner, Jones explained, was fellowship, good nourishment, and sparing the worker's wife the effort and cost of making an extra lunch. A cooperative insurance program was in effect by which 1 percent of a man's wages would be deducted and matched by the company. And at the end of the year Jones gave each employee a 5 percent Christmas dividend on his total wages for the year. In his annual Christmas message a year later Jones announced a plan by which his employees, if they wished, could exchange their 5 percent dividend for shares in the company. His intent, he said, was to eliminate the distinction between employer and employee and to create a truly cooperative experiment by equal division of all earnings among all members of the company community.

There was more. Jones needed a foundry, but when he acquired the property adjacent to his factory he turned the land into Golden Rule Park instead. The park was made available to his workers and their families. They met there evenings and Sunday afternoons to picnic, listen to speeches, and enjoy concerts performed by the Golden Rule Band. A large room in the factory was converted into a meeting room, Golden Rule Hall, where various factory clubs met and where the workers could hear speakers such as Lloyd, Herron, Gladden, Debs, Jane Addams, and other reformers whom Jones attracted to Toledo. A typical meeting in Golden Rule Hall was held in October 1899, near the completion of Jones's gubernatorial campaign. The hall was filled with workers. The meeting opened with the singing of Jones's "Industrial Freedom" by the Acme Chorus Club:

> With justice done to everyone, then happy shall we be,

> Poverty will disappear, the prisoners will be free;
> The right to work, the right to live, the love of liberty—
> All God's best gifts to the people.

George Herron then spoke for an hour on the new collective economy presaged by Jesus. The Chorus sang "Divide the Day," followed by an address by Jones on "A Golden Rule Government." The meeting concluded with the singing of Jones's "The Man Without a Party."

Jones went beyond specific factory reforms by seeking to instill self-respect in his employees. He refused to ask questions about a job applicant's past; he regularly hired ex-criminals, gamblers, and tramps. He fully believed that "every tramp is a good citizen spoiled" by the demoralizing effects of looking for work and that "social conditions at present make it a hundred times easier for a man to do wrong than right." An employee once broke three sets of castings in a week and a foreman asked Jones what to do about him. Jones inquired into how long the man had been working and with how much vacation. Upon learning that he had had five days off in two years, Jones gave him a two-week paid vacation. The absence of rules or time clocks in the factory was an indication of Jones's trust in his workers. He encouraged criticisms of his policies and often chided his employees for not using the suggestion box. His innumerable assurances of the equality and dignity of all men and women were confirmed when he told his workers that the death of a nineteen-year-old employee in early October 1901 was to be mourned equally with the death of President McKinley three weeks earlier. When Jones announced the 5 percent Christmas dividend he wrote that "this is not intended as a charitable gift; it is an expression of good will, a recognition of faithful service, and an admission that the present wage system is not scientific, therefore not a just system." He continually reassured his workers that his apparently benevolent reforms were not charity but justice. His will provided for $10,000 worth of stock to be given to trustees elected by the employees of the company to do with as they wished. Jones had a realistic, self-ironic awareness of the relationship between his reforms and his profit margin. "Most manufacturers . . . keep about eight out of every ten dollars which their employees earn for them," he said. "I keep only about seven, and so they call me 'Golden Rule' Jones."

Because he occupied a respectable position in the community as a businessman and because his eccentric views were not yet widely known, Jones was nominated as a compromise Republican candidate for mayor of Toledo in the spring of 1897. The party machine tried to force him to campaign on the issue of abolishing the saloon, but he refused, preferring to establish his own issues. These included municipal ownership of utilities and street railway companies, support for labor and the unemployed, and the application of the golden rule to government as he had already begun to apply it to industry. His victory was a narrow one—518 votes out of some 21,000. In a letter of gratitude to Lloyd for his help in the campaign, Jones noted proudly that the ward surrounding his factory had given McKinley a majority of 132 votes in 1896 but had overwhelmingly voted for him by a majority of 435 votes. "It only goes to show," he wrote, "that the common people are quick to respond to just a little touch of Golden Rule fair play."

In his First Annual Message to the Common Council, Jones announced his program. He would support a publicly owned natural gas plant (an old and controversial issue in Toledo), municipal ownership of lighting, home rule for Ohio cities, more public parks and playgrounds, and free music for the people. In addition, he advocated a day-labor plan rather than the contract system for street improvement workers, a higher wage for shorter hours for all city employees, and the municipal responsibility of caring for tramps by providing them with "a bath, a good bed and wholesome food." These men, Jones said, should be required to work for their food and lodging, thus "restoring their manhood—in many cases well nigh crushed by the hopelessness of the despair into which they have fallen." In his succeeding years as mayor, Jones also endorsed the municipal ownership of all utilities, a merit system

for hiring and promotion, complete nonpartisanship in all city offices, free public baths and pools, free public skating rinks and sleigh rides for children, and municipal free vocational education and kindergartens. He did not in any way seek more power for his own office; rather, he endorsed a referendum instead of the mayor's veto on actions of the Common Council. He donated his salary as mayor to charity.

Jones's accomplishments were mixed. He fared best in instituting most of the free public services he wanted, in providing lodging and public works employment for tramps and vagrants, and in improving wages and hours for city employees. He failed in his attempts for home rule and municipal ownership of all utilities. He neither abolished the saloon, as some of his supporters had hoped, nor bowed to the dictates of the local party machine, which was furious with him for his repudiation of traditional patronage appointments. Jones admitted in a letter to Lloyd only seven months into his first term that "we have not done very much that is radical in the way of reform in city government." He realized, however, that "a good deal has been done in the way of reforming public sentiment in Toledo and starting it in the right direction." His style was unique and his enthusiasm was irrepressible. Lincoln Steffens, after visiting with Jones, was so overwhelmed by his ambitious efforts that he exploded to Brand Whitlock: "why, that man's program will take a thousand years!"

The most publicized and controversial practices of Jones's tenure as mayor were in the areas of law enforcement and penal reform. He improved the conditions of Toledo's jails. He took away the policeman's side arms and heavy clubs, replacing them with light canes. "I would be glad," he said once, "to see every revolver and every club in the world go over Niagara Falls, or better still, over the brink of Hell." He was strongly in favor of abolition of capital punishment and told Crosby once how proud he was of the warden of the Ohio penitentiary who had resigned rather than preside over an electrocution. Jones was decisively influenced by Tolstoy's severe indictment of the Russian penal system in

Resurrection. Like Tolstoy, Jones fully believed that drunkards, gamblers, prostitutes, tramps, and petty thieves were victims of an unjust social order and that only the poor went to jail for drunkenness or gambling. Once fined for contempt of court, he pulled out his checkbook and paid the fine in order to show that "the only crime our civilization punishes is the crime of being poor." His political enemies often charged that his lenient policies encouraged crime in Toledo and made the city a haven for criminals and prostitutes. Although these accusations were untrue, Jones did everything he could to encourage them by his unorthodox behavior as a police magistrate.

On Monday mornings Jones often presided in police court, as the mayor was empowered to do in the absence of the police judge. He and his secretary, Whitlock, competed with each other to see who could dismiss more prisoners arrested during the weekend. Jones once discharged two men arrested for petty larceny after lecturing them—and the many visitors who crowded into the courtroom to watch him—on the inadequate rehabilitation provided at the state penitentiary. One day a drunken tramp in possession of a pistol was arrested. Jones preached on the evils of "hellish" weapons and sentenced the man to smash the pistol to bits with a sledge hammer. He was particularly sympathetic to the prostitute's plight. He told Elbert Hubbard that whenever a woman of the streets was brought before him he fined each man present in the courtroom ten cents and himself a dollar for permitting prostitution to exist. When an irate delegation of Toledo's wealthy and prominent ladies came to his office to demand that he drive the prostitutes out of their city, he gently asked them where he should send them. "Over to Detroit or to Cleveland, or merely out into the country? They have to go somewhere, you know." Then he proposed to them that if each promised to take one prostitute into her home and care for her until she found honest work, he would do the same for two of the most hardened harlots in the city. As Whitlock reported the incident, the ladies "looked at him,

then looked at each other, and seeing how utterly hopeless this strange man was, they went away."

In a letter to Crosby, Jones justified his lenient policies as a judge by saying that he had no right to do anything as a judge that he would not do as a man, a principle that Crosby thoroughly understood. "I found no difficulty in disposing of these cases," he wrote, "by the application of the law of love." In Jones's office hung a plaque with the inscription "Judge not that ye be not judged." In a letter to a Toledo newspaper, he said that his actions in court were based on the golden rule. "There are two methods of dealing with people whose liberty makes them a menace to society— on the one hand, prisons, penalties, punishment, hatred and hopeless despair; and on the other, asylums, sympathy, love, help and hope." His method seemed to work. Although the outraged leading citizens of the city charged Jones with encouraging crime, under his merciful policies the number of crimes and arrests in Toledo, a notoriously sinful city, appreciably decreased. By 1902, however, a bill, framed by his opponents in Toledo preventing the mayor from sitting as a police magistrate, was passed by the Ohio state legislature.

Although he had been a reluctant candidate for mayor in 1897, Jones eagerly announced in February 1899 that he was a candidate for reelection as "a Lincoln Republican." His party, however, distressed with his eccentricities and furious with his disregard for the party machine, refused to renominate him. On March 4, therefore, Jones declared that he would run as an independent. The ensuing one-month campaign, according to an Ohio historian, was the "wildest in Toledo's history, and one of the wildest in the country." Jones's quest for reelection was bitterly opposed by both major party machines, business leaders (especially the utility and traction companies), the newspapers, and every minister in the city except two. His enemies called him "Millionaire Jones" and the "Golden Sucker Man." The Toledo Pastors Union arranged for the revivalist Samuel P. Jones to come to Toledo in late March, just prior to the election, ostensibly to preach against the saloon. His real purpose, however, as his revival sermons revealed, was to charge the mayor with abetting crime, prostitution, and drinking by his policies. On the last day of the revival, Samuel P. Jones openly attacked Samuel M. Jones as a "devil mayor" who had instituted a rule of hate rather than of love in Toledo. The revivalist argued that he was for the "Golden Rule up to a certain point and then I want to take up the shotgun and the club." The mayor responded by stating that in his version of Christianity there was no place whatsoever for either the shotgun and the club or anti-Christian revivalism. Despite the organized strength and financial resources of his opposition, Jones won the election in a landslide. He received 70 percent of the votes, four times as many as his nearest competitor, and won every precinct but one. His victory, he said, represented "a great triumph for the common people." He was right; almost no one else had supported him.

No sooner had he won than a movement commenced to elect him governor of Ohio in the fall of 1899. In late August, Jones declared his candidacy as an independent under the banner of "equality of opportunity for all." In many respects, Jones's program was a typically progressive one, similar to Robert La Follette's in Wisconsin at the same time. He called for nonpartisan politics, home rule for cities, referendums and initiatives, public ownership of utilities, improved standards of work for labor, the abolition of the contract system for public works projects, and the relief of unemployment as a positive responsibility of the state. Although running formally on this platform, he campaigned much of the time as an anti-imperialist. He lost the election, carrying only Cleveland and, to his particular happiness, Toledo. In a public statement after the election, he indicated that he was gratified by the more than 100,000 votes he received and interpreted "the non-partisan vote in Ohio . . . as favoring a Christian policy towards the Philippines." Privately, however, he wrote to Lloyd, somewhat despondently, that "I must . . . let others do the fighting." He understood his loss to mean that political justice and social peace could not be won by political action alone, but also needed "an awakened social conscience and an enlightened intellect."

Characteristically, Jones wrote another "Freedom Song" for his gubernatorial campaign, "The Man without a Party," which went in part:

> My party's 'all the people'—their rights I will proclaim.
>   Struggling for liberty and freedom;
> I'll cast my vote for principle, not for a party name,
>   Struggling for liberty and freedom.

Jones held a distinct distaste for partyism of any kind and scorned all political labels. Before 1899 he had been a Republican, but as he constantly reminded audiences, he had been a Republican like Lincoln, Garrison, and John Brown, and not like Mark Hanna, his bitter foe in Ohio politics. At times he thought he was probably a socialist, but as he wrote to Lloyd in 1897 he believed only in the "kind of socialism that is taught in the new testament." Two years later he wrote that "I think I am a socialist," but was just as willing "to be called a collectivist, mutuelist [sic], or Brotherhood man." Throughout the election year of 1900, he refused to commit himself, much to the distress of Bryan and Debs, each of whom expected his support. Jones preferred, as he said, to be "a man without a party, for how can I believe in all of the people, of whom I am one, and belong to a *part* or a party of them?" Debs's response to this was that he, too, was for all the people in theory, but in practice was for workers and the oppressed; he pointedly signed his letter to Jones, "a Man With a Party." Bryan's firm anti-imperialist stand and the influence of Ernest Crosby, however, finally persuaded Jones to support the Democrat. He wrote to Bryan to express sympathy after his defeat, and added that "your ideals are far and away ahead of the time." To his distress, so were his own, as he was increasingly finding out.

Although discouraged with nonpartisan political action, Jones ran again for mayor in 1901 and won, with 56 percent of the total vote, a 14 percent decline in two years. Because of illness and the street railway franchise contest, his last campaign in 1903 was a bitter one. Many of his old followers—tired of his unorthodox leadership—had left him. He was hurt seriously from persecution by churches, civic leaders, and the newspapers, none of which would publish his platform and principles or report on his campaign. He campaigned virtually alone, driving around Toledo in a buggy drawn by an old mare, with his son blowing a saxophone to attract crowds. He won the election, but with only 44 percent of the vote. He fought the renewal of the street railway franchise for most of the next year and died halfway through this fourth and unhappiest term. A few years after Jones's death a general strike paralyzed Toledo. Although the workers in the S. M. Jones Company, as it had been called since 1903, were also on strike, their factory was conspicuously one of the few firms in the city not picketed. When Whitlock asked a labor leader why not, he answered, "Oh well, you know—Mayor Jones. We haven't forgotten him and what he was."

The "Golden Rule Man" was not easily forgotten. For ten years he had put his words into deeds by a practical application of the golden rule to economic and political life in Toledo. His policies had improved the quality of life in concrete ways for the workers in his oil fields and factory: a higher wage, an eight-hour day, job security, safer, happier working conditions, paid vacations, and Christmas dividends. The quality of life for the poorer, outcasted citizens of Toledo had also been enhanced: a job, a new chance, a dismissed arrest, a bath, a meal, and a night's lodging. More importantly, he treated each person he encountered with dignity and respect. His trust and love were returned by those whose lives he had enriched.

Nor was Jones easily forgotten or ignored by the other Christian intellectual reformers in the new religious movement. In 1899 he described his platform, by design, in the broadest terms: "Love is the law of life. Co-operation is the social method of love. Competition is war. Parties are warring armies. Punishment is brutal. You can trust the people. The right to work is inalienable.

Art is the expression of pleasure in work." In this statement of principles he expounded with simplicity if not precision the several ideals of the crusade and its intellectual inspirers. With Tolstoy and Crosby he made love the operating law of his life, abhorred war and government by force, and sought to overcome evil by good. With Mazzini, Markham, and Whitman he believed in brotherhood, association, and democratic trust in the people. With Howells and Lloyd he condemned competition as war and argued that the solution to the trust and labor questions was in profit-sharing and cooperation. With Ruskin and Scudder he believed not only that a person has an inalienable right to work but also that his labor should be pleasurable and aesthetically rewarding. With Bliss and Flower he shared an optimistic faith in the inevitability of progress, believing that the signs of the times pointed to the "coming of a wonderful awakening of the social conscience of the world." With Herron and Rauschenbusch he was convinced that "unless we find heaven here . . . I very much fear we shall not realize a heaven hereafter."

Jones understood that one fulfilled these elevated ideals to the extent that one embodied them in action. He pulled himself up toward the skies by lifting his city up an inch. And yet, in spite of his practical applications, he was not entirely immune to the kinds of self-doubts, guilt, and unhappiness that plagued the other knights of the golden rule. He often quoted Mazzini's comment that "we admire martyrdom but do not adopt it" and was discouraged with his inability to martyr himself in some significant way. He thought, for example, that he should "prove the sincerity of [his] convictions by simply going out and willingly becoming poor, as did Jesus, St. Francis, and many others." And no matter how much good he did, it was never enough. In a letter to Lloyd in 1899 he wrote: "We must all understand the gospel of DO. I know well enough how to practice the Golden Rule; the difficulty comes in my unwillingness to do it entirely, with my halfway doing it." Two years later, after giving a talk at Golden Rule Hall on how genuine Tolstoy was, he wrote to his close friend N. O. Nelson that "the cause of all my soul distress—and I have lots of it, comrade—might be found in the one fact that I am yet lacking the backbone to go and do as Tolstoi does." At this point in the letter Jones's soul distress over his failures was similar to the guilt and pain that Howells, Crosby, or Scudder felt in their inability to emulate Tolstoy or Ruskin. But Jones went on, as the others did not and could not do: "Still, I am plugging away in that direction, and I . . . may even yet do something that is genuine and that is worth while." In fact, he already had, as the others recognized, if he himself did not.

Jones's determination and success in "plugging away" in Tolstoyan directions distinguished him from the others in the movement. Despite the self-recriminations caused by Mazzini and Tolstoy, he escaped the paralyzing effects of the guilt that so often grieved Howells, Crosby, and Scudder. He was, in short, a free person. Although acknowledging the influence of others, Jones insisted that he was "not a Whitmanite, nor a Tolstoyan. . . . Somehow I want to be free. I do not want to 'belong' to anybody or anything." And because he understood this desire in himself, he was able to understand it in others. False altruism and the worship of saviors, he said, was unjustified, a folly. "Neither Moses nor Jesus nor Lincoln nor any other man or woman ever saved the people. All they could do or did was to live the ideal life that each one must live in order to save himself or to be free." Jones sought similarly not to save others but to live *his* ideal life in order to save himself, that he might be free. He was therefore able to be himself and did not try, like Howells or Crosby, to be someone else. This enabled him to retain the self-respect and psychic freedom which is necessary for a healthy, functioning, effective life, particularly as a reformer.

In his practical accomplishments and self-respect Jones achieved what the other knights sought to achieve and could not, except perhaps for Lloyd. More than to any other person, they pointed to Jones as the embodiment of the golden rule in action and, consequently, as the unofficial hero of the movement, an honor he consistently repudiated. Lloyd, Markham, and Herron all

went to Ohio to campaign for him, and Crosby wrote a short, eulogistic biography of him. These four, as well as Howells, Bliss, Flower, and Rauschenbusch, all corresponded with Jones and frequently offered their best wishes and admiration for his achievements. Only Vida Scudder, cloistered at Wellesley and Denison House, seems not to have crossed paths with the Toledo mayor. Jones's relationship with the others illustrates not only his ability to perform deeds, and inversely, their inability, but also reflects again their own respective roles and failures as intellectual reformers. Each reformer, it must be added, performed that function most consistent with his temperament, training, and talents. Each person, after all, is what he is.

William Dean Howells was one of the elder statesmen of the movement, often peripherally connected with it, obligated as he was to fulfill his demanding and prestigious role as the dean of American letters. Many young writers and reformers sought him out for praise and encouragement; Jones, however, was sought out by Howells. In December 1898 he received an unsolicited letter from Howells, commending Jones's Second Annual Message as mayor for its humanity and wishing him long years of service to his city. Jones was delighted with Howells's note, proudly published it in his book, and wrote immediately to his well-wisher to thank him. In the letter Jones praised *A Traveller from Altruria,* which he had been reading, and told Howells that "the question of social reform is, after all, a question of moral reform," a vagueness of position that the Altrurian romanticist understood well. During his last campaign, Jones received another letter of encouragement from Howells, who wrote to bolster Jones's spirits in his most difficult campaign. "You may not be elected," Howells predicted incorrectly, "but I know you cannot be defeated." In these brief exchanges Howells was doing what he did best: encouraging others in their efforts to perform deeds which, to his distress, he knew he could not perform himself. His role was a sad, but necessary one.

The relationship between Jones and Henry

Demarest Lloyd, both midwesterners and both more active as reformers than Howells, was much closer. As Jones wrote to Lloyd in 1897, "I know there is very much in common between us." Their correspondence was regular and marked by the frankness of genuine friendship. The two had met as early as 1893, again at a meeting of Social Gospel clergymen in the summer of 1896 at Crosbyside, and six months later at a conference at Hull House. Jones often acknowledged his intellectual debt to Lloyd. He wrote to his friend in 1900 that he was "thoroughly in line with your philosophy" of love and social self-interest in the closing chapters of *Wealth against Commonwealth.* As a solution to social problems, Jones could see "no hope in any other." And in his speech at the Lloyd memorial meeting in 1903, Jones recalled Lloyd's profound influence in making him "a golden rule man."

But Lloyd's relationship to Jones was practical as well as inspirational, reflecting his supportive function to unions and other cooperative efforts. Lloyd often went to Toledo to speak on Jones's behalf, sent him money for his campaigns, offered advice on municipal and corporate problems, and wrote letters upon Jones's request to persons of influence in Toledo who were critical of the mayor. Lloyd was a wise and critical counselor; he frequently chastised his friend for allowing his emotions and eccentricities to interfere with his political wisdom. In the summer of 1899, for example, he was angry with Jones for his excessively "kindly tone" in combating the oil trust and advised him to be more stern. And in August 1899, after Jones declared his candidacy for governor, Lloyd wrote to warn him not to make a martyr of himself unwisely, as he later thought Herron had done in resigning from Iowa College. Quoting the Bible, Lloyd cautioned: "we must not only love [sic] as doves, but be as wise as serpents." He charged Jones with wasting too much money in the campaign, and wrote: "Keep yourself well in hand; be as cool in your head as you are hot in your heart. Remember that money is the sinews of war, and that, if you keep possession of the means, you can carry on not only this campaign but a score of campaigns to follow." In

a postscript Lloyd noted that he was enclosing, as he said, "a little of the sinews of war." Lloyd even refused to speak in Ohio for his friend during the gubernatorial attempt. As he wrote to Gladden, "it seems to me that the campaign in his [Jones's] hands is so unique that no outside influence could do anything but mar it." Jones had his own unorthodox style and approach to social questions, and as Lloyd implied, his uniqueness both earned the admiration of others in the movement and sometimes drove them away. Above all, however, his singularity was in his practical action, equaled in the movement only, perhaps, by Lloyd himself.

Benjamin Flower saw this same uniqueness in Jones. In an editorial in the *Coming Age* on the significance of Jones's mayoralty election in 1899, Flower asserted that Jones was "living nearer to the Golden Rule than any other public official." His victory, Flower wrote in one of his usual hyperbolic outbursts, was "one of the most important and encouraging events of the closing years of our century. It is a positive step toward a truer democracy than the world has yet known." The correspondence between the two men was largely devoted to letters of support from Flower and requests for articles for his several magazines. Jones said of the *New Time* that it was "one of the best things in the line of progressive literature that we have"; he was, however, generally unreceptive or otherwise engaged to meet Flower's insistent requests for articles. Jones's preference for 5 percent dividends and free public facilities rather than Flower's idealistic monthly discussions of issues suggests the major difference between them.

The correspondence between Jones and William Dwight Porter Bliss was similar, and it was just as discouraging for Bliss as for Flower that the busy mayor failed to produce articles for his many journalistic ventures. Jones was generally sympathetic with most of Bliss's attempts to effect unity among Christian reformers, though he disagreed vigorously with Bliss's temptation in 1899 to start a new party. Jones attended the Buffalo conference, which he compared to the gathering of early Christians in the upper room, and consented to let Bliss use his name as a vice president of the Social Reform Union. "I am in," Jones wrote abruptly, "God bless you." Bliss returned the favor by reporting regularly on Jones's political campaigns in the *Social Forum* and *Social Unity* and happily announced Jones's mayoralty victory in 1899: "Blessing on Jones! May his tribe increase!" Bliss eventually came around to Jones's position that nonpartisanship was preferable to a new party. He pointed out, however, that Jones's solitary success as a nonpartisan officeholder was an exception to his belief that organization in the form of a national Christian socialist union was essential to the overall success of the reform movement. Jones, of course, dissented. He wrote to Bliss that he served Christian socialist principles more effectively without any labels, badges, or organizational limits on his freedom. He repudiated Bliss's implicit elitism, saying: "The mass is good enough for me. . . . I do not propose to wait for socialism or brotherhood. To the extent of my ability . . . I am practising both now." Again, this was the basic difference between Jones and others such as Bliss and Flower, who seemed content to wait for the millennium. Jones was more effective than they were because his attempted range of practical impact was limited. He was effective in Toledo; when he widened his scope to include state action, he failed. The efforts of Bliss and Flower for national unity and influence were spread too thin, and their failures were as large as their expectations.

George Herron was one of the earliest influences on Jones, whose library contained well-marked copies of Herron's many books. To an injunction by Herron to arise and obey the summons of Jesus to love others, Jones responded: "*I will.*" At the end of the *New Redemption,* which he read in 1897, Jones wrote: "*So may it be* every word of it." He wrote to Herron in October that whatever good he had done for his fellow men and women "is due very largely to the inspiration to activity that came from the study of the books you have written." Two years later he told George Gates that the teachings of Herron and Gates at Grinnell and in the *Kingdom* had helped him to realize that "our only hope for real free-

dom lies in the application of the Christ philosophy to the affairs of every day life." On June 14, 1899, in the midst of the attempt of the Iowa College trustees to force Herron's resignation, Jones delivered the commencement address at Grinnell, as Lloyd had done four years earlier. In reporting the address the next day a Des Moines newspaper said that Jones's speech "pleased nearly every one. . . . He may be a crank, but if he is there ought to be more of them," kinder words than the paper usually had for Herron.

Jones and Herron gradually moved farther apart, partly because of differences of style and partly for political reasons. As early as February 1898 Jones indicated that he found Herron not constructive enough, a more than valid insight. And they disagreed about the national election of 1900. In October, Jones told Herron that he thought the socialist movement was hopeless and that he was going to campaign for Bryan. Part of Jones's disenchantment with Herron and socialist parties derived from the kind of help Herron gave him during his gubernatorial campaign in 1899. Herron made several speeches for Jones in Ohio, but his controversial dogmatism and increasing militancy, according to an Iowa newspaper, probably hurt rather than helped. As Lloyd had perceptively observed, Jones's uniqueness precluded outside help, especially when provided by the impatient, angry, and tainted Herron.

Walter Rauschenbusch and Jones shared an optimistic confidence in social progress already achieved toward the creation of the kingdom of heaven on earth. They corresponded briefly in 1897, as the New York minister sought Jones's help in persuading Crosby to run for mayor of New York. Rauschenbusch also asked Jones to speak at the summer meeting of the Brotherhood of the Kingdom at Marlborough; Jones planned to speak on "The Golden Rule in Business," but pressures of his work in Toledo prevented him from attending. There is little doubt what he would have said. From his detached and professorial position a few years later, Rauschenbusch commended Jones as a civic leader who courageously fought private municipal interests. In *Christianizing the Social Order* he praised Jones,

Henry George, Hazen Pingree of Detroit, and Tom Johnson of Cleveland, all of whom deserved to have a "civic crown on their graves. They fought for us." He particularly admired Jones and Johnson, both rich men, as embodiments of Jesus' message to men of wealth. Both had earned their place in heaven, Rauschenbusch wrote, "by proclaiming their own wealth to be derived from injustice and by leading the people to an assault on the sources of it." Little is known about what Jones thought about Rauschenbusch, since the mayor died before any of the prominent theologian's major books were published.

Besides Lloyd, Jones's closest personal friendships among the members of the new religious movement were with the poets, Markham and Crosby. Beginning in 1899, Edwin Markham and Jones exchanged books and carried on a correspondence lauding each other's work. They shared a faith in spiritual and social man, as well as in the efficacy of the application of the golden rule to social questions. They also shared a gentleness of style missing in their mutual friend, George Herron. When Markham initiated the friendship by sending the mayor a copy of "The Man with the Hoe," Jones replied by telling him that he already had memorized the poem. "I see The Man With the Hoe in every mis-shapen child of God that I meet upon the street," Jones wrote, expressing the hope that he would meet the poet soon. They met within a month at Buffalo. Shortly after their encounter, Jones began using stationery in which Millet's painting and part of Markham's poem appeared in the letterhead. A framed picture of the painting and poem hung in his office. When Markham wrote to praise *The New Right,* which Jones had sent him, Jones replied, "I do not know of any other endorsement that could touch me as yours has." Markham reciprocated Jones's enthusiasm in his work as a poet by taking an interest in Jones's "noble work" as mayor. In two different newspaper articles in August 1899, Markham pointed to Jones as an exemplary man, "seeking for a clew to the secret of social salvation—trying to make the Golden Rule a working principle." That same month the poet wrote Jones, "I stand squarely with you,"

and followed the letter with a visit to Ohio to campaign for his friend. Markham capped this mutual love affair by telling Jones that he was "a God-quickened man. . . . The work you are doing for human welfare is far larger than the orbit in which you move: it is an object lesson to the world." The noble poet, however, did not indicate how Jones's work was an object lesson for himself.

Jones's good friend Ernest Crosby saw the same distinctive qualities in Jones and yet, unlike Markham, was not afraid to measure his own life's work against Jones's high standard. In his biography of the mayor, Crosby wrote that Jones "never uttered a harsh word against anyone, and he gently expostulated with me for being too inconsiderate." He was a man totally without pretense, pride, or illusions. "Day to day," Crosby wrote, Jones "did the best thing that he saw was practicable." He was so different that Crosby thought of him "as a sort of visitor from some other planet where brotherhood and harmony have been realized in the common life, dropped down here in a semi-barbarous world and calmly taking his place in the midst of its crude and cruel institutions." Alone among reformers, according to Crosby, Jones not only "pointed out the iniquities of our organized social life" but also "was sowing the seed of a new harvest."

The friendship between the two began during the conferences at Crosbyside and Hull House in 1896 when, as Crosby wrote, he was struck with "the open and childlike way in which [Jones] expressed his extreme democratic views to everyone," including a crippled janitor at Hull House whom he befriended. Jones and Crosby shared an intense admiration for Tolstoy, Whitman, and Carpenter, were in accord in their dedicated opposition to war, judicial judgments, and penal injustices, and both repudiated political labels. In a letter to Crosby in 1898 Jones thanked the New Yorker for teaching him that he was, like Garrison and Tolstoy, "truly a non-resistant." Crosby continued the lesson by pointing out in his reply that he preferred not to call his position one of nonresistance, which sounded too negative, but rather one of "overcoming evil with good," a phrase Jones eagerly adopted. Two months later Jones sought out Crosby for Tolstoy's address in order that he might "write to him and tell the dear old man for myself how much good his books have done me." They talked often about Tolstoy, and Crosby found a picture of the Russian for Jones's office. Crosby's influence and the Filipino insurrection were decisive in persuading Jones to support Bryan in 1900. In April of that year Jones wrote to Crosby that he was surprised that his friend was going to support the Democrat rather than Debs. By August he wrote a friend that Crosby was going to vote for Bryan as an anti-imperialist, and that "possibly that may be the best thing for the rest of us to do." Within a month Jones committed himself to Bryan.

Crosby helped his friend with definitions, details, and political decisions; he also helped him in a much more profound and significant way, one that illustrates the fundamental difference between them, and, for that matter, between Jones and the other knights of the golden rule. In the late winter of 1902 Jones wrote to Crosby, as he was increasingly writing to others, that he was tired of his active involvement in the city and yearned for rural quietude. His enormous energy, sapped for years by asthma and catarrh, had begun to diminish. And so also had his spirits. As the bitterness of his battles with the interests of Toledo intensified during his last two terms in office, and as he read more of Tolstoy and Thoreau, Jones increasingly wanted to abandon his factory for the simple life in the fields, hoeing beans and digging potatoes, as he told Crosby in his letter.

Crosby's impassioned reply argued that despite the apparent attractiveness of his own serene life at Crosbyside, Jones's hectic life was by far the more personally satisfying and socially useful. "I have nothing to repent," Crosby wrote, but nevertheless "go on marking time." He advised Jones that "it would be a mistake for you to give up manufacturing for potato-digging. Tolstoy's mistake is in not seeing that machinery may be made a blessing to all men." The major problem of material development, which in the main was fine, he wrote, was "how to wed it to

. . . spiritual development." For Jones to give up manufacturing to "become a farmhand is to avoid the social problem & not to answer it." This was the fallacy, Crosby pointed out, in Tolstoy's and his own life. As "a maker of machinery" Jones was in a unique position to "show how wealth-producing can be civilised," as he had already been doing. "Pay yourself only $2. a day if you please," Crosby beseeched, "but don't throw away your position in the producing world—a position which I envy you."

Jones followed his friend's pleading advice and stayed in the producing world. But it was not easy. He continued to write sad and wistful letters about his weariness and yearnings for the simple rural life. In August 1902 he told Jane Addams, after a month's vacation in northern Michigan, that the simple life of Tolstoy and Thoreau seemed to him the only way to live. In June 1903 he wrote to a friend that he was "tired of books, tired of reading, tired of talk, tired of libraries and lectures, tired of respectability." He desired instead a pure life in the open air, "working with my hands rather than by working my jaw." Two months later he wrote to Nelson that he was more and more inclined to "do as Tolstoi did in effect —die to the ownership of property or things; give it away to those who want to own it." The point here is that despite his desires, Jones renounced neither his factory, nor his wealth (what was left of it after his generous giving), nor his political office. He continued to write the letters, but he also continued to fight the private traction company, continued to provide free public services and new opportunities for the citizens of his city, and continued to increase the benefits for the workers in his factory.

Eight months after the exchange with Crosby, Jones announced the profit-sharing experiment in his annual Christmas message to the employees in his factory. But the new proposal seemed almost like an afterthought, following a lengthy and curious discourse on good health, exercise, and outdoor living, including a review of Jones's own medical history and the prescriptions he had been following: "I take lots of fresh air, sleep with windows wide open in all kinds of weather, get up at six o'clock, take ten or fifteen minutes of lively exercise, cold bath, walk two miles to the shop, and I feel best when I do a few hours' real hard work. However, I keep busy until 11:30, when I have a good, keen hunger for the first meal of the day; I eat absolutely nothing before that. During the last two months, I have cut out meat, and I think I notice a marked improvement in my feelings since doing so." Jones thereby combined his personal yearnings for hard work and Tolstoyan simplicity with a continuation of his public service in the producing world, as Crosby had advised. Arguing from his own feelings of unhappiness and guilt over his withdrawal to Crosbyside and his ineffectiveness as a reformer, Crosby had helped to convince his friend to escape his own sad plight. His crucial argument was in helping Jones understand that to salve one's conscience by renouncing the world was really to avoid solving the problems of the world and, worse yet, to act selfishly. Although Jones did not admit it, he understood the message. To flee to green hills and potato-digging, however appealing that life seemed, was an evasion of his responsibilities, and Jones knew it.

What Crosby did not understand about Jones, however, was that his standards of personal behavior and excellence were so high that he was incapable of genuine and complete happiness no matter how much good he accomplished. In the Christmas message in 1902 he admitted that as he acted on the golden rule to enhance the happiness of others he was made even more aware of all those whose happiness he had not enhanced. Moreover, he felt personally responsible for good work undone and therefore believed that he deserved to be miserable: "while I leave undone one thing that is in my power to do to enhance the real happiness of the least or lowest man or woman on the planet, my own claim to happiness is defective, and I shall be miserable and I ought, for the same law that entitles me to share in the happiness that I produce condemns me to share in the unhappiness for which I am responsible, whether it be caused by what I have either done or left undone." With a standard of perfection for personal happiness and self-worth like that, one wonders why Crosby envied Jones so much. The point, however, is that he did.

12

WOMAN'S PLACE IS AT THE TYPEWRITER: THE FEMINIZATION OF THE CLERICAL LABOR FORCE

MARGERY W. DAVIES

To mention the word *secretary* is to call to mind an image of a woman sitting in front of a typewriter or office computer. But as Margery Davies makes clear in this essay, this was not always the case. Before the late nineteenth century nearly all office workers were men. Women either worked at home, in factories, or as school teachers.

Beginning in the late 1870s American business entered a new phase of expansion. Production increased dramatically and factories and firms expanded in size, squeezing out small, family-run firms. Large business organizations, now employing hundreds and sometimes thousands of workers, required new means of coordination and control. Over the course of the late nineteenth and early twentieth centuries American business found this new means of control in the creation of bureaucratic procedures and organizations. These business bureaucracies in turn required large numbers of educated and cheap workers to compile, organize, and disseminate the increased amounts of information upon which large-scale industry depended. As Davies shows, American businessmen found this new labor force in the growing number of high-school-educated women who were seeking employment at the turn of the century.

How important do you think the reestablishment of patriarchy was in the creation of the predominantly female clerical labor force? How do you think female clerical workers would have responded to the birth control movement, described by Linda Gordon in Reading 15?

A large proportion of the recent historical research about women in the labor force has focused on industrial workers, using their specific factory experiences as a model for viewing the class as a whole. On the other hand, relatively little attention has been given to clerical workers. This is surprising: in 1968 for example, over 40 percent of women in the U.S. labor force were employed as clerical and sales workers, while only 16.5 percent were employed in the industrial workforce. This essay is a contribution to a discussion aimed first at clarifying the role of a "secretarial proletariat," and secondly at broadening the definition of the working class to include other than those in industrial production. In particular, there are millions of low-level clerical workers, most of them women, who form an important segment of the working class.

The essay is historical in scope and focuses on the feminization of the clerical labor force. Women now form the majority of the clerical workforce, but this was not always the case. How did women enter and come to dominate clerical work? How did the ideology with respect to women office workers change? What are the connections between a sexual segmentation of the clerical labor force and hierarchical relations in the office? The first step in answering these questions is to look at the "19th-century office."

The Nineteenth-Century Office

> Mr. Vhole's office, in disposition retiring and in situation retired, is squeezed up in a corner, and blinks at a dead wall. Three feet of knotty floored dark passage bring the client to Mr. Vhole's jet black door, in an angle profoundly dark on the brightest midsummer morning, and encumbered by a black bulk-head of cellerage staircase, against which belated civilians generally strike their brows. Mr. Vhole's chambers are on so small a scale, that one clerk can open the door without getting off his stool, while the other who elbows him at the same desk has equal facilities for poking the fire. A smell as of unwholesome sheep, blending with the smell of must and dust, is referable to the nightly (and often daily) consumption of mutton fat in candles, and to the fretting of parchment forms and skins in greasy drawers. The atmosphere is otherwise stale and close.

Two of the basic characteristics of 19th-century offices, in the United States as well as Dickensian England, are that they were small and staffed almost exclusively by men. Census data for 1870, for example, show that out of 76,639 office workers in the United States, women numbered only 1869; men were 97.5 percent of the clerical labor force. With the exception of a few banks, insurance companies and governmental branches, most offices in the United States prior to the Civil War usually contained about two or three clerks. This is not surprising, since most capitalist firms were also relatively small until the last decades of the 19th century. For example, in *Bartleby,* Herman Melville described a Wall Street lawyer's office of the 1850's which consisted of the lawyer, three copyists and an errand boy.

The small size of offices at this time meant that the relationship between employer and employee tended to be a very personalized one. The clerks worked under the direct supervision, and often the direct eyesight, of their employers. Although the tasks of a clerk were generally well-defined— the job of the copyists in *Bartleby* was to tran-

scribe legal documents—they were also often asked to do numerous other tasks by their employers. It was clearly the employer who set the limits of the clerk's job—there was no question here of the clerk being ruled by the inexorable pace of a machine.

The personal benevolence of an employer could go a long way toward making the hierarchical relations within an office more tolerable. An employer who spoke nicely to his clerks, let them leave early if they were feeling sick, or gave them a Christmas goose helped to create working conditions against which the clerks were not likely to rebel. By treating his clerks with kindness or politeness, a paternalistic employer was also likely to be able to get them to work harder for him.

This personalization of the work relationship between the clerk and his employer in the 19th-century office lies at the root of the phenomenon of employees being "devoted to the firm." A clerk who spent forty or fifty years of his life working for the same small office of an insurance company did not necessarily work so long and so hard out of a belief in the importance of promoting that particular company's kind of insurance. The source of the devotion of this hypothetical employee was much more likely the network of personal relations he had built up in the office over the years. It was probably more important to the employee to "produce" a good working relationship with his boss, with whom he was in constant contact, than to produce, for example, improvements in the insurance company's filing system. Needless to say that that good working relationship no doubt depended in part on the employee producing improvements in the filing system. But whether the employee cared more about the selling of insurance or his personal relationship with his employer, the end result tended to be the same: the clerk became a "devoted employee of the firm" who was not likely to rebel or go out on strike.

Not all clerks in the 19th-century office spent all their working days in clerical positions. A clerkship also served as an apprenticeship for a young man who was "learning the business" before he moved on to a managerial position. These young men were often nephews, sons, or grandsons of the firm's managers and owners—the "family business" trained its sons by having them work as clerks for a period of time. Most clerks, however, ended up with gold watches instead of managerial posts in return for their years of devoted service.

Thus the clerks in an office at any particular time came from different class backgrounds and were likely to have very different occupational futures. (Sons of entrepreneurs and professionals would work as clerks for only a short period of time before going on to managerial jobs. Men from the working classes, sons of artisans or low-level clerks, would probably work as clerks for the rest of their lives; few would be promoted to managerial positions.

Political-Economic Changes

In the last few decades of the 19th century, American corporations underwent a period of rapid growth and consolidation. These changes, which marked the rise of modern industrial capitalism, had been signalled by developments in banks, insurance companies and public utilities; they had spread to manufacturing enterprises by the turn of the century. As business operations became more complex, there was a large increase in correspondence, record-keeping, and office work in general. This expansion of record-keeping and the proliferation of communications both within and between firms created a demand for an expanded clerical labor force. In 1880 there were 504,454 office workers who constituted 3 percent of the labor force; by 1890 there were 750,150 office workers. The number of office workers has been increasing ever since. (See Table 1.) In order to fill the need for clerical workers, employers turned to the large pool of educated female labor.

As early as the 1820's, women had been receiving public high school educations: Worcester, Massachusetts opened a public high school for girls in 1824; Boston and New York City did so in 1826. In 1880, 13,029 women graduated from high school in the United States, as compared to only 10,605 men. The figures for 1900 show an even greater disparity: 56,808 female high school graduates and 38,075 male.

Until the end of the 19th century, schools were the main place of employment for these educated women. The feminization of elementary and secondary teaching had taken place with the introduction of compulsory public education and consequent increase in teaching jobs. In 1840 men were 60 percent of all teachers, and in 1860 they made up only 14 percent. Women were hired in education because they were a cheap replacement for the dwindling supply of male teachers. "As Charles William Eliot observed some years after the feminization of primary school teaching was largely completed: 'It is true that sentimental reasons are often given for the almost exclusive employment of women in the common schools; but the effective reason is economy. . . . If women had not been cheaper than men, they would not have replaced nine tenths of the men in American public schools.' "

But teaching was about the only job that drew on the pool of educated female labor in substantial numbers. The "professions"—law, medicine, business, college teaching—both excluded women and did not employ large numbers of people. The 1890 census, for instance, counted only 200 women lawyers. Social work was still the preserve of moral reformers like Jane Addams; the growth of social work as an occupation with government funding did not come until the 20th century. Nursing was beginning to employ some women by the end of the 19th century: in 1900 there were 108,691 nurses and midwives, although only 11,000 of them had become graduate nurses and achieved professional status.

In the last decades of the 19th century, the situation was, then, the following. There were more women than men graduating from high school every year. These women constituted a pool of educated female labor which was being drawn upon only by elementary and secondary schools. Consequently, there were literally thousands of women with training that qualified them for jobs that demanded literacy, but who could not find such jobs. Excluded from most of the professions, these women were readily available for the clerical jobs that started to proliferate at the end of the 19th century. The expansion and consolidation of enterprises in the 1880's and

Table 1
Feminization of the Clerical Labor Force

		Bookkeepers, accountants, and cashiers	Messengers, errand and office boys and girls	Stenographers, typists, and secretaries	Shipping and receiving clerks	Clerical and kindred Workers	Office machine operators
1870	Total	39,164	7,820			29,655	
	Female	893	46			930	
	% female	2%	.6%			3%	
1880	Total	75,688	12,447			64,151	
	Female	4,295	228			2,315	
	% female	6%	2%			4%	
1890	Total	160,968	45,706			219,173	
	Female	28,050	1,658			45,553	
	% female	17%	4%			21%	
1900	Total	257,400	63,700			357,100	
	Female	74,900	3,800			104,400	
	% female	29%	6%			29%	
1910	Total	491,600	95,100			1,034,200	
	Female	189,000	6,400			386,800	
	% female	38%	7%			37%	
1920	Total	742,000	99,500			2,092,000	
	Female	362,700	8,100			1,038,400	
	% female	49%	8%			50%	
1930	Total	940,000	79,500	2,754,000			36,200
	Female	487,500	5,100	1,450,900			32,100
	% female	52%	6%	53%			89%
1940	Total	931,300	60,700	1,174,900	229,700	1,973,600	64,200
	Female	475,700	3,000	1,096,400	9,100	702,500	55,100
	% female	51%	5%	93%	4%	36%	86%
1950	Total	—	59,000	1,629,300	297,400	2,354,200	146,200
	Female	—	10,600	1,538,000	20,700	1,252,900	120,300
	% female	—	18%	94%	7%	53%	82%
1960	Total	—	63,200	2,312,800	294,600	3,016,400	318,100
	Female	—	11,200	2,232,600	25,000	1,788,700	236,400
	% female	—	18%	96%	8%	59%	74%

1890's created a large demand for clerical labor; the large pool of educated female labor constituted the supply.

Women Enter The Office

Prior to the Civil War there were no women employed in substantial numbers in any offices, although there were a few women scattered here and there who worked as bookkeepers or as copyists in lawyers' offices. During the Civil War, however, the reduction of the male labor force due to the draft moved General Francis Elias Spinner, the U.S. Treasurer, to introduce female clerical workers into government offices. At first women were given the job of trimming paper money in the Treasury Department, but, they gradually moved into other areas of clerical work. The experiment proved successful and was continued after the end of the war. Commenting upon this innovation in 1869, Spinner declared "upon his word" that it had been a complete success: "Some of the females (are) doing more and better work for $900 per annum than many male clerks who were paid double that amount." At the time, men clerks were being paid from $1200 to $1800 per year.

Although women started to work in government offices during the Civil War, it was not until the 1880's that women began to pour into the clerical work force. In 1880, the proportion of women in the clerical labor force was 4 percent; in 1890 it had jumped to 21 percent. By 1920, women made up half of the clerical workers: 50 percent of all low-level office workers (including stenographers, typists, secretaries, shipping and receiving clerks, office machine operators, and clerical and kindred workers not elsewhere classified) were women. In 1960, 72 percent of them were. (See Table 1.) This tremendous increase in the number of women office workers has changed the composition of the female labor force. While in 1870 less than 0.05 percent of the women in the labor force were office workers, by 1890 1.1 percent of them were. In 1960, 29.1 percent of all women in the labor force were office workers.

When women were hired to work in government offices in Washington during the Civil War, a precedent was established. This precedent facilitated the entrance of women in large numbers into the clerical labor force at the end of the 19th century. Women had gotten a foot in the office door in the Civil War, and the prejudices against women working in offices had already started to deteriorate by 1880. A second factor which eased women's entrance into the office was the invention of the typewriter. By the 1890's the typewriter had gained widespread acceptance as a practical office machine.

Various American inventors had been working on "writing machines" since the 1830's. They had generally been thought of as crackpots by capitalists and the general public alike, and had seldom if ever been able to get anyone to underwrite their attempts to develop a manufacturable machine.

By the early 1870's, an inventor named Christopher Latham Sholes had managed to produce a fairly workable machine. The Remington family, which had manufactured guns, sewing machines and farm machinery, bought the rights to start making typewriters. But they did not sell very well. People bought them out of curiosity for their own private use, but businesses were not yet willing to commit themselves. When asked to write a testimonial for the machine he bought in 1875, Mark Twain replied:

> Gentlemen: Please do not use my name in any way. Please do not even divulge the fact that I own a machine. I have entirely stopped using the Typewriter, for the reason that I never could write a letter with it to anybody without receiving a request by return mail that I would not only describe the machine but state what progress I had made in the use of it, etc., etc. I don't like to write letters, and so I don't want people to know that I own this curiosity breeding little joker.
>
> Yours truly,
>
> Saml L. Clemens

People were curious about the typewriter, but it was not until the last two decades of the 19th century that businesses began to buy the machines in large quantities.

It seems fairly clear that it was not until businesses began to expand very rapidly that employers saw the usefulness of a mechanical writing machine. Changes in the structure of capitalist enterprises brought about changes in technology: no one was interested in making the typewriter a workable or manufacturable machine until the utility of having such a machine became clear. But the typewriter no doubt also gave rise to changes in office procedure. Writing was faster on a typewriter. The increase in correspondence and record-keeping was caused in part by the existence of the machine. For example, Robert Lincoln O'Brien made the following comment in the *Atlantic Monthly* in 1904:

> The invention of the typewriter has given a tremendous impetus to the dictating habit. . . . This means not only greater diffuseness, inevitable with any

lessening of the tax on words which the labor of writing imposes, but it also brings forward the point of view of the one who speaks.

The typewriter also facilitated the entrance of women into the clerical labor force. Typing was "sex-neutral" because it was a new occupation. Since typing had not been identified as a masculine job, women who were employed as typists did not encounter the criticism that they were taking over "men's work." In fact, it did not take long for typing to become "women's work": in 1890, 63.8 percent of the 33,418 clerical workers classified as stenographers and typists were women; by 1900, that proportion had risen to 76.7 percent. (See Table 2.) The feminization of low-level clerical work proceeded extremely rapidly.

It is important to determine why women wanted to become office workers. Most women at the end of the 19th century probably worked out of economic necessity. This holds true for the unmarried single woman of middle-income origins who worked until she married and was supported by her husband as well as for the immigrant working-class woman, single or married, who worked to keep her family from starving.

Clerical work attracted women because it paid better than did most other jobs that women could get. In northeastern American cities at the end of the 19th century clerical wages were relatively high: domestic servants were paid $2 to $5 a week; factory operatives, $1.50 to $8 a week; department store salesgirls, $1.50 to $8 a week; whereas typists and stenographers could get $6 to $15 a week. Also, clerical work enjoyed a relatively high status. A woman from a middle-

income home with a high school education was much more likely to look for clerical work than for work as a house servant or as a factory girl making paper boxes, pickles or shoes. And, as the passage below excerpted from *The Long Day* shows, a clerical position was coveted by working-class women, who usually could find work only in sweatshops, factories or department stores.

The Long Day, the autobiography of Dorothy Richardson, is a good example of the way in which some 19th-century working women regarded clerical work. Richardson came from western Pennsylvania to New York City as a young woman—she is very vague about her background, but the hints she drops lead to the conclusion that she came from a middle-income family that had fallen into bad financial straits. For several months she went from job to job, making paper boxes, shaking out newly-washed laundry, etc. Her account of those days is told in a tone of dismay about the long hours and poor working conditions and a tone of contemptuous pity for the loose morality of the other "working girls." Richardson finally went to secretarial school and got a position as a secretary, clearly a step up in the occupational structure as far as she was concerned:

I had often thought I would like to learn shorthand and typewriting. . . . I went to night school five nights out of every week for exactly sixty weeks, running consecutively save for a fortnight's interim at the Christmas holidays, when we worked nights at the store. . . .

When I had thoroughly learned the principles of

Table 2
Stenographers and Typists, for the United States and by Sex, 1870–1930

	Total	Male	Female	% female
1870	154	147	7	4.5%
1880	5,000	3,000	2,000	40.0
1890	33,400	12,100	21,300	63.8
1900	112,600	26,200	86,400	76.7
1910	326,700	53,400	263,300	80.6
1920	615,100	50,400	564,700	91.8
1930	811,200	36,100	775,100	95.6

my trade and had attained a speed of some hundred and odd words a minute, the hardest task was yet before me. This task was not in finding a position, but in filling that position satisfactorily. My first position at ten dollars a week I held only one day. I failed to read my notes. This was more because of fright and self-consciousness, however, than of inefficiency. My next paid me only six dollars a week, but it was an excellent training school, and in it I learned self-confidence, perfect accuracy, and rapidity. Although this position paid me two dollars less than what I had been earning brewing tea and coffee and handing it over the counter, and notwithstanding the fact that I knew of places where I could go and earn ten dollars a week, I chose to remain where I was. There was method in my madness, however, let me say. I had a considerate and conscientious employer, and although I had a great deal of work, and although it had to be done most punctiliously, he never allowed me to work a moment overtime. He opened his office at nine in the morning, and I was not expected before quarter after; he closed at four sharp. This gave me an opportunity for further improving myself with a view to eventually taking not a ten-dollar, but a twenty-dollar position. I went back to night-school and took a three months' "speed course," and at the same time continued to add to my general education and stock of knowledge by a systematic reading of popular books of science and economics. I became tremendously interested in myself as an economic factor, and I became tremendously interested in other working girls from a similar point of view.

However, despite the fact that women were pouring into offices at the end of the 19th century, they still met with disapproval. An engraving of 1875 shows a shocked male government official opening the door on an office that has been "taken over by the ladies." The women are preening themselves before a mirror, fixing each other's hair, reading *Harper's Bazaar,* spilling ink on the floor—in short, doing everything but working. The engraving makes women working in an office seem ludicrous: women are seen as frivolous creatures incapable of doing an honest day's work.

Outright contempt was not the only negative reaction to the entrance of women into the office. Bliven cites the following passage from *The Typewriter Girl,* a novel by Olive Pratt Rayner whose

heroine is an American typist fallen on hard financial times in London:

Three clerks (male), in seedy black coats, the eldest with hair the color of a fox's, went on chaffing one another for two minutes after I closed the door, with ostentatious unconsciousness of my insignificant presence. . . . The youngest, after a while, wheeled around on his high stool and broke out with the chivalry of his class and age, "Well, what's your business?"

My voice trembled a little, but I mustered up courage and spoke. "I have called about your advertisement. . . ."

He eyed me up and down. I am slender, and, I will venture to say, if not pretty, at least interesting looking.

"How many words a minute?" he asked after a long pause.

I stretched the truth as far as its elasticity would permit. "Ninety-seven," I answered. . . .

The eldest clerk, with the foxy head, wheeled around, and took his turn to stare. He had hairy hands and large goggle-eyes. . . . I detected an undercurrent of double meaning. . . . I felt disagreeably like Esther in the presence of Ahasuerus—a fat and oily Ahasuerus of fifty. . . . He perused me up and down with his small pig's eyes, as if he were buying a horse, scrutinizing my face, my figure, my hands, my feet. I felt like a Circassian in an Arab slavemarket. . . .

The overtones of sexuality in the passage from *The Typewriter Girl* are hard to miss. The implication here seems to be that a decent girl is risking her morality if she tries to invade the male preserve of the office. Whether or not such sensationalism was backed up by many instances of seduction or corruption, the message seems clear: the office was a dangerous place for a woman of virtue.

Even in 1900, some people counselled women to leave the office and return to their homes, where they rightfully belonged. The editor of the *Ladies' Home Journal,* Edward Bok, gave just such advice in the pages of his magazine in 1900:

A business house cannot prosper unless each position has in it the most competent incumbent which it is possible to obtain for that particular position. And, although the statement may seem a hard one, and will unquestionably be controverted, it nevertheless is a plain, simple fact that women have shown themselves naturally incompetent to fill a great many of the business positions which they have sought to occupy. . . . The fact is that not one woman in a hundred can stand the physical strain of the keen pace which competition has forced upon every line of business today. . . . This magazine has recently made a careful and thorough investigation and inquiry of the hospitals and sanitariums for women, and the results verify and substantiate the most general statement that can be made of the alarming tendency among business girls and women to nervous collapse. No such number of patients has ever been received by these institutions during any previous period of their existence as in the last year or two. . . .

I have recently been interested in ascertaining the definite reasons why employers have felt that the positions in their establishments were not most effectively filled by women. . . . In times of pressure women clerks were found to be either necessarily absent or they invariably gave out. The lack of executive ability was given as the main reason in positions of trust, and the friction caused by the objection of women subordinates to receive orders from one of their own sex. Pending or impending matrimonial engagements were also a very pronounced cause. The proprieties also came in for their share, the merchant not feeling that he could ask his female secretary or clerk to remain after business hours. The trader felt that he could not send a woman off on a mission which required hasty packing and preparations for travel at an hour's notice. Then, too, women do not care to travel alone. The newspaper editor felt that he could not give his female reporter indiscriminate assignments or send her out alone at all hours of the night. . . . Illness in the family, which would not necessitate a man's absence at the office, keeping the woman at home, was another reason. . . . And as I carefully went over the reasons each pointed to simply one thing: the unnatural position of women in business. It was not mental incompetence. But God had made her a woman and never intended her for the rougher life planned out for man, and each step she took proved this uncontrovertible fact to her. It was not man that stood in her path; it was herself.

The Shift in Ideology

However, sixteen years after Bok used the pages of the *Ladies Home Journal* to admonish women to return home, another writer in the same magazine not only took for granted the fact that women worked in offices, but also found that certain "feminine" qualities were particularly suited to clerical work. "The stenographer plus" was described:

I should describe the equipment of the ideal stenographer as follows: Twenty percent represents technical ability—that is, the ability to write and read shorthand and to typewrite rapidly and accurately; thirty percent equals general information—that is, education other than that in shorthand and typewriting; and the last and most important fifty percent I should ascribe to personality. . . .

There are two kinds of personality—concrete and abstract: the one you can see, the other you can feel. The concrete side is that which the stenographer sees when she looks in the mirror. The stenographer who wins must look good—not in the sense that she must be beautiful, for dividends are never declared on pink cheeks and classic features; but she should make the very most of her personal equipment. . . .

That other kind of personality—the abstract kind—is the more important element in the stenographer's equipment, for it involves her temperament. Thousands of stenographers stay in mediocre positions because they lack the ability to adapt their conduct to those fixed principles of harmony and optimism which must prevail in all big undertakings.

A large employer of stenographic help said to me once:

"I expect from my stenographer the same service that I get from the sun, with this exception: the sun often goes on a strike and it is necessary for me to use artificial light, but I pay my stenographer to work six days out of every seven, and I expect her all the while to radiate my office with sunshine and sympathetic interest in the things I am trying to do."

It is the spirit in which the stenographer lives and works as well as the volume of her work that makes her profitable. She must be adaptable, agreeable, courteous. Perhaps no single word so under-writes her success as "courtesy"; this is the keyword in all of our new gospels of salesmanship and efficiency. Our great enterprises are showing us to what extent courtesy can be capitalized.

Fortune magazine, in a series of unsigned articles on "Women in Business," carried the argument a step further and equated secretaries with wives:

The whole point of the whole problem, in other words, is that women occupy the office because the male employer wants them there. Why he wants them there is another question which cannot be answered merely by saying that once there they take to the work very nicely. It is doubtless true that women take to the work nicely. Their conscious or subconscious intention some day to marry, and their conscious or subconscious willingness to be directed by men, render them amenable and obedient and relieve them of the ambition which makes it difficult for men to put their devotion into secretarial work. But that fact only partially explains the male employer's preference. It indicates that women and by virtue of some of their most womanly traits are capable of making the office a more pleasant, peaceful, and homelike place. But it does not indicate why the employer desires that kind of office rather than an office full of ambitious and pushing young men intent upon hammering their typewriters into presidential desks. To get at that problem pure speculation is the only tool.

One might well speculate somewhat as follows: the effect of the industrial revolution was the de-domestication of women. In the working classes the substitute for domestic servitude was factory servitude. In the well-to-do classes, to which the office employer's wife belongs, the substitute for domestic responsibility was no responsibility—or no responsibility to speak of. Consequently, in the well-to-do classes, women were presented first with idleness, then with discontent with idleness, and finally with that odd mixture of rebellion and independence which changed the face of American society in the years that followed the War. In the process the upper-class home, as the upper-class home was known to the Victorians, disappeared. The male was no longer master in his own dining room and

dreadful in his own den nor did a small herd of wives, daughters, and sisters hear his voice and tremble. He was, on the contrary, the more or less equal mate of a more or less unpredictable woman. And he resented it.

He resented the loss of his position. He regretted the old docility, the old obedience, the old devotion to his personal interests. And finding himself unable to re-create the late, lost paradise in his home he set about re-creating it in his office. What he wanted in the office was not the office mistress described at least fifty-two times a year by American short-story writers. His very pretty and very clever and very expensive wife was already mistress enough and to spare. What he wanted in the office was something as much like the vanished wife of his father's generation as could be arranged—someone to balance his checkbook, buy his railroad tickets, check his baggage, get him seats in the fourth row, take his daughter to the dentist, listen to his side of the story, give him a courageous look when things were blackest, and generally know all, understand all. . . .

Whether or not any such speculative explanation of the male desire for a female office is sound there can be no doubt that the desire exists and that it is the male employer who is chiefly responsible for the female secretary.

In 1900, the *Ladies' Home Journal* warned women that they could not stand the physical strain of working in a fast-paced business office, that business girls and women were apt to suffer a nervous collapse. But by 1916 the *Journal* was comparing the faithful female secretary to some heavenly body who "radiated the office with sunshine and sympathetic interest." It had not taken very long for the ideology to shift and for people to accept the presence of women in offices. Bok had argued in 1900 that women, by virtue of their "nature," were unsuited to the office. But only a few years later, the *Journal* came close to arguing that the "natural" temperament of women made them good stenographers. And by 1935, *Fortune* had concocted a full-fledged historical justification for the assertion that "woman's place was at the typewriter."

Women, so the argument went, are by nature

adaptable, courteous, and sympathetic—in a word, passive. This natural passivity makes them ideally suited to the job of carrying out an endless number of routine tasks without a complaint. Furthermore, their docility makes it unlikely that they will aspire to rise very far above their station. Thus their male boss is spared the unpleasant possibility that his secretary will one day be competing with him for his job.

The image of the secretary as the competent mother-wife who sees to her employer's every need and desire was a description which most fitted a personal secretary. Here certain "feminine" characteristics ascribed to the job of personal secretary—sympathy, adaptability, courtesy—made women seem the natural candidates for the job. Not all clerical workers were personal secretaries. For the large proportion of clerical workers who were stenographers, typists, file clerks and the like, another ideological strain developed, emphasizing the supposed greater dexterity of women. These workers were seldom assigned to one particular boss, but instead constituted a pool from which any executive could draw as he wished. In the case of these low-level clerical workers, personal characteristics such as sympathy and courtesy seemed less important. Dexterity—the ability to do work quickly and accurately—was much more important. Not long after the typewriter began to be used as a matter of course in business offices, people started to argue that women, endowed with dextrous fingers, were the most fitting operators of these machines. Elizabeth Baker states that "women seemed to be especially suited as typists and switchboard operators because they were tolerant of routine, careful, and manually dextrous."

Woman's Place in the Office Hierarchy

Whether it was for the warmth of their personalities or the dexterity of their fingers, women came to be seen as "natural" office workers. Why did this ideology develop?

The ideology is obviously connected to the fem-
inization of the clerical labor force. If women were employed in large numbers in offices, then it was not surprising that an ideology justifying their presence there developed. Women were originally employed in offices because they were cheaper than the available male labor force. As corporations expanded at the end of the 19th century, they were forced to draw on the pool of educated females to meet their rapidly increasing demand for clerical workers. But the expansion of capitalist firms did not entail a simple proliferation of small, "19th-century" offices. Instead, it meant a greatly-expanded office structure, with large numbers of people working in a single office. The situation was no longer that of the 19th-century office, where some of the clerks were in effect apprenticing managers. The expanded office structure, on the contrary, brought with it a rapid growth of low-level, dead-end jobs.

It was primarily women who filled those low-level jobs. By 1920, for instance, women made up over 90 percent of the typists and stenographers in the United States. (See Table 2.) Women—whose "natural" docility and dexterity made them the ideal workers for these jobs on the bottom of the office hierarchy. By harping upon the docility of the female character, writers like Spillman in the *Ladies' Home Journal* provided a convenient rationalization for the fact that most low-level clerical workers in dead-end jobs were women.

It is important to point out that differentiating office workers by sex is not the same as dividing them into groups distinguished, say, by eye color. The sexual division of labor in the office—where men hold the majority of managerial positions and women fill the majority of low-level, clerical jobs—is a division which is strengthened by the positions which men and women hold outside the office.

When the ideology of passive female labor first manifested itself in the early 20th century, the United States was, by and large, a patriarchal society. Patriarchal relations between men and women, in which men made decisions and women followed them, were carried over into the office.

These patriarchal social relations meshed very conveniently with office bureaucracies, where the means by which the workers were told what to do was often an extremely personalized one. For although the number of clerical workers was large, they were often divided into small enough groups so that five or six typists, stenographers or file clerks would be directly accountable to one supervisor. And if that supervisor was a man (as was generally the case in the early 20th century) and those clerical workers were women, it is easy to see how patriarchal patterns of male-female relations would reinforce the office hierarchy.

The segmentation of the office work force by sex thus promoted a situation where a docile mass of clerical workers would follow without rebellion the directives of a relatively small group of managers. The ideology that women, by virtue of their "feminine docility", were naturally suited to fill the low-level clerical jobs, can be seen as an important buttress of the stability of the hierarchical office structure.

13

WELFARE, REFORM, AND WORLD WAR I

ALLEN F. DAVIS

The progressive movement of the early twentieth century was one of America's most important reform movements. Not only did progressive measures such as the Children's and Women's bureaus signal the acceptance of national government intervention in social issues, but nearly every aspect of society was brought under rational, "scientific" scrutiny by progressive social workers, journalists, and social scientists. Under the umbrella of progressivism, settlement houses were established to house the destitute, mental hospitals were brought into line with advanced mental hygiene practices, city governments were cleansed of machine politics and politicians, and the political system was further democratized by the addition of measures for popular recall and referendum.

Yet for all of its accomplishments, the progressive movement seemed to vanish into the quagmire of World War I. With American commitment to the war in 1917 and the consequent military mobilization, progressive programs and goals faded into the background as national attention was focused on preparations for the war in Europe.

But, as Allen F. Davis shows in this essay, what appeared to be the disappearance of the progressive movement often became its continuation in a new form. As the nation mobilized for war, progressives entered the government as administrators, consultants, and advisors, taking their reform ideas with them. Ironically perhaps, the war powers of the federal government gave the progressives a greater opportunity to apply their ideas than they ever had under peacetime conditions.

Compare this essay with that of Howard Gillette in Reading 9. What was the importance of wartime conditions in the development of the progressive movement? Why were such conditions so conducive to progressivism? How does progressivism compare with other reform movements, such as those discussed by Melvyn Dubofsky, Lawrence C. Goodwyn, Linda Gordon, and Dominic J. Capeci in this reader?

Only a decade ago historians were satisfied with the simple generalization that World War I killed the progressive movement, or that the crusade to make the world safe for democracy absorbed the reforming zeal of the progressive era and compounded the disillusionment that followed. "Participation in the war put an end to the Progressive movement," Richard Hof- stadter announced. "Reform stopped dead," Eric Goldman decided. It is now obvious that the relationship between social reform and World War I is more complex. Henry May has demonstrated that some of the progressive idealism had cracked and begun to crumble even before 1917, while Arthur Link and Clarke Chambers have discovered that a great deal of

Reprinted from *American Quarterly*, 19 (Fall 1967): 516–533. Copyright 1967, the Trustees of the University of Pennsylvania. Reprinted with the permission of the author and the *American Quarterly*.

progressivism survived into the 1920s. At the same time several historians have shown that for the intellectuals associated with the *New Republic* the war seemed something of a climax to the New Nationalism. And William Leuchtenburg has argued that the economic and social planning of World War I was a much more important model for the New Deal than anything that happened during the progressive era.

It is an overworked truism that there were many progressive movements, but one of the most important and interesting was the social justice movement. Led by social workers, ministers and intellectuals, the social justice movement, in broadest terms, sought to conserve human resources and to humanize the industrial city. The social justice reformers tried to improve housing, abolish child labor, limit the hours of work for both men and women, build parks and playgrounds and better schools. Like all progressives they believed that by altering the environment it was possible to reconstruct society. They combined optimism and a large amount of moral idealism with an exaggerated faith in statistics, efficiency and organization. Of course the social justice reformers did not always agree among themselves; prohibition, immigration restriction and the war itself caused divisions within the group.

The optimism and the idealism of the social justice reformers had been tempered before 1917. In a real sense the formation of the Progressive Party with its platform of industrial minimums had seemed the climax to their crusade. The collapse of the Progressive party coming almost simultaneously with the outbreak of war in Europe led to shock and disillusionment and to many pronouncements that the war had ended social reform. The shock wore off quickly, though some of the disillusionment remained. Many reformers continued to promote social welfare legislation. They lobbied for the La Follette Seaman's bill, and early in 1916 helped to force a reluctant Wilson into supporting a national child labor law. Most of the social justice reformers voted for Wilson in 1916 but without a great deal of enthusiasm. The specter of war hung over

them as it hung over all Americans, but for many of them the acceptance or rejection of war was an especially difficult, and in some cases, a shattering experience. A few, like Jane Addams, Lillian Wald and Alice Hamilton, were consistent pacifists. Most of them opposed the preparedness movement and America's entry into the war, and they played important roles in organizations like the American Union Against Militarism. But when the United States declared war most of them went along with the decision, with fear and trembling but with loyalty. They feared that the crisis of war would cancel the victories they had won, that civil liberties would be abridged, that education and recreation and health standards would be neglected, that child labor and long hours for men and women would be resumed in the name of national need. Yet gradually, to their own surprise, many of them came to view the war, despite its horror and its dangers, as a climax and culmination of their movement for social justice in America.

Few of the reformers saw the war as a great crusade to make the world safe for democracy, at least in the beginning, but they were soon caught up in the feverish activity and enthusiasm for action that marked the first months of the war. Part of the excitement came from the thrill of being listened to after years of frustration, of plotting and planning and lobbying. "Enthusiasm for social service is epidemic . . . ," Edward T. Devine, the General Secretary of the New York Charity Organization Society, wrote in the summer of 1917, "a luxuriant crop of new agencies is springing up. We scurry back and forth to the national capital; we stock offices with typewriters and new letterheads; we telephone feverishly, regardless of expense, and resort to all the devices of efficient 'publicity work.' . . . It is all very exhilarating, stimulating, intoxicating." The reformers went to Washington; they also joined the Red Cross or the YMCA and went to France. For a time during the war the capital of American social work and philanthropy seemed to have been transferred from New York to Paris. Devine, who in 1918 was in Paris working for the Red Cross, wrote:

We have moved our offices to 12 Boissy d'Anglas, the Children's Bureau is on the ground floor; the Tuberculosis Bureau with the Rockefeller Foundation was already on the third . . . , the rest of the Department of Civil Affairs is on the first floor, Bureau Chiefs and Associate Chiefs being marshalled along the street side in an imposing array, with Mr. [Homer] Folks and Mr. [John] Kingsbury at one end and Miss Curtis and myself at the other.

John Andrews, Secretary of the American Association for Labor Legislation, surveyed the new kind of administrator being employed by the government, many of them social workers and college professors, and decided that "Perhaps aggressive competition with Germany is having a beneficial effect on bureaucratic Washington." Andrews had gone to Washington in October 1917 to try to get the House to pass a bill, already approved by the Senate, providing workmen's compensation for longshoremen. With Congress ready to adjourn everyone assured him there was no chance for passage. But he went to see President Wilson, and the next day the bill passed the House under the unanimous consent rule. Andrews was amazed and found himself with a great stack of unused facts and statistics. "Usually before our bills are passed, we wear our facts threadbare," he remarked. "Perhaps this is not the most democratic way to secure urgently needed labor laws, but it is effective."

Not everyone of course shared the enthusiasm for war, nor the confidence that war would lead to great social gain. There was some truth in Randolph Bourne's charge that the intellectuals who saw so much good coming out of war were deceiving themselves and falling victim to the worst kind of chauvinism and rationalization. "It is almost demonical," Helena Dudley, a Boston settlement worker, wrote to Jane Addams, "the sweep toward conscription and these enormous war loans which Wall Street is eager to heap on: and labor so passive and the socialists broken up, and the social workers lining up with the bankers." Another woman reported from Seattle that there "the men who feel 'the call to arms' and the women who feel 'the call to knit' for the Red Cross are the men and women generally opposed to labor legislation and all progressive movements to increase the rights and well being of the many." But these were minority views.

Most of the social justice reformers joined John Dewey, Thorstein Veblen and the *New Republic* progressives and applauded the positive action of the Wilson administration in taking over the railroads, mobilizing industry and agriculture. They looked forward to sweeping economic reforms and contemplated the "social possibilities of war." "Laissez-faire is dead," one of them wrote, "Long live social control: social control, not only to enable us to meet the rigorous demands of the war, but also as a foundation for the peace and brotherhood that is to come." Some of them, inspired by the promise of the Russian Revolution and wartime socialism in England, looked forward to a kind of "democratic collectivism."

But the social justice reformers were concerned with more than an extension of the New Nationalism, and their primary interest was not in economic planning. They wanted to continue their crusade for social justice. Nothing was more important to them than the rights of the workingman, and the working woman and child. More than most progressives they had supported the cause of organized labor, and they were cheered by the rights won by labor during the war. The National War Labor Policies Board, the United States Employment Service and other wartime agencies recognized collective bargaining, the minimum wage and the eight-hour day, improved conditions of work and reduced the exploitation of women and children in industry. "One of the paradoxes of the war is the stimulus it is giving to human conservation," a writer in *The Survey* noted. The social justice reformers spent a large amount of time making sure labor standards were not weakened, and that women and children were not exploited during the war. Yet even the invalidation of the National Child Labor Law by the Supreme Court failed to dim their enthusiasm. The National Child Labor Committee set to work to design another and better law, and Congress responded by passing a bill that levied a 10 per cent tax on products produced by children under fourteen. A Supreme Court decision did not seem very important when Secretary of War Newton Baker and other members of the Wilson administration were saying publicly: "We cannot afford, when we are losing boys in France to lose children in the United States at the same time . . . , we cannot afford when this nation is having a drain upon the life of its young manhood . . . , to have the life of women workers of the United States depressed."

The crisis of war also stimulated the movement to improve urban housing. The housing movement was central to the social justice movement and intertwined with all other reforms from child labor legislation to progressive education. Much of the prewar movement, led by men like Lawrence Veiller, was devoted to passing restrictive legislation, but the war brought the first experiment with public housing. Borrowing something from the English example and spurred to action by the crucial need for housing war workers, the Federal Government, operating through the United States Shipping Board and the Department of Labor, built or controlled dozens of housing projects during the war. For many who had been working to improve urban housing for decades the government experiments seemed like the climax to the movement. Lawrence Veiller himself drew up the "Standards for Permanent Industrial Housing Developments" that were followed by the government agencies. The result was that the projects were much better designed and safer than those built by commercial builders. In addition the architects of the developments, influenced by the English Garden City Movement and by the settlement ideal of neighborhood unity, experimented with row houses, curved streets, recreation and shopping areas. Thus the public housing experiment of World War I was clearly the product of the city planning as well as of the housing movement of the progressive era.

The war also provided a climax to the social insurance movement, which had won very little support in the United States before 1910. Many states had passed workmen's compensation laws by 1917, but they were inadequate and filled with loopholes, and the philosophy of the movement was only gradually being accepted by many reformers, let alone the general public, when the United States became involved in World War I. Consequently the Military and Naval Insurance Act, which became law October 6, 1917, was hailed as a great victory by the leaders of the movement. The act, which was drawn up by Judge Julian Mack with the aid of experts like Lee Frankel and Julia Lathrop, required each enlisted man to make an allotment to his family, which the government supplemented. It also provided compensation in case of death or disability, and re-education in case of crippling injury. The architects of the plan hoped that it would prevent the demands for pensions and bonuses that had followed every American war, but more important to those who had fought for social insurance was the fact that the government had assumed the extra hazard involved in military service and guaranteed a minimum standard of subsistence to the soldier's family. The act was slow to get into operation, indeed some families did not receive their allotments until after the Armistice. It also put a heavy burden on the Red Cross, which tried to advance the money to needy families, but at the time the act seemed to mark a victory for an important progressive measure.

Health insurance had made even less progress in the United States before 1917 than had workmen's compensation, but a group of social workers in 1915 picked it as the next great reform. "Health Insurance—the next step in social progress," became their slogan. A few states had amended their workmen's compensation laws to include industrial diseases, and New York, New Jersey, Massachusetts and a few other states were investigating the possibility of compulsory, contributory workmen's health insurance when the war came. The war seemed to increase the need. The New Jersey commission on old age insurance, in urging the government to enact a health insurance law, declared that "health protection . . . has been raised by the war from a position deserving of humanitarian consideration to one demanding action if we are to survive as a nation." But compulsory health insurance quickly aroused the opposition of the insurance companies and the medical profession, as well as of other groups who denounced it as "Prussianism." Not even the reminder that most of the British troops were protected by government health insurance could stop the opposition.

While health insurance fell victim to the war, or perhaps more accurately to a combination of circumstances, the movement to improve the nation's health was stimulated by the conflict. "War makes sanitation a common cause," Alice Hamilton announced. "We suddenly discovered that health is not a personal matter, but a social obligation," Owen Lovejoy remarked. Early fears that the war, by drawing doctors and nurses into the Army, would lead to a rise in infant mortality, tuberculosis and other diseases proved groundless as a variety of agencies, volunteers and the Federal Government rallied to the cause. Lillian Wald, who opposed American participation in the war, served on the Red Cross Advisory Committee, traveled frequently to Washington as a consultant on health matters, and labored long and hard to keep the district nurses in New York functioning at top efficiency even during the influenza epidemic at the end of the war. Part of the stimulus to the health movement during the war came from the massive attempt to control venereal disease, part came from shock, especially over the rejection of 29 per cent of those drafted as physically unfit for service. But it was more than shock. As one social worker expressed it: "far from arresting public health progress, the war has suddenly defined America's public health problem. And the aroused public conscience has promptly enacted measures which a few months ago would have been tabled by leisurely officials and classed as visionary schemes. Into a year has been packed the progress of a decade."

Other reform movements seemed to make great strides during the war. The use of industrial education in rehabilitation work pleased the supporters of progressive education, while the mental hygiene movement approved the use of psychiatrists and psychiatric tests by the Army. The use of schools as community centers by the Coun-

cil of National Defense led to the climax of the school social center movement, and the development of community councils and war chests stimulated community organization and led to acceptance of the federated fund drive.

Women also profited from the war. Out of necessity they achieved a measure of equal rights. They entered hundreds of occupations formerly barred to them, and their presence led to the establishment of the Women in Industry Service and ultimately to the Women's Bureau of the Department of Labor. "Wonderful as this hour is for democracy and labor—it is the first hour in history for the women of the world," Mrs. Raymond Robins, the President of the National Women's Trade Union League, announced in 1917. "This is the woman's age! At last after centuries of disabilities and discriminations, women are coming into the labor and festival of life on equal terms with men." The war also seemed to accelerate the movement for woman suffrage. Eight additional states gave women the vote, at least on some issues, during 1917. Wilson, after years of opposition, came out in favor of women voting, and the House of Representatives passed a woman suffrage amendment in January 1918.

The Negro and the immigrant often fell victim to racist hysteria during the war and did not gain as much as other groups. But the war seemed to hold hope even for the disadvantaged. Negroes were drafted and enlisted in the Army in great numbers and often served with distinction. All the training camps, recreation facilities and even the YMCA buildings were segregated, and there were many incidents of racial bitterness and a few of violence. Yet many of the social justice progressives, who had always been more sympathetic to the Negro's plight than had most reformers, hoped that the Negro's willingness to serve and what he learned in the Army would help lead to better conditions after the war. They were cheered by the appointment of Emmett J. Scott, Secretary of Tuskegee Institute, as Special Assistant to the Secretary of War, and by the emergence of a number of young leaders within the Negro community. "We may expect to see the walls of prejudice gradually crumble before the onslaught of common sense and racial progress," a writer in *The Crisis* predicted.

It was hard to forget the bloody battle of East St. Louis and the race riot in Houston for which thirteen Negro soldiers were executed. It was easy to dwell on a thousand incidents of prejudice and on the lynchings that continued during the war, but many agreed with William E. B. DuBois when he called in July 1918 for the Negro to close ranks, support the war effort and put aside special grievances. "Since the war began we have won: Recognition of our citizenship in the draft; One thousand Negro officers; Special representation in the War and Labor Departments; Abolition of the color line in railway wages; Recognition as Red Cross Nurses; Overthrow of segregation ordinances; A strong word from the President against lynching. . . . Come fellow black men," DuBois urged his critics, "fight for your rights, but for god's sake have sense enough to know when you are getting what you fight for."

The war did not end the grievances, but it seemed to improve the Negro's lot. It also stimulated a massive migration. A large number of Negroes had moved north even before 1914 but the war and the lure of jobs increased the flow. Many Negroes did find employment, but they also encountered prejudice and hate. Social workers and a few other reformers continued to struggle against increasing odds to aid the Negro. Yet during the war the problems and the prejudice seemed less important than the promise for the future. The migration north and the large numbers who joined the Army also seemed to create improved wages and better treatment for Negroes in the South. The story of the migration might be told in terms of crime and corruption, of drift and hate, a writer in *Survey* noted but "Against it, there is a story of careful adjustment to new circumstances, of stimulation to self-help, of education . . . , of job findings and vocational guidance. . . ."

The story of the treatment of the immigrant and alien during the war was also not entirely bleak. German-Americans were attacked as radicals, pacifists and traitors, and wartime hysteria led to the development of super-patriotism and the decline of civil liberties. Yet at the time the patriotic enthusiasm seemed in some cases to accelerate the process of Americanization. The sight of many different ethnic groups joining enthusiastically to support Liberty Bond drives and other war activities led one observer to predict that the war would "weld the twenty-five or thirty races which compose our population into a strong, virile and intelligent people . . . ," into "a splendid race of new Americans." The war also strengthened the movement to restrict immigration. In February 1917, a bill requiring a literacy test for the first time passed Congress and became law. There had always been disagreement among social justice progressives on the matter of restriction; some had argued that to help those already here it was necessary to reduce the flow, but the war seemed to end the debate. Not all reformers greeted the new law as a victory for progressivism, but no one, not even the Immigrant Protective League, launched an effective protest against the bill. The National Committee for Constructive Immigration Legislation, formed in 1918, and supported by a great variety of reformers, tried only to soften and define the restrictive legislation.

Despite occasional setbacks reform seemed to triumph in many areas during the war, but perhaps the most impressive victory came with the progressive take-over of the training camps. The Commission on Training Camp Activities was a product of the minds of Newton Baker and Raymond Fosdick. Baker, of course, had been a municipal reformer, and progressive mayor of Cleveland before becoming Secretary of War. Fosdick had been a settlement worker and Commissioner of Accounts in New York and an expert on American and European police systems. As Chairman of the Commission Fosdick picked men like Joseph Lee of the Playground Association, Lee Hanner of the Russell Sage Foundation and John Mott of the YMCA to serve with him. With the aid of several other private agencies the Commission on Training Camps set out to apply the techniques of social work, recreation and community organization to the problem of mobilizing, entertaining and protecting the American serviceman at home and abroad. They organized community singing and baseball, post exchanges and theaters, and even provided university extension courses for the troops. They moved out into the communities near the military bases and in effect tried to create a massive settlement house around each army camp. No army had seen anything like it before, but it provided something of a climax to the recreation and community organization movement and a victory for those who had been arguing for creative use of leisure time, even as it angered most of the career army men.

The Commission on Training Camp Activities also continued the progressive crusades against alcohol and prostitution. Clearly a part of the progressive movement, both crusades sought to preserve the nation's human resources, and were stimulated by a mixture of moral indignation and the latest medical knowledge. The prohibition movement had a long history, of course, but in its most recent upsurge it had been winning converts and legislative victories since the 1890s. The fight was led by the Anti-Saloon League and the Woman's Christian Temperance Union, but was supported by many social workers and social justice reformers who saw prohibition as a method of improving social conditions in the cities. But many of them had refused to go all the way with the crusade against alcohol. In New York a group of settlement workers had agitated against the Sunday closing of saloons; they appreciated that the saloon served as a social center. The most successful municipal reformers, including Newton Baker in Cleveland, carefully avoided enforcing some of the liquor laws, realizing how easy it was to antagonize the urban masses. The war stimulated the movement and brought it to a climax; it also ended the lingering doubts among many reformers. It became patriotic to support prohibition in order to save the grain for food, and for the first time in 1917 the National Conference of Social Work came out in favor of prohibition. But it was more than patriotism, for temperance was one key to social advance. Edward T. Devine announced after returning from Russia in 1917 that "the social revolution which followed

the prohibition of vodka was more profoundly important and more likely to be permanent than the political revolution which abolished autocracy." Robert Woods, who had long supported prohibition, predicted in 1919 that the 18th amendment would reduce poverty, nearly wipe out prostitution and crime, improve labor organization and "substantially increase our national resources by setting free vast, suppressed human potentialities."

The progressive era also saw a major attack on prostitution, organized vice and the white slave trade, which seemed closely allied with the liquor traffic. Although the progressive vice reformer concentrated his attack on the madams and pimps and business interests which exploited the natural sex instincts of others, he also denied the time-honored defense of the prostitute, that it was necessary for the unmarried male to "sow his wild oats." Using the latest medical statistics, he argued that continence was the best defense against the spread of venereal disease.

Progressive attitudes toward alcohol and prostitution were written into sections twelve and thirteen of the Military Draft Act. They prohibited the sale of liquor to men in uniform and gave the President power to establish zones around all military camps where prostitution and alcohol would be outlawed. There was opposition from a few military commanders, a number of city officials and from at least one irate citizen who protested that red-light districts were "God-provided means for prevention of the violation of innocent girls, by men who are exercising their 'God-given passions.'" But Raymond Fosdick, with the full cooperation of the government, launched a major crusade to wipe out sin in the service; "Fit to Fight" became the motto. It was a typical progressive effort—a large amount of moral indignation combined with the use of the most scientific prophylaxis. Josephus Daniels, the Secretary of the Navy, disapproved of Fosdick's methods. He believed that urging the men to avoid sexual contact was the best and only way to reduce disease; "Men must live straight if they would shoot straight," he told the sailors on one occasion. But when the disease rate in the Navy became the highest in the service he gave in to Fosdick's demand that science as well as moralism be used. The crusade was successful, for by the end of 1918 every major red-light district in the country had been closed, and the venereal disease rate had been lowered to produce what one man called, "the cleanest Army since Cromwell's day."

To protect the health of the soldiers was not enough, however; "We must make these men stronger in every sense, more fit, morally, mentally and physically than they have ever been in their lives . . . ," one recreation worker announced. "These camps are national universities —training schools to which the flower of American youth is being sent." When the boys go to France, "I want them to have invisible armour to take with them," Newton Baker told a conference on War Camp Community Service. "I want them to have armour made up of a set of social habits replacing those of their homes and communities."

France provided a real test for the "invisible armour" of the American soldier. He was forbidden to buy or to accept as gifts any alcoholic beverage except light wine and beer. Despite hundreds of letters of protest from American mothers, Fosdick and Baker decided it would be impossible to prevent the soldiers from drinking wine in France. But sex posed a more serious threat, for both the British and French armies had tried to solve the problem of venereal disease by licensing and inspecting prostitutes. Clemenceau could not understand the American attempt to outlaw prostitution and even accused the American Army of spreading disease among the French civilian population. He graciously offered to provide the Americans with licensed prostitutes. General Pershing considered the offer "too hot to handle" and gave it to Fosdick. When Fosdick showed it to Baker, the Secretary of War remarked, "For God's sake, Raymond, don't show this to the President or he'll stop the war." The Americans never accepted Clemenceau's invitation and he continued to be baffled by the American progressive mind.

One of the overriding assumptions of those

who sought to protect the American soldier at home and abroad was that he would learn from his experience and return to help make a better America after the war. Indeed one of the major reasons for the optimism of the social justice reformers was their confidence that the experiments and social action of the war years would lead to even greater accomplishments in the reconstruction decade ahead. Robert Woods surveyed the positive actions of the federal government during wartime in the spring of 1918 and asked, "Why should it not always be so? Why not continue in the years of peace this close, vast, wholesome organism of service, of fellowship, of constructive creative power?" Even Jane Addams, who saw much less that was constructive about war than did many of her colleagues, lectured for Herbert Hoover's Food Administration, and looked ahead with confidence and hope for the future. Paul Kellogg, editor of *The Survey,* also mirrored some of the hope for continuing the reform that the war had accelerated when he wrote to his subscribers in September 1918:

With hundreds of people for the first time shaken out of their narrow round of family and business interests and responding to public service as a patriotic call, with American help going out to the far ends of the earth as at no time since the early stages of the missionary movement; with federal action affecting housing, labor relations, community life, as never before; with reconstruction plans afoot in England and France . . . we feel that *The Survey* has never before faced such a great obligation and such a great opportunity.

Of course the enthusiasm for the present and optimism for the future was sometimes tempered by doubts. There was the occasional glimpse of the horror of war, especially by those who went overseas. There was the abridgment of the freedom of speech and the persecution of radicals and aliens and pacifists. There was the fear that opposition or apathy would arise after the war to strike down the gains, and that the American labor movement, led by Gompers, was too conservative to take advantage of the opportunity for labor advance. There was even a lingering worry about the very enthusiasm for reform that made the war years exciting, concern over the disappearance of the opposition and even the decline of debate over immigration restriction, prohibition and other measures. But the doubts were few and far between. Most of the social justice reformers surveyed the success of social reform at home and looked confidently toward the future. For them the war was not so much a war to make the world safe for democracy as it was a war that brought to a climax their crusade for reform at home.

Yet the progressives deluded themselves. They were the victims of their own confidence and enthusiasm, for the social reforms of the war years were caused more by the emergency situation than by a reform consensus. Quickly after the war, the Wilson administration abandoned public housing and social insurance, and withdrew the government from positive participation in many areas. The gains for labor and the Negro proved ephemeral, and the dream that the newly enfranchised women, together with a generation of young men educated on the battlefields and in the training camps, would lead a great crusade to reconstruct America turned out to be idealistic in the extreme.

By 1920 there was little left from wartime social reform except prohibition, immigration restriction and racist hysteria. The disillusionment that followed can be explained in part by the false hopes raised by the war. Many social justice progressives had been discouraged by the failure of the Progressive Party, then rescued by the excitement of the wartime social experiments. The collapse of the dreams fostered by the war changed American reformers irrevocably. They would never again be quite as optimistic and enthusiastic. Their faith in statistics and their confidence that the American people really wanted reform were shattered. Yet the despair was not complete—it never reached the depths that marked the group of young intellectuals which Ernest Hemingway came to symbolize. Their disillusionment was tempered by a lingering vision of social justice, a vision of government action to protect the rights of labor, and especially the working woman and child, of public housing and social insurance, of equal opportunity for the Negro and other minorities.

A number of social justice progressives worked quietly and sometimes forlornly during the twenties preparing to battle for the success of some of their plans in the 1930s and after. Very often their point of reference was World War I. It is no longer possible to say simply that the war ended the progressive movement. It was not the war itself which killed reform, but rather the rejection afterward of the wartime measures which seemed at the time to constitute the climax to the crusade for social justice. Yet scholars interested in the collapse and survival of progressivism should examine the war years, for here were raised some of the hopes that were later dashed and some of the dreams that were later fulfilled.

14

W. E. B. DU BOIS: DUSK OF DAWN

LERONE BENNETT

By the beginning of the twentieth century many black Americans and their leaders despaired of ever achieving equality in American society. In the South, where the majority of blacks lived at the turn of the century, disenfranchisement, the legal discrimination of the Black Codes, the terrorism of lynchings, and the intimidation and violence of the Ku Klux Klan served notice that white society meant to keep black Americans separate and unequal. The manifest racial discrimination that southern blacks encountered when they traveled north only served to reinforce the conclusion that the Thirteenth and Fourteenth Amendments to the Constitution, which guaranteed black citizenship and voting rights, were hollow phrases that would never be realized in practice.

It was against this background of profound racial domination that black leaders argued over "the Negro problem" and the proper course to be taken by their people. Two of the most famous and powerful of these leaders were Booker T. Washington and W. E. B. Du Bois. Faced with the fact of deep-seated racial antagonism and with little prospect for immediate accommodation, Washington urged his people to forget integration into white society and to concentrate their energies on the intellectual, moral, and economic development of their race. To accomplish the "civilization" of what he called "the Negro peasant," Washington proposed a program that would promote black business, provide vocational education for the majority of black children, and provide a separate black world that would parallel that of whites. To accomplish these goals Washington founded the Tuskegee Institute as a technical college that would train young black people in the skills needed to meet the demands of a modern business-oriented society. With great success, Washington appealed to the giants of the financial and business world for funds to build and operate Tuskegee and to make it a shining example of black abilities in a hostile white world.

Not all black leaders were willing to follow the path of Booker T. Washington however. As Lerone Bennett points out in this essay, resistance to Washington's accommodation with American racism became manifest with the rise of the Niagara Movement and the founding of the National Association for the Advancement of Colored People (NAACP) in the first decade of the twentieth century. At the center of this opposition was the man who organized the Niagara Movement and helped found the NAACP, W. E. B. Du Bois. Surveying the history and present circumstances of black people, Du Bois concluded that the active integration of black people into the mainstream of American life was the only realistic goal to follow.

Considering the deep-running racism of American society, as described by Law-

Reprinted by permission from Lerone Bennett Jr., *Pioneers in Protest.* © 1968 Johnson Publishing Company, Inc.

rence C. Goodwyn in Reading 7, Elizabeth Bethel in Reading 1, and Jack Chen in Reading 3, do you think Washington's or Du Bois' strategy the most effective? How does the course of the black movement in the early twentieth century compare with that of the birth control movement discussed in Reading 15?

On Thursday night, February 23, 1893, a young black student performed an extraordinary ceremony in a small room in Berlin.

He was alone in the room. No one knew what he was doing or why. No one knew then that it would be important later—no one, that is, except the black student who answered to the name of William Edward Burghardt Du Bois.

A solitary black pebble on the hot white sand of Berlin, a cultural pinnacle of triumphant Western civilization, Du Bois was completing a graduate course at the University of Berlin. The prospects before him were not promising. He was an orphan, he was poor, and he had more pride than could be profitably used. Most important of all, he was black, and this was an age of unbridled racism. In that year, in the heyday of Victoria and Leopold and "Pitchfork" Ben Tillman, the white man bestrode the earth like a colossus and the future was white with the promise of endless Western expansion. No one knew then that Western civilization was about to unravel at the seams. No one knew then that the bubble was about to burst—no one, that is, except W. E. B. Du Bois, who celebrated his twenty-fifth birthday on that faraway night by vowing to become the Moses of the black people of Africa and America. To seal that vow, he improvised a ritual of regeneration, using Greek wine, candles, oil, and oranges. In the stillness of the small room, he prayed, sang, "cried &c." Then he made "a sacrifice to the *Zeitgeist* of Work, God, and Mercy." Later that night, before closing his eyes, W. E. B. Du Bois wrote strange words in his diary:

I am glad I am living. I rejoice as a strong man to run a race, and I am strong—is it egotism is it assurance—or is it the silent call of the world spirit that makes me feel that I am royal and that beneath my sceptre a world of kings shall bow? The hot dark blood of that black forefather born king of men—

is beating at my heart, and I know that I am either a genius or a fool.

I wonder what I am—I wonder what the world is—I wonder if life is worth the striving. I do not know—perhaps I shall never know; but this I do know: be the Truth what it may I shall seek it on the pure assumption that it is worth seeking—and Heaven nor Hell, God nor Devil shall turn me from my purpose till I die. . . .

I am striving to make my life all that life may be —and I am limiting that strife only in so far as that strife is incompatible with others of my brothers and sisters making their lives similar. The crucial question now is where this limit comes . . . God knows I am sorely puzzled . . . I therefore take the work that the Unknown lays in my hands & work for the rise of the Negro people, taking for granted that their best development means the best development in the world.

This night before my life's altar I reiterate, what my heart has—

The tumbling flow of words breaks off here and resumes with this promise:

These are my plans: to make a name in science, to make a name in literature and thus to raise my race. Or perhaps to raise a visible empire in Africa thro' England, France, or Germany.

I wonder what will be the outcome? Who knows?

I will go unto the King—which is not according to the law & if I perish—I *perish*.

When, seventy years later, W. E. B. Du Bois perished, having gone up to the King, in spite of and in defiance of law, he had made a name in science and in literature and had lifted his race by founding the modern black protest movement and the Pan-African movement. In Africa, at his death, there was a "visible empire"; and, in America, there were two visible monuments—the NAACP, which he helped to found in 1909, and the Freedom movement, which is the reverberating echo of the new ideas he articulated between 1903 and 1933.

But in death, as in life, Du Bois is a figure of controversy. On the edge of the grave, disillusioned and disheartened, he made two decisions that will doubtless exercise future historians. In 1961, at the age of ninety-three, he became a member of the Communist party. Two years later, shortly before his ninety-fifth birthday, he became a citizen of Ghana. Some Americans contend that "overzealous" defenders of the status quo hounded Du Bois out of America and into the Communist party. However he came to his ordeal, his life—particularly the last period—was a bitter parable of a bitter time.

Parables apart, this fact remains. Du Bois was a mountain no Afro-American, or white man, for that matter, can ignore. It can be said, in fact, that no one can understand the Afro-American who does not understand the early Du Bois.

In 1934, the Board of Directors of the NAACP said: ". . . the ideas which he propounded [in the *Crisis*] and in his books and essays transformed the Negro world as well as a large portion of the liberal white world, so that the whole problem of the relation of black and white races has ever since had a completely new orientation. He created, what never existed before, a Negro intelligentsia, and many who have never read a word of his writings are his spiritual disciples and descendants. Without him the Association could never have been what it was and is."

Du Bois, who cared nothing for convention and always spoke the Truth (his capital) as he saw it, agreed.

"I think I may say without boasting," he wrote, "that in the period from 1910 to 1930 I was a main factor in revolutionizing the attitude of the American Negro toward caste. My stinging hammer blows made Negroes aware of themselves, confident of their possibilities and determined in self-assertion. So much so that today common slogans among the Negro people are taken bodily from the words of my mouth."

Who was this man who spoke with such immodesty, such eloquence—and such truth?

Almost despite himself, Du Bois was the Columbus of the Negro's New World. An intellectual giant, probably the largest mind produced in black America, an actionist, a seer, a prophet, he discovered the shores beyond the Europeanized West. He was perhaps the first black man to say with all his heart and all his soul that the world did not belong to white people. He was perhaps the first black man to say in action that God had placed the Negro in the midst of Western civilization to civilize it. *Negritude,* the African personality, protest, Africa for Africans, the sociology of the slums, *The Gifts of Black Folk, The Souls of Black Folk,* the sorrow songs: all found a place in the world view of the prophet who said in 1903: "The problem of the twentieth century is the problem of the color line—the relation of the darker to the lighter races of men in Asia and Africa, in America and the islands of the sea."

Du Bois was a product of the rising tide of color he symbolized. He was one month old when Grant became President, eight years old when Victoria became Empress of India, nine when white men with guns nullified Reconstruction and the Fourteenth and Fifteenth amendments, sixty-two when Gandhi marched to the sea, and ninety-five when he died on the eve of the March on Washington.

Born February 23, 1868, in the shadow of slavery, Du Bois was the son of Alfred and Mary Du Bois, two members of the small free black elite in the town of Great Barrington in western Massachusetts. There was in his veins, he said, "a flood of Negro blood, a strain of French, a bit of Dutch, but, thank God, no Anglo-Saxon." Du Bois grew up with a strong sense of family and place. The Du Boises were poor but proud and they tended, Du Bois recalled later, to look down on the poor white immigrants who composed the bulk of the working class of Great Barrington.

Du Bois spent the first seventeen years of his life in this climate of genteel poverty. His father died while he was quite young and his mother died soon after he finished high school. As a result, the future leader spent part of his early life as the ward of relatives.

Despite his vulnerable position, Du Bois decided quite early that he was destined for big things. How he learned this is a mystery, but we catch him at the age of fifteen in an extraordinary and, considering the circumstances, somewhat immodest pursuit: collecting and annotating his papers for posterity.

Small-boned, intense, pugnacious, Du Bois made an excellent record at the predominantly white Great Barrington public schools. Although there was little overt racism in Great Barrington, he perceived early that he was beyond the pale and he reacted with the cold fury that would characterize his later life. He has written that "the sky was bluest when I could beat my mates at examination-time, or beat them at a foot-race, or even beat their stringy heads."

With the help of a church scholarship, Du Bois went in the fall of 1885 to Fisk University in Nashville, Tennessee. This was the first of several turning points in his life. He had never really known black people before. Now suddenly he was plunged into "the whole gorgeous color gamut of the American Negro world. . . ." Du Bois said later that his first day on the Fisk campus was something of a religious experience. He wandered, exhilarated, across the campus, sampling the colors—"bronze, mahogany, coffee, gold." At the first dinner at Fisk, he sat opposite a girl "of whom I have often said, no human being could possibly have been as beautiful as she seemed to my eyes that far-off September night of 1885." Ever afterwards, Du Bois would be fascinated by the beauty of black skin color and astonished by the inability of white Americans to perceive that beauty.

After graduation from Fisk, Du Bois moved on to Harvard, where he repeated part of his college work and earned M.A. and Ph.D. degrees in history. His Ph.D. dissertation, the first of nineteen works of non-fiction and fiction, was entitled *The Suppression of the African Slave Trade.* Du Bois later received a scholarship from the Slater Fund and went off for two additional years of study at the University of Berlin.

There are men in every group who will accept life on no other basis except absolute equality, men who present the hardness of their spirit to the hardness of the world, asking no favors and giving none. Du Bois was such a man. He expected, anticipated, even provoked, the hostile

consciousness of the white Other; and one can imagine him smiling disdainfully when the hostility came. He had, he said, "an island within." He was Du Bois—he needed no one.

The two years in Europe changed Du Bois' perspective. His human contacts, both at the university and in European cities, were singularly free of the collective contempt he experienced in America. He went sailing on the Rhine with a German family and spent happy holidays with French, English, and German boys and girls. When a fraulein, "blue-eyed Dora," confessed her readiness to marry him *"gleich!"* Du Bois told her "frankly and gravely" that it would be unfair to himself and cruel to her for a colored man to take a white bride to America."

As a result of his experiences in Europe, Du Bois developed a more complex view of life and race. "I became more human," he said, "[and] learned the place in life of 'Wine, Women, and Song'; I ceased to hate or suspect people simply because they belonged to one race or color. . . ."

In July, 1894, having dedicated himself to the liberation of colored peoples, Du Bois returned to America and began his academic career at Wilberforce, where he taught Latin and Greek for two years and met Nina Gomer, "the slender, quiet and dark-eyed girl who became Mrs. Du Bois in 1896." That same year, 1896, he went to the University of Pennsylvania and made the first in-depth study of an urban Negro community, *The Philadelphia Negro.* The next year, 1897, he entered on his "life plan" as a professor of economics and history at Atlanta University, where he organized a series of annual conferences on the urban Negro, and produced a series of studies that gave a new orientation to the Negro situation in America.

At this point, Du Bois was at the height of his considerable powers. Trim, agile, with chiseled features and a Van Dyke beard, Du Bois presented a picture of fastidious determination. He was seldom seen without the cane and gloves of a German student. "I doubtless strutted," he said, "and I certainly knew what I wanted. My redeeming features were infinite capacity for work, and terrible earnestness, with appalling and tactless frankness."

Although Du Bois was probably the best-educated and most gifted scholar in Atlanta, he was proscribed as a pariah. Because of the humiliation that awaited him off-campus, Du Bois lived as though the city of Atlanta did not exist. He never rode a streetcar, never entered a movie or a concert hall.

While the Du Boises were living in Atlanta, a son, Burghardt, and a daughter, Yolanda, were born to them. The girl survived but Burghardt, the first-born, died eighteen months after birth. In a house still ringing with the cries of a bereaved mother, Du Bois sat down and wrote the most searing essay in the history of race relations. In this essay, "On the Passing of the First Born," Du Bois expressed an "awful gladness" that his son had "escaped" the horrors of living the life of a black male in America. Many years later, a young man attempted to read this essay aloud. He stumbled along until he came to the words "awful gladness." Then, sobbing, he flung the book across the room and said: "No man has a right to utter such terrible sorrow."

He died at eventide, when the sun lay like a brooding sorrow above the western hills, veiling its face; when the winds spoke not, and the trees, the great green trees he loved, stood motionless. . . .

We could not lay him in the ground there in Georgia, for the earth there is strangely red; so we bore him away to the northward, with his flowers and his little folded hands. In vain, in vain!—for where, O God! beneath thy broad blue sky shall my dark baby rest in peace,—where Reverence dwells, and Goodness, and a freedom that is free?

All that day and all that night there sat an awful gladness in my heart,—nay, blame me not, if I see the world thus darkly through the Veil, and my soul whispers ever to me, saying, "not dead, not dead, but escaped, not bond, but free." No bitter meanness now shall sicken his baby heart till it die a living death. . . .

By the turn of the century, events in Atlanta and in the outer world had changed Du Bois' mind about the nature of racial reality. He re-called later that there were five lynchings a week during this period and "each death was a scar on my soul." The depth of Du Bois' emerging despair can be gauged by his passionate arraignment of God in the *Litany* he wrote after the brutal Atlanta riots of 1906.

Doth not his justice of hell stink in Thy nostrils, O God. How long shall the mounting flood of innocent blood roar in Thine ears and pound on our hearts for vengeance? Pile the pale frenzy of blood-crazed brutes, who do such deeds, high on Thine Altar, Jehoveh Jireh, and burn it in hell forever and forever!

Forgive us, good Lord; we know not what we say!

Bewildered we are and passion-tossed, mad with the madness of a mobbed and mocked and murdered people; staring at the armposts of Thy Throne, we raise our shackled hands and charge Thee, God, by the bones of our stolen fathers, by the tears of our dead mothers, by the very blood of Thy Crucified Christ: what meaneth this? Tell us the plan; give us the sign!

Keep not thou silent, O God!

Sit not longer dumb, Lord God, deaf to our prayers and dumb to our dumb suffering. Surely, Thou, too, are not white, O Lord, a pale, bloodless, heartless thing!

Du Bois' efforts as a poet and professor were based on a belief that racism was caused by ignorance. His remedy then was Truth. As the years wore on and as outrage piled on outrage, Du Bois came to see that the old saw, "The truth will set you free," is only true in the very, very long run. For Du Bois, analysis was always a step toward or away from action. Having decided that the truth was not enough, he descended from his ivory tower and tried "with bare hands to lift the earth."

Beginning in 1903 with the publication of his book, *The Souls of Black Folk,* a group of essays that had an impact on its age not unlike that of James Baldwin's *The Fire Next Time* sixty years later, Du Bois began to attack the program and policies of Booker T. Washington. To Washington's program of accommodation and submission, Du Bois opposed a program of "ceaseless agitation and insistent demands for equality," involving "the use of force of every sort: moral suasion, propaganda and . . . even physical resistance." To Washington's philosophy of "individual education," Du Bois opposed a program of higher education with special emphasis on the Talented Tenth, an elite group which would lead, inspire, exalt, serve, and guide the masses.

Taking the offensive two years later, Du Bois helped organize the germinal Niagara movement, an NAACP-like organization composed of black professionals and intellectuals. Although this group made few concrete gains, it prepared the way for the NAACP and educated black people in a strategy of protest and litigation. Du Bois and the Niagara cadre played a pivotal role in the organization of the NAACP, which merged the forces of black militancy and white liberalism in 1909. In 1910, Du Bois, then forty-two, resigned from Atlanta University and became director of publications of the new organization and editor of its organ, the *Crisis.* As *Crisis* editor, Du Bois set the tone for organization and educated a whole generation of black people in the art of protest. Many people in fact believed Du Bois and the *Crisis* were the NAACP, a belief Du Bois did nothing to dispel. By 1918, William Edward Burghardt Du Bois was by far the most prominent black man in all America.

Du Bois was not a natural leader. He despised, he said, "the essential demagoguery" of personal leadership. He could not "slap people on the back and make friends of strangers. I could not easily break down an inherited reserve; or at all times curb a biting, critical tongue." As a result, Du Bois won influence, not power. His, as he said, was a leadership solely of ideas.

Du Bois' life style caused considerable tension at the NAACP, where he operated the *Crisis* as a personal fief and reserved the right to criticize the Association in its own journal. Another source of conflict was Du Bois' racial program which differed considerably from the program of the Association. Du Bois, for example, championed what he called "economic democracy." He was also an exponent of what is now called

Negritude. Negroes, he said, had a special mission in the world. What he envisioned was a "new and great Negro ethos." To create this ethos, Negroes, he said, had to channel their power— physical, political, economic, and spiritual— through the whole Negro group. What was required, he said in a 1915 article, was "conscious self-realization and self-direction." The NAACP was essential in this effort, he said. But larger black control was necessary. "We must not only support but control this and similar organizations and hold them unswervingly to our objects, and our ideals."

World War I, which Du Bois called "the climacteric of my pilgrimage," created a new Du Bois with a "vaster conception of the role of black men in the future of civilization." Disillusioned by massacres at home and blatant racism in many army camps abroad, Du Bois began to move further away from his white liberal and black militant supporters. "Fools," he said—"yes, that's it. Fools. All of us fools fought a long, cruel, bloody and unnecessary war and we not only killed our boys— boys—we killed Faith and Hope." Convinced now that colonialism and racial imperialism were the root causes of war, Du Bois began to see himself not only as a black leader but as a leader of all the colored peoples of the world. In 1919, he organized a pioneer Pan-African Congress in Paris. In the twenties, he held a series of Pan-African congresses—in London and Brussels in 1921, in London and Lisbon in 1923, in New York in 1927.

With the coming of the Great Depression, Du Bois reevaluated his whole program and decided that the protest tradition he had spawned was doomed to futility. "By 1930," he said, "I had become convinced that the basic policies and ideals [of the NAACP] must be modified and changed; that in a world where economic dislocation has become so great as in ours, a mere appeal based on the old liberalism, a mere appeal to justice and further effort at legal decision, was missing the essential need; that the essential need was to guard and better the chances of Negroes, educated and ignorant, to earn a living, safeguard their income, and raise the level of their employ-

ment. I did not believe that a further prolonga-
tion of looking for salvation from the whites was
feasible. So far as they were ignorant of the results
of race prejudice, we had taught them; but so far
as their race prejudice was built and increasingly
built on the basis of the income which they enjoyed and their anti-Negro bias consciously or
unconsciously formulated in order to protect
their wealth and power, in so far our whole program must be changed, and we must seek to increase the power and particularly the economic
organization among Negroes to meet the new situation. . . ."

Du Bois was not then a Communist. Although
he was impressed by the Russian "experiment,"
he had nothing but contempt for the American
Communist party which was led, he said, "by a
group of pitiable mental equipment, who gave no
thought to the intricacies of the American situation, the vertical and horizontal divisions of the
American working classes, and who plan simply
to raise hell on any and all occasions, with
Negroes as shock troops—these offer in reality
nothing to us except social equality in jail." Du
Bois was equally contemptuous of the American
labor movement, white liberalism, and the black
elite. The only hope, he said, was "a magnificent
crusade" based on a great leap by the black
masses.

Beginning in January, 1934, Du Bois began to
spell out the details of the crusade in the columns
of the *Crisis.* Black people, he said, must use
segregation to smash segregation. He called for
the establishment of a "cooperative commonwealth" in the black ghetto, the organization of
producer and consumer cooperatives, the socialization of the professional services of black doctors and lawyers, and a new ethic of leadership
which would limit black leaders to small salaries.
This program, which was in essence an anticipation of the Black Power movement, horrified
NAACP leaders, who attacked Du Bois in the
Crisis and were answered by Du Bois in the
Crisis. The whole controversy became extremely
heated, and Du Bois resigned in a huff and returned to Atlanta University.

Ideology apart, this was an act of extraordi-

nary intellectual courage. For what Du Bois did
now was to turn his back on twenty-five years of
his life. He said that he now regarded the "in-
come-bearing value of race prejudice" as "the
cause not the result of prejudice" and "this conviction I had to express or spiritually die."

Although he was now sixty-six, Du Bois entered what was essentially his third career with a
spurt of energy that would have distinguished a
man half his age. During ten productive years at
Atlanta University, he wrote two books, including the seminal *Black Reconstruction,* started
work on an Afro-American encyclopedia, wrote
a weekly newspaper column, founded *Phylon,*
and lectured widely. He received a flood of tributes in these years, but he remained a disturbing
and controversial figure. In 1944, his contract at
Atlanta University was abruptly terminated and
he returned to the NAACP with the vague title of
director of special research. In this position,
Du Bois gave special attention to colonial affairs.
At the founding of the United Nations, he served
as an associate counsel to the American delegation. After the San Francisco meeting, he revived
the Pan-African movement, holding a very successful conference in London in October, 1945.
This meeting, which was a milestone in the history of the colored peoples of the world, was
attended by representatives from sixty nations
and colonies, including Jomo Kenyatta and
Kwame Nkrumah.

Throughout this period, Du Bois was the center of a series of internal disputes at NAACP
headquarters. Two months before the 1948 election, in which he supported the Progressive party
candidate, Du Bois was discharged from the
NAACP with a pension.

There is no reason to think that Du Bois was
right and his adversaries wrong in the intermina-
ble feuds that dotted his life. Du Bois was not an
organization man. He was not an easy person to
know or to work with. His presence in an organization, any organization, even his own organization, guaranteed internal strife. The old warrior
said once that he loved a good fight, and he was
not above going out of his way to pick one.

After leaving the NAACP, Du Bois abandoned the path of protest he had virtually invented and entered into an alliance with "progressive" and left-wing forces. In the next few years, he became an open advocate of "some form" of socialism, but he did not join the Communist party. "With my particular type of thinking and impulse," he said in 1948, "it was impossible for me to be a party man." Yet, he said openly that he would be a "fellow-traveler with Communist or capitalist, with white man or black" as long as "he walks towards the truth."

It seems that Du Bois maintained his independence in the left-wing camp. Biographer Francis L. Broderick noted that Du Bois "stubbornly rebuffed Communist efforts to induce him to testify at their trial" and turned thumbs down on other efforts to use him in ways not of his own choosing. Moreover, Du Bois' definition of socialism remained curiously unorthodox. He said on one occasion that the New Deal was just another name for socialism. Broderick concluded that Du Bois "appears to have remained master of his own thoughts—The Party did not set them for him. The alliance continued, at least until 1951, on Du Bois' own terms. On major issues—control of atomic energy, civil rights, the Korean War, the Marshall Plan—Du Bois sounded like an echo of the party's. Yet in all probability, Du Bois cooperated with Communists because on major issues they agreed with his independent views. . . . After all, Du Bois had been wary of white imperialism before the Russian Revolution of 1917; he had been thinking favorably about socialism at least as early as 1907; he had gone on record as a pacifist many times."

In 1949, Du Bois attended a series of international peace conferences. In 1950, he ran unsuccessfully as an American Labor party candidate in the New York senatorial race. That same year, 1950, he became chairman of the Peace Information Center, which was organized to agitate for peace and to secure American signatures on the "Stockholm Appeal," which demanded the absolute banning of atomic weapons. In 1951, Du Bois and four of his associates were indicted by a federal grand jury for failing to register the Peace Information Center as an alleged American agent of a foreign principal. Though Du Bois

was acquitted at the trial, he was deeply affected by the whole episode and by the refusal of the government to permit him to travel to several events abroad (because of his failure to sign a non-Communist affidavit), including the Ghana independence celebration.

Out of pride perhaps or even perversity, Du Bois refused to modify his philosophy. In fact, as Broderick noted, he "deliberately" avoided "softening his line—no compromises, no equivocation," for, as Du Bois himself said: "I wanted to dispel in the minds of the government and of the public any lingering doubt as to my determination to think and speak freely on the economic foundations of the wars and the frustrations of the twentieth century."

To the end, Du Bois maintained a keen interest in the Freedom movement. He was particularly encouraged by the audacity of the black youth who initiated the sit-in age in 1960. Asked if he had any advice for the sit-in students, Du Bois said: "They don't need any advice from me. Perhaps I need some from them."

After the Supreme Court invalidated the non-Communist affidavit provision, Du Bois left America and wandered across the face of the world. "In my own country," he said, "for nearly half a century I have been nothing but a nigger." Old, weary, ninety-three years of age, he entered the Communist party.

On the invitation of President Nkrumah, who considered him "the father of Pan-Africanism," Du Bois moved to Accra, Ghana. With his second wife, author Shirley Graham, whom he married in 1951 after the death of his first wife, Du Bois settled down in a comfortable cottage and began work on an *Encyclopedia Africana*. There, at the end of the trail, on the eve of the mammoth March on Washington, W. E. B. Du Bois died at 10:40, Tuesday night, August 27, 1963. The next day, the *Ghanaian Times* printed a bold black headline:

THIS DAY A MIGHTY TREE
HAS FALLEN IN AFRICA

A long way from the white snow of Great Barrington, a long way from the peach trees of

Atlanta, in a new land he called home, Du Bois was laid to rest in a plot of ground where the surf meets the sea that carried his forefathers to America decades ago. It was a gesture that would have pleased the poet. The wheel had come full cycle—from Africa to Africa, from freedom to Freedom.

Large in life, even larger in death, Du Bois received memorial tributes from left-wingers and right-wingers, liberals and conservatives, Tories and radicals. In a radio tribute, President Kwame Nkrumah of Ghana said: "The essential quality of Dr. Du Bois' life and achievement can be summed up in a single phrase—intellectual honesty and integrity." Thirty prominent Americans (James Baldwin, John Hope Franklin, John Haynes Holmes, Roy Wilkins and others) who sponsored a memorial tribute to Du Bois in Carnegie Hall perceived similar qualities in the old fighter's life. The aim of the memorial tribute, as stated by actor and playwright Ossie Davis, was "to secure to the Afro-American consciousness the personality, image, and cultural significance of the most illustrious Afro-American scholar of our time, and to present to Americans at large a proper sense of Dr. Du Bois' intellectual contribution to American life."

Even in death, Du Bois characteristically had the last word. Feeling death coming, he had written, six years before, his last message to the world. The message was read at his funeral.

It is much more difficult in theory than actually to say the last goodbye to one's loved ones and friends and to all the familiar things of this life.

I am going to take a long, deep and endless sleep. This is not a punishment but a privilege to which I have looked forward for years.

I have loved my work. I have loved people and my play but always I have been uplifted by the thought that what I have done well will live long and justify my life: that what I have done ill or never finished can now be handed on to others for endless days to be finished, perhaps better than I could have done. And that peace will be my applause.

One thing alone I charge you as you live and believe in life. Always human beings will live and progress to greater, broader and fuller life. The only possible death is to lose belief in this truth simply because the great end comes slowly; because time is long.

Goodbye.

15

BIRTH CONTROL AND SOCIAL REVOLUTION

LINDA GORDON

By the turn of the twentieth century the American women's movement had compiled over a half century of hard-won experience in fighting for the equality of women. Women had been prominent in the antislavery campaigns of the mid-nineteenth century, had organized trade unions, participated in the populist and socialist movements, and had been instrumental in bringing about protective legislation for women and child workers. Yet, in spite of their many accomplishments, women entered the present century as second-class citizens.

One way of measuring women's inferior status is to observe their political status. In 1900 a handful of western states offered women the right to vote, but in most places women—fully half of the adult population of the country—were denied a voice in the selection of those who would set local, state, and national policy. It was not until 1918 that the Nineteenth Amendment granting suffrage to women passed the House of Representatives and not until 1920 that American polls were opened to women.

Another way of measuring women's status in early twentieth-century America is to look, as Linda Gordon suggests in this essay, at the degree of control that women had over their own bodies. As early twentieth-century feminists claimed, a fundamental condition for women's full participation in social life is their ability to control their reproductive lives. This idea, which is commonplace today, was at the beginning of the century a radical, even revolutionary, notion. As Gordon shows, the idea of fully liberated women was a threat, not only to conservative men but to moderate and radical males as well. Birth control was in the beginning a very political idea.

How do you think the progressives discussed above by Howard Gillette and Allen F. Davis in Readings 9 and 13, respectively, would have responded to the birth control movement? Would the women of the Southern Farmers' Alliance, discussed by Julie Roy Jeffrey in Reading 6, have subscribed to Margaret Sanger's movement as well? How important was the availability of reliable birth control to the emergence of the New Feminism, as described below by Jane DeHart Mathews in Reading 25?

The movement that first coalesced around the slogan "birth control," a phrase invented by Margaret Sanger in 1915, was a force of people fighting for their own immediate needs, and because of this it had an intensely personal dimension for its participants. The fact that the birth controllers often stood to gain immediately in their personal lives from legalization of birth control did not narrow their vision but strengthened their commitment. They united their personal experience and emotional understanding with political thought and action. They created a politics based on women's shared experience which had the potential to unite masses of women. At the

From *Women's Body, Women's Rights* by Linda Gordon. Copyright © 1974, 1976 by Linda Gordon. Reprinted by permission of Viking Penguin, Inc.

same time the birth controllers transcended women's immediate needs. They were not seeking incremental improvements in their sex lives or medical care; they did not view birth control as primarily a sexual or medical reform at all, but as a social issue with broad implications. They wanted to transform the nature of women's rights —indeed, of human rights—to include free sexual expression and reproductive self-determination.

In challenging the traditional limits of people's control over their own lives, they used birth control to make a revolutionary demand, not a reform proposal. They did not want just to limit their pregnancies; they wanted to change the world. They believed that birth control could alleviate much human misery and fundamentally alter social and political power relations, thereby creating greater sexual and class equality. In this they shared the voluntary-motherhood analysis —that involuntary motherhood was a major prop of women's subjection—and added a radical version of a Neo-Malthusian analysis—that overlarge families weakened the working class in its just struggle with the capitalist class. They also demanded sexual freedom.

The birth controllers were putting forward these demands at a time when American radicalism was at one of its peaks of strength and breadth. Indeed, the birth-control movement that began in 1914 was a part of a general explosion of resistance to economic and social exploitation. Joining that resistance, birth controllers appealed for support to the powerless, particularly to women and to working-class and poor people in general, because they believed that lack of control over reproduction helped perpetuate an undemocratic distribution of power.

Strategically their analysis tried to draw together the women's movement and the working-class movement. The leading birth controllers between 1914 and 1920 were both feminists and socialists and wanted to unite their respective goals and constituencies. Many of them came to the birth-control cause from multi-issue reform or revolutionary movements, ranging from the suffrage organizations to the IWW. Few were

themselves working class, although some important leaders—Margaret Sanger is only one—had working-class origins. Their experience of the common oppression of women in sexual and reproductive matters convinced them that they could transcend their class differences and create a movement that would fight for the interests of the least privileged women.

They failed in this grand intention, but that does not mean that their analysis and strategy were completely wrong or that their experiences are useless to us today. Their belief that birth control could create a new freedom and dignity for women and a new right for all people was not wrong just because it was incompletely realized.

By 1914 the radical movement in the United States was unified to a large extent in a single Socialist party. From 10,000 members in 1901 it grew to include 118,000 in 1912. Its voting strength was many times greater—almost 6 per cent of the total in 1912—and by 1912 it had elected twelve hundred public officials and regularly published over three hundred periodicals. No other political party in American history has ever fought as consistently for women's rights (such as woman suffrage, employment opportunities, equal legal rights). Especially after 1910 many feminists entered the Party and began agitating for more active political work by and for women. Women's committees were organized in many locals, socialist woman-suffrage societies were created, and a few women were elected to the National Executive Committee.

The Socialist party's conception of what women's rights were, however, agreed in all respects with those advocated by liberal feminists. Like suffragists, most socialists accepted the conventional definition of woman's proper sphere and activities—home, motherhood, housework, and husband care. There was no general support in the Socialist party for birth control or for any reforms that threatened to alter or even to question traditional sexual roles and division of labor. In clinging to their traditional views of the family, socialists often cited as their authority the early Marxist view that drawing women out of their homes was one of the evils of capitalism that socialism would put right. The revolutionaries in the Socialist party, more inclined to reject the conventions, were concerned even more exclusively than the rest of the Party with class struggle in the workplace, and consequently had little interest in questions of domestic relations. The Party's women's journal, *Socialist Woman,* published in Girard, Kansas, did not have a single article that discussed the principle of voluntary motherhood before 1914. (Indeed, even when the journal got a letter asking them to take up the question, the editors declined to publish it.) Socialist women concerned with sexual issues, even regular contributors to Party periodicals, published their writings on birth control elsewhere.

Despite its great influence in the birth-control movement, the Socialist party never formally endorsed birth control. Indeed, before 1912 the issue was never the subject of major debate within the Party, so great was the disapproval of creating internal divisions. The rejection of anything but the most limited feminist goals by the Socialist-party majority reflected a larger split in the whole U.S. radical and reform community between socialism and the women's movement. That split deepened in the early twentieth century. Previously, almost all supporters of birth control had been socialists of a sort. Voluntary-motherhood advocates of the 1870s had been critical of capitalist values and social organization, as had utopian communitarians who practiced birth control; many American feminists by the end of the nineteenth century had concluded that women's emancipation would require a higher level of economic justice than capitalism could provide; most European sex radicals were socialists. But as Marxian scientific socialism began to dominate, and the organized socialist movement gained a working-class constituency, emphasis on class differences and class struggle tended to diminish the importance of sex equality as a program. Many feminists although thoroughly anticapitalist, refused to follow socialist theory into a denial of their own experience of sex oppression.

This ideological split occurred under condi-

tions of industrialization which deepened class differences among women as among men. A feminist analysis that in the 1870s seemed broad enough to include all women, by the early twentieth century could appeal only to upper-class women. By 1910 working-class women were more distant from the suffrage organizations in their point of view as well as in their actual political loyalties than they had been in the 1870s. On the other hand, the Marxian socialist movement in America had rejected many of the feminist and sex-radical traditions of utopian and other romantic socialisms. Furthermore, within the Marxist organizations, the tendency to emphasize unions and organizing at the workplace left men without pressing reasons to appeal to women, most of whom remained outside the labor force. The complaints of even the most antifeminist of socialist women leave no doubt that arrogance and disrespectful attitudes toward women were widespread among socialist men. Thus anyone trying to formulate a socialist *and* feminist theory about the importance of birth control faced serious difficulties: a conservative and elite woman-suffrage movement and a rather blindly antifeminist Socialist party.

Despite its limitations, however, the existence of the Socialist party was one of the most important, probably necessary, conditions for the emergence of the radical birth-control movement in the second decade of the century, in that it brought together almost all radicals and reformers in touch with the working class or concerned with working-class power. Without this opportunity to reach and to learn from working-class women, the sex radicals would have continued to pursue sterile, theoretical formulations, contributing at most to a bohemian life style among urban intellectuals. On the other hand, the sexual conservatism of the Party's male leadership could not contain the growing restlessness produced among women by their changed circumstances. . . .

In this period sex education was not merely action but militant action because it involved breaking the law. The Comstock law still barred "obscene" materials from the mails, and most noneuphemistic sex discussion—such as naming the human genitalia—was considered obscene. Defying such laws was a form of what the IWW called direct action, people acting directly against state and capitalist power, not petitioning or negotiating but taking what they needed. Women needed sex education. Feminists and sexual-freedom advocates agreed that women's ignorance of their bodies was debilitating and that deference to conventions about what was good for "ladies" to know deepened their passivity and political fearfulness.

In the United States a campaign of sex education formed a bridge between pro-birth-control ideas and an organized movement for birth control. Sex manuals had been plentiful since the mid-nineteenth century, but their style had begun to change in the 1900s. Even the conservative writers, while remaining moralistic, introduced detailed physiological descriptions and sometimes drawings of reproductive anatomy. Midwestern socialists and feminists of Virginia Butterfield's tradition had been the first to appreciate the importance of sex education and had written dozens of books in the first decades of the twentieth century. Somewhat later, demands for sex education appeared within the Socialist party itself. One particularly effective spokeswoman and practitioner of sex and birth-control education was Antoinette Konikow, a Russian immigrant physician. She had been one of the founding members of the Socialist party and later of the five members of its Women's Commission. She practiced medicine in Boston after her graduation from Tufts Medical School in 1902; and although Boston was then as now an overwhelmingly Catholic city, with little support even within its radical community for sexual unconventionality, she was outspoken for birth control and probably did abortions. Kronikow wrote for the *New York Call,* a daily socialist newspaper, arguing that sex education was an important task for socialists. Dr. William Jo. Robinson also wrote for the *Call* on sex hygiene; he and Kronikow were the first to focus their sex-education articles on birth control.

The most notorious for her outspokenness on

sexual questions was Emma Goldman. Goldman, more than any other person, fused into a single ideology the many currents that mingled in American sex radicalism. She had connections with European anarchism, syndicalism, and socialism; she knew and was influenced by American utopian anarchists and free lovers such as Moses Harman; she was also familiar with American feminism and with dissident doctors such as Robinson. In 1900 she had attended the secret conference of Neo-Malthusians in Paris and had even smuggled some contraceptive devices into the United States. In New York Goldman was tremendously influential on other women radicals, as a role model and a practitioner of the new morality. One woman strongly influenced by Goldman was Margaret Sanger. Sanger later tried to hide that influence. Always needing recognition and fearing rivals for power and importance, Sanger underestimated Goldman's contribution to birth control in her later writings. Sanger met Goldman when Goldman was a magnetic and dominating figure nationally and Sanger an insecure young woman lacking a cause and a political identity. Sanger still clung to more conservative sexual ideas, and Goldman must have been shocking to her, at the least.

Moving to New York City in 1911 and searching for something to do, Sanger's background as a nurse made it natural for her to take an interest in sex education. She began writing articles for the *New York Call.* At about the same time she was hired as an organizer for the Women's Commission of the Socialist party (with a small salary) and elected secretary of the Harlem Socialist Suffrage Society. In both capacities she began making speeches and was so enthusiastically received when she spoke on health and sex topics that she began to specialize in these areas. Questions and responses at the meetings and letters to the *Call* gave Sanger reinforcement and a sense of appreciation.

On the other hand, Sanger was disappointed in her more "orthodox" socialist organizing, working with striking laundry workers and trying to garner support for a legislative campaign for a wages-and-hours bill. She resigned as an organizer in January 1912. But her dissatisfaction with her Socialist-party work did not at first push her more deeply into sex-education activities; rather she was drawn, as were so many radical intellectuals at the time, toward the greater militancy of the IWW, with its direct-action tactics. When the strike of Lawrence, Massachusetts, textile workers, supported by the IWW, broke out in January 1912, Sanger became involved in support work for the strikers, which she continued until June 1912.

Sanger resumed her articles in the *Call* in November 1912 with a series, "What Every Girl Should Know." It was more daring than the first series, which had been called "What Every Mother Should Know" and had been designed to help mothers tell their children about sex and reproduction, largely through analogy to flowers and animals. The second series spoke more fully of human physiology, especially the female sexual and reproductive apparatus, and argued that the "procreative act" was something natural, clean, and healthful. But when Sanger turned to the problem of venereal disease, which had for decades been discussed in public only with euphemisms such as the "social problem" and "congenital taint," the Post Office could take no more. They declared the article unmailable under the Comstock law. The *Call* responded by printing the headline of the column—"What Every Girl Should Know"—and in a big, blank box underneath it, the words, "*NOTHING,* by order of the Post-Office Department." (The Post Office ban was lifted two weeks later on orders from Washington and the article actually appeared in the *Call* on March 2. In one of the finer ironies produced by the rapid changes in attitudes of those years, this very article was reprinted—without credit to the author—by the U.S. government and distributed among troops during World War I.)

Up until this time, however, Sanger had not discussed birth control in writing. Her sex-education work was again interrupted by a more urgent demand for her services—the Paterson silk-workers' strike that began in February 1913. The workers asked the IWW for help, and Big Bill

Haywood sent Sanger and Jessie Ashley (a socialist, feminist lawyer later to be active in birth control) to Paterson to organize picket lines. Sanger worked there until the strike's failure in the summer. She did not write anything further on sexual hygiene that year, and in October sailed for Europe with her husband and children. In Paris she began the first stage of her "research" into birth control—the sociological phase. Not yet interested in libraries and sexual theory, she spoke with her neighbors, with the French syndicalists that Bill Haywood (also then in Paris) introduced her to, with druggists, midwives, and doctors. She collected contraceptive formulas. She discovered that birth control was respectable, widely practiced, and almost traditional in France. Women told her that they had learned about contraception from their mothers. In fact, birth-control advocates in the United States such as William J. Robinson had been publishing articles about the low birth rate and widespread contraceptive use in France for years. Emma Goldman knew these facts about France. All this, however, was new to Sanger in 1913. For the rest of her life, birth control was to be her single, exclusive passion.

What were the sources of this decision, or conversion, of Sanger's? Years later she herself portrayed it as a rather sudden conversion and attributed it to an incident that had happened a year earlier in her work as a visiting nurse: an encounter with a poor Jewish family in which a beloved wife died from one pregnancy too many. She also wrote that before going to Paris she had already spent a year in New York libraries and the Library of Congress futilely searching for contraceptive information. Apparently, Bill Haywood himself urged her to go to France to learn. There can be no doubt that she was hearing about birth control frequently and that it had the basic approval of people she respected. Even in the Paterson strike it was in the air. Elizabeth Gurley Flynn recalled a meeting for women strikers at which Carlo Tresca, an IWW organizer, "made some remarks about shorter hours, people being less tired, more time to spend together and jokingly he said: 'More babies.' The women did not look amused. When Haywood interrupted and said: 'No, Carlo, we believe in birth control—a few babies, well cared for!' they burst into laughter and applause."

One key difference between Sanger and her radical friends who saw the importance of birth control was that she was dissatisfied with her role as a rank-and-file socialist organizer and was searching for something more like a career. Many biographers have commented on Sanger's drive for recognition. Among men in most situations that kind of drive would have seemed so commonplace that it would have gone unmentioned. Sanger instinctively understood that the recognition she needed required a special cause, a specialization. As a nurse, she felt comfortable building on expertise and experience she already had.

But the reason she chose contraception rather than venereal disease or sex education was her recognition of the potential historical and political meaning of birth control. Most American socialists at this time, primarily oriented to class relations, saw birth control in Neo-Malthusian terms, that is, in terms of economics. They were concerned to help raise the standard of living of workers and thus increase their freedom to take political control over their own lives. Measured against this goal, birth control was at most an ameliorative reform. Seen in terms of sexual politics, however, birth control was revolutionary because it could free women entirely from the major burden that differentiated them from men, and made them dependent on men. Sanger did not originally have this perspective. Although female and concerned about women's rights, her political education had been a male-defined one. She gained this perspective in Europe from the sexual-liberation theorists like Havelock Ellis. Ellis literally tutored Sanger. His idealism about the potential beauty and expressiveness of human sexuality and his rage at the damage caused by sexual repression fired Sanger with a sense of the overwhelming importance, urgency, and profundity of the issue of birth control, a sense lacking in most other American radicals.

The entire future course of birth control in the United States was influenced by Sanger's Euro-

pean "education" on birth control. And yet the conviction, curiosity, and drive that led her to her research in Europe would almost certainly have led someone else there if Margaret Sanger had been diverted. Sanger's European trips took place in the midst of a flurry of activity for sexual change in the United States which began before Sanger's influence was great and which would inevitably have led to a birth-control campaign before long. Sanger was stimulated by it and returned to shape it, but in all respects she was a part of a movement, not its inventor. . . .

After about 1910 Emma Goldman regularly included a birth-control speech on her tour offerings. In it she placed birth control in the context of women's rights and opposition to conventional legal marriage. Like all radicals of her era, she used eugenic arguments: "Woman no longer wants to be a party to the production of a race of sickly, feeble, decrepit, wretched human beings. Instead she desires fewer and better children. . . ." On the other hand, she also spoke about homosexuality, criticizing social ostracism of the "inverts," as homosexuals were commonly called at that time. Her sexual and feminist theories were not only far more radical than those of the birth controllers who followed her, but also far more systematic, integrated into her whole politics. "To me anarchism was not a mere theory for a distant future; it was a living influence to free us from inhibitions . . . and from the destructive barriers that separate man from man." Reitman was himself a birth-control campaigner, not a mere companion to Goldman, and he did indeed, as he claimed, serve sixty days shoveling coal on Blackwell's Island and six months in an Ohio workhouse for distributing birth-control leaflets.

Goldman and Reitman distributed a small, four-page pamphlet called *Why and How the Poor Should Not Have Many Children*. It may have been written by Goldman or Reitman, or possibly by William J. Robinson. It described condoms, instructing the user to check them for leaks by blowing them up with air; recommended rubber cervical caps, diaphragms (also called pessaries or womb veils; in the early twentieth century there was no standard nomenclature for these various devices), which could be bought in drugstores, but urged fitting by a physician for reliability. It suggested three contraceptive methods that could be homemade: suppositories, douches, a cotton ball dipped in borated vaseline. (It advised against relying on the rhythm method but unfortunately still defined the safe period as the two weeks between menstrual periods.) The political argument of the pamphlet was brief: although normal people love and want children, society today is a "wretched place" for poor children, who are not only a burden to their mothers and families, but also "glut the labor market, tend to lower wages, and are a menace to the welfare of the working class. . . . If you think that the teaching of the prevention of conception will help working men and women, spread the glad tidings."[1] American sex radicals, despite their militant rhetoric, had not so far defied law and convention by publishing such explicit contraceptive advice. Goldman and Reitman's ideas about birth control were not new. Their sense of the political importance of taking risks to spread it was, however.

Though Goldman and her associates were the first radicals since the free lovers to act in defiance of the law, they were not able to make birth control a mass cause. Goldman's connections made her seem the right person for that task. But Goldman was also an extremist, and as a result she was often isolated. Partly because she took outrageous positions and partly because she was personally egocentric, Goldman left most of her admirers behind. If they were feminists, they were often from the educated classes, individualist by habit and ultimately more deeply committed to professional and artistic careers than to full-time revolutionary organizing. If they were revolutionaries, they were often men, skeptical about the importance of sexual and women's rights issues.

Though she began later, Margaret Sanger was much more effective as an *organizer* for birth

control. Lacking Goldman's intellectual daring and originality, she drew supporters to her, at first, through assuming a role in which she was more convincing than Goldman: that of victim. In the first years of her career, people frequently commented on Sanger's apparent fragility and vulnerability; only as they came to know her did her stamina, tenacity, and personal power impress them. Intellectuals repelled by the abrasive style of Goldman and her comrades could adore Margaret Sanger. Max Eastman, for example, hailed Sanger as a hero in *The Masses* but refused to speak at a Carnegie Hall meeting to welcome Goldman out of jail after she had served sixty days for distributing birth-control pamphlets, because, he said, he would not appear with Ben Reitman. "Reitman was a white-fleshed, waxy-looking doctor, who thought it was radical to shock people with crude allusions to their sexual physiology." Nevertheless, Sanger's debut as a birth-control activist was tactically and substantively right within the pattern plotted out by Goldman and the IWW. Sanger began with provocative, illegal action, and, once arrested, organized support for her defense.

The key difference between Sanger's and Goldman's strategies in 1914 was that Sanger chose to act independently of any leftist organization—indeed, independently of even any close collaborators. The path that led the Sanger-inspired birth-control movement away from the Left thus began with Sanger's first actions, though they may not have been consciously intended in that direction. When Sanger's divergence from the organized Left led to total separation, it was as much because the Left had rejected birth control as because Sanger and her followers had rejected the Left. Nevertheless, the roots of the split can be found at the beginnings of the birth-control movement itself.

Sanger returned from Paris to New York in December 1913, deeply influenced by her discovery that birth control was widely accepted in Europe and by support for birth control among some French syndicalists. She did not return to Socialist-party work but decided instead to publish an independent, feminist paper. *The Woman*

---

[1]Note that this pamphlet was written before the term "birth control," coined by Sanger, was in use.

Rebel, which appeared seven times in 1914 until it was suppressed by the Post Office, emphasized birth control but was not a single-issue journal. It raised other problems of women's sexual liberation: "The marriage bed is the most degenerating influence of the social order, as to life, in all of its forms—biological, psychological, sociological— for man, woman and child." Although concerned with the whole gamut of injustices that the capitalist system created, *The Woman Rebel* focused mainly on its effects on women. But it also sharply attacked the nonsocialist suffrage movement and various "bourgeois feminists." For example, of Katherine Bement Davis, then New York City Commissioner of Corrections (and later, ironically, a sociologist of sexual behavior who worked with Sanger on several sex-education projects), *The Woman Rebel* wrote: "We have no respect for the type of so-called "modern" and "advanced" woman who becomes a willing and efficient slave of the present system, the woman who curries favors of capitalists and politicians in order to gain power and the cheap and fulsome praise of cheaper and more fulsome newspapers." Also characteristic of the journal was a supermilitancy, surpassing even the IWW in its rhetorical support of violence. An editorial asked women to send rifles instead of messages of solidarity to striking miners in Colorado. An article in the July issue was the last straw that led the Post Office to declare the journal unmailable, although when Sanger was indicted, two counts of obscenity were also brought against her.

The Woman Rebel did not represent a tendency in American feminism or socialism at this time. It was rather a singular, unrepeated attempt by Sanger to combine her IWW-influenced commitment to direct action with her deepened feminism and sense of the radical potential of birth control. At any rate, it did not last long—and its sudden demise may well have been in part Sanger's intention. She claimed that she wanted to be arrested in order to force a legal definition of what was "obscene." In fact, she may have recognized the journal's lack of political viability.

But *The Woman Rebel* had given Sanger space and stimulus for further political exploration. She was able to correspond with leading European and American feminists in the name of a publication; rejected by many of them, she discovered the pro-birth-control tradition among many quasi-religious groups such as spiritualists and theosophists. She coined the phrase "birth control." When prevented from mailing the journal, Sanger drafted a detailed birth-control pamphlet, *Family Limitation,* and got IWW member Bill Shatoff to print one hundred thousand copies. She got a few hundred dollars to pay for it from a free-speech lawyer who administered a fund left by Edward Bond Foote (Sanger called him "A certain Dr. Foote," again illustrating her ignorance of the American birth-control tradition). Sanger arranged that the *Family Limitation* pamphlets would be sent out by IWW comrades on receipt of a prearranged signal from her. She thought thereby to release the provocative information they contained after she was already in jail. This would make an effective effective climax to her work, for *The Woman Rebel* was never able to print actual contraceptive information. The pamphlet not only recommended and explained a variety of contraceptive methods— douches, condoms, pessaries, sponges and vaginal suppositories—but even gave a suggestion for an abortifacient. While promising that birth control would make abortion unnecessary, she nevertheless defended women's rights to abortion, something she was never to do at any later time. In this period her attitude toward sexual issues was consistent with her general militance. Still using IWW anarcho-syndicalist rhetoric, she wrote in the pamphlet, "The working class can use direct action by refusing to supply the market with children to be exploited, by refusing to populate the earth with slaves."

But when her case came to trial, Sanger changed her strategy. Fearing that she would lose publicity because of the dominance of war news, and perhaps also that juries would be unsympathetic at this time, she decided to flee and went via Canada to London under an assumed name. In the United States the illegal pamphlets were mailed out as she had planned. With them went a letter asking that the pamphlets be passed on to "poor working men and women who are overburdened with large families. . . . Thousands of women in the cotton states bearing twelve to sixteen children request me to send them this pamphlet. Thousands of women facing the tortures of abortion . . . Three hundred thousand mothers who lose their babies every year from poverty and neglect . . . Are the cries of these women to be stifled? Are the old archaic laws to be respected above motherhood, womanhood! The mothers of America answer no. The women of America answer no!"

Sanger remained in Europe from October 1914 to October 1915. She spent that time researching the history, philosophy, technology, and practice of birth control, working in archives and libraries and visiting clinics and doctors in Holland, France, and England. Havelock Ellis directed and encouraged her work in a relationship made only more intense and nourishing to her because it was a love affair. Ellis had sympathy for neither revolution nor the working class. His influence in diminishing Sanger's attraction to the revolutionary Left was communicated to her not only through his political views, but also through the life style and charm of the British Neo-Malthusians she met through him. (In Britain the sex radicals did not have connections with a revolutionary, class-conscious Left.) After she returned she herself never resumed the consistently revolutionary posture she had held until 1914. In this second trip to Europe, the basic outlines of Sanger's entire future work took shape. She became committed unwaveringly to birth control as a single issue. She would offer feminist or pro-working-class arguments for birth control when they were helpful, along with many other arguments, but she never again saw her identity as mainly within a socialist, or even a generally radical, movement. For all its rhetoric, *The Woman Rebel* had already been a step away from the radical community.

Her reputed radicalism hereafter became more specifically the sex radicalism she learned from Ellis and his circle. But this radicalism was not the hedonistic sex-for-enjoyment ideology of the mid-twentieth century. Sanger's sexual views always remained within the romantic school of thought that had reached her from the European sex radicals and American free lovers. Her orientation was always to treat sexual activity as a form of communication, expressing love through extrasensory impulses. In their desire to rescue sexuality from its degraded reputation under the reign of prudery, Sanger and the sex radicals, better called sex romantics, virtually reversed the Victorian view of sexuality: from an animal passion it became a spiritual one, at least potentially. There were degrees of the development of one's sexual nature which presumably were determined by more than technical expertise. The stages of development represented depth of communication and emotional intensity which in turn reflected men's consideration of women. (This consideration was necessary because Sanger did not argue for women's equal assertiveness in sexual encounters.) In Sanger's own sex manual, published in 1926, she entitled intercourse "sex communion," the use of a religious term revealing her tendency to spiritualize the sexual act. "At the flight, body, mind and soul are brought together into the closest unity. 'No more are they twain, but one flesh,' in the words of the Bible."

> . . . sex-communion should be considered as a true union of souls, not merely a physical function for the momentary relief of the sexual organs. Unless the psychic and spiritual desires are fulfilled, the relationship has been woefully deficient and the participants degraded and dissatisfied. . . . the sexual embrace not only satisfies but elevates both participants. The physical demands are harnessed for the expression of love.

Sanger's work in sex education helped to alleviate the guilt of married couples and to give women an ideology with which to encourage—but hardly to demand—that men be considerate and proceed more slowly. But this sex education could hardly be considered radical in that it did nothing to challenge the conventional Victorian structure of sex relations, which were confined to the nuclear family and rested on male assertiveness and female passivity.

Furthermore Sanger's politics did not tend toward a socialist, and certainly not toward a Marxist, feminism but rather toward a mystique about womanliness, the successor to nineteenth-century feminist notions of the moral superiority of women (a precursor of what is known as "radical feminism" in the 1970s). Sanger believed in the "feminine spirit," the motive power of woman's nature. It was this spirit, coming from within, rather than social relations that drove women to revolt. She often thought of women as fundamentally different from men. She wanted to help poor women but had no particular commitment to the working class as a class, not even to its female half, let alone its male; she simply did not see class relations, the relations of production, as fundamental to women's problems.

If any leader could have drawn Socialist party and feminist support together behind birth control, Sanger was not the one. Of course, Sanger's relative social and sexual conservatism greatly contributed to the acceptance of birth control as a specific reform. Similarly, her narrow focus and single-mindedness contributed to its legalization. But in 1914 neither the ultimate dominance of this conservative, single-issue approach nor the central role of Sanger was yet evident.

Before Sanger returned to the country, a spontaneous and decentralized movement of birth-control agitation and organization appeared in the Eastern, Midwestern and Western United States. It was stimulated by the news of Sanger's indictment, which was carried in newspapers through the country, in such distant places as Pittsfield, Massachusetts, and Reno, Nevada. Some newspapers described Sanger as an IWW editor. Local socialist groups were distributing Sanger's and other birth-control leaflets. Local birth-control organizations were established in several places in 1915 long before Sanger's return to the United States and her first speaking tour.

Two kinds of political groups were primarily responsible for the birth-control agitation in 1915: women's Socialist-party groups and IWW locals. In many places people had been introduced by Emma Goldman to Sanger's pamphlet, Sanger's name, and sometimes *The Woman*

Rebel, just as later Goldman was to raise money for Sanger's defense on her speaking tours. Elizabeth Gurley Flynn spoke about birth control in the Northwest and pledged local IWW and other anarchist support if Sanger would go on a speaking tour there. Socialists saw Sanger, or adopted her, as one of their own and flooded her with letters of support and, inevitably, advice. Eugene Debs was one of the first to write and promised her the support of a "pretty good-sized bunch of revolutionists." Goldman, in her motherly way, wanted to take Sanger under her wing, not only recommending a tactical plan for Sanger's trial but suggesting, "Hold out until I come back the 23rd of this month. Then go away with me for 2 weeks to Lakewood or some place . . . we'd both gain much and I would help you find yourself. . . ." Others like Kate Richards O'Hare, Rose Pastor Stokes, Georgia Kotsch, Caroline Nelson, Rockwell Kent, Alexander Berkman, William J. Robinson, Jessie Ashley, and many lesser-known socialist organizers sent her messages of support and spoke on her behalf. Liberals supported her too: for example, *The New Republic* published several editorials in her favor after March 1915. In May 1915 birth-control supporters held a large meeting at the New York Academy of Medicine, urging public birth-control clinics. Many liberals spoke there. But in March 1915, when a primarily liberal group organized the National Birth Control League (despite its name, the NBCL was never more than a New York City group), they would not support Sanger or any law-defying tactics. (They also excluded Goldman and other radicals.) To the end of 1915 at least, those who supported Sanger and did local birth-control organizing everywhere except New York City were socialists.

In September 1915 William Sanger, Margaret's estranged husband, was tried for distributing her *Family Limitation* pamphlet. (He had been entrapped by a Post Office agent who requested a pamphlet.) Sanger was convicted in a dramatic trail in which he defended himself. The trial was dominated by radicals, who shouted at the judge until he ordered the police to clear the courtroom. Messages of support came from various parts of the country. From Portland, Oregon, a strong IWW city that was a veritable hotbed of birth-control fervor, came a handwritten petition:

1. A woman has the right to control her own body even to the extent of deciding when she will become a mother.
2. Unwelcome or unfit children ought not to be born into the world.
3. Motherhood is dignified and noble only when it is desired and a joy. . . .
4. Scientific knowledge of sex-physiology can never be classified as impure or obscene. Those who do so classify it, proclaim only the impurity of their own minds.

The first signer added after his name: "The industrial system which needs children as food for powder or factories may desire unlimited propagation, but the masses who suffer in poverty have no right to add sufferers to the already too many competing for bread." In these phrases were summarized fifty years of different birth-control arguments as they had reached the grass roots in the United States: women's rights, hereditarian social thought, social purity transformed by a faith in science and human dignity, and Neo-Malthusianism. It was such letters that made William Sanger believe his trial a great success, making "birth control a household word [*sic*]." The responses that flowed in to the Sangers showed that the concept of birth control, if not the term, was already widely known and supported. It was as if people had been waiting for leadership to ask them for help.

Margaret Sanger came home from London soon after her husband's trial. Seeking support for the trial she faced, she found that her husband's confrontational conduct at his trial had aroused many strong opinions as to how she should conduct her trial. The flurry of letters offering to tell her how to run the trial emerged from gallant but male-chauvinist assumptions that she was in need of help. Most of her friends urged her not to follow her husband's example (pleading not guilty and acting as his own lawyer) but to plead guilty and use a lawyer. Goldman,

on the other hand, begged her to resist those counsels, branding that line of defense cowardly. One of her medical "supporters" preached to her about her duty to her children. Sanger stood firm in her plant to plead not guilty.

The differences among birth-control supporters over what Sanger's trial tactics should be repeated differences that had become evident within the organization of the NBCL. In that original split it seemed that Sanger herself belonged to the ultra-left faction identified with the IWW. But Sanger's own public-relations activities in the fall of 1915 were not ultra-left at all. She had a "distinguished-guests-only" dinner at the Brevoort Hotel and in her speech gave an apologia for her militant tactics, explaining that her methods had been unorthodox merely in order to secure publicity. Instead of devoting time to preparing her defense, she worked on publicity; and the steady growth of public support for her led to the government's dismissing the charges against her on February 18, 1916. On April 1 Sanger left for a three-and-a-half-month speaking tour across the country. By its conclusion she was nationally famous. Newspaper coverage of her speeches was copious and often enthusiastic. Her occasional misadventures were usually transformed into successes: refused halls in Akron and Chicago, arrested and jailed in Portland, Oregon, and locked out of her hall in St. Louis by Catholic Church pressure, she responded like a seasoned political campaigner, turning always from the defense to the offense. She turned birth control into a free-speech as well as a sexual-liberation issue and won support from important liberal civil libertarians. She sought to establish effective coalitions of liberal and radical groups for birth control.

Still, the grass-roots work in organizing for birth control was being done by radicals. In Cleveland (the first major city to organize a birth-control group, and a place where the birth-control campaign was later to be especially successful), workers' groups sponsored Sanger's tremendously successful speeches and led the birth-control movement. In St. Paul the Women's Socialist Club led the birth-control movement, and in Ann

Arbor, Agnes Inglis, a socialist activist, organized a group. Even the relatively staid Massachusetts Birth Control League was led by socialists. In small towns as well as big cities socialists were organizing for birth control. And although Sanger varied her appeals to particular audiences, she made several sharp attacks on the conservatism of privileged groups. When the snobbish Chicago Women's Club cancelled her speaking engagement, she attacked it, saying she did not care to speak to a "sophisticated" audience anyway. "I want to talk to the women of the stock yards, the women of the factories—they are the victims of a system or lack of system that cries out for corrections. I am interested in birth control among working women chiefly."

In 1916 birth control in the United States was a radical movement and a large movement. Birth control as a political demand had demonstrated an ability to involve not only educated but also working-class women in a participatory social movement. Elizabeth Gurley Flynn wrote to Sanger that she found everywhere in the country the "greatest possible interest" in birth control. . . . one girl told me the women in the stockyards District [Chicago] kissed her hands when she distributed [Sanger's birth-control pamphlet]." In 1913 in Tampa, Florida, Flynn had visited a cigar factory with Spanish-speaking workers where the reader[2] was reading aloud a pamphlet on birth control. Letters from women all over the country came pouring in not only to Sanger but also to others who were identified in newspapers as birth-control activists, letters asking for contraceptive information and thanking them for the fight they were making. Often they were fearful: "I nearly had nervous prostration after I had mailed you my letter asking for that 'information'. . . ." Or: "Please send me one of your Papers on birth control, I have had seven children and cannot afford any more. Please don't give my name to the Papers." Usually they poured out the difficulties of their lives, with their most intimate sexual problems and most externally caused eco-

nomic problems intermingled—as they indeed always are in real life.

> I was married at the age of eighteen. Now I am married for seven years and I have four children. . . . I am a little over twenty-four and already skinny, yellow and so funny looking and I want to hold my husband's love. . . . He tried to help me but somehow I got caught anyway and a baby came. We didn't have any money to get rid of it and now when I look on her little innocent, red face I am glad I didn't kill it. . . . When you was in Chicago I wanted to go to see you but I had no nice clothes and I knew I would make you feel ashamed if I went dressed shabbily. . . .

Many of the letters expressed exasperation at the class injustice behind the fact that they were deprived of birth control information. "Tell me how it is the wealthier class of people can get information like that and those that really need it, can't?" And many others plunged immediately into political action, like Mrs. Lulu MacClure Clarke of St. Louis, who wrote to Sanger:

> I have been through suffrage wrangles all my adult life, in backwoods communities and [among] the vicious of a city and I know how very chivalrous indeed men can be when any new freedom is asked for by women, and this is harder for them to swallow. . . . But even if women can't help much, don't know how to speak in public or write for the press, etc., yet they are awakening up all over the nation and waiting for someone to lead the way. I think—in fact, I know—there is a well-spring of gratitude to you—that they think you are fighting for them and they wait hoping and praying. . . . I am glad you have a husband who is a help and not a hindrance. And oh, Please dont give up or get discouraged. . . .

Not only was there a potentially large movement here, but its people were ready for action. What they wanted personally, the *minimum* demand, was to be given information in defiance of the law. Beyond that, women in many places quickly moved to a strategy that logically followed—opening illegal birth-control clinics to give that illegal information to others. There was

---

[2]Cigar makers traditionally pooled their money to employ readers to entertain them as they worked.

a practical reason for this: the best contraceptive —a vaginal diaphragm—required a private fitting. Sanger was already convinced of the efficacy of "direct action." She gained support for this plan by what she learned on her national tour. In many ways that tour was as much a learning experience for Sanger as a teaching one. In Ann Arbor, Michigan, socialist Agnes Inglis had a de facto clinic functioning before Sanger returned to New York. In St. Paul socialist women announced plans for a clinic in June. Sanger herself dreamed of a "glorious 'chain' of clinics" throughout the country.

Returning to New York City in July 1916, Sanger organized a clinic of her own in the Brownsville section of Brooklyn. Brownsville was then a Jewish and Italian immigrant neighborhood, an extremely poor slum. Sanger worked with her sister Ethel Byrne, also a nurse, and Fania Mindell, whom Sanger had recruited in Chicago. The three women rented an apartment and gave out to every family in the district a handbill printed in English, Yiddish, and Italian. They were not prepared to fit women with contraceptives, but only to "give the principles of contraception, show a cervical pessary to the women, explain that if they had had two children they should have one size and if more a larger one."

Women were lined up outside when the clinic opened on October 16. As many Catholics came as Jews. Sanger asked one Catholic woman what she would say to the priest at confession. "It's none of his business," she answered. "My husband has a weak heart and works only four days a week. He gets twelve dollars, and we can barely live on it now. We have enough children." Most of the neighbors were friendly and supportive. The baker gave them free doughnuts and the landlady brought them tea. By the end of nine days, the clinic had 464 case histories of women on file.

Then, inevitably, one of the patients turned out to be a policewoman. She seemed prosperous; Fania Mindell suspected her but did not turn her away. The next day she returned as Officer Margaret Whitehurst, arrested the three women, and confiscated all the equipment and case histories. Tried separately, Ethel Byrne was sentenced to thirty days on Blackwell's Island. Byrne immediately announced her intention to go on a hunger strike. (The hunger strikes of British suffragists were at this time an international symbol of feminist resistance.) Like the British suffragists, she was force-fed by tubes through the nose; the combination of her starvation and the brutality of the force-feeding left her so weakened she required a year to recuperate. At Sanger's trial women who had visited the clinic testified. Although legally they supported the prosecution, giving evidence that they had indeed received contraceptive advice without medical indication, politically they helped the birth-control cause by the clear testimonials to the misery of involuntary pregnancy. Sanger also was sentenced to thirty days but conducted herself cooperatively. When she was released on March 6 her friends met her singing "The Marseillaise." . . .

Commitment to action was strong among these birth controllers. As socialists, most of them believed that working-class strength was the key to political progress, and thus they wanted above all to reach working-class people with their message and service. As feminists, they wanted to improve the position of women. They believed that the subjugation of women supported capitalism directly by creating profit, and indirectly by weakening the socialist movement: depriving it of half its potential constituency and allowing socialist men to cling to privileges that corrupted. All of them, even the non-Marxists, shared an interest in improving the lives of poor people in the present and did not try to fob them off with promises of postrevolutionary paradise. Their work in trying to reach working-class women was made more difficult by their own class origins. Most of the leadership of this movement was from professional, even capitalist, backgrounds. Their superior confidence and articulateness often made them better talkers than listeners. But their humanitarianism, their desire to eliminate material misery, was not a symptom of elitism. Indeed it was shared by those among them of "lower" origins—like Stokes, Goldman,

Equi, and Sanger. It was also a conscious tactical choice, a rejection of the myth that greater misery makes workers more revolutionary.

Similarly, the plan to agitate among working-class people, particularly women, on an issue so private and so removed from production was a conscious tactical choice, one based on political experience. Sanger had been struck by the strongly positive reaction among socialist constituencies to her writing and speaking on sexual hygiene. Flynn and Bloor had worked with women, sometimes women who were not wage workers themselves but workers' wives, in many strike situations and had perceived the deep connections between family support and workers' militancy. Robinson had been receiving for over a decade the kind of personal letters that began flooding in to Sanger and the birth-control organizations after 1915—letters attesting to the mutually reinforcing nature of sexual, economic, and political helplessness. A systematic evaluation of five thousand such letters sent to Margaret Sanger after the publication of her *Woman and the New Race* in 1920 showed that they were overwhelmingly from working-class and poor women. The most common occupation given for husbands was "laborer," the most common salary fifteen dollars per week. One-third of the women were themselves wage-earners, as compared to the over-all national average of 23 per cent in 1920. Eighty per cent of the writers had married before the age of twenty, and averaged five children. These organizers thought birth control could improve the economic situations and family stability of the poor and give women in particular more free choice and greater alternatives. Focusing on the connection between the sexual and economic oppression of working-class women was a strategy for organizing. Its goal was to create a significant women's force within a socialist movement.

Socialist feminist birth controllers in the pre-war years developed educational propaganda that used birth control as a political issue. For example, Rose Pastor Stokes wrote a didactic script, "Shall the Parents [sic] Decide?" which tried to capture the revolutionary impact that birth control could have. In it a factory owner, who has already attacked birth control for its threat to deprive him of cheap labor, fires his worker, Mrs. Jones, for coming late. Mrs. Jones is burdened with many children to take care of and was late becaue of her grief over the death of one of her children! Helen, another worker in the plant, is incensed at the firing and organizes a wildcat strike to demand Jones's job back. The owner orders his friend the police chief to have Helen arrested, but Helen sneaks out her back door, with the help of her mother, because she is scheduled to speak at a birth control rally. Accidentally meeting the owner's mistress, Helen gives her emotional support when she is rejected and offers a political analysis of her unhappy position. When the factory owner tries to buy off his mistress with money, she gives it to Helen for her bail. The themes of women's solidarity and women's sexual exploitation were both important in the writings of many of these early birth controllers. Sanger had written a short story in 1912, before her conversion to birth control, about a young nurse whose first employer tries to rape her. It concluded with a plea for working girls to stick together and defend one another.

From their earliest efforts, however, these organizers learned that this task would not be easy. As early as June 1915 Caroline Nelson spelled out in a letter to Sanger the difficulties she had already encountered:

> It seems strange, but it is almost impossible to interest the workers in this. . . . So that our League here consists mostly of professional people. . . . I myself think that if the Leagues are ever to amount to anything, they must send trained nurses into the workers' districts, who speak the language of the district, whatever that may be. . . . I still hold that it would be beneficial to change the name. You know the workers are so afraid of being suspected of immorality, and they love the word—Moral—with an affection worthy of something better than it stands for today. That is why I cling to the name of—New Moral. . . . Yes, dear Margaret, this is the mere beginning of working women to do our work. The working men have gone around in a vicious circle, until today they are engaged in the very lawful occu-

pation of killing each other, and where they are not killing each other they are running around begging for a job to feed their starved families. All this, after seventy-five years of revolutionary propaganda and scientific economy and academic discussion that the working woman had [no] interest in, chiefly because they were not practical, and did not touch her life, and the radical woman is chiefly an echo of the radical man, even in the sex question. . . .

But Nelson's frank appraisal of the difficulties did not diminish her commitment. Indeed, her analysis led to the conclusion that there was no choice but to continue to fight for birth control, for she seemed convinced that unless women of the working class could be aroused to assuming some political leadership the entire cause of socialism would be doomed. Though not a feminist, Nelson had developed in her thinking from two years previously when she still saw birth control primarily in socialist Neo-Malthusian terms: the rich have birth control but try to keep it from the working class. By 1915 she saw birth control not merely as an economic device but as fundamental to women's liberation. Thus, like many other birth-control activists, though members of the Socialist party, she also looked to the woman-suffrage movement for approval and support of her work. Though they were successful to an extent—the first to be interested in birth control did indeed recruit from within the ranks of the Party and even of NAWSA—they also met with disapproval and even opposition from both sources.

When Sanger published her sexual-hygiene articles in the *New York Call,* many readers protested. "I for one condemn the idea where a mother should show through the columns of a newspaper her nakedness to her children," Mrs. L. B. of Greenpoint, Brooklyn, wrote. Caroline Nelson had met these attitudes since 1915:

. . . while they want to get the information in secret, they cannot discuss it in public without giggling and blushing and this holds good to our very learned radical men, or at least some of them. . . . I must say with great shame to our labor editors that the capitalist editors in many instances have been much

more liberal and sensible on this question than they have, which shows that our class is not yet out of the woods of gullibility with its sewage minds, and sewage minds are not clear instruments of thinking.

These antisexual attitudes were hard to separate from outright male chauvinism. Most socialists were not prepared to acknowledge the existence of male supremacy within the working class. They often disguised their defense of male privilege with criticisms of population control as a capitalist plot. One typical letter argued:

Will you kindly question yourself and see that it is better to relieve the poor than to bring more destruction. Naturally we all-appreciate the fact that we would be free from having children, but it only brings a more adulterous generation and gives married women a freedom to wander more into the sin of the world.

Some socialist leaders opposed birth-control propaganda because they hoped that eschewing sexual radicalism would make their economic radicalism more palatable. That is, socialist economics combined with defense of family, home, and motherhood would presumably make a wider appeal to the American public. Here again, socialist tactical thinking was not so different from that of the suffragists, who also wished to avoid association with antifamily doctrines. Both socialism and suffragism had been charged with advocating free love in the late nineteenth and early twentieth centuries; both socialism and suffragism had defended themselves by condemning free love.

The free-love charge was a constant thorn to the birth controllers. Margaret Sanger was frequently accused of free loveism, and always denied it. The origins of birth control as a women's movement *were* in free love. Some socialists not only recognized this but thought it best to accept that legacy, trying perhaps to redefine it. Those who took this view were inclined to the perception that youth involved in sexual rebellion might be an important socialist constituency. Others believed that refusing to face the necessity for fundamental change in family and sexual norms would ultimately betray the interests of women. Josephine Conger-Kaneko of the Socialist party argued that women and the whole Party had to give up "bourgeois respectability" in order to make a thoroughgoing women's rights struggle.

But most Socialist-party people feared being forced back into isolation by attacks from the Right branding them as immoral. They felt this danger because changes in sexual behavior had made free love a real threat. Because the sexual revolution meant increased sexual activity among women, many men stood to lose from it. It threatened to rob them not only of the pleasures of exclusive privilege, but of the security of women's dependency on marriage.

Birth control was an easy focus for all this fear of sexual change. The attack was strong enough to prevent birth control from becoming an official program of either the Socialist party or any national women's rights organization.

At the same time other factors caused a rapid diminution of the power of socialist and women's rights movements. This political shift affected the future course of birth control greatly. The decline of women's rights movement was probably hastened by its one victory—the woman suffrage amendment to the Constitution. The National American Woman Suffrage Association had mobilized a powerful lobby, its work orchestrated by an excellent politician, Carrie Chapman Catt, and focused on the single issue, suffrage. But the narrowing focus of women's rights had weakened the movement. Large social changes created a distinctly antifeminist mood among the American middle classes in the 1920s. The sexual revolution itself was partly responsible in that the increased sexual orientation of women made political activity seem even more unacceptable than usual to many of them. Greatly expanded commodity production and advertising industries appealed to women as consumers in two roles primarily—housewives and beauty objects—thus contributing to make other activities seem uncomfortable to women. The false ideology of prosperity added to the unfashionableness of appearing discontented. Within the remnant women's organizations, the controversy over an

equal-rights amendment to the Constitution (first introduced in Congress in 1923) ended by pushing feminism even further into a minority corner, as the majority of socially concerned women opposed the equal-rights amendment for fear of jeopardizing protective labor legislation for women. A false dichotomy was set up which opposed feminism to progressive labor reform.

Organized feminism was also weakened by repression of socialism which began with the First World War. So virulent was the patriotic hysteria that any views critical of American society appeared disloyal; in this regard feminists were only slightly better than socialists. Many feminists and some socialists supported the war, but this did not help the reputation of their causes, especially since some feminists and socialists were outspoken critics of the war. The patriotism led to jingoism, not only against Germans but to some extent against all non-WASP immigrants. Many radicals, including Goldman, were deported. Dr. Robinson, a pacifist, was ostracized in his profession. Dr. Equi was jailed. There were also many local persecutions and even lynchings of antiwar radicals. Calculating men of power, long anxious for a tool to check the increasing strength of their class enemies, stimulated and guided antiradical hysteria to a systematic and effective attack on socialist leaders and organizations.

Under attack the socialist movement could not respond effectively because it was split between pro-war and antiwar politics. After November 1917 another division—regarding attitudes toward the Russian Revolution—rapidly led to a final split. Furthermore, the Russian Revolution and Civil War helped antisocialists brand socialist ideas as alien and violent.

Thus two separate factors pushed the birth-control movement away from the organized Left —the attacks on birth control by socialists and feminists and the independent decline of socialism and feminism.[3] These two factors together

[3]Perhaps that decline was not so independent; perhaps had the socialist and feminist organizations taken more supportive positions toward birth control, they would have been rewarded with the increased allegiance of neglected but large constituencies, particularly women and young people. But these are mere speculations.

forced the birth-control movement to assume the form of independent organizations, local and national. That independence meant that even though large numbers of socialists and feminists were committed to birth control, they were unable to bring with them into the movement the benefits of the large world view and broad constituency of their movements of origin. Organizational connections with such groups as the Socialist party, the IWW, NAWSA, the Women's Party, the socialist suffrage leagues, and the WTUL could have brought political experience and discipline into the birth-control movement. Organizational estrangement from such groups and their constituencies made the task of creating a socialist-feminist politics in the birth-control movement extremely difficult. Birth control as an issue presented problems new to socialist and feminist organizers. It required efforts to change the law, efforts to seek favorable court rulings, tactics of breaking the law, and above all the means to provide services—birth-control information and devices. Outside of utopian communities and ill-fated workers' cooperatives, the American Left had had little experience with the provision of services through counterinstitutions like birth-control clinics. Fundamentally, birth-control advocates were confused and ambivalent about whether they felt that the practice of birth control or the illegal agitation for birth control was the factor that would do most to change the society; they therefore had difficulty setting their own priorities for political action.

16

WHAT THE DEPRESSION DID TO PEOPLE

EDWARD R. ELLIS

The American economy has a long history of cyclical recessions and depressions dating back to the eighteenth century. But none of the depressions could compare in severity or longevity to that which struck Americans between 1929 and 1941. Following a decade of unprecedented prosperity, which saw the rapid expansion of consumer goods production and the introduction of consumer credit to pay for it, the Great Depression took Americans by surprise. What had gone wrong?

Modern historians and economists now view the Depression as the consequence of underconsumption, that is, the overproduction of goods for sale and the lack of buyers with sufficient wages to purchase them. But to the unemployed workers, the dispossessed farmers and their families, the Depression, whatever its cause, was the most disastrous event of their lives. By 1931 over 11 million workers, nearly a third of the labor force, were unemployed, and average farm income had declined to 60 percent of 1929 levels. In this essay Edward Ellis provides a wide panorama of life during the Depression, surveying its effects on the rich as well as the poor. Whatever their social class, the Great Depression scarred the lives and shaped the outlook of everyone who lived through it.

Ellis paints a picture of everyday despair and survival; but what about organized attempts to redress popular grievances? Did they have a role to play in everyday life during the Depression? The succeeding essay by Barton Bernstein (Reading 17) and the earlier essay by Allen F. Davis (Reading 13) offer some possible answers.

The Depression smashed into the nation with such fury that men groped for superlatives to express its impact and meaning.

Edmund Wilson compared it to an earthquake. It was "like the explosion of a bomb dropped in the midst of society," according to the Social Science Research Council Committee on Studies in Social Aspects of the Depression.

Alfred E. Smith said the Depression was equivalent to war, while Supreme Court Justice Louis D. Brandeis and Bernard Baruch declared that it was worse than war. Philip La Follette, the governor of Wisconsin, said: "We are in the midst of the greatest domestic crisis since the Civil War." Governor Roosevelt agreed in these words: "Not since the dark days of the Sixties have the people of this state and nation faced problems as grave, situations as difficult, suffering as severe." A jobless textile worker told Louis Adamic: "I wish there would be war again." In a war against a foreign enemy all Americans might at least have felt united by a common purpose, and production would have boomed.

Poor and rich alike felt anxious and helpless.

Steel magnate Charles M. Schwab, despite his millions and the security of his Manhattan palace, freely confessed: "I'm afraid. Every man is afraid." J. David Stern, a wealthy newspaper

Reprinted by permission of the Putnam Publishing Group from *A Nation in Torment* by Edward R. Ellis.
Copyright © 1970 by Edward R. Ellis.

publisher, became so terrified that he later wrote in his autobiography: "I sat in my back office, trying to figure out what to do. To be explicit, I sat in my private bathroom. My bowels were loose from fear." Calvin Coolidge dolorously told a friend: "I can see nothing to give ground for hope."

Herbert C. Pell, a rich man with a country estate near Governor Roosevelt's, said the country was doomed unless it could free itself from the rich, who have "shown no realization that what you call free enterprise means anything but greed." Marriner Eccles, a banker and economist who had *not* lost his fortune, wrote that "I awoke to find myself at the bottom of a pit without any known means of scaling its sheer sides." According to Dwight W. Morrow, a Morgan associate, diplomat and Senator: "Most of my friends think the world is coming to an end—that is, the world as we know it." Reinhold Niebuhr, the learned and liberal clergyman, said that rich "men and women speculated in drawing-rooms on the best kind of poison as a means to oblivion from the horrors of revolution."

In Youngstown, Ohio, a friend of Mayor Joseph L. Heffernan stood beside the mayor's desk and said: "My wife is frantic. After working at the steel mill for twenty-five years I've lost my job and I'm too old to get other work. If you can't do something for me, I'm going to kill myself." Governor Gifford Pinchot of Pennsylvania got a letter from a jobless man who said: "I cannot stand it any longer." Gan Kolski, an unemployed Polish artist from Greenwich Village, leaped to his death from the George Washington Bridge, leaving this note: "To All: If you cannot hear the cry of starving millions, listen to the dead, brothers. Your economic system is dead."

An architect, Hugh Ferriss, stood on the parapet of a tall building in Manhattan and thought to himself that the nearby skyscrapers seemed like monuments to the rugged individualism of the past. Thomas Wolfe wrote: "I believe that we are lost here in America, but I believe we shall be found," Democratic Senator Thomas Gore of Oklahoma called the Depression an economic disease. Henry Ford, on the other hand, said the Depression was "a wholesome thing in general."

Obviously, the essence of a depression is widespread unemployment. In one of the most fatuous remarks on record, Calvin Coolidge said: "The final solution of unemployment is work." He might have added that water is wet. Senator Robert Wagner of New York called unemployment inexcusable.

A decade before the Crash the British statesman David Lloyd George had said: "Unemployment, with its injustice for the man who seeks and thirsts for employment, who begs for labour and cannot get it, and who is punished for failure he is not responsible for by the starvation of his children—that torture is something that private enterprise ought to remedy for its own sake." Winston Churchill now used the same key word, "torture," in a similar comment: "This problem of unemployment is the most torturing that can be presented to a civilized society."

Before Roosevelt became President and named Frances Perkins his secretary of labor, she was so pessimistic that she said publicly it might take a quarter century to solve the unemployment problem. A Pennsylvania commission studied 31,159 workless men and then reported that the typical unemployed man was thirty-six years old, native-born, physically fit and with a good previous work record. This finding contradicted Henry Ford's belief that the unemployed did not want to work.

However, the Pennsylvania study was *not* typical of the unemployed across the entire nation. Negroes and aliens were the last hired and the first fired. Young men and women were graduated from high schools and colleges into a world without jobs. Mississippi's demagogic governor and sometime Senator, Theodore G. Bilbo, vowed the unemployment problem could be solved by shipping 12,000,000 American blacks to Africa. The United Spanish War Veterans, for their part, urged the deportation of 10,000,000 aliens—or nearly 6,000,000 more than the actual number of aliens in the United States. Some noncitizens, unable to find work here, voluntarily returned to their homelands. With the deepening of the Depression, immigration dropped until something strange happened in the year 1932: More than three times as many persons left this country as entered it. No longer was America the Promised Land.

The Depression changed people's values and thus changed society.

The Chamber of Commerce syndrome of the Twenties became a mockery in the Thirties. Business leaders lost their prestige, for now it had become apparent to all Americans that these big shots did not know what they were talking about when they said again and again and again that everything would be all right if it were just left to them. Worship of big business was succeeded by greater concern for human values. The optimism of the speculative decade was replaced by the pessimism of the hungry decade, by anguished interest in the problem of having enough food on the table.

People eager to make a big killing in the stock market had paid scant attention to politics, but now they wondered about their elected representatives and the kind of political system that could permit such a catastrophe to happen. Indifference gave way to political and social consciousness. Dorothy Parker, the sophisticate and wit, cried: "There is no longer I. There is WE. The day of the individual is dead." Quentin N. Burdick, who became a Senator from North Dakota, said long after the Depression: "I guess I acquired a social conscience during those bad days, and ever since I've had the desire to work toward bettering the living conditions of the people." Sylvia Porter, who developed into a financial columnist, said that while at Hunter College she switched from English to economics because of "an overwhelming curiosity to know why everything was crashing around me and why people were losing their jobs."

People lost their houses and apartments.

Franklin D. Roosevelt said: "One of the major disasters of the continued depression was the loss of hundreds of thousands of homes each year from foreclosure. The annual average loss of

urban homes by foreclosure in the United States in normal times was 78,000. By 1932 this had increased to 273,000. By the middle of 1933, foreclosures had advanced to more than 1,000 a day."

In New York City, which had more apartments than private houses, there were almost 200,000 evictions in the year 1931. During the first three weeks of the following year there were more than 60,000 other evictions. One judge handled, or tried to handle, 425 eviction cases in a single day! On February 2, 1932, the New York *Times* described the eviction of three families in the Bronx:

Probably because of the cold, the crowd numbered only about 1,000, although in unruliness it equalled the throng of 4,000 that stormed the police in the first disorder of a similar nature on January 22. On Thursday a dozen more families are to be evicted unless they pay back rents.

Inspector Joseph Leonary deployed a force of fifty detectives and mounted and foot patrolmen through the street as Marshal Louis Novick led ten furniture movers in to the building. Their appearance was the signal for a great clamor. Women shrieked from the windows, the different sections of the crowd hissed and booed and shouted invectives. Fighting began simultaneously in the house and in the street. The marshal's men were rushed on the stairs and only got to work after the policemen had driven the tenants back into their apartments.

In that part of New York City known as Sunnyside, Queens, many homeowners were unable to meet mortgage payments and were soon ordered to vacate. Eviction notices were met with collective action, the residents barricading their doors with sandbags and barbed wire, flinging pepper and flour at sheriffs who tried to force their way inside. However, it was a losing battle; more than 60 percent of Sunnyside's householders lost their homes through foreclosure.

Harlem Negroes invented a new way to get enough money to pay their rent. This, as it came to be called, was the house-rent party. A family would announce that on Saturday night or Thursday night they would welcome anyone and everyone to their home for an evening of fun.

Sometimes they would print and distribute cards such as this: "There'll be plenty of pig feet/And lots of gin;/Jus' ring the bell/An' come on in." Saturday night, of course, is the usual time for partying, while Thursday was chosen because this was the only free night for sleep-in black domestics who worked for white people. Admission to a house-rent party cost 15 cents, but more money could be spent inside. A festive mood was established by placing a red bulb in a light socket, by serving food consisting of chitterlings and pigs' feet and by setting out a jug of corn liquor. These parties often went on until daybreak, and the next day the landlord got his rent. The innovation spread to black ghettos in other big cities across the land, and some white people began imitating the Negroes.

In Chicago a crowd of Negroes gathered in front of the door of a tenement house to prevent the landlord's agent from evicting a neighborhood family, and they continued to stand there hour after hour, singing hymns. A Chicago municipal employee named James D. O'Reilly saw his home auctioned off because he had failed to pay $34 in city taxes at the very time the city owed him $850 in unpaid salary.

A social worker described one pathetic event: "Mrs. Green left her five small children alone one morning while she went to have her grocery order filled. While she was away the constable arrived and padlocked her house with the children inside. When she came back she heard the six-weeks-old baby crying. She did not dare to touch the padlock for fear of being arrested, but she found a window open and climbed in and nursed the baby and then climbed out and appealed to the police to let her children out."

In widespread areas of Philadelphia no rent was paid at all. In this City of Brotherly Love evictions were exceedingly common—as many as 1,300 a month. Children, who saw their parents' distress, made a game of evictions. In a day-care center they piled all the doll furniture in first one corner and then another. One tot explained to a teacher: "We ain't got no money for the rent, so we's moved into a new house. Then we got the constable on us, so we's moving' again."

In millions of apartments, tension mounted and tempers flared toward the end of each month, when the rent was due. Robert Bendiner, in his book *Just Around the Corner,* wrote about conditions in New York City:

Evictions and frequent moves to take advantage of the apartment market were as common in middle-income Washington Heights as in the poor areas of town, and apartment hopping became rather a way of life. My own family moved six times in seven years. . . . Crises occurred monthly, and several times we were saved from eviction by pawning left-over valuables or by my mother's rich talent for cajoling landlords. On one more than routinely desperate occasion she resorted to the extreme device of having one of us enlarge a hole in the bathroom ceiling and then irately demanding repairs before another dollar of rent should be forthcoming.

In moving from one place to another, some families left their furniture behind because it had been bought on the installment plan and they were unable to meet further payments. Time-payment furniture firms owned warehouses that became crammed with tables and chairs and other items reclaimed from families without money. Whenever a marshal, sheriff or constable evicted a family from a house or apartment, the landlord would simply dump the furniture on the sidewalk. If the installment company failed to pick it up, each article would soon be carried away by needy neighbors.

What happened to people after they were dispossessed? Many doubled up with relatives—or even tripled up, until ten or twelve people were crammed into three or four rooms. Human beings are like porcupines: they like to huddle close enough to feel one another's warmth, but they dislike getting so close that the quills begin pricking. Now, in teeming proximity to one another, the quills pricked, and relatives quarreled bitterly.

The Depression strained the family structure and sometimes shattered it. Well-integrated families closed ranks in the face of this common danger and became ever more monolithic. Loosely knit families, on the other hand, fell apart when the pressures on them became too great.

After a man lost his job, he would trudge from factory to factory, office to office, seeking other employment, but after weeks of repeated rejections he would lose heart, mutely denounce himself as a poor provider, shed his self-respect and stay at home. Here he found himself unwelcome and underfoot, the target of puzzled glances from his children and hostile looks from his wife. In the early part of the Depression some women simply could not understand that jobs were unavailable; instead, they felt there was something wrong with their men. In Philadelphia one unemployed man begged a social worker: "Have you anybody you can send around to tell my wife you have no job to give me? She thinks I don't want to work."

The idle man found himself a displaced person in the household, which is woman's domain, and in nameless guilt he crept about uneasily, always finding himself in the way. He got on his wife's nerves and she on his, until tension broke in endless wrangles. If the man tried to help by washing dishes and making beds, he lost status in the eyes of the rest of the family.

The Depression castrated some men by dethroning them from their position as the breadwinner and the head of the family. Ashamed, confused and resentful, they became sexually impotent. In Western culture a man tends to think of himself in terms of the work he does, this self-identity being what Jung calls his persona. Man does. Woman is. To rob a man of his work was to rob him of his idea of himself, leaving him empty and without much reason for living. The displacement of the man as the head of the family and the way some women moved in to fill this vacuum were described sensitively by John Steinbeck in his novel *The Grapes of Wrath*. This great book tells the story of the flight of the Joad family from the dust bowl of Oklahoma to the green valleys of California:

"We got nothin', now," Pa said. "Comin' a long time—no work, no crops. What we gonna do then? How we gonna git stuff to eat? . . . Git so I hate to think. Go diggin' back to a ol' time to keep from thinkin'. Seems like our life's over an' done."

"No, it ain't," Ma smiled. "It ain't, Pa. An' that's one more thing a woman knows. I noticed that. Man, he lives in jerks—baby born an' a man dies, an' that's a jerk—gets a farm an' loses his farm, an' that's a jerk. Woman, it's all one flow, like a stream, little eddies, little waterfalls, but the river, it goes right on. Woman looks at it like that. We ain't gonna die out. People is goin' on—changin' a little maybe, but goin' right on."

Some adolescent girls felt their fathers' agony and tried to comfort them with lavish expressions of love, much to the embarrassment of the man and the uneasiness of his wife. This did emotional damage to father, mother and the young girl, whose fixation on her father retarded her normal interest in boys her own age.

Strife between parents, together with the realization that it cost money to marry and have babies, resulted in a decision by many young people to postpone their weddings. One young man joined the Communist Party and swore he never would marry or have children under "the present system." Unable to repress their human needs, however, young men and women made love secretly and guiltily, regarding pregnancy as a disaster. Despite an increase in the sale of contraceptives, the abortion rate rose, and so did venereal disease. The birthrate dropped.

It has been estimated that the Depression postponed 800,000 marriages that would have occurred sooner if it had not been for hard times. Margaret Mead, the noted anthropologist, argued that there was nothing wrong about letting girls support their lovers so they could marry sooner. Surprisingly, there even was a decline in marriages among members of the *Social Register*. Liberals and feminists pointed out that half of all births were in families on relief or with incomes of less than $1,000 a year; they strongly advocated birth control. Who could afford babies when a sixty-one-piece layette cost all of $7.70? Gasps of horror arose when it was reported in Illinois that a sixteenth child had been born to a family on relief.

Housewives suffered as acutely as their husbands. Many had to send their kids to live with relatives or friends. Others took part-time jobs, while a few wives actually became temporary whores to earn enough money to keep the family going. Lacking money for streetcars and buses, without the means to buy clothes to keep them looking attractive, they remained cooped up in their homes until their nerves screamed and they had nervous breakdowns.

All too often their men simply deserted them. A California woman said: "My husband went north about three months ago to try his luck. The first month he wrote pretty regularly. . . . For five weeks we have had no word from him. . . . Don't know where he is or what he is up to."

A young man who lived in the French Quarter of New Orleans was solicited by five prostitutes during a ten-block stroll, each woman asking only 50 cents. In Houston a relief worker, curious about how the people were getting along, was approached by one girl after another. For the benefit of an insistent streetwalker, the man turned his pockets inside out to prove that he had no money. Looking at him ruefully, she said: "It doesn't cost much—only a dime!"

The close relationship between poverty and morals shocked Franklin D. Roosevelt, who told reporters about an investigator who went to southeastern Kentucky: "She got into one of those mining towns," Roosevelt said, "and started to walk up the alley. There was a group of miners sitting in front of the shacks, and they pulled down their caps over their faces. As soon as she caught sight of that she walked up and said, 'What are you pulling your caps down for?' They said, 'Oh, it is all right.' 'Why pull your caps down?' They said, 'It is sort of a custom because so many of the women have not got enough clothes to cover them.'"

The Depression made changes in the country's physical appearance.

Fewer pedestrians were to be seen on the streets since many men did not go to work and women shopped less frequently; for lack of warm clothing and fuel, many people stayed in bed most of the day during winter. The air became cleaner over industrial cities, for there was less smoke from factory chimneys. The downtown business districts of most cities had long rows of empty shops and offices. Trains were shorter, and only rarely did one see a Pullman car. However, gas stations multiplied because millions of Americans drove their battered family cars here and there in endless quest of work. In conflicting attempts to solve their problems, farmers moved into town while city folks moved into the country to build their own houses and grow their own food. More and more blacks were seen in northern cities as desperate Negroes fled from the hopeless South. Telephones were taken out of homes, and mail deliveries were lighter. Houses and stores, parks and fences sagged and lapsed into unpainted, flaked ugliness for want of money to make repairs.

In his novel called *You Can't Go Home Again,* Thomas Wolfe described a comfort station in front of New York City Hall:

. . . One descended to this place down a steep flight of stairs from the street, and on bitter nights he would find the place crowded with homeless men who had sought refuge there. Some were those shambling hulks that one sees everywhere, in Paris as well as in New York. . . . But most of them were just flotsam of the general ruin of the time—honest, decent, middle-aged men with faces seamed by toil and want, and young men, many of them mere boys in their teens, with thick, unkempt hair. These were the wanderers from town to town, the riders of freight trains, the thumbers of rides on highways, the uprooted, unwanted male population of America. They drifted across the land and gathered in the big cities when winter came, hungry, defeated, empty, hopeless, restless, driven by they knew not what, always on the move, looking everywhere for work, for the bare crumbs to support their miserable lives, and finding neither work nor crumbs. Here in New York, to this obscene meeting place, these derelicts came, drawn into a common stew of rest and warmth and a little surcease from their desperation.

Heywood Broun devoted a column to a description of a slum in San Antonio, Texas:

. . . The Church of Guadalupe stands upon the fringe of what had been described to me as the most fearsome slum in all America. It covers four square miles. At first I thought that the extreme description might have been dictated by local pride. It was my notion to protest and say, "Why, we in New York City know worse than that." But after we had gone up the third back alley I had to confess defeat gracefully.

You can see shacks as bad as these in several States, but I do not know of any place where they have been so ingeniously huddled together. This is flat, sprawling country, and there is much of it, and so it seems devilish that one crazy combination of old lumber and stray tin should be set as a flap upon the side of another equally discreditable. I did not quite comprehend the character of the alley until I discovered that what I took to be a toolhouse was a residence for a family of eleven people.

And these are not squatter dwellings. People pay rent for them, just as if a few rickety boards and a leaky roof constituted a house. They even have evictions and go through the solemn and obscene farce of removing a bed and a frying pan as indication that the landlord's two-dollars-and-a-half rent has not been forthcoming. . . .

Back at the Church of Guadalupe, the priest said, "I have other letters from those who fight federal housing because they like their rents." He tossed over an anonymous message, which read, "I could start a story that there is a priest who writes love letters to young girls and gives jewels to women of his congregation."

"Doesn't this worry you?" one of us asked.

"No," said the priest. "Last month we buried thirty-nine persons, mostly children, from this little church alone.

"I am worried," he said, "about people starving to death."

Louis Adamic and his wife were living with her mother in New York City in January, 1932. Born in Yugoslavia, now a naturalized American, he was a writer, a tall young man with a look of eager curiosity in his eyes. One cold morning at seven forty-five the doorbell rang, and Adamic, thinking it was the postman, opened the front door. In his book called *My America,* he told what happened next.

There stood a girl of ten and a boy of eight.

They had schoolbooks in their arms, and their clothing was patched and clean, but hardly warm enough for winter weather. In a voice strangely old for her age, the girl said: "Excuse me, mister, but we have no eats in our house and my mother she said I should take my brother before we go to school and ring a doorbell in some house"—she swallowed heavily and took a deep breath—"and ask you to give us . . . something . . . to eat."

"Come in," Adamic said. A strange sensation swept over him. He had heard that kids were ringing doorbells and asking for food in the Bronx, in Harlem and in Brooklyn, but he had not really believed it.

His wife and her mother gave the children some food. The girl ate slowly. Her brother bolted his portion, quickly and greedily.

"He ate a banana yesterday afternoon," said his sister, "but it wasn't ripe enough or some-thing', and it made him sick and he didn't eat anything since. He's always like this when he's hungry and we gotta ring doorbells."

"Do you often ring doorbells?"

"When we have no eats at home."

"What made you ring our bell?"

"I don't know," the girl answered. "I just did."

Her name was Mary, and her brother's name was Jimmie. They lived in a poor neighborhood five blocks away.

Mary said: "We used to live on the fourth floor upstairs and we had three rooms and a kitchen and bath, but now we have only one room downstairs. In back."

"Why did you move downstairs?"

The boy winced.

"My father," said the girl. "He lost his job when the panic came. That was two years ago. I was eight and Jimmie was six. My father he tried to get work, but he couldn't, the depression was so bad. But he called it the panic."

Adamic and the two women were astonished at her vocabulary: "panic" . . . "depression."

"What kind of work did your father do?"

"Painter and paperhanger. Before things got so bad, he always had jobs when his work was in season, and he was good to us—my mother says so, too. Then, after he couldn't get any more jobs, he got mean and he yelled at my mother. He couldn't sleep nights and he walked up and down and talked, and sometimes he hollered and we couldn't sleep, either."

"Was he a union man?"

"No, he didn't belong to no union."

"What did your father holler about?"

"He called my mother bad names."

At this point in the conversation, Adamic wrote, the little girl hesitated, and her brother winced again. Then she continued: "Uh . . . he was angry because my mother, before she married him, she was in love with another man and almost married him. But my mother says it wasn't my father's fault he acted mean like he did. He was mean because he had no job and we had no money."

"Where's your father now?"

"We don't know. He went away four months ago, right after Labor Day, and he never came back, so we had to move downstairs. The landlord didn't want to throw us out, so he told my mother to move in downstairs."

Between sips of milk the girl said her mother did household work whenever she could find a job, but earned very little money this way. A charity organization had been giving her $2.85 a week, but lately it had stopped. Mary did not know why. Her mother had applied for home relief, but had not yet received anything from that source.

The boy stopped eating, turned to his sister and muttered: "You talk too much! I told you not to talk!"

The girl fell silent.

Adamic said: "It's really our fault, Jimmie. We're asking too many questions."

The little boy glared and said: "Yeah!"

In Detroit someone gave another little girl a nickel, which seemed like such a fortune to her that she agonized three full days about how best to spend it.

In Erie, Pennsylvania, a seven-year-old boy named Tom received a tiny yellow chick as an Easter present. Using some old chicken wire, he built a coop for his pet beneath the back step to the house and fed and tended it carefully. His father was an unemployed molder, and the family often ate nothing but beans. Time passed. Now the little chick had grown into a full-sized chicken. One day Tom's father announced that the boy's pet would have to be killed and served for Sunday dinner, since everyone was hungry. Tom screamed in horrified protest but was unable to prevent his father from taking his chicken into the backyard and chopping off its head. Later that day the family sat around the table feasting on fowl, while the boy hunched in his chair, sobbing.

There was another boy who never forgot a scene from his childhood days during the Depression. He lived in a small town in Iowa. Every so often a train would stop there for a few minutes, and a man would get out carrying bags of buttons. He would distribute these buttons to waiting farmers and their wives, collect the cards to which they had sewn other buttons, pay them a meager sum for their labor, get back into the train and depart. This trivial piecework provided them with the only income they could get.

President Hoover was foolish enough to let himself be photographed on the White House lawn feeding his dog. This picture did not sit well with Americans who were hungry, suffering from malnutrition or even starving to death. Several times Hoover denied that there was widespread undernourishment in the nation, but he depended on unreliable statistics. Comedian Groucho Marx, who was closer to the people, said he knew things were bad when "the pigeons started feeding the people in Central Park." However, it was no laughing matter.

In Oklahoma City a newspaper reporter was assigned to cover state relief headquarters. Walking into the building one morning, he ran into a young man he had met through his landlady. This fellow offered the reporter some candy. The reporter did not want the candy but accepted it lest he hurt the other's feelings. As they stood and chewed, a social worker approached them.

"We don't allow any eating in here," she said.

The reporter, who thought she was jesting, made a wisecrack.

"We don't allow any eating in here," she repeated sternly. "Some of these applicants haven't had any breakfast. We make it a rule among ourselves never to eat or to drink Cokes in front of them."

Ashamed of himself, the reporter mumbled an apology and slunk behind a beaver-board wall. He wanted to throw away the morsel of candy remaining in his hand but felt that this would be even more sinful with hungry people so near.

Arthur Brisbane, the rich columnist and editor, walked into a Manhattan restaurant and ordered two lamb chops. When he had finished the first one, he looked longingly at the second but was too full to eat it, too. After much thought he summoned a waiter.

"What happens if I don't eat this chop?" Brisbane asked. "Will you take it back?"

"No, sir. We can't do that, sir."

"But what will you do with it? Will it be thrown away?"

"Not at all, sir. We give the leftovers to poor people."

Brisbane sighed in relief, nodded approvingly, paid his check and left.

In 1933 the Children's Bureau reported that one out of every five children in the nation was not getting enough of the right things to eat. A teacher in a coal-mining town asked a little girl in her classroom whether she was ill. The child said: "No. I'm all right. I'm just hungry." The teacher urged her to go home and eat something. The girl said: "I can't This is my sister's day to eat." In the House of Representative, during a debate about appropriations for Indians living on reservations, a Congressman said that eleven cents a day was enough to feed an Indian child. A Senate subcommittee learned that the president of a textile firm had told his workers they should be able to live on six cents a day.

AFL President William Green said: "I warn the people who are exploiting the workers that they can only drive them so far before they will turn on them and destroy them. They are taking no account of the history of nations in which governments have been overturned. Revolutions grow out of the depths of hunger."

Sidney Hillman, president of the Amalgamated Clothing Workers of America, appeared at a Senate hearing in 1932 and was told that it was not yet time to give federal relief. Angrily, he cried: "I would ask by what standards are we to gauge that time! Must we have hundreds of thousands of people actually dead and dying from starvation? Must we have bread riots? What is necessary to convince them that there is a need for federal and speedy relief?"

The Communists took up the slogan: "Starve or fight!"

At the University of Pennsylvania a prim audience was shocked to hear Daniel Willard, president of the B & O Railroad, say: "While I do not like to say so, I would be less than candid if I did not say that in such circumstances I would steal before I would starve."

Obviously, less fortunate Americans agreed. Petty thievery soared. Children hung around grocery stores begging for food. Customers emerging from groceries had bundles snatched from their arms by hungry kids, who ran home with the food or ducked into alleys to gobble it as fast as they could. Small retail stores had their windows smashed and their display goods stolen. Grown men, in groups of two and three, walked into chain store markets, ordered all the food they could carry and then quietly walked out without paying for it. Chain store managers did not always report these incidents to the police for fear that publicity would encourage this sort of intimidation. For the same reason the newspapers engaged in a tacit conspiracy of silence.

However, newspapers did not mind reporting that in Manhattan a debutante supper for 600 guests at the Ritz-Carlton cost $4,750. On nearby Park Avenue, beggars were so numerous that a well-dressed man might be asked for money four or five times in a ten-block stroll. President Hoover not only denied that anyone was starving, but said: "The hoboes, for example, are better fed than they ever have been. One hobo in New York got ten meals in one day."

People of means thought up ways to protect

themselves from panhandlers and from begging letters. Boston's mayor, James M. Curley had a male secretary named Stan Wilcox, who was adept at brushing off approaches. Whenever a beggar asked if he had a quarter, Wilcox would reply: "Heavens, no! I wouldn't dream of taking a drink at this hour!" Alfred E. Smith received the following letter from Milwaukee: "This is unusual, but I am in need. Would you send me $2,500, as this is the amount I am in need of. I will give you as collateral my word of honor that I will repay you if possible. If not, let the good Lord repay you and he will also pay better interest."

Governor Gifford Pinchot of Pennsylvania flatly declared that starvation was widespread. Among the many pathetic letters he received was this one: "There are nine of us in the family. My father is out of work for a couple of months and we haven't got a thing eat [sic] in the house. Mother is getting $12 a month of the county. If mother don't get more help we will have to starve to death. I am a little girl 10 years old. I go to school every day. My other sister hain't got any shoes or clothes to wear to go to school. My mother goes in her bare feet and she crys every night that we don't have the help. I guess that is all, hoping to hear from you."

Bernard Baruch, who felt burdened by the thought of his wealth, got a desperate letter from his cousin, Fay Allen Des Portes, who lived in his home state of South Carolina. "The horrible part of the whole situation," she wrote to him, "is these poor starving people here in our midst. The banks can't let anyone have money, the merchants are all broke; the farmers can't let the poor Negroes on the farm have anything to eat. I don't know what is going to happen. I have about four hundred Negroes that are as absolutely dependent upon me as my two little boys, but I can't help them any more and God knows what is going to happen to them."

John L. Lewis, president of the United Mine Workers, once said to a group of mine operators: "Gentlemen, I speak to you for my people. I speak to you for the miners' families in the broad Ohio valley, the Pennsylvania mountains and the black West Virginia hills. There, the shanties lean over as if intoxicated by the smoke fumes of the mine dumps. But the more pretentious ones boast a porch, with the banisters broken here and there, presenting the aspect of a snaggle-toothed child. Some of the windows are wide open to flies, which can feast nearby on garbage and answer the family dinner call in double-quick time. But there is no dinner call. The little children are gathered around a bare table without anything to eat. Their mothers are saying, 'We want bread.' "

A writer named Jonathan Norton Leonard described the plight of Pennsylvania miners who had been put out of company villages after losing a strike: "Reporters from the more liberal metropolitan papers found thousands of them huddled on the mountainsides, crowded three or four families together in one-room shacks, living on dandelion and wild weedroots. Half of them were sick, but no local doctor would care for the evicted strikers. All of them were hungry and many were dying of those providential diseases which enable welfare workers to claim that no one has starved."

In 1931 four New York City hospitals reported 95 deaths from starvation. Two years later the New York City Welfare Council said that 29 persons had died from starvation, more than 50 others had been treated for starvation, while an additional 110 individuals—most of them children—had perished of malnutrition. In one routine report the council gave this picture of the plight of one family in the Brownsville section of Brooklyn: "Family reported starving by neighbors. Investigator found five small children at home while mother was out looking for vegetables under pushcarts. Family had moved into one room. Father sleeping at Municipal Lodging House because he could get more to eat there than at home and frequently brought food home from there in pockets for children and wife. Only other food they had for weeks came from pushcarts."

A family of fourteen was on relief in Kewanee, Illinois, the hog-raising center of the Midwest. The family was given $3 worth of groceries a week, and of course this food soon ran out. After giving the last crumbs to the children, the adults would exist on nothing but hot water until they received their next grocery allotment.

In Chicago a committee investigated city garbage dumps and then reported: "Around the truck which was unloading garbage and other refuse were about 35 men, women and children. As soon as the truck pulled away from the pile all of them started digging with sticks, some with their hands, grabbing bits of food and vegetables."

Edmund Wilson described another Chicago scene: "A private incinerator at Thirty-fifth and La Salle Streets which disposes of garbage from restaurants and hotels, has been regularly visited by people, in groups of as many as twenty at a time, who pounce upon anything that looks edible before it is thrown into the furnace. The women complained to investigators that the men took unfair advantage by jumping on the truck before it was unloaded; but a code was eventually established which provided that different sets of people should come at different times every day, so that everybody would be given a chance."

A ballad called "Starvation Blues" was sung by some of the poor people of America during the Depression.

Prentice Murphy, director of the Children's Bureau of Philadelphia, told a Senate committee: "If the modern state is to rest upon a firm foundation, its citizens must not be allowed to starve. Some of them do. They do not die quickly. You can starve for a long time without dying."

Scientists agree that a person can starve a long time without dying, but this is what it is like to starve to death: After a few days without food the stomach cramps and bloats up. Later it shrinks in size. At first a starving child will cry and eat anything to ease hunger pains—stuffing his mouth with rags, clay, chalk, straw, twigs, berries and even poisonous weeds. Then, as the child weakens, his cries change to whimpers. He feels nauseated. All the fat is being burned from his body. This burning produces acidosis. The fruity odor of acetone can be smelled on the breath, and it also appears in the urine. When starvation reaches this point, nature becomes kinder. The child grows listless and sleepy. The bulging eyes are sad and dull. Now body proteins have been depleted, while the water and electrolyte balance has been destroyed. Degeneration of the vital organs, such as the liver and kidneys, proceeds in earnest. By this time the child lacks all resistance to diseases and may be killed by some infection.

John Steinbeck has told how he survived the early part of the Depression before he became a famous author. "I had two assets," he wrote. "My father owned a tiny three-room cottage in Pacific Grove in California, and he let me live in it without rent. That was the first safety. Pacific Grove is on the ocean. That was the second. People in inland cities or in the closed and shuttered industrial cemeteries had greater problems than I. Given the sea, a man must be very stupid to starve. That great reservoir is always available. I took a large part of my protein food from the ocean.

"Firewood to keep warm floated on the beach daily, needing only handsaw and ax. A small garden of black soil came with the cottage. In northern California you can raise vegetables of some kind all year long. I never peeled a potato without planting the skins. Kale, lettuce, chard, turnips, carrots and onions rotated in the little garden. In the tide pools of the bay, mussels were available and crabs and abalones and that shiny kelp called sea lettuce. With a line and pole, blue cod, rock cod, perch, sea trout, sculpin could be caught."

The sale of flower seeds shot up as Americans, tired of the ugliness of their lives, turned to the beauty of homegrown flowers. As might have been expected, there was widespread cultivation of vegetable gardens. Many did this on their own, while others received official encouragement. Big railroads rented garden plots for their workers. The United States Steel Corporation used social workers and faculty members of Indiana University to develop an extensive garden project for its workers in Gary, Indiana. In New York State, in the summer of 1933, jobless men and women were tending 65,000 gardens. The city of Detroit provided tools and seed for "thrift gardens" on empty lots, an idea which Mayor Frank Murphy said he had borrowed from Hazen S. Pingree. During the Panic of 1893 Pingree had been the mayor of Detroit, and confronted with a city of jobless men, he provided them with gardens to cultivate—"Pingree's Potato Patches" receiving national attention.

Now, in the present emergency, Henry Ford ordered all his workmen to dig in vegetable gardens or be fired. Out of his imperious command there developed what the Scripps-Howard Washington *News* called 50,000 "shotgun gardens." Rough-grained Harry Bennett, chief of Ford's private police, supervised this vast project and kept a filing system on all Ford employees. If a man had no garden in his own backyard or on some neighborhood lot, he was assigned a patch of earth somewhere on Ford's 4,000 acres of farmland around Dearborn, Michigan. Each workman had to pay fifty cents to have his strip plowed.

More than one-third of the men employed in Ford's Dearborn plant lived 10 to 20 miles away, and some protested that since they did not own a car they would have to spend an extra two hours daily just traveling to and from their allotted patches. A Bennett henchman would snarl: "Why don't-cha buy a car? You're makin' 'em, ain't-cha?" Bone-weary workmen who simply couldn't muster the energy to toil on their garden plots soon were brought into line by Bennett's personal deputy, Norman Selby, the former boxer "Kid McCoy."

In the spring of 1932 the Community Council of Philadelphia ran out of private funds for the relief of needy families. Eleven days elapsed before this relief work could be resumed with public funds, and many families received no help during this interim. A study was made to find out what had happened when food orders stopped.

One woman borrowed 50 cents from a friend and bought stale bread at 3½ cents per loaf. Except for one or two meals, this was all she could serve her family throughout those eleven days.

A pregnant mother and her three children could afford only two meals a day. At eleven o'clock in the morning she would serve breakfast,

which consisted of cocoa, bread and butter. This left everyone so hungry that the mother began advancing the time of their evening meal, which was just one can of soup.

Another woman scoured the docks, picking up vegetables that fell from produce wagons. Fish vendors sometimes gave her a fish at the end of the day. On two separate occasions her family went without food for a day and a half.

On the day the food orders stopped, one family ate nothing all day. At nine o'clock that night the mother went to a friend's house and begged for a loaf of bread. Later she got two days' work at 75 cents a day. With this pittance she bought a little meat. Then, adding vegetables picked up off the street, she made a stew which she cooked over and over again each day to prevent spoilage.

One family ate nothing but potatoes, rice, bread and coffee, and for one and a half days they were totally without food.

Hunting jackrabbits to feed the family became a way of life among farmers and ranchers. This gave birth to a Depression joke reported by John Steinbeck in *The Grapes of Wrath.* One man said to another: "Depression is over. I seen a jackrabbit, an' they wasn't nobody after him." The second man said: "That ain't the reason. Can't afford to kill jackrabbits no more. Catch 'em and milk-'em and turn 'em loose. One you seen prob'ly gone dry."

Audie Murphy was born on a Texas farm five years before the Crash, the son of very poor parents. Almost as soon as he could walk, he began hunting game for the family. Since shells were expensive, every shot had to count. Aware of this, Audie Murphy developed into an expert marksman—so expert that when he was a GI during World War II, he killed 240 Nazis and emerged as the most decorated American soldier of the war.

Wheat growers, bankrupted by drought, talked about heading for Alaska to kill moose to fill their growling bellies. In the timberlands of the great Northwest some desperate men set forest fires so that they would be hired to extinguish them, while in big cities other men prayed for heavy snowfalls to provide them with shoveling jobs. When some Pittsburgh steel mills reopened briefly, the steelworkers called back to their jobs were too weak from hunger to be able to work.

At the age of eleven Cesar Chavez, who later won renown as a Mexican-American labor leader, fished and cut mustard greens to help keep his family from starving.

Charles H. Percy, who wound up a multimillionaire and a United States Senator, never forgot what it was like to be a poor boy in Chicago during the Depression: "I remember a great feeling of shame when the welfare truck pulled up to our house. And you talk about cheating! Once they delivered us 100 pounds of sugar by mistake. My father wanted to return it, but my mother said, 'God willed us to have it,' and she wouldn't give it up." She swapped some of the sugar for flour and helped tide the family over by baking cookies that little Chuck Percy peddled door to door.

Americans under the stress of the Depression behaved with a dignity that varied in terms of their religious backgrounds, their mental images of themselves and their rigidity or flexibility. Brittle people snapped, while the pliant bent and survived.

In Georgia a blind Negro refused all relief, harnessed himself to a plow like a mule and tilled the fields, day after day. In Pittsburgh a father with starving children stole a loaf of bread from a neighbor, was caught, hanged himself in shame. In Youngstown, Ohio, a father, mother and their four sons preferred to starve rather than accept charity. Before they died, their condition was discovered by a neighbor who happened to be a newspaper reporter. They were existing on fried flour and water.

Charles Wayne also lived in Youngstown. He had been a hot mill worker for the Republic Iron and Steel Company until he was laid off. For the next two years he was unable to get any kind of work. Now a fifty-seven-year-old man, workless, hopeless, unable to feed his wife and ten children, he climbed onto a bridge one morning. He took off his coat, folded it neatly, then jumped into the swirling Mahoning River below. Instinct caused

him to swim a few strokes, but then he gave up and let himself drown. Later his wife sobbed to reporters: "We were about to lose our home and the gas and electric companies had threatened to shut off the service."

An elderly man receiving $15-a-week relief money for his large family went out each day, without being asked, to sweep the streets of his village. "I want to do something," he said, "in return for what I get." A graduate of the Harvard Law School, now old and almost deaf, gladly took a $15-a-week job as assistant caretaker at a small park.

Rather than accept charity, a New York dentist and his wife killed themselves with gas. He left this note: "The entire blame for this tragedy rests with the City of New York or whoever it is that allows free dental work in the hospital. We want to get out of the way before we are forced to accept relief money. The City of New York is not to touch our bodies. We have a horror of charity burial. We have put the last of our money in the hands of a friend who will turn it over to my brother."

John Steinbeck wrote: "Only illness frightened us. You have to have money to be sick—or did then. And dentistry also was out of the question, with the result that my teeth went badly to pieces. Without dough you couldn't have a tooth filled."

Shoes were a problem. Upon reaching home, poor people took off their shoes to save wear and tear. Middle-class people bought do-it-yourself shoe-repair kits. Those unable to afford the kits would resole their shoes with strips of rubber cut from old tires. Some wore ordinary rubbers over shoes with holes in their bottoms. A miner's son, Jack Conroy, told what a hole in a shoe could mean to a man walking the streets looking for work: "Maybe it starts with a little hole in the sole; and then the slush of the pavements oozes in, gumming sox and balling between your toes. Concrete whets Woolworth sox like a file, and if you turn the heel on top and tear a pasteboard inner sole, it won't help much. There are the tacks, too. You get to avoiding high places and curbstones because that jabs the point right into the heel. Soon the tack has calloused a furrowed hole, and you don't notice it unless you strike something unusually high or solid, or forget and walk flat-footed. You pass a thousand shoe-shops where a tack might be bent down, but you can't pull off a shoe and ask to have *that* done—for nothing."

Keeping clean was also a problem, since soap cost money. Steinbeck washed his linen with soap made from pork fat, wood ashes and salt, but it took a lot of sunning to get the smell out of sheets. As the sale of soap declined across the nation, its production was reduced. Procter & Gamble did not lay off its workers, as it might have done under the circumstances, but put them to work cutting grass, painting fences and repairing factories until soap production began to rise again.

Steinbeck wrote a short story called "Daughter" about a sharecropper who shot and killed his own daughter because he had no food to give her. This could not be shrugged off as mere fiction, for in Carlisle, Pennsylvania, a starving man named Elmo Noakes actually suffocated his three small daughters rather than see them starve.

The Depression scarred many young men and women who later became celebrities or who already were well known. Jack Dempsey, former heavy-weight boxing champion of the world, became so strapped for money that at the age of thirty-six he got himself sufficiently back into shape to fight fifty-six exhibition bouts. Babe Ruth, always a big spender, tried to supplement his income by opening a haberdashery on Broadway but lost his own shirt after five months.

Clifford Odets wrote his first play while living on ten cents a day. Lillian Hellman, who later became a renowned playwright, earned $50 a week as a script reader for Metro-Goldwyn-Mayer. William Inge, who also won fame as a playwright, acted in tent shows during the Depression, long afterward recalling: "We actors considered ourselves fortunate if we earned five dollars a week. Sometimes the farmers of Kansas would bring in flour and meat as barter for admission to Saturday matinees."

Songwriter Frank Loesser learned from his parents that they had lost all their money. He took any job he could get, including screwing the tops on bottles of an insecticide. He also worked as a spotter for a chain of restaurants, getting seventy-five cents a day plus the cost of each meal for reporting on the food and service. Later he reminisced: "I used to eat twelve times a day. When you're poor, you're always hungry from walking around so much."

Danny Thomas performed in saloons, but finally even this kind of work came to an end. The chance of getting another job seemed so slim that he considered giving up show business. In desperation, he prayed to St. Jude, the patron saint of the hopeless, and the next day he landed a job in Chicago that proved to be the turning point of his career.

Ralph Bellamy almost starved to death in the basement of a Greenwich Village apartment. Cary Grant was working in Hollywood as an extra. Dana Andrews worked four years as a gas station attendant in Van Nuys, California. Robert Young was employed as a soda jerk, grease monkey and truck driver. Ray Milland, living on credit in Hollywood, was about to go to work in a garage when he landed a part in a movie called *Bolero*. In Chireno, Texas, a twelve-year-old girl named Lucille Ann Collier began dancing professionally to help the family finances; later she grew into a long-legged beauty and won fame under the name of Ann Miller. In the Bronx a four-year-old girl named Anna Maria Italiano sang for WPA men working on a nearby project; today she is known as Anne Bancroft.

Victor Mature set out for Hollywood in 1935 at the age of seventeen, with $40 in cash and a car loaded with candy and chewing gum. He drove for five days and slept in his automobile each night, and by the time he reached the film capital he was almost broke. To his father in Louisville he wired: ARRIVED HERE WITH 11 CENTS. His father, an Austrian scissors grinder who had taken up refrigerator selling, wired back: FORTY-THREE YEARS AGO I ARRIVED IN NEW YORK WITH FIVE CENTS. I COULD NOT EVEN SPEAK ENGLISH. YOU ARE SIX CENTS UP ON ME.

The effect of the Depression on Hollywood extras was told by Grover Jones to an amused courtroom in a trial concerning Metro-Goldwyn-Mayer. Jones, once an extra and then a script-writer, gave this entertaining testimony: "They wanted eighty Indians, and I got the job only because I knew how to put on what they called bolamania—burnt umber and raw umber mixed. But they made me a chief. That meant I didn't have to go naked. I could wear a suit, you see. And at that time I was convinced I was fairly smart. So there were now eighty-one Indians. I had never seen a camera during all those months, because I was always in the background, waiting over in back of the hill for the call to come over the hill on the horses to rescue the child. And I had never been on horses. So we sat on these horses, each confiding in the other, and none of them had ever been on horses, except we were all hungry. Finally the man said, 'Now look, when you hear shooting I want you all to come over the hills, and I want some of you to fall off the horses.' Well, in those days they paid three dollars extra for a man who would fall off a horse, because it is quite a stunt. So we waited until finally we got the call to come over the hill, and somebody shot a gun off—and eighty-one Indians fell off their horses."

There was nothing surprising about the fact that men would risk injury or death by falling off a horse to earn an extra $3 a day. People felt that if they could just live through the Depression, they could endure anything else life had to offer. To *endure* was the main thing. Many took pay cuts without a murmur. A young man just out of college with a Bachelor of Journalism degree accepted a job on a newspaper at exactly *nothing* per week; a month later he was grateful to be put on the payroll at $15. Graduate engineers worked as office boys. College graduates of various kinds ran elevators in department stores. Unemployed architects turned out jigsaw puzzles. One jobless draftsman, Alfred Butts, used his spare time to invent the game of Scrabble.

Young men who might have grown into greatness chose, instead, to seek the security of civil service jobs, becoming policemen, firemen, garbage collectors. Fewer sailors deserted from the Navy. Enlistments rose in all branches of the nation's military establishment. When Congress voted a 10 percent pay cut for all federal employees, President Hoover secretly asked the Senate to make an exception for soldiers and sailors, because he did not wish to rely on disgruntled troops in case of internal trouble.

Women and children toiled for almost nothing in the sweatshops of New York City, welfare workers reporting these grim examples:

- A woman crocheted hats for 40 cents a dozen and was able to make only two dozen per week.
- An apron girl, paid 2½ cents per apron, earned 20 cents a day.
- A slipper liner was paid 21 cents for every seventy-two pairs of slippers she lined, and if she turned out one slipper every forty-five seconds she could earn $1.05 in a nine-hour day.
- A girl got half a cent for each pair of pants she threaded and sponged, making $2.78 a week.

Connecticut's state commissioner of labor said that some sweatshops in that state paid girls between 60 cents and $1.10 for a fifty-five-hour week. In Pennsylvania men working in sawmills were paid 5 cents an hour, men in tile and brick manufacturing got 6 cents per hour, while construction workers earned 7½ cents an hour. In Detroit the Briggs Manufacturing Company paid men 10 cents and women 4 cents an hour, causing auto workers to chant: "If poison doesn't work, try Briggs!" Also in Detroit, the Hudson Motor Car Company called back a small-parts assembler and then kept her waiting three days for a half hour of work, forcing her to spend 60 cents in carfare to earn 28 cents.

Two Marine fishermen put out to sea at four o'clock one morning and did not return to port until five o'clock that afternoon. During this long day of toil they caught 200 pounds of hake and 80 pounds of haddock. They burned up eight gallons of gas at 19 cents a gallon and used 100 pounds of bait costing two cents a pound. For their catch they were paid one cent a pound for the hake and four cents a pound for the haddock. Thus they earned less than two cents an hour for their day's work.

Meantime, Henry Ford was declaring: "Many families were not so badly off as they thought; they needed guidance in the management of their resources and opportunities." Ford needed no guidance. He managed to transfer 41½ percent of stock in the Ford Motor Company to his son, Edsel, without paying a cent in inheritance or estate taxes.

Ford, who liked to boast that he always had to work, declared in 1930 that "the very poor are recruited almost solely from the people who refuse to think and therefore refuse to work diligently." Roger W. Babson, the statistician, pontificated two years later: "Better business will come when the unemployed change their attitude toward life." Most rich men were quick to moralize.

The concept of hard work was central to capitalism and the Protestant ethic. Americans had been raised on a diet of aphorisms praising work and self-reliance. Benjamin Franklin said: "God helps them that help themselves." The Bible insisted: "In the sweat of thy face shalt thou eat bread." Thomas Carlyle said: "All work, even cotton-spinning, is noble; work alone is noble." Elizabeth Barrett Browning wrote: "Whoever fears God, fears to sit at ease." It was either Bishop Richard Cumberland or George Whitefield (no one is sure) who first said: "Better to wear out than to rust out." Most Americans agreed, but now in these Depression times men did sit at home and rust, through no fault of their own, losing the fine edge of their skills.

Idle, dispirited, hungry, defeated, withdrawn, brooding—people began to feel that somehow they were to blame for everything, that somehow, somewhere, they had failed. Maybe the Depression was punishment for their sins. After all, Protestant Episcopal Bishop John P. Tyler attributed it to the lack of religion. Perhaps Christians, if they wished to be good Christians, should bow to fate by accepting Christ's words that "to everyone that hath shall be given; and from him

that hath not, even that which he hath shall be taken from him." But some found it difficult to find comfort in a sermon preached by the Reverend William S. Blackshear, an Episcopalian clergyman, in the bleak year of 1932. Blackshear said in part: "Christ was happy to be at the banquets of the rich. It was at such a place that the woman broke the vial of costly ointment and anointed His feet. There were those who cried out for the improvident and rebuked the woman, saying that this should have been converted into cash and given to the poor. It was then that Christ spoke on the economic plan, 'The poor ye have always with you.' "

This kind of sermon, representing conservative Protestantism, offended liberal clergymen. Forced by the Depression to rethink their values, they began searching for a new theology. Some began with the premise that if the church were to serve any purpose or perform realistically, it had to divorce itself from economic and political values. This developing viewpoint was expressed with crystal clarity by H. Richard Niebuhr, a pastor and a brother of Reinhold Niebuhr. He wrote:

The church is in bondage to capitalism. Capitalism in its contemporary form is more than a system of ownership and distribution of economic goods. It is a faith and a way of life. It is faith in wealth as the source of all life's blessings and as the savior of man from his deepest misery. It is the doctrine that man's most important activity is the production of economic goods and that all other things are dependent upon this. On the basis of this initial idolatry it develops a morality in which economic worth becomes the standard by which to measure all other values and the economic virtues take precedence over courage, temperance, wisdom and justice, over charity, humility and fidelity. Hence nature, love, life, truth, beauty and justice are exploited or made the servants of the high economic good. Everything, including the lives of workers, is made a utility, is desecrated and ultimately destroyed. . . .

Other dissenters noted the supremacy of capitalism over every other value in the fact that church property was exempt from taxation.

State constitutions and special statutes declared that no real estate taxes could be levied on church-owned properties, such as the church building itself, parochial schools, parsonages, the parish house and cemeteries. Why? A Missouri Supreme Court decision said that "no argument is necessary to show that church purposes are public purposes."

But was this really true? The United States of America was a Christian nation nominally, but not legally. No single religion, sect or church was recognized as the established church. Although the phrase "separation of church and state" does not appear in the Constitution of the United States or in that of any state but Utah, the idea for which it stands is found in the constitutional provisions against religious tests and in the words of the First Amendment: "Congress shall make no law respecting an establishment of religion. . . ."

During the Depression some liberal Christians, agnostics, atheists and others fretted about the special status given churches and church property. A few scholars recalled that President Ulysses S. Grant had said: "I would suggest the taxation of all property equally, whether church or corporation, exempting only the last resting place of the dead, and possibly, with proper restrictions, church edifices." Dissenters objected on principle to the exemption of church property, regarded this as an indirect subsidy by the state to religion and pointed out that personal taxes might be less if churches bore their share of the tax burden.

They got nowhere. At the core of capitalism was the belief that God looked with favor on the rich. This idea had been expressed as long ago as 1732 by one of J. P. Morgan's ancestors, the Reverend Joseph Morgan, who sermonized: "Each man coveting to make himself rich, carries on the Publick Good: Thus God in His Wisdom and Mercy turns our wickedness to Publick Benefit. . . . A rich Man is a great friend of the Publick, while he aims at nothing but serving himself. God will have us live by helping one another; and since Love will not do it, Covetousness shall."

J. P. Morgan himself flatly told a Senate committee: "If you destroy the leisure class you destroy civilization." When reporters pressed for a definition of the leisure class, Morgan said it included all who could afford a maid. In 1931, according to *Fortune* magazine, there still were 1,000,000 families with servants. One wealthy family announced that it had solved its Depression problem by discharging fifteen of its twenty servants—although the family members showed no curiosity or concern about the fate of the unemployed fifteen.

John Jacob Astor came of age in 1933 and thereupon inherited about $4 million. Nonetheless, he dabbled at a job in a downtown Manhattan brokerage house. Before long he quit with the explanation: "I didn't finish until five o'clock and by the time I got uptown it was six. And then I had to get up early the next morning." At a later date Astor was employed briefly by a shipping firm, and when he quit this second job, he commented: "I have discovered that work interferes with leisure." He was a representative of that leisure class which Morgan felt must be maintained to save civilization.

When Dwight Morrow was running for governor of New Jersey, he said: "There is something about too much prosperity that ruins the fiber of the people. The men and women that built this country, that founded it, were people that were reared in adversity." Morrow made this statement and died before Adolf Hitler declared: "It was poverty that made me strong." Joseph P. Kennedy, a busy member of the leisure class, felt that the rich had to make some sacrifices. Writing about the Depression, Kennedy said: "I am not ashamed to record that in those days I felt and said I would be willing to part with half of what I had if I could be sure of keeping, under law and order, the other half."

One member of the enormously wealthy Du Pont family seems to have been out of touch with reality. An advertising agency wanted his company to sponsor a Sunday afternoon radio program, but this Du Pont rejected the idea, saying: "At three o'clock on Sunday afternoons everybody is playing polo."

Everybody except the millions of Americans gobbling the last morsel of food from their plates in the fear that it might be their last meal —a habit that persisted in some people down through the next three decades. As Sinclair Lewis commented in his novel *It Can't Happen Here,* people were so confused, insecure and frustrated that they hardly could do anything more permanent than shaving or eating breakfast. They were tortured with feelings of inadequacy and guilt.

A young Alabama school teacher with eight years of tenure was fired after the Wall Street Crash. Eager to work, willing to take any job however low in the social scale, she became a maid in a private home. However, upon learning that she would be expected to work seven days a week, getting room and board but no wages, she quit. Then she took a job in a convalescent home which paid her room and board and $3 a week, but soon the home closed for lack of funds. The gentle schoolteacher completely lost faith in herself, confessing to a caseworker: "If, with all the advantages I've had, I can't make a living, then I'm just no good, I guess!"

Forty experienced secretaries found work after being unemployed a year, but the first few days on the job they were unable to take dictation from their bosses without weeping from sheer nervousness. After seeking employment for a long time, a man finally landed a job and became so overwrought with joy that he died of excitement. A corporation executive was given the nasty chore of firing several hundred men. A kind and compassionate person, he insisted on talking to each of them personally and asking what plans each had for the future. In a few months the executive's hair had turned gray.

The Depression began to erode freedom.

Some Americans, a little more secure than others, asked harsh questions. How about fingerprinting everyone on relief? Was it proper for a man on relief to own a car—even if he needed it to try to find work? Wasn't it wrong to sell liquor to the head of a family on relief? Did anyone owning a life insurance policy deserve relief?

Should reliefers be allowed to vote? Did they deserve citizenship?

In New Orleans a federal judge denied citizenship to four qualified persons because they were on relief and therefore, in the judge's words, "unable financially to contribute to the support of the government." In California another judge withheld citizenship from Jacob Hullen; in response to the judge's questions Hullen had said he believed in municipal or federal ownership of public utilities.

In New York City, one cold and rainy day, the police arrested 38 men who had taken shelter in the Pennsylvania Railroad's ferry terminal on Cortlandt Street. All were marched to the nearest police station. Fifteen of them, able to prove that they had a few nickels and dimes in their pockets, were released. The other 23 men, who did not have a cent on them, were led before a magistrate, who sentenced them to jail for vagrancy. Newspaper stories about this obvious injustice raised such a hullabaloo, however, that the 23 prisoners soon were freed.

Robert Morss Lovett, a professor of English literature at the University of Chicago, wrote in his autobiography:

An example of the injustice meted out to foreign-born workers involved a Yugoslav named Perkovitch. When conditions were at their worst in 1932–33 the unemployed on the West Side [of Chicago] were in the habit of crossing the city to the South Side where food was sometimes available from bakeries, disposing of yesterday's bake, and where, at least, the garbage was more lavish.

One morning these itinerants were picked up by the police and held at the station house on the absurd pretext that a revolution was planned. Perkovitch told me that he and about one hundred others were kept in the basement all day without food. Once a lieutenant with a bodyguard of patrolmen raged through the room, striking and kicking the men in an ecstasy of sadism. At six the prisoners were released with no charges.

Paul D. Peacher, the town marshal of Jonesboro, Arkansas, arrested a group of Negro men without cause and forced them to work on his farm. A federal grand jury indicted him under Title 18 of the Anti-Slavery Act of 1866 for "causing Negroes to be held as slaves" on a cotton plantation. This was the first case ever tried under the slavery statute. A county grand jury absolved Peacher, but the federal Department of Justice would not drop the case. Now the marshal was forced to stand trial—this time before a *federal* jury. Taking the witness chair in his own behalf, he denied that he had done anything wrong. However, the jury disagreed with him and found him guilty. Peacher was sentenced to two years in prison and fined $3,500. He appealed, lost his appeal, paid the fine and accepted a two-year probationary sentence.

Someone asked Eugene Talmadge, the governor of Georgia, what he would do about the millions of unemployed Americans. Talmadge snarled: "Let'em starve!" It made him happy when the city fathers of Atlanta put unwanted nonresidents in chain gangs. When some textile workers went on strike in Georgia the governor had barbed-wire concentration camps built and threw pickets into them. Frank Hague, the mayor and ruthless boss of Jersey City, called for the erection in Alaska of a concentration camp for native "Reds."

Wise and temperate men worried about the growing loss of liberty in America, the land of the free and the home of the brave. George Boas, a professor of philosophy, sadly said: "It is taken for granted that democracy is bad and that it is dying." Will Durant, busy writing his many-volumed *Story of Civilization,* asked rhetorically: "Why is it that Democracy has fallen so rapidly from the high prestige which it had at the Armistice?"

17

THE NEW DEAL: THE CONSERVATIVE ACHIEVEMENTS OF LIBERAL REFORM

BARTON BERNSTEIN

Most historians view Franklin D. Roosevelt's New Deal as a watershed in American history. In a sharp break with the past, they argue, Roosevelt and his advisors began to fashion a distinctively American welfare state to combat the worst abuses of the Depression. The New Deal record was an impressive one: it established price supports in agriculture, fashioned a National Recovery Administration to direct new industrial growth, provided jobs for the unemployed through the Civilian Conservation Corps and the Works Progress Administration, insured bank deposits, and established social welfare programs through the Social Security Administration. The New Deal, these historians claim, tamed capitalism and paved the way for further liberal reforms during the next two decades.

Not all historians agree with this interpretation however. As Barton J. Bernstein suggests in this essay, the New Deal can be seen as something less than revolutionary. The principle of government involvement in the economy and the idea of a welfare state emerged in the 1880s and was foreshadowed in the progressive movement at the turn of the century. New Deal reforms were important, but it can be argued that they did more to help the middle and upper classes than the poor. And the evidence clearly demonstrates that it was World War II, not the New Deal, that rescued America from the Depression. For Bernstein the New Deal was not always the watershed that historians have made it. If it brought the power of the state into social reform, he argues, it was only in order to save capitalism.

How does Bernstein's argument about the conservative nature of the New Deal compare with Edward R. Ellis's description of its social effects in Reading 16? Were there similarities between the progressive reforms discussed by Allen F. Davis in Reading 13 and those of the New Deal? Between the Populist platform discussed by Lawrence C. Goodwyn in Reading 7 and the New Deal?

Writing from a liberal democratic consensus, many American historians in the past two decades have praised the Roosevelt administration for its nonideological flexibility and for its far-ranging reforms. To many historians, particularly those who reached intellectual maturity during the depression, the government's accomplishments, as well as the drama and passion, marked the decade as a watershed, as a dividing line in the American past.

Enamored of Franklin D. Roosevelt and recalling the bitter opposition to welfare measures and restraints upon business, many liberal historians have emphasized the New Deal's discontinuity

Reprinted from *Towards a New Past: Dissenting Essays in American History*, edited by Barton Bernstein. © 1968 by Random House, Inc. Reprinted by permission of Pantheon Books, a division of Random House, Inc.

with the immediate past. For them there was a "Roosevelt Revolution," or at the very least a dramatic achievement of a beneficent liberalism which had developed in fits and spurts during the preceding three decades. Rejecting earlier interpretations which viewed the New Deal as socialism or state capitalism, they have also disregarded theories of syndicalism or of corporate liberalism. The New Deal has generally commanded their approval for such laws or institutions as minimum wages, public housing, farm assistance, the Tennessee Valley Authority, the Wagner Act, more progressive taxation, and social security. For most liberal historians the New Deal meant the replenishment of democracy, the rescuing of the federal government from the clutches of big business, the significant redistribution of political power. Breaking with laissez faire, the new administration, according to these interpretations, marked the end of the passive or impartial state and the beginning of positive government, of the interventionist state acting to offset concentrations of private power, and affirming the rights and responding to the needs of the unprivileged.

From the perspective of the late 1960s these themes no longer seem adequate to characterize the New Deal. The liberal reforms of the New Deal did not transform the American system; they conserved and protected American corporate capitalism, occasionally by absorbing parts of threatening programs. There was no significant redistribution of power in American society, only limited recognition of other organized groups, seldom of unorganized peoples. Neither the bolder programs advanced by New Dealers nor the final legislation greatly extended the beneficence of government beyond the middle classes or drew upon the wealth of the few for the needs of the many. Designed to maintain the American system, liberal activity was directed toward essentially conservative goals. Experimentalism was most frequently limited to means; seldom did it extend to ends. Never questioning private enterprise, it operated within safe channels, far short of Marxism or even of native American radicalisms that offered structural critiques and structural solutions.

All of this is not to deny the changes wrought by the New Deal—the extension of welfare programs, the growth of federal power, the strengthening of the executive, even the narrowing of property rights. But it is to assert that the elements of continuity are stronger, that the magnitude of change has been exaggerated. The New Deal failed to solve the problem of depression, it failed to raise the impoverished, it failed to redistribute income, it failed to extend equality and generally countenanced racial discrimination and segregation. It failed generally to make business more responsible to the social welfare or to threaten business's pre-eminent political power. In this sense, the New Deal, despite the shifts in tone and spirit from the earlier decade, was profoundly conservative and continuous with the 1920s.

Rather than understanding the 1920s as a "return to normalcy," the period is more properly interpreted by focusing on the continuation of progressive impulses, demands often frustrated by the rivalry of interest groups, sometimes blocked by the resistance of Harding and Coolidge, and occasionally by Hoover. Through these years while agriculture and labor struggled to secure advantages from the federal government, big business flourished. Praised for creating American prosperity, business leaders easily convinced the nation that they were socially responsible, that they were fulfilling the needs of the public. Benefitting from earlier legislation that had promoted economic rationalization and stability, they were opponents of federal benefits to other groups but seldom proponents of laissez faire.

In no way did the election of Herbert Hoover in 1928 seem to challenge the New Era. An heir of Wilson, Hoover promised an even closer relationship with big business and moved beyond Harding and Coolidge by affirming federal responsibility for prosperity. As Secretary of Commerce, Hoover had opposed unbridled competition and had transformed his department into a vigorous friend of business. Sponsoring trade associations, he promoted industrial self-regulation and the increased rationalization of business. He had also expanded foreign trade, endorsed the regulation of new forms of communications, encouraged relief in disasters, and recommended public works to offset economic declines.

By training and experience, few men in American political life seemed better prepared than Hoover to cope with the depression. Responding promptly to the crisis, he acted to stabilize the economy and secured the agreement of businessmen to maintain production and wage rates. Unwilling to let the economy "go through the wringer," the President requested easier money, self-liquidating public works, lower personal and corporate income taxes, and stronger commodity stabilization corporations. In reviewing these unprecedented actions, Walter Lippmann wrote, "The national government undertook to make the whole economic order operate prosperously."

But these efforts proved inadequate. The tax cut benefitted the wealthy and failed to raise effective demand. The public works were insufficient. The commodity stabilization corporations soon ran out of funds, and agricultural prices kept plummeting. Businessmen cut back production, dismissed employees, and finally cut wages. As unemployment grew, Hoover struggled to inspire confidence, but his words seemed hollow and his understanding of the depression limited. Blaming the collapse on European failures, he could not admit that American capitalism had failed. When prodded by Congress to increase public works, to provide direct relief, and to further unbalance the budget, he doggedly resisted. Additional deficits would destroy business confidence, he feared, and relief would erode the principles of individual and local responsibility. Clinging to faith in voluntarism, Hoover also briefly rebuffed the efforts by financiers to secure the Reconstruction Finance Corporation (RFC). Finally endorsing the RFC, he also supported expanded lending by Federal Land Banks, recommended home-loan banks, and even approved small federal loans (usually inadequate) to states needing funds for relief. In this burst of activity, the President had moved to the very limits of his ideology.

Restricted by his progressive background and insensitive to politics and public opinion, he stopped far short of the state corporatism urged by some businessmen and politicians. With capitalism crumbling he had acted vigorously to save it, but he would not yield to the representatives of business or disadvantaged groups who wished to alter the government. He was reluctant to use the federal power to achieve through compulsion what could not be realized through voluntary means. Proclaiming a false independence, he did not understand that his government already represented business interests; hence, he rejected policies that would openly place the power of the state in the hands of business or that would permit the formation of a syndicalist state in which power might be exercised (in the words of William Appleman Williams) "by a relatively few leaders of each functional bloc formed and operating as an oligarchy."

Even though constitutional scruples restricted his efforts, Hoover did more than any previous American president to combat depression. He "abandoned the principles of laissez faire in relation to the business cycle, established the conviction that prosperity and depression can be publicly controlled by political action, and drove out of the public consciousness the old idea that depressions must be overcome by private adjustment," wrote Walter Lippmann. Rather than the last of the old presidents, Herbert Hoover was the first of the new.

A charismatic leader and a brilliant politician, his successor expanded federal activities on the basis of Hoover's efforts. Using the federal government to stabilize the economy and advance the interests of the groups, Franklin D. Roosevelt directed the campaign to save large-scale corporate capitalism. Though recognizing new political interests and extending benefits to them, his New Deal never effectively challenged big business or the organization of the economy. In providing assistance to the needy and by rescuing them from starvation, Roosevelt's humane efforts also protected the established system: he sapped organized radicalism of its waning strength and of its

potential constituency among the unorganized
and discontented. Sensitive to public opinion and
fearful of radicalism, Roosevelt acted from a mixture of motives that rendered his liberalism cautious and limited, his experimentalism narrow.
Despite the flurry of activity, his government was
more vigorous and flexible about means than
goals, and the goals were more conservative than
historians usually acknowledge.

Roosevelt's response to the banking crisis em-
phasizes the conservatism of his administration
and its self-conscious avoidance of more radical
means that might have transformed American
capitalism. Entering the White House when
banks were failing and Americans had lost faith
in the financial system, the President could have
nationalized it—"without a word of protest,"
judged Senator Bronson Cutting. "If ever there
was a moment when things hung in the balance,"
later wrote Raymond Moley, a member of the
original "brain trust," "it was on March 5, 1933
—when unorthodoxy would have drained the last
remaining strength of the capitalistic system." To
save the system, Roosevelt relied upon collaboration between bankers and Hoover's Treasury officials to prepare legislation extending federal assistance to banking. So great was the demand for
action that House members, voting even without
copies, passed it unanimously, and the Senate,
despite objections by a few Progressives, approved it the same evening. "The President," remarked a cynical congressman, "drove the
money-changers out of the Capitol on March 4th
—and they were all back on the 9th.'

Undoubtedly the most dramatic example of
Roosevelt's early conservative approach to recovery was the National Recovery Administration
(NRA). It was based on the War Industries
Board (WIB) which had provided the model for
the campaign of Bernard Baruch, General Hugh
Johnson, and other former WIB officials during
the twenties to limit competition through industrial self-regulation under federal sanction. As
trade associations flourished during the decade,
the FTC encouraged "codes of fair competition"
and some industries even tried to set prices and
restrict production. Operating without the force

of law, these agreements broke down. When the
depression struck, industrial pleas for regulation
increased. After the Great Crash, important business leaders including Henry I. Harriman of the
Chamber of Commerce and Gerard Swope of
General Electric called for suspension of antitrust
laws and federal organization of business collaboration. Joining them were labor leaders, particularly those in "sick" industries—John L. Lewis of
the United Mine Workers and Sidney Hillman of
Amalgamated Clothing Workers.

Designed largely for industrial recovery, the
NRA legislation provided for minimum wages
and maximum hours. It also made concessions to
pro-labor congressmen and labor leaders who demanded some specific benefits for unions—recognition of the worker's right to organization and to
collective bargaining. In practice, though, the
much-heralded Section 7a was a disappointment
to most friends of labor. (For the shrewd Lewis,
however, it became a mandate to organize: "The
President wants you to join a union.") To many
frustrated workers and their disgusted leaders,
NRA became "National Run Around." The
clause, unionists found (in the words of Brookings economists), "had the practical effect of placing NRA on the side of anti-union employers in
their struggle against trade unions. . . . [It] thus
threw its weight against labor in the balance of
bargaining power." And while some far-sighted
industrialists feared radicalism and hoped to forestall it by incorporating unions into the economic
system, most preferred to leave their workers
unorganized or in company unions. To many
businessmen, large and independent unions as
such seemed a radical threat to the system of
business control.

Not only did the NRA provide fewer advantages than unionists had anticipated, but it also
failed as a recovery measure. It probably even
retarded recovery by supporting restrictionism
and price increases, concluded a Brookings study.
Placing effective power for code-writing in big
business, NRA injured small businesses and contributed to the concentration of American industry. It was not the government-business partnership as envisaged by Adolf A. Berle, Jr., nor

government managed as Rexford Tugwell had hoped, but rather, business managed, as Raymond Moley had desired. Calling NRA "industrial self-government," its director, General Hugh Johnson, had explained that "NRA is exactly what industry organized in trade associations makes it." Despite the annoyance of some big businessmen with Section 7a, the NRA reaffirmed and consolidated their power at a time when the public was critical of industrialists and financiers.

Viewing the economy as a "concert of organized interests," the New Deal also provided benefits for farmers—the Agricultural Adjustment Act. Reflecting the political power of larger commercial farmers and accepting restrictionist economics, the measure assumed that the agricultural problem was overproduction, not underconsumption. Financed by a processing tax designed to raise prices to parity, payments encouraged restricted production and cutbacks in farm labor. With benefits accruing chiefly to the larger owners, they frequently removed from production the lands of sharecroppers and tenant farmers, and "tractored" them and hired hands off the land. In assisting agriculture, the AAA, like the NRA, sacrificed the interests of the marginal and the unrecognized to the welfare of those with greater political and economic power.

In large measure, the early New Deal of the NRA and AAA was a "broker state." Though the government served as a mediator of interests and sometimes imposed its will in divisive situations, it was generally the servant of powerful groups. "Like the mercantilists, the New Dealers protected vested interests with the authority of the state," acknowledges William Leuchtenburg. But it was some improvement over the 1920s when business was the only interest capable of imposing its will on the government. While extending to other groups the benefits of the state, the New Deal, however, continued to recognize the pre-eminence of business interests.

The politics of the broker state also heralded the way of the future—of continued corporate dominance in a political structure where other groups agreed generally on corporate capitalism and squabbled only about the size of the shares. Delighted by this increased participation and the absorption of dissident groups, many liberals did not understand the dangers in the emerging organization of politics. They had too much faith in representative institutions and in associations to foresee the perils—of leaders not representing their constituents, of bureaucracy diffusing responsibility, of officials serving their own interests. Failing to perceive the dangers in the emerging structure, most liberals agreed with Senator Robert Wagner of New York: "In order that the strong may not take advantage of the weak, every group must be equally strong." His advice then seemed appropriate for organizing labor, but it neglected the problems of unrepresentative leadership and of the many millions to be left beyond organization.

In dealing with the organized interests, the President acted frequently as a broker, but his government did not simply express the vectors of external forces. The New Deal state was too complex, too loose, and some of Roosevelt's subordinates were following their own inclinations and pushing the government in directions of their own design. The President would also depart from his role as a broker and act to secure programs he desired. As a skilled politician, he could split coalitions, divert the interests of groups, or place the prestige of his office on the side of desired legislation.

In seeking to protect the stock market, for example, Roosevelt endorsed the Securities and Exchange measure (of 1934), despite the opposition of many in the New York financial community. His advisers split the opposition. Rallying to support the administration were the out-of-town exchanges, representatives of the large commission houses, including James Forrestal of Dillon, Read, and Robert Lovett of Brown Brothers, Harriman, and such commission brokers as E. A. Pierce and Paul Shields. Opposed to the Wall Street "old guard" and their companies, this group included those who wished to avoid more radical legislation, as well as others who had wanted earlier to place trading practices under federal legislation which they could influence.

Though the law restored confidence in the securities market and protected capitalism, it alarmed some businessmen and contributed to the false belief that the New Deal was threatening business. But it was not the disaffection of a portion of the business community, not the creation of the Liberty League, that menaced the broker state. Rather it was the threat of the Left—expressed, for example, in such overwrought statements as Minnesota Governor Floyd Olson's: "I am not a liberal . . . I am a radical. . . . I am not satisfied with hanging a laurel wreath on burglars and thieves . . . and calling them code authorities or something else." While Olson, along with some others who succumbed to the rhetoric of militancy, would back down and soften their meaning, their words dramatized real grievances: the failure of the early New Deal to end misery, to re-create prosperity. The New Deal excluded too many. Its programs were inadequate. While Roosevelt reluctantly endorsed relief and went beyond Hoover in support of public works, he too preferred self-liquidating projects, desired a balanced budget, and resisted spending the huge sums required to lift the nation out of depression.

For millions suffering in a nation wracked by poverty, the promises of the Left seemed attractive. Capitalizing on the misery, Huey Long offered Americans a "Share Our Wealth" program —a welfare state with prosperity, not subsistence, for the disadvantaged, those neglected by most politicians. "Every Man a King": pensions for the elderly, college for the deserving, homes and cars for families—that was the promise of American life. Also proposing minimum wages, increased public works, shorter work weeks, and a generous farm program, he demanded a "soak-the-rich" tax program. Despite the economic defects of his plan, Long was no hayseed, and his forays into the East revealed support far beyond the bayous and hamlets of his native South. In California discontent was so great that Upton Sinclair, food faddist and former socialist, captured the Democratic nomination for governor on a platform of "production-for-use"—factories and farms for the unemployed. "In a cooperative society," promised Sinclair, "every man, woman, and child would have the equivalent of $5,000 a year income from labor of the able-bodied young men for three or four hours per day." More challenging to Roosevelt was Francis Townsend's plan— monthly payments of $200 to those past sixty who retired and promised to spend the stipend within thirty days. Another enemy of the New Deal was Father Coughlin, the popular radio priest, who had broken with Roosevelt and formed a National Union for Social Justice to lead the way to a corporate society beyond capitalism.

To a troubled nation offered "redemption" by the Left, there was also painful evidence that the social fabric was tearing—law was breaking down. When the truckers in Minneapolis struck, the police provoked an incident and shot sixty-seven people, some in the back. Covering the tragedy, Eric Sevareid, then a young reporter, wrote, "I understood deep in my bones and blood what fascism was." In San Francisco union leaders embittered by police brutality led a general strike and aroused national fears of class warfare. Elsewhere, in textile mills from Rhode Island to Georgia, in cities like Des Moines and Toledo, New York and Philadelphia, there were brutality and violence, sometimes bayonets and tear gas.

Challenged by the Left, and with the new Congress more liberal and more willing to spend, Roosevelt turned to disarm the discontent. "Boys —this is our hour," confided Harry Hopkins. "We've got to get everything we want—a works program, social security, wages and hours, everything—now or never. Get your minds to work on developing a complete ticket to provide security for all the folks of this country up and down and across the board." Hopkins and the associates he addressed were not radicals: they did not seek to transform the system, only to make it more humane. They, too, wished to preserve large-scale corporate capitalism, but unlike Roosevelt or Moley, they were prepared for more vigorous action. Their commitment to reform was greater, their tolerance for injustice far less. Joining them in pushing the New Deal left were the leaders of industrial unions, who, while also not wishing to transform the system, sought for workingmen higher wages, better conditions, stronger and larger unions, and for themselves a place closer to the fulcrum of power.

The problems of organized labor, however, neither aroused Roosevelt's humanitarianism nor suggested possibilities of reshaping the political coalition. When asked during the NRA about employee representation, he had replied that workers could select anyone they wished—the Ahkoond of Swat, a union, even the Royal Geographical Society. As a paternalist, viewing himself (in the words of James MacGregor Burns) as a "partisan and benefactor" of workers, he would not understand the objections to company unions or to multiple unionism under NRA. Nor did he foresee the political dividends that support of independent unions could yield to his party. Though presiding over the reshaping of politics (which would extend the channels of power to some of the discontented and redirect their efforts to competition within a limited framework), he was not its architect, and he was unable clearly to see or understand the unfolding design.

When Senator Wagner submitted his labor relations bill, he received no assistance from the President and even struggled to prevent Roosevelt from joining the opposition. The President "never lifted a finger," recalls Miss Perkins. ("I, myself, had very little sympathy with the bill," she wrote.) But after the measure easily passed the Senate and seemed likely to win the House's endorsement, Roosevelt reversed himself. Three days before the Supreme Court invalidated the NRA, including the legal support for unionization, Roosevelt came out for the bill. Placing it on his "must" list, he may have hoped to influence the final provisions and turn an administration defeat into victory.

Responding to the threat from the left, Roosevelt also moved during the Second Hundred Days to secure laws regulating banking, raising taxes, dissolving utility-holding companies, and creating social security. Building on the efforts of states during the Progressive Era, the Social Se-

curity Act marked the movement toward the welfare state, but the core of the measure, the old-age provision, was more important as a landmark than for its substance. While establishing a federal-state system of unemployment compensation, the government, by making workers contribute to their old-age insurance, denied its financial responsibility for the elderly. The act excluded more than a fifth of the labor force leaving, among others, more than five million farm laborers and domestics without coverage.

Though Roosevelt criticized the tax laws for not preventing "an unjust concentration of wealth and economic power," his own tax measure would not have significantly redistributed wealth. Yet his message provoked an "amen" from Huey Long and protests from businessmen. Retreating from his promises, Roosevelt failed to support the bill, and it succumbed to conservative forces. They removed the inheritance tax and greatly reduced the proposed corporate and individual levies. The final law did not "soak the rich." But it did engender deep resentment among the wealthy for increasing taxes on gifts and estates, imposing an excess-profits tax (which Roosevelt had not requested), and raising surtaxes. When combined with such regressive levies as social security and local taxes, however, the Wealth Tax of 1935 did not drain wealth from higher-income groups, and the top one percent even increased their shares during the New Deal years.

Those historians who have characterized the events of 1935 as the beginning of a second New Deal have imposed a pattern on those years which most participants did not then discern. In moving to social security, guarantees of collective bargaining, utility regulation, and progressive taxation, the government did advance the nation toward greater liberalism, but the shift was exaggerated and most of the measures accomplished far less than either friends or foes suggested. Certainly, despite a mild bill authorizing destruction of utilities-holding companies, there was no effort to atomize business, no real threat to concentration.

Nor were so many powerful businessmen disaffected by the New Deal. Though the smaller businessmen who filled the ranks of the Chamber of Commerce resented the federal bureaucracy and the benefits to labor and thus criticized NRA, representatives of big business found the agency useful and opposed a return to unrestricted competition. In 1935, members of the Business Advisory Council—including Henry Harriman, outgoing president of the Chamber, Thomas Watson of International Business Machines, Walter Gifford of American Telephone and Telegraph, Gerard Swope of General Electric, Winthrop Aldrich of the Chase National Bank, and W. Averell Harriman of Union Pacific —vigorously endorsed a two-year renewal of NRA.

When the Supreme Court in 1935 declared the "hot" oil clause and then NRA unconstitutional, the administration moved to measures known as the "little NRA." Reestablishing regulations in bituminous coal and oil, the New Deal also checked wholesale price discrimination and legalized "fair trade" practices. Though Roosevelt never acted to revive the NRA, he periodically contemplated its restoration. In the so-called second New Deal, as in the "first," government remained largely the benefactor of big business, and some more advanced businessmen realized this.

Roosevelt could attack the "economic royalists" and endorse the TNEC investigation of economic concentration, but he was unprepared to resist the basic demands of big business. While there was ambiguity in his treatment of oligopoly, it was more the confusion of means than of ends, for his tactics were never likely to impair concentration. Even the antitrust program under Thurman Arnold, concludes Frank Freidel, was "intended less to bust the trusts than to forestall too drastic legislation." Operating through consent degrees and designed to reduce prices to the consumer, the program frequently "allowed industries to function much as they had in NRA days." In effect, then, throughout its variations, the New Deal had sought to cooperate with business.

Though vigorous in rhetoric and experimental in tone, the New Deal was narrow in its goals and wary of bold economic reform. Roosevelt's sense of what was politically desirable was frequently more restricted than others' views of what was possible and necessary. Roosevelt's limits were those of ideology; they were not inherent in experimentalism. For while the President explored the narrow center, and some New Dealers considered bolder possibilities, John Dewey, the philosopher of experimentalism, moved far beyond the New Deal and sought to reshape the system. Liberalism, he warned, "must now become radical. . . . For the gulf between what the actual situation makes possible and the actual state itself is so great that it cannot be bridged by piece-meal policies undertaken *ad hoc.*" The boundaries of New Deal experimentalism, as Howard Zinn has emphasized, could extend far beyond Roosevelt's cautious ventures. Operating within very safe channels, Roosevelt not only avoided Marxism and the socialization of property, but he also stopped far short of other possibilities—communal direction of production or the organized distribution of surplus. The President and many of his associates were doctrinaires of the center, and their maneuvers in social reform were limited to cautious excursions.

Usually opportunistic and frequently shifting, the New Deal was restricted by its ideology. It ran out of fuel not because of the conservative opposition, but because it ran out of ideas. Acknowledging the end in 1939, Roosevelt proclaimed, "We have now passed the period of internal conflict in the launching of our program of social reform. Our full energies may now be released to invigorate the processes of recovery in order to preserve our reforms. . . ."

The sad truth was that the heralded reforms were severely limited, that inequality continued, that efforts at recovery had failed. Millions had come to accept the depression as a way of life. A decade after the Great Crash, when millions were still unemployed, Fiorello LaGuardia recommended that "we accept the inevitable, that we are now in a new normal." "It was reasonable to expect a probable minimum of 4,000,000 to 5,000,000 unemployed," Harry Hopkins had concluded. Even that level was never reached, for business would not spend and Roosevelt refused to countenánce the necessary expenditures. "It was in economics that our troubles lay," Tugwell wrote. "For their solution his [Roosevelt's] progressivism, his new deal was pathetically insufficient. . . ."

Clinging to faith in fiscal orthodoxy even when engaged in deficit spending, Roosevelt had been unwilling to greatly unbalance the budget. Having pledged in his first campaign to cut expenditures and to restore the balanced budget, the President had at first adopted recovery programs that would not drain government finances. Despite a burst of activity under the Civil Works Administration during the first winter, public works expenditures were frequently slow and cautious. Shifting from direct relief, which Roosevelt (like Hoover) considered "a narcotic, a subtle destroyer of the human spirit," the government moved to work relief. ("It saves his skill. It gives him a chance to do something socially useful," said Hopkins.) By 1937 the government had poured enough money into the economy to spur production to within 10 percent of 1929 levels, but unemployment still hovered over seven million. Yet so eager was the President to balance the budget that he cut expenditures for public works and relief, and plunged the economy into a greater depression. While renewing expenditures, Roosevelt remained cautious in his fiscal policy, and the nation still had almost nine million unemployed in 1939. After nearly six years of struggling with the depression, the Roosevelt administration could not lead the nation to recovery, but it had relieved suffering. In most of America, starvation was no longer possible. Perhaps that was the most humane achievement of the New Deal.

Its efforts on behalf of humane *reform* were generally faltering and shallow, of more value to the middle classes, of less value to organized workers, of even less to the marginal men. In conception and in practice, seemingly humane efforts revealed the shortcomings of American liberalism. For example, public housing, praised as evidence of the federal government's concern for the poor, was limited in scope (to 180,000 units) and unfortunate in results. It usually meant the consolidation of ghettos, the robbing of men of their dignity, the treatment of men as wards with few rights. And slum clearance came to mean "Negro clearance" and removal of the other poor. Of much of this liberal reformers were unaware, and some of the problems can be traced to the structure of bureaucracy and to the selection of government personnel and social workers who disliked the poor. But the liberal conceptions, it can be argued, were also flawed for there was no willingness to consult the poor, nor to encourage their participation. Liberalism was elitist. Seeking to build America in their own image, liberals wanted to create an environment which they thought would restructure character and personality more appropriate to white, middle-class America.

While slum dwellers received little besides relief from the New Deal, and their needs were frequently misunderstood, Negroes as a group received even less assistance—less than they needed and sometimes even less than their proportion in the population would have justified. Under the NRA they were frequently dismissed and their wages were sometimes below the legal minimum. The Civilian Conservation Corps left them "forgotten" men—excluded, discriminated against, segregated. In general, what the Negroes gained—relief, WPA jobs, equal pay on some federal projects—was granted them as poor people, not as Negroes. To many black men the distinction was unimportant, for no government had ever given them so much. "My friends, go home and turn Lincoln's picture to the wall," a Negro publisher told his race. "That debt has been payed in full."

Bestowing recognition on some Negro leaders, the New Deal appointed them to agencies as advisers—the "black cabinet." Probably more dramatic was the advocacy of Negro rights by Eleanor Roosevelt. Some whites like Harold Ickes and Aubrey Williams even struggled cautiously to break down segregation. But segregation did not yield, and Washington itself remained a segregated city. The white South was never challenged, the Fourteenth Amendment never used to assist Negroes. Never would Roosevelt expend political capital in an assault upon the American caste system. Despite the efforts of the NAACP to dramatize the Negroes' plight as second-class citizens, subject to brutality and often without legal protection, Roosevelt would not endorse the anti-lynching bill. ("No government pretending to be civilized can go on condoning such atrocities," H. L. Mencken testified. "Either it must make every possible effort to put them down or it must suffer the scorn and contempt of Christendom.") Unwilling to risk schism with Southerners ruling committees, Roosevelt capitulated to the forces of racism.

Even less bold than in economic reform, the New Deal left intact the race relations of America. Yet its belated and cautious recognition of the black man was great enough to woo Negro leaders and even to court the masses. One of the bitter ironies of these years is that a New Dealer could tell the NAACP in 1936: "Under our new conception of democracy, the Negro will be given the chance to which he is entitled. . . ." But it was true, Ickes emphasized, that "The greatest advance [since Reconstruction] toward assuring the Negro that degree of justice to which he is entitled and that equality of opportunity under the law which is implicit in his American citizenship, has been made since Franklin D. Roosevelt was sworn in as President. . . ."

It was not in the cities and not among the Negroes but in rural America that Roosevelt administration made its (philosophically) boldest efforts: creation of the Tennessee Valley Authority and the later attempt to construct seven little valley authorities. Though conservation was not a new federal policy and government-owned utilities were sanctioned by municipal experience, federal activity in this area constituted a challenge to corporate enterprise and an expression of concern about the poor. A valuable example of regional planning and a contribution to regional prosperity, TVA still fell far short of expectations. The agency soon retreated from social planning. ("From 1936 on," wrote Tugwell, "the TVA should have been called the Tennessee Val-

ley Power Production and Flood Control Corporation.") Fearful of antagonizing the powerful interests, its agricultural program neglected the tenants and the sharecroppers.

To urban workingmen the New Deal offered some, but limited, material benefits. Though the government had instituted contributory social security and unemployment insurance, its much-heralded Fair Labor Standards Act, while prohibiting child labor, was a greater disappointment. It exempted millions from its wages-and-hours provisions. So unsatisfactory was the measure that one congressman cynically suggested, "Within 90 days after appointment of the administrator, she should report to Congress whether anyone is subject to this bill." Requiring a minimum of twenty-five cents an hour ($11 a week for 44 hours), it raised the wages of only about a half-million at a time when nearly twelve million workers in interstate commerce were earning less than forty cents an hour.

More important than these limited measures was the administration's support, albeit belated, of the organization of labor and the right of collective bargaining. Slightly increasing organized workers' share of the national income, the new industrial unions extended job security to millions who were previously subject to the whim of management. Unionization freed them from the perils of a free market.

By assisting labor, as well as agriculture, the New Deal started the institutionalization of larger interest groups into a new political economy. Joining business as tentative junior partners, they shared the consensus on the value of large-scale corporate capitalism, and were permitted to participate in the competition for the division of shares. While failing to redistribute income, the New Deal modified the political structure at the price of excluding many from the process of decision making. To many what was offered in fact was symbolic representation, formal representation. It was not the industrial workers necessarily who were recognized, but their unions and leaders; it was not even the farmers, but their organizations and leaders. While this was not a conscious design, it was the predictable result of conscious policies. It could not have been easily avoided, for it was part of the price paid by a large society unwilling to consider radical new designs for the distribution of power and wealth.

In the deepest sense, this new form of representation was rooted in the liberal's failure to endorse a meaningful egalitarianism which would provide actual equality of opportunity. It was also the limited concern with equality and justice that accounted for the shallow efforts of the New Deal and left so many Americans behind. The New Deal was neither a "third American Revolution," as Carl Degler suggests, nor even a "half-way revolution," as William Leuchtenburg concludes. Not only was the extension of representation to new groups less than full-fledged partnership, but the New Deal neglected many Americans—share-croppers, tenant farmers, migratory workers and farm laborers, slum dwellers, unskilled workers, and the unemployed Negroes. They were left outside the new order. As Roosevelt asserted in 1937 (in a classic understatement), one third of the nation was "ill-nourished, ill-clad, ill-housed."

Yet, by the power of rhetoric and through the appeals of political organization, the Roosevelt government managed to win or retain the allegiance of these peoples. Perhaps this is one of the crueller ironies of liberal politics, that the marginal men trapped in hopelessness were seduced by rhetoric, by the style and movement, by the symbolism of efforts seldom reaching beyond words. In acting to protect the institution of private property and in advancing the interests of corporate capitalism, the New Deal assisted the middle and upper sectors of society. It protected them, sometimes, even at the cost of injuring the lower sectors. Seldom did it bestow much of substance upon the lower classes. Never did the New Deal seek to organize these groups into independent political forces. Seldom did it risk antagonizing established interests. For some this would constitute a puzzling defect of liberalism; for some, the failure to achieve true liberalism. To others it would emphasize the inherent shortcomings of American liberal democracy. As the nation prepared for war, liberalism, by accepting private property and federal assistance to corporate capitalism, was not prepared effectively to reduce inequities, to redistribute political power, or to extend equality from promise to reality.

PART THREE
AN ENDURING PEOPLE

18

THE DECISION FOR MASS EVACUATION OF THE JAPANESE-AMERICANS

ROGER DANIELS

From 1939, when World War II broke out in Europe, to December 1941 mainstream opinion in America was avowedly isolationist. This war was thought to be a European concern, the price which European states had to pay for their "corrupt" system of power politics. But when Japanese naval aircraft attacked and destroyed much of the American fleet at Pearl Harbor on December 7, 1941, popular isolationism quickly changed to demands for prompt retaliation.

In Washington, Franklin D. Roosevelt responded quickly to the Japanese attack, asking Congress on December 9 for a declaration of war. But America was unprepared militarily to proceed against the Japanese, for much of its Pacific forces had been destroyed at Pearl Harbor. Moreover, America's European allies were in desperate straits by 1942; excepting Switzerland and Luxembourg, all of continental Europe was under Axis control and Germany was poised for a major assault upon a staggering Britain.

Faced with this situation, Roosevelt saw America's first duty as the rescue of Britain and the defeat of the Fascist forces in Europe. Only then, reasoned Roosevelt, would the United States have sufficient time to arm itself for a concentrated campaign against Japan. But Roosevelt had also to respond to the growing public clamor for an immediate military response to the Japanese attack.

Caught between these conflicting demands, Roosevelt looked to symbolic attacks against the Japanese to satisfy domestic demands and to gain support for his war strategy. Thus, in early 1942, Roosevelt authorized air raids on Tokyo, and in February of the same year he signed an executive order giving the Army authority to remove all people of Japanese descent, many of whom were American citizens, from the western United States.

How does the public attitude about Japanese removal in 1942 compare with that toward the Indian removals of the nineteenth century, discussed by Mary Young in *Retracing the Past: Volume One,* Reading 18. Refer back to the essays by Jack Chen (Reading 3) and Leonard M. Pitt (*Volume One,* Reading 24). How do contemporary attitudes toward the Japanese compare with those directed toward the Chinese a century earlier? Toward the Chicanos in the same period?

December 1941 was a month of calamities which saw West Coast opinion harden against the Japanese; during January, as the war news got worse and worse and it became apparent that the Japanese audacity at Pearl Harbor would not be quickly avenged, the national climate of opinion,

Reprinted from Roger Daniels, *Concentration Camps, North America: Japanese in the United States and Canada during World War II* (Malabar, Fla.: Robert E. Krieger, 1981), by permission of the author.

and Congressional opinion in particular, began to veer toward the West Coast view. That this climate had to be created is shown by an examination of the *Congressional Record*. Not only was there no concerted strong feeling exhibited against the Japanese Americans, but in the first weeks after Pearl Harbor members of the California delegation defended them publicly. (The only trace of hostility shown by a California solon in early December was a telephone call that the junior senator, Democrat Sheridan Downey, made to the Army on the night of December 7 suggesting that De Witt prompt Governor Olson to declare some sort of curfew on "Japs.") On December 10, for example, Bertrand W. Gearhart, a four-term Republican congressman from Fresno and an officer of the American Legion, read a telegram professing loyalty to the United States from an Issei leader in his district whom Gearhart described as an "American patriot." Five days later, when John Rankin (D-Miss.), the leading nativist in the lower house, called for "deporting every Jap who claims, or has claimed, Japanese citizenship, or sympathizes with Japan in this war," he was answered by another Californian, Leland M. Ford, a Santa Monica Republican:

These people are American-born. They cannot be deported . . . whether we like it or whether we do not. This is their country. . . . [When] they join the armed forces . . . they must take this oath of allegiance . . . and I see no particular reason at this particular time why they should not. I believe that every one of these people should make a clear, clean acknowledgement.

Despite the lack of Congressional concern, by the end of December momentum was gathering for more drastic action against the Japanese and against enemy aliens generally. On December 30 the Justice Department made the first of many concessions to the military, concessions that had little to do either with due process or the realities of the situation. On that date Attorney General Biddle informed the Provost Marshal General's office that he had authorized the issuance of

search warrants for any house in which an enemy alien lived, merely on the representation that there was reasonable cause to believe that there was contraband on the premises. Contraband had already been defined to include anything that might be used as a weapon, any explosive (many Issei farmers used dynamite to clear stumps), radio transmitters, any radio that had a short-wave band, and all but the simplest cameras. For the next few months thousands of houses where Japanese lived were subjected to random search. Although much "contraband" was found (most of it in two Issei-owned sporting goods stores), the FBI itself later stipulated that none of it was sinister in nature and reported that there was no evidence at all that any of it was intended for subversive use. But the mere fact of these searches, widely reported in the press, added to the suspicion with which the Japanese were viewed. These searches, like so much of the anti-Japanese movement, were part of a self-fulfilling prophecy: one is suspicious of the Japanese, so one searches their houses; the mere fact of the search, when noticed ("the FBI went through those Jap houses on the other side of town"), creates more suspicion.

For individual Japanese families, these searches intensified the insecurity and terror they already felt. One fifteen-year-old girl in San Jose, California reported what must have been an all-too-routine occurrence:

One day I came home from school to find the two F.B.I. men at our front door. They asked permission to search the house. One man looked through the front rooms, while the other searched the back rooms. Trembling with fright, I followed and watched each of the men look around. The investigators examined the mattresses, and the dresser and looked under the beds. The gas range, piano and sofa were thoroughly inspected. Since I was the only one at home, the F.B.I. questioned me, but did not procure sufficient evidence of Fifth Columnists in our family. This made me very happy, even if they did mess up the house.

Concurrent with its more stringent search order, the Department of Justice and the Provost

Marshal General's office decided to send representatives to De Witt's headquarters in San Francisco; the two men sent—James Rowe, Jr., Assistant Attorney General and a former Presidential assistant, and Major (later Colonel) Karl R. Bendetsen, chief of the Aliens Division, Provost Marshal General's office—were key and mutually antagonistic figures in the bureaucratic struggle over the fate of the West Coast Japanese. Rowe, during his short visit in California, exercised a moderating influence on the cautious General De Witt, who often seemed to be the creature of the last strong personality with whom he had contact. Bendetsen represented a chief (Gullion) who wanted not only exclusion of the Japanese from the West Coast but also the transfer of supervisory authority over all enemy aliens in the United States from the civilian control of the Department of Justice to the military control of his office. Bendetsen soon became the voice of General De Witt in matters concerning aliens, and was well rewarded for his efforts. A graduate of Stanford Law School, he had gone on to active duty as a captain in 1940, and in the process of evacuating the Japanese he would gain his colonel's eagles before he turned thirty-five. After Bendetsen's arrival, Gullion arranged with De Witt that the West Coast commander go out of normal channels and deal directly with the Provost Marshal on matters concerning aliens. The result of this seemingly routine bureaucratic shuffle was highly significant; as Stetson Conn has pointed out, the consequence of this arrangement was that "the responsible Army command headquarters in Washington [that is, Chief of Staff George C. Marshall and his immediate staff] had little to do during January and February 1942 with the plans and decisions for Japanese evacuation."

Telephone conversations and correspondence between De Witt's headquarters and the Provost Marshal General's office in late December and early January reveal the tremendous pressures that the soldiers were putting on the civilians. According to General Gullion, the Justice Department's representatives, James Rowe, Jr., and Edward J. Ennis, were apologetic about the slowness of the Justice Department, an apparent criticism of their chief, the Attorney General. At about the same time Gullion was complaining that "the Attorney General is not functioning" and threatened to have Secretary Stimson complain to the President. De Witt was, as usual, vacillating. Within the same week he told the Provost Marshal General's office that "it would be better if . . . this thing worked through the civil channels," but a few days later insisted that "I don't want to go after this thing piecemeal. I want to do it on a mass basis, all at the same time."

The arrival of Bendetsen at De Witt's San Francisco headquarters seemed to strengthen the West Coast commander's resolve. Before Bendetsen left Washington he had drafted an Executive Order transferring authority over aliens to the War Department, but the Provost Marshal General's office felt that since the Justice Department's representatives were so apologetic, it "wasn't quite fair" to take over without giving them a chance to come up to the Army's standards. Shortly after his arrival in San Francisco, Bendetsen drafted a memo that quickly became the guideline for De Witt's policy. It called for an immediate and complete registration of all alien enemies, who were to be photographed and fingerprinted. These records were to be kept in duplicate, one set to be kept in the community in which the alien resided, the other in a central office. The purpose was to set up what Bendetsen called a "Pass and Permit System." Doubtful that the Attorney General would agree to this, Bendetsen's memo concluded with what had become the refrain of the Provost Marshal General's men: if Justice won't do it, the War Department must.

The next day, January 4, in a conference at his Presidio headquarters attended by Rowe, Bendetsen, and representatives of other federal departments and officials in local government, De Witt made some of his position clear, stressing, as he always did to civilians, what he called the military necessity.

We are at war and this area—eight states—has been designated as a theater of operations. I have approximately 240,000 men at my disposal.... [There are] approximately 288,000 enemy aliens ... which we have to watch. ... I have little confidence that the enemy aliens are law-abiding or loyal in any sense of the word. Some of them yes; many, no. Particularly the Japanese. I have no confidence in their loyalty whatsoever. I am speaking now of the native born Japanese—117,000—and 42,000 in California alone.

One result of this conference was that the Department of Justice agreed to go further than it had previously: enemy aliens were to be re-registered under its auspices, the FBI would conduct large-scale "spot" raids, something De Witt was particularly eager for, and, most significantly, a large number of restricted, or Category A, zones would be established around crucial military and defense installations on the Pacific Coast. Entry to these zones would be on a pass basis. Assistant Secretary of War John J. McCloy later described this program as "the best way to solve" the West Coast alien problem.

... establish limited restricted areas around the airplane plants, the forts and other important military installations ... we might call these military reservations in substance and exclude everyone—whites, yellows, blacks, greens—from that area and then license back into the area those whom we felt there was no danger to be expected from ... then we can cover the legal situation ... in spite of the constitution. ... You may, by that process, eliminate all the Japs [alien and citizen] but you might conceivably permit some to come back whom you are quite certain are free from any suspicion.

In addition to the Category A zones, there were to be Category B zones, consisting of the rest of the coastal area, in which enemy aliens and citizen Japanese would be allowed to live and work under rigidly prescribed conditions. Although De Witt and the other Army people were constantly complaining about the slowness of the Justice Department, they quickly found that setting up these zones was easier said than done. De Witt did not forward his first recommendations for Category A areas to the War Department

until January 21, more than two weeks after the San Francisco conference.

On January 16 Representative Leland Ford, the Santa Monica Republican who had opposed stern treatment for the Japanese on the floor of the House in mid-December, had changed his mind. Ford had received a number of telegrams and letters from California suggesting removal of Japanese from vital coastal areas—the earliest seems to have been a January 6 telegram from Mexican American movie star Leo Carillo—and by mid-January had come around to their point of view. He urged Secretary of War Henry L. Stimson to have "all Japanese, whether citizens or not, . . . placed in inland concentration camps." Arguing that native-born Japanese either were or were not loyal to the United States, Ford developed a simple test for loyalty: any Japanese willing to go to a concentration camp was a patriot; therefore it followed that unwillingness to go was a proof of disloyalty to the United States. Stimson and his staff mulled over this letter for ten days, and then replied (in a letter drafted by Bendetsen, now back from the Pacific Coast) giving the congressman a certain amount of encouragement. "The internment of over a hundred thousand people," Stimson wrote, "involves many complex considerations." The basic responsibility, Stimson pointed out, putting the finger on his Cabinet colleague Francis Biddle, has been delegated to the Attorney General. Nevertheless, the Secretary continued, "the Army is prepared to provide internment facilities in the interior to the extent necessary." Assuring Ford that the Army was aware of the dangers on the Pacific Coast, Stimson informed him that the military were submitting suggestions to the Justice Department, and advised him to present his views to the Attorney General.

The same day that Ford wrote Stimson, January 16, another federal department became involved in the fate of the West Coast Japanese. Agriculture Secretary Claude Wickard, chiefly concerned with increasing farm production—"Food Can Win the War" was his line—called a meeting in his office at which the War, Labor, Navy, Justice, and Treasury Departments were represented. He had become alarmed over investigative reports from his agents on the West Coast, who were concerned both about the fate of the Japanese and the threat to food production. Wickard had been informed that although violence against the Japanese farmers was an isolated phenomenon, greatly exaggerated by the press, nevertheless it was quite clear that the Japanese rural population was "terrified."

> They do not leave their homes at night, and will not, even in the daytime, enter certain areas populated by Filipinos. The police authorities are probably not sympathetic to the Japanese and are giving them only the minimum protection. Investigation of actual attacks on Japanese have been merely perfunctory and no prosecutions have been initiated.

The federal officials then concluded that the whole "propaganda campaign" against the Japanese was essentially a conspiracy designed to place Japanese-owned and leased farm lands into white hands; the real aim was to "eliminate Japanese competition." Wickard's West Coast representatives urged him to take positive steps both to maintain agricultural production and to preserve and protect the property and persons of the Japanese farmers.

Wickard's action was not exactly along the lines recommended by the men in the field. He did urge immediate federal action "so that the supply of vegetables for the military forces and the civilian population will not be needlessly curtailed." But Wickard also felt that the fears and suspicions of the general public—particularly the West Coast public—should be taken into account. He seemed to envision a sort of large agricultural reservation in the central valleys of California on which the Japanese could "carry on their normal farming operations" after being removed from "all strategic areas." In this way, Wickard felt, the country could protect itself from "possible subversive Japanese activities," provide "limited protection to all Japanese whose conduct is above suspicion," and at the same time "avoid incidents that might provide an excuse for cruel treatment for our people in Japanese occu-

pied territory." As for the agricultural lands in the coastal area which the Japanese had tilled, Wickard suggested that Mexicans might be brought in to replace them.

Also, by mid-January, the urban Japanese, if not terrorized as were their rural cousins, were feeling more and more hopeless and demoralized. An occasional militant like James Y. Sakamoto, a Japanese American Citizen League (JACL) official in Seattle, could indignantly protest against Representative Ford's evacuation proposal which went out on the Associated Press wire on January 21.

"This is our country," Sakamoto pointed out, "we were born and raised here . . . have made our homes here . . . [and] we are ready to give our lives, if necessary, to defend the United States." Ford's drastic measures, he insisted, were not in the best interests of the nation. But even a Nisei leader like Sakamoto felt compelled to admit that there was some kind of subversive danger from the older generation of Japanese. The Seattle Nisei, he stated, were "actively cooperating" with the authorities "to uncover all subversive activity in our midst" and, if necessary, he concluded, the Nisei were "ready to stand as protective custodians over our parent generation to guard against danger to the United States arising from their midst." One of the standard complaints quite properly raised by Americans in denouncing totalitarian regimes is that their police states turn children against their parents; it is rarely remarked that, in this instance at least, such too was the function of American democracy.

But for those really in charge, the agonizing distinctions between father and son, between alien and citizen, were essentially irrelevant. By mid-January, perhaps as a way of answering the points made by Representative Ford, Chief of Staff George C. Marshall ordered the Provost Marshal General's office to prepare a memorandum on the West Coast Japanese situation. Bendetsen, the natural drafter for such a report, called General De Witt to ask what his attitude would be if "the Department of Justice still fails to do what we think they ought to do?" De Witt, who felt that things would work out, was never-

theless apprehensive about the continuing potentialities for sabotage and other subversive activities. "We know," he told Bendetsen, "that they
are communicating at sea. . . ." De Witt actually
knew no such thing, as no evidence existed of
such communication, but he undoubtedly believed it. Then, in a classic leap in what Richard
Hofstadter has styled the paranoid style, the West
Coast commander insisted that "the fact that we
have had [not even] sporadic attempts at sabotage
clearly means that control is being exercised
somewhere." Here then was the "heads I win,
tails you lose" situation in which this one Army
officer was able to place more than 100,000 innocent people. There had been no acts of sabotage,
no real evidence of subversion, despite the voices
that De Witt kept hearing at sea. Yet, according
to this military logician, there was a conspiracy
afoot not to commit sabotage until America
dropped its guard. Ergo, evacuate them quickly
before the conspiracy is put into operation.

The next day, January 25, the long-awaited
report on the attack on Pearl Harbor made by the
official committee of inquiry headed by Supreme
Court Justice Owen J. Roberts was released to the
press just in time for the Sunday morning papers,
though it is dated two days earlier. In addition to
its indictment of the general conditions of un-
readiness in the Hawaiian command, the board
reported, falsely, as it turned out, that the attack
was greatly abetted by Japanese spies, some of
whom were described as "persons having no open
relations with the Japanese foreign service." It
went on to criticize the laxity of counterespionage
activity in the Islands, and implied that a too
close adherence to the Constitution had seriously
inhibited the work of the Federal Bureau of Investigation. The publication of the report was
naturally a sensation; it greatly stimulated already prevalent rumors that linked the disaster to
wholly imaginary fifth column activities by resident Japanese. Perhaps the most popular was the
yarn that University of California class rings had
been found on the fingers of Japanese pilots shot
down in the raid. Even more ridiculous was the
story that the attacking pilots had been aided by
arrows, pointing at Pearl Harbor, which had been

hacked into the cane fields the night before by
Japanese workers. The absurdity of this device—
a large natural harbor containing dozens of war
vessels, large and small, is highly visible from the
air—seems to have occurred to few. The Roberts
Report provided a field day for those who had
long urged more repressive measures and a more
effective secret police unfettered by constitutional
restrictions. Congressmen like Martin Dies of
Texas, then head of the House Committee on
Un-American Activities, insisted, in and out of
Congress, that if only people had listened to
them, the disaster at Pearl Harbor could have
been averted. More significantly, it gave an additional argument to those who were pressing for
preventive detention and must have given pause
to some who had been urging restraint.

On January 25 Secretary Stimson forwarded
to Attorney General Biddle recommendations
that General De Witt had made four days earlier,
calling for total exclusion of enemy aliens from
eighty-six Category A zones and close control of
enemy aliens in eight Category B zones on a pass
and permit system. As this proposal involved
only aliens, the Justice Department quickly
agreed and made the first public, official announcement of a mass evacuation on January 29,
to be effective almost a month later, on February
24. This relatively modest proposal would have
moved only about 7000 aliens in all, and fewer
than 3000 of these would have been Japanese. At
about the same time it announced the appointment of Tom C. Clark (who later became
Attorney General under Truman and then an
Associate Justice of the Supreme Court) as Coordinator of the Alien Enemy Control Program
within the Western Defense Command. Clark
flew to the West Coast the next day.

A few days before Stimson's recommendation
to Biddle, the top echelons of military command,
for the first time, began to become aware of the
kinds of proposals that were emanating from De
Witt's headquarters. General Mark W. Clark
(then a brigadier on the General Staff and later a
major commander in the European Theater) was
instructed to prepare a memorandum for the
President on the subject of "enemy aliens" in the

Western Theater of Operations. The day after Stimson's letter to Biddle requesting the announcement of Category A and B areas, General Clark recommended that no memorandum be sent unless the Attorney General's action should "not be all that is desired." Clark's memorandum was read by Chief of Staff George C. Marshall, who noted on it "hold for me until Feb. 1." The top brass was satisfied with a very modest program, involving the forced removal, without detention, of a very few aliens. Clark's memorandum made no mention of citizens at all.

But if the top brass were satisfied, De Witt, Bendetsen, and Gullion were not. And neither were the leading public officials in California. On January 27 De Witt had a conference with Governor Culbert Olson and related to Washington, probably accurately:

> There's a tremendous volume of public opinion now developing against the Japanese of all classes, that is aliens and non-aliens, to get them off the land, and in Southern California around Los Angeles— in that area too—they want and they are bringing pressure on the government to move all the Japanese out. As a matter of fact, it's not being instigated or developed by people who are not thinking but by the best people of California. Since the publication of the Roberts Report they feel that they are living in the midst of a lot of enemies. They don't trust the Japanese, none of them.

Two days later, De Witt talked with Olson's Republican Attorney General Earl Warren. (De Witt thought his name was Warner.) The California Attorney General, who was then preparing to run for governor against Olson in November, was in thorough agreement with his rival that the Japanese ought to be removed. This was not surprising. Warren was heir to a long anti-Japanese tradition in California politics and the protégé of U. S. Webb, a long-time Attorney General of California (1902–1939) and the author of the 1913 California Alien Land Act. Warren had been intimately associated with the most influential nativist group in the state, the Joint Immigration Committee, but shortly after he became Attorney General in 1939 he prudently arranged to

have his name taken off the Committee's letterhead, although he continued to meet with them and receive copies of all documents and notices. Because of his later prominence, some have tried to make too much of Warren's very minor role in pressing for an evacuation. He did add his voice, but it was not yet a very strong one and it is almost inconceivable that, had any other politician held his post, essentially the same result would not have ensued.

On the very day of Biddle's formal announcement of the A and B zones, De Witt and Bendetsen worked out a more sweeping scheme, which Bendetsen would present to an informal but influential meeting of congressmen the next day. After a rambling conversation—De Witt was rarely either concise or precise—Bendetsen, always the lawyer in uniform, summed it up neatly:

> BENDETSEN: . . . As I understand it, from your viewpoint summarizing our conversation, you are of the opinion that there will have to be an evacuation on the west coast, not only of Japanese aliens but also of Japanese citizens, that is, you would include citizens along with alien enemies, and that if you had the power of requisition over all other Federal agencies, if you were requested you would be willing on the coast to accept responsibility for the alien enemy program.
> DE WITT: Yes I would. And I think it's got to come sooner or later.
> BENDETSEN: Yes sir, I do too, and I think the subject may be discussed tomorrow at the congressional delegation meeting.
> DE WITT: Well, you've got my viewpoint. You have it exactly.

The next day, January 30, the Japanese question was discussed in two important meetings, one in the White House and one on Capitol Hill. In the Cabinet meeting fears were expressed about the potentially dangerous situation in Hawaii. General Marshall penned a short memo to General Dwight D. Eisenhower, then a member of his staff, telling him that Stimson was concerned about "dangerous Japanese in Hawaii." Justice Roberts had told the War Secretary that "this point was regarded by his board as most serious." Several Cabinet members, but particularly Navy Secretary Frank Knox, were greatly disturbed at what they considered the laxity with which the Hawaiian Japanese were treated. As early as December 19, a previous Cabinet meeting had decided that all Japanese aliens in the Hawaiian Islands should be interned, and put on some island other than Oahu, where the major military installations were located.

At the other end of Pennsylvania Avenue, the focus was on the West Coast Japanese. Bendetsen, along with Rowe and Ennis from the Justice Department, attended a meeting of the Pacific Coast House delegation. (A joint meeting between the congressmen and the six senators was already scheduled for the following Monday.) The subject was what to do about the Japanese. Although Bendetsen officially reported to his superiors that he "was present as an observer," it is clear from his telephone conversations with General De Witt, both before and after the meeting, that he went as an advocate for the policies that he and his boss, General Gullion, had been proposing. Bendetsen called De Witt right after the meeting and told him what they both considered good news.

They asked me to state what the position of the War Department was. I stated that I could not speak for the War Department. . . . They asked me for my own views and I stated that the position of the War Department was this: that we did not seek control of the program, that we preferred it be handled by the civil agencies. However, the War Department would be entirely willing, I believed, [to assume] the responsibility provided they accorded the War Department, and the Secretary of War, and the military commander under him, full authority to require the services of any federal agency, and required that that federal agency was required to respond.

De Witt liked this. "That's good," he responded. "I'm glad to see that action is being taken . . . that someone in authority begins to see the problem." What he particularly liked was the delegation to himself of full power over civilian agencies. He had had problems with civilians already, particularly civilians in the Federal Bureau of Investigation whose West Coast agents, as we have seen, refused to respond positively to De Witt's imaginary alarms and excursions. As De Witt envisioned it, "Mr. [J. Edgar] Hoover himself as head of the F.B.I. would have to function under the War Department exactly as he is functioning under the Department of Justice."

Bendetsen, naturally, encouraged De Witt to grab for power. "Opinion is beginning to become irresistible, and I think that anything you recommend will be strongly backed up . . . by the public." De Witt and Bendetsen agreed that protestations of loyalty from the Nisei were utterly worthless. As De Witt put it:

"There are going to be a lot of Japs who are going to say, 'Oh, yes, we want to go, we're good Americans and we want to do everything you say,' but those are the fellows I suspect the most."

"Definitely," Bendetsen agreed. "The ones who are giving you only lip service are the ones always to be suspected."

The Congressional recommendations were immediately sent to Secretary Stimson by the senior California representative, Clarence Lea, a Santa Rosa Democrat first elected in 1916. Although they did not specifically call for removal of American citizens of Japanese ancestry, the delegation did ask that mass evacuation proceed for "all enemy aliens and their families," which would have included most of the Nisei. Later the same day, Provost Marshal General Gullion called De Witt to get some details straight. He was chiefly interested in how far De Witt proposed to move the evacuees. De Witt did not know, but he did point out to Gullion that within California "one group wanted to move them entirely out of the state," whereas another wanted "them to be left in California." After receiving these assurances from De Witt, Gullion began to wonder where the Army was going to put 100,-000 people, and, perhaps for the first time, fleetingly realized that "a resettlement proposition is quite a proposition." The following day, Bendetsen, acting for his chief, had the Adjutant Gen-

eral dispatch telegrams to Corps Area commanders throughout the nation asking them about possible locations for large numbers of evacuees.
Bendetsen suggested some possible sites: "agricultural experimental farms, prison farms, migratory labor camps, pauper farms, state parks,
abandoned CCC camps, fairgrounds."

By the end of the month De Witt was able to
make his position a little clearer. When Bendetsen asked whether or not he contemplated moving citizens, De Witt was emphatic.

> I include all Germans, all Italians who are alien
> enemies and all Japanese who are native-born or
> foreign born . . . evacuate enemy aliens in large
> groups at the earliest possible date . . . sentiment is
> being given too much importance. . . . I think we
> might as well eliminate talk of resettlement and
> handle these people as they should be handled
> . . . put them to work in internment camps. . . . I
> place the following priority. . . . First the Japanese,
> all prices [?sic] . . . as the most dangerous . . . the
> next group, the Germans . . . the third group, the
> Italians. . . . We've waited too long as it is. Get them
> all out.

On Sunday, February 1, exactly eight weeks
after Pearl Harbor, Assistant Secretary of War
John J. McCloy, Gullion, and Bendetsen went to
a meeting in Attorney General Francis Biddle's
office. Biddle, who was seconded by James Rowe,
Jr., Edward J. Ennis, and J. Edgar Hoover, had
been concerned about the increasing pressure for
mass evacuation, both from the military and from
Congress, and about a crescendo of press criticism directed at his "pussyfooti·g," some of
which was undoubtedly inspired by the military.
Biddle presented the Army men with a draft of
what he hoped would be a joint press release. Its
crucial sentences, which the military refused to
agree to, were

> The Department of War and the Department of
> Justice are in agreement that the present military
> situation does not *at this time* [my emphasis] re-
> quire the removal of American citizens of the Japa-
> nese race. The Secretary of War, General De Witt,
> the Attorney General, and the Director of the Fed-

eral Bureau of Investigation believe that appropriate steps have been and are being taken.

Biddle informed McCloy and the others that
he was opposed to mass evacuation and that the
Justice Department would have nothing to do
with it. Rowe, remembering his early January
visit to De Witt's headquarters, said that the
West Coast commander had been opposed to
mass evacuation then and wondered what had
changed his mind. According to Gullion, Rowe,
after some uncomplimentary remarks about Bendetsen, complained about the hysterical tone of
the protests from the West Coast, argued that the
western congressmen were "just nuts" on the subject, and maintained that there was "no evidence
whatsoever of any reason for disturbing citizens."
Then Biddle insisted that the Justice Department
would have nothing at all to do with any interference with civilians. Gullion, admittedly "a little
sore," said: "Well, listen, Mr. Biddle, do you
mean to tell me if the Army, the men on the
ground, determine it is a military necessity to
move citizens, Jap citizens, that you won't help
us?"

After Biddle restated his position, McCloy,
again according to Gullion, said to the Attorney
General: "You are putting a Wall Street lawyer
in a helluva box, but if it is a question of the safety
of the country [and] the Constitution. . . . Why
the Constitution is just a scrap of paper to me."

As the meeting broke up, it was agreed that the
Army people would check with the "man on the
ground," General De Witt. As soon as they got
back to their office, Gullion and Bendetsen made
a joint phone call to the West Coast commander.
They read him the proposed press release and,
when the crucial sentences were reached, De Witt
responded immediately: "I wouldn't agree to
that." When asked specifically whom he did want
to evacuate, the answer was "those people who
are aliens and who are Japs of American citizenship." Then Gullion cautioned De Witt:

> Now I might suggest, General, Mr. McCloy was in
> the conference and he will probably be in any subse-
> quent conference . . . he has not had all the benefit

of conversations we have had with you—if you could give us something, not only in conversation but a written thing . . . stating your position.

De Witt agreed to do this. Then Bendetsen summarized the Justice Department's point of view:

> . . . they say . . . if we recommend and it is determined that there should be an evacuation of citizens, they said hands off, that is the Army's job . . . they agree with us that it is possible from . . . a legal standpoint. . . . They agree with us that [the licensing theory] could be . . . the legal basis for exclusion. . . . However we insist that we could also say that while all whites could remain, Japs can't, if we think there is military necessity for that. They apparently want us to join with them so that if anything happens they would be able to say "this was the military recommendation."

De Witt stated, "they are trying to cover themselves and lull the populace into a false sense of security."

When questioned about the details of the evacuation, De Witt blustered: "I haven't gone into the details of it, but Hell, it would be no job as far as the evacuation was concerned to move 100,000 people."

Actually, of course, it was a tremendous job, and even in such a relatively simple matter as the designation of Category A (prohibited to aliens) and Category B (restricted to aliens) zones, De Witt's staff had botched the job. Bendetsen had to call Western Defense Command headquarters and point out that although they had permitted limited use by enemy aliens of the San Francisco–Oakland Bay Bridge (the bridge itself was Category B), all the approaches to the bridge were classified Category A, and thus prohibited.

Two days after the conference in Biddle's office both Assistant Secretary of War McCloy and General George C. Marshall made separate calls to De Witt. McCloy, and presumably Stimson and Marshall, had become concerned that De Witt and the Provost Marshal's office were committing the Army to a policy that the policy makers had not yet agreed to. McCloy was blunt:

. . . the Army, that means you in the area, should not take the position, even in your conversations with political figures out there [favoring] a wholesale withdrawal of Japanese citizens and aliens from the Coast. . . . We have about reached the point where we feel that perhaps the best solution of it is to limit the withdrawal to certain prohibited areas.

Then, incredibly to anyone who has read the transcripts of his conversations with Gullion and Bendetsen (which were apparently not then available to McCloy), General De Witt denied that he had done any such thing: "Mr. Secretary . . . I haven't taken any position."

This, of course, was a palpable lie. What the cautious commander knew, however, was that he had never put any recommendations on paper, and that General Gullion was not likely to produce the telephone transcripts because they showed him and his subordinates pressing for a policy that had not yet been officially sanctioned.

General Marshall's call was terse and businesslike; the extract of it which he furnished to the Secretary of War is worth quoting in full, both because of what it does and what it does not say.

> MARSHALL: Is there anything you want to say now about anything else? Of course we're on an open phone.
> DE WITT: We're on an open phone, but George I can talk a little about this alien situation out here.
> MARSHALL: Yes.
> DE WITT: I had a conference yesterday [February 2] with the Governor [Olson] and several representatives of the Department of Justice [Tom C. Clark] and the Department of Agriculture with a view to removal of the Japanese from where they are now living to other portions of the state.
> MARSHALL: Yes.
> DE WITT: And the Governor thinks it can be satisfactorily handled without having a resettlement somewhere in the central part of the United States and removing them entirely from the state of California. As you know the people out here are very much disturbed over these aliens, and want to get them out of the several communities.
> MARSHALL: Yes.
> DE WITT: And I've agreed that if they can get

them out of the areas limited as the combat zone, that it would be satisfactory. That would take them about 100 to 150 miles from the coast, and they're going to do that I think. They're working on it.

MARSHALL: Thank you.

DE WITT: The Department [of Justice] has a representative out here and the Department of Agriculture, and they think the plan is an excellent one. I'm only concerned with getting them away from around these aircraft factories and other places.

MARSHALL: Yes. Anything else?

DE WITT: No, that's all.

MARSHALL: Well, good luck.

That same day, February 3, there was an hour-and-a-half meeting between Stimson, McCloy, Gullion, and Bendetsen. (It is not clear whether the phone conversations between McCloy and De Witt and Marshall and De Witt preceded, followed or straddled this meeting.) The next day Provost Marshal Gullion reported, somewhat dejectedly: ". . . the two Secretaries [Stimson and McCloy] are against any mass movement. They are pretty much against it. And they are also pretty much against interfering with citizens unless it can be done legally."

What had apparently happened was that De Witt, understanding from the McCloy and Marshall phone calls that the War Department was, as he put it, "afraid that I was going to get into a political mess," and under great pressure from Governor Olson and Tom C. Clark to allow a limited, voluntary, compromise evacuation within California, trimmed his position accordingly. Clark, a strong and vigorous personality, seemed to have great influence over the general, who described him as "a fine fellow . . . the most cooperative and forceful man I have ever had to deal with. He attacks a problem better than any civilian I have ever had contact with."

Clark was clearly playing an independent role, and his position was somewhere between that of the Provost Marshal's office and that held by his own chief, the Attorney General. The plan that he sponsored or supported in the February 2 conference in Sacramento with Governor Olson and De Witt called for a conference between Governor Olson and leading Japanese Americans which would result in a voluntary resettlement in the central valleys of California where the Japanese could augment agricultural production. As De Witt explained the Clark-Olson plan to an unhappy Gullion:

> Well, I tell you, they are solving the problem here very satisfactorily. . . . I have agreed to accept any plan they propose to put those people, Japanese Americans and Japanese who are in Category A area in the Category B area on farms. . . . We haven't got anything to do with it except they are consulting me to see what areas I will let them go into. . . . Mr. Clark is very much in favor of it . . . the people are going to handle it locally through the Governor and they are going to move those people to arable and tillable land. They are going to keep them in the state. They don't want to bring in a lot of negroes and mexicans and let them take their place. . . . They just want to put them on the land out of the cities where they can raise vegetables like they are doing now.

The Provost Marshal General's men were disgusted with this turn of events. Not only were their plans being thwarted by the civilians who ran the Army—Stimson and McCloy, who were thinking in terms of creating "Jap-less" islands of security around a few key installations like the Consolidated-Vultee aircraft plant in San Diego, the Lockheed and North American plants in Los Angeles, and the Boeing plant in Seattle—but even their former ally, General De Witt, the all-important man on the ground who alone could make authoritative statements about "military necessity," had now deserted their cause. As Colonel Archer Lerch, Gullion's deputy, put it:

> I think I detect a decided weakening on the part of Gen. De Witt, which I think is most unfortunate. . . . The idea suggested to Gen. De Witt in his conference with Gov. Olson, that a satisfactory solution must be reached through a conference between the Governor and leading Jap-Americans, savors too much of the spirit of Rotary and overlooks the necessary cold-bloodedness of war.

If pressure for evacuation within the Army seemed to be weakening, stronger and stronger outside forces were being brought into play. On February 2 and 3, in separate meetings, representatives and senators from all three Pacific Coast states agreed to coordinate their efforts. Serving as coordinator of these anti-Japanese efforts was Senator Hiram W. Johnson of California, who, in the mid-1920s, had masterminded a similar joint Congressional effort which brought about elimination of a Japanese quota in the Immigration Act of 1924. Johnson was actually more concerned about the defense of the West Coast—he feared a Japanese invasion—and complained bitterly to one of his political intimates that "the keenness of interest in the Japanese question far overshadowed the general proposition of our preparedness."

Back in California, Governor Culbert Olson went on the air on February 4; his speech could only have further inflamed public opinion. Disseminating false information that probably came from his conference two days previously with General De Witt and Tom Clark, he warned the already frightened people of California that

it is known that there are Japanese residents of California who have sought to aid the Japanese enemy by way of communicating information, or have shown indications of preparation for fifth column activities.

Loyal Japanese, he insisted, could best prove their loyalty by cooperating with whatever the authorities asked them to do. Then, in a vain attempt to reassure the public, he went on to say that everything would be all right. He told of his conference with De Witt and announced, without of course giving any specifics, that

general plans [have been] agreed upon for the movement and placement of the entire adult Japanese population in California at productive and useful employment within the borders of our state, and under such surveillance and protection . . . as shall be deemed necessary.

The next day the mayor of Los Angeles, Fletcher Bowron, outdid the governor in attempting to arouse passions. After pointing out that the largest concentration of Japanese was in Los Angeles, he turned on the venom:

Right here in our own city are those who may spring to action at an appointed time in accordance with a prearranged plan wherein each of our little Japanese friends will know his part in the event of any possible attempted invasion or air raid.

He then argued that not only Japanese aliens but citizens of Japanese descent, some of whom were "unquestionably . . . loyal," represented a threat to Los Angeles. Disloyal Nisei, he argued, would loudly proclaim their patriotism. "Of course they would try to fool us. They did in Honolulu and in Manila, and we may expect it in California." Bowron's answer, of course, was mass internment for all Japanese, citizens and aliens alike. From favorable references to Tom Clark, he seems to have been willing to go along with the De Witt–Olson–Clark plan of labor camps within California. Bowron also tried to take care of constitutional and ethical scruples:

If we can send our own young men to war, it is nothing less than sickly sentimentality to say that we will do injustice to American-born Japanese to merely put them in a place of safety so that they can do no harm. . . . We [in Los Angeles] are the ones who will be the human sacrifices if the perfidy that characterized the attack on Pearl Harbor is ever duplicated on the American continent.

In a follow-up statement the next day, Bowron put forth the interesting proposition that one of the major reasons that Japanese could not be trusted was that Californians had discriminated against them:

The Japanese, because they are unassimilable, because the aliens have been denied the right to own real property in California, because of [immigration discrimination against them], because of the marked differences in appearance between Japanese and Caucasians, because of the generations of training and philosophy that makes them Japanese and nothing else—all of these contributing factors set the Japanese apart as a race, regardless of how many generations have been born in America. Undoubtedly many of them intend to be loyal, but only each individual can know his own intentions, and when the final test comes, who can say but that "blood will tell"? We cannot run the risk of another Pearl Harbor episode in Southern California.

And, that same week, in Sacramento, Attorney General Earl Warren presided over a meeting of some one hundred and fifty law enforcement officers, mostly sheriffs and district attorneys. According to a federal official who attended the meeting:

> In his opening remarks, Mr. Warren cautioned against hysteria but then proceeded to outline his remarks in such a fashion as to encourage hysterical thinking. . . . Mr. [Isidore] Dockweiler, Los Angeles District Attorney . . . , asserted that the United States Supreme Court had been packed with leftist and other extreme advocates of civil liberty and that it was time for the people of California to disregard the law, if necessary, to secure their protection. Mr. Dockweiler finally worked himself into such a state of hysteria that he was called to order by Mr. Warren. . . . The meeting loudly applauded the statement that the people of California had no trust in the ability and willingness of the Federal Government to proceed against enemy aliens. One high official was heard to state that he favored shooting on sight all Japanese residents of the state.

Despite relative calm in the press until the end of January, a government intelligence agency (the civilian Office of Government Reports) informed Washington that "word of mouth discussions [continue] with a surprisingly large number of people expressing themselves as in favor of sending all Japanese to concentration camps." By the end of January, the press "flared up again" with demands growing "that positive action be taken by the Federal Government. This awakening of the press has increased the verbal discussions that never ceased." By early February the Los Angeles *Times,* never friendly to the Japanese Americans, as we have seen, could no longer find human terms to describe them. All Japanese Americans, the *Times* insisted editorially, were at

least potentially enemies: "A viper is nonetheless a viper wherever the egg is hatched—so a Japanese-American, born of Japanese parents—grows up to be a Japanese, not an American."

Henry McLemore, the nationally syndicated columnist, put into words the extreme reaction against Attorney General Francis Biddle, whom Californians (probably with some prompting from the military and militant congressmen) had made the chief target of their ire. Biddle, McLemore reported, couldn't even win election as "third assistant dog catcher" in California. "Californians have the feeling," he explained, "that he is the one in charge of the Japanese menace, and that he is handling it with all the severity of Lord Fauntleroy."

With this kind of encouragement in the background, Provost Marshal Gullion and his associates continued to press for mass action against the West Coast Japanese despite the fact that the officers of General Headquarters, directly under Marshall, were now trying to moderate anti-Japanese sentiment among members of Congress. On February 4, an impressive array of military personnel attended the meeting of West Coast congressmen: Admiral Harold R. Stark, Chief of Naval Operations; Brigadier General Mark W. Clark of General Headquarters (who had become Marshall's "expert" on the West Coast Japanese, even though just hours before he was to appear at the meeting he had to ask Bendetsen, "Now what is this Nisei?"); Colonel Hoyt S. Vandenberg of the Army Air Corps; and Colonel Wilton B. Persons, Chief of the (Congressional) Liaison Branch. According to Colonel Persons' report, Senator Rufus Holman of Oregon was the chief spokesman, and in pressing for an evacuation, he stressed the point that the people on the West Coast were "alarmed and terrified as to their person, their employment, and their homes." Clark then gave the congressmen the first truly military appraisal of the situation that they had received. Summarizing General Headquarters' findings, he told them that they were "unduly alarmed" and speculated that, at worst, there might be a sporadic air raid or a commando attack or two, and that while an attack on Alaska "was not a fantastic idea," there was no likelihood of a real onslaught on the West Coast states.

The day after General Clark's moderate presentation, the Provost Marshal began to try to bring Assistant Secretary of War McCloy around to his point of view. On February 5 he wrote McCloy that although De Witt had changed his mind, he (Gullion) was still of the view that mass evacuation was necessary. The De Witt–Olson–Tom Clark idea of voluntary cooperation with Japanese American leaders, the Provost Marshal General denounced as "dangerous to rely upon. . . ." In a more detailed memo the following day (February 6) he warned McCloy of the possible grave consequences of inaction:

> If our production for war is seriously delayed by sabotage in the West Coastal states, we very possibly shall lose the war. . . . From reliable reports from military and other sources, the danger of Japanese inspired sabotage is great. . . . No half-way measures based upon considerations of economic disturbance, humanitarianism, or fear of retaliation will suffice. Such measures will be "too little or too late."

This shrewd appeal—"too little and too late" was a journalistic slogan that all too accurately described the general tenor of anti-Axis military efforts to that date—was followed by a concrete program that had been drawn up by Gullion and Bendetsen, and that the Provost Marshal General formally recommended. Somewhat short of total evacuation, it still would have involved moving the vast majority of West Coast Japanese. The plan consisted of four steps, as follows:

> *Step 1.* Declare restricted areas from which all alien enemies are barred. [This had already been done by Biddle, although it would not go into effect until February 24.]
> *Step 2.* Internment east of the Sierra Nevadas of *all* Japanese aliens, accompanied by such citizen members of their families as may volunteer for internment. [Since a majority of the Nisei were minors this would have included most of the citizen generation.]
> *Step 3.* The pass and permit system for "military

reservations." [This would result, according to Gullion, in excluding citizens of Japanese extraction, "without raising too many legal questions."]
> *Step 4.* Resettlement. [Neither Gullion nor anyone else, as we shall see, had worked this out in any detail. According to the Provost Marshal General, it was "merely an idea and not an essential part of the plan."]

By February 10, however, Gullion and Bendetsen, the latter now back on the West Coast to strengthen General De Witt's resolve, seemed to have convinced McCloy, somehow, that a mass evacuation was necessary, although Secretary Stimson still clung to the idea of creating islands around strategic locations, an idea that the Provost Marshal General's men were sure he had gotten from General Stilwell. Bendetsen insisted that safety "islands" would not prevent sabotage: "if they wanted to sabotage that area, they could set the outside area on fire. They could still cut water lines and power lines." According to Bendetsen he had been over that ground twice with McCloy, who seemed to agree, and who had told Bendetsen that he would call him back after he had had another talk with the Secretary.

The next day, February 11, 1942, was the real day of decision as far as the Japanese Americans were concerned. Sometime in the early afternoon, Secretary Stimson telephoned Franklin Roosevelt at the White House. Shortly after that call, McCloy phoned Bendetsen at the Presidio to tell him the good news. According to McCloy:

> . . . we talked to the President and the President, in substance, says go ahead and do anything you think necessary . . . if it involves citizens, we will take care of them too. He says there will probably be some repercussions, but it has got to be dictated by military necessity, but as he puts it, "Be as reasonable as you can."

McCloy went on to say that he thought the President would sign an executive order giving the Army the authority to evacuate. He also indicated there was at least some residual reluctance on the part of Secretary Stimson, who wanted to make a start in Los Angeles, concentrating on areas around the big bomber plants. McCloy indicated that he thought he could convince the Secretary that the limited plan was not practicable. In his conversation with McCloy, Bendetsen had talked about evacuating some 61,-000 people, but in talking to Gullion about an hour later, he spoke of evacuating approximately 101,000 people.

By February 11 the Provost Marshal's men had the situation all their own way. Assistant Secretary McCloy, who had been "pretty much against" their view just a week before, had been converted, and through him, Secretary Stimson and the President, although the latter probably did not take too much persuading. Bendetsen was again in San Francisco, and helping General De Witt draft what the Western Defense commander called "the plan that Mr. McCloy wanted me to submit." Although, in retrospect, it seems clear that the struggle for mass evacuation was over by then, not all the participants knew it yet.

Among those in the dark were the staff at General Headquarters, particularly General Mark Clark who had been assigned to make the official military report on the advisability of mass evacuation. Early on February 12 he called De Witt, and when told that an evacuation, to include citizens of Japanese descent, was in the works, he expressed disbelief. His own official memorandum, completed at about that time, had reached opposite conclusions, and deserves quoting at length, because it alone represents official military thinking on the subject. General Clark's report concluded:

I cannot agree with the wisdom of such a mass exodus for the following reasons:

(a) We will never have a perfect defense against sabotage except at the expense of other equally important efforts. The situation with regards to protecting establishments from sabotage is analogous to protecting them from air attack by antiaircraft and barrage balloons. We will never have enough of these means to fully protect these establishments. Why, then, should we make great sacrifices in other efforts in order to make them secure from sabotage?

(b) We must weigh the advantages and disadvan-

tages of such a wholesale solution to this problem. We must not permit our entire offensive effort to be sabotaged in an effort to protect all establishments from ground sabotage.

I recommend the following approach to this problem:

(a) Ascertain and designate the critical installations to be protected in each area and list them according to their importance.

(b) Make up our minds as to what means are available for such protection and apply that protection as far as it will go to the most critical objectives, leaving the ones of lesser importance for future consideration, or lesser protection.

(c) Select the most critical ones to be protected and delimit the essential areas around them for their protection.

(d) Eject all enemy aliens from those areas and permit entrance of others by pass only.

(e) Only such installations as can be physically protected in that manner should be included in this category. For example, it is practicable to do this in the case of the Boeing Plant, Bremerton Navy Yard and many other similar vital installations. In other words we are biting off a little at a time in the solution of the problem.

(f) Civilian police should be used to the maximum in effecting this protection.

(g) Federal Bureau of Investigation should be greatly augmented in counter-subversive activity.

(h) Raids should be used freely and frequently.

(i) Ring leaders and suspects should be interned liberally.

(j) This alien group should be made to understand through publicity that the first overt act on their part will bring a wave of counter-measures which will make the historical efforts of the vigilantes look puny in comparison.

It is estimated that to evacuate large numbers of this group will require one soldier to 4 or 5 aliens. This would require between 10,000 and 15,000 soldiers to guard the group during their internment, to say nothing of the continuing burden of protecting the installations. I feel that this problem must be attacked in a sensible manner. We must admit that we are taking some chances just as we take other chances in war. We must determine what are our really critical installations, give them thorough protection and leave the others to incidental means in the hope that we will not lose too many of them—

and above all keep our eye on the ball—that is, the creating and training of an offensive army.

Here was truly "stern military necessity." The General Staff officer, who probably reflected Marshall's real view, would have moved very few Japanese, not because he was a defender of civil liberty, or even understood what the probabilities for sabotage really were, but because, it did not seem to him, on balance, that the "protection" which total evacuation would provide was worth its cost in military manpower and energy. But military views, as we have seen, were not the determinants of policy; political views were. The real architects of policy were the lawyers in uniform, Gullion and Bendetsen. Their most highly placed supporters, McCloy and Stimson, were two Republican, Wall Street lawyers.

Very late in the game, and often after the fact, a very few New Dealers tried to influence the President to take a more consistently democratic approach to the Japanese. On February 3 Archibald MacLeish, then Director of the Office of Facts and Figures, a predecessor of the Office of War Information, wrote one of Roosevelt's confidential secretaries suggesting that the President might want to try to hold down passions on the West Coast. His office, he said, was "trying to keep down the pressure out there." He enclosed, for the President, a statement of Woodrow Wilson's that he thought might be useful. During the other world war, Wilson had said, in a statement highly appropriate to the West Coast situation:

> . . . I can never accept any man as a champion of liberty either for ourselves or for the world who does not reverence and obey the laws of our beloved land, whose laws we ourselves have made. He has adopted the standards of the enemies of his country, whom he affects to despise.

Getting no response from the White House, MacLeish tried the Army six days later. "Dear Jack," the libertarian poet wrote McCloy, "In my opinion great care should be taken not to reach a grave decision in the present situation on the representations of officials and pressure groups alone. The decision may have far-reaching effects."

MacLeish's efforts were, of course, fruitless. Much more influential was the authoritarian voice of America's chief pundit, Walter Lippmann. Writing from San Francisco in a column published on February 12, the usually detached observer who has so often been on the unpopular side of issues, was, in this instance, merely an extension of the mass West Coast mind. In an essay entitled "The Fifth Column on the Coast," Lippmann wrote:

> . . . the Pacific Coast is in imminent danger of a combined attack from within and without. . . . It is a fact that the Japanese navy has been reconnoitering the coast more or less continuously. . . . There is an assumption [in Washington] that a citizen may not be interfered with unless he has committed an overt act. . . . The Pacific Coast is officially a combat zone: Some part of it may at any moment be a battlefield. And nobody ought to be on a battlefield who has no good reason for being there. There is plenty of room elsewhere for him to exercise his rights.

The pundit's thinkpiece drew a lot of notice. Westbrook Pegler, delighted at finding a respectable man urging what he had long urged, chortled:

> Do you get what he says? This is a high-grade fellow with a heavy sense of responsibility. . . . The Japanese in California should be under armed guard to the last man and woman right now [even Pegler didn't like to talk about children]—and to hell with habeas corpus until the danger is over. . . . If it isn't true, we can take it out on Lippmann, but on his reputation I will bet it is all true.

In the War Department, Marshall sent a copy of Lippmann's column to Stimson, and Stimson sent it to McCloy, and it was undoubtedly read in the White House. It was read in the Justice Department too. Long-suffering Attorney General Francis Biddle, former law clerk to Justice Holmes, civil libertarian and New Dealer, was finally stirred to respond by Lippmann's column.

In his memoirs, published in 1962, deeply regretting the whole affair, Biddle wrote:

> . . . if, instead of dealing almost exclusively with McCloy and Bendetsen, I had urged [Stimson] to resist the pressure of his subordinates, the result might have been different. But I was new to the Cabinet, and disinclined to insist on my view to an elder statesman whose wisdom and integrity I greatly respected.

What Biddle did not reveal, however, was that he himself had given Stimson a kind of green light. In a letter written on February 12, the Attorney General voiced his distaste for the proposed evacuation, particularly of citizens, but assured Stimson that

> I have no doubt that the Army can legally, at any time, evacuate all persons in a specified territory if such action is deemed essential from a military point of view. . . . No legal problem arises when Japanese citizens are evacuated, but American citizens of Japanese origin could not, in my opinion, be singled out of an area and evacuated with the other Japanese.

Then Biddle, Philadelphia lawyer that he was, told Stimson how he thought it could be done.

> However, the result might be accomplished by evacuating all persons in the area and then licensing back those whom the military authorities thought were not objectionable from a military point of view.

Five days later, on February 17, Biddle addressed a memorandum to the President, a memorandum that was, in effect, a last-gasp effort to stop the mass evacuation that was being planned. Biddle apparently was unaware that Roosevelt had given Stimson and McCloy the go-ahead signal almost a week before. The Attorney General opened with a statement about the various West Coast pressure groups and congressmen who were urging the evacuation. He then singled out Lippmann and Pegler, and argued that their concern about imminent invasion and sabotage was not borne out by the facts. Biddle then maintained, rather curiously, that "there [was] no dispute between the War, Navy and Justice Departments," and warned that the evacuation of 93,000 Japanese in California would disrupt agriculture, require thousands of troops, tie up transportation, and raise very difficult questions of resettlement. Then, in an apparent approval of evacuation, Biddle wrote, "If complete confusion and lowering of morale is to be avoided, so large a job must be done after careful planning."

Then, in a parting blast, directed specifically at Lippmann, Biddle attacked columnists acting as "Armchair Strategists and Junior G-Men," suggested that they were essentially "shouting FIRE! in a crowded theater," and warned that if race riots occurred, Lippmann and the others would bear a heavy responsibility.

But Biddle could have directed his attack much closer to home. Not only his Cabinet colleagues but some of his subordinates were doing more than shouting. Three days before the Attorney General's letter, Tom C. Clark, of his staff, assured a Los Angeles press conference that the federal government would soon evacuate over 200,000 enemy aliens and their children, including all American-born Japanese, from areas in California vital to national defense.

On February 13, the Pacific Coast Congressional delegation forwarded to the President a recommendation for evacuation that was fully in line with what Stimson and McCloy were proposing. They recommended, unanimously:

> the immediate evacuation of all persons of Japanese lineage and all others, aliens and citizens alike, whose presence shall be deemed dangerous or inimical to the defense of the United States from all strategic areas . . . such areas [should] be enlarged as expeditiously as possible until they shall encompass the entire strategic areas of the states of California, Oregon and Washington, and the Territory of Alaska.

Finally, on Thursday, February 19, 1942, a day that should live in infamy, Franklin D. Roosevelt signed an Executive Order that gave the Army, through the Secretary of War, the authority that Gullion and Bendetsen had sought so long. Using as justification a military necessity for "the successful prosecution of the war," the President empowered the military to designate "military areas" from which "any or all persons may be excluded" and to provide for such persons "transportation, food, shelter, and other accommodations as may be necessary . . . until other arrangements are made." The words Japanese or Japanese Americans never even appear in the order; but it was they, and they alone, who felt its sting.

The myth of military necessity was used as a fig leaf for a particular variant of American racism. On the very day that the President signed the order, a conference at General Headquarters heard and approved an opposite opinion. Army Intelligence reported, officially, that it believed "mass evacuation unnecessary." In this instance, at least, the military mind was superior to the political: the soldiers who opposed the evacuation were right and the politicians who proposed it were wrong. But, why did it happen?

Two major theories have been propounded by scholars which ought to be examined. Almost as the evacuation was taking place, administrators and faculty at the University of California at Berkeley took steps to set up a scholarly study of the relocation in all its aspects. With generous foundation support and with the cooperation of some of the federal officials most responsible for the decision (for example, John J. McCloy), the "Japanese American Evacuation and Resettlement Study" was set up under the directorship of Dorothy Swaine Thomas, then a University of California Professor of Rural Sociology and a skilled demographer. Her staff included a broad spectrum of social scientists, but curiously did not include either professional historians or archivists. Professor Thomas' own volumes did not seek to determine responsibility for the evacuation, but two volumes that flowed out of the project did: Morton Grodzins, *Americans Betrayed* (Chicago, 1949) and Jacobus tenBroek, Edward N. Barnhart, and Floyd Matson, *Prejudice, War, and the Constitution* (Berkeley and Los Angeles, 1954). Grodzins felt that the major cause of the evacuation was the pressure exerted by special interest groups within California and on the Pacific Coast generally. The "western group," he wrote, "was successful in having a program molded to its own immediate advantage made national policy." Professors tenBroek, Barnhart, and Matson vigorously disputed the Grodzins thesis: for them, the responsibility was General De Witt's, and, they argued, his decision was based essentially on his "military estimate of the situation."

Five years later a professional historian, Stetson Conn, then a civilian historian for the Department of the Army and later the Army's Chief of Military History, published an authoritative account of what really happened, as far as the military was concerned. He found in the contemporary evidence "little support for the argument that military necessity required a mass evacuation" and pointed, accurately, to the machinations of Gullion and Bendetsen and their success in bending the civilian heads of the War Department to their will.

The question that remains to be answered is why the recommendation of Stimson and McCloy was accepted by the nation. Grodzins' pressure groups were, of course, important, but even more important than the peculiar racism of a region was the general racist character of American society. The decision to evacuate the Japanese was popular, not only in California and the West, but in the entire nation, although only on the West Coast was it a major issue in early 1942.

The leader of the nation, was, in the final analysis, responsible. It was Franklin Roosevelt, who in one short telephone call, passed the decision-making power to two men who had never been elected to any office, saying only, with the politician's charm and equivocation: "Be as reasonable as you can." Why did he agree? Probably for two reasons: in the first place, it was expedient; in the second place, Roosevelt himself harbored deeply felt anti-Japanese prejudices.

As to expediency, it is important to remember what the war news was like in early 1942. It was a very bad time for the military fortunes of the United States and its allies. The Japanese had landed on the island of Singapore on February 8, on New Britain on the 9th, and were advancing rapidly in Burma. Roosevelt was concerned, first of all with winning the war, and secondly with unity at home, so that he, unlike his former chief, Woodrow Wilson, could win the peace with the advice and consent of the Senate. He could read the Congressional signs well and knew that cracking down on the Japanese Americans would be popular both on the Hill and in the country generally. And the last thing he wanted was a rift with establishment Republicans like Stimson and McCloy; New Dealers like Biddle and MacLeish could be counted on not to rock the boat.

But, in addition, Franklin Roosevelt was himself convinced that Japanese, alien and citizen, were dangerous to American security. He, along with several members of his Cabinet and circle of advisers, persistently pushed for mass internment of the Hawaiian Japanese-Americans long after the military had wisely rejected such a policy. And there was a kind of rationale for such a policy. If Japanese were a threat to security in California, where they represented fewer than 2 percent of the population, certainly in wartorn Hawaii, where they were more than a third of the population, they should have constituted a real menace. But it is one thing to incarcerate a tiny element of the population, as was done on the West Coast, and quite another to put away a sizable fraction of the whole. Apart from the sheer size of the problem, relatively and absolutely, there was the question of the disruption that such a mass evacuation would cause in the local economy. Referring to Oahu alone, Lieutenant General Delos C. Emmons, the Army commander there, pointed out to the War Department in January 1942 that Japanese provided the bulk of the main island's skilled labor force and were indispensable unless replaced by an equivalent labor force from the mainland. In addition, the logistical problems of internment in the islands were so great that Emmons recommended that any evacuation and relocation be to the mainland.

At the Cabinet level, however, different views were held. On February 27, for example, Navy Secretary Knox, the most vocal Japanophobe in the Cabinet, suggested rounding up all the Japanese on Oahu and putting them under Army guard on the neighboring island of Molokai, better known as a leper colony. Stimson concurred as to the danger, but insisted that if they were to be moved they be sent to the states. (The shipping situation, for all practical purposes, made this impossible.) The President, according to Stimson, clearly favored Knox's plan. The President and his Navy Secretary continued to press for this policy well into 1942, but eventually were forestalled by a strongly worded joint recommendation to the contrary signed by both Chief of Staff Marshall and Chief of Naval Operations Admiral Ernest J. King. In other words, real rather than imaginary military necessity governed in Hawaii. Although Hawaii was the first real theater of war, fewer than 2000 of the territory's 150,000 Japanese were ever deprived of their liberty.

19

THE ATOMIC BOMB AND
THE ORIGINS OF THE COLD WAR

MARTIN J. SHERWIN

International politics has always created strange alliances, but none as unique as that of the Big Three during World War II. Faced with a powerful and successful Fascist onslaught, Stalin joined forces with Churchill and Roosevelt to defeat German hopes for domination in Europe. Thus were joined one of Britain's most conservative politicians, a reforming American president, and the leader of the Communist world.

What united these three improbable allies, however, was not merely the German war threat. From 1942 onward these three leaders were increasingly concerned with the shape of the postwar world and with establishing and maintaining their respective spheres of influence within it. Breaking with the American isolationist past, Roosevelt joined with Churchill and Stalin in secret agreements designed to partition the world, dividing it into Russian and Anglo-American zones where each was to have military and political control.

As Martin Sherwin demonstrates in this essay, however, relations between the Big Three were not always free of conflict. One of the most divisive issues faced by this alliance was the question of the atomic bomb. Since the early 1940s, when British and American intelligence operatives reported German experiments with nuclear weaponry, British and American scientists had been engaged in their own intensive nuclear program. The critical question, as Sherwin points out, was who among the allies was to share in the knowledge and production of the allies' atomic bomb. It was Churchill and Roosevelt's decision to exclude Stalin from their atomic club that precipitated the climate of distrust which characterized the Cold War that followed World War II.

In light of subsequent events, do you think that Churchill and Roosevelt made the right decision in not sharing their nuclear research with Stalin? How do Roosevelt's attitudes toward the Soviets compare with those of "the McCarthy era" discussed by Robert Griffith in Reading 20?

During the Second World War the atomic bomb was seen and valued as a potential rather than an actual instrument of policy. Responsible officials believed that its impact on diplomacy had to await its development and, perhaps, even a demonstration of its power. As Henry L. Stimson, the secretary of war, observed in his memoirs: "The bomb as a merely probable weapon had seemed a weak reed on which to rely, but the bomb as a colossal reality was very different." That policy makers considered this difference before Hiroshima has been well documented, but whether they based wartime diplomatic policies upon an anticipated successful demonstration of the bomb's power remains a source of controversy. Two questions delineate the issues in this debate. First, did the development of the atomic bomb affect the way American policy makers conducted diplomacy with the Soviet Union? Second, did diplomatic considerations related to the Soviet Union influence the decision to use the atomic bomb against Japan?

These important questions relating the atomic bomb to American diplomacy, and ultimately to the origins of the cold war, have been addressed almost exclusively to the formulation of policy during the early months of the Truman administration. As a result, two anterior questions of equal importance, questions with implications for those already posed, have been overlooked. Did diplomatic considerations related to Soviet postwar behavior influence the formulation of Roosevelt's atomic-energy policies? What effect did the atomic legacy Truman inherited have on the diplomatic and atomic-energy policies of his administration?

To comprehend the nature of the relationship between atomic-energy and diplomatic policies that developed during the war, the bomb must be seen as policy makers saw it before Hiroshima, as a weapon that might be used to control postwar diplomacy. For this task our present view is conceptually inadequate. After more than a quarter century of experience we understand, as wartime policy makers did not, the bomb's limitations as a diplomatic instrument. To appreciate the profound influence of the unchallenged wartime assumption about the bomb's impact on diplomacy we must recognize the postwar purposes for which policy makers and their advisers believed the bomb could be used. In this effort Churchill's expectations must be scrutinized as carefully as Roosevelt's, and scientists' ideas must be considered along with those of politicians. Truman's decision to use the atomic bomb against Japan must be evaluated in the light of Roosevelt's atomic legacy, and the problems of impending peace must be considered along with the exigencies of war. To isolate the basic atomic-energy policy alternatives that emerged during the war requires

that we first ask whether alternatives were, in fact, recognized.

What emerges most clearly from a close examination of wartime formulation of atomic-energy policy is the conclusion that policy makers never seriously questioned the assumption that the atomic bomb should be used against Germany or Japan. From October 9, 1941, the time of the first meeting to organize the atomic-energy project, Stimson, Roosevelt, and other members of the "top policy group" conceived of the development of the atomic bomb as an essential part of the total war effort. Though the suggestion to build the bomb was initially made by scientists who feared that Germany might develop the weapon first, those with political responsibility for prosecuting the war accepted the circumstances of the bomb's creation as sufficient justification for its use against any enemy.

Having nurtured this point of view during the war, Stimson charged those who later criticized the use of the bomb with two errors. First, these critics asked the wrong question: it was not whether surrender could have been obtained without using the bomb but whether a different diplomatic and military course from that followed by the Truman administration would have achieved an earlier surrender. Second, the basic assumption of these critics was false: the idea that American policy should have been based primarily on a desire not to employ the bomb seemed as "irresponsible" as a policy controlled by a positive desire to use it. The war, not the bomb, Stimson argued, had been the primary focus of his attention; as secretary of war his responsibilities permitted no alternative.

Stimson's own wartime diary nevertheless indicates that from 1941 on, the problems associated with the atomic bomb moved steadily closer to the center of his own and Roosevelt's concerns. As the war progressed, the implications of the weapon's development became diplomatic as well as military, postwar as well as wartime. Recognizing that a monopoly of the atomic bomb gave the United States a powerful new military advantage, Roosevelt and Stimson became increasingly anxious to convert it to diplomatic advantage. In December 1944 they spoke of using the "secret" of the atomic bomb as a means of obtaining a *quid pro quo* from the Soviet Union. But viewing the bomb as a potential instrument of diplomacy, they were not moved to formulate a concrete plan for carrying out this exchange before the bomb was used. The bomb had "this unique peculiarity," Stimson noted several months later in his diary; "Success is 99% assured, yet only by the first actual war trial of the weapon can the actual certainty be fixed." Whether or not the specter of postwar Soviet ambitions created "a positive desire" to ascertain the bomb's power, until that decision was executed "atomic diplomacy" remained an idea that never crystallized into policy.

Although Roosevelt left no definitive statement assigning a postwar role to the atomic bomb, his expectations for its potential diplomatic value can be recalled from the existing record. An analysis of the policies he chose from among the alternatives he faced suggests that the potential diplomatic value of the bomb began to shape his atomic-energy policies as early as 1943. He may have been cautious about counting on the bomb as a reality during the war, but he nevertheless consistently chose policy alternatives that would promote the postwar diplomatic potential of the bomb if the predictions of scientists proved true. These policies were based on the assumption that the bomb could be used effectively to secure postwar diplomatic aims; and this assumption was carried over from the Roosevelt to the Truman administration.

Despite general agreement that the bomb would be an extraordinarily important diplomatic factor after the war, those closely associated with its development did not agree on how to use it most effectively as an instrument of diplomacy. Convinced that wartime atomic-energy policies would have postwar diplomatic consequences, several scientists advised Roosevelt to adopt policies aimed at achieving a postwar international control system. Churchill, on the other hand, urged the president to maintain the Anglo-American atomic monopoly as a diplomatic counter against the postwar ambitions of other nations—particularly against the Soviet Union. Roosevelt fashioned his atomic-energy policies from the choices he made between these conflicting recommendations. In 1943 he rejected the counsel of his science advisers and began to consider the diplomatic component of atomic-energy policy in consultation with Churchill alone. This decision-making procedure and Roosevelt's untimely death have left his motives ambiguous. Nevertheless it is clear that he pursued policies consistent with Churchill's monopolistic, anti-Soviet views.

The findings of this study thus raise serious questions concerning generalizations historians have commonly made about Roosevelt's diplomacy: that it was consistent with his public reputation for cooperation and conciliation; that he was naive with respect to postwar Soviet behavior; that, like Wilson, he believed in collective security as an effective guarantor of national safety; and that he made every possible effort to assure that the Soviet Union and its allies would continue to function as postwar partners. Although this article does not dispute the view that Roosevelt desired amicable postwar relations with the Soviet Union, or even that he worked hard to achieve them, it does suggest that historians have exaggerated his confidence in (and perhaps his commitment to) such an outcome. His most secret and among his most important long-range decisions—those responsible for prescribing a diplomatic role for the atomic bomb—reflected his lack of confidence. Finally, in light of this study's conclusions, the widely held assumption that Truman's attitude toward the atomic bomb was substantially different from Roosevelt's must also be revised.

Like the Grand Alliance itself, the Anglo-American atomic-energy partnership was forged by the war and its exigencies. The threat of a German atomic bomb precipitated a hasty marriage of convenience between British research and American resources. When scientists in Britain proposed a theory that explained how an atomic bomb might quickly be built, policy makers had to assume that German scientists were building one. "If such an explosive were made," Vannevar Bush, the director of the Office of Scientific Research and Development, told Roosevelt in July 1941, "it would be thousands of times more powerful than existing explosives, and its use might be determining." Roosevelt assumed nothing less. Even before the atomic-energy project was fully organized he assigned it the highest priority. He wanted the program "pushed not only in regard to development, but also with due regard to time. This is very much of the essence," he told Bush in March 1942. "We both felt painfully the dangers of doing nothing," Churchill recalled, referring to an early wartime discussion with Roosevelt about the bomb.

The high stakes at issue during the war did not prevent officials in Great Britain or the United States from considering the postwar implications of their atomic-energy decisions. As early as 1941, during the debate over whether to join the United States in an atomic-energy partnership, members of the British government's atomic-energy committee argued that the matter "was so important for the future that work should proceed in Britain." Weighing the obvious difficulties of proceeding alone against the possible advantages of working with the United States, Sir John Anderson, then lord president of the council and the minister responsible for atomic-energy research, advocated the partnership. As he explained to Churchill, by working closely with the Americans British scientists would be able "to take up the work again [after the war], not where we left off, but where the combined effort had by then brought it."

As early as October 1942 Roosevelt's science advisers exhibited a similar concern with the potential postwar value of atomic energy. After conducting a full-scale review of the atomic-energy project, James B. Conant, the president of Harvard University and Bush's deputy, recommended discontinuing the Anglo-American partnership "as far as development and manufacture is concerned." Conant had in mind three considerations when he suggested a more limited arrangement with the British: first, the project had been transferred from scientific to military control; second, the United States was doing almost all the developmental work; and third, security dictated "moving in a direction of holding much more closely the information about the development of this program." Under these conditions it was difficult, Conant observed, "to see how a joint British-American project could be sponsored in this country." What prompted Conant's recommendations, however, was his suspicion— soon to be shared by other senior atomic-energy administrators—that the British were rather more concerned with information for postwar industrial purposes than for wartime use. What right did the British have to the fruits of American labor? "We were doing nine-tenths of the work," Stimson told Roosevelt in October. By December 1942 there was general agreement among the president's atomic-energy advisers that the British no longer had a valid claim to all atomic-energy information.

Conant's arguments and suggestions for a more limited partnership were incorporated into a "Report to the President by the Military Policy Committee." Roosevelt approved the recommendations on December 28. Early in January the British were officially informed that the rules governing the Anglo-American atomic-energy partnership had been altered on "orders from the top."

By approving the policy of "restricted interchange" Roosevelt undermined a major incentive for British cooperation. It is not surprising, therefore, that Churchill took up the matter directly with the president and with Harry Hopkins, "Roosevelt's own, personal Foreign Office." The prime minister's initial response to the new policy reflected his determination to have it reversed: "That we should each work separately," he threatened, "would be a sombre decision."

Conant and Bush understood the implications of Churchill's intervention and sought to counter its effect. "It is our duty," Conant wrote Bush, "to see to it that the President of the United States, in writing, is informed of what is involved in these decisions." Their memorandums no longer concentrated on tortuous discussions differentiating between the scientific research and the manufacturing stages of the bomb's development but focused on what to Conant was "the major consideration . . . that of *national security and postwar strategic significance.*" Information on manufacturing an atomic bomb, Conant noted, was a "military secret which is in a totally different class from anything the world has ever seen if the potentialities of this project are realized." To provide the British with detailed knowledge about the construction of a bomb "might be the equivalent to joint occupation of a fortress or strategic harbor in perpetuity." Though British and American atomic-energy policies might coincide during the war, Conant and Bush expected them to conflict afterward.

The controversy over the policy of "restricted interchange" of atomic-energy information shifted attention to postwar diplomatic considerations. As Bush wrote to Hopkins, "We can hardly give away the fruits of our developments as a part of postwar planning except on the basis of some overall agreement on that subject, which agreement does not now exist." The central issue was clearly drawn. The atomic-energy policy of the United States was related to the very fabric of Anglo-American postwar relations and, as Churchill would insist, to postwar relations between each of them and the Soviet Union. Just as the possibility of British postwar commercial competition had played a major role in shaping the U.S. policy of restricted interchange, the specter of Soviet postwar military power played a major role in shaping the prime minister's attitude toward atomic-energy policies in 1943.

"We cannot," Sir John Anderson wrote Churchill, "afford after the war to face the future without this weapon and rely entirely on America should Russia or some other power develop it." The prime minister agreed. The atomic bomb was an instrument of postwar diplomacy that Britain had to have. He could cite numerous reasons for his determination to acquire an independent atomic arsenal after the war, but Great Britain's postwar military-diplomatic position with respect to the Soviet Union invariably led the list. When Bush and Stimson visited London in July,

Churchill told them quite frankly that he was "vitally interested in the possession of all [atomic-energy] information because this will be necessary for Britain's independence in the future as well as for success during the war." Nor was Churchill evasive about his reasoning: "It would never do to have Germany or Russia win the race for something which might be used for international blackmail," he stated bluntly and then pointed out that "Russia might be in a position to accomplish this result unless we worked together." In Washington, two months earlier, Churchill's science adviser Lord Cherwell had told Bush and Hopkins virtually the same thing. The British government, Cherwell stated, was considering "the whole [atomic-energy] affair on an after-the-war military basis." It intended, he said, "to manufacture and produce the weapon." Prior to the convening of the Quebec Conference, Anderson explained his own and Churchill's view of the bomb to the Canadian prime minister, Mackenzie King. The British knew, Anderson said, "that both Germany and Russia were working on the same thing," which, he noted, "would be a terrific factor in the postwar world as giving an absolute control to whatever country possessed the secret." Convinced that the British attitude toward the bomb would undermine any possibility of postwar cooperation with the Soviet Union, Bush and Conant vigorously continued to oppose any revival of the Anglo-American atomic-energy partnership.

On July 20, however, Roosevelt chose to accept a recommendation from Hopkins to restore full partnership, and he ordered Bush to "renew, in an inclusive manner, the full exchange of information with the British." A garbled trans-Atlantic cable to Bush reading "review" rather than "renew" gave him the opportunity to continue his negotiations in London with Churchill and thereby to modify the president's order. But Bush could not alter Roosevelt's intentions. On August 19, at the Quebec Conference, the president and the prime minister agreed that the British would share the atomic bomb. Despite Bush's negotiations with Churchill, the Quebec Agreement revived the principle of an Anglo-American atomic-energy partnership, albeit the British were reinstated as junior rather than equal partners.

The president's decision was not a casual one taken in ignorance. As the official history of the Atomic Energy Commission notes: "Both Roosevelt and Churchill knew that the stake of their diplomacy was a technological breakthrough so revolutionary that it transcended in importance even the bloody work of carrying the war to the heartland of the Nazi foe." The president had been informed of Churchill's position as well as of Bush's and Conant's. But how much closer Roosevelt was to Churchill than to his own advisers at this time is suggested by a report written after the war by General Leslie R. Groves, military director of the atomic-energy project. "It is not known what if any Americans President Roosevelt consulted at Quebec," Groves wrote. "It is doubtful if there were any. All that is known is that the Quebec Agreement was signed by President Roosevelt and that, as finally signed, it agreed practically in toto with the version presented by Sir John Anderson to Dr. Bush in Washington a few weeks earlier."

The debate that preceded the Quebec Agreement is noteworthy for yet another reason: it led to a new relationship between Roosevelt and his atomic-energy advisers. After August 1943 the president did not consult with them about the diplomatic aspects of atomic-energy policy. Though he responded politely when they offered their views, he acted decisively only in consultation with Churchill. Bush and Conant appear to have lost a large measure of their influence because they had used it to oppose Churchill's position. What they did not suspect was the extent to which the president had come to share the prime minister's view.

It can be argued that Roosevelt, the political pragmatist, renewed the wartime atomic-energy partnership to keep relations with the British harmonious rather than disrupt them on the basis of a postwar issue. Indeed it seems logical that the president took this consideration into account. But it must also be recognized that he was perfectly comfortable with the concept Churchill advocated—that military power was a prerequisite to successful postwar diplomacy. As early as August 1941, during the Atlantic Conference, Roosevelt had rejected the idea that an "effective international organization" could be relied upon to keep the peace; an Anglo-American international police force would be far more effective, he told Churchill. By the spring of 1942 the concept had broadened: the two "policemen" became four, and the idea was added that every other nation would be totally disarmed. "The Four Policemen" would have "to build up a reservoir of force so powerful that no aggressor would dare to challenge it," Roosevelt told Arthur Sweetser, an ardent internationalist. Violators first would be quarantined, and, if they persisted in their disruptive activities, bombed at the rate of a city a day until they agreed to behave. The president told Molotov about this idea in May, and in November he repeated it to Clark Eichelberger, who was coordinating the activities of the American internationalists. A year later, at the Teheran Conference, Roosevelt again discussed his idea, this time with Stalin. As Robert A. Divine has noted: "Roosevelt's concept of big power domination remained the central idea in his approach to international organization throughout World War II."

Precisely how Roosevelt expected to integrate the atomic bomb into his plans for keeping the peace in the postwar world is not clear. However, against the background of his atomic-energy policy decisions of 1943 and his peace-keeping concepts, his actions in 1944 suggest that he intended to take full advantage of the bomb's potential as a postwar instrument of Anglo-American diplomacy. If Roosevelt thought the bomb could be used to create a more peaceful world order, he seems to have considered the threat of its power more effective than any opportunities it offered for international cooperation. If Roosevelt was less worried than Churchill about Soviet postwar ambitions, he was no less determined than the prime minister to avoid any commitments to the Soviets for the international control of atomic energy. There could still be four policemen, but only two of them would have the bomb.

The atomic-energy policies Roosevelt pursued during the remainder of his life reinforce this interpretation of his ideas for the postwar period. The following three questions offer a useful framework for analyzing his intentions. Did Roosevelt make any additional agreements with Churchill that would further support the view that he intended to maintain an Anglo-American monopoly after the war? Did Roosevelt demonstrate any interest in the international control of atomic energy? Was Roosevelt aware that an effort to maintain an Anglo-American monopoly of the atomic bomb might lead to a postwar atomic arms race with the Soviet Union?

An examination of the wartime activities of the eminent Danish physicist, Niels Bohr, who arrived in America early in 1944 as a consultant to the atomic-bomb project, will help answer these questions. "Officially and secretly he came to help the technical enterprise," noted J. Robert Oppenheimer, the director of the Los Alamos atomic-bomb laboratory, but "most secretly of all . . . he came to advance his case and his cause." Bohr was convinced that a postwar atomic armaments race with the Soviet Union was inevitable unless Roosevelt and Churchill initiated efforts during the war to establish the international control of atomic energy. Bohr's attempts to promote this idea in the United States were aided by Justice Felix Frankfurter.

Bohr and Frankfurter were old acquaintances. They had first met in 1933 at Oxford and then in 1939 on several occasions in London and the United States. At these meetings Bohr had been impressed by the breadth of Frankfurter's interests and, perhaps, overimpressed with his influence on Roosevelt. In 1944 the Danish minister to the United States brought them together, once again, at his home in Washington. Frankfurter, who appears to have suspected why Bohr had come to America and why this meeting had been arranged, had learned about the atomic-bomb project earlier in the war when, as he told the story, several troubled scientists had sought his advice on a matter of "greatest importance." He therefore invited Bohr to lunch in his chambers and, by dropping hints about his knowledge, encouraged Bohr to discuss the issue.

After listening to Bohr's analysis of the postwar alternatives—an atomic armaments race or some form of international control—Frankfurter saw Roosevelt. Bohr had persuaded him, Frankfurter reported, that disastrous consequences would result if Russia learned on her own about the atomic-bomb project. Frankfurter suggested that it was a matter of great importance that the president explore the possibility of seeking an effective arrangement with the Soviets for controlling the bomb. He also noted that Bohr, whose knowledge of Soviet science was extensive, believed that the Russians had the capability to build their own atomic weapons. If the international control of atomic energy was not discussed among the Allies during the war, an atomic arms race between the Allies would almost certainly develop after the war. It seemed imperative, therefore, that Roosevelt consider approaching Stalin with a proposal as soon as possible.

Frankfurter discussed these points with the president for an hour and a half, and he left feeling that Roosevelt was "plainly impressed by my account of the matter." When Frankfurter had suggested that the solution to this problem might be more important than all the plans for a world organization, Roosevelt had agreed. Moreover he had authorized Frankfurter to tell Bohr, who was scheduled to return to England, that he might inform "our friends in London that the President was most eager to explore the proper safeguards in relation to X [the atomic bomb]." Roosevelt also told Frankfurter that the problem of the atomic bomb "worried him to death" and that he was very eager for all the help he could have in dealing with it.

The alternatives placed before Roosevelt posed a difficult dilemma. On the one hand, he could continue to exclude the Soviet government from any official information about the development of the bomb, a policy that would probably strengthen America's postwar military-diplomatic position. But such a policy would also encourage Soviet mistrust of Anglo-American intentions and was bound to make postwar cooperation more difficult. On the other hand, Roosevelt could use the atomic-bomb project as an instrument of cooperation by informing Stalin of the American government's intention of cooperating in the development of a plan for the international control of atomic weapons, an objective that might never be achieved.

Either choice involved serious risks. Roosevelt had to balance the diplomatic advantages of being well ahead of the Soviet Union in atomic-energy production after the war against the advantages of initiating wartime negotiations for postwar cooperation. The issue here, it must be emphasized, is not whether the initiative Bohr suggested would have led to successful international control, but rather whether Roosevelt demonstrated any serious interest in laying the groundwork for such a policy.

Several considerations indicate that Roosevelt was already committed to a course of action that precluded Bohr's internationalist approach. First, Frankfurter appears to have been misled. Though Roosevelt's response had been characteristically agreeable, he did not mention Bohr's ideas to his atomic-energy advisers until September 1944, when he told Bush that he was very disturbed that Frankfurter had learned about the project. Roosevelt knew at this time, moreover, that the Soviets were finding out on their own about the development of the atomic bomb. Security personnel had reported an active Communist cell in the Radiation Laboratory at the University of California. Their reports indicated that at least one scientist at Berkeley was selling information to Russian agents. "They [Soviet agents] are already getting information about vital secrets and sending them to Russia," Stimson told the president on September 9, 1943. If Roosevelt was indeed worried to death about the effect the atomic bomb could have on Soviet-American postwar relations, he took no action to remove the potential danger, nor did he make any effort to explore the possibility of encouraging Soviet postwar cooperation on this problem. The available evidence indicates that he never discussed the merits of the international control of atomic energy with his advisers after this first or any subsequent meeting with Frankfurter.

How is the president's policy of neither discussing international control nor promoting the idea to be explained if not by an intention to use the bomb as an instrument of Anglo-American postwar diplomacy? Perhaps his concern for maintaining the tightest possible secrecy against German espionage led him to oppose any discussion about the project. Or he may have concluded, after considering Bohr's analysis, that Soviet suspicion and mistrust would be further aroused if Stalin were informed of the existence of the project without receiving detailed information about the bomb's construction. The possibility also exists that Roosevelt believed that neither Congress nor the American public would approve of a policy giving the Soviet Union any measure of control over the new weapon. Finally Roosevelt might have thought that the spring of 1944 was not the proper moment for such an initiative.

Though it would be unreasonable to state categorically that these considerations did not contribute to his decision, they appear to have been secondary. Roosevelt was clearly, and properly, concerned about secrecy, but the most important secret with respect to Soviet-American relations was that the United States was developing an atomic bomb. And that secret, he was aware, already had been passed on to Moscow. Soviet mistrust of Anglo-American postwar intentions could only be exacerbated by continuing the existing policy. Moreover an attempt to initiate planning for international control of atomic energy would not have required the revelation of technical secrets. Nor is it sufficient to cite Roosevelt's well-known sensitivity to domestic politics as an explanation for his atomic-energy policies. He was willing to take enormous political risks, as he did at Yalta, to support his diplomatic objectives.

Had Roosevelt avoided all postwar atomic-energy commitments, his lack of support for international control could have been interpreted as an attempt to reserve his opinion on the best course to follow. But he had made commitments in 1943 supporting Churchill's monopolistic, anti-Soviet position, and he continued to make others in 1944. On June 13, for example, Roosevelt and Churchill signed an Agreement and Declaration of Trust, specifying that the United States and Great Britain would cooperate in seeking to control available supplies of uranium and thorium ore both during and after the war. This commitment, taken against the background of Roosevelt's peace-keeping ideas and his other commitments, suggests that the president's attitude toward the international control of atomic energy was similar to the prime minister's.

Churchill had dismissed out of hand the concept of international control when Bohr talked with him about it in May 1944. Their meeting was not long under way before Churchill lost interest and became involved in an argument with Lord Cherwell, who was also present. Bohr, left out of the discussion, was frustrated and depressed; he was unable to return the conversation to what he considered the most important diplomatic problem of the war. When the allotted half hour elapsed, Bohr asked if he might send the prime minister a memorandum on the subject. A letter from Niels Bohr, Churchill bitingly replied, was always welcome, but he hoped it would deal with a subject other than politics. As Bohr described their meeting: "We did not even speak the same language."

Churchill rejected the assumption upon which Bohr's views were founded—that international control of atomic energy could be used as a cornerstone for constructing a peaceful world order. An atomic monopoly would be a significant diplomatic advantage in postwar diplomacy, and Churchill did not believe that anything useful could be gained by surrendering this advantage. The argument that a new weapon created a unique opportunity to refashion international affairs ignored every lesson Churchill read into history. "You can be quite sure," he would write in a memorandum less than a year later, "that any power that gets hold of the secret will try to make the article and this touches the existence of human society. This matter is out of all relation to anything else that exists in the world, and I could not think of participating in any disclosure to third or fourth parties at the present time."

Several months after Bohr met Churchill, Frankfurter arranged a meeting between Bohr and Roosevelt. Their discussion lasted an hour and a half. Roosevelt told Bohr that contact with the Soviet Union along the lines he suggested had to be tried. The president also said he was optimistic that such an initiative would have a "good result." In his opinion Stalin was enough of a realist to understand the revolutionary importance of this development and its consequences. The president also expressed confidence that the prime minister would eventually share these views. They had disagreed in the past, he told Bohr, but they had always succeeded in resolving their differences.

Roosevelt's enthusiasm for Bohr's ideas was more apparent than real. The president did not mention them to anyone until he met with Churchill at Hyde Park on September 18, following the second wartime conference at Quebec. The decisions reached on atomic energy at Hyde Park were summarized and documented in an *aide-mémoire* signed by Roosevelt and Churchill on September 19, 1944. The agreement bears the markings of Churchill's attitude toward the atomic bomb and his poor opinion of Bohr. "Enquiries should be made," the last paragraph reads, "regarding the activities of Professor Bohr and steps taken to ensure that he is responsible for no leakage of information particularly to the Russians." If Bohr's activities prompted Roosevelt to suspect his loyalty, there can be no doubt that Churchill encouraged the president's suspicions. Atomic energy and Britain's future position as a world power had become part of a single equation for the prime minister. Bohr's ideas, like the earlier idea of restricted interchange, threatened the continuation of the Anglo-American atomic-energy partnership. With such great stakes at issue Churchill did not hesitate to discredit Bohr along with his ideas. "It seems to me," Churchill wrote to Cherwell soon after Hyde Park, "Bohr ought to be confined or at any rate made to see that he is very near the edge of mortal crimes."

The *aide-mémoire* also contained an explicit rejection of any wartime efforts toward international control: "The suggestion that the world should be informed regarding tube alloys [the atomic bomb], with a view to an international agreement regarding its control and use, is not accepted. The matter should continue to be regarded as of the utmost secrecy." But Bohr had never suggested that the world be informed about the atomic bomb. He had argued in memorandums and in person that peace was not possible unless the Soviet government—not the world—was officially notified only about the project's existence before the time when any discussion would appear coercive rather than friendly.

It was the second paragraph, however, that revealed the full extent of Roosevelt's agreement with Churchill's point of view. "Full collaboration between the United States and the British Government in developing tube alloys for military and commercial purposes," it noted, "should continue after the defeat of Japan unless and until terminated by joint agreement." Finally the *aide-mémoire* offers some insight into Roosevelt's intentions for the military use of the weapon in the war: "When a bomb is finally available, it might perhaps, after mature consideration, be used against the Japanese, who should be warned that this bombardment will be repeated until they surrender."

Within the context of the complex problem of the origins of the cold war the Hyde Park meeting is far more important than historians of the war generally have recognized. Overshadowed by the Second Quebec Conference on one side and by the drama of Yalta on the other, its significance often has been overlooked. But the agreements reached in September 1944 reflect a set of attitudes, aims, and assumptions that guided the relationship between the atomic bomb and American diplomacy during the Roosevelt administration and, through the transfer of its atomic legacy, during the Truman administration as well. Two alternatives had been recognized long before Roosevelt and Churchill met in 1944 at Hyde Park: the bomb could have been used to

initiate a diplomatic effort to work out a system for its international control, or it could remain isolated during the war from any cooperative initiatives and held in reserve should cooperation fail. Roosevelt consistently favored the latter alternative. An insight into his reasoning is found in a memorandum Bush wrote following a conversation with Roosevelt several days after the Hyde Park meeting: "The President evidently thought he could join with Churchill in bringing about a US-UK postwar agreement on this subject [the atomic bomb] by which it would be held closely and presumably to control the peace of the world." By 1944 Roosevelt's earlier musings about the four policemen had faded into the background. But the idea behind it, the concept of controlling the peace of the world by amassing overwhelming military power, appears to have remained a prominent feature of his postwar plans.

In the seven months between his meeting with Churchill in September and his death the following April Roosevelt did not alter his atomic-energy policies. Nor did he reverse his earlier decision not to take his advisers into his confidence about diplomatic issues related to the new weapon. They were never told about the Hyde Park agreements, nor were they able to discuss with him their ideas for the postwar handling of atomic-energy affairs. Though officially uninformed, Bush suspected that Roosevelt had made a commitment to continue the atomic-energy partnership exclusively with the British after the war, and he, as well as Conant, opposed the idea. They believed such a policy "might well lead to extraordinary efforts on the part of Russia to establish its own position in the field secretly, and might lead to a clash, say 20 years from now." Unable to reach the president directly, they sought to influence his policies through Stimson, whose access to Roosevelt's office (though not to his thoughts on atomic energy) was better than their own.

Summarizing their views on September 30 for the secretary of war, Bush and Conant predicted that an atomic bomb equivalent to from one to ten thousand tons of high explosive could be "demonstrated" before August 1, 1945. They doubted that the present American and British monopoly could be maintained for more than three or four years, and they pointed out that any nation with good technical and scientific resources could catch up; accidents of research, moreover, might even put some other nation ahead. In addition atomic bombs were only the first step along the road of nuclear weapons technology. In the not-too-distant future loomed the awesome prospect of a weapon perhaps a thousand times more destructive—the hydrogen bomb. Every major center of population in the world would then lie at the mercy of a nation that struck first in war. Security therefore could be found neither in secrecy nor even in the control of raw materials, for the supply of heavy hydrogen was practically unlimited.

These predictions by Bush and Conant were more specific than Bohr's, but not dissimilar. They, too, believed that a nuclear arms race could be prevented only through international control. Their efforts were directed, however, toward abrogating existing agreements with the British rather than toward initiating new agreements with the Soviets. Like Bohr they based their hope for Stalin's eventual cooperation on his desire to avoid the circumstances that could lead to a nuclear war. But while Bohr urged Roosevelt to approach Stalin with the carrot of international control before the bomb became a reality, Bush and Conant were inclined to delay such an approach until the bomb was demonstrated, until it was clear that without international control the new weapon could be used as a terribly effective stick.

In their attempt to persuade Roosevelt to their point of view Bush and Conant failed. But their efforts were not in vain. By March 1945 Stimson shared their concerns, and he agreed that peace without international control was a forlorn hope. Postwar problems relating to the atomic bomb "went right down to the bottom facts of human nature, morals and government, and it is by far the most searching and important thing that I have had to do since I have been here in the office

of Secretary of War," Stimson wrote on March 5. Ten days later he presented his views on postwar atomic-energy policy to Roosevelt. This was their last meeting. In less than a month a new president took the oath of office.

Harry S. Truman inherited a set of military and diplomatic atomic-energy policies that included partially formulated intentions, several commitments to Churchill, and the assumption that the bomb would be a legitimate weapon to be used against Japan. But no policy was definitely settled. According to the Quebec Agreement the president had the option of deciding the future of the commercial aspects of the atomic-energy partnership according to his own estimate of what was fair. Although the policy of "utmost secrecy" had been confirmed at Hyde Park the previous September, Roosevelt had not informed his atomic-energy advisers about the *aide-mémoire* he and Churchill signed. Although the assumption that the bomb would be used in the war was shared by those privy to its development, assumptions formulated early in the war were not necessarily valid at its conclusion. Yet Truman was bound to the past by his own uncertain position and by the prestige of his predecessor. Since Roosevelt had refused to open negotiations with the Soviet government for the international control of atomic energy, and since he had never expressed any objection to the wartime use of the bomb, it would have required considerable political courage and confidence for Truman to alter those policies. Moreover it would have required the encouragement of his advisers, for under the circumstances the most serious constraint on the new president's choices was his dependence upon advice. So Truman's atomic legacy, while it included several options, did not necessarily entail complete freedom to choose from among all the possible alternatives.

"I think it is very important that I should have a talk with you as soon as possible on a highly secret matter," Stimson wrote to Truman on April 24. It has "such a bearing on our present foreign relations and has such an important effect upon all my thinking in this field that I think you ought to know about it without further delay."

Stimson had been preparing to brief Truman on the atomic bomb for almost ten days, but in the preceding twenty-four hours he had been seized by a sense of urgency. Relations with the Soviet Union had declined precipitously during the past week, the result, he thought, of the failure of the State Department to settle the major problems between the Allies before going ahead with the San Francisco Conference on the United Nations Organization. The secretary of state, Edward R. Stettinius, Jr., along with the department's Soviet specialists, now felt "compelled to bull the thing through." To get out of the "mess" they had created, Stimson wrote in his diary, they were urging Truman to get tough with the Russians. He had. Twenty-four hours earlier the president met with the Soviet foreign minister, V. M. Molotov, and "with rather brutal frankness" accused his government of breaking the Yalta Agreement. Molotov was furious. "I have never been talked to like that in my life," he told the president before leaving.

With a memorandum on the "political aspects of the S-1 [atomic bomb's] performance" in hand and General Groves in reserve, Stimson went to the White House on April 25. The document he carried was the distillation of numerous decisions already taken, each one the product of attitudes that developed along with the new weapon. The secretary himself was not entirely aware of how various forces had shaped these decisions: the recommendations of Bush and Conant, the policies Roosevelt had followed, the uncertainties inherent in the wartime alliance, the oppressive concern for secrecy, and his own inclination to consider long-range implications. It was a curious document. Though its language revealed Stimson's sensitivity to the historic significance of the atomic bomb, he did not question the wisdom of using it against Japan. Nor did he suggest any concrete steps for developing a postwar policy. His objective was to inform Truman of the salient problems: the possibility of an atomic arms race, the danger of atomic war, and the necessity for international control if the United Nations Organization was to work. "If the problem of the proper use of this weapon can be solved," he

wrote, "we would have the opportunity to bring the world into a pattern in which the peace of the world and our civilizations can be saved." To cope with this difficult challenge Stimson suggested the "establishment of a select committee" to consider the postwar problems inherent in the development of the bomb. If his presentation was the "forceful statement" of the problem that historians of the Atomic Energy Commission have described it as being, its force inhered in the problem itself, not in any bold formulations or initiatives he offered toward a solution. If, as another historian has claimed, this meeting led to a "strategy of delayed showdown," requiring "the delay of all disputes with Russia until the atomic bomb had been demonstrated," there is no evidence in the extant records of the meeting that Stimson had such a strategy in mind or that Truman misunderstood the secretary's views.

What emerges from a careful reading of Stimson's diary, his memorandum of April 25 to Truman, a summary by Groves of the meeting, and Truman's recollections is an argument for overall caution in American diplomatic relations with the Soviet Union: it was an argument against any showdown. Since the atomic bomb was potentially the most dangerous issue facing the postwar world and since the most desirable resolution of the problem was some form of international control, Soviet cooperation had to be secured. It was imprudent, Stimson suggested, to pursue a policy that would preclude the possibility of international cooperation on atomic-energy matters after the war ended. Truman's overall impression of Stimson's argument was that the secretary of war was "at least as much concerned with the role of the atomic bomb in the shaping of history as in its capacity to shorten the war." These were indeed Stimson's dual concerns on April 25, and he could see no conflict between them.

Despite the profound consequences Stimson attributed to the development of the new weapon, he had not suggested that Truman reconsider its use against Japan. Nor had he thought to mention the possibility that chances of securing Soviet postwar cooperation might be diminished if Stalin did not receive a commitment to international control prior to an attack. The question of why these alternatives were overlooked naturally arises. Perhaps what Frankfurter once referred to as Stimson's habit of setting "his mind at one thing like the needle of an old victrola caught in a single groove" may help to explain his not mentioning these possibilities. Yet Bush and Conant never raised them either. Even Niels Bohr had made a clear distinction between the bomb's wartime use and its postwar impact on diplomacy. "What role it [the atomic bomb] may play in the present war," Bohr had written to Roosevelt in July 1944, was a question "quite apart" from the overriding concern: the need to avoid an atomic arms race.

The preoccupation with winning the war obviously helped to create this seeming dichotomy between the wartime use of the bomb and the potential postwar diplomatic problems with the Soviet Union raised by its development. But a closer look at how Bohr and Stimson each defined the nature of the diplomatic problem created by the bomb suggests that for the secretary of war and his advisers (and ultimately for the president they advised) there was no dichotomy at all. Bohr apprehended the meaning of the new weapon even before it was developed, and he had no doubt that scientists in the Soviet Union would also understand its profound implications for the postwar world. He was also certain that they would interpret the meaning of the development to Stalin just as scientists in the United States and Great Britain had explained it to Roosevelt and Churchill. Thus the diplomatic problem, as Bohr analyzed it, was not the need to convince Stalin that the atomic bomb was an unprecedented weapon that threatened the life of the world but the need to assure the Soviet leader that he had nothing to fear from the circumstances of its development. By informing Stalin during the war that the United States intended to cooperate with him in neutralizing the bomb through international control, Bohr reasoned that its wartime use could be considered apart from postwar problems.

Stimson approached the problem rather differently. Although he believed that the bomb

"might even mean the doom of civilization or it might mean the perfection of civilization" he was less confident than Bohr that the weapon in an undeveloped state could be used as an effective instrument of diplomacy. Until its "actual certainty [was] fixed," Stimson considered any prior approach to Stalin as premature. But as the uncertainties of impending peace became more apparent and worrisome, Stimson, Truman, and the secretary of state-designate, James F. Byrnes, began to think of the bomb as something of a diplomatic panacea for their postwar problems. Byrnes had told Truman in April that the bomb "might well put us in a position to dictate our own terms at the end of the war." By June, Truman and Stimson were discussing "further *quid pro quos* which should be established in consideration for our taking them [the Soviet Union] into [atomic-energy] partnership." Assuming that the bomb's impact on diplomacy would be immediate and extraordinary, they agreed on no less than "the settlement of the Polish, Rumanian, Yugoslavian, and Manchurian problems." But they also concluded that no revelation would be made "to Russia or anyone else until the first bomb had been successfully laid on Japan." Truman and Stimson based their expectations on how they saw and valued the bomb; its use against Japan, they reasoned, would transfer this view to the Soviet Union.

Was an implicit warning to Moscow, then, the principal reason for deciding to use the atomic bomb against Japan? In light of the ambiguity of the available evidence the question defies an unequivocal answer. What can be said with certainty is that Truman, Stimson, Byrnes, and several others involved in the decision consciously considered two effects of a combat demonstration of the bomb's power: first, the impact of the atomic attack on Japan's leaders, who might be persuaded thereby to end the war; and second, the impact of that attack on the Soviet Union's leaders, who might then prove to be more cooperative. But if the assumption that the bomb might bring the war to a rapid conclusion was the principal motive for using the atomic bomb, the expectation that its use would also inhibit Soviet

diplomatic ambitions clearly discouraged any inclination to question that assumption.

Policy makers were not alone in expecting a
military demonstration of the bomb to have a
salubrious effect on international affairs. James
Conant, for example, believed that such a demonstration would further the prospects for international control. "President Conant has written
me," Stimson informed the news commentator
Raymond Swing in February 1947, "that one of
the principal reasons he had for advising me that
the bomb must be used was that that was the only
way to awaken the world to the necessity of abolishing war altogether." And the director of the
atomic-energy laboratory at the University of
Chicago made the same point to Stimson in June
1945: "If the bomb were not used in the present
war," Arthur Compton noted, "the world would
have no adequate warning as to what was to be
expected if war should break out again." Even
Edward Teller, who has publicly decried the attack on Hiroshima and declared his early opposition to it, adopted a similar position in July 1945.
"Our only hope is in getting the facts of our
results before the people," he wrote to his colleague, Leo Szilard, who was circulating a petition among scientists opposing the bomb's use.
"This might help to convince everybody that the
next war would be fatal," Teller noted. "For this
purpose actual combat use might even be the best
thing."

Thus by the end of the war the most influential
and widely accepted attitude toward the bomb
was a logical extension of how the weapon was
seen and valued earlier—as a potential instrument of diplomacy. Caught between the remnants of war and the uncertainties of peace, scientists as well as policy makers were trapped by the
logic of their own unquestioned assumptions. By
the summer of 1945 not only the conclusion of
the war but the organization of an acceptable
peace seemed to depend upon the success of the
atomic attacks against Japan. When news of the
successful atomic test of July 16 reached the president at the Potsdam Conference, he was visibly
elated. Stimson noted that Truman "was tremendously pepped up by it and spoke to me of it again

and again when I saw him. He said it gave him
an entirely new feeling of confidence." The day
after receiving the complete report of the test
Truman altered his negotiating style. According
to Churchill the president "got to the meeting
after having read this report [and] he was a
changed man. He told the Russians just where
they got on and off and generally bossed the
whole meeting." After the plenary session on July
24 Truman "casually mentioned to Stalin" that
the United States had "a new weapon of unusual
destructive force." Truman took this step in response to a recommendation by the Interim Committee, a group of political and scientific advisers
organized by Stimson in May 1945 to advise the
president on atomic-energy policy. But it is an
unavoidable conclusion that what the president
told the premier followed the letter of the recommendation rather than its spirit, which embodied
the hope that an overture to Stalin would initiate
the process toward international control. In less
than three weeks the new weapon's destructive
potential would be demonstrated to the world.
Stalin would then be forced to reconsider his diplomatic goals. It is no wonder that upon learning
of the raid against Hiroshima Truman exclaimed:
"This is the greatest thing in history."

As Stimson had expected, as a colossal reality
the bomb was very different. But had American
diplomacy been altered by it? Those who conducted diplomacy became more confident, more
certain that through the accomplishments of
American science, technology, and industry the
"new world" could be made into one better than
the old. But just how the atomic bomb would be
used to help accomplish this ideal remained unclear. Three months and one day after Hiroshima was bombed Bush wrote that the whole
matter of international relations on atomic energy "is in a thoroughly chaotic condition." The
wartime relationship between atomic-energy
policy and diplomacy had been based upon the
simple assumption that the Soviet government
would surrender important geographical, political, and ideological objectives in exchange for
the neutralization of the new weapon. As a result of policies based on this assumption Ameri-

can diplomacy and prestige suffered grievously: an opportunity to gauge the Soviet Union's response during the war to the international control of atomic energy was missed, and an atomic-energy policy for dealing with the Soviet government after the war was ignored. Instead of promoting American postwar aims, wartime atomic-energy policies made them more difficult to achieve. As a group of scientists at the University of Chicago's atomic-energy laboratory presciently warned the government in June 1945: "It may be difficult to persuade the world that a nation which was capable of secretly preparing and suddenly releasing a weapon as indiscriminate as the [German] rocket bomb and a million times more destructive, is to be trusted in its proclaimed desire of having such weapons abolished by international agreement." This reasoning, however, flowed from alternative assumptions formulated during the closing months of the war by scientists far removed from the wartime policy-making process. Hiroshima and Nagasaki, the culmination of that process, became the symbols of a new American barbarism, reinforcing charges, with dramatic circumstantial evidence, that the policies of the United States contributed to the origins of the cold war.

20

AMERICAN POLITICS AND
THE ORIGINS OF "McCARTHYISM"

ROBERT GRIFFITH

More than any other event, the post-World War II world has been dominated by the geo-political and ideological contest between the United States and the Soviet Union. Beginning, as we have just seen, during World War II itself, the Cold War made its first public appearance with Winston Churchill's "Iron Curtain" speech of 1946. That speech, which warned Americans of the imminent threat that Soviet communism posed to the "free world," joined with Harry Truman's Cold War policies to create an atmosphere of tension and misunderstanding in Soviet-American relations.

It was from this atmosphere of profound distrust between the Soviet Union and the United States that the phenomenon known as "McCarthyism" rose to dominate the American media and the minds of many historians of the era. McCarthy, a little known senator until his anti-Communist campaign made him famous, used the power of congressional inquiry to intimidate and harass political enemies and liberal intellectuals alike. Employing deceit, innuendo, falsification, and badgering, McCarthy called scores of Americans before his committee to ferret out "Communists" in all walks of life. By the time he had finished McCarthy violated nearly every civil liberty and principle of due process that undergirded American political life. In the process he destroyed the careers of thousands of government workers, writers, academics, and intellectuals. And, for all his years of persecution, he found not a single "Communist" or "Red" working to undermine American life.

The question of how the anti-American "Americanism" of McCarthy was possible has long fascinated historians. How, they have asked, were the Constitution and the civil liberties it protects so easily abrogated by a demagogue like McCarthy? Why were the American people, who had just fought a war to defend the principles of democracy, so pursuaded by the authoritarianism and intolerance of McCarthy? As Robert Griffith argues in this revisionist essay, perhaps historians have been looking in the wrong places for the answer to McCarthyism. Perhaps, he suggests, McCarthyism was not a popular movement at all.

How does Griffith's argument about the origins of McCarthyism compare with Roger Daniels' account, in Reading 18, of the decision to evacuate the Japanese during World War II? Were similar attitudes and actions apparent?

For nearly two decades American scholars and journalists have described "McCarthyism" in terms of a popular uprising, a mass movement of the "radical right" that threatened the very fabric of American society. Inchoate, irrational, it swept across the political landscape like an ele-

Reprinted from *The Specter* by Robert Griffith (New York: New Viewpoints, 1974), by permission of the publisher.

mental force of nature carrying all before it. Its sources, these scholars maintained, lay not so much in the emergent cold war, but in the "social strains" and status tensions produced by a century of modernization. McCarthyism, like populism, was seen as an attack by paranoid provincials upon the educated and the wealthy. Politicians, in this view, were but the passive instruments of the popular will, reflecting the hysteria that welled up from the grass roots. McCarthy himself, of course, was something of an exception. He was "the most gifted" demagogue in American history, succeeding where others had failed in arousing the American masses and inciting them to action "outside of and against the established channels of constitutional government."

But was McCarthyism really a popular movement? Probably not. To be sure, anti-Communism was an element in the American political culture, and popular attitudes toward Communism, conditioned as they were by several decades of misinformation and strident propaganda, were mostly negative. It is also true that public opinion polls showed a rather high level of support for McCarthy (around 35 percent for most of 1953–54), combined with frequently intolerant attitudes toward nonconformists and dissenters. But popular intolerance and anti-Communism, however important, have tended to be constants. Even in the supposedly radical thirties, for example, most Americans seemed to favor denying freedom of speech, press, and assembly to native Communists. What needs to be explained, therefore, is not the mere existence of such attitudes, but how, during the late 1940's and early 1950's, they were mobilized and became politically operational.

Second, as even Seymour Martin Lipset and other proponents of the "radical right" thesis admit, intense negative feelings about McCarthy were usually more common than strongly favorable ones. McCarthy aroused more opposition than support. Third, as Nelson Polsby has suggested in a critique of the radical right thesis, the most common characteristic of McCarthy sup-

porters was not class, religion, or ethnicity, but political affiliation. Support for McCarthy was strongest among Republicans. Socioeconomic factors were not unimportant—when party affiliation was held constant, those with lower status, less education, and of the Catholic faith tended to support McCarthy disproportionately. But these last factors seem clearly less significant than party. There was, moreover, no continuity between populism and McCarthyism, as some historians have argued. Indeed, as Michael Paul Rogin has shown, nearly the reverse was true—agrarian radicalism, where cohesive, contributed not to the Republican right, but to the constituency of Democratic liberalism.

Fourth, while the polls did show substantial support for McCarthy and extremely negative feelings about Communism, as well as a low level of support for the civil liberties of Communists and other political dissidents, the intensity of these feelings was apparently not very strong. When people were asked, for example, whether they favored allowing Communists to teach in their schools, the response (both in the thirties and in the fifties) was largely and unsurprisingly negative. But in 1953, at the height of the McCarthy era, when people were asked a simple, nondirective question ("What kinds of things do you worry about most?"), less than 1 percent listed the threat of Communism as a major concern and only 8 percent mentioned the tangentially related area of world problems. Even when the interviewer sought to lead the respondent ("Are there other problems you worry about or are concerned about, especially political or world problems?"), the level of concern was not great. The number expressing anxiety about Communism increased only from 1 percent to 6 percent. The number concerned over international affairs rose more substantially, from 8 percent to 30 percent. Significantly, more than half of those so questioned added nothing to their initial response. Thus, as Samuel Stouffer concluded in his 1954 study, *Communism, Conformity and Civil Liberties,* Americans were not very deeply concerned over domestic Communism. The "picture of the average American as a person with the jitters, trembling lest he find a Red under the bed, is clearly nonsense."

Finally, what is all too often overlooked is the congruence between popular attitudes toward Communism and the attitudes of influential public figures. Many prominent Republicans, for example, were constantly accusing the Roosevelt and Truman Administrations of selling out to Communism at home and abroad. Nor were such charges limited to conservatives. Some liberal Republicans, such as Senator Ralph Flanders of Vermont who would later lead the movement to censure McCarthy, believed that "our late departed saint Franklin Delano Roosevelt was soft as taffy on the subject of Communism and Uncle Joe." Even Democrats such as Massachusetts Congressman John F. Kennedy attacked the Truman Administration's foreign policies, charging that "what our young men saved [in World War II], our diplomats and our President have frittered away." The Truman Administration itself used the Red issue against Henry Wallace and the Progressives and occasionally even against the Republicans. McCarthy, the President charged at one point, was the Kremlin's "greatest asset." In denouncing Communism, then, Joe McCarthy, despite his occasional attacks on "the bright young men who are born with silver spoons in their mouths," was adopting a political issue already sanctioned by much of the nation's political leadership.

The commonly accepted portrait of McCarthyism as a mass movement and McCarthy as a charismatic leader is, thus, badly overdrawn. People were less concerned about the threat of Communism and less favorably inclined toward McCarthy than is generally thought. Support for McCarthy, moreover, was closely identified with partisan Republicanism. Finally, popular attitudes about Communism generally mirrored the views of many prominent political leaders, and McCarthy's use of the issue was unexceptional.

But if McCarthyism is not to be understood primarily in terms of popular passion, then how do we explain the contentious and tumultuous politics of the mid-twentieth century? A partial answer to this problem involves a political definition of McCarthyism and, as Michael Paul Rogin has suggested, the actions and inactions of political elites. McCarthyism may not have been only a political phenomenon; it may indeed have reflected the "social strains" of modern American society, as Talcott Parsons and others have maintained. But it was primarily a product of the political system and its leaders. The latter did not simply respond to popular protest, but rather helped to generate the very sense of concern and urgency that came to dominate the decade.

This is not to argue that the politics of McCarthyism was born solely of the postwar period. There was a long history of anti-radicalism in America, a history produced both by conservative resistance to social change and by nativist fears of strangers in the land. It was not a history created by protean mass movements, however, but by the complicated interplay of political manipulation and popular myth and stereotype. The Red Scare of 1919–20 is instructive in this regard both as analogy and as legacy.

The Red Scare was made possible by hostile popular attitudes toward Communists and other radicals—what has been called the "anti-Communist persuasion." The intolerant atmosphere of World War I politics, the triumph of the Bolsheviks in Russia, the organization of the American Communist Party, and widespread labor unrest all served as proximate causes. The Red Scare itself was created, however, by the vigorous activities of conservative businessmen, organized veterans, patriotic societies, and by ambitious politicians in Congress and especially in the federal government. Business organizations such as the National Association of Manufacturers, the National Metal Trades Association, the National Founders Association all worked hard to stir up public opinion against labor unions as part of their crusade for the "American plan," as they called the open shop. Conservative patriotic groups, such as the National Security League, the American Defense Society, the American Protective League, and the National Civil Federation, sought to promote 100 percent Americanism, as did the newly organized American Legion. Even the American Federation of Labor (AFL) joined the crusade, partially to stifle leftist activities within the labor movement and partially to deflect conservative attacks from the AFL. Sensational reporting by conservative newspapers, a category that included most of the American press, further aroused popular anxieties. Finally, the impulses created by these and other groups were mobilized by such politicians as Attorney General A. Mitchell Palmer and translated into political action—the Palmer raids, deportation of alien radicals, and a flood of sedition bills including one designed to attack what Palmer called "the real menace of evil-thinking." Following the federal lead, more than thirty states hurriedly passed criminal syndicalism, criminal anarchy, and red flag laws.

The Red Scare finally subsided, of course. Most Americans were probably not deeply troubled by the imminence of a red revolution and were aroused only fitfully by politicians and the press. The Red Scare left as its legacy, however, both a substantial body of law and precedent and a reinforced set of popular myths and stereotypes susceptible to future manipulation by interest groups and politicians.

During the depression thirties the rise of domestic radicalism and the reform programs of the New Deal prompted nervous conservatives to again raise the specter of Communism. Anti-Communism, of course, was a traditional tactic of conservative opponents of social reform—used in response to the general railroad strike of the 1870's, the Populists in the 1890's, and the IWW in the early 1900's. During the thirties it simply became sound conservative doctrine to attack the New Deal as the forerunner of an American bolshevism. "If Roosevelt is not a Communist today," charged Robert A. Taft of Ohio, "he is bound to become one." Roosevelt, echoed the Republican National Committee in 1936, was "the Kerensky of the American Revolutionary Movement."

In 1930 and again in 1934, Congress launched investigations into "un-American activities," and in 1938 Congressman Martin Dies, with the support of Democratic House leaders Sam Rayburn and William B. Bankhead and the endorsement of Vice President John Nance Garner, proposed the creation of a Special Committee on Un-American Activities. Approved by a vote of 191 to 41, the committee, under Dies's flamboyant leadership, set out on a celebrated search for Communists in the Roosevelt Administration. In the process it pioneered almost all of the techniques that would later be associated with Senator McCarthy. The committee's activities were generously reported by the press, and popular reaction appeared to be generally favorable. Liberal opposition to the committee, never very potent, virtually disintegrated; and by the end of the decade one-time critic John M. Coffee (Democrat-Washington) was campaigning on the slogan "The Dies Committee endorses John Coffee's reelection."

At the same time, growing concern over domestic radicalism, combined with increasing international tensions, led to a mass of anti-radical and anti-alien bills, three of which were finally enacted into law. The first of these was the McCormack Act of 1938, which required all agents of foreign governments to register with the Department of Justice and which later served as partial precedent for the Communist registration section of the McCarran Internal Security Act of 1950. The following year Congress passed the Hatch Act, which was primarily intended to restrict the political activities of federal employees, but which also excluded from federal employment members of any organization that advocated the forcible overthrow of the government. Finally, the Smith Act of 1940, designed mainly to compel the registration of aliens, also made it illegal to advocate the overthrow of the government by force or violence.

Most of these measures were sponsored and supported by anti-New Deal conservatives. The Roosevelt Administration itself, however, was an indifferent champion of civil liberties. Thus Secretary of Labor Frances Perkins confined her testimony on the Smith bill to relatively minor points, while the Justice Department, under whose jurisdiction the sedition provisions fell, did not testify at all. The Navy Department, which was responsible for placing in the bill a section aimed at pacifists that made it illegal to interfere with or influence adversely the loyalty, morale, or discipline of the armed forces, warmly supported the measure. Roosevelt himself defended the bill's sedition provisions, replying to a critic that "they can hardly be considered to constitute an improper encroachment of civil liberties in the light of the present world conditions."

The activities of the federal government inspired imitation at the state and local level. These activities peaked, as did their national models, during the "little Red Scare" of the mid-thirties and again toward the end of the decade. Spurred on by the American Legion and other zealously anti-Communist groups, a half dozen states initiated investigations of "un-American activities," and several passed bills requiring loyalty oaths for teachers. A few states sought to exclude Communists from the ballot, while others attempted, following the example of the Hatch Act, to bar from public office anyone thought to advocate the violent overthrow of the government.

Although the success of such activities often depended on the acquiescence or even passive support of liberals, the anti-Communist impulse of the thirties remained primarily anti-reformist, the product of conservative Republican and Democratic attacks on the New Deal. Its appeal was, therefore, always limited by the widespread popularity of the Roosevelt program. All this changed, however, with the advent of the cold war and the subsequent shift from domestic to international concerns.

The cold war transformed the climate of American politics, overlaying traditional political issues with a new and emotionally charged set of concerns. The growing power of the Soviet Union and its challenge to American supremacy served to focus previously diffuse fears and anxieties over Communism. So did the arrest of men and women accused of spying for the U.S.S.R. But the anti-Communist protest of the late 1940's was more than a simple response to external events. It also sprang from the goals that American leaders set for postwar foreign policy, the manner in which they perceived the Soviet challenge to that policy, and the methods they chose to meet that challenge.

For a variety of reasons—idealism, self-interest, the hubris of the very powerful—American leaders defined United States policy in sweeping terms: the creation of a global system of stability, peace, and prosperity. The Soviet challenge to this new order was seen as a threat to world peace and to American relevance. The Chamber of Commerce, for example, through its Committee on Socialism and Communism, prepared and distributed a series of pamphlets designed to expose Communists in government and labor, to discredit New Deal social legislation, and to help businessmen reassert themselves at the community level. The American Legion was even more active. Led by its Americanism Division and active at both the state and federal levels, the Legion campaigned vigorously to arouse the nation to the perils of Communism. The Legion played an important role in creating and sustaining the Special House Committee on Un-American Activities and in the establishment of "little Dies Committees" in the states. The Legion lobbied hard for new anti-Communist legislation, supporting the Mundt-Nixon Communist registration bill as well as a wide variety of restrictive measures at the state level. Finally, the Legion became deeply involved in the colorful crusade against Communism in Hollywood and in the subsequent spread of blacklisting in the film, radio, and television industries.

The Legion and the Chamber of Commerce were only two among a welter of anti-Communist organizations, which included patriotic societies such as the Daughters of the American Revolution, Catholic groups such as the Knights of Columbus and the Catholic War Veterans, ethnic groups such as the Polish-American Congress, and a host of smaller right-wing organizations. The activities of these groups included lobbying, propaganda, and on occasion picketing and other forms of public protest. The concerns of such groups were amplified by the press. The conservative McCormick, Hearst, and Gannett chains were especially active in this undertaking, though overwrought anti-Communism was not limited to them alone. As early as 1945, for example, *Life* magazine complained that "The 'fellow traveler' is everywhere, in Hollywood, on college faculties, in government bureaus, in publishing companies, in radio offices, even on the editorial staffs of eminently capitalistic journals." From here it was but a short step to the demand that such "fellow travelers" be purged from American life.

This was not, of course, "mass" politics but "interest group" politics, a typical expression of the American political culture and not an aberrational one. The group base of American politics was not aligned, as earlier scholars have suggested, against a mass politics of anti-Communism. Instead, interest groups themselves lay at the heart of the anti-Communist politics of the era.

The aggressive actions of right-wing interest groups were not, moreover, met by countervailing pressures from the left. Instead, the same broad forces that lent strength and legitimacy to the postwar right served to undermine and destroy the postwar left. In 1945 the American left was a relatively large and potentially powerful movement, which included a wide assortment of liberals, socialists, and Communists. Though scarred by the memory of past betrayals and sharply divided among themselves, these leftists nevertheless shared a consensus on two fundamental points: the necessity for radical social change at home and for a conciliatory and pacific foreign policy abroad. The rise of the cold war and the resurgence of conservatism, however, led to bitter divisions within the left over American policy toward the Soviet Union and over the role of Communism in American life. The precarious unity of the popular front was shattered, both by the Communists who repudiated the wartime leadership of Earl Browder and by cold-war liberals who supported the foreign policies of the Truman Administration and sought to purge Communists from labor unions, political parties, and other voluntary associations. The overwhelming rejection of Henry Wallace in the 1948 campaign and the emergence of Americans for Democratic

Action (ADA) marked the beginning of a new political era in which the left was in virtual eclipse and in which the distinction between liberals and conservatives became one of method and technique, not fundamental principle. Divided, demoralized, and after 1948 led by men who shared many of the anti-Communist assumptions of the right, the American left was unable to withstand the mounting demands of McCarthyite conservatives.

The political climate of postwar America was thus shaped by the cold war, by the agitation of conservative interest groups, and by the disintegration of liberalism. It remained, however, for politicians to mobilize the support necessary for a politics of anti-Communism. Foremost among such politicians were those Republican and Democratic conservatives who had championed the anti-Communist issues since the thirties and who had maintained all along that Democratic liberalism was leading the country down the road to Communism. After 1945, however, this anti-reformist impulse was joined with the new foreign policy and internal security issues bred by the cold war. Congressional conservatives now charged that the Roosevelt and Truman Administrations were "soft" on Communism abroad and tolerant of subversion and disloyalty at home; and beginning in 1945 they launched a series of investigations into Communist activities designed in part to embarrass the government.

The frequency of such investigations was one measure of the rise of the Communist issue in American politics. There were four investigations during the 79th Congress (1945–47); twenty-two during the Republican 80th Congress (1947–49); twenty-four during the 81st Congress (1949–51); thirty-four during the 82nd Congress (1951–53); and fifty-one, an all-time high, during the Republican 83rd Congress (1953–55). Throughout the forties most of these investigations were conducted by the House Committee on Un-American Activities, led, following the retirement of Martin Dies, by J. Parnell Thomas (Republican-New Jersey) and by John S. Wood (Democrat-Georgia). More important, the focus and character of these investigations changed. Before December 1948 most of HUAC's investigations seemed to be linked to domestic concerns —the committee's primary targets were left-wing New Deal personnel, New Deal agencies such as the Federal Theatre Project and the Office of Price Administration, trade unions whose leadership included Communists, and Hollywood. But after 1948, the year in which Whittaker Chambers accused Alger Hiss first of having been a Communist and then, later, of having spied for the Soviet Union, the committee began increasingly to emphasize the internal security issues of espionage, subversion, and "Communists in government."

The Communist issue was injected into the 1946 elections and was apparently a factor in the Republican triumph, especially among urban Catholics. In 1947–48 the Truman Administration responded to these pressures by justifying its foreign policies with a crusading anti-Communist rhetoric, by instituting a federal loyalty-security program, by prosecuting Communist party leaders under the Smith Act, and in general by stressing its own firm anti-Communist credentials. Indeed, by 1948 the Administration had succeeded, if only temporarily, in using the Communist issue to its own advantage against both the Progressives and the Republicans. Crusades, however, are more easily begun than halted, and by early 1950 those conservative politicians whom Truman had sought to outflank once again held the initiative, now denouncing the Administration for the "loss" of China and demanding a sweeping purge within the government.

The rise of anti-Communism as an issue in national politics was accompanied by the growth of a derivative anti-Communist politics at the state and local levels. In part this was because many of the organizations that had agitated for restrictive measures at the federal level were also active in the states and in the communities. Some of these groups, the Chamber of Commerce and the American Legion, for example, labored not only to arouse others to the menace of Communism, but also to popularize techniques and methods for combating it. The Chamber sponsored anti-Communist seminars for local businessmen, while the American Legion held conferences for state legislators anxious to learn what the federal government and other states were doing to safeguard the Republic. Catholic Church groups and the conservative Hearst press also helped agitate the issue, as did the coterie of staff and witnesses that surrounded the House Committee on Un-American Activities.

More important, state legislatures responded almost slavishly to the force of federal law and precedent and to the anxieties aroused by national leaders. Anti-radical legislation was not, of course, new to most states. Yet what was remarkable about the great outpouring of the late forties was that so many legislatures acted at the same time and in the same way. In 1949, for example, the Maryland legislature passed a Subversive Activities Act, popularly known as the Ober Law. There was little original in the new law, however, for it had been drawn from the Smith Act of 1940, from Truman's Loyalty Program of 1947, and from portions of the Mundt-Nixon bill then pending before Congress. The Ober Law was in turn copied in part or entirely by the states of Mississippi, New Hampshire, Washington, and Pennsylvania. In the case of Pennsylvania, the legislature in 1951 established as the criteria for dismissing state employees not the Ober Law's standard—"reasonable grounds . . . to believe that any person is a subversive person"—but instead "reasonable doubt as to the loyalty of the person involved." The Maryland law had followed the criteria set forth in Truman's March 1947 loyalty order (Ex. Order 9835); the Pennsylvania legislature incorporated a generally unheralded but highly significant change in that criteria, in effect reversing the burden of proof, which Truman had ordered in April 1951 (Ex. Order 10241).

During the late forties, nearly thirty states enacted laws seeking to bar from public employment those who advocated the violent overthrow of the government, or who belonged to organizations which so advocated. In only one instance did such a state statute predate the Truman loyalty order; all of them, of course, came after the

1939 Hatch Act, which had provided such restrictions for federal employment. The Attorney General's list, institutionalized by Truman's 1947 loyalty order, was quickly adopted as a test of loyalty by states (including Arizona, New York, Michigan, Texas, Oklahoma), by municipalities (among them Detroit and New York City), and even by private employers (including the Columbia Broadcasting System). Following the passage in September 1950 of the McCarran Internal Security Act, more than a half dozen states rushed to enact so-called Communist Control Laws. Even cities passed municipal ordinances directed against Communists.

Thus state and local anti-Communist legislation, though widespread, is best understood as a reflection, not a cause, of national priorities. Unlike populism, the impact of which was felt first at the local and state level and only later at the national level, the politics of anti-Communism originated at the national level and then spread to the states.

By 1950, then, political leaders had succeeded, through the manipulation of popular myths and stereotypes, in creating a mood conducive to demagogues such as Joseph R. McCarthy. The Wisconsin senator's crude attacks on American policy and policymakers resonated through the political system not because of their uniqueness, but because of their typicality. To call this political impulse "McCarthyism," however, is to exaggerate the senator's importance and to misunderstand the politics that he came to symbolize. McCarthy was the product of anti-Communist politics, not its progenitor. Had he never made that speech in Wheeling, West Virginia, had his name never become a household word, what people came to call "McCarthyism" would nevertheless have characterized American politics at the mid-century.

21

THE NEW FREEDOM: LOS ANGELES SINCE 1920

SAM BASS WARNER

The 1920 federal population census revealed an important fact about America: for the first time in its history the majority of Americans lived in cities rather than rural communities. This announcement of an urbanized America was received by many people with considerable foreboding. What would this shift in the population distribution mean? What would become of the rural values of individual choice and independence that had fortified American culture since colonial days?

In part these concerns were a result of the peculiar nature of urban geography in America. Until the mid-nineteenth century most American cities were dense clusters of homes, shops, and warehouses where men and women of different races, classes, and ethnic groups were in daily public contact with one another. Then, with the development of street railways in the third quarter of the nineteenth century, elite and middle-class urban dwellers moved into the suburban complexes that grew up along the trolley routes. By the turn of the twentieth century this exodus left the central city and industrial areas to the immigrant working classes whose low wages precluded their escape to the suburbs. Thus, when Americans conjured up images of an urban America in 1920, their referent was the increasingly dilapidated and impoverished inner-city ghettos that the "streetcar suburbs" had created.

If early twentieth-century urban residents were prisoners of the geography of their cities, forced to live and work in close proximity to mass transit lines, urban growth in the West offered an alternative line of development. As Sam Bass Warner argues in this essay, Los Angeles lacked the feature most typical of eastern and mid-western cities: a central, downtown area. Reflecting the more diverse and decentralized culture of southern California, Los Angeles was more a collection of local communities than a traditional city. As Warner suggests, this decentralized structure and the freeway system it encouraged made possible a greater freedom in the choice of residence, place of work, and avenues of recreation than was possible in the old-style centralized city. Los Angeles became the prototype for a new type of modern urban community.

Do you think that life in Los Angeles, as portrayed by Warner, was indeed more free than that in Toledo under Samuel "Golden Rule" Jones, described by Peter Frederick in Reading 11, or in Boss Cox's Cincinnati, as depicted by Zane L. Miller in Reading 5? How do Warner's proposals for federal planning and control of urban development stand up to today's political realities? What do his proposals tell us about the period of the late 1960s and early 1970s when this essay was written?

Our great urban conglomerations offer to the mass of people who inhabit them an illusively wide range of choices, whether of a way of life or of work among a diversity of social institutions. A high level of choice has always been a peculiar attraction of cities, and the wealthy have long flocked to them to enjoy the stimulation of variety and the satisfactions of freedom of personal expression. Even in colonial times the planters of South Carolina built town houses in Charleston, and mill owners and mining czars moved to New York and Chicago to escape the constrictions of the towns in which they had founded their fortunes. For the masses, however, whether white-collar or blue-, urban life was always severely constrained by long working hours, tight schedules of time and commutation, and the strict conformity required to hold a steady job, advance a career, or belong in a "nice" neighborhood. As a nation we have not yet traveled far from these conditions, and the blacks and the poor still struggle within this old framework to be admitted to the freedom of our cities. These are the unique qualities and terrible failures of our urban areas. Nevertheless in many basic structures of today's cities there is the potential of a range of personal choices and social freedoms for all city dwellers if we would only extend the paths of freedom that our urban system has been creating.

In brief, since 1920 the basic technology, transportation, urban markets, business institutions, and land-use structures of the growing national network of cities have all expanded by means of successive inventions and investments until the entire elaborate modern urban complex has begun to reveal an increased potentiality for personal and social choices. The automobile did not by any means initiate the suburbanization of the American city, but it did enable suburbanization to take on a new low-density, multicentered form. Neither did the truck build the nation's manufacturing belts, but by lengthening the distance of cheap short-haul freight traffic it did enable the manufacturing belts to be reorganized into the far-flung communication regions we now identify as megalopolises. The corporation was very much a product of the nineteenth century, but its lusty growth in the soil of national urban markets brought decentralization with it, thereby placing more authority and autonomy in the hands of some of its employees. The turn of the national economy toward services from production began with the introduction of machine manufacture, but in our own time the proliferation of urban services has promoted and sustained a giant middle class without forcing it into a single role of corporate bureaucracy.

During the past half century these extensions from the past have mired our society in a series of contradictions and confusions which we must now come to understand if we are to find policies that will enable us to realize humane solutions. Every component of the forces that bear upon the American urban system, as well as the system itself, harbors twin potentials—for mass repression or for the expansion of popular freedoms. Science and technology can be directed toward war and manipulation or toward services for everyday living; the multiple ways of modern transportation can be either an escape route for the affluent or a means of expanding everyone's horizons; the service economy can be directed toward world domination or toward everyday human needs; the national network of cities can be linked only to the enrichment of local business and political elites or can become the foundation for broadened employment and equalized living standards; the reach and complexity of urban markets can be tied only to private profit or can provision a universal public; private and public corporations can be instruments for bureaucratic control or levers to release personal and group autonomy; the abundant land of the megalopolis can be restricted to the present unequal contest between the classes and races or can become the site of humane physical environments. Our history shows that the capacity of the American urban system for war production, private profit, and inequality, and for the ignoring and infliction of deprivation and suffering is seemingly limitless and certainly enduring. What is new in our time is the enlarged potential of the system to promote the freedom of all the groups within it. . . .

The proliferation of technology and transportation has strongly influenced both the national economy and its network of cities. The continued application of science and technology to agriculture and mining has brought an increasingly dramatic decline in employment in that sector of the economy and a concomitant strong outmigration from the rural United States. The sheer productivity of mechanized manufacture, despite the multiplication of products and the vast increase in the volume of factory-made goods for producers and consumers, has allowed the ratio of the labor force engaged in that sector to fall slightly too. Trade, services, transportation, and government have become the hallmarks of today's economy because two-thirds of the labor force is engaged in these activities. Science, technology, and transportation have made possible the service and military economy that now obtains.

The changing focus of the national economy has meant a corresponding adjustment in the network of cities. Urbanization in general was encouraged because the growing trade-service-transport-government activities were themselves the specialties of cities. Thus the population of the United States, North and South, East and West, grew increasingly metropolitanized. Ports and trading centers, on both coasts and along the Great Lakes and in the South, prospered in particular. If we measure the size of cities solely in terms of the inhabitants within their formal political boundaries, Houston rose to be the nation's sixth most populous city, Dallas the eighth, and San Antonio passed Boston and St. Louis, while the size of Memphis, New Orleans, Seattle, and Phoenix each exceeded that of Pittsburgh—the archetypical city of the former era of the industrial metropolis. . . .

The complexity of manufacturing in the new economy was compatible with the dispersal of urban population from old central cities, but at the same time it fostered a concentration of population within large multicity regions. Thus the old manufacturing belts of the Northeast and Midwest, and the new one in southern California, prospered as the urbanized manufacturing regions of the United States. The major trend in manufacturing locations since 1920 has been to seek sites near the final markets for consumer goods and to search out effective placement in the midst of regions where producers' goods can be bought and sold easily. Both trends favored the old manufacturing belts because these were huge agglomerations of individual consumers and also buyers and sellers of producers' goods. The mass migration to southern California and the succession of wars since 1941 have transformed that region into another such belt. The diffusion of population and enterprise within these three regions has altered their former patterns of mill town and industrial metropolis established in the railroad era. The megalopolis, a gigantic continuous band of urbanized territory with towns, cities, and metropolises embedded within it, is the emergent urban manifestation of the new economy and new transportation. The Boston–New York–Washington megalopolis has functioned at least since 1950 as a regional city; the Pittsburgh–Cleveland–Detroit–Chicago megalopolis seems to be a recrudescence of the old Midwestern manufacturing belt but in a form that favors growth along the path of the region's largest metropolises; while the third, stretching from San Diego through Los Angeles to San Francisco, has become recognizable as a growing entity only in the last decade. The megalopolises are of about equal length. Each of them extends 454 to 470 miles, and all of them are abundantly provided with transportation. They are in every case industrially diversified and encompass thousands of specialized firms so that the benefits of complementarity obtain for almost any economic enterprise, from steel mills to toy manufacture, throughout the regions.

The channeling of national metropolitan growth into the formation of the three megalopolises has had two effects upon the organization of urban business: first, corporate enterprise has expanded and altered its management form; second, the service economy has nurtured an enormous class of urban professionals and small businessmen—retailers, furniture dealers, doctors, lawyers, insurance agents, and every kind of home and business service establishment. Both developments contain possibilities for a more humane urban society and equally for the further concentration of power exercised for the benefit of a minority.

The large corporation, as it added more products and services and reached ever farther afield for customers, was forced to abandon its traditional centralized, departmentalized form. Instead it adopted various adjustments that resulted in a general way in a hierarchy where a central office of staff executives assessed and assisted a series of semiautonomous divisions. This decentralized, divisional structure owed its origins to a management crisis of the 1920s. In the four cases that have been studied in detail (General Motors, Du Pont, Standard Oil of New Jersey, and Sears, Roebuck) a growing diversity of operations finally broke the centralized form. General Motors made many different models of cars—unlike Ford with its Model T—and also turned out refrigerators, electrical equipment, and an extensive line of parts and accessories. Du Pont branched out in the first years of the century from gunpowder and blasting materials into chemicals and paints. Standard Oil of New Jersey undertook international oil prospecting, oil transport, and refining, along with the domestic and foreign marketing of a full range of petroleum products from automobile gasolines to fuel oils and the old staple, kerosene. Sears, Roebuck, already a profitable mail-order house, in 1925 established a national chain of retail outlets to offset declining sales and to reach out to the growing suburban markets. . . .

Decentralization today takes a number of forms. The semiautonomous divisional style of the 1920s is favored by the new conglomerates, which are aggregations of capital assembled by a team of central-office executives who seek to purchase independent businesses for profitable investment. If the newly acquired business proves to be well managed, its executives continue their work as an autonomous division of the conglomerate. This is true for instance, of Litton Industries of Beverly Hills, California, a firm that began in 1954 in electronics and now deals in typewriters, calculators, office furniture and

equipment, surgical instruments, X-ray machines, motion-picture cameras, and automatic revenue-collecting machines, and also operates paper mills, printing plants, and Great Lakes shipping lines. It manages its diverse affairs through fifty separate divisions, each largely autonomous.

The reach to the ultimate consumer has meant market-oriented decentralization for manufacturing firms as well as for retailers. The goal of management has been to adjust production to sales as closely as possible and thereby to reduce losses sustained by the accumulation of unwanted and slow-moving inventories. Abundant long-haul transportation enabled manufacturing firms to maintain specialized production plants, each located for its specialty's best advantage, where components could be manufactured and then assembled into the final product near the final markets. Cheap intracity transportation encouraged such a strategy; one sales-warehousing-assembly plant could serve an entire metropolis or a cluster of them. Thus a famous brand of St. Louis beer no longer travels by refrigerator car from a single brewery to scattered urban markets but is brewed in Tampa, Newark, Houston, and Los Angeles and marketed regionally from these points. Chevrolets are assembled at Arlington (Texas), Baltimore (Maryland), Doraville (Georgia), Janesville (Wisconsin), Leeds and St. Louis (Missouri), South Gate and Van Nuys (California), North Tarrytown (New York), Willow Run (Michigan), and Wilmington (Delaware). Here, then, were some of the multitude of plants and offices that have sought suburban locations since World War II. Retail chains like Sears, Roebuck and Montgomery Ward have evolved a commercial style that they call metropolitan management. A metropolis like Los Angeles may have a dozen retail stores belonging to one of these chains, each store located in a regional shopping center. The sheer volume of Los Angeles sales, as well as the peculiarities of that particular market as opposed to the Chicago or New York demands, justified the establishment of a metropolitan management team responsible for operations in that area. For general merchandising, unlike the distribution and sales of a limited range of products like automobiles or beer, the metropolis has proved to be a more feasible unit than the sprawling megalopolis.

In these cases of decentralization it is easy to see how a measure of public responsibility could be introduced into the national corporate structure. The special interests of the metropolis or megalopolis in employment, plant, office, and store location, and the need of workers and managers for autonomy, could be expressed in management committees of public officials and employees without disrupting the efficiency of the corporation since the current dispersal of the company mirrors the structure of the national network of cities. . . .

The outcome of five decades of these contradictory decentralized and centralized business trends is a mixture of benefit and condemnation for the urban worker and city dweller. Thanks to the sheer growth of big business, industrial work, which in the preceding century was the scene of the most unrestrained exploitation of workers, has now become bureaucratized. Planned production, market power, and manipulation even out the employment season for corporate workers so that they can be reasonably sure of an approximate yearly income. National unions, such as the United Auto Workers, represent their members as they confront the giant corporations in conflicts over wages, local plant discipline, mechanization, and working conditions. The countervailing union power, however, suffers all the problems of responsibility that confront its corporate adversary. The key issues revolve around working conditions in the individual plants, and they find their expression in the union locals. In recent years large national and international unions have proved cumbersome and inadequate to negotiate these issues for their members. Strikes that have been settled to the satisfaction of the central union office and the corporate headquarters have dragged on for weeks and months in scattered plants around the country. Moreover, most unions have been reluctant to enter in a positive way into the decisions of plant location and production design and prefer to content

themselves with a responsive role, approving or disapproving each individual innovative machine or job description. Yet the high level of modern technology offers many alternative paths to efficient production. The assembly line is not the only way to make cars, cut meat, or assemble TV sets. Although no group or institution in the nation, the megalopolis, or the metropolis takes as its charge the establishment of more humane working conditions, the riots and strikes of the past and the boredom, absenteeism, and local union rebellions of the present repeatedly emphasize that working conditions are and always have been one of the three or four determinants of the quality of urban life.

White-collar workers, although not usually unionized, have profited most from the trends of the economy over the past half century. Opportunities abounded as white-collar jobs rapidly increased. Large-scale production and sales required more and more research, engineering, cost accounting, advertising, and promotion, and the white-collar force has accordingly advanced at a reasonably regular pace in the nation's corporate bureaucracies. Scientific management, especially for middle management, has also come to the aid of the white-collar worker. Social scientists have demonstrated that when decisions must be made in an environment of rapid change, efficiency is promoted by individual and group autonomy, open communications from those lower in status to those above, and a general climate of trust and cooperation. Modern business thrives in situations of rapid change, and management jobs have accordingly multiplied, much to the pleasure and profit of the middle-class city dwellers who work in them. The problem for the city and the society as a whole has been that these benign and inherently more pleasurable working roles have not been extended more widely. Bureaucratic routine and mechanized production are the rule for most tasks in American business and government, and they are successful after their fashion. Autonomous, responsible white- and blue-collar work for nonmanagers will not become generally available until the masses of the office and factory workers insist upon it. In fact, so long as Americans regard their working hours as an unavoidably unpleasant period by which they purchase evening and weekend pleasures, they will not find the civility and autonomy in their jobs that they insist upon in their leisure and home environments. One need only contemplate the human impairment and cultural poverty of a large industrial city like Detroit to appreciate the enormous costs of our present methods of doing business.

The disadvantages of today's style are notorious. Although our plants, offices, and schools may be less harsh than their predecessors, more uniform and equitable in their treatment of people, less authoritarian and more temperate, a fog of boredom tinged with resentment fills the factories, salesrooms, and offices of the metropolis. Much work is dull routine. Much work in sales and supervision consists of selling one's own personality and manipulating those of others. Indeed, some of the new findings in social science have been used to manipulate employees for the benefit of management. Thompson Ramo Wooldridge Systems, for instance, is currently using T-groups, a technique of social psychology, as a means of reducing payrolls. In the factory, close tolerances and repetitive tasks make for ceaseless discipline without the compensating psychological release that might be provided by control over one's pace or by self-determination through one's craft. Everywhere there is an acceptance of real personal powerlessness and a dependence upon the pecking order of bureaucratically defined jobs. Sociologists speak of the alienation of the modern American; radio and television trumpet the fun culture. The advertising and market manipulation that ensures the corporate worker's position seeks also to alleviate his alienation by urging him to deaden his complaints in repeated consumerism. . . .

Just as Americans have failed to make full use of the flexibility of the dispersed metropolis, so they have failed to realize the social opportunities of the corporate society. The modern corporation has all the organized power necessary for the democratic and socially responsible organization of its enterprise. The capacity of the central staff to control accounting, planning, engineering,

product design, market research, and capital allocation demonstrates that our society could manage the whole range of planned production. The successful splitting of the centralized firm into semiautonomous divisions suggests that the worst features of mindless uniformity could be overcome by giving more divisional authority to workers and regions where the corporation operates. In the last half century, while the corporations have been maturing, the missing element has been the urge on the part of citizens to make the private corporations public. Yet it seems clear that if we are to regain control of our society we must find ways to make our corporations into public enterprises.

Underlying the whole issue of the relationship between private corporations and urban life runs the unanswered question of legitimacy. What are the legitimate goals of these ubiquitous institutions and to whom should they be held responsible? Hitherto Americans have subscribed to the belief that the function of private enterprises was to make money for their managers and investors. Over the years unions and government regulations have defined limits within which this activity should take place, yet neither unions nor government agencies deny that profit is the ultimate justification for corporate endeavor. Corporations are now too important to society to be allowed to continue in this limited direction; profit should be but one test of their effectiveness. So long as profit remains the ultimate measure of achievement, the products and services of corporations will fail to build a humane society because they will take on only those tasks in the society which are profitable and will indeed rush toward those that are most profitable to the exclusion of essential considerations. Thus in the midst of urban racism, poverty, and neglect, unemployment, housing shortages, malfunctioning education and health services, world starvation, and a host of other social ills which call out for attention, General Mills has decided that its future prosperity lies in developing a line of games and hobbies. The decision may be logical enough, given the company's past organization, present talents, and the likelihood of a large middle-class market, but it hardly sets in motion an activity to which society at the moment needs to devote its managerial talent or inherited capital. So it is down through the list of corporate contributions to our consumer society. Most products are harmless, and each of them is useful and satisfying in its own way, yet the sum of all the new cosmetics, cake mixes, lawn foods, appliances, home and office furnishings, and sports cars constitutes a vast misapplication of human resources and accumulated capital. The high but extremely uneven standard of living which the corporations have helped to create represents—like the corporations themselves—an appalling default in bringing about the humane and inclusive urban society that might be appearing.

The already large class of professionals and small businessmen has expanded with the rising standard of living, and the shift of the economy into retailing and services has helped to screen private corporations from public notice. For example, in metropolitan Los Angeles in 1967 there were 801,000 proprietors and employees engaged in operating small shops and services: lumber companies, hardware stores, groceries, restaurants, gasoline stations, clothing, furniture and appliance and drug stores, motels and laundromats, dry cleaners, travel and real-estate agencies, bowling alleys, and so forth. The same year, 982,000 persons were engaged in manufacturing enterprises, but they were laboring in establishments with an average of fifty-two employees, while the retailers were working in establishments that averaged 7.3 and the service people five. In other words, besides the highly organized manufacturing workers in the modern metropolis stands a group of workers, almost as numerous, who follow the working patterns of the early nineteenth-century city. This modern petty-bourgeois class is deeply antisocialist, and it regards all social regulation and control as a threat to its personal and economic freedom. As C. Wright Mills observed some years ago, this class of professionals and businessmen defends the managers of large plants and offices in the local chambers of commerce and before local government agencies. It uncritically supports the

use of public money for the assistance of business as a boon to prosperity and progress, obstructing all efforts toward local and regional planning which might deny a firm its desires. As a class it opposes national economic planning unless it takes the form of public works, tax write-offs, and subsidies. Thus today's urban business institutions present an ugly paradox—the corporate form holds a real potential for successful public ownership or public management, while the growing retail and service sector continues in the mold of the ideology of the early nineteenth century. The corporation is susceptible to dedication to public goals; but the second group, although it could be a key element in a revived localism, is opposed to every effort to make public goals the aim of successful economic enterprise.

The form of the corporation has always been and will continue to be determined by the ways in which the society and the economy are developing. We stand at a moment of unique opportunity. If strong steps are not taken now to socialize these institutions, it seems probable that the personnel of government and private management will merge into interlocking bureaucracies placed beyond the reach of democratic supervision. Such at least is the tendency today; it is the meaning of the outcry against the military-industrial complex and the reason for the frustration of consumer and ecological reforms. If we fail to socialize soon we will have lost, through foolish devotion to our cherished myth of private property, a historic opportunity to gain social responsibility for and democratic control of the building of our society and its cities.

Los Angeles, city of war material, swimming pools, and smog, wonderfully exemplifies the urban consequences stemming from the change in structure of the national economy and its institutions. It is par excellence a city of the past half century. In 1920 the city proper had grown to be the tenth largest in the nation, about the same size as Pittsburgh (Los Angeles, 577,000; Pittsburgh, 588,000), and its metropolitan population had reached almost a million. Thanks largely to the prosperity and land rush of the twenties, the metropolitan area sustained a population of 2,-785,000 on the eve of World War II, and the wartime infusion of business and workers raised this figure to 9,475,000 in 1970. Today Los Angeles is the second largest cluster of population and the third largest manufacturing center in the United States (Chicago Consolidated Statistical Area 7,612,000; New York CSA 16,179,000). It has now become the economic capital of the Pacific and the Southwest, the heart of the fast-growing San Diego–San Francisco megalopolis.

Like all great American cities, Los Angeles grew not by accretion of economic functions taken from other cities but by being geographically located in the center of new developments. Chicago rose with the settlement of the Midwest, Los Angeles with the waves of migration to California and the Southwest. Moreover, new resources and industries fired its growth. The railroads, the prairie farms, the forests of Michigan and Wisconsin, and Lake Superior ore had made Chicago a center for transportation, food processing, lumber, steel, and machinery. Similarly oil, a warm sunny climate, and the airlines made Los Angeles the capital of petroleum refining, of the national distribution of fruit and vegetables, and of movies, as well as the focal point of the nation's aircraft, aerospace, and war-research industries. Migrants added banks, stores, and residentiary industries of all kinds, and the local specialties encouraged complementary industries, until by the fifties the city was functioning as a widely diversified metropolis given over to manufacturing, commerce, service, and war production.

During the twenties and thirties, irrigated agriculture, oil discoveries, the motion-picture boom, and waves of Midwestern and Texas migrants seeking a pleasant place to live and work swelled the city's size. Oil revenues in part financed the construction of an ocean port at Long Beach, and favorable rail connections to the Southwest and the East (the city lies a few miles closer to Chicago than San Francisco does) made Los Angeles a preferred site for warehouses and branch plants of national corporations. During the twenties, for example, both Ford and Goodyear built Pacific plants there, and many other firms followed suit. But the city was handicapped by the circumstance that its factories were some two thousand miles from the western edge of the Midwestern manufacturing belt at St. Louis. Therefore the sectors of the metropolitan economy devoted to general machinery and metal-working—sectors of vital importance to a fully elaborated industrial region—did not develop during these years. Los Angeles in 1940, for all its impressive size, was not yet committed to manufacturing.

Thirty years of almost continuous hot and cold wars ended this anomaly. Tremendous aircraft orders from the federal government not only caused that particular industry to shoot ahead, but federal sponsorship of aerospace research and all sorts of war material fostered supportive manufacturing, until today the city is the only fully diversified manufacturing region outside the belts of the Northeast and Midwest. To be sure, Los Angeles still has its agricultural, aircraft, electronic, and movie specialties, just as Chicago still concentrates on steel, machinery, and printing and New York on garments, leather, printing, electrical equipment, and national offices, but since the 1950s a full range of complementarities has been available in Los Angeles to boost further expansion.

Three special characteristics of the Los Angeles metropolis stand out by comparison with the earlier examples of New York and Chicago: its high degree of spatial freedom, its potential for a more equitable and inclusive class and racial society, and its growth in response to deliberate federal programs.

The land-use and transportation structure of Los Angeles gives glimpses of a more humane environment than we have yet enjoyed. The special factor of the city's social geography is its low density of settlement, the ease and scope of movement of the overwhelming proportion of its citizens, and its comparative lack of domination by a single downtown area. It has thus escaped the rigid core, sector, and ring structure of business and residential occupation that tyrannized the industrial metropolis and from which older cities are only now beginning to extricate themselves.

Los Angeles is an amorphous metropolis, and vast tracts of it have a rather uniform low-density settlement of five to twenty-four persons per acre. Along the Pacific in the Santa Monica and Long Beach areas and in a crescent of housing from Santa Monica through Beverly Hills to the old core city there are apartment houses and multiple-dwelling neighborhoods that resemble those in Chicago or New York. Also scattered through the metropolis, especially along its shopping strips, stand many of the motel-like courts that are the contemporary slum-tenement style of the American city; but the single-family dwelling has long been the glory of Los Angeles and the expression of its design for living. Sixty-four percent of all its occupied housing in 1967 was given over to single-family dwelling units.

The plan for a metropolis composed of single-family houses did not emerge from the drawing boards of freeway engineers; their constructions followed an already entrenched preference of the Angelenos. During the twenties three social factors had converged to establish the Los Angeles plan: the cultural preference of Americans for detached private homes, the need to supply water for burgeoning land development, and the sheer pleasure and freedom bestowed by the automobile.

Three out of four of the army of migrants who came into southern California during the early part of the twentieth century were white native-born Americans from the cities to the east and from the farms and small towns of the Midwest. City dwellers and farmers alike brought with them an ingrained tradition of the single-family house as the measure of a home and of Main Street or suburbia as the measure of satisfactory living. The American has often had to share his housing with others—in rented rooms, in two-family houses, in tenements of three, six, or more flats—but given the opportunity he has customarily sought a house of his own. Moreover, just as in the case of Chicago's middle class, in the Los Angeles region no thirst for the big-city life of skyscrapers, restaurants, and theaters has tempted him to sacrifice the privacy of a tree-shaded lawn and garden for apartment luxury or

for the urban habits of the nineteenth-century inhabitants of European or American industrial cities. In sum, people came to southern California, seeking a warm, sunlit, home-town city.

To provide these amenities in the first decades of the twentieth century in the face of the aridity of Los Angeles, residential property carried high land-preparation costs and so had to be developed in tracts of considerable size. An expensive water supply had to be meshed with public transportation to a degree unheard-of in the modest subdivisions common in Eastern cities. Speculators capitalized on the situation by building a wide-range complex of electric interurban streetcars. They hoped that their initial investment in lines that stretched from twenty to thirty-five miles out from the downtown area would be justified by massive profits from future land development and ensuing heavy traffic on their routes. Los Angeles in 1920, compared to other cities of the period, was extraordinarily extended into large-scale suburban development.

The automotive boom of the twenties carried these trends toward diffusion to modern proportions. The general ownership of automobiles and their use in commuting allowed developers to open up smaller tracts beyond walking distance from the interurbans. When these lines began to lose money from competition with automobiles and when traffic jams in downtown Los Angeles became intolerable, the municipality called for the construction of a rapid-transit system to alleviate traffic, revitalize the street railways, and save the downtown. Other cities had voted for subways in the twenties, but Los Angeles did not follow the precedents; its citizens voted down the proposals. Their city was so new and open that they had no image before them of a desirable downtown, and they had no habit of listening to the appeals of downtown business leaders. Then, too, their tradition told them that happiness lay in another style of life.

During the Great Depression the public transportation system cut back its service, and after World War II the interurban lines closed down; today the public bus lines handle a small volume of passengers—400,000 fewer than in 1939. Without the discipline of street railways, commerce drained from the core city to spread out along strips of land like Wilshire Boulevard. Suburban towns like Glendale and Pasadena established their own downtowns, and suburban shopping centers and office clusters have sprung up to form a multicentered metropolis.

The key decision in the determination of the spatial freedom of its residents came in 1939, when the Los Angeles Freeway plans were settled into a multicentered pattern. A failing public transit, serious traffic jams, and a new state statute that permitted construction of limited-access highways had prompted the City of Los Angeles to commission still another study of its transportation problems. The Works Progress Administration of the federal government carried out a traffic census, and on the basis of these findings the City of Los Angeles Transportation and Engineering Board made its recommendations; freeways would be the solution to the region's traffic difficulties. The unusual multicity and multicounty membership of the advisory board may have accounted for its metropolitan orientation. Besides Los Angeles officials, representatives from such scattered places as Glendale, Beverly Hills, Redondo Beach, Huntington Beach, Whittier, Pasadena, and the San Fernando and San Gabriel valleys sat on the board. The 1939 plan called for limited-access express highways to be laid out in the form of a giant grid, which would be capable of carrying automobile traffic both into and out of the overcrowded Los Angeles central business district and would guide it across the city without the necessity of its going through the downtown area. The principal justification for this plan was the board's recognition of the already highly dispersed character of the region. Many of its alignments were to follow the much-traveled state highways that crisscrossed the area. The report may well have reflected too the politics of the Transportation Board itself. Although no record survives of its discussions, it seems highly probable that the members from the more distant areas would not have accepted the conventional hub-and-wheel design that was at this time being proposed for old American single-core

cities, since such a plan would have drawn business away from their own centers. The board did expect, however, that Los Angeles would eventually grow to be a conventional single-centered city and that in time commuter railroads and subways would be required.

The 1939 proposal for freeways derives its historical importance from the fact that it was subsequently adopted and adapted in a succession of plans and projects. The first undertakings, begun in 1940 with the Pasadena Freeway, all converged on the downtown (the Hollywood, San Bernardino, Santa Ana, and Harbor Freeways), thereby beginning a radial scheme for serving the downtown, but wartime and postwar planning studies continued to repeat the basic grid strategy of the 1939 report. Then in 1956, when the federal government passed its Interstate Highway law, the California legislature set up a committee to establish routes for the state. The routes that were then adopted incorporated the 1939 proposal for a grid system of metropolitan freeways, and many such highways have been built in the ensuing years. The grid is still being extended at its outer margins in order to keep up with the spread of the metropolis, and it is being added to at the center to relieve traffic congestion further, but for many years now Los Angeles has enjoyed a transportation system that permits its residents to move swiftly from subcenter to subcenter over the entire region without having to go through the downtown or any lesser center.

The social consequences of the multicentered, low-density metropolitan region are manifold and are important to our urban future. First and foremost was the increase in the job choices offered the urban resident. In 1967 there were three automobiles for every seven persons in the Los Angeles region; 41 percent of the households had access to one vehicle, 44 percent had access to two or more vehicles, and only 15 percent of the households lacked a car. Such a distribution of automobiles and freeways gives the Los Angeles employee the widest choice of job opportunities ever possible in an American city. An hour's drive from any point in the region makes hundreds of possible employers accessible. A man can live in the San Fernando Valley and work in the old industrial sector of southeast Los Angeles, or he can commute from the old core-city neighborhoods to the new steel mills at Fontana. These are extreme commuting distances, to be sure, but recent studies show that blue-collar workers in particular are crisscrossing the whole area in search of the best jobs. In the past urban workers were pinned down to living next to their mills, or they purchased their economic freedom by commuting from crowded core-city working-class and slum districts along the radial lines of the streetcar system. These journeys were long, the cars crowded and slow, and transfers and waits in the cold and wet often necessary. Such trials cannot be compared with the ease of an hour's run today in a private car or car pool. In Los Angeles most commuters go directly from their home to the company parking lot, and the majority travel alone; more than 70 percent of all weekday automobile trips are taken by a single driver.

To this economic freedom must be added the social advantages that have accrued to the Los Angeles public. The greater number of car trips are not work-related at all but are undertaken for social or recreational purposes or for shopping. Thus scattered friends and relatives, long shopping strips and outlying shopping centers, the Pacific beaches, and national parks are all within easy reach of most families. At the same time the city is able to grow by continuing to build in its low-density popular single-family or low-rise apartment-court style.

Like all American cities, the Los Angeles automobile metropolis does not extend its amenities equally to all its residents but reinforces sharp differences governed by class and race. Boyle Heights, an early twentieth-century neighborhood in East Los Angeles, offers some of the attractions of small-town life to its Mexican-American residents. Watts and the black ghetto have many of the same features. Yet the poor, lacking cars and perhaps also fearful of their reception in other parts of the metropolis, do not travel over large sections of the region as residents of the San Fernando Valley might do.

Women and old people especially suffer from a dearth of cars. The women thus lack access to jobs that would boost family income, and to essential shopping and health services. For the men, transportation doesn't seem to be the problem. Once they find employment they seem to be able to purchase cars on time.

The solution to the disadvantaged position of those without cars is neither difficult nor expensive, but like all our cities Los Angeles remains heedless of the needs and suffering of its poor, its blacks, its Mexican-Americans, and its old people. After the Watts riot the transportation problems of the poor were made plain, and the state of California, with federal funding, set up a demonstration project in southeast Los Angeles to attempt to deal with the problem. A social science team intervened in behalf of the poor in several ways. They became the spokesmen of the neighborhoods before the bus companies; they waged campaigns to have route maps printed and distributed and to persuade the companies to post the schedules at the bus stops. They discovered that the last bus might leave a factory's gates a few minutes before the men finished their daily shifts; they discovered routes that could be instituted or altered to reflect the commuting habits of the residents. It seems clear from the findings of this team that the cost cutting of private and public bus companies should be monitored in every city by a political agency representing the transportation interests of those outside the circle of the automobile world. The altering of existing public transportation, however, was not sufficient. The women needed short runs along shopping strips and to shopping centers and they needed long trips in every direction to reach scattered job sites. To this end the experimental rented buses for some new regular routes and also used station wagons and cars for a kind of metropolitan taxi service to jobs at such widely dispersed destinations as Lockheed in Burbank, Douglas Aircraft at Long Beach, Torrance, and Santa Monica, American Electric at La Mirada, and Sergent-Fletcher in El Monte. The cost of these services was high, but could have been much reduced if established permanently. The demonstration project was a success, but in 1971, when the funds were gone, predictably the grant by the federal government was not renewed and the service closed down.

Judging from this experience, a few millions of dollars a year spent in maintaining an agency to represent the carless and offer its own flexible small-bus service would redress the worst of the access problems attendant on Los Angeles' unequal distribution of family income. To be sure, those without cars are the ones who suffer most from low wages, from job discrimination against women, old people, blacks, and the ill-educated, and from regional and national callousness toward the unemployed and the underemployed, but even a modest effort would be far more useful to the poor than the currently fashionable enthusiasm for rail lines. Railroads by their very nature offer high-volume service only along their own narrow strip. Los Angeles is neither a linear nor a radial city; it is a multicentered city that calls for multidestination public transportation.

Finally, although Los Angeles does not have the problem of choking traffic jams and hard-to-reach areas like those of New York, it does have a serious air-pollution problem. In view of the enormous investment and great social success of the freeways, it seems foolish not to try to eliminate the smog in similar terms. Surely the technology of the moon era is capable of manufacturing low-emission engines as an alternative to the present disgraceful pollution created by Los Angeles' 4.5 million automobiles.

Since all of the metropolises and the three megalopolises of the United States are growing into the form of Los Angeles, it is important that we understand the social potential of this diffuse layout of building. The open character of Los Angeles has resulted in a land-use structure more favorable for the achievement of racial and class justice than any that has so far existed in any large American city. This structure is only a potential for justice, however, and remains far from realization.

Los Angeles is no better than most cities when it comes to racial discrimination, segregation, and disadvantages for its poor. The county population is 10.8 percent black, 13.5 percent of Spanish surname. The isolation of blacks is almost as extreme as in Chicago. The Mexican-Americans are less rigidly segregated from the Anglo-Americans than are the blacks but nonetheless they are highly segregated. When the frustration of the black community exploded with the Watts riots of 1965, a national chain reaction was set in motion, and since that time there have been a number of Mexican-American riots expressing the conflicts of another disadvantaged community. All the hostility and failings of our society, so fully documented in 1968 by the Kerner Commission and in other reports, are part of Los Angeles as well. But if it wishes to build a more inclusive society, it has a special advantage in the availability of land for redevelopment and in abundant fringe land for new construction. The prerequisite for making good use of the land in terms of its society is a commitment by the national government and the Los Angeles public and its officials to make a decent house and neighborhood open to every resident. With such a commitment, new housing can become the framework for an inclusive urban society, rejecting the city's present mechanism for class, racial, and ethnic segregation.

The original low density of Los Angeles' construction has saved it from mortgaging its future. Its built-up areas are not so crammed with structures that new construction in old areas brings serious dislocation of present residents, as is the case in Chicago or New York. There is vacant land all over the Los Angeles region. This land is in the form of weedy lots and unused spaces, some large enough for development in their own right, some requiring some demolition of adjacent houses. If public agencies were to build on five-acre tracts they would find land, either vacant or sparsely occupied, by the hundreds of parcels all over the city. Such land is ideal for the design and construction of low-rise apartments, two-family housing, and town houses. In other words, existing styles of housing could become the basis for a massive public housing program that would not disrupt the physical fabric of the city. Federal programs for land clearance, housing, and rent subsidies allow such housing to be offered today to the fourth of the Los Angeles population who cannot afford decent housing at present prices. Such federal programs, however, would have to be so funded as to allow for a large-scale and sustained undertaking.

At least three important social consequences would be derived from such a small-parcel program. First, the chronic shortage of low-income housing would be relieved. Second, the abundance of scattered sites would enable blacks, Mexican-Americans, and the poor to choose to settle either near their present neighborhoods or in new distant sections of the city. The degree of social pioneering undertaken by any family would be according to their own choice and would not depend on the decision of public authorities. Third, the five-acre tracts would have to be designed to fit into the styles prevailing in their environs or else face strong local opposition. Perhaps this requirement that design attain at least the levels of popular taste would save the projects from the degradation of some of the philanthropic architectural styles that now stigmatize public housing.

At its fringes the Los Angeles freeway brings large tracts of vacant land within the reach of commuters. This same situation prevails in the Eastern and Midwestern megalopolis and all metropolises. Here publicly sponsored or managed new towns of 50,000 to 200,000 residents could be used as a device for increasing the residential options of black and low-income families. The key advantage of the new-town concept, or entire-city building scheme, over the conventional suburban subdivision lies in its coordination of public facilities with employment and housing. The new town can be built around industries to provide jobs for a range of skills and classes. The schools and health services can be built in the beginning so that the residents do not create unnecessary conflict by overloading small local community services. Finally, because these would be large projects, the social engineering of building at all class levels would become feasible. Los Angeles is currently building a beautiful new town at Irvine. Its extent is 53,000 acres, and it

will ultimately hold 430,000 inhabitants. It has jobs, recreation, an airport, and community facilities laid out in such a way that the native California land form is undisturbed. It is a brilliant example of the advantage of large-scale new-town development over the spread of subdivisions. Despite all this, Irvine is a social scandal— an all-white, upper-middle-class enclave. It is exactly the sort of project that at once shows the high potential of the new metropolis and its bigoted, class-bound failure to realize that potential.

Finally, Los Angeles should be understood as an outstanding example of regional and national planning. Its port at Long Beach, its interstate water-supply system, and its national parks and forests are excellent examples of well-designed and coordinated large-scale planning. Its war-stimulated growth is of interest precisely because it demonstrates an important but as yet little exercised capability of the federal government to influence the prosperity of a metropolitan region. The Los Angeles experience shows that we have depressed cities and depressed regions only because we have chosen to let them go unattended.

Several principles governing a successful national urban policy can be derived from the federal sponsorship in Los Angeles. First, federal orders for products and services, direct intervention in the construction of plants, and long-term aid in the building of water and electric facilities encouraged and sustained its growth. In the case of huge aircraft orders and the subsequent erection of aircraft plants with federal funds, the investment helped an industry that had already taken root to settle in more firmly. The additional contracts in the fields of aerospace and war material were instrumental in bringing the blossoming electronics industry into the city from the East.

Second, the magnitude of orders and assistance exceeded any later federal attempts to foster business in depressed areas through favored purchasing, small-business loans, and Office of Economic Opportunity programs. Aside from the money spent for war material, tools were being forged here for a national policy directed to urban growth and regional employment guidance, but our low-key use of these tools and our compulsion to tie them to the Congressional pork barrel have rendered them ineffective.

Third, the federal infusion of capital into the area continued over a long period—at least thirty years—without serious interruption, so that the war specialties of Los Angeles have been consistently nourished.

Fourth, the Los Angeles case showed that special institutions could be used to upgrade a regional labor force that had been neither particularly skilled nor outstandingly intelligent. The government sponsored here the foundation of nonprofit research and development corporations, such as RAND and the Systems Development Corporation, to supplement the educational and research capabilities of the California Institute of Technology, the University of Southern California, and the University of California. These additional institutions, by attracting scientists and engineers to the region, did much to accelerate the city's movement into higher levels of technology, and at a pace more rapid than would have prevailed if the city had depended only upon its universities and the technical staffs of resident aircraft and electronic concerns. In the Boston metropolitan region, similar paramilitary institutions helped raise the level of a management and labor force formerly connected to the dragging textile industry, and it seems probable that the Houston Manned Spacecraft Center will have the same effect in Texas. These instances suggest that the federal government could create research and service institutions for civilians as a device to upgrade the industries and labor forces of such places as Atlanta, Chicago, Detroit, and New York.

Fifth and finally, the federal investment in Los Angeles, moved by an unconscious planning wisdom, supplemented and stimulated an existing trend. There was no effort to reverse the path of popular migration or to go against the locational trends of the economy as might have been the case in such places as Appalachia or East St. Louis, Illinois. It is obvious that to roll with the economy, to relieve temporary distress, and to help people to move is a prerequisite for national urban programs.

What the federal effort in Los Angeles lacked was self-conscious dedication. The United States has the tools to plan its regional and national urban growth through the twin job-awarding devices of the giant corporation and the federal budget. Since World War II the magnitude of the corporate and federal effort has in large measure determined the national location of jobs; it has designated the industries and places where jobs would be plentiful and where they would be sparse. The depressed condition of the core of New York City is a casualty of the federal and corporate concentration on war just as surely as the prosperity of Los Angeles is its hero. If we are to mitigate the appalling human waste and suffering of our cities, both institutions must be made to act as self-conscious agents of urban reordering. The federal government must follow European examples by adopting a carefully considered, politically viable policy for urban growth so that the modernization of our cities and our economy can go forward more humanely; the corporations must be socialized to the point at which they can be held accountable for the public consequences of their behavior. Like the legitimate demands for decent work, comfortable housing, and an open inclusive society, the promise of today's economy and its cities will not be realized unless the American public demands that government and business serve the goals of a humane society.

22

FROM HARLEM TO MONTGOMERY: THE BUS BOYCOTTS AND LEADERSHIP OF ADAM CLAYTON POWELL, JR., AND MARTIN LUTHER KING, JR.

DOMINIC J. CAPECI, JR.

One of the most dramatic and important social movements of the twentieth century is the civil rights movement of the 1950s and 1960s. After centuries of servitude, discrimination, and oppression black Americans began a campaign to gain for themselves a measure of economic, political, and social equality that had been denied them by white America.

But while attention is easily drawn to the Montgomery, Alabama, bus boycott of 1956, to the March On Washington and Martin Luther King's "I Have A Dream" speech of 1963, and to the final passage of the Civil Rights and Voting Rights acts of 1964 and 1965, the success of the modern civil rights movement rested upon the firm ground of earlier struggles for black equality. As we have seen, black Americans struggled for freedom from the early days of slavery, but a continuous movement for black equality was the product of the twentieth century. Beginning with Du Bois' Niagara Movement and the founding of the NAACP and Urban League early in the century, black Americans and their liberal white supporters were able to maintain an organized response to the predominant racism of American society.

But, as Dominic J. Capeci points out, it is easy to forget the less publicized local battles for black equality in the glare of dramatic national battles. It was, however, from local struggles, such as the Harlem bus boycott of 1941 discussed in this essay and the more recent Memphis sanitation worker's strike of 1968 that a feeling of power and an ability to change social conditions developed among black Americans. It was these local struggles that provided the basis for successful struggles on the national level.

How do the outlook and strategies of Adam Clayton Powell and Martin Luther King compare with those of W. E. B. Du Bois, discussed by Lerone Bennett in Reading 14? How were the tactics of the anti-Vietnam War protests, discussed by Allen J. Matusow in Reading 24, similar to or different from those of the Harlem and Montgomery bus boycotts?

While much has been written about Martin Luther King, Jr., and the Montgomery Bus Boycott of 1956, historians have ignored Adam Clayton Powell, Jr., and the Harlem Bus Boycott of 1941. The two boycotts were marked by similar leadership and occurred in decades of despair but in periods of major socioeconomic change. Although it was much smaller in size and more local in impact, a study of the Harlem boycott yields important information on Powell's leadership before his political career and, more significantly, on earlier protest philosophies and tactics. A comparison of the boycotts reveals both the continuity and unity in black protest and leadership

Reprinted from *The Historian*, 41 (1979): 721–37, by permission of *The Historian*.

and the diversity that marks different eras and locales.

Though Powell and King came of age in different generations and regions, they experienced similar formative influences that ultimately led them to nonviolent protest. Both were named after their fathers, each of whom had risen from sharecropping to become renowned Baptist ministers in Harlem and Atlanta, respectively. Reverend Adam Clayton Powell, Sr., and Reverend Martin Luther King, Sr., were assertive, protective parents. Thus young Powell was spoiled "utterly and completely," while King, Jr., enjoyed life's comforts in "an extraordinarily peaceful and protected way." Both were precocious, entering college in their mid-teens and earning advanced degrees in religion. More significant, both underwent serious racial and religious growing pains. As a youngster, Powell had been roughed up by blacks for being "white" and by whites for being "colored." Later at Colgate University he passed for white until his father came to lecture on race relations. The negative reaction of Powell's white roommate to his true identity was a "tremendous" shock. Perhaps the trauma was almost as great as the earlier, unexpected death of his sister Blanche, which triggered in Powell a religious reaction: "The church was a fraud, my father the leading perpetrator, my mother a stupid rubber stamp." King, too, was scarred during his early years. When the mother of his white playmates informed King (then six years old) that as they grew older they could no longer play together, he ran home crying. Although never estranged from his father, as a teenager King considered the church irrelevant and wondered whether religion "could serve as a vehicle for modern thinking."

As young adults, Powell and King overcame these problems. At Colgate, Powell experienced a revelation, which led to his ordination in 1931. He served as assistant pastor of his father's Abyssinian Baptist Church and earned a master's degree in religious education at Columbia University. In 1937, he succeeded his father as pastor. Adopting the elder Powell's commitment to the social gospel, he forged his congregation into "a

mighty weapon" and led numerous nonviolent direct action protests for black employment opportunities during the Great Depression. As part of the larger "Jobs-for-Negroes" movement, Powell joined with Reverend William Lloyd Imes of the St. James Presbyterian Church and A. Philip Randolph of the Brotherhood of Sleeping Car Porters to organize the Greater New York Coordinating Committee for Employment. By 1941 Powell overestimated that four years of picketing by the committee had brought Harlem "ten thousand jobs." This commitment and leadership earned him enormous popularity and, among church women, the title "Mr. Jesus."

King matured along similar lines, for Dr. Benjamin E. Mays and others at Morehouse College successfully molded his concept of religion. King was ordained and became the assistant pastor at his father's Ebenezer Baptist Church. He then attended Crozer Theological Seminary and received a doctorate in theology from Boston College. Although the elder King was only infrequently involved in organized protest, he and Alberta King had instilled dignity and pride in their son. King remembered his father admonishing a policeman for calling him "boy"; pointing to his son, the elder King ejaculated, "That's a boy there. I'm Reverend King." Eventually, King drew on nonviolent direct action for the Montgomery boycott and became immensely popular. "L. L. J.," or "Little Lord Jesus" as church women called him, had moved to the center stage of black leadership.

While Powell and King, then, experienced similar upbringings, a comparison of the bus boycotts in Harlem and Montgomery provides an opportunity to analyze their leadership, protest philosophies, and tactics.

The Harlem bus boycott of 1941 was prompted by black degradation, rising expectations, and a heritage of black protest. Throughout the 1930s, black New Yorkers subsisted on marginal economic levels. As late as 1940, 40 percent of the city's black population received relief or federal monies for temporary jobs. Moreover, most blacks were relegated to menial positions. In Harlem, the largest black community of over two hundred thousand persons, hope was generated, nevertheless, as black leaders and white officials —like Mayor Fiorello H. La Guardia—pressed for change and as World War II held out promise for greater black employment opportunities.

Blacks had a longstanding grievance against the Fifth Avenue Coach Company and the New York Omnibus Corporation. In 1935, the Mayor's Commission on Conditions in Harlem reported that the Coach Company was "fixed in its policy of the exclusion of Negroes from employment." At the time of the bus boycott six years later, the Coach Company and the Omnibus Corporation together employed only sixteen blacks, mostly as janitors, none as drivers or mechanics, out of a labor force of thirty-five hundred persons. Hence, on March 10, 1941, when the Transportation Workers Union (TWU), under the leadership of Michael J. Quill, went on strike against the bus companies, black leaders moved quickly to the union's support. The National Negro Congress, for example, "wholeheartedly" supported the strike, which lasted for twelve days and halted the service of thirteen hundred buses.

Under Roger Straugh's leadership, the Harlem Labor Union (HLU) began picketing local bus stops before the TWU strike had ended, demanding the employment of black bus drivers and mechanics. The Greater New York Coordinating Committee for Employment led by Powell and the Manhattan Council of the National Negro Congress directed by Hope R. Stevens joined with HLU to form the United Bus Strike Committee (UBSC). The formal boycott, however, did not begin until March 24, four days after TWU had agreed to arbitration and two days after bus service had resumed. Moreover, Powell emerged as the spokesman for the boycotters, providing, in Urban Leaguer Elmer A. Carter's estimation, "dynamic leadership."

Before the boycott began, Powell received a quid pro quo from Quill. In return for black support of the TWU strike, the boycott would receive union backing. Later, on March 24, Quill assured Powell that blacks employed by the bus companies would be considered for union membership so long as they had clean records and had never been scabs. That evening, over fifteen hundred persons gathered at the Abyssinian Baptist Church and agreed to boycott the buses until blacks were hired as drivers and mechanics.

Powell's tactics drew from the Jobs-for-Negroes movement, in which many members of the United Bus Strike Committee had participated. Picket lines surrounded Harlem's bus stops, soup kitchens fed volunteers, and black chauffeurs and mechanics were registered. An "emergency jitney service" of privately owned automobiles transported some boycotters, but the key to the boycott's success was New York City's subway system and taxi companies which provided efficient, relatively inexpensive alternative transportation. Before the boycott terminated, volunteers painted placards, donated approximately $500, and gave the use of their automobiles. The month-long campaign kept sixty thousand persons off the buses each day at a loss of $3,000 in daily fares. It also drew together five hundred persons from various backgrounds and both races, as bandleaders, ministers, postal clerks, housewives, beauticians, and nurses walked the picket line. Celebrities, like musician Duke Ellington, actively supported the boycott.

Well aware of the significance of the church in black society, Powell made the Abyssinian Baptist Church one of two boycott headquarters. It was the location of the first and second boycott rallies. It provided volunteers experienced in protest, communications, and physical resources and, of course, became the base of Powell's operations and the center of his power.

Powell stressed the philosophy of nonviolent direct action. Blacks were to use only peaceful, legal avenues of redress. By appealing to "the Grace of God" and "the power of the masses," Powell combined religious and political themes; this combination of righteousness and self-help would enable "a black boy . . . to roll a bus up Seventh Avenue." Picket lines, as well as Powell's rhetoric, however, implied militancy. Those flouting the boycott, he declared, should be converted, "one way or another." Three years after the boycott, Powell summarized his nonviolent, though strident, philosophy in *Marching*

Blacks: "No blows, no violence, but the steady unrelenting pressure of an increasing horde of people who knew they were right" would bring change.

The boycott was threatened first by violence and then by a misleading newspaper story. Following a UBSC rally at the Abyssinian Baptist Church on March 31, individuals hurled objects at several buses along Lenox Avenue. Fifty patrolmen dispersed those responsible, some of whom had attended the rally. "FEAR ANOTHER HARLEM RIOT," screamed the *Age*'s headlines. Of more concern to Powell and others was the *Amsterdam News* story of April 5. It announced that the bus companies had agreed to employ over two hundred black drivers and mechanics, providing that TWU waive the seniority rights of more than three hundred former bus employees waiting to be rehired. Such an agreement had been discussed, but no final decision had been reached. UBSC leaders moved quickly to maintain the boycott. They labeled the story "a lie," reorganized pickets, distributed leaflets, asked ministers to inform their congregations of "the true facts," and planned a mass meeting.

Despite crisis, the boycott and negotiations continued. Once Ritchie agreed to hire blacks, the major obstacle was TWU seniority policies. On April 17, Powell informed five thousand persons at the Golden Gate Ballroom that an agreement was imminent. Signed twelve days later, the agreement waived the seniority rights of all except ninety-one TWU drivers furloughed by the bus companies; after these men were reinstated, one hundred black drivers were to be hired. The next seventy mechanics employed would also be black, and thereafter, blacks and white would be taken on alternately until 17 percent of the companies' labor force—exclusive of clerical staff— was black. This quota represented the percentage of black residents in Manhattan. Black workers would be enrolled as TWU members, although the bus companies exercised "sole discretion as to the type of Negro employees to be hired." The agreement would not take precedence over prior management-labor commitments provided they were nondiscriminatory. Of course, all boycott

activities would cease. Powell declared that the agreement was made possible by new TWU contracts providing shorter hours and by additional municipal franchises enabling the bus companies to employ three hundred more persons.

Several factors made the Harlem boycott successful. Powell's agreement with Quill prevented bus company officials from playing blacks against whites in the TWU strike and the bus boycott. Throughout the strike, Quill raised the possibility of the bus companies employing strikebreakers. Blacks traditionally had been exploited as scabs, and some of the bus terminals were strategically located in Harlem. Indeed, at least one Harlem correspondent informed Mayor La Guardia that two thousand black men could "start the bus lines in 5, 10, or 20 hours." Powell's agreement significantly reduced the possibility of TWU's strike being broken by force, and reciprocally, it assured that the bus boycott would not fail because of traditional union opposition toward blacks.

Powell's agreement with Quill also held out the hope that blacks would support labor in the upcoming subway negotiations between La Guardia and TWU leaders. During the previous June, the municipal government had bought and unified the Brooklyn-Manhattan Transit Corporation and the Interborough Rapid Transit Company, which had been operated by TWU and the Brotherhood of Locomotive Engineers. When La Guardia contended that neither the right to strike nor a closed shop could be permitted among civil service employees, labor officials reported that the mayor had reneged on his obligations and anticipated a precedent-breaking conflict with the municipal government when the original contract expired on June 20, 1941. TWU leaders believed that mayoral reference to the bus strike as "bull-headed, obstinate and stupid" was designed to weaken their position in the coming subway negotiations. Obviously, public opinion would be crucial in that dispute. Hence, some blacks, like the *Age* editor, saw TWU support for the bus boycott as a trade-off for black support in the forthcoming union battle with the mayor.

Changing opinions and the impact of World

War II helped make the Powell-Quill agreement possible. The racial attitudes of TWU leaders had been improving since 1938 when the union unsuccessfully sent blacks to be employed as drivers at the World's Fair. By World War II, Powell understood how uncomfortable society was in opposing a totalitarian, racist Nazi regime while practicing racial discrimination. "America," he stated later, "could not defeat Hitler abroad without defeating Hitlerism at home." Of equal importance, TWU leadership could pare seniority lists by three hundred unemployed members and make room for black employees because defense orders stimulated the economy and selective service calls reduced union ranks. According to the *Afro-American* editor, the difficulty in finding bus drivers and mechanics provided blacks with unforeseen opportunities.

The boycott assured those opportunities. By early May, seven black mechanics had been hired by the bus companies and ten blacks were expected to begin chauffeur training within a week. Six months later, forty-three blacks had been employed in various classifications, including mechanic's helpers. Finally, on February 1, 1942, after all the ninety-odd furloughed white operators had been given opportunity for reemployment, the first ten black drivers employed by the Coach Company and the Omnibus Corporation began their routes.

That victory was historical. It drew blacks, labor, and management together in a successful effort to break down discriminatory employment practices in privately owned bus companies, and indirectly, it accelerated a similar trend that had already begun in the municipally owned transportation systems under La Guardia's leadership. The boycott also held out promise for "Negro-labor solidarity." Moreover, it effectively utilized the tactics and philosophies of the Jobs-for-Negroes movement, focused on the concept of equal opportunity, established the idea of a quota system, and provided safeguards for protecting blacks in their newly won jobs. All these elements were also attempted in the 1930s and 1960s, indicating the continuum in black protest that links militant means with traditional ends and nonvio-

lent direct action tactics with greater participation in larger society. By exploiting both TWU ambitions and war manpower exigencies, Powell, Straugh, and Stevens created numerous jobs for black workers. But it was Powell who played the leading role, as he had done for the past decade, speaking out and organizing protests that brought approximately seventeen hundred jobs to Harlem. Exactly because of that record, blacks enthusiastically supported his successful candidacy for City Council in November 1941. His delivery of tangible gains merits mention, for as councilman and later, congressman he had the reputation for imparting only catharsis to his constituents. Finally, Powell's boycott sparked other protests; numerous blacks agreed with the editor of the *Pittsburgh Courier,* who said, "If this can be done in New York, it can be done in other cities." Indeed, in May the National Association for the Advancement of Colored People launched a nationwide picket campaign against defense industries that held government contracts but refused to hire blacks; Powell journeyed to Chicago to help the Negro Labor Relations League launch a jobs campaign; and the Colored Clerks Circle of St. Louis prepared to boycott a local cleaning company. Official entry of the United States into World War II prevented the emergence of what might have been widespread black protest akin to that of the 1950s and 1960s.

Nearly fifteen years later, when Rosa Parks refused to give up her seat to a white passenger on the Montgomery Bus Line, another phase of black protest began. It was led by Martin Luther King, Jr., who was unknown and inexperienced when leadership of the Montgomery Improvement Association was thrust on him in December of 1955. When he arrived in Montgomery during the previous year to accept the pastorate of the Dexter Avenue Baptist Church, it was "the cradle of the Confederacy." Of one hundred and thirty thousand residents, blacks comprised 40 percent. Segregated and scattered throughout the city, they were exploited economically and lacked even the semblance of geographic, political, or social unity. Jim Crow practices prevailed, particularly on the bus lines where operators possessed police powers for enforcing segregation. A long history of passenger abuse by bus drivers was well known to blacks who had been beaten, ridiculed, and stranded. Coretta Scott King accurately contended that black passengers were treated worse than cattle, "for nobody insults a cow." Earlier efforts to protest this treatment had failed because of black disunity and white power.

Juxtaposed to years of degradation, however, were rising expectations. If the United States Supreme Court's decision against segregated public school systems in *Brown* v. *Topeka* (1954) did not affect Montgomery immediately, it signaled a major change in race relations. More immediate, however, was the emergence of what King termed "a brand new Negro" whose struggle for dignity was obstructed by self-deceiving whites who continued to live in the past. Hence some blacks and many whites were surprised when the arrest of Rosa Parks triggered protest. During the eighteen years that he had lived in the South, columnist Carl Rowan "had never seen such spirit among a group of Negroes."

That spirit was mobilized by the Montgomery Improvement Association (MIA) which grew out of the efforts of E. D. Nixon, a pullman porter who presided over the local NAACP, and Jo Ann Robinson, an English professor at Alabama State College and president of the Women's Political Council. They arranged a meeting of black ministers, who adopted Reverend Ralph Abernathy's idea of the MIA, elected King as its president, and organized a mass meeting of black residents. On Sunday, December 5, over four thousand people crammed into the Holt Street Baptist Church to endorse a boycott until the bus lines guaranteed (1) courteous treatment, (2) a first-come-first-served seating arrangement (blacks in the rear, whites in the front), and (3) employment of black operators on predominantly black routes. Moderate, mostly symbolic, alterations in the Jim Crow system were sought.

The MIA tactics resembled those of earlier black protest movements, including Powell's. As Lawrence D. Reddick has pointed out, Montgomery was "ideally fitted" for a bus boycott: its

sizable black population comprised 70 percent of all bus passengers, while its layout of 27.9 square miles enabled residents to reach most places by foot. An effective boycott, however, needed alternative means of transportation. In its initial stages, black cab companies agreed to carry black passengers for the price of the ten cents bus fare. A car pool supplemented the taxi service, becoming the major mode of transportation after municipal officials outlawed the lower taxi fares. Over three hundred automobiles moved in and out of forty-eight dispatch and forty-two collection stations. Financial support originated among the protestors, but as their efforts drew national and international attention, donations came from various sources. In one year, the MIA had spent $225,000. From December 5, 1955, to December 21, 1956, the boycott cost the Montgomery Bus Lines over a quarter of a million dollars in fares, the City of Montgomery several thousand dollars in taxes, and the downtown white merchants several million dollars in business. It also boosted black businesses and reduced the social distance between classes within the black society.

It was no coincidence that the protest spirit emanated from the church, southern black society's most independent institution and primary means of communication. It became routine for blacks to share a ride or walk daily and attend mass meetings at a different church each Monday and Thursday. The boycott became inseparable from the secular and religious life of black society, maximizing the participation of everyone from domestic to clergymen. Not surprisingly, church-owned vehicles in the car pool were dubbed 'rolling churches'.

Emphasizing the concepts of love and justice, King forged a philosophy of nonviolent direct action, stressing self-help, condemning violence, focusing on evil—rather than evil-doers—and espousing "love for America and the democratic way of life." He realized the limits of black power, the history of white repression, and the need for legitimacy in the eyes of white America. Perhaps for these reasons, MIA leaders originally sought a first-come-first-served seating arrangement "under segregation" and watched those blacks who might have resorted to violence. Both the demands for desegregation in seating arrangements and the Gandhian dimension of King's philosophy evolved after the boycott had begun. Nonviolence, already implicit in the Christian teaching that underlay the boycott, was formally articulated by King as a result of the influences of Bayard Rustin and the Reverend Glenn E. Smiley of the Fellowship of Reconciliation.

Despite solid organization and philosophical appeal, the boycott confronted several problems. King later admitted having been "scared to death by threats against myself and my family." Indeed, on January 30, 1956, as Coretta King and baby Yolanda inhabited the premises, the King home was bombed. In addition, King had to deal with a legal system that sanctioned Jim Crow. As a result of Title 14, Section 54, of the Alabama Code prohibiting boycotts, King and eighty-eight others were convicted of unlawful activities. Later the car pool was halted by court injunction. What saved the boycott was the slow wit of the municipal officials and the federal injunction banning segregated buses which was upheld by the United States Supreme Court. Nor did the boycott receive meaningful support from the white community. A handful of whites, like Reverend Robert Graetz, pastor of the black Lutheran Trinity Church, "paid dearly" for participating in the boycott. Other whites assisted the protest unwittingly by chauffeuring their domestics to and from work. For the most part, however, whites either opposed the boycott or, if sympathetic to it, were afraid to say so publicly.

Internal pressures also proved troublesome. Early in the boycott, as abusive phone calls, long hours of work, and relentless efforts to maintain unity began to mount, King despaired and confided in God, "I've come to the point where I can't face it alone." At this time King experienced a revelation, which enabled him "to face anything." Jealousy on the part of some black ministers threatened the boycott periodically. The gravest incident occurred on January 21 when King was informed that Mayor W. A. Gayle and three black ministers had agreed on a settlement to end the boycott. That evening and

the following Sunday morning, MIA leaders successfully alerted the black community to this hoax.

These pressures notwithstanding, the boycott was successful, with support coming from numerous quarters. Congressman Adam Clayton Powell, Jr., for example, pressed President Dwight D. Eisenhower to protect the eighty-odd blacks indicted for boycott activities. When Eisenhower refused to comply, Powell publicly chided him for "trying to wash his hands like Pilate of the blood of innocent men and women in the Southland." He then organized a "National Deliverance Day of Prayer" for March 28, which was commemorated in several cities, including Atlanta, Chicago, and New York. Powell collected and sent $2,500 to MIA. Early the next month, he asked all members of the House of Representatives for contributions to help rebuild seven black churches in Montgomery that had been bombed by terrorists, and later recorded that only two Congressmen honored his request. Before the year ended, he and several other nationally known blacks spoke in Montgomery. In sum, the Montgomery bus boycott brought to the surface black awareness that had been stirring since World War II.

As significant was the recent shift in the United States Supreme Court under Chief Justice Earl Warren. Just as Mayor Gayle had deduced that the boycott could be crushed by enjoining the car pool for being unlicensed, the higher court upheld a United States District Court decision that laws in Alabama requiring segregation on buses were unconstitutional. This decision of November 13, 1956, meant victory for MIA, but King continued the boycott until a federal order arrived in Montgomery six weeks later; on December 21, MIA leaders rode the bus in victory.

That victory sparked the Civil Rights Movement. The Montgomery bus boycott provided a leader in King, a philosophy in nonviolence, a tactic in direct action, and, as important, a tangible triumph. Blacks were poised for change, needing, in Lerone Bennett's worlds, "an act to give them power over their fears." The boycott, of course, did much more, for under King's leadership it achieved legitimacy and prepared both races for a prolonged assault on inequality. That King succeeded in the South, and succeeded with the United States Supreme Court's assistance, underscored a major theme for the coming decade. That the Montgomery City Bus Line so adamantly and successfully refused any agreement regarding the hiring of black bus drivers indicated both the obstacles and limits for changes that lay ahead. Nevertheless, the boycott spawned the Southern Christian Leadership Conference, "a sustaining mechanism," and elevated the struggle for racial equality to the national level.

The Harlem boycott of 1941 came nowhere near achieving this, for it was much smaller and failed to sustain a national protest movement. Nor was it supported throughout the black community. Yet similarities between it and the Montgomery experience abound, particularly those dealing with leadership. Powell and King came from deeply Christian, middle-class families that provided physical security while imposing high parental expectations. As precocious youngsters, both Powell and King experienced anxiety and guilt. Each questioned his father's vocation, perhaps feeling incapable of living up to the parental reputation or, as most likely in Powell's case, repressing hostility toward a domineering father. Each tried to escape: Powell by passing for white and King by engaging in masochistic tendencies. (King jumped out of an upstairs window once, blaming himself for an accident involving his grandmother; at another time, he blamed himself for being at a parade when she died of illness.) As young adults, however, both men sublimated this inner turmoil and embraced the church and their fathers, becoming independent from the latter, yet reflecting them. Perhaps, as psychoanalyst Erich Fromm has theorized about other historical figures, their long-sought-after personal independence emerged in their struggle for collective black liberation.

Powell and King believed that collective liberation could only come through the black church with its "enormous reservoirs of psychic and social strength." Such liberation would free both races, for blacks possessed the divinely inspired mission of achieving equality through the redemption of white society. As the largest black Protestant church in the United States, the Abyssinian Baptist Church boasted a membership of thousands, which provided Powell with impressive human and financial resources. King's Dexter Avenue Baptist Church, however, was more representative of black congregations, comprising one thousand persons and limited finances. In order to be effective, Powell and King successfully established coalitions with other religious and secular groups.

If the church became the vehicle for change, it was black folk religion that provided the sinew for protest. Powell and, more directly King, converted traditional black religiosity into "a passion for justice." Speaking to northern, urban congregations, Powell, avoided "Valley-and-Dry-Bones sermons," stressing instead "nicely chosen Negro idioms about every day issues." Powell could be moved by his own words and weep publicly. King spoke a more "religious language" that struck at the heart of southern black culture. Reverend Andrew Young, a member of the Southern Christian Leadership Conference, observed that no one could have mobilized black southerners by arguing about segregation and integration, but when King preached about "leaving the slavery of Egypt" or "dry bones rising again" everybody understood his language. Both Powell and King possessed what historian Joseph R. Washington, Jr., has called "that Baptist hum which makes what is said only as important as how it is said." The inflections of their voices, the cadence of their deliveries, the nuances of their messages, the animation of their gestures were eagerly anticipated and instinctively understood by multitudes who shared a special cultural and historical relationship with their preachers. Powell and King, then, mobilized black people and became their surrogates, "interpreting their innermost feelings, their passions, their yearnings" as well as channeling their emotions into viable protest.

Protestant theology and Gandhian tactics provided the means by which Powell and King could channel the passion for justice. Both men advocated the social gospel, contending that any religion ignoring the socioeconomic conditions that shackle humanity was, in King's rhetoric, "a dry-as-dust religion." Nonviolent direct action was not a new tactic in black protest, but it was one that permitted Powell, King, and their supporters to become social gospel activists. Following King's successful boycott, blacks increasingly favored an active role by the church in social and political issues during the years 1957 to 1968.

If the boycotts shared a similar religious heritage, they also reflect the respective personality characterizations of Powell and King. Political scientist Hanes Walton, Jr., notes that Powell used nonviolence for practical reasons as "a potent, energetic tool," while King embraced it as "an end in itself, endowed with superior moral qualities." Powell did not advocate violence, but on occasion his rhetoric was intimidating and implied the use of intimidation. King, of course, would tolerate no such deviation from passive resistance. King's commitment notwithstanding, Powell more accurately reflected the reasons for which blacks utilized nonviolent direct action. In the aftermath of the Montgomery boycott, for example, over 70 percent of the black respondents surveyed in that city recognized the usefulness of nonviolence since black people lacked the "power to use violence successfully." According to sociologist E. Franklin Frazier, "Gandhism as a philosophy and a way of life is completely alien to the Negro"; black religious heritage accounts for the presence of nonviolent direct action in the civil rights movement.

That King much more than Powell envisaged —as did Mahatma Gandhi—"a life of service to humanity on a level which called for a self-discipline of rare order" was partly due to socioecological factors. Even in 1941, Harlem, the "Negro Mecca" of the world, was a more secure environment for black people than was Montgomery fifteen years later. Powell had been raised in that security and had successfully used the avenues of redress that were available in the North. King had been brought up in southern segregation, where survival depended upon staying in one's place and where protest efforts had little result.

Powell never experienced the pressures and fears that haunted King daily; Powell had enemies, but none who threatened his family or bombed his home. Exactly because of his own background and fears, King understood the need to allay southern white fears if blacks were to avoid pogroms and race relations were to progress: "If you truly love and respect an opponent, you respect his fears too."

King's upbringing emphasized inner control, the kind that enabled him to bear parental whippings with "stoic impassivity." Reverend King, Sr., stressed discipline, and the precarious social environs demanded self-regulation. Hence King originally questioned the emotionalism in the black church and later, in the boycott, took great pains to direct it into safe arenas. Finally, the religious and secular elements in the southern black church appear to have been much more interdependent than elsewhere, which partly accounts for King's commitment to nonviolence as a way of life. This commitment may have been—as in Gandhi's experience—marked by ambivalence, for King stressed love partly for the purpose of controlling hate (perhaps his own). In Powell's case, the opposite was true. As a child, he was spoiled, and lived in an environment that did not demand inner control for survival. He never led a humble life but, rather, publicly flouted the racial mores of white society. Nor was his religion as all-encompassing as King's; it was more secular and compartmentalized, reflecting the tremendous impact that migration and urbanization had had upon the northern black church. Powell released anger more directly by stressing direct action, while King tended to displace it by putting emphasis on nonviolence or, more precisely, on what Gandhi called Satyagraha—love-force. It is, then, no coincidence that Powell later singled out Marcus Garvey as the greatest mass leader, demonstrated his independence by clearly identifying an enemy, and spoke militantly of change. King, however, referred only to Booker T. Washington in his first major address in the boycott— "Let no man pull you so low as to make you hate him," stressed racial reconciliation by describing forces of evil, and prayed for opponents. Hence it is not surprising that the name of Powell's organization, the United Bus Strike Committee, projected an assertive, challenging image and that the Harlem boycott focused on the tangible bread-and-butter issue of jobs. By contrast, King's efforts emphasized uplift, as implied in the title, Montgomery Improvement Association, and sought more symbolic, civil rights objectives.

Powell had undertaken the Harlem boycott as his last major protest as a social gospel activist at the end of the Jobs-for-Negroes campaign. He would soon begin a political career as councilman in New York City, and World War II would soon reduce protest to rhetoric as black leaders feared that their efforts would be labeled traitorous.

King was thrust into the Montgomery boycott, his first meaningful protest, which began the civil rights movement. Larger and more significant historically than anything that Powell had done, King embraced that movement and its principles until they died together on April 4, 1968. While the contributions of King are obvious, those of Powell have been forgotten by many. Nevertheless, King knew of Powell's efforts. "Before some of us were born, before some of us could walk or talk," King recalled in the 1960s, "Adam Powell wrote *Marching Blacks,* the charter of the black revolution that is taking place today." One can imagine Powell, in his accustomed modesty, ejaculating an "Amen."

23

MIRACLE IN DELANO

DICK MEISTER AND ANNE LOFTIS

In the course of the late nineteenth and twentieth centuries skilled craftsmen, semi-skilled machine operators, and clerical workers formed unions to represent and protect their interests as workers. Employers fought bitterly against these unions until the post-World War II era, when collective bargaining became a widely accepted standard for employer-employee relations. This new era of industrial relations was also facilitated by the role which the federal government played in stabilizing these relations. Beginning with the establishment of the National Labor Relations Board in 1935, the federal government became increasingly involved in every aspect of industrial relations, until today labor law constitutes a separate field of legal scholarship and practice.

Yet, in spite of widespread unionization and the involvement of government in labor relations, many sectors of the labor force were left unprotected. One of the largest groups of these forgotten workers were America's agricultural laborers. Not only were agricultural laborers thought to be unorganizable because of their migratory status, but the National Labor Relations Act specifically excluded agricultural workers from its statutes. Ignored by the union movement and the government as well, farm workers were left at the mercy of growers who cared little for their welfare. It was not surprising, then, that in his classic expose of postwar American poverty, *The Other America* (1963), Michael Harrington found migratory farm workers to be among the poorest of America's poor. Migrating from state to state as they followed the harvest season, living without adequate housing, food, or medical care, and paid the lowest wages of any American workers, the farm workers lived a life of extreme deprivation and poverty amidst widespread American prosperity. As Dick Meister and Anne Loftis show, it was to remedy this situation that Cesar Chavez organized the United Farm Workers of America (UFW).

How do the methods and outlook of Chavez and the UFW compare with earlier attempts by William Haywood and the IWW to organize farmers, as discussed by Melvyn Dubofsky in Reading 10? What part do you think that racism played in the struggle against the farmworkers' union? The essays by Lerone Bennett (Reading 14), Lawrence Goodwyn (Reading 7), and Jack Chen (Reading 3) may be useful in answering this question. What similarities or differences do you find in the farmworkers' movement and the civil rights movement as described by Dominic J. Capeci in Reading 22?

Grower attempts to undermine the NFWA's [National Farm Workers Association] new urban support were extremely ineffectual. They did most of their arguing in local farm areas, where they formed community groups to join them in red-baiting and other tactics of the political right, which only reinforced the views of the NFWA's liberal supporters. Growers denounced the strike for being a civil rights movement, attacked the strikers' clerical helpers as radical "apostles of discord" whose churches were in danger of losing financial support, and brought in the National Right to Work Committee to proclaim that the whole thing was an onslaught on "personal freedom." The John Birch Society concluded that it was a subversive plot hatched in Saul Alinsky's "School of Revolution."

Growers hoped to get at least as much from the California Senate's Committee on Un-American Activities; but though the committee dutifully found that the strike was supported by "known members of the Communist Party," and "new left and subversive organizations," it reported that the strikers themselves were unsubversively aiming at nothing more than that great American goal of "better wages and working conditions."

One of the more bizarre attempts to discredit the NFWA was disclosed six years later when Jerome Ducote, a private investigator active in right-wing causes, offered to sell the union files he admitted stealing from NFWA offices between 1966 and 1968. Ducote claimed growers hired him to uncover material that would link the NFWA to "subversives," and although he didn't find any such documents, he did come away with mailing lists, financial records and boycott plans that were important to the union. The NFWA notified the FBI immediately after Ducote offered to sell the files back, but he wasn't arrested until seventeen months later—nine years after the first burglaries. He was charged with grand theft, but though growers admitted giving him money for information and other help in fighting the NFWA, they denied his assertions that they had asked him to engage in burglaries.

Growers got plenty of encouragement from the agricultural establishment in opposing the NFWA. Buck up, the California Farm Bureau Federation told them, a picket line actually could be a blessing in disguise—"a means of sorting the good, loyal worker from the undesirable." The Farm Bureau advised that tighter supervision by

growers would take care of most problems, but that growers might want to make a few concessions, since "the only deterrent to unions is worker satisfaction." The Bureau suggested this wouldn't take much more than supplying water and paper drinking cups on the job and, to really do it up right, "coffee and doughnuts." Growers could rid themselves of "misfits" who might still be dissatisfied by issuing identification cards that "reliable and responsible employees" could present when seeking work.

Mobilization of strike support continued at a rapid pace, with a strong assist from Senator Robert Kennedy and California's Roman Catholic bishops. They spoke up at hearings that the Senate's Subcommittee on Migratory Labor held in the vineyard region just three months after the boycott began. Nearly 1000 farm workers, waving colorful, hand-lettered placards, jammed into a sweltering high school auditorium for the hearing in Delano, while 300 others milled outside anxiously.

Except for James Vizzard and some other individual priests willing to brave the censure of their superiors, the church to which most of the strikers belonged had played only a small role in the strike. But pressures on the church hierarchy had become irresistible, and the farm workers broke into loud cheers at the testimony of Hugh Donohoe, the slight, white-haired Bishop of Stockton. He announced, with just a touch of brogue, that all seven of the state's Catholic bishops would support the proposal of Subcommittee Chairman Harrison Williams to extend the labor laws to farm workers; and, Bishop Donohoe added, they would support the strikers' demand for unionization. The bishops believed the strikers were merely "seeking a basic right," and were now convinced "that unless farm workers are given the chance to organize, they are going to become the wards of the state."

Kennedy took a similar position. "When you're talking about having meals to feed your children and money to buy clothes and continue an education," Kennedy told grower witnesses who insisted their workers didn't want to strike, "then you'll have to make the judgment of whether you're going to be able to go on strike or whether you're going to have to go to work." And if the growers were so certain their employees didn't want a union, why not "permit the people to vote and decide for themselves"?

Kennedy also turned attention to Kern County's curious law enforcement practices in an exchange with Sheriff Leroy Galyen, a rotund figure in a rumpled suit whose manner was as distinctly small-town lawman as Kennedy's was urbane Bostonian. Kennedy looked genuinely astonished as Galyen testified that he had arrested more than three dozen pickets for being *potential* troublemakers."

"How can you arrest someone if they haven't violated the law?" Kennedy demanded.

"Well, I heard some of the people out in the fields were going to cut up the pickets. So I arrested the pickets . . . for unlawful assembly."

Kennedy suggested acidly that the sheriff "read the Constitution of the United States."

Kennedy's support was among the most important the strikers were ever to receive; it brought them into the highest circles of liberal wealth and political influence, and it buoyed their self-esteem immeasurably. Political motives played a part in Kennedy's support—there were political motives in *everything* Robert Kennedy did. But his support was deep and sincere; and it was unflagging until he was assassinated two years later while walking down a Los Angeles hotel corridor just a few feet ahead of Dolores Huerta and Paul Schrade, after delivering the speech in which he had singled out the farm workers for helping provide his small margin of victory in California's presidential primary. "Whenever we needed him, wherever we asked him to come," said Chavez, "we knew he would be there. He approached us with love; as people, not as subjects for study . . . as equals, not as objects of curiosity. . . . His were *hechos de amor.* Deeds of love."

The NFWA made its most dramatic bid for support immediately after adjournment of the Senate subcommittee hearings, when 100 farm workers and supporters set out from Delano on a 300-mile march to the state capitol in Sac-ramento. They were to arrive on Easter Sunday, twenty-five days later, to demand that Governor Brown and the state legislature grant farm workers "justice, freedom and respect" in the form of the legal rights that would make their struggle on the picket lines unnecessary. The marchers did not get what they wanted; the governor, fearful of alienating powerful agricultural interests, refused even to meet with them, much less call the special legislative session their demand required. But they gained valuable support as they tramped through the San Joaquin Valley, demonstrating the breadth and dedication of the coalition that had formed around the strike and bringing a sense of hope and solidarity to the farm workers who joined them en route.

The workers provided marchers with money, food and lodging, and participated in nightly Masses, rallies and meetings where they learned what had been happening in Delano, and how they might do the same thing in their own areas. It wasn't all inspirational talk; perhaps the most effective organizing was done through satirical skits, presented by the NFWA's theatrical group, El Teatro Campesino. They laid out the issues in broad simple terms and turned the weapon of ridicule against the growers, whom many workers had passively regarded as unassailable.

By day, they marched beside the flat, green fields of the valley, waving brilliant red banners and chanting, always chanting—dark-skinned farm workers; intense young students; union men and women from the cities; black civil rights workers; nuns in flowing habits; priests and ministers in somber black suits; children, squirming uncomfortably in the broiling sun. Among the marchers, tall and patriarch-like, was Chavez' father Librado, now eighty-two. They were led by men carrying the flags of Mexico and the United States, a wooden cross with the word "*Huelga*" burned into it, and, like those who led the peasant armies of Emiliano Zapata, an embroidered image of *La Virgen de Guadalupe.* It was patterned quite consciously after the Lenten *peregrinacións* of Mexico, the pilgrimages that combine penance with protests by the poor.

The 52 marchers who covered the entire route

from Delano were joined by more than 3000 supporters for the final five-mile leg of the journey, and 5000 more were waiting as they paraded boldly through tree-lined Capitol Park and onto the marble steps of the capitol. They were greeted by dozens of leading churchmen, AFL-CIO and Teamster officials, Democratic officeholders and candidates, and chief representatives of the state's Mexican-American and civil rights organizations. Governor Brown's decision to spend Easter Sunday with his family, at the home of singer Frank Sinatra in Palm Springs, angered but did not dismay the enthusiastic crowd. The protest rally was turned into a celebration of the NFWA's first victory, achieved just a week earlier when Schenley Industries agreed to negotiate a union contract.

Schenley had easily harvested its grapes despite the strike; but the boycott, said a Schenley vice president, raised "a threat of serious damage to our business on a nationwide scale." NFWA supporters were flooding the country with publicity depicting Schenley as a corporate giant oppressing a tiny band of poor farm workers, Teamsters were refusing to distribute Schenley's liquors in northern California, and there was a rumor that bartenders in Los Angeles were about to stop pouring Schenley. The initial reaction of Schenley's board chairman, Lewis Rosensteil, was to order his West Coast representative, Sidney Korshak, to sell the firm's vineyard. But Korshak convinced Rosensteil there was a better way to salvage Schenley's reputation.

Chavez was summoned from the march, a recognition agreement was reached quickly with the help of AFL-CIO officials and, shortly afterward, Chavez signed one of the few contracts ever negotiated by a farm union outside Hawaii. Schenley, which had already joined other growers to raise base pay to $1.40 an hour in hopes of easing union pressure, agreed to raise pay another 35 cents, and to grant rights that were unheard of among most farm workers. They included a union shop, which required all Schenley field workers to join the NFWA, and requirements that Schenley go first to the union when seeking new workers and consult with the union before changing any work

procedures or continuing operations the workers claimed to be hazardous.

DiGiorgio tried to escape the NFWA's growing pressure by offering to hold a union representation election, but under conditions that would give the corporation the maximum advantage. The NFWA would have to call off its strike and boycott against DiGiorgio immediately, allow the ballot to include a grower-controlled employee association that had been formed since the strike began, and agree that if the NFWA did win the election it would not resume the strike, even if subsequent contract negotiations broke down. Chavez rejected the offer; but however devious the proposal, it was a major concession, and a sign that stepped-up boycott pressure might result in a legitimate offer.

The mere threat that the boycott might be extended to other firms brought the NFWA a rapid series of victories at a half-dozen of the state's major wineries, including two—Christian Brothers and Novitiate—that were operated by Catholic orders. The wineries held elections or checked the union membership cards of their employees to determine if they wanted NFWA representation, and then negotiated contracts similar to the Schenley agreement with a minimum of fuss.

DiGiorgio wouldn't fall so easily and, as lettuce grower Bud Antle had done in the Salinas Valley five years earlier, would use the Teamsters Union against the organizers. The NFWA tried for two months to reach an agreement with DiGiorgio on election procedures: then, in the midst of the negotiations, DiGiorgio abruptly announced that the corporation would hold an election on its own, under rules the NFWA negotiators had opposed. Striking NFWA members would not be allowed to vote, and though AWOC was not demanding representation rights at DiGiorgio, AWOC would be on the ballot along with the NFWA and the Teamsters. That would split the vote badly and possibly swing the election to the Teamsters, which had begun organizing DiGiorgio field workers with the corporation's active support. The NFWA applied heavy pressure through the AFL-CIO and supporters in the

Catholic hierarchy to get regional Teamster leaders to order the organizers to withdraw, but the organizers convinced them to reverse the order.

The Teamsters Union represented DiGiorgio cannery workers and was conducting an organizing drive in citrus groves to the north in conjunction with AWOC's Al Green; that, the union asserted, explained its presence in DiGiorgio's vineyards. But if the Teamsters weren't there on the direct invitation of DiGiorgio, they certainly were there with the corporation's blessing. DiGiorgio supervisors and foremen escorted Teamster organizers; helped pass out Teamster petitions, dues authorization forms and literature that attacked the NFWA as a collection of "beatniks, out-of-town agitators and do-gooders"; sent pro-Teamster letters to employees and, on several occasions, fired or laid of NFWA sympathizers.

Given these circumstances, the NFWA didn't even try to win the union representation election that DiGiorgio had set up. It decided, rather, to discredit the election by documenting DiGiorgio's pro-Teamster activities, getting a court order that removed AWOC and the NFWA from the ballot and urging DiGiorgio employees to boycott the voting.

NFWA representatives talked with workers at their homes, circulated among them at lunch breaks while Teamsters wooed them with free beer and soft drinks, and greeted them on election day with a line of 300 pickets shouting, "Don't vote!" As anticipated, the Teamsters got most of the votes cast—201 of 385. But 347 DiGiorgio employees didn't vote—almost half of those eligible. That and charges of unfair electioneering made against DiGiorgio and the Teamsters by the NFWA, AFL-CIO and a group of clergymen was enough for the NFWA to successfully demand another election.

The NFWA took its demands to Governor Brown, who was in a tough reelection campaign against Republican Ronald Reagan. Brown still was fearful of alienating conservative grower interests; but he needed the liberals within his party, and extensive lobbying by the NFWA and its allies had won the support of several liberal Democratic organizations for a new election at DiGiorgio.

Brown agreed to an investigation by Ronald Haughton, one of the country's most respected arbitrators. Haughton, co-director of labor studies at the University of Michigan and Wayne State University in Detroit, pointedly declined to make any charges of his own, but recommended that a new election be held in order to settle the dispute "fair and equitably." It took Haughton almost two months to set up the election because of a dispute with the Teamsters over ground rules. He got the NFWA to suspend its strike and boycott as a precondition, and DiGiorgio to agree that those who had struck could vote, even if not currently employed at DiGiorgio. It was also agreed that the election winner would not strike to enforce unresolved contract demands, but submit them to Haughton and another arbitrator for decision after forty-five days. DiGiorgio nevertheless refused to agree to an election because the Teamsters would not accept the preconditions. Haughton recommended that the election be held anyway, and the NFWA and its allies staged a series of demonstrations at DiGiorgio's San Francisco headquarters to demand that Haughton's recommendation be followed.

But DiGiorgio wouldn't budge, and the other grape growers meanwhile arranged a hearing of the state senate's Fact-Finding Committee on Agriculture to try to discredit the NFWA with another session of red-baiting and employer testimony that the vineyard workers really didn't want to be unionized. The committee had a list of 5000 "outsiders" who had been in Delano, thanks to the diligence of the Kern County Sheriff's Department in taking down the license numbers of every car seen near the picket lines or NFWA headquarters. One of those outsiders, the committee reported darkly, was Mickey Lima, the northern California chairman of the Communist Party. Lima was subpoenaed, but testified that, although his car had been in Delano, he had never been there; it was his daughter who had driven in the car to the strike area.

Undaunted, the committee summoned Saul Alinsky, whom grower witnesses had portrayed as the clandestine guiding hand behind the NFWA. The vineyard strike, declared one witness, was "an Alinsky-inspired attempt to sow distrust, racial and religious discord and economic disaster . . . attempted revolution." Alinsky, peering through thick glasses, cheek on one hand, a cigarette in the other, calmly informed the committee that "I am not now and never have been a member of the John Birch Society, the Ku Klux Klan, the Minute Men, the DiGiorgio Corporation or the Communist Party." Besides, Alinsky hadn't contacted Chavez or anyone else in the NFWA since they began attempting to organize farm workers— "not by spiritual séance or in any other way."

DiGiorgio finally had to agree to the election after the Teamsters withdrew and thus removed the corporation's excuse for further delay. Heavy public pressure from Catholic leaders and others had made it clear an election would inevitably be held, with or without Teamster agreement on the preconditions; and the precondition allowing NFWA strikers to vote faced the Teamsters with almost certain defeat. For the NFWA had rounded up hundreds of DiGiorgio strikers scattered throughout the Southwest, paying their transportation back and in some cases finding them local jobs or financially supporting them. To add to the heavy odds, the NFWA had merged with AWOC to form a single organization, the United Farm Workers Organizing Committee, which would present a united front against the Teamsters.

The merger had been coming since 1965, when AFL-CIO President George Meany appointed Bill Kircher, an old opponent of Walter Reuther within the Auto Workers Union, as the AFL-CIO's national director of organization with the primary assignment of organizing farm workers. Kircher, strapping, outspoken and pragmatic, soon was convinced that the NFWA's way was the only way; that the NFWA was going to organize farm workers with or without the AFL-CIO's help. He got ready agreement from Meany, who was moved as well by the AFL-CIO's rivalry with the independent Teamsters Union. Suddenly, Meany was saying thing like "the only

effective farm workers union will be one built by the farm workers themselves," and Kircher was offering Chavez the strength and protection of the AFL-CIO, and openly defying the wishes of some AWOC leaders by taking a prominent part in the march to the state capitol and other NFWA activities the AWOC leaders scorned as "civil rights demonstrations."

It took Kircher five months to convince Chavez; the NFWA wanted the use of the AFL-CIO's extensive resources, but wanted independence even more. Chavez was finally swayed by Kircher's offer of a monthly organizing budget of $10,000, on-the-scene help from Kircher and other AFL-CIO leaders and freedom to continue operating in the NFWA manner, albeit without some of those volunteers who greeted AFL-CIO affiliation with charges of "sellout."

Kircher immediately closed AWOC's office in Stockton and shunted aside Al Green and others who objected to the NFWA's methods. Operations were moved to Delano, where the merged organization, known as UFWOC, was run by an executive board consisting of four former NFWA officers headed by Chavez, and three of AWOC's Filipino leaders headed by Larry Itliong. Nearly fifty AFL-CIO organizers were assigned to work on the DiGiorgio election campaign with Fred Ross, whom Chavez had lured from semiretirement to become UFWOC's director of organization.

The election was UFWOC's first victory. Strikers came from as far away as Texas and Mexico to mark ballots that asked simply if they wanted "to be represented by UFWOC." More than 1300 of the 2000 eligible voters went to the polls; 813 said "yes," 530 "no."

The victory against one of the country's most prominent foes of farm unionization inspired organizing activities and strikes throughout California and nine other states, most notably in Texas, where Chavez led a march on the state capitol. But UFWOC had to concentrate on defeating the rest of the Delano growers, and lacking the local resources, leadership and advance work of the farm workers in California, most of the outside movements died quickly under the heavy pressure of powerful growers and their allies in law enforcement and political office.

The contract eventually won from DiGiorgio, in part through arbitration, went beyond even the pioneering Schenley agreement. It set up an employer-financed health and welfare fund, for instance, based layoffs and promotions on seniority, and granted holiday pay, vacations and unemployment benefits. But DiGiorgio was soon to dispose of its farm properties, in accord with an order from the Bureau of Reclamation. The Bureau had responded to pressure from land reform groups by ruling that a provision of the reclamation laws, largely unenforced until then, required growers getting federally subsidized water to sell any holdings in excess of 160 acres. UFWOC argued for a contract clause that would have bound buyers of DiGiorgio's 47,000 acres of excess land to honor the contract and the union recognition it conferred. But the arbitrators ruled in favor of DiGiorgio's argument that the land could not be sold under those circumstances, since the potential buyers were Delano grape growers who were still opposing the union. By the time the last of thirty-one parcels of land was sold in early 1969, less than two years after the DiGiorgio contract was signed, UFWOC's victory had disappeared, and with it the precedent that the contract might have set. For none of the buyers would recognize UFWOC.

Nor did the DiGiorgio settlement end UFWOC's problems with the Teamsters Union. A short time later, while UFWOC was trying to negotiate a settlement with another major Delano grower, Perelli-Minetti, the firm announced it would sign a contract with the Teamsters. Perelli-Minetti suddenly discovered its employees wanted to be represented by the Teamsters; for good reason: the Teamsters had recruited many of those employees and brought them to work across UFWOC picket lines, sometimes after violent confrontations. UFWOC immediately called a boycott against the bulk and bottled wines and brandies that were widely distributed by Perelli-Minetti, and again turned church pressure on the Teamsters. Within a few months, an interfaith committee of California clergymen arranged a peace treaty between the AFL-CIO and the Teamsters. The Teamsters promised to stay within their customary jurisdiction in canneries and processing plants and leave field workers to UFWOC. The Teamsters abandoned their contract with Perelli-Minetti, aptly described as a "sweetheart agreement" that granted a pay raise but little else to workers, and UFWOC was to negotiate a contract with the firm on its own terms. The Teamsters also dropped a challenge they had raised to UFWOC's recognition by Gallo, the world's largest winery.

Despite the unprecedented victories, UFWOC's concrete gains were slight: a dozen contracts covering only about 5000 of California's 250,000 farm workers, most of them employed by growers of wine grapes, whose operations were highly mechanized and required comparatively few workers. UFWOC's pressures had forced an increase of 25 cents an hour in the base pay of most other vineyard workers, but otherwise the union had barely touched the more numerous growers of table grapes; and now was the time to do it. UFWOC started with the biggest, the giant Giumarra Corporation. "If we can crack Giumarra," declared Dolores Huerta, "we can crack them all."

UFWOC reiterated its demand for a union election among Giumarra's 3000 workers, concentrated most of its pickets on the corporation's vast holdings and geared up its boycott machinery to try to halt the sale of Giumarra grapes. But Giumarra easily recruited replacements for employees who joined the picket lines, got a court order that neutralized the pickets by forcing them to stand 50 feet apart, and tried to escape the boycott by shipping grapes under 100 different labels supplied by other growers in California and Arizona. UFWOC had little choice but to declare a boycott against all grapes. "It was the only way we could do it," Chavez recalled. "We had to take on the whole industry. The grape itself had to become a label."

The grape became, certainly, one of the best-known symbols in the country as the target of what developed into the most extensive and most successful boycott in U.S. history. It began in

January of 1968, when Huerta and sixty UFWOC members set out in an old bus for a 3000-mile trip to New York City, the largest single market for western grapes. Some of the farm workers got out along the way to work with volunteers on setting up boycott committees in more than thirty other cities. Eventually, 200 strikers and their families were working with 500 full-time volunteers on committees in more than 400 communities across the United States and Canada.

Strikers had to leave their homes, and sometimes their families, to live for extended periods in the totally unfamiliar urban surroundings, and were paid only $5 a week and minimal expenses. But their presence was essential if the farm workers were to continue building their own union, and it dramatized their cause in a way that outsiders working alone could never have done.

The most dramatic act was performed by Chavez himself, a month after the farm workers began the difficult task of seeking help in the cities. Chavez provided them and their potential supporters an extreme example of sacrifice by undertaking a twenty-five-day fast which he dedicated to reaffirming the principles of nonviolence. Chavez wanted to focus maximum attention on the farm workers' effort, but he was also sincerely concerned that the strikers' frustrations were turning them toward violence. There had been no serious violence in the strike yet, despite a spate of minor attacks and extreme provocations for which union and grower forces blamed each other; but there was danger that Chavez, emerging as the Martin Luther King of the newly aroused Mexican-Americans, might be supplanted by men from the Southwest who were preaching a "brown power" version of the call to arms being raised in riot-torn ghettos by black militants. "Some of our people accused us of cowardice," Chavez said. "They told me: 'If you go out and kill a couple of growers and blow up some cold storage plants and trains, the growers will come to terms. This is the history of labor; this is how things are done.' "

Chavez now feared that "someone would hurt someone" if picketing continued at the struck vineyards, and was well aware, too, that victory would come from urban boycott activities rather than from the picketing. He called off the pickets, sent some strikers back to work to ease the strain on UFWOC finances, and retired to a storeroom at UFWOC headquarters to fast, pray and read the Bible and the writings of Gandhi. Chavez announced the fast and its purpose six days after it began. "No union movement," he declared, "is worth the death of one farm worker or his child or one grower and his child. . . . Social justice for the dignity of man cannot be won at the price of human life."

The storeroom became almost a religious shrine. Tents were erected outside to shelter UFWOC members and supporters who came in pilgrimage from all over the state. They celebrated daily Masses conducted by a young Franciscan priest who wore vestments fashioned of burlap and the red and black banners of UFWOC and offered "union-made wine" to communicants, held prayer vigils and stood in line for hours to talk with Chavez as he lay on a cot in the small, white-walled storeroom. Some refused to accept his sacrifice and tried to force food on him; but all were sent away with the same message: "Go home and organize!"

Giumarra inadvertently helped publicize the fast and generate more support for the boycott by insisting that UFWOC be held in contempt of court for previous violations of orders against mass picketing. Chavez tottered into court weakly on the arms of two aides, his path lined by 1000 farm workers kneeling in silent prayer, to get the judge to postpone the hearing in deference to his condition. It was not a scene that would win growers much sympathy from the public which was being asked to bypass their grapes, and Giumarra quietly dropped the contempt charge for fear of being trapped into such a situation again.

Chavez broke the fast before 4000 supporters at an ecumenical mass in Delano's city park. Robert Kennedy was at his side as he slumped in a chair and nibbled feebly at a tiny bit of bread handed him by a priest. Senator Kennedy took a portion from the same home-baked loaf, then hailed Chavez as "one of the heroic figures of our time," endorsed UFWOC's legislative goals, and congratulated those who were "locked with Cesar in the struggle for justice for the farm workers and for justice for Spanish-speaking Americans." Chavez reminded his followers, in a message read by an aide, that "we have our bodies and spirits and the justice of our cause as our weapons." He was convinced, Chavez said later, that the fast had turned his followers from the violent path that militants everywhere else were trodding and had made UFWOC's nonviolent position clear to the public, "ourselves and our adversaries."

The ordeal sent Chavez to a hospital, where he lay immobilized for three weeks with severe back pains attributed to a lack of calcium in his diet, and for much of the next eight months he directed the union from a hospital bed at home. Chavez became a near-fanatic vegetarian who praised the virtues of carrot and celery juice to just about anyone within hearing; but the pain did not subside until Dr. Janet Travell, a physician who had treated John F. Kennedy, correctly diagnosed that Chavez was suffering from the same back problems as the late President. His spine was twisted out of alignment because one leg was shorter than the other. Dr. Travell, who treated Chavez at the request of Senator Edward Kennedy, had Chavez perform special exercises, put a lift in one shoe and, like President Kennedy, sit in a rocking chair when working at his desk.

The fast focused increased attention on the boycott, and the UFWOC members who had been sent to the cities found thousands of allies, in barrios, on college campuses and in churches, synagogues, and union halls, to give them food, money, lodging and other support. Supporters contributed $20,000 a month to supplement the $10,000 UFWOC was getting directly from the AFL-CIO, made untold thousands of posters, signs and bumper strips demanding that shoppers "boycott California grapes," and engaged in an astounding variety of well-publicized activities. Students at Holy Angels School in Sacramento held a cupcake sale that raised $5 for the cause; Ethel Kennedy held a glittering cocktail party in

New York that raised $20,000; supporters dumped grapes into Boston Harbor in a latter-day version of the Boston Tea Party; prominent entertainers held benefit concerts; labor, political and religious leaders spoke out at news conferences, before legislative committees and in newspaper advertisements, arranged rallies and church services in behalf of the farm workers, and joined the picket lines that were at the heart of the boycott.

Boycott committees kept in close contact with each other, and it was rare for a shipment of grapes to enter a city without being greeted by pickets who had been dispatched from commune-like "boycott houses," along with supporters who were on call for such occasions. They demonstrated at produce terminals, then followed the grapes to supermarkets—picketing, singing, chanting, leafletting customers, confronting store managers with their demand for removal of the grapes. Other grape shipments were followed to the waterfront, where pickets urged sympathetic longshoremen not to load them onto ships that were to carry them to Europe and the Far East.

Entire supermarket chains quit stocking grapes; student supporters had grapes stricken from the menus of cafeterias and university dining halls; church leaders kept them from their schools and hospitals and urged their millions of followers to cease buying them; the union-oriented mayors of three dozen industrial cities, including New York, proclaimed support for the boycott and in some cases ordered municipal agencies to stop buying grapes. Legal action forced longshoremen to load the overseas shipments, but there also were boycott committees in major cities abroad, backed by the World Council of Churches and major European unions.

In New York, where growers normally sold about 20 percent of their crop, sales plummeted 90 percent during the summer of 1968 and wholesale prices dropped by as much as one-third. Shippers were forced to put tons of grapes into cold storage or ship them to other areas, creating a surplus that helped drive prices down and cut sales nationally by 12 percent. Overall sales returned the growers about $2.5 million less than they had anticipated for the summer, and the antiboycott campaign, importation of workers to replace strikers and other new expenses were steadily increasing their costs.

Growers could have stopped it all by simply agreeing to union representation elections; but they still were unwilling to give up *any* of their unilateral authority in labor relations. The growers got strong backing from the Farm Bureau Federation, whose statewide president called the boycott "the worst crisis that California agriculture has ever faced," and from others in the agricultural establishment who feared that unionization in California's vineyards would lead to unionization on farms throughout the country. Growers expanded their markets to the South and elsewhere outside liberal eastern and midwestern cities and frightened off some boycott supporters with damage suits alleging violations of the law against secondary boycotts by industrial unions. Then they joined with their anxious allies to get help from newspapers, chambers of commerce and other business groups, and from conservative figures in government and politics who depended on their support.

The grower interests spent more than $2 million on an advertising and public relations campaign directed by Whitaker & Baxter, the firm that had previously waged the major campaigns against Medicare and reapportionment of rural-dominated legislatures. Bumper strips urged people to "Eat California Grapes, the Forbidden Fruit," and newspaper ads said they could "feel better in all respects" by "buying and enjoying fresh California grapes." Other ads, and editorials and columns, charged that UFWOC was undermining "consumer rights" and violating its own precept of nonviolence chiefly to extract dues from well-paid workers whom it did not actually represent.

The John Birch Society and National Right to Work Committee formed so-called consumer groups to spread the message and dire warnings that UFWOC sought "control of America's food supply." Giumarra and thirteen other growers secretly set up and financed an "Agricultural Workers Freedom to Work Association." The association had very few members, but it did have an "executive secretary" who was sent on speaking tours to claim he represented a large body of farm workers who opposed unionization, and to win praise from conservative legislators and columnists for being "a true farm worker."

Growers got strong support from California's new governor, Republican Ronald Reagan, who announced at the height of the boycott that he had "probably eaten more grapes during the past year than ever." Reagan resisted all efforts to grant union bargaining rights to farm workers; appointed growers to run the state's Farm Placement Service; joined the state Board of Agriculture in waging an antiboycott campaign, and provided growers with convict help and welfare recipients, until blocked by a state Supreme Court ruling. It held, in significant contrast to the attitudes of Reagan and governors before him, that the "interests of the growers are private, not public."

Richard Nixon proved to be at least as firm a grower ally during and after his successful presidential race in 1968. He gleefully plopped grapes into his mouth during campaign rallies and declared, in one of his more misleading public statements, that the boycott was illegal and unnecessary. Nixon said that was because "we have laws on our books to protect workers who wish to organize . . . a National Labor Relations Board to impartially supervise the election of collective bargaining agents and to safeguard the rights of organizers." Nixon knew farm workers were excluded from these laws; he, of course, had been a member of the congressional subcommittee that had recommended their continued exclusion after hearings during the DiGiorgio strike in 1949. But Nixon was not one to let down his supporters or miss an opportunity to condemn his Democratic opponent, Hubert Humphrey, for supporting "lawbreaking" by endorsing the boycott as the only way for farm workers to win bargaining rights.

As President, however, Nixon didn't overlook the farm workers' exclusion from the National Labor Relations Act. He had said during the campaign that "the law must be applied equally to all"; and once elected he moved to apply it to farm workers—but only those parts of it that prohibited secondary boycotts and allowed the President to block serious strikes for eighty-day "cooling-off periods."

Nixon's efforts were part of a legal campaign that centered on a "Consumer Food Protection Act" introduced by another major grower ally, Senator George Murphy. The measure, described by Democratic Congressman Phillip Burton of San Francisco as "one of the worst union-busting bills of the twentieth century," would have outlawed the boycott, made it illegal to strike at any time a grower could be hurt and put farm labor relations under a presidential board. But though the legislation failed, so did bills by liberal Democrats to extend the NLRA in its entirety to farm workers.

Supermarket chains began resisting the boycott strongly, now that heavy pressure was being exerted by their natural allies in government and business. Retailers also set up "consumer rights committees," and placed ads that proclaimed their "neutrality" and support for free enterprise. If a customer didn't want to buy grapes, that was the customer's concern, but food stores had a moral obligation to make grapes available. "No one has the right to tell our customers that they cannot buy a product because one group wants to put bargaining pressure on another," declared a typical ad. "Our customers should have the 'freedom of choice.'"

This did not appreciably increase domestic grape sales, however. Growers needed more substantial help; and they got it from the Department of Defense. The Department also professed "neutrality," but felt it a patriotic duty to take advantage of the availability of large quantities of grapes at lowered prices. Department grape purchases shot up from 6.9 million pounds in the 1967–68 fiscal year to 11 million pounds in 1968–69, partly because of an increase of 350 percent in shipments to U.S. troops in Vietnam. The Vietnam shipments jumped from 500,000 to 2.5 million pounds over the year—enough grapes to provide eight pounds to each and every serviceman.

Department representatives were summoned

before the Senate Subcommittee on Migratory Labor to explain what members felt to be a deliberate undercutting of the boycott. The Department spokesmen cited increased "troop acceptance" of grapes, alleged shortages of other fresh fruit, the superior "caloric value" of grapes and a need for menu planners to follow the dictates of "objective and systematic management" without regard to such external matters as labor disputes. Democratic Senator Alan Cranston of California asked angrily whether the Department officer in charge of food procurement, Dale Babione, had ever seen an order from Defense Secretary Melvin Laird that called for the Department to show "a social consciousness . . . in evaluating the domestic impact of all its actions." Babione said he hadn't heard of the order, and believed, in any case, that the Department was obliged to continue its current rate of grape purchases, whatever the domestic consequences. The Department maintained that position, despite the insistence of Cranston and others in Congress that neutrality dictated cutting back purchases to preboycott levels.

But though the Defense Department did a great deal to shore up growers who were weakening under boycott pressures, it also gave UFWOC another attention-grabbing issue. The union waged a major campaign against the government purchases, in part through a hyperactive legal department. Previous farm union organizers had not even tried to match the growers' heavy and often decisive use of court action against them; but growers and their supporters were hit with a steady barrage of lawsuits by young attorneys who worked with UFWOC all over California, many as volunteers, none for anything but a bare minimum salary.

Grower suits to limit or halt picketing were met with suits charging growers with assault and harassment of pickets, illegal use of alien workers and violations of laws requiring safe and sanitary working conditions and guaranteeing freedom of assembly and association. Damage suits charging boycotters with restraint of trade were met with countersuits charging growers with violating antitrust laws by conspiring to block union contract negotiations, dividing up the grape market among themselves, maintaining artificially high prices and low wages, illegally using federally subsidized water and so forth.

Few of the lawsuits came to a decision, but they exposed grower tactics and provided UFWOC members and supporters a continuous flow of issues to keep them active, militant and highly visible.

UFWOC increased its pressures considerably by exposing the growers' heavy use of poisonous pesticides. The union's concern helped prompt a survey by the California Department of Public Health indicating that at least 15 of every 100 farm workers suffered from pesticide poisoning, and that the rate would grow now that the organic phosphates causing "serious disabling illnesses" and deaths were being widely substituted for DDT.

Grape pickers commonly exhibited the flu-like symptoms of poisoning by the chemicals that were applied to vineyards according to standards determined almost solely by the pesticide manufacturers, and when an increasing number began coming to UFWOC clinics for treatment, the union went to Kern County's agricultural commissioner to determine which chemicals had caused the illness and how they had been applied. But the commissioner refused to disclose the data. He said the records were "trade secrets" entrusted to him by the firms that applied the pesticides and he was not about to give UFWOC ammunition for "phony lawsuits" against growers and the companies. The union immediately filed suit in the county's superior court; but though the court acknowledged that many pesticides could cause serious illness and death, it also refused public access to the records, on grounds that UFWOC was merely seeking publicity to use in the boycott.

The court's refusal was enough to give UFWOC plenty of publicity anyway. The union got even more when boycotters discovered a batch of grapes in a Washington, D.C., supermarket that supposedly carried a heavy residue of Aldrin, a pesticide that has since been banned because of signs that it might produce cancer.

The boycotters presented the Senate's Subcommittee on Migratory Labor a laboratory analysis showing the grapes carried eighteen times the maximum residue allowed by the Federal Drug Administration. Senator Murphy and other grower supporters challenged the test results as false; but neither they nor the boycotters could conclusively prove their conflicting claims because of the extreme difficulty of accurately testing for Aldrin. But true or not, UFWOC's claim gave some shoppers still another reason to avoid grapes. It also aided the union in its drive to help ban DDT and other dangerous pesticides and force growers to agree to contract provisions giving workers a strong voice in use of the chemicals whose dangers previously had been regarded indifferently by workers and growers alike.

Chavez weakened UFWOC's growing support by changing his stand on extension of the NLRA to farm workers. UFWOC and its political allies had argued for several years that farm workers merely sought equal rights—that they wanted no more than industrial workers were granted under the act. But though this meant farm workers would be covered by the original provisions of the act, which granted the legal right to union recognition, it meant they also would be covered by later amendments that prohibited secondary boycotts. The boycott had become UFWOC's only effective weapon, and by early 1969, Chavez saw that the union could not give it up. Getting a grower to recognize the union was one matter, but getting him to agree to a contract would take heavy pressure, which UFWOC could mount only through a boycott.

Hence Chavez argued that only the original provisions of the NLRA should be extended to farm workers. The NLRA had been amended in 1947 only *after* industrial unions had used the freer provisions of the original act to firmly establish themselves over a twelve-year period. The act had been intended for just that purpose and, Chavez reasoned, "We, too, need our decent period of time to grow strong under the life-giving sun of a public policy which affirmatively favors the growth of farm unionism . . . what has proved beneficial to the nation in the past when unions were weak and industry strong." Chavez argued as well for a special provision that the fledgling industrial unions had not needed. The provision would have made it illegal "for a grower to employ anyone during a strike or lockout who has not actually established a permanent residence in the United States."

Chavez' logic was irrefutable. His argument, however, was raised at a time when the AFL-CIO and other UFWOC allies were pressing hard for passage of legislation to extend the NLRA to farm workers in its current form. Chavez was still arguing for equal rights, yet many of his supporters failed to grasp the difference between what industrial unions had been granted and what they now had under the act. AFL-CIO leaders knew the difference; but they were angered that Chavez had not consulted them before changing his position and felt they couldn't sell the idea of what seemed to be special treatment to Congress or to their own members—especially not to those who worked in the retail trades that could be hurt by a secondary boycott. As a result, the AFL-CIO continued to lobby for simply extending the NLRA to farm workers in its entirety and ignored Chavez' call for special legislation. With union forces taking conflicting approaches, however, the odds for passage of any farm labor legislation became prohibitive.

As if to try to prove Chavez' contention that UFWOC would be better off without NLRA coverage, the union moved ahead with an extensive secondary boycott against Safeway Stores, the West's largest food chain. Growers relied heavily on Safeway—Giumarra marketed fully one-fifth of its grapes through the chain, for instance—and if UFWOC could cut Safeway's patronage to the point that the chain quit stocking grapes, or at least reduce its grape sales substantially, the growers would be under great pressure to bargain with the union.

Chants of "Boycott Safeway! Boycott Safeway!" rang out in front of supermarkets and at rallies and demonstrations in 100 cities as the boycott was launched at the start of the 1969 grape harvest. On the same day, a group of UFWOC members began a 100-mile march to the

Mexican border to mark an extension of the vineyard strike to the Coachella Valley and to try to convince Mexican nationals not to act as strikebreakers. The activities were coordinated to put maximum pressure on the highly vulnerable Coachella Valley growers who depended on getting their crop to market before arrival of the later-maturing grapes grown elsewhere.

Safeway's board of directors, which included directors of major agricultural corporations, banks and others closely associated with farming, held firm against the demand to clear grapes from the chain's markets. But the board did make the significant concession of endorsing NLRA coverage for farm workers. As intended, that helped ease the direct pressure on Safeway.

Growers had far less success in their attempts to counter the boycott. Early-season sales of Coachella Valley grapes dropped 15 percent below the previous year and grapes that had sold for as high as $7 a box were selling for as low as $3. Tons of fresh grapes were put into cold storage, sold at even lower prices to wine makers and food processors, or just left in the vineyards.

The break finally came midway through the harvest. A spokesman for ten growers who produced one-third of the Coachella Valley's grapes —15 percent of the state's entire crop—suddenly announced, "We are ready to negotiate tomorrow." The message was sent to the federal Mediation and Conciliation Service by Lionel Steinberg, a prominent Democrat who served on the state Board of Agriculture and operated three of the valley's largest vineyards. Although Steinberg was one of the few political liberals among growers, it was not liberalism that moved him. He was as conservative as his fellow growers in labor matters; but, he declared, "it is costing us more to produce and sell our grapes than we are getting paid for them and the boycott is the major factor in this ridiculous situation. . . . We are losing maybe 20 percent of our market." The boycott is "illegal and immoral," Steinberg added, "but it also is a fact and we must recognize it and try to deal with it in a manner fair to both sides."

Strictly speaking, the Mediation and Conciliation Service had no jurisdiction in farm labor disputes, and was directed by a Nixon appointee. "As a public service," however, three government mediators were dispatched to Los Angeles to oversee contract negotiations between representatives of UFWOC and the ten growers. For more than three weeks the mediators moved between two rooms where union and grower negotiators separately drafted demands and offers. They sometimes went at it fourteen hours a day, but could hardly get the parties together in a single room, much less get them to agree on contract terms.

UFWOC negotiators were extremely cautious. An agreement with these few growers would be a major breakthrough, but it also would weaken the boycott against hundreds of other growers because shoppers would have difficulty distinguishing between nonunion grapes and those from vineyards under union contract. The union wanted contracts with the entire table grape industry, and purposely sought to prolong the negotiations in hopes of forcing other anxious growers to the bargaining table through an intensified boycott.

UFWOC demanded nothing less than the contract terms agreed to previously by wine grape growers. But that was asking too much of the Coachella Valley growers; despite their economic distress, they could not yet conceive of granting UFWOC such rights as virtual control over hiring and, especially, the right to veto use of some pesticides and help determine how others were to be applied to their vineyards.

Heavy pressure was put on to keep the ten growers from weakening. Alan Grant, head of the state Farm Bureau and now chairman as well of the Board of Agriculture, rushed to the Coachella Valley to hold a news conference. He assured the growers that the boycott would soon be over because of new efforts to pass bills outlawing boycotts by farm workers. Senator Murphy, who was carrying the major bill, demanded an investigation of possible "collusion" between UFWOC and the ten growers, and the California Grape and Tree Fruit League tried to discredit them further by issuing an imaginative report claiming the boycott actually had been a "total failure."

Stronger, wealthier Delano growers who had been close personal friends deliberately snubbed the ten, and though one of the most influential of the Delano growers joined the negotiations, there were suspicions he was merely spying. On the very day he joined the talks, eighty-one of the other growers filed a $75 million damage suit against UFWOC, which sought to outlaw the boycott as a violation of the Sherman Anti-trust Act. That was the last straw. Within hours, mediators concluded that neither side would ever budge on even the most minor contract issues and so called off the "hopelessly deadlocked" negotiations.

Steinberg tried to settle on his own, but he did not offer UFWOC nearly enough to make it worthwhile to sign with just one table grape grower, however prominent. The other nine growers asked President Nixon to appoint a fact-finding committee to recommend a settlement, but UFWOC would not subject itself to such pressure from Nixon appointees.

Steinberg estimated that Coachella Valley growers lost $3 million during the 1969 harvest. But the standoff continued until just before the start of the next year's harvest, when the unrelenting force of the boycott and the mediation efforts of a committee from the National Conference of Catholic Bishops brought Steinberg back to the negotiating table in a mood to bargain. UFWOC also was ready to settle, since other growers had told the bishops' committee privately that if Steinberg could reach an agreement they would follow him rather than face another losing year. First came another Coachella Valley grower, K. K. Larson, who insisted that UFWOC submit to an election. Larson had been on a grower "truth squad" that toured the country declaring that vineyard workers did not want UFWOC representation; but he quickly agreed to a contract after his employees voted 152–2 for UFWOC.

Agreements were reached rapidly with most of the other Coachella Valley growers, and with three of the most influential growers in the major vineyard areas to the north. They included Hollis Roberts, who grew eighteen fruit and nut crops on 46,000 acres of corporate holdings spread across five San Joaquin Valley counties, and two Delano growers, Anthony Bianco and Bruno Dispoto, who had been among UFWOC's most outspoken opponents. Roberts had been forced to virtually abandon grape growing, Bianco declared bankruptcy and, like many of the other growers, Dispoto was feeling the pinch of banks and other creditors. Dispoto didn't believe the creditors "were much in favor of continuing to finance growers who were doing nothing about the union. . . . Sometimes you have to make decisions that you are not too happy about, but if that decision will keep your business alive, you make it."

By mid-July of 1970, the rest of the Delano growers were calling for peace. Their harvest would start soon and they, too, wanted agreements before their grapes got to the supermarkets where many shoppers were now demanding "union grapes." There were twenty-six growers, men who produced half of California's entire grape crop and employed 8000 workers. They now were convinced, said John Giumarra Jr., "that unionism has finally come to this industry and there's no sense pretending it will go away. The thing to do is to come to the best possible terms."

The growers tried to disarm UFWOC at the last minute by having Governor Reagan offer to hold state-supervised union elections and then by announcing they would negotiate only if the boycott was called off. But UFWOC would neither agree to elections whose rules would be designed to defeat the union, nor give up the only weapon it could use in negotiations.

Within a week Giumarra and other growers were meeting secretly with Chavez and other UFWOC and AFL-CIO representatives, a committee of farm workers who insisted on being involved in every detail, and members of the bishops' committee who had spent the past two months persuading growers to agree to the peace talks. A contract agreement was reached after two weeks, on terms similar to those accepted previously by other growers. Base pay, currently $1.65 an hour, was to be raised immediately to $1.80, go up to $1.95 in 1971 and to $2.05 in 1972. Another 12 cents an hour would finance the first health and welfare benefits ever granted these workers, and there would be a 5-cent increase in the piece-rate bonus of 15 cents for each of the three to four boxes of grapes the average worker picked hourly.

It was not the economic provisions that marked the contract as a victory for the farm workers, however. They had not struggled five years merely for pay raises and fringe benefits, as important as those were to their well-being; nor had growers absorbed millions of dollars in losses for purely economic reasons. The growers had been fighting to maintain complete control over the working lives of their employees, but now they were agreeing to get their workers from a union hiring hall, to set up joint worker-grower committees to regulate pesticides and to create machinery through which employees could effectively press grievances against them. An auto worker or steel worker would consider all this routine. But it was downright revolutionary in an industry that had languished for a century in the dark ages of labor relations.

The Delano growers, on that hot July day when they signed the contracts in UFWOC's crowded hiring hall, put a stamp of permanence on the movement that had brought agriculture into the twentieth century. The farm workers who led the way had "lost all their worldly possessions," as Cesar Chavez told the joyous crowd, "but in struggling for justice, they found themselves."

"What's happened here is a miracle," added Dolores Huerta. "But it didn't come about by magic."

24

THE VIETNAM WAR, THE LIBERALS, AND THE OVERTHROW OF LBJ

ALLEN J. MATUSOW

The Vietnam War dominated much of American life in the decade between 1964 and 1974. With an active draft supplying the bulk of the quarter of a million American troops and advisors fighting in Vietnam, three presidents—Kennedy, Johnson, and Nixon—sought to project American military power into Southeast Asia in an effort to "contain communism."

Between 1954, when the United States assumed the role of supporter of the corrupt but anti-Communist South Vietnamese regime, and the early 1960s American involvement in Vietnam was limited to small numbers of military and civilian advisors. But beginning in 1962, when President John F. Kennedy created the Green Berets, a special counter-insurgency force, American involvement in the region took the path of escalation. Slowly at first, but with increasing speed after the mid-1960s, the American military presence grew until daily reports from the war zone dominated the nightly television news.

As the war drew on with little evidence of success or purpose, growing numbers of Americans began to question the propriety of the war. At the same time students and other Americans, including many church leaders, organized the most effective antiwar movement in American history. By the late 1960s antiwar protest took on epic proportions as tens of thousands of Americans—men and women, young and old alike —marched across the country to end the war and bring American troops home.

One of the Vietnam War's more famous casualties was President Lyndon B. Johnson. In the arrogance of his belief that he could convert the peasants of Vietnam into his image of upwardly mobile American farmers, Johnson escalated U.S. involvement. Mindless of local conditions and the history of the Vietnamese people, Johnson and his advisors committed billions of dollars to a war that many military analysts agreed could not be won. As Allen J. Matusow shows in the essay, this arrogance cost Johnson the support of American liberals and ultimately the presidency itself.

What do you think accounts for America's initial commitment to war in Vietnam? Do you find any similarities between the American occupation of Cuba, described by Howard Gillette in Reading 9, and that of Vietnam? Was the war in Vietnam in America's national interest?

In April 1965, three months after Lyndon Johnson made his decision to bomb North Vietnam, Democratic Senator Wayne Morse of Oregon predicted that Johnson's war policy would send him "out of office the most discredited President in the history of .he nation." Given the popularity of both the war and the president at the time, Morse's prophecy seemed absurd on its face. But, as Vietnam dragged on month after month, it did indeed become an acid eroding Johnson's political base, until in the end it destroyed his presidency. The first constituency to be alienated by Vietnam—and the most dangerous opponent of Johnson's war policy—proved to be the liberal intellectuals.

At first glance the split between the president and the intellectuals seemed surprising. He was, after all, attempting to govern in the liberal tradition not only in his conduct of domestic policy but in foreign affairs as well. They must hate him, he came to believe, not really for anything he did but because of who he was—a crude Texas cowboy without a Harvard degree. What he failed to understand was that his liberalism and theirs—apparently so similar in 1964—thereafter rapidly diverged, his remaining rooted in the ideas of the 1950s, theirs moving far beyond.

The root of the difficulty was the breakup of the Cold War consensus. In the 1950s, of course, liberal intellectuals typically had embraced the Cold War as a holy crusade, becoming in the process staunch defenders of the American way of life. Even after Sputnik in 1957, when the intellectuals began denouncing the nation for its materialism and complacency, they did so primarily to goad the people into greater sacrifice for the struggle against world Communism. The first sign of restlessness began to appear around 1960. That was the year, for example, when Norman Podhoretz, a New York intellectual who had been a dutiful Cold War liberal but now felt the old ideas going stale, "going dead," became editor of the influential magazine *Commentary.* Daring to open his early issues to dissident voices, he discovered among the intellectuals who wrote for his magazine and read it "a hunger for something new and something radical." Radicalism was hardly the term to describe the outlook of the intellectuals in the Kennedy era, but they were more open to novelty, more willing to acknowledge the flaws in American society, than they had been for years. In 1963, when Kennedy and Khrushchev moved toward détente following the

Cuban missile crisis, the international tension that for so long had sustained the Cold War mentality began to dissipate, the old obsession to bore. Liberal intellectuals supported Johnson's 1964 presidential campaign because they believed he shared not only their renewed commitment to social justice but their growing willingness to reach an accommodation with the Russians.

Strains in Johnson's relations with the liberals first appeared in February 1965 when Johnson launched his air war over North Vietnam. Immediately the *New Republic,* a leading journal of liberal opinion, and the Americans for Democratic Action (ADA), the leading liberal organization, condemned the bombing and called for a negotiated settlement. Johnson was perplexed by the criticism since he correctly believed that he was merely applying in Vietnam the doctrine of containment so recently espoused by the liberals themselves. He did not grasp that that doctrine had suddenly fallen from fashion. Among the prominent liberal intellectuals who attempted to account for the shifting views of their community were Hans Morgenthau, an academic specialist in foreign affairs, member of the ADA board, and an early and formidable war critic; Reinhold Niebuhr, the renowned theologian and a founder of ADA, ailing but still influential; Arthur Schlesinger, Jr., a historian, former White House aide to Kennedy and Johnson, half-hearted defender of the war in 1965, but a leading foe by 1966; John Kenneth Galbraith, the Harvard economist, Kennedy's ambassador to India, and in 1967 the ADA chairman; Richard Goodwin, a precocious speech writer for Johnson till September 1965, and a war critic by the following spring; and Richard Rovere, the prestigious political correspondent of *The New Yorker,* a late but important convert to the dove side of the war argument.

The liberal intellectuals did not apologize for their past support of the Cold War. So long as Communist parties everywhere had subordinated themselves to the malign purposes of the Soviet Union, every Communist gain threatened American security. But times had changed, the liberals said. The Communist world was now "polycentric" (many-centered), a situation resulting from the Sino-Soviet split and the emergence of conflicting national aspirations among Communist states. Wrote Schlesinger, "Communism is no longer a unified, coordinated, centralized conspiracy." According to Rovere, since Tito's break with Stalin in 1948, the U.S. should have known that "international Communism" was a myth, "that national interest was more powerful than ideology, and that while we might on occasion find it advisable to resist the outward thrust of certain Communist nations, it made absolutely no sense to have a foreign policy directed against an alliance that did not exist." In short, it was no longer necessary to oppose every Communist initiative on every part of the globe.

With the exception of Morgenthau, who favored recognizing spheres of influence, these intellectuals continued to advocate containing China. But they denied that the war in Vietnam followed logically from this policy. Secretary of State Dean Rusk's opinion to the contrary, China was not the enemy there. The war in South Vietnam, they argued, was primarily a civil war, pitting indigenous revolutionaries against the corrupt and repressive regime in Saigon. If the Communists won, Vietnam might well become a bulwark against the spread of Chinese influence in the region. As a practical matter, the U.S. could not win. Escalation on the ground in the South could easily be offset by the enemy and would do nothing to remedy the defects of the Saigon government. Bombing the North would merely strengthen the enemy's will to fight. If Johnson proceeded on the course of escalation, he would destroy the country he was trying to save or else provoke war with China.

The war, the liberals said, was not a result of American imperialism but a mistake of policy deriving from obsolete assumptions about international Communism. Unfortunately, it was a mistake not easily remedied. Liberals rejected unilateral withdrawal on the grounds that it would mean abandonment of America's friends in the South, a blow to U.S. prestige, and maybe even the rise at home of a new Joe McCarthy to exploit the frustrations attending defeat. The liberal solution was a negotiated settlement—the middle course, they called it. Stop the foolish bombing in the North, since Hanoi demanded it as a precondition for negotiations. Convince Ho Chi Minh that the U.S. could not be dislodged by force. Offer the Vietcong a seat at the conference table and a role in the postwar political life of South Vietnam. It was possible, of course, that negotiations would fail. In that event, said Galbraith, "We must be prepared to defend for the time being the limited areas that are now secure." Indeed, on close inspection, it turned out that the liberals were waist deep in the Big Muddy along with LBJ and were no more certain than he of getting back to shore. The difference was that they thought the war was all a big mistake, and he was there on principle.

As opposition to the war among the intellectuals mounted, so did their impatience with the administration's response to the great racial and urban crisis that was tearing the country apart. As they never would have done during the American celebration that had characterized the heyday of the Cold War, liberals were now earnestly discussing the menace of corporate monopoly, redistribution of income, and a Marshall Plan for the cities. In its January 1967 issue *Commentary* ran both a long article by Theodore Draper attacking Johnson's foreign policy for its "willingness to use and abuse naked military power" and an essay by the Keynesian economist Robert Lekachman summarizing the case of many liberal intellectuals against the president's domestic policies. Lekachman wrote:

> Possibly Mr. Johnson went just about as far as a conservative politician in a conservative, racist country could have gone. The Great Society has distributed the nation's income even less equally than it was distributed before 1960. It has enlarged the prestige and influence of the business community. It has lost its token bouts with racism and poverty. The Great Society, never a giant step beyond the New Deal which was President Johnson's youthful inspiration, has ground to a halt far short of a massive attack on urban blight, far short of the full integration of Negroes into American society, and far short of a genuine assault upon poverty and deprivation.

Where liberal intellectuals led, liberal politicians usually followed. But politicians skeptical of the war in Vietnam initially hesitated to tangle with a president to whom most were bound by ties of party loyalty and whose vindictive character was legend. In 1965 even senators held their tongues, excepting of course Oregon's Wayne Morse and Alaska's Ernest Gruening, the lone opponents of the 1964 Gulf of Tonkin Resolution. Among those who privately worried but publicly acquiesced in Johnson's war policy were Senators Mike Mansfield, George McGovern, Frank Church, Joseph Clark, Eugene McCarthy, and J. William Fulbright. Fulbright was the pivotal figure. If he moved into the open against Johnson, the rest would follow.

A senator from the ex-Confederate state of Arkansas, Fulbright was a gentleman of inherited wealth, excellent education, and illiberal record on matters of race and social reform. But for more than twenty years, on matters of foreign policy, Fulbright had been the leading spokesman in Congress for the views of the liberal community. Though he had had his share of arguments with presidents, he was by nature a contemplative rather than a combative man, a Senate club member who played by the rules. Fulbright's early opinions on Vietnam were hardly heretical. In March 1964, in a wide-ranging speech attacking Cold War mythology, he paused over Vietnam long enough to make a few hawkish observations. The allies were too weak militarily to obtain "the independence of a non-Communist South Vietnam" through negotiations, he said. The only "realistic options" were to hasten the buildup of the regime in the South or to expand the war, "either by the direct commitment of large numbers of American troops or by equipping the South Vietnamese Army to attack North Vietnamese territory." In August 1964 Fulbright sponsored the Gulf of Tonkin Resolution, which gave Johnson authority to expand the war.

For reasons unknown, Fulbright had second thoughts about escalation once it actually began. Publicly in the spring of 1965 he backed Johnson's policy, though he called for a temporary bombing halt to induce Hanoi to negotiate. Privately, he warned his old friend in the White House against waging war on North Vietnam and tempted him with the vision of a Communist Vietnam hostile to China. Johnson seemed bored by Fulbright's conversation. Fulbright gave a Senate speech in June that both criticized the bombing and praised Johnson's statesmanship. In July Johnson began the massive infusion of ground troops into South Vietnam.

Fulbright's first real attack on the Johnson administration was occasioned not by Vietnam but by policy in the Dominican Republic. In April 1965 Johnson sent U.S. troops into the midst of a developing civil war, ostensibly to protect Americans but really to prevent a possible Communist takeover. Fulbright brooded over this intervention, held secret hearings on it, and finally in September delivered a powerful Senate speech attacking the administration's conduct as ruthless and lacking in candor. The president promptly ended all pretense of consulting the chairman of the Foreign Relations Committee and cut him socially.

As Fulbright edged toward open rebellion on the issue of the war, so did the other Senate doves, almost all of whom were liberal Democrats. This was probably one reason why Johnson halted the bombing of North Vietnam on Christmas Eve, 1965, and launched a well-advertised peace offensive allegedly to persuade Hanoi to negotiate. The State Department moved closer to Hanoi's conditions for negotiations in early January, and both sides scaled down ground action in South Vietnam. Diplomats in several capitals worked to bring the wary antagonists together. But on January 24, 1966, Johnson hinted to a group of congressional leaders that he might soon resume the bombing. Two days later fifteen senators, all of them liberal Democrats, sent a letter to Johnson urging him to continue the pause. Fulbright and Mansfield did not sign but were on record with similar views. On January 29, Johnson ordered the air attack to recommence. The episode convinced many liberals that Johnson's talk about peace masked his private determination to win total military victory.

In February 1966 Fulbright held televised

hearings on the war. The scholar-diplomat George Kennan and the retired general James Gavin argued the case against it on grounds of American self-interest. Dean Rusk and General Maxwell Taylor parried the thrusts of liberal committee members now openly critical of Johnson's policy. Neither side drew blood in debate, but by helping legitimize dissent, the Fulbright hearings were a net loss for Johnson. Fulbright, meantime, was reading, talking to experts, and rethinking first principles. In the spring of 1966 he took to the lecture platform to hurl thunderbolts at orthodoxy. Revised and published as a book later in the year, Fulbright's lectures were a critique of American foreign policy far more advanced than any yet produced by the liberal academicians.

"Gradually but unmistakably America is showing signs of that arrogance of power which has afflicted, weakened, and in some cases destroyed great nations in the past," Fulbright said. Harnessing her might to a crusading ideology, America had overextended herself abroad and was neglecting vital tasks at home. Americans meant well overseas, Fulbright conceded, but they often did more harm than good, especially in the Third World. A conservative people, Americans supported necessary social revolutions in traditional societies only if they were peaceful, that is, in "our own shining image." To violent revolutions, which "seem to promise greater and faster results," Americans reacted with automatic hostility or panic. Fulbright was hardly an apologist for revolutions, but neither would he oppose them, even if they were led by Communists. Fulbright dared to find much that was praiseworthy in Castro's Cuba and even extended sympathy to the aims of the Chinese revolutionaries, whose regime he would recognize de facto. In Vietnam, he said, the U.S. had blundered into a war against Communism in the only country in the world "which won freedom from colonial rule under communist leadership." Fulbright favored a negotiated settlement that would provide self-determination for South Vietnam through the mechanism of a referendum.

President Johnson had expected his main trouble to come from hawks who wanted to escalate faster than he did. Stung by the sweeping attacks of Fulbright and other doves, he resorted to a scoundrel's last refuge. Before a friendly audience of Democratic politicians in Chicago mid-May 1966, Johnson defended the war as a patriotic effort to secure lasting peace by punishing aggression and then said, "There will be some 'Nervous Nellies' and some who will become frustrated and bothered and break ranks under the strain, and some will turn on their leaders, and on their country, and on our own fighting men. . . . But I have not the slightest doubt that the courage and the dedication and the good sense of the wise American people will ultimately prevail." The attack failed to silence the critics. The majority of the people still backed the war, but not with the passion aroused by wars of the past. Fulbright continued to assault the premises of American foreign policy and, indirectly, the president who was acting on them. Confronted with irreconcilable views of world politics, members of the liberal public in ever-increasing numbers deserted the president and sided with the senator.

To make matters worse for Johnson, he faced a personal as well as an intellectual challenge to his party leadership. When Robert Kennedy emerged from mourning in early 1964, he discovered a remarkable fact. Despite his squeaky voice, diffident public manner, private shyness, and reputation as a ruthless backroom operator, he was the sole beneficiary of his brother's political estate. In him resided the hopes of millions who believed in the myth of Camelot and longed for a Kennedy restoration. Robert Kennedy believed the myth himself and shared the longing. Lyndon Johnson, however, despised Kennedy personally and made himself the great obstacle to the younger man's ambitions. After Johnson denied him the vice-presidential nomination in 1964, Kennedy repaired to New York, where he successfully ran for the Senate. Soon there grew up around him what the political columnists called the Kennedy party—Kennedy loyalists still in the bureaucracy, some senators, New Frontiersmen out of favor, and lesser politicians, lawyers, and professors scattered around the country. Most of the Kennedy loyalists were liberals, but by no means all liberals were Kennedy loyalists. Robert Kennedy, after all, had been an ally of Joe McCarthy, an advocate of wiretapping, too zealous a pursuer of the Teamster chief Jimmy Hoffa, and a frequent offender of liberal sensibilities. But liberals unhappy with Johnson needed a popular leader, and Kennedy needed to broaden his party base. The one issue guaranteed to bring them together was Vietnam.

The issue posed problems for Kennedy. As a Cabinet officer, he had been an enthusiastic student of guerrilla warfare and strong supporter of his brother's counterinsurgency program in South Vietnam. When Johnson escalated in 1965, Kennedy questioned less the attempt to rescue South Vietnam by force of arms than the tendency to subordinate political to military considerations in fighting the war. Speaking at the graduation ceremony of the International Police Academy in July, he said, "I think the history of the last 20 years demonstrates beyond doubt that our approach to revolutionary war must be political—political first, political last, political always." To avoid offending Johnson, he excised from his prepared text the view that "victory in a revolutionary war is won not by escalation but by de-escalation." Kennedy waited one whole year after escalation before putting real distance between his position and Johnson's. It bothered Kennedy that, when Fulbright asked Rusk during the televised hearings of February 1966 to state the options other than "surrender or annihilation" that he was offering the Vietcong, Rusk had replied, "They do have an alternative of quitting, of stopping being an agent of Hanoi and receiving men and arms from the North." The war could go on forever if this was the American requirement for peace. So Kennedy decided to propose another option. On February 19, 1966, he became the first senator to suggest a negotiated settlement that would give the Vietcong "a share of power and responsibility"—in what he did not say. Assuming he meant the government of Vietnam, the administration dismissed the idea contemptuously. Kennedy's proposal, said Vice President Humphrey, would be like putting "a fox in the chicken coop" or "an arsonist in a fire department." Kennedy spent the next week clarifying and qualifying, and though he retreated some, he was clearly moving toward the peace wing of his party.

Strange things were happening to Bobby Kennedy. Perhaps prolonged grief deepened his social sympathies, perhaps he was trying in his own life to vindicate his brother's legend—or outdo it. Whatever the cause, Kennedy plunged into the currents of change that were swirling through America in the mid-1960s, currents that were altering the perspective of liberalism and passing Johnson by. Kennedy opened a running dialogue with students, made a friend of Tom Hayden, felt the yearnings of the poor and the black for power and dignity, and took unnecessary political risks. Blood donations for the Vietcong? Burial for a Communist war hero in Arlington Cemetery? Why not? he asked. Kennedy went to South Africa in mid-1966 to aid the opponents of apartheid. He attacked administration witnesses at Senate hearings in August for unresponsiveness to the poor. He flew to California to stand with Cesar Chavez in his fight to unionize the grape pickers. A man who risked his life scaling mountains and defying tropical storms on the Amazon, Kennedy was becoming an existentialist in politics, defining himself in action and moving where his heart told him to go.

As Kennedy and Johnson edged closer toward political combat, their personal relations worsened. In February 1967 *Newsweek* erroneously reported that Kennedy had brought back from a recent trip to Paris a peace feeler from Hanoi. The story enraged Johnson, who, believing it was planted by Kennedy, called him to the White House for a tongue lashing. According to *Time*'s colorful account, Johnson told Kennedy, "If you keep talking like this, you won't have a political future in this country within six months," warned him that "the blood of American boys will be on your hands," and concluded, "I never want to see you again." Uncowed, Kennedy called Johnson an s.o.b. and told him, "I don't have to sit here and take that——."

Whether Kennedy really used vulgarity was a matter of some dispute, but there was no doubt that the gist of the conversation had been accurately reported. Less than a month later (March 2, 1967) Kennedy gave a major Senate speech calling for a halt to the bombing and a compromise settlement through negotiations. A few party malcontents, especially in the liberal wing, permitted themselves a small hope that maybe the crown prince of the Democratic party would claim his inheritance sooner than expected.

In the summer of 1967 gloom descended on the camp of the liberals. In August Johnson sent 45,000 more troops to Vietnam and asked for higher taxes to finance the war. And, though Defense Secretary Robert McNamara himself voiced public criticism of the bombing, day after day the bombs continued to fall. Liberals who had once viewed it merely as politically stupid watched in horror as the carnage mounted and now pronounced the war morally wrong as well. Meanwhile domestic insurrectionaries were gutting great American cities, the War on Poverty was bogging down, and the long-awaited white backlash finally arrived. Among those surrendering to despair that summer was Senator Fulbright. Speaking to the American Bar Association in August, he said, "How can we commend democratic social reform to Latin America when Newark, Detroit, and Milwaukee are providing explosive evidence of our own inadequate efforts at democratic social reform? How can we commend the free enterprise system to Asians and Africans when in our own country it has produced vast, chaotic, noisy, dangerous and dirty urban complexes while poisoning the very air and land and water?" Fulbright called the war "unnecessary and immoral" and blamed it for aggravating grave domestic problems. The country "sickens for lack of moral leadership," he said, and only the idealistic young may save us from the "false and dangerous dream of an imperial destiny."

Fulbright's charges about the damage done at home by the war were confirmed in the autumn. Driven by hatred of the war, new left students began acting out their guerrilla fantasies, and major campuses were threatened by chaos. No less disturbing to liberals was the fever of discontent rising in intellectual circles. Some of the nation's most brilliant writers and artists were concluding, as had their counterparts in France during the Algerian war, that they now had no choice but to resist the state.

From the beginning a minority of the nation's intellectual elite—call them radicals—saw the war as more than a blunder in judgment. Most of these radicals had life histories punctuated by episodes of dissent but had stayed aloof from politics during the Cold War. Vietnam brought them back to political awareness and gave focus to their inchoate alienation. To people like the novelists Norman Mailer and Mary McCarthy, the critics Susan Sontag and Dwight Macdonald, *New York Review of Books* editor Robert Silvers, the linguist Noam Chomsky, the anarchist writer Paul Goodman, and the poet Robert Lowell, America appeared to be in the hands of a technological elite that was debauching the American landscape and lusting after world dominion. Morally revolted by the imperial war against the peasants of Vietnam, the radicals found traditional politics insufficient to express their opposition. The war was a matter of conscience, and good men would act accordingly.

Their first impulse was to avoid complicity with the crime. Thus when Johnson invited a group of writers and artists to participate in a White House Festival of the Arts in June 1965, Robert Lowell refused to come. Scion of a distinguished American family, perhaps the best of living American poets, and a draft resister in World War II, Lowell sent a letter to the president, saying, "Every serious artist knows that he cannot enjoy public celebration without making subtle public commitments. . . . We are in danger of imperceptibly becoming an explosive and suddenly chauvinistic nation, and we may even be drifting on our way to the last nuclear ruin. . . . At this anguished, delicate and perhaps determining moment, I feel I am serving you and our country best by not taking part." Robert Silvers took the lead in circulating a statement in support of his friend Lowell and in two days attracted the signatures of twenty of the nation's most prominent writers and artists, among them Hannah Arendt, Lillian Hellman, Alfred Kazin, Dwight Macdonald, Bernard Malamud, Mary McCarthy, William Styron, and Robert Penn Warren. Johnson was so angry at "these people," these "sonsofbitches" that he almost canceled the festival.

By 1967 the radicals were obsessed by the war and frustrated by their impotence to affect its course. The government was unmoved by protest, the people were uninformed and apathetic, and American technology was tearing Vietnam apart. What, then, was their responsibility? Noam Chomsky explored this problem in February 1967 in the *New York Review,* which had become the favorite journal of the radicals. By virtue of their training and leisure, intellectuals had a greater responsibility than ordinary citizens for the actions of the state, Chomsky said. It was their special responsibility "to speak the truth and to expose lies." But the "free-floating intellectual" who had performed this function in the past was being replaced by the "scholar-expert" who lied for the government or constructed "value-free technologies" to keep the existing social order functioning smoothly. Chomsky not only enjoined the intellectuals once again "to seek the truth lying behind the veil of distortion"; he concluded by quoting an essay written twenty years before by Dwight Macdonald, an essay that implied that in time of crisis exposing lies might not be enough. "Only those who are willing to resist authority themselves when it conflicts too intolerably with their personal moral code," Macdonald had written, "only they have the right to condemn." Chomsky's article was immediately recognized as an important intellectual event. Along with the radical students, radical intellectuals were moving "from protest to resistance."

The move toward resistance accelerated through 1967. Chomsky announced in the *New York Review* that for the second consecutive year he was withholding half his income taxes to protest the war. Paul Goodman invited federal pros-

ecution by acknowledging his efforts to aid and abet draft resistance. Mary McCarthy, back from a trip to Vietnam, said that "to be in the town jail, as Thoreau knew, can relieve any sense of imaginary imprisonment." On the cover of its issue of August 24, 1967, the *New York Review* put a diagram of a Molotov cocktail, while inside Andrew Kopkind, in the midst of dismissing Martin Luther King for having failed to make a revolution, wrote, "Morality, like politics, starts at the barrel of a gun." (Some intellectuals never forgave the *New York Review* for that one.) On October 12, 1967, the *New York Review* published a statement signed by 121 intellectuals and entitled "A Call to Resist Illegitimate Authority." The statement denounced the war on legal and moral grounds and pledged the signers to raise funds "to organize draft resistance unions, to supply legal defense and bail, to support families and otherwise aid resistance to the war in whatever ways may seem appropriate."

A few days later Stop the Draft Week began. This was an event whose possibilities excited radical intellectuals as well as radical students. Paul Goodman kicked the week off with a speech at the State Department before an audience of big business executives. "You are the military industrial of the United States, the most dangerous body of men at the present in the world," Goodman declaimed. On Friday, October 20, 1967, Lowell and Mailer spoke on the steps of the Justice Department prior to the efforts of the Reverend William Sloane Coffin to deliver to the government draft cards collected from draft resisters across the country earlier in the week. (This occasion provided evidence for later federal charges of criminal conspiracy against Coffin, Dr. Benjamin Spock, and three other antiwar activists.) Saturday began with speeches at the Lincoln Memorial ("remorseless, amplified harangues for peace," Lowell called them), and then the march across the bridge toward the Pentagon. Lowell, Mailer, and Macdonald, described by Mailer as "America's best poet? and best novelist??, and best critic???," walked to the battle together. Lowell wrote of the marchers that they were

. . . like green Union recruits
for the first Bull Run, sped by photographers,
the notables, the girls . . . fear, glory, chaos,
rout . . .
our green army staggered out on the miles-long
    green fields,
met by the other army, the Martian, the ape, the
    hero,
his new-fangled rifle, his green new steel helmet.

At the Pentagon Mailer was arrested, much to his satisfaction, but Lowell and Macdonald failed of their object. Noam Chomsky, also present, had not intended to participate in civil disobedience, feeling its purpose in this occasion too vague to make a point. Swept up by the events of the day, Chomsky found himself at the very walls of the fortress, making a speech. When a line of soldiers began marching toward him, he spontaneously sat down. Chomsky spent the night in jail with Mailer.

In his brilliant book *The Armies of the Night,* Mailer probed for the meaning of these apocalyptic events. For him the siege of the Pentagon was a rite of passage for the student rebels, for the intellectuals, for himself. The few hundred fearful youths who sat on the Pentagon steps till dawn on Sunday were a "refrain from all the great American rites of passage when men and women manacled themselves to a lost and painful principle and survived a day, a night, a week, a month, a year." The battle at the Pentagon was a pale rite of passage, he thought, compared to that of the immigrants packed in steerage, Rogers and Clark, the Americans "at Sutter's Mill, at Gettysburg, the Alamo, the Klondike, the Argonne, Normandy, Pusan." But it was a true rite of passage nonetheless, the survivors having been reborn and rededicated to great purpose. On departing from jail Sunday morning, Mailer felt as Christians must "when they spoke of Christ within them." For Mailer and many other radical intellectuals, American institutions seemed so illegitimate that a moral man could find redemption only in resisting them. As for the liberals, they could only wonder what would happen to America if Lyndon Johnson was not stopped.

Signs of a liberal revolt against Johnson's renomination were plentiful in the fall of 1967. Reform Democrats in New York, the liberal California Democratic Council, party factions in Minnesota, Michigan, Wisconsin, and elsewhere were preparing to oppose him. In late September the ADA national board implicitly came out against him by promising to back the candidate who offered "the best prospect for a settlement of the Vietnam conflict." The *New Republic* explicitly rejected his candidacy in an editorial that same week. And Allard Lowenstein, thirty-eight-year-old liberal activist and ADA vice-chairman, opened an office in Washington and began organizing a movement on campuses, in the peace movement, and among dissident Democratic politicians to "dump Johnson."

Lowenstein wanted Robert Kennedy to be his candidate. And the existentialist Bobby was tempted. Kennedy worried about the frustration building up in the antiwar movement and had himself come to view the war as morally repugnant. "We're killing South Vietnamese, we're killing women, we're killing innocent people because we don't want to have the war fought on American soil, or because they're 12,000 miles away and they might get 11,000 miles away," he said on *Face the Nation* late in November 1967. But Bobby the professional hated losing, and in his view he could not defeat Johnson in a fight for the nomination, and neither could anybody else. On that same TV program he stated flatly that he would not be a candidate. If he were, he said, "it would immediately become a personality struggle," and the real issues would be obscured. Asked about some other Democrat, such as Senator Eugene McCarthy of Minnesota, taking on the president, Kennedy replied, "There could be a healthy element in that." He would endorse neither Johnson nor McCarthy but support whoever was the eventual party nominee.

Eugene McCarthy had become convinced that someone would have to raise the issue of the war in the party primaries in 1968. When Kennedy and other leading doves rejected Lowenstein's pleas to be the candidate, McCarthy agreed to run. Explaining his purpose at a press conference on November 30, 1967, he said, "There is growing evidence of a deepening moral crisis in America—discontent and frustration and a disposition to take extralegal if not illegal actions to manifest protest. I am hopeful that this challenge . . . may alleviate at least in some degree this sense of political helplessness and restore to many people a belief in the processes of American politics and of American government." In other words, McCarthy was offering his candidacy as an alternative to radicalism.

Only an unusual politician would undertake what no one else would dare. In truth McCarthy, who had spent eight months of his youth as a novice in a Benedictine monastery, was in the political world but not of it. He was a senator bored by the Senate, an office seeker who disdained intrigue and self-advertisement, a professional who valued honor more than influence. In recent years he had seemed more interested in Thomistic theology and writing poetry than in the business of government. His career, it appeared, would not fulfill its early promise. But the political crisis in the United States in late 1967 provided McCarthy with an opportunity perfectly suited to his self-conception. Like his hero Thomas More, he would play the martyr in a historic confrontation between conscience and power.

McCarthy's candidacy prospered beyond anyone's expectation, even his own. Though Johnson's rating on the Gallup poll was only 41 percent in November, the professionals were mesmerized by the cliché that no president could be denied renomination by his own party. The war was the biggest cause of Johnson's unpopularity. Hawks and doves disagreed on how best to end the war but otherwise had much in common: both disliked the war, wanted its early termination, and tended to blame Lyndon Johnson for dragging it on. It was the public's declining confidence in Johnson's ability to conclude the war that made him vulnerable to McCarthy's candidacy.

What little confidence still existed in the president's war leadership was shattered on January 31, 1968, when the Vietnamese Communists launched a massive attack in the midst of a truce called for the Tet holiday. Sixty-seven thousand enemy troops invaded more than one hundred of South Vietnam's cities and towns. The allies recaptured most urban areas after a few days and inflicted huge casualties on the attackers. But the Tet Offensive had astounded military men by its scope and daring. It showed that no place in South Vietnam was secure, not even the American embassy, whose walls had been breached in the first hours of the attack. And it temporarily derailed the pacification program in the countryside by drawing allied troops into the cities. Coming after recent administration assurances that the war was being won, the Tet Offensive dealt Johnson's credibility its crowning blow. When he and the U.S. commander in Vietnam, General William Westmoreland, issued victory statements after the offensive ended, few took them seriously, though militarily they were right. The chief political casualty of the Tet Offensive, therefore, was Lyndon Johnson.

In the six weeks after Tet, such pillars of establishment opinion as Walter Cronkite, *Newsweek,* the *Wall Street Journal,* and NBC News gave way and called for de-escalation. High officials in the government finally dared express their private doubts about the war to the president. The Gallup poll reported a seismic shift in public opinion: in February self-described hawks had outnumbered doves 60 percent to 24 percent; in March it was hawks 41 percent, doves 42 percent. And on March 10, two days before the New Hampshire primary, the *New York Times* set off waves of national anxiety by reporting a secret request from the generals to the president for 206,000 more troops for the war.

Meanwhile, in New Hampshire, the first primary state, McCarthy was proving an eccentric candidate. A lazy campaigner, he often did not return phone calls, would not court potential contributors, and avoided local politicians. His manner on the stump was uninspired, and even his references to the war were low-key. (McCarthy opposed unilateral withdrawal and advocated a negotiated settlement.) But McCarthy had an insight denied to his detractors: he mattered less in this campaign than the movement he represented. At the climax of the campaign there were so many student volunteers in the tiny state (3,000, or one for every 25 Democratic voters) that McCarthy's lieutenants begged potential workers to stay home. Scrubbed and shaven, the students ran a canvassing operation that was the envy of the professionals. Even McCarthy's peculiar style proved to be an asset. At a time when the country was fed up with politicians, shrill voices, and the hard sell, there was something reassuring in McCarthy's unhurried, dignified manner. He did not frighten people. He seemed safe.

Governor John W. King, one of the inept managers of Johnson's write-in campaign in New Hampshire, said in the beginning that McCarthy would get 5 percent of the vote. McCarthy himself predicted 30 percent. On March 12, 1968, 49 percent of New Hampshire's Democratic voters wrote in the name of the president of the United States, and 42 percent marked their ballots for a senator of whom days before few had heard. Poll data showed that more McCarthy voters in New Hampshire were hawks than doves. McCarthy's remarkable showing, then, was not a victory for peace, merely proof that Lyndon Johnson, who could neither pacify the ghetto, speak the plain truth, lick inflation, nor above all end the war, was a mighty unpopular president indeed.

McCarthy had done more than demonstrate Johnson's vulnerability. As he had hoped, his candidacy drained off some of the discontent flowing into illegal protest. Thousands of students who might otherwise have joined SDS got "clean for Gene." Intellectuals who had flirted with resistance a few months before became the senator's avid fans. McCarthy's traveling companion through much of New Hampshire was Robert Lowell—a symbolic relationship whose significance was probably lost on neither of these famous poets.

It had been a hard winter for Robert Kennedy. He realized after the Tet Offensive that his refusal to run had been a mistake. Throughout February 1968, while McCarthy's New Hampshire campaign was getting started, Kennedy and his advisers wrestled again with the problem of his candidacy. Kennedy was ready to go early in March and set in motion machinery for a campaign. But still he found reason to delay a public announcement. By the time he declared on March 16, 1968, the results of the New Hampshire primary had already electrified the country. Much of the constituency that would have been his now belonged to McCarthy. Lyndon Johnson, however, took Kennedy's candidacy more seriously than McCarthy's. He knew, even if the students did not, that Kennedy was the one man in the party who might beat him.

McCarthy refused to step aside for Kennedy and moved on to the Wisconsin primary, whose date was April 2. Early in March the president's men in Wisconsin had been confident of victory. But McCarthy arrived with more students, money, and prestige than he had had in New Hampshire, and by mid-month the Johnson managers knew their man was in trouble. On March 28 Postmaster Larry O'Brien, an old political pro, returned from a look around the state to tell Johnson that his cause there was hopeless.

While the political storms raged around them, Johnson and his advisers were deep into a momentous review of war policy. General Earl Wheeler, chairman of the Joint Chiefs of Staff, had blundered in late February when he privately requested 206,000 additional troops for Vietnam. Since General Westmoreland was in no danger of being overrun, there was never much chance that Johnson would dispatch massive reinforcements. The tax money to pay for escalation was not there, and neither was the political support. Wheeler's request had one unintended result. By asking so much, it forced policy makers to resolve the basic ambiguity that had characterized America's policy since 1965. Militarily, Johnson had been seeking victory over the Vietcong. Diplomatically, he paid lip service to a negotiated settlement, which implied compromise. Since his generals were in effect telling him that they needed more troops than he could furnish to win, Johnson had no choice now except to opt for negotiation. Accounts differ on how Johnson reached this conclusion in March 1968. But in the end those of his advisers urging some steps in the direction of de-escalation prevailed. On March 31 Johnson went on television to announce that he was stopping the bombing over most of North Vietnam and would end it entirely if Hanoi demonstrated comparable restraint. Johnson called on the North Vietnamese to respond to his partial bombing halt by accepting his invitation to negotiate. A few days later they did so.

Johnson announced another decision in this speech. For some time he had been dropping hints among friends and advisers that he might not run in 1968. Only at the last minute did he determine not to make his 1968 State of the Union Message the occasion for announcing his retirement. But his mood seemed to change after that, and he took steps to organize a re-election campaign. Even after the ambush in New Hampshire, Johnson authorized Larry O'Brien to meet with Cabinet officers and give them marching orders for the political battle ahead.

Though most Johnson intimates believed he would run, he had compelling reasons not to. Exhausted, haunted by fear of another heart at-tack, bitter at the vilification he had suffered, the man had had enough. "The only difference be-tween the [John F.] Kennedy assassination and mine," he said in this period, "is that I am alive and it has been more torturous." There were other reasons too. Politically he faced a Congress opposed to his programs, a public that had lost confidence in his leadership, a defeat at the hands of McCarthy in the Wisconsin primary, and an uncertain contest with Robert Kennedy. On the diplomatic front, he wished to take a step toward peace, which his opponents, domestic and for-eign, would probably dismiss as insincere if he remained a potential candidate. In his speech of March 31, Johnson spoke of "division in the American house" and declared his intention to keep the presidency above partisanship in this election year. "Accordingly," he told a stunned nation, "I shall not seek, and I will not accept, the nomination of my party for another term as your President." The liberals, with an assist from the peace movement, the attackers of Tet, and war-weariness, had dumped Johnson.

25

THE NEW FEMINISM AND THE DYNAMICS OF SOCIAL CHANGE

JANE DeHART MATHEWS

The civil rights movement of the 1950s and 1960s produced more than a demand for equality among black Americans. The sit-ins, marches, and voter registration drives that characterized the movement also produced a consciousness of inequality in American life that would be taken up by other oppressed people. Hispanics, Native Americans, Asian-Americans, the poor, the elderly, and homosexuals watched the civil rights movement and saw in it a call to fulfill the democratic promise of America.

The group most influenced by the civil rights movement was not, however, a minority in American society. American women had borne the yoke of inequality since colonial days, and though they had gained the right to vote in 1920, by the 1960s women continued to suffer discrimination at home, at work, and in society as a whole. Following in the steps of the civil rights movement, where many of them had gained firsthand experience, groups of American women began to organize their own movement in the mid-1960s to demand an end to their second-class status in society.

As Jane DeHart Mathews shows in this essay, at the forefront of this renewed women's movement was a new generation of feminists who sought to move beyond the reform of job and income inequality championed by the middle-class oriented National Organization of Women (NOW) to encompass a more fundamental revolution in gender relations. Following in the footsteps of nineteenth- and early twentieth-century feminists, the vanguard of this renewed movement sought to analyze the sources of gender inequality, to locate the means by which such inequality was reproduced in everyday life, and to bring about an end to discrimination against women.

How do the ideas of the new feminists compare with those of their turn-of-the-century counterparts discussed by Linda Gordon in Reading 15? Compare the women's rights activists and the women's liberationists discussed by Jane DeHart Mathews in Reading 25. Which group do you think is most likely to succeed in ending gender inequality?

Fifty years after gaining the right to vote, women who had been suffragists and women young enough to be their great-granddaughters embarked on a new quest. Their motive: to change not only laws and institutions, but values, patterns of behavior, personal relationships, and ultimately themselves. Their goal: equality. This new feminist movement was vigorous, diffuse, and highly controversial. In order to understand its origins and goals, its opponents, and, most important, its potential for changing society, it is necessary to examine the long-term economic

Reprinted from Jane DeHart Mathews and Linda K. Kerber, eds., *Women's America: Refocusing the Past* (New York: Oxford University Press, 1982). Copyright © 1982 by Oxford University Press, Inc. Reprinted by permission.

and social changes that created an environment within which the movement could emerge. It is important also to appreciate the ferment of the 1960s that provided feminism with its ideological core, vitality, and impetus. To explore such origins is also to explore the sense in which contemporary feminists confronted issues an earlier generation had left unresolved.

Unfulfilled Expectations

By winning the vote in 1920, many women believed that the decisive battle in the long struggle for sexual equality had been won. The atmosphere was electric with a sense of achievement and expectation generated by the euphoria of the moment. The fact that enfranchisement had come on the heels of other reforms identified with women seemed evidence of their growing influence. Congress had passed legislation to protect women in industry, outlaw child labor, and enact prohibition—measures important to those who believed that women and children were the primary victims of exploitative employment and alcohol-related abuse. Champions of women's rights also celebrated gains in education and employment. Since 1900 female enrollment had shot up 100 percent in public colleges and universities and nearly 500 percent in private ones. As ambitious graduates gained access to advanced training, the proportion of women in the professions climbed by 1920 to an unprecedented 11.9 percent. During World War I women in record numbers had moved into skilled jobs and administrative positions formerly held by men.

These very real achievements had been won by a movement that was successful only so long as large numbers of women remained committed to each other and to common goals. This collective commitment had secured the vote and corrected some of the wrongs associated with women's exclusion from full participation in the public sphere of ballot box and marketplace. Few suffragists and reformers, however, were prepared to confront the barriers to equality in the domestic sphere of family. Most women as well as men still accepted as one of the few unchanging facts of life

the conviction that woman's primary duty was to be "the helpmeet, the housewife, and the mother." Feminists who hoped to provide additional, complementary, or alternative possibilities gradually found themselves a diminishing minority. Since their understanding of the many kinds of change yet required to ensure full emancipation was shared by so few women, enfranchisement failed to create a bloc of female voters prepared to use the ballot to remove additional barriers to equality. Like their male counterparts, they found issues of class, race, and ethnicity more compelling than the need to improve women's status. The collective power of the "woman's vote" through which suffragists had hoped to achieve further gains never fully materialized in the decade ahead.

Part of the reason for this failure lay in the physical and emotional fatigue of the suffragists themselves. The fight for the ballot, compounded by the stress of World War I, had taken its toll. As one suffragist explained: "After we [got] the vote, the crusade was over. It was peacetime and we went back to a hundred different causes and tasks that we'd been putting off all those years. We just demobilized." For those who still had the energy, there were new causes. Pacifism and disarmament acquired an added urgency not only for prewar pacifists such as Crystal Eastman and Jane Addams but also for more recent enthusiasts such as suffragist leader Carrie Chapman Catt, who established the National Conference on the Cause and Cure of War. Other women, whose feminist sympathies and political activism had been tenuous even in the yeasty reformist milieu of the progressive era, gradually yielded to the political conservatism of the 1920s. They could not be effectively mobilized for protest even when the Supreme Court in 1922 and 1923 invalidated two of the major legislative gains of the prewar women's movement—minimum wages for women and the abolition of child labor. Younger women who might have become new recruits found old visions of female equality less exciting than the personal gratification associated with the relaxed social and sexual mores and affluence of the new consumer culture.

As these and other disappointments mounted, divisions developed within the movement itself. The organizations most responsible for winning the vote, the National American Woman Suffrage Association (NAWSA) and its militant offshoot, the Congressional Union, had regrouped under new names. The Congressional Union, under Alice Paul's leadership became the National Woman's Party. It enrolled between four and five thousand members, many of them professional women, whose first priority was improvement of women's status. Many NAWSA members moved in a different direction, finding their way into the new League of Women Voters created in 1919 to educate women for citizenship. The league represented the persistence of a broad progressive impulse along with the commitment to the advancement of women. Its bipartisan concern for "good government" and legislation protecting women and children made it the more broadly reformist of the two organizations. Disagreement over tactics during the suffrage campaign continued in the debate over the next tactic in the struggle for equality. The Woman's Party advocated a constitutional amendment to guarantee equality before the law. The league and other organizations—such as the General Federation of Women's Clubs, the Women's Trade Union League, the Young Women's Christian Association, and the American Association of University Women—preferred to deal with the many discriminatory aspects of the law through a state-by-state effort to change specific statutes.

The league's preference derived in part from fears that an equal rights amendment would jeopardize legislation regulating hours, wages, and working conditions for thousands of unskilled, nonunionized female workers. Their health and safety, insisted the league, required the special protection of government. The courts, having denied this legislation to men on the ground that such laws interfered with their "freedom of contract," permitted it to women workers only because of their traditional role as mothers. Women workers, opponents of the amendment argued, could ill afford to surrender their concrete gains for the abstract principle of equality.

By the end of the 1920s the league and its allies could point to a few transitory gains in the area of maternal and infant health care and to the easing of legal strictures affecting marriage, divorce, property holding, and contracts. But they failed to shake the unswerving conviction of Woman's Party loyalists that the key to equality lay in amending the Constitution. As a result of these disagreements, intense and acrimonious debate persisted throughout years of fragmentation and frustration. Feminism as an organized movement virtually disappeared. Individually feminists might cling to egalitarian goals. Collectively, however, they were simply too few and too powerless to achieve those goals. As a result, the fundamental circumstances of women's lives remained little changed.

For working-class women life was still one of constant toil—on farms, in factories and mills, or in other women's homes. The factory job that had promised escape from poverty or the drudgery of farm work or the servility of domestic service often carried with it new problems. To be sure, increases in productivity during the 1920s allowed a handful of companies to initiate a five-day workweek, the eight-hour day, or a two-week annual vacation with pay. But low wages, long hours, frequent layoffs, monotony, noise, dirt, and danger still characterized many industrial jobs, especially in the nonunionized South. Moreover, wage work brought no escape from domestic duties.

For married women with children, the burden was especially heavy, as Grace Elliott's experience graphically demonstrates. An ambitious young textile worker, she worked as a weaver at the East Marion Manufacturing Company in Marion, North Carolina, during the 1920s. Earning $16 a week, she paid $5 for a cook and $2 for laundry. Because the $9 remaining seemed "such a slow path to home and furniture," she decided to do her own housework, getting up at 4:00 A.M., preparing breakfast and dinner, milking the cow, getting the children's clothes ready for them to wear to school before rushing to the mill for the 5:40 shift. Breaking at noon, she walked home for a cold lunch and then rushed back to the mill where she worked until 6:00 P.M. Returning home, she cooked supper, sometimes sewing after the children had gone to bed. Her schedule was "very hard" but, she insisted, "I had to keep the children in school." For all of her determination, the physical strain was too much. Like so many of her fellow workers, Grace Elliott was exhausted and ill at the end of four years. Struggling with wage labor, housework, illness, pregnancy, and poverty, such women seemed as powerless to control the conditions in which they lived and worked as did their voteless predecessors.

Middle-class women fared better than their working-class counterparts. More advantaged economically, they had easier access to birth control devices and to the educational and professional opportunities that would equip them to function in the world outside the home. Yet if progress is measured by achievements in business, professional, and political life, middle-class women made few gains in the postsuffrage decades. The proportion of women attending colleges and universities actually declined between 1920 and 1960, as did the proportion of women on college faculties. In 1920, one out of every seven doctoral degrees was awarded to a woman; in 1956, only one in ten. By 1960 only 4 percent of the lawyers and judges in this nation were women, only 6 percent of the medical doctors, and less than 1 percent of the architects. Percentages, of course, can be misleading in that they indicate a share rather than absolute numbers. For example, although the percentage of women awarded the Ph.D. in 1920 was 15 percent as opposed to 10.5 percent in 1960, indicating a decline of one-third, the actual number of women receiving the doctorate had increased from 90 in 1920 to 1,090 in 1960. In certain areas of business, notably real estate, women had increased in both numbers and percentage. In the final analysis, however, there was no escaping the fact that women were still excluded from the higher echelons of business, government, and the professions. The number of women elected to Congress throughout this entire forty-year period totaled a mere three in the Senate and forty-four in the House. The number of female cabinet members was a scant two. A seat on the stock exchange was as difficult to come by as a seat on the president's cabinet. Boards of directors of major corporations were also a male preserve. Veteran champions of equality of the sexes had to admit a certain element of truth in the phrase that is the despair of radicals and the hope of conservatives: *plus ça change, plus c'est la même chose.*

Unresolved Issues

The discrepancy between feminists' expectations and the actual accomplishments of women in the postsuffrage decades is a measure of how effectively internal and external barriers interacted to bind women to the traditional pattern of domesticity. That so many women rejected the new possibilities of public life for the old expectations of a private one when the former *seemingly* offered more challenging and potentially rewarding options is testimony both to the power of cultural constraints that undermined real freedom of choice and to the reality of external barriers that denied women equality in the workplace. Although women themselves may have thought they chose "freely," few were actually in a position to do so. Most had grown up in an atmosphere of profound conditioning that from infancy through adulthood assigned individuals of each sex social roles defined essentially by gender.

The cumulative impact of this socialization shaped young women's sense of themselves as females and the options open to them by the time they reached college. There, as in high school, the curriculum reinforced established patterns. Students taking home economics courses learned about the tasks that awaited them as consumer, homemaker, and mother. By the 1940s and 1950s many sociology courses portrayed the "normal" family as one based on a sexual division of labor and "sex-determined" behavioral characteristics. If the campus served as an environment within which to pursue a husband rather than an independent intellectual life or preprofessional training, that acknowledged a basic reality. Getting a man, especially one with bright prospects, was itself a vocational objective, one preferable to others.

The reason was that in a sexually segregated labor force positions filled predominantly by women carried little pay and prestige—to the financial detriment of the few males involved as well as the many females. Fields such as business, engineering, architecture, law, medicine, and university teaching were only slightly open to women. Female applicants to professional schools were usually confronted with admission quotas limiting the number of women, often to 5 percent. University faculties frequently assumed that female students would marry, get pregnant, and drop out, or, if they did graduate, never practice the profession for which they had been trained. Those young women who persisted, ultimately receiving the Ph.D. or the M.D., could expect continued discrimination in hiring, pay, or promotion once their active work life began.

They also had to face the problem of combining work and family in a society governed by traditional assumptions relating to both. Many business and professional women in the early years of the twentieth century solved the problem by staying single. Successive generations, less attracted to that option, had to find husbands willing to have a spouse pursue an active work life outside the home in an era in which a working wife was thought to reflect poorly on a man's ability to provide for his family. Even if husbands consented, those holding management positions in major corporations were expected by their companies to relocate frequently if they wished to move up the executive ladder. Wives of such men often found it difficult to establish their own vocational roots. Those who were able to do so had to contend with still other problems. Nagging fears that successful careers were inconsistent with marital happiness—at least for women—found reinforcement in Hollywood movies, women's magazines, and scholarly studies. The conventional assumption that an achieving woman would lose "her chance for the kind of love she wants" was criticized by the anthropologist Margaret Mead in 1935 to no avail. Twelve years later the sociologist Ferdinand Lundberg and the psy-

chiatrist Marynia Farnham were adamant in their insistence that "the 'successful woman" is only occasionally successful as a woman." In this context, women whose personal and professional lives provided refutation of such assertions were simply too few to make a difference. For those younger women who did persist, the self-doubt and confusion that are a part of role conflict sometimes remained long after the conflict had been resolved.

Parenting complicated the situation even further, creating practical problems and compounding internal anxieties. To be a lawyer and a father in America was to be "normal"; to be a lawyer and a mother was to be "deviant" because motherhood was assumed to be a full-time occupation, especially in middle-class circles. How to cope with the physical and psychological demands of family while simultaneously meeting the performance criteria and competitive pressures of work challenged even the most dedicated and resourceful woman. Pregnancy and child care leaves, tax benefits for child care expenses, public day care centers with strong programs to encourage physical and intellectual growth; these measures had become well established in advanced European nations such as Sweden. But they were never fully incorporated into the structure of American society during the first three-quarters of this century.

Families, too, were ill prepared to accommodate the special needs of women who worked outside the home. With kin networks often scattered about in distant cities and towns, it was difficult to find a grandparent or aunt who could take care of children during an emergency. Husbands, even when supportive in principle, often proved reluctant in practice to assume additional responsibilities at home. To have done so would have pitted them against conventional expectations, especially if their own schedules were full and job-related responsibilities demanding. Energetic women motivated by ambition or poverty somehow managed. They devised suitable child care arrangements, revised household priorities, and balanced work demands and personal needs. That in the process they often acquired a reputation for being "superwomen" was itself indication of the inequities inherent in a sex role system that allowed men the option of combining career and family while denying it to women.

For the vast majority of middle-class women the problems of combining work and family were simply too great. Moreover, their social position was such that most of the working women they knew—clerks, beauticians, domestics—were lower-middle and working-class people. *Not* working for pay outside the home indicated the high status so important to millions of Americans. As internal constraints and external constraints reinforced each other, most middle-class women concluded that they would have a better chance for security and status as wives and mothers than as workers. Economic dependency seemed a small price to pay for the pleasures of domesticity and the rewards of community activism so integral to suburban life. Paying this price was not a conscious decision so much as the unconscious transaction of investing in roles patterned after those of their mothers. The little girls who donned women's clothes on rainy afternoons while "playing house" were also donning attitudes and habits. In doing so, they indicated their "agreement" to contracts yet to be made with little boys who were learning how to be aggressive, independent, and successful. The sentimental myths surrounding middle-class family life created an almost sacred place within which children could take an idyllic apprenticeship in adulthood. This inviolability protected the family from widespread criticism. Champions of women's rights, concentrating on legal and political disabilities that deprived women of a full public life, never effectively challenged the pervasive cultural constraints binding women to dependency. To have raised such issues in the suffrage crusade would have been to play directly into the hands of opponents who were already predicting that giving women the vote would be the undoing of the family.

There were, to be sure, achieving women whose lives were not defined only by domesticity —Helen Keller, Amelia Earhart, Mary McLeod Bethune, and Eleanor Roosevelt. But this was a culture that, while celebrating the "exceptional woman," endlessly romanticized domesticity, extolling the joys of the housewife-mother who lovingly tended her garden and a bumper crop of children. Even the heroines hawked by Hollywood fell into two categories: sex objects and wives. The former were voluptuous if vacuous— the sexually alluring blonde whom "gentlemen preferred," as Marilyn Monroe so sensationally demonstrated during what one film critic dubbed the "mammary madness" of the 1950s. The latter, invariably played by Doris Day or Debbie Reynolds, were bland, childish, but amusing in a peppy, well-scrubbed, but unmistakably feminine way that projected them from girl-next-door to suburban wife. The message of the culture was clear. To be a woman in this society was to be "feminine"; to be a feminist was to be "neurotic."

The Growing Gap Between Ideology and Reality

The apparent retreat from feminism into domesticity after 1920 hid a more complex reality. Impersonal economic, scientific, and demographic forces were subtly undermining old patterns and assumptions. Although in themselves these new developments did not produce a resurgence of feminism, they did add impetus to the growing gap between conventional attitudes and changing conditions. This in turn lent credibility to a feminist critique of society.

One of the economic realities of modern American has been that many women were never fully in their "place"—the home. They have long been part of a paid labor force. Their numbers increased significantly throughout the twentieth century. Even during the Depression the proportion of women in the work force remained constant. This occurred despite the fact that many employers, including local school boards and the federal civil service, sought to deny employment to married women, assuming, often mistakenly, that their husband's earnings were adequate to support the family and that, as working women, they took jobs away from other men with families to support. But if hard times forced some women back into the home, others were forced out. Many mothers desperately needed even meager wages to keep the family afloat at a time when one out of every five children in this country was not getting enough nourishing food to eat.

As the nation shifted from fighting economic depression to waging global war, women responded by the millions to patriotic appeals to get a war job so as to bring their men home sooner. Between 1940 and 1945 the proportion of women in the work force rose from 25 percent to 36 percent. Money as well as patriotism was involved. The women who flocked to factories were beneficiaries of New Deal legislation governing wages and hours for both sexes. They also benefited from the Congress of Industrial Organization's (CIO) successful unionization effort during the 1930s and became the first generation of female industrial employees to receive good wages. Not surprisingly many were reluctant to return home when "Rosie, the Riveter," that symbol of women war workers, was told to put down her riveting machine at the return of peace. Forced out of well-paying "male" jobs, many women returned to low-paying "female" jobs in restaurants, laundries, shops, and offices. Moreover, their wartime experience seemingly had little impact on public attitudes. When asked whether married women whose husbands made enough to support them should be allowed to hold jobs if they wanted to, the majority of Americans responded with a resounding no. Yet as white-collar and clerical jobs expanded rapidly in the postwar years, so did the number of working women.

By 1960 some 40 percent of American women were employed in full- or part-time jobs. Moreover, those who worked outside the home were no longer predominantly young, single, or poor. Nearly half were mothers of school-age children; many of them were middle-class. When asked why they worked most responded that they regarded their jobs as an extension of family responsibilities as well as a matter of economic need. A second salary made possible a family vacation, a large home better suited to the children's needs, savings for college tuition, or simply a color television set for the family room. During the period when all America seemed about to become one great shopping mall, the definition of economic need was clearly changing. But even if one allows for a rising level of expectations consistent with the consumer culture of the 1950s, the fact remains that, while rhetoric still conformed to the old domestic ideology, the presence of women in the work force did not.

The gap between the old ideology of home and family and the new reality of office and work widened still further as medical advances resulted in improved birth control devices and longer life expectancy. Referring to the extent to which women's lives had been determined by their reproductive role, Sigmund Freud had observed tnat "anatomy is destiny." But as women gained the ability to control "destiny"—to decide whether to have children, when and how many— they were no longer victims of biological processes. Use of condoms and diaphragms, widespread especially among middle-class couples, made birth control a reality even before the introduction in 1960 of an oral contraceptive—"the pill." As medical science also devised new weapons against disease, the years during which one could expect to function as a healthy, active adult increased accordingly. For example, the average woman in 1900, marrying at twenty-two years of age and having her last child at the age of thirty-two, could expect to live to fifty-one, which was about the time her youngest reached maturity. By 1960, however, the average woman, marrying at the age of twenty, could expect to live until she was sixty-five. If she completed childbearing by the age of thirty, staying home while her children were small, she faced by the age of thirty-five nearly half of her life ahead of her in a house empty of children—empty at first during school hours; empty ultimately for many years after the last child had moved out.

The implications were enormous. That they were not immediately grasped is not surprising for a generation seeking in the private world of home and family the security unavailable in a public world wracked successively by economic depression, world war, and the threat of global annihilation. Throughout the 1950s specialists in marketing techniques continued to fuse the role of homemaker and mother with that of consumer, stressing that true feminine fulfillment lay in maternity, domesticity, and purchase of the "right" products. Yet by glorifying women as homemakers and mothers at precisely the same time important changes were occurring that served to undermine those roles, advertising people were unwittingly helping to sharpen the discrepancy between the domestic myth and the new reality of many women's lives. The gap between reality (change) and ideology (popular notions) was not yet great enough in the early 1960s for large numbers of women to be shocked into recognition of it. But it was there.

The gap could be ignored initially because it was at first a "bad fit." It was an oval peg in a round hole, a size six foot in a five-and-one-half shoe—a small discomfort with which people thought they could live. Social scientists did report slight deviations in the domestic image: daughters tended to regard working mothers as positive role models; husbands were more likely to accord them a greater voice in financial decisions; and families provided more help with household chores. But new developments were incorporated into old patterns even as women felt the pinch and stress. They still had difficulty seeing themselves as permanent members of the work force. Many seemed reluctant to join unions or press for equal pay, perhaps because they saw themselves as supplementary breadwinners or as housewives whom misfortune had trapped in monotonous, low-paying jobs. That so many women continued to see themselves, and their work primarily as serving family needs is hardly surprising in a culture in which homemaking was described as "the most important and difficult profession any woman can have." But the bad fit was there: the unfairness of unequal pay for the same work, the low value placed on jobs women performed, the double burden of housework and wage work. Those women who sensed the growing discrepancy between the traditional private world of domesticity and new realities in the public world of work needed a new way of looking at things that would allow them to examine afresh the condition of their lives, moving from grudg-

ing acceptance to confrontation and change. They needed, in short, a feminist consciousness.

The Creation of a Feminist Consciousness

Revolutions are seldom started by the powerless. The feminist revolution of the 1960s was no exception. It was begun largely by educated, middle-class women whose diverse experiences had sharpened their sensitivity to the fundamental inequality between the sexes at a time when America had been thrust into the throes of self-examination by a movement for racial equality. Some were young veterans of the civil rights movement and the new left, steeped in a commitment to equality and the techniques of protest. Others were young professionals increasingly aware of their secondary status, and still others were older women with distinguished careers as professionals or as activists. To explore how they came self-consciously to appraise women's condition as one demanding collective action is to explore the process of radicalization that helped to create a new feminist movement.

In its early state that movement consisted of two different groups—women's rights advocates and women's liberationists. Although the differences between the two groups began to blur as the movement matured, initial distinctions were sharp. Women's rights advocates were likely to have been older, to have had professional training or work experience, to have been more inclined to form or join organized feminist groups. Reform oriented, these organizations used traditional pressure group tactics to achieve changes in laws and public policy that would guarantee women equal rights. Emphasis on "rights" meant extending to women in life outside the home the same "rights" men had, granting them the same options, privileges, and responsibilities that men enjoyed. There was little suggestion initially of personal or cultural transformation.

Women's liberationists were younger women, less highly educated, whose ideology and political style, shaped in the dissent and violence of the 1960s, led them to look at women's predicament differently. Instead of relying upon traditional organizational structure and lobbying techniques, they developed a new style of politics. Instead of limiting their goals to changes in public policy, they embraced a transformation in private, domestic life as well. They sought liberation from ways of thinking and behaving that they believed stunted or distorted women's growth and kept them subordinate to men. Through the extension of their own personal liberation they hoped to remake the male world, changing it as they had changed themselves. For women's liberationists as for women's rights advocates, however, the first step toward becoming feminists demanded a clear statement of women's position in society, one that called attention to the gap between the egalitarian ideal and the actual position of women in American culture. There also had to be a call to action from women themselves, *for* women, *with* women, *through* women. Redefining themselves, they had to make being a woman a political fact; and, as they did so, they had to live with the radical implications of what could only be called a rebirth.

The Making of Feminists: Women's Rights Advocates

For some women, the process of radicalization began with the appointment of a Presidential Commission on the Status of Women in 1961. Presidents, Democrat and Republican, customarily discharged their political debt to female members of the electorate, especially to those who had loyally served the party, by appointing a few token women, usually party stalwarts, to highly visible posts. John Kennedy was no exception. He was, however, convinced by Esther Petersen that the vast majority of women would be better served if he also appointed a commission charged with investigating obstacles to the full participation of women in society. Assistant secretary of labor and head of the Women's Bureau, Petersen believed that the report of such a commission could sensitize the public to barriers to equality just as her own experience as a labor organizer had sensitized her to the particular problems confronting women workers. Citizens thus informed could then be mobilized on behalf of governmental efforts at reform. Accordingly,

the commission was appointed with Eleanor Roosevelt serving as chair until her death a year later. Its report, *American Women* (1963), was conservative in tone, acknowledging the importance of women's traditional roles within the home and the progress they had made in a "free democratic society." It also provided extensive documentation of discriminatory practices in government, education, and employment, along with substantial recommendations for change. Governors, replicating Kennedy's move, appointed state commissions on the status of women. In these commissions hundreds of men and women encountered further evidence of the economic, social, and legal disabilities that encumbered the nation's "second sex." For some, the statistics were old news; for others, they were a revelation.

Although there were variations from state to state, the pattern documented by the North Carolina Commission soon became increasingly familiar to a small but growing number of women throughout the nation. According to that commission's report, women workers, who made up over one-third of the state's labor force, suffered economically from job segregation and pay inequities. Of the 600,000 women employed outside the home in 1960, most (68 percent) were concentrated in blue-collar jobs or in traditionally low-paying "female" professions such as teaching and nursing. Whatever their occupational level, women earned significantly less than their male counterparts with comparable skills, experience, and responsibilities. They also had fewer opportunities for advancement. (Female mill operatives, for example, earned nearly 30 percent less than male operatives.)

Educational experience, seemingly more equitable, actually foreshadowed economic inequities. At the graduate level, women constituted only a tiny fraction of those enrolled in schools training future members of high-paying professions such as medicine. At the undergraduate level female students clustered in the humanities, avoiding the math and science courses necessary for providing greater career choice. Whatever their educational level, most women lacked access to diversified vocational training, enlightened career guidance, and the kind of role models provided by women, especially minority women, holding important nontraditional jobs. Worse still, they lacked expert, readily available child care. (Licensed day care facilities had only one space available for every seventeen preschool children of working mothers.)

Legally women in North Carolina, as elsewhere, were handicapped not only by hundreds of discriminatory federal statutes but also by state laws denying them equal treatment under the law. For example, married women still lacked complete control over their own property; state law required the written assent of the husband before a wife could convey her real property to someone else. Nor did women function as political equals. In North Carolina, as in other states, women were less likely to vote than men and far less likely to hold elective office or significant policymaking jobs. Especially disturbing to the commission was the failure of most women to understand "the direct connection between their own active and informed participation in politics . . . and the solution to many of their most pressing problems."

Some women, however, could make that connection. Aroused by growing evidence of "the enormity of our problem," members of state commissions gathered in Washington in 1966 for the Third National Conference of the Commissions on the Status of Women. Individuals who were coming to know and rely on one another as they pooled their growing knowledge of widespread inequities, they were a network in the making. They were also women who wanted something done. This time they encountered a situation that transformed at least some of those present into activists in a new movement for women's equality. The catalyst proved to be a struggle involving Representative Martha Griffiths and the Equal Employment Opportunity Commission (EEOC), the federal agency in charge of implementing the Civil Rights Act of 1964.

Despite the fact that the law proscribed discrimination on the basis of sex as well as race, the commission refused to take seriously the problem of sexual discrimination. The first executive director of EEOC, knowing that "sex" had been injected into the bill by opponents seeking to block its passage, regarded the sex provision as a "fluke" best ignored. Representative Griffiths from Michigan thought otherwise. While the bill was still in Congress she encouraged a small group of women in the House to become part of an unlikely alliance with legislative opponents of a federal civil rights act in order to keep the sex provision in the bill. Liberals objected, fearing that so encumbering a bill would prevent passage of much-needed legislation on behalf of racial equality. But despite such objections—and the ridicule of many of her male colleagues—Griffiths persisted. Once the bill passed she was determined to see the new law enforced in its entirety. When EEOC failed to do so, she lambasted the agency for its inaction in a biting speech delivered on the House floor only days before the Conference of the Commissions on the Status of Women met.

Griffiths's concern was shared by a group of women working within EEOC. They argued that the agency could be made to take gender-related discrimination more seriously if women had a civil rights organization as adept at applying pressure on their behalf as was the National Association for the Advancement of Colored People (NAACP) on behalf of blacks. Initially the idea was rejected. Conference participants most upset by EEOC's inaction decided instead to propose a resolution urging the agency to treat sexual discrimination with the same seriousness it applied to racial discrimination. When the resolution was ruled inappropriate by conference leaders, they were forced to reconsider. After a whispered conversation over lunch they concluded the time for discussion of the status of women was over. It was time for action. Before the day was out twenty-eight women had paid five dollars each to join the National Organization for Women (NOW), including author Betty Friedan who happened to be in Washington at the time of the conference.

Friedan's presence in Washington was auspicious; her involvement in NOW, virtually inevitable. The author of a brilliant polemic published in 1963, she not only labeled the resurgent domestic ideology of recent decades but exposed the groups perpetuating it. Editors of women's magazines, advertising experts, Freudian psychologists, social scientists, and educators—all, according to Friedan, contributed to a romanticization of domesticity she termed "the feminine mystique." The result, she charged, was the infantilization of intelligent women and the transformation of the suburban home into a "comfortable concentration camp." Harsh words, they rang true to those who found the creativity of homemaking and the joys of motherhood vastly exaggerated. Sales of the book ultimately zoomed past the million mark.

By articulating heretofore inarticulated grievances, *The Feminine Mystique* had advanced a process initiated by more dispassionate investigations of women's status and the discriminatory practices which made that status inferior. That process, was the collective expression of discontent. It is not surprising that those who best expressed that discontent initially were overwhelmingly white, educated, and middle or upper middle class. College women who regarded themselves the equals of male classmates by virtue of intellect and training were, as Jo Freeman points out, more likely to develop expectations they saw realized by their male peers but not, in most cases, by themselves. The frustrations were even greater for women with professional training. The very fact that many had sought advanced training in fields not traditionally "female" meant that they were less likely to find in traditional sex roles the identity and self-esteem such roles provided other women. Moreover, when measuring themselves against fellow professionals who happened to be men, the greater rewards enjoyed by their male counterparts seemed especially galling. Privileged though they were, such women *felt* more deprived in many cases than did those women who were in reality less privileged. By 1966 this sense of deprivation had been sufficiently articulated and shared and the networks of like-minded women sufficiently developed so that collective discontent could be translated into

collective action. The formation of NOW signaled the birth of a new feminist movement.

The three hundred men and women who gathered in October for the organizational meeting of NOW were in the main professionals, some of them veterans of commissions on the status of women. Adopting bylaws and a statement of purpose, they elected officers, naming Friedan president. Her conviction that intelligent women needed purposeful, generative work of their own was reflected in NOW's statement of purpose, which attacked "the traditional assumption that a woman has to choose between marriage and motherhood on the one hand and serious participation in industry or the professions on the other." Determined that women should be allowed to develop their full potential as human beings, the organization's goal was to bring them into "full participation in the mainstream of American society NOW, exercising all the privileges and responsibilities thereof in truly equal partnership with men." To that end NOW developed a Bill of Rights, adopted at its 1967 meeting, that exhorted Congress to pass an equal rights amendment to the Constitution, called on EEOC to enforce antidiscrimination legislation, and urged federal and state legislators to guarantee equal and unsegregated education. To ensure women control over their reproductive lives, these new feminists called for removal of penal codes denying women contraceptive information and devices as well as safe, legal abortions. To ease the double burden of working mothers, they urged legislation that would ensure maternity leaves without jeopardizing job security or seniority, permit tax deductions for child care expenses, and create public, inexpensive day care centers. To improve the lot of poor women, they urged reform of the welfare system and equality with respect to benefits, including job-training programs.

Not content simply to call for change, NOW leaders worked to make it happen. Using persuasion, pressure, and even litigation, they, with other newly formed women's rights groups such as the Women's Equity Action League (WEAL), launched a massive attack on sex discrimination.

By the end of the 1960s NOW members had filed legal suits against newspapers listing jobs under the headings "Help Wanted: Male" and "Help Wanted: Female," successfully arguing that such headings discouraged women from applying for jobs they were perfectly capable of doing. Building on efforts begun in the Kennedy administration such as the passage of the Equal Pay Act, they pressured the federal government to intensify its commitment to equal opportunity. They urged congressmen and labor leaders to persuade the Department of Labor to include women in its guidelines designed to encourage the hiring and promotion of blacks in firms holding contracts with the federal government. They persuaded the Federal Communications Commission to open up new opportunities for women in broadcasting. Tackling the campus as well as the marketplace, WEAL filed suit against more than three hundred colleges and universities, ultimately securing millions of dollars in salary raises for women faculty members who had been victims of discrimination. To ensure that women receive the same pay men received for doing the same work, these new feminists lobbied for passage of a new Equal Employment Opportunity Act that would enable EEOC to fight discrimination more effectively.

NOW also scrutinized the discriminatory practices of financial institutions, persuading them to issue credit to single women and to married women in their own—not their husband's—name. WEAL, in turn, filed charges against banks and other lending institutions that refused to grant mortgages to single women, or in the case of married couples, refused to take into account the wife's earning in evaluating the couple's eligibility for a mortgage. Colleges and universities that discriminated against female students in their sports programs came under fire, as did fellowship programs that failed to give adequate consideration to female applicants.

While NOW and WEAL attacked barriers in industry and education, the National Women's Political Caucus (NWPC) focused on government and politics. Formed in 1971, the caucus was initiated by Friedan, New York congress-

woman Bella Abzug and Shirley Chisholm—both outspoken champions of women's rights—and Gloria Steinem, soon to become founding editor of the new mass-circulation feminist magazine *Ms.* Especially concerned about the small numbers of women in government, the caucus concentrated on getting women elected and appointed to public office while also rallying support for issues such as the Equal Rights Amendment. . . . Meanwhile women in the professions, aware of their small numbers and inferior status, began to organize as well. Physicians, lawyers, and university professors fought for equal opportunity in the meetings of such overwhelmingly male groups as the American Medical Association, the American Association of University Professors, and the American Historical Association.

Collectively such protests served notice that more women were becoming feminists. The particular combination of events that transformed women into feminists varied with the individual. A southern legislator, describing the process that brought home the reality of her own second-class citizenship, wrote:

> As a State Senator, I succeeded in getting Mississippi women the right to sit on juries (1968); the opposition's arguments were appalling. When women began hiring me in order to get credit, I became upset at the discrimination I saw. After I was divorced in 1970, I was initially denied a home loan. The effect was one of the worst traumas I've suffered. Denial of a home loan to one who was both a professional and a member of the legislature brought things to a head.

Although the number of women who understood what it meant to be the "second sex" were still only a tiny minority, they were nonetheless a minority whose energy, talents, and experience enabled them to work for changes necessary to ensure equal rights.

The Making of Feminists: Women's Liberation
The process of radicalization that transformed some individuals into women's rights advocates

occurred simultaneously—but in different fashion and with somewhat different results—among a younger generation of women. Many of them veterans of either the civil rights movement or the new left, these were the activists who would become identified with the women's liberation branch of the women's movement. Differing in perspective as well as style, they would ultimately push many of their older counterparts beyond the demand for equal rights to recognition that true emancipation would require a far-reaching transformation of society and culture.

The experiences awakening in this 1960s generation a feminist consciousness have been superbly described by Sara Evans in her book, *Personal Politics.* "Freedom, equality, love and hope," the possibility of new human relationships, the importance of participatory democracy —letting the people decide—were, as Evans points out, part of an egalitarian ideology shared by both the southern-based Student Nonviolent Coordinating Committee (SNCC) in its struggle for racial equality and the Students for a Democratic Society (SDS) in its efforts to mobilize an interracial organization of the urban poor in northern ghettos. Membership in both organizations—"the movement"—thus reinforced commitment to these ideals among the women who joined. In order to translate ideals into reality, however, young, college-age women who had left the shelter of middle-class families for the hard and dangerous work of transforming society found themselves doing things that they would never have thought possible. Amidst the racial strife of the South, they joined picket lines, created freedom schools, and canvassed for voter registration among blacks, often enduring arrest and jailing. SDS women from affluent suburbs entered decaying tenements and were surrounded by the grim realities of the ghetto. They trudged door-to-door in an effort to reach women whose struggle to survive made many understandably suspicious of intruding strangers. Summing up the feelings of hundreds, one young woman wrote: "I learned a lot of respect for myself for having gone through all that." A heightened sense of self-worth and autonomy, Evans argues,

was not all they acquired. They also learned the skills of movement building and the nuts and bolts of organizing.

Particularly important was the problem of getting people, long passive, to act on their own behalf. SDS women began by encouraging ghetto women together to talk about their problems. This sharing of experiences, they believed, would lead these women to recognize not only that their problems were common but that solutions required changes in the system. In the process of organizing, the organizers also learned. They began to understand the meaning of oppression and the valor required of those who fought it. They found new role models, Evans suggests, in extraordinary southern black women whose courage never wavered in the face of violence and in those welfare mothers of the North who confronted welfare bureaucrat and slum lord after years of passivity.

But if being in the movement brought a new understanding of equality, it also brought new problems. Men who were committed to equality for one group were not necessarily committed to equality for another group. Women in SNCC, as in SDS, found themselves frequently relegated to domestic chores and refused a key voice in the formulation of policy. Moreover, the sexual freedom that had been theirs as part of the cultural revolution taking place in the 1960s soon began to feel more like sexual exploitation as they saw their role in the movement spelled out in the draft resister's slogan: "Girls Say Yes to Guys Who Say No." Efforts to change the situation were firmly rebuffed. When SNCC leader Stokeley Carmichael announced, "The only position for women in SNCC is prone," he spoke for white males in the new left as well. Evans concludes: "The same movement that permitted women to grow and to develop self-esteem, energy, and skills generally kept women out of leadership roles and reinforced expectations that women would conform to tradition as houseworkers, nurturers, and sex objects." By 1967 the tensions had become so intense that women left the movement to organize on behalf of their own "liberation."

They did not leave empty handed. As radicals, they were accustomed to challenging prevailing ideas and practices. As movement veterans, they had acquired a language of protest, an organizing tactic, and a deep-seated conviction that the personal was political. How that legacy would shape this burgeoning new feminist movement became evident as small women's liberation groups began springing up spontaneously in major cities and university communities across the nation.

Structure, Leadership, and Consciousness-Raising

Initially, at least, the two branches of the new feminism seemed almost to be two different movements, so unlike were they in structure and style. Linked only by newsletters, notices in underground newspapers, and networks of friends, women's liberation groups rejected both traditional organizational structure and leadership. Unlike NOW and other women's rights groups, they had no central headquarters, no elected officers, no bylaws. There was no legislative agenda and little of the activism that transformed the more politically astute women's rights leaders into skilled lobbyists and tacticians. Instead this younger generation of feminists, organizing new groups wherever they found themselves, concentrated on a kind of personal politics rooted in movement days. Looking back on male-dominated meetings in which, however informal the gathering, a few highly verbal, aggressive men invariably controlled debate and dictated strategy and left less articulate and assertive women effectively excluded, they recalled the technique they had used in organizing the poor. They remembered how they had encouraged those women to talk among themselves until the personal became political, that is, until problems which, at first glance, seemed to be personal were finally understood to be social in cause—rooted in society rather than in the individual—and political in solution. Applying this same process in their own informal "rap groups," women's liberationists developed the technique of "consciousness raising." Adopted by women's rights groups such as

local chapters of NOW, consciousness-raising sessions became one of the most important innovations of the entire feminist movement.

The immediate task of the consciousness-raising session was to bring together in a caring, supportive, noncompetitive setting women accustomed to relating most intimately not with other women but with men—husbands, lovers, "friends." As these women talked among themselves, exchanging confidences, reassessing old options, and mentally exploring new ones, a sense of shared problems began to emerge. The women themselves gradually gained greater understanding of how profoundly their lives had been shaped by the constraints of culture. Personal experience with those constraints merged with intellectual awareness of women's inferior status and the factors that made it so. By the same token, new understanding of problems generated new determination to resolve them. Anger, aggression, and frustration formerly turned inward in unconscious self-hatred began to be directed outward, becoming transformed into new energy directed toward constructive goals. If society and culture had defined who women were through their unconscious internalization of tradition, they could reverse the process, and, by redefining themselves, redefine society and culture. At work was a process of change so fundamental that the individuals undergoing it ultimately emerged in a very real sense as different people. Now feminists, these were women with a different understanding of reality—a new "consciousness," a new sense of "sisterhood," and a new commitment to change.

Consciousness raising was an invigorating and sometimes frightening experience. As one young woman wrote, "This whole movement is the most exhilarating thing of my life. The last eight months have been a personal revolution. Nonetheless, I recognize there is dynamite in this and I'm scared shitless." "Scared" or not, such women could no longer be contained. Veterans of one rap group fanned out, creating others. For the feminist movement, this mushrooming of groups meant increased numbers and added momentum. For some of the women involved, it meant confronting and articulating theoretically as well as personally what "oppression," "sexism," and "liberation" really meant; in short, developing a feminist ideology.

Toward a Feminist Ideology: Oppression, Sexism, and Change

The development of feminist ideology was not a simple process. Women's rights advocates were essentially pragmatic, more interested in practical results than in theoretical explanations. Even among feminists who were more theoretically oriented, intellectual perspectives reflected differences in experience, temperament, style, and politics. Manifestos, position papers, and books began to pile up as feminists searched for the historical origins of female oppression. Socialist feminists debated nonsocialist feminists as to whether socialism was a prerequisite for women's liberation. Lesbian feminists argued that the ultimate rejection of male domination meant the rejection of intimacy with men. Other feminists insisted that rigid sex-role differentiation oppressed men as well as women and that their goal should be restructuring male-female relations in ways that would encourage greater mutuality and fulfillment for both sexes in all aspects of life. Given such a variety of perspectives, it is almost impossible to talk about a feminist ideology in the sense of a unified theory to which all members of the women's movement subscribe. At the risk of considerable oversimplification, however, it is possible to talk about a critique of society. Owing much to the liberationists, this critique has come to be shared by many in the movement, including many women's rights advocates who started out with the initial belief that equality meant simply giving women the same "rights" men enjoyed.

Although feminists differ as to the historical roots of oppression, they agree that men have been the dominant sex and that women as a group are oppressed. Explanations for the perpetuation of oppression in present-day society also vary. Feminists whose socialism was forged in the new left of the 1960s see oppression as the inevitable result of a capitalist system that permits employers, in effect, to hire two workers for the price of one (men being paid wages with their unpaid wives performing the services necessary to enable them to perform their jobs). Women also working outside the home function as a cheap labor force enabling employers to keep wages low and profits high. Other feminists, including members of women's rights groups such as NOW, WEAL, and NWPC, believe the continuation of male domination and female oppression is perpetuated by sex role socialization and cultural values that continue to confer on males higher status, greater options, and greater power, by virtue of their sex. This preference, conscious and unconscious, for whatever is "masculine," feminists term *sexism*. Not surprisingly, they reject the traditional assumption that biology—sexual dichotomy—dictates distinct spheres, status, roles, or personality types. To put the matter most simply, feminists reject the notion that the bearing of children creates for women "natural" roles as wives and mothers, a rightful "place" limited to the home, a subordinate status, and behavior patterns of self-denying submissiveness and service to others. The persistence of gender-based determinism, they believe, continues to limit options resulting in female dependency and the vapid, trivialized image of feminity associated with such dependency—the feminity of the "Total Woman" with its mixture of sexuality and submissiveness. The fact that so many women continue to rely on men not only for financial support but also for social status and even self-esteem, feminists argue, deprives such women of the economic and psychological freedom to determine their own lives, to make real choices, to be judged as individuals on the basis of their own merit and accomplishments, not those of fathers or husbands.

Just as traditional male roles provide access to power and independence in a sexist society, whereas female roles do not, so masculine values define what attributes are admired and rewarded. Thus masculine qualities are associated with strength, competence, independence, and rationality, while female qualities are associated with fragility, dependence, passivity, and emotionalism. These qualities, however, are not intrinsically "male" or "female" in the sense that they are biologically inherent. Rather, feminists argue, they are an extension of the training that is part of sex role socialization. The very fact that masculine values are those Americans of both sexes regard more highly and also constitute the standard by which mental health is judged has implications feminists find distressing. Women, internalizing these sexist judgments and feeling themselves lacking in competence, tend to undervalue themselves (and women in general) and therefore lack self-esteem. Moreover, society also undervalues the female qualities that are positive, such as nurturing, supportiveness, and empathy. *All* of these qualities—those considered "male" and those considered "female"—feminists insist are shared human qualities. Those that are desirable, such as competence, independence, supportiveness, and nurturing, should be encouraged in both men and women.

Such changes, however, demand the eradication of sexism. And sexism, feminists believe, is persistent, pervasive, and powerful. It is internalized by women as well as men. It is most dramatically evident in the programmed-to-please women who search for happiness through submissiveness to men and in the men who use their power to limit women's options and keep them dependent. It is also evident in a more subtle fashion among women who emulate male models and values, refusing to see those aspects of women's lives that are positive and life affirming, and among men who are unaware of the unconscious sexism permeating their attitudes and actions. Internalized in individuals, sexism is also embedded in institutions—the family, the educational system, the media, politics, the law, and even organized religion.

Given the pervasiveness of sexism, many feminists see no possibility for real equality short of transformation not only of individuals but also of social institutions and cultural values. Even what was once seen as the relatively simple demand of women's rights advocates for equal pay for equal work no longer seems so simple. What seemed to be a matter of obtaining equal rights *within* the existing system in reality demands changes that *transform* the system. Involved is:

a reevaluation of women as workers, of women as mothers, of mothers as workers, of work as suitable for one gender and not for the other. The demand implies equal opportunity and thus equal responsibilities. It implies a childhood in which girls are rewarded for competence, risk taking, achievement, competitiveness and independence—just like boys. Equal pay for equal work means a revision in our expectations about women as equal workers and it involves the institutional arrangements to make them so.

"There is nothing small here," observes a noted feminist scholar. And indeed there is not.

Feminism in Action

While the contemporary women's movement contains under its broad umbrella women who differ significantly in the degree of their radicalism, the changes implied in achieving sexual equality are of such scope as to make radical by definition those who genuinely understand what is involved in equality and, beyond that, emancipation. Feminism is not for the fainthearted. To clarify frustration and rage so as to understand problems accurately and then to use that understanding in ways that permit growth and change in one's self are to engage in a process requiring considerable courage and energy. To reform society so that women can achieve legal, economic, and social parity requires even greater commitment—commitment that has to be sustained over time and through defeat. To work for cultural transformation of a patriarchal world in such a way as to benefit both men and women requires extraordinary breadth of vision as well as sustained energy and dedication. Yet despite the obstacles, thousands of women during the past decade have participated in the process.

For some the changes have consisted largely of private actions—relationships renegotiated, careers resumed. Others, preferring to make public statements of new commitments, used flamboyant methods to dramatize the subtle ways in which society so defined woman's place as to deny not only her full participation but also her full humanity. As part of the confrontational politics of the 1960s, feminists picketed the 1968 Miss America contest, protesting our national preoccupation with bust size and "congeniality" rather than brain power and character. (In the process they were dubbed "bra burners," despite the fact that no bras were burned.) Activists pushed their way into all-male bars and restaurants as a way of forcing recognition of how these bastions of male exclusivity were themselves statements about "man's world/woman's place." They sat in at the offices of *Ladies' Home Journal* and *Newsweek* protesting the ways in which the media's depiction of women perpetuated old stereotypes at the expense of new realities.

Still other feminists chose to work for social change in a different fashion. They created nonsexist day care centers, wrote and published nonsexist children's books, monitored sex stereotyping in textbooks, lobbied for women's studies programs in high schools and colleges, and founded women's health clinics. They worked for reform of abortion laws so that women would not be forced to continue pregnancies that were physically or psychologically hazardous but could instead have the option of a safe, legal abortion. They formed rape crisis centers so that rape victims could be treated by caring females; they agitated for more informed, sympathetic treatment on the part of hospital staffs, the police, and the courts. Feminists also lobbied for programs to retrain displaced homemakers so that such women could move from economic dependency to self-support. Feminist scholars used their talents to recover and interpret women's experience, opening new areas for research and in the process furthering change. Feminist legislators sponsored bills, not always successful, to help housewives to secure some form of economic recognition for work performed, to enable women workers to obtain insurance that would give them the same degree of economic security afforded male coworkers, and to secure for battered wives protection from the physical violence that is the most blatant form of male oppression. Black feminists, speaking out on the "double jeopardy" of being black and female—"the most pressed down of us

all"—lent their support to feminist measures of especial importance to minority women. Actions, like voices, differed. Such diversity, however, was basic to the movement.

Feminism: The Public Impact

In a society in which the media create instant awareness of social change, feminism burst upon the public consciousness with all the understated visibility of a fireworks display on the Fourth of July. The more radical elements of the movement with their talk of test tube conception, the slavery of marriage, and the downfall of capitalism might be dismissed out of hand. But it was hard to ignore the presence of *Ms.* magazine on newsstands, feminist books on the best-seller lists, women in hard hats on construction jobs or the government-mandated affirmative action programs that put them there. It was harder still to ignore the publicity that accompanied the appointment of women to the Carter cabinet, the enrollment of coeds in the nation's military academies, and the ordination of women to the ministry. A Harris poll of December 1975 reported that 63 percent of the women interviewed favored most changes designed to improve the status of women, although some were quick to insist that they were not "women's libbers."

Evidence of changing views was everywhere. The list of organizations lined up in support of ratification of the Equal Rights Amendment included not only such avowedly feminist groups as NOW, WEAL, and NWPC as well as longtime supporters such as the National Woman's Party and the National Federation of Business and Professional Women's Clubs, but also "mainstream" women's organizations such as the General Federation of Women's Clubs, the American Association of University Women, the League of Women Voters, the National Council of Jewish Women, and National Council of Negro Women, and the YWCA. Included, too, were the Girl Scouts of America, along with a host of churches and labor organizations. Even more potent evidence that feminism had "arrived" was the 1977 National Women's Conference in Houston. Before over two thousand delegates from every state and territory in the United States and twenty thousand guests, three First Ladies—Lady Bird Johnson, Betty Ford, and Rosalyn Carter—endorsed the Equal Rights Amendment and the goals of the Houston Conference, their hands holding a lighted torch carried by women runners from Seneca Falls where, in 1848, the famous Declaration of Sentiments had been adopted. Confessing that she once thought the women's movement belonged more to her daughters than to herself, Lady Bird Johnson added, "I have come to know that it belongs to women of all ages." Such an admission, like the presence of these three women on the platform, proclaimed a message about feminists that was boldly printed on balloons throughout the convention hall: "We Are Everywhere!"

Opposition to Feminism

For some women the slogan was not a sign of achievement but of threat. Gathered at a counter-convention in Houston and proudly wearing "Stop ERA" buttons were women who shared neither the critique nor the goals of the women's movement. They were an impressive reminder that social change generates opposition and that opposition to feminism had crystallized in the struggle for ratification of the Equal Rights Amendment. ERA—as the amendment is called—is a simple statement: "Equality of rights under the law shall not be denied or abridged by the United States or by any State on account of sex." It was first suggested in 1923 as the logical extension of suffrage. Not all feminists embraced the amendment, however. Some, fearing it would be used to strike down laws to protect women in the workplace, preferred to look for constitutional guarantees of equality through the extension of judicial interpretation of the Fifth and Fourteenth Amendments. By the 1960s sentiments had shifted. NOW called for passage of the amendment as part of its legislative agenda. The President's Task Force on the Status of Women and the Citizen's Advisory Council on the Status of Women endorsed the amendment, as did Presi-

dents Johnson and Nixon. Persuasive feminists helped to bring aboard such historic opponents as the Women's Bureau and organized labor. Arguing in support of the amendment, they pointed out that New Deal legislation provided a basis for protection of both sexes that had not existed in the 1920s. They also pointed out that many state laws granting protection only to women had already been voided by Title VII of the Civil Rights Act of 1964. With unions and many women's organizations thus persuaded, NOW turned its attention to Congress itself, asking legislators to pass a constitutional amendment removing sexual bias from common, statutory, and constitutional law. In the spring of 1972 the Senate finally joined the House and sent ERA to the states for ratification by a lopsided vote of eighty-four to eight. Almost immediately twenty-one states rushed to ratify. By the spring of 1973, however, opponents of ratification had begun a counter-attack that ultimately stalled the number of ratified states at thirty-five, three short of the needed three-fourths majority. They even induced some ratifying states to rescind their approval. Early successes indicated that a majority of Americans favored ERA—but not a large enough majority.

Opposition to ERA is starkly paradoxical. A constitutional amendment proposed especially to benefit women was opposed by many of them. The dimensions of paradox are suggested by the reasons sometimes given for taking a position on the issue. Women opposed the amendment because they wanted to protect the family; other women supported it because they, too, wanted to protect the family. Women resisted ERA because some could not trust men to treat women fairly; and others supported it, giving precisely the same reason.

The paradox is resolved in part by remembering that conservatives of both sexes are often suspicious of the principle of equality, especially when identified with specific controversial federal policies. This is especially true of programs to bus school children in order to achieve equality through "racial balance" in the public schools. The policy was believed by some parents to be a denial of their right to educate their children how and where they pleased. Proponents of busing saw it as an issue of public policy, having nothing to do with private relationships. But opponents believed that education was an extension of the private relationships between parents and children. The moving of children literally from their parents' door to a faraway school was an act reinforcing the sense of losing one's children. Busing, therefore, was seen as an intrusion into the private domain of family, subverting the influence and values of parents. Other federal policies seemed to do the same thing. Attempts to break up segregated housing, for example, were seen as an assault on the right to live in neighborhoods that reflected the private, family lives of the people who lived there. Since ERA was perceived both as a continuation of previous governmental commitment to equality *and* as a symbol of feminism, it was attacked for attempting to give the federal bureaucracy power to change relationships within the family. Opposition to ERA expressed a diffuse anger with federal intervention in "private" relationships. As one woman wrote her U.S. senator: "Forced busing, forced mixing, forced housing. Now forced women! No thank you!"

Opposition to ERA also expressed an elemental response to what many people believe to be a threat to cherished values. "The drug revolution, the sexual revolution, gay liberation, students' rights, children's rights, and the civil rights and the Native American and Latino movements"—to borrow the list of one observer—all challenged basic middle-class values. Above all, there was the women's movement. Feminists believed that theirs was a struggle for justice and liberation—liberation from social roles and cultural values that denied rights and limited autonomy. To require all women to conform to patterns of behavior dictated not by biology but by culture was, from the standpoint of feminists, to deny freedom and self-determination to half the population simply because they were born female. To women who did not believe they were oppressed, however, feminists' efforts at liberation appeared *not* as an attack on unjust constraints but rather

as an attack on familiar patterns that provide security. To women who had internalized traditional female roles, feminism, with its demands to rethink what it means to be a man or a woman, was perceived not just as an assault upon them personally but as symbolic of every other threat to their identity and traditions. Because ERA has been seen as the instrument through which feminists could achieve goals regarded by antifeminists as Utopian and threatening, the amendment itself has come to symbolize to its opponents both the danger and absurdity inherent in this latest drive for equality of the sexes. Indeed the very idea of oppression seems preposterous to women who believe that they have benefited from being treated as "the fairer sex" and "the better half." Their experience, even if not the ideal of wedded bliss, nevertheless seems to them to be at odds with that of feminists who seem to antifeminists to be attacking women for behaving like women.

From this point of view feminists appear silly for wanting to use *Ms.* instead of the traditional *Mrs.* or *Miss,* tasteless for intruding where men do not want them to be, eccentric for celebrating the filly who won the Kentucky Derby. Worse still, feminists, in the eyes of antifeminists, appear to be women-who-want-to-be-men. The accusation that ERA would require men and women to use the same public toilets is not therefore to be taken literally so much as symbolically. It represents the intrusion of men and of women-who-want-to-be-men into the privacy of women-who-are-proud-to-be-women. The accusation that ERA would destroy the family should also be understood as a way of defending the social significance and indispensability of traditional female roles. Underlying everything is the theme of purity (traditional female roles) against danger and corruption (social disintegration). The result of this formulation of the issue of equality has been to enable antifeminist women to develop a consciousness of their own. The free-floating anxiety aroused by the enormity of the social change inherent in feminism thus acquired a concrete focus. ERA became an issue in which what seemed to be at stake for opponents was their very identity as women—and the fate of society.

Predictions of the terrible consequences that would result from ratification of the amendment were not so important as was the function such statements seemed to serve—that is, the reaffirmation of traditional sex roles identified with social stability. The indictment of feminism and of ERA is an indictment of what Phyllis Schlafly, the chief female opponent of ratification, persistently calls the "unisex society." By rallying women to this danger, Schlafly has revealed that the issue was not whether or not women should stay at home minding the children and cooking the food—Schlafly herself did not do that. The issue was the *meaning* of sexual differences between men and women.

Many feminists minimize those differences, believing that traditional roles are not only oppressive but outmoded because reproductive control and work in the public sector have made women's lives more like men's. Antifeminists inflate those differences. Their response is a measure both of their belief that women are "eternal in their attributes and unchanged by events" and their anger and distress at changes that have already occurred. It is a reminder, too, of how far the feminist movement has still to go to achieve the political and legal reforms it seeks, much less its more far-reaching goals.

New Progress and Old Problems

There were gains during the 1970s to be sure. New reproductive freedom came with the Supreme Court's liberalization of abortion laws that removed the danger of the illegal, back alley abortions so long the recourse of desperate women. Sexual preference and practice became less an occasion for denial of civil rights and more a matter of individual choice. Evidence of expanding educational and employment opportunities seemed to be everywhere. Women assumed high level posts in government, the judiciary, the military, business, and labor. From an expanding population of female college graduates, younger women moved in record numbers into professional schools, dramatically changing enrollment patterns in such fields as law, medicine, and business. Their blue-collar counterparts, completing job training programs, trickled into the construction industry and other trades, finding in those jobs the decent wage that had eluded them as waitresses, hairdressers, sales clerks, or domestics. Political participation also increased. Women emerged from years of lobbying for ERA with a new understanding of the political process. (So, too, did their opponents.) More female candidates filed for office and more female politicians worked themselves into positions of power. Revision of discriminatory statutes, while by no means completed, brought a greater measure of legal equality. A heightened public consciousness of sexism ushered in other changes. School officials began admitting boys to home economics classes, girls to shop. Some employers transformed maternity leaves into child care leaves, making them available to fathers as well as mothers. Liberal religious leaders talked of removing gender-related references from the Bible.

Such gains, while in some cases smacking of tokenism, are not to be minimized. Most required persistent pressure from feminists, from government officials, and often from both. They were by no means comprehensive, however. As in the case of the civil rights movement, the initial beneficiaries of the feminist movement were predominantly middle-class, often highly educated, and relatively young. The increase in the number of single women, the older age at which women married for the first time, the declining birth rate—changes characteristic of the entire female population during the 1970s—were especially characteristic of a younger generation of career-oriented women. But even for these women and their spouses, financial as well as personal costs were sometimes high: couples living apart for some portion of the week or year in order to take advantage of career opportunities; married women devoting virtually all of their salaries to domestic and child care costs, especially during their children's preschool years. Perhaps the personal recognition, independence, and sense of fulfillment associated with career success made the costs "affordable"—especially given the alternatives.

The women who stand to gain most from the

implementation of feminists' efforts to change the nation's economic and social structure are not those who are young, talented, and educated but those who are less advantaged. Yet the latter could with good reason argue that over a decade of feminist activity had left their lives little changed in ways that really count. While the number of women in the work force continues to rise from less than 20 percent in 1920 to a projected 54 to 60 percent by 1990, working women in the 1970s saw the gap between male and female income widen rather than narrow. Female workers earned 59 cents for every dollar earned by males. Although the gap is smaller among business and professional women than among blue-collar workers, a recent study of alumni of such prestigious graduate business schools as Stanford, Harvard, and the University of Pennsylvania indicated that women graduating in 1977 and 1978 were earning on the average $4,000 less a year than their male classmates. Part of the explanation for this persistent gap lies in pay inequities. More fundamental, however, is the continuation of occupational segregation and the undervaluation of work done by women. Around 80 percent of all working women still cluster in gender-segregated occupations in which wages are artificially low. At American Telephone and Telegraph, for example, a 1976 court case revealed that 97 percent of the middle management jobs were held by men, while 98 percent of all telephone operators and 94 percent of all clerical workers were women. Moreover, as inflationary pressures drive more women into the work force, competition for jobs in traditionally "female" fields enables employers to keep wages low.

With the dramatic rise in the number of female-headed households, the continuation of this occupational ghetto has disturbing implications not only for women workers but also for their children. Female heads of households, often lacking both child care facilities and skills that would equip them for better-paying jobs if such jobs were available, earn enough to enable only one in three to stay above the poverty level. Their struggle for economic survival is shared by other women, especially older women—widows or divorcees whose years of housework have left them without employable skills. Thus ironic as it may seem, the decade that witnessed the revival of the feminist movement also saw the feminization of poverty. By the end of the 1970s, two out of every three poor persons in the United States were female.

Ironic, too, given the feminist insistence that child care and household responsibilities should be shared by working spouses, is the persistence of the double burden borne by women working outside the home. According to a recent national survey, in 53 percent of the couples interviewed both husband and wife agreed that, even though the wife held a job, she should also do the housework. Not surprisingly, working women continue to do 80 to 90 percent of the chores related to running a household, with husbands and children "helping out." For all the talk about the changing structure of family roles, major shifts occurred slowly, even in households in which women were informed and engaged enough to be familiar with current feminist views. Although some fathers, especially among the middle class, have become more involved in parenting, the primary responsibility for children still remains the mother's. And working mothers still receive little institutional help despite the fact that by 1980 nearly half of all mothers with children under six worked outside the home. Without a fundamental rethinking of both work and family, women will continue to participate in the labor force in increasing numbers while, at the same time, remaining in its lower echelons as marginal members.

In sum, economic and demographic change has been the basis of important changes in attitudes and behavior. As a result, life is more challenging for many women, but the feminization of poverty reminds the nation of its failures. We have yet to see the new social policies necessary to create the egalitarian and humane society envisioned by feminists. Indeed, in the climate of political conservatism of the 1980s feminists have had to fight hard to maintain gains already won. The reproductive freedom of poor women had already been eroded by limitations on federal funding of abortions, and the reproductive freedom of all women had been threatened by Congressional opponents of legalized abortion. Governmental enforcement of legislation mandating equal opportunity is effective only if a commitment to eradicate discrimination is backed with the funds and personnel necessary to do the job. Without an equal rights amendment requiring legislators to revise the discriminatory statutes that remain, the impetus will come not from the governments—state and local—but from individual women and men genuinely committed to equality before the law. Thus the need for collective action on the part of feminists is as great in the 1980s as it was in the 1970s.

Social change is complex and results from the interplay of many factors. Nowhere is this truer than in the women's movement. The swiftness with which a resurgent feminism captured the imagination of millions of American women dramatized the need for change. The inability of feminists to win ratification of ERA dramatized the limits of change. The irony of the polarization, however, was that the failure of ERA did not and could not stop feminism in its tracks and that antifeminist women, in mobilizing to fight the amendment, were themselves assuming a new role whether they acknowledged that fact or not. They organized lobbies, political action committees, and conventions; they also ran for and won public office. Where feminists have led, antifeminists would not be too far behind, defining themselves within the context of change they could not stop. But the rhetoric of liberation that had been so important to the awakening and maturation of women in the 1970s seemed by 1980 to be less appealing. Women could happily benefit from the achievements of feminism without understanding or embracing its critique and style. As a result, old patterns of sexual differentiation persisted. They had hindered efforts of women to establish a public role in the nineteenth century; they had restricted that public role once it was won. The same patterns, so indelible even under attack, continue to obstruct contemporary efforts to redefine social roles in the drive for equality. The tension between past position and future possibility, however, demands of all women—not merely feminists—a definition of self that extends beyond definitions of the past.